MAP OF NON-MEMBER COUNTRIES OF ASEAN

SOUTHEAST ASIA IN SEARCH OF AN ASEAN COMMUNITY

The **Institute of Southeast Asian Studies (ISEAS)** was established as an autonomous organization in 1968. It is a regional centre dedicated to the study of socio-political, security and economic trends and developments in Southeast Asia and its wider geostrategic and economic environment.

The Institute's research programmes are the Regional Economic Studies (RES, including ASEAN and APEC), Regional Strategic and Political Studies (RSPS), and Regional Social and Cultural Studies (RSCS).

ISEAS Publishing, an established academic press, has issued more than 1,000 books and journals. It is the largest scholarly publisher of research about Southeast Asia from within the region. ISEAS Publications works with many other academic and trade publishers and distributors to disseminate important research and analyses from and about Southeast Asia to the rest of the world.

SOUTHEAST ASIA IN SEARCH OF AN ASEAN COMMUNITY

Insights from the former ASEAN Secretary-General

Rodolfo C. Severino

INSTITUTE OF SOUTHEAST ASIAN STUDIES
Singapore

First published in Singapore in 2006 by
ISEAS Publishing
Institute of Southeast Asian Studies
30 Heng Mui Keng Terrace
Pasir Panjang
Singapore 119614

E-mail: publish@iseas.edu.sg
Website: <http://bookshop.iseas.edu.sg>

All rights reserved. No part of this publication may be reproduced, stored in a retrieval system, or transmitted in any form or by any means, electronic, mechanical, photocopying, recording or otherwise, without the prior permission of the Institute of Southeast Asian Studies.

© 2006 Institute of Southeast Asian Studies, Singapore.

The responsibility for facts and opinions in this publication rests exclusively with the author and his interpretations do not necessarily reflect the views or the policies of ISEAS or its supporters.

ISEAS Library Cataloguing-in-Publication Data

Severino, Rodolfo C.
  Southeast Asia in search of an ASEAN Community.
  1. ASEAN.
  2. Southeast Asia—Politics and government—1945–
  3. National security—Southeast Asia.
  4. Southeast Asia—Economic integration.
  5. Southeast Asia—Foreign economic relations.
  6. Southeast Asia—Foreign relations.
  I. Title.
JZ5333.5 A9S49   2006

ISBN-13: 978-981-230-388-2 (soft cover — 13 digit)
ISBN-10: 981-230-388-X (soft cover — 10 digit)

ISBN-13: 978-981-230-389-9 (hard cover — 13 digit)
ISBN-10: 981-230-389-8 (hard cover — 10 digit)

Typeset by Superskill Graphics Pte Ltd
Printed in Singapore by Utopia Press Pte Ltd

CONTENTS

Foreword by Tommy Koh — ix

Introduction — xi

About the Author — xiii

Acknowledgements — xv

Glossary — xix

1. The "ASEAN Way": Its Nature and Origins — 1
   - Southeast Asia is Not Western Europe — 4
   - Diversity and Fragile Relations — 6
   - Informality and Loose Arrangements — 11
   - "A Pace Comfortable to All" — 18
   - Institutions Following Substance — 23
   - Vulnerability and Mutual Suspicions — 24
   - Who is ASEAN's Leader? — 26
   - A Question of Equality — 32
   - The Way of Consensus — 34
   - Fruits of the ASEAN Way — 35
   - Time for Change? — 37

2. Who Belongs in ASEAN? The Question of Membership — 41
   - Burmese and Cambodian Refusal — 43
   - Sri Lanka's Bid for Inclusion — 45
   - Opening to Indochina — 47
   - Unconditional Membership — 50
   - The Admission of New Members — 53

	Laos and Myanmar	55
	Delay in Cambodia's Admission	57
	A Two-Tier ASEAN?	67
	Integrating the Newer Members	70
	What About Timor-Leste?	75
	A Diversity of Members	80
3	The Issue of Non-Interference	85
	The Financial Crisis 1997–98	96
	Haze and SARS	107
	East Timor	121
	Myanmar	131
	Human Rights	148
	"A Community of Caring Societies"	154
4	Regional Security: The ASEAN Role	161
	The Sabah Question	164
	Zone of Peace, Freedom and Neutrality	166
	Treaty of Amity and Cooperation	167
	A Nuclear Weapons-Free Zone	168
	Opposing Vietnam	170
	The Indochinese Asylum-Seekers	174
	The South China Sea	180
	The ASEAN Regional Forum	189
	International Terrorism	198
	The New Members and Regional Security	201
	ASEAN+3, ASEAN Plus India, and the East Asia Summit	202
	Forum of Defence Ministers	205
	The ASEAN Security Community	206
5	Integrating the Regional Economy	212
	Before AFTA	213
	The ASEAN Free Trade Area	222
	Services	231
	Customs	233
	Product Standards	236
	Transport	237
	Tourism	240
	Labour	243
	Investments	244

	Stumbling on the Road to Integration	245
	On to the ASEAN Economic Community	250
6	**ASEAN and the World**	**256**
	ASEAN+3	264
	The East Asia Summit	269
	China	274
	India	290
	Japan	294
	Korea	307
	Australia	309
	New Zealand	315
	Australia-New Zealand Closer Economic Relations	317
	Russia	321
	The United States	325
	The European Union	329
	Canada	336
7	**The ASEAN Community: Is It for Real?**	**342**
	An Economic Community	342
	Getting Serious About Market Integration?	344
	Concrete Measures and Short Deadlines	347
	ASEAN Minus X and Two Plus X	352
	Empowered Regional Institutions	353
	An ASEAN Customs Union?	354
	The Security Community: Its Contents	355
	Setting New Norms	357
	Maritime Security	361
	Weapons of Mass Destruction	362
	Terrorism and Transnational Crime	364
	Defence Cooperation	364
	The ASEAN Regional Forum	365
	Cooperating with the UN	366
	The Security Community: Its Prospects	367
	A Socio-Cultural Community — Is It Necessary?	368
8	**What Kind of Future for ASEAN?**	**372**
	Of Institutions and Values	377
	An ASEAN Charter	381
	Moving ASEAN Now	384

Appendices

A.	The ASEAN Declaration	389
B.	Treaty of Amity and Cooperation in Southeast Asia	392
C.	Agreement on the Common Effective Preferential Tariff Scheme for the ASEAN Free Trade Area	402
D.	ASEAN Vision 2020	411
E.	ASEAN at a Crossroads	416
F.	Declaration of ASEAN Concord II	420
G.	Recommendations of the High-Level Task Force on ASEAN Economic Integration	429
H.	ASEAN Security Community Plan of Action	440
I.	The ASEAN Socio-Cultural Community (ASCC) Plan of Action	450

Interviews   463

Index   471

FOREWORD

I have great pleasure in writing this Foreword.

First, I am an old friend and admirer of the author, Rodolfo Severino. I admire the good work he did as ASEAN Secretary-General. I admire his accomplishments as a skilful diplomat of his country's foreign service. I admire him as a gentleman, a peace-maker and a man of goodwill. Recently, we had the pleasure of working together in the ASEAN–China Group of Eminent Persons. Rod, as we affectionately call him, Jusuf Wanandi of Indonesia and I were able to collaborate closely in the Group and to make a modest contribution to its work.

Second, this important book is being published at an important moment in the life of ASEAN. After thirty-eight successful years, the Association has recently established a Group of Eminent Persons (EPG) to make recommendations for an ASEAN Charter. The members of the EPG will find many thoughtful essays in this book on issues which are on their agenda, for example, should all ASEAN decisions continue to be made by consensus, should Timor-Leste be admitted into ASEAN, how to bridge the gap between the older and more developed members and the newer and less developed ones, should the principle of non-interference be watered down, should ASEAN become a more formal, more legal, more rule-based organization, how to accelerate the pace, breadth and depth of ASEAN integration?

Third, this book is also relevant to the increasingly important role which ASEAN plays in bringing the region together and in bringing the region and its external stakeholders together. The major powers of the region, China, India and Japan do not enjoy a high comfort level with one another. For this reason, it is not possible for any one of them to launch an initiative without arousing the suspicion of the others. ASEAN is not allied to any and is acceptable to all of them. ASEAN is also acceptable to the external stakeholders, such as the United States, EU, Australia, Canada and New Zealand. This is why ASEAN finds itself in the driver's seat of the ASEAN Regional Forum and of the newly inaugurated East Asia Summit. It is a great responsibility to be the driver, the architect of the evolving regional order. Rod Severino has several constructive ideas on how ASEAN can live up to this responsibility in Chapters 6 and 7 of the book.

In conclusion, I wish to congratulate Rodolfo Severino for writing this timely and important book. I am happy to commend it to the many constituencies of ASEAN. I wish the book success.

Tommy Koh
Singapore
21 February 2006

INTRODUCTION

I decided to write this book in order to contribute to a better understanding of the Association of Southeast Asian Nations. I believe that such a better understanding is important. From the beginning, the five founding countries of ASEAN — Indonesia, Malaysia, the Philippines, Singapore and Thailand — saw the need to band together as a region, not just by themselves but, ultimately, with the rest of Southeast Asia, so that they would no longer go into confrontation with one another, so that their disputes would not turn into conflict, and so as to have greater weight in an increasingly complicated and still dangerous world. More recently, with the admission of five additional members — Brunei Darussalam in 1984, Vietnam in 1995, Laos and Myanmar in 1997, and Cambodia in 1999, they have begun to realize that they must progressively, steadily integrate their economies if they are to remain competitive in the scramble for markets, including their own, and for investment capital. And then there are the problems that are regional in scope, transcending national boundaries, and, therefore, call for regional action — environmental degradation, communicable diseases, transnational crime, and natural disasters. Yet, there remains much misunderstanding about what ASEAN is and how it does things, what it has been meant to be and do, what it has done and what it has failed to do, what it can and cannot do, and the promise of what it could yet become and accomplish.

The purpose of this book, then, is to seek to clarify some of these things in the hope that people will come to appreciate not only the value of ASEAN but also what it could still do. To live up to its potential, ASEAN needs not only the vision and drive of Southeast Asia's leaders but also the understanding and pressure of a wider segment of its people.

The book does not narrate a chronology of ASEAN's development. It does not analyse the association or any of its endeavours within the framework of a theoretical construct. It does not probe deeply and in great detail into specific aspects of ASEAN or Southeast Asia. Many others have done these much more competently than I ever could, and I try not to duplicate their work. It does not attempt to cover the whole range of ASEAN cooperation — in labour, health, the environment, education, and transnational crime, for example — which is broad and still growing. Nor is this book my memoirs of my years in the ASEAN Secretariat. My life is much too uninteresting for that. Neither is it a tell-all account. ASEAN is remarkably free of salacious scandal. It also has few secrets.

What the book does is deal with individual issues that have been controversial or at least are interesting for people who take a serious interest in ASEAN and in Southeast Asian affairs. It deals, one by one, with the so-called "ASEAN Way", the question of membership, including the two-tier ASEAN that is supposed to have resulted from the entry of the four new members, the issue of non-interference, the role of ASEAN in regional security, regional economic integration, ASEAN's relations with external powers, the concept of an ASEAN Community, and what possibilities lie ahead for ASEAN. The book does not treat these issues as discrete subjects but strives to present them as inter-related elements of a coherent whole. Each chapter, however, can be read by itself, according to the reader's particular interests.

The book draws knowledge and insights not from the "literature", as more scholarly works do, but from my own experience and exposure and from interviews with personalities closely involved with ASEAN affairs. It is this knowledge and these insights that I wish to share.

Upon learning that I was working on this book, Professor Tommy Koh, Singapore's pre-eminent ambassador for all seasons, asked me what the readership was that I had in mind. I can say, in delayed response, that the book is for people who have some knowledge of Southeast Asia and are interested in it. Among them are academics, of course, both teachers and students, but not necessarily specialists. It is meant also for journalists, other persons concerned with the region or with public affairs in general, and, hopefully, policy-makers in Southeast Asia and elsewhere.

ABOUT THE AUTHOR

Rodolfo C. Severino is Visiting Senior Research Fellow at the Institute of Southeast Asian Studies in Singapore and a frequent speaker at international conferences in Asia and Europe. He writes articles for journals and for the press. He was Secretary-General of the Association of Southeast Asian Nations from 1998 to 2002. His speeches and other statements were published in *ASEAN Today and Tomorrow*. As a member of the faculty at the Asian Institute of Management in the Philippines in the school year 2003–04, he lectured on regional economic cooperation, the elements of competitiveness, and leadership in the management of change. Before assuming the position of ASEAN Secretary-General, Severino was Undersecretary of Foreign Affairs of the Philippines. In the Philippine Foreign Service, Severino was Ambassador to Malaysia from 1989 to 1992, chargé d'affaires at the Philippine Embassy in Beijing from 1975 to 1978, Consul General in Houston, Texas, and an officer at the Philippine Embassy in Washington, D.C. Between overseas postings, he worked as special assistant to the Undersecretary of Foreign Affairs and as Assistant Secretary for Asian and Pacific Affairs at the Department of Foreign Affairs. He twice served as ASEAN Senior Official for the Philippines. Before joining the Philippine Government, Severino worked at the United Nations and with Operation Brotherhood-Laos. He has a Bachelor of Arts degree in the humanities from the Ateneo de Manila University and a Master of Arts degree in international relations from the Johns Hopkins University School of Advanced International Studies. He has lived in six of the ten ASEAN member-nations, including his native country.

ACKNOWLEDGEMENTS

I said earlier that the purpose of this book was to share my knowledge of and insights into ASEAN and Southeast Asia. This presumes that I have learned something worth sharing about the region and about ASEAN.

For this, I am deeply indebted to the officers and staff of the ASEAN Secretariat, those who are still there and those who have since moved on, from whom I acquired an inestimable store of knowledge about ASEAN and who shared their insights with me during my tenure as Secretary-General from the beginning of 1998 to the end of 2002. Now led by Secretary-General Ong Keng Yong, members of the Secretariat and their newer colleagues helped in countless ways in the writing of this book. I learned much simply by living for five years among the people of Indonesia and by interacting with the Indonesian Government — under four Presidents — and many sectors of Indonesian society. I am, of course, grateful to the heads of government of the ASEAN member-countries and to their ministers and officials, from whom I learned a great deal, and to the business leaders and the activists in non-governmental organizations, who have prodded ASEAN to live up to its potential, including during my service in the ASEAN Secretariat.

I learned much about ASEAN also from my colleagues in the Department of Foreign Affairs and other agencies of the Philippine Government when I served as ASEAN Senior Official for the Philippines in 1987–89 and 1992–97 and as Ambassador to Malaysia in 1989–92. Needless to say, my interaction with the government and people of Malaysia during my tour in Kuala Lumpur added substantially to what I know about the region. Living in Phnom Penh in the first half of 2003, as adviser to the Ministry of Foreign Affairs and International Cooperation, was extremely useful for the same purpose.

In particular relation to the writing of this book, I am extremely grateful to the Institute of Southeast Asian Studies, under the leadership of its director, Ambassador K. Kesavapany, a long-time friend and colleague, for the support, in many forms, that it gave me in writing this book during my fellowship at the Institute from December 2003 to February 2004, and since May 2004. The atmosphere at the Institute, at once relaxed and intense, was ideal for intellectual pursuits, including work on contemporary affairs. The library, with its half a million items, is a paradise for any researcher on Southeast Asia. The presence of so many learned and helpful scholars in the institute was, of course, a great advantage. I am grateful to them for their help, encouragement and friendship. I am thankful, too, to Triena Ong and her colleagues in the ISEAS Publications Unit for shepherding the book to the light of day with great professionalism, competence and creativity.

Beyond ISEAS, the active intellectual life in Singapore and the many opportunities to interact with scholars and other people concerned with Southeast Asia, resident and visiting, were of enormous value.

I thank the Ministry of Foreign Affairs of Singapore, under the leadership of Professor S. Jayakumar, and in particular Brigadier General Tan Chin Tiong, then Permanent Secretary and now Ambassador to Japan, followed by Brigadier General (NS) George Yeo and Peter Ho, respectively, for endorsing my fellowship at ISEAS and for other forms of support.

I deeply appreciate the time and facilities that the Asian Institute of Management in Makati made available to me in the year that I was on the faculty of AIM. I owe a debt of gratitude to many in AIM, but I wish to mention specifically its President, Roberto de Ocampo, the Dean of the Institute at the time, Nieves Confesor, and Sophia Noreen S. Castillo, my research assistant for this book during that period.

I owe special thanks to the many people who gave so much of their time and insights in interviews with me. It is not only the time and the trouble that they took for which I am grateful; it is, above all, their willingness to share their views, their candor, and their wisdom. The list of the interviewees is at the end of the book. If I have omitted any of them, I apologize.

I am deeply indebted to Professor Tommy Koh for taking the time and trouble to write the Foreword, a major contribution to the book's purposes. I am grateful, too, to the colleagues and friends who expended time and effort to make detailed and incisive comments on parts of the draft and pointed out its inaccuracies, including Ong Keng Yong, Nugroho Wisnumurti, Sheng Lijun, Tin Maung Maung Than, Robert H. Taylor, and K. Kesavapany. Needless to say, none of them is to blame for the many shortcomings of the book, for which I alone am responsible.

Far from least, I am profoundly grateful to my wife, Weng, who, for many months, looked after our daughter Rhoda in Manila and dealt by herself with other family concerns for much of the time that I was on the fellowship in Singapore and in many other ways gave me the space, the support, the encouragement and the love without which the book could not have been done.

GLOSSARY

AADCP	ASEAN Australia Development Cooperation Programme
AAECP	ASEAN Australia Economic Cooperation Programme
ADB	Asian Development Bank
ADMM	ASEAN Defence Ministers Meeting
AEC	ASEAN Economic Community
AEM	ASEAN Economic Ministers
AEMM	ASEAN-EU Ministerial Meeting
AFP	Agence France-Presse
AFTA	ASEAN Free Trade Area
AHTN	ASEAN Harmonized Tariff Nomenclatures scheme
AIA	ASEAN Investment Area
AIC	ASEAN Industrial Complementation scheme
AICO	ASEAN Industrial Cooperation program
AIJV	ASEAN Industrial Joint Ventures
AIP	ASEAN Industrial Projects
AMBDC	ASEAN Mekong Basin Development Cooperation
AMEICC	AEM-METI Economic and Industrial Cooperation Committee
AMM	ASEAN Ministerial Meeting
APEC	Asia Pacific Economic Cooperation
APRIS	ASEAN Programme for Regional Integration Support (EU)
ARF	ASEAN Regional Forum
ARF SOM	ASEAN Regional Forum Senior Officials Meeting
ASA	Association of Southeast Asia
ASC	ASEAN Standing Committee

ASEAN	Association of Southeast Asian Nations
ASEAN-4	ASEAN's four newer members: Cambodia, Laos, Myanmar and Vietnam
ASEAN-6	ASEAN's six older members: Brunei Darussalam, Indonesia, Malaysia, the Philippines, Singapore and Thailand
ASEAN+3	ASEAN and China, Japan and the Republic of Korea
ASEAN CCI	ASEAN Chambers of Commerce and Industry
ASEAN-ISIS	ASEAN Institutes of Strategic and International Studies
ASEANAPOL	ASEAN Chiefs of Police
ASEF	Asia Europe Foundation
ASEM	Asia Europe Meeting
ATF	ASEAN Tourism Forum
AU	African Union
BCII	Bali Concord II or Declaration of ASEAN Concord II
BIMP EAGA	Brunei Darussalam-Indonesia-Malaysia-Philippines East ASEAN Growth Area
B-to-B	Brand-to-Brand Complementation scheme
BWC	Biological Weapons Convention
CEP	Closer Economic Partnership (between ASEAN and Australia and New Zealand)
CEP	Comprehensive Economic Partnership (between ASEAN and Japan)
CEPT	Common Effective Preferential Tariff scheme for AFTA
CER	Closer Economic Relations (between Australia and New Zealand)
CGDK	Coalition Government of Democratic Kampuchea
CLMV	Cambodia, Laos, Myanmar and Vietnam
COMECON	Council for Mutual Economic Cooperation
CPP	Cambodian People's Party
CSCAP	Council for Security Cooperation in the Asia Pacific
CWC	Chemical Weapons Convention
DSM	Dispute Settlement Mechanism
EAEC	East Asia Economic Caucus
EAEG	East Asia Economic Group
EAS	East Asia Summit
EASG	East Asia Study Group
EAVG	East Asia Vision Group
EC	European Community, European Communities, or European Commission

EEC	European Economic Community
EAI	Enterprise for ASEAN Initiative (U.S.)
ESCAP	UN Economic and Social Commission for Asia and the Pacific
EU	European Union
EURATOM	European Atomic Energy Community
FAO	Food and Agriculture Organization of the United Nations
FDI	Foreign direct investment
FTA	Free trade area
FUNCINPEC	Front Uni National pour un Cambodge Indépendant, Neutre, Pacifique et Coopératif (National United Front for an Independent, Neutral, Peaceful and Cooperative Cambodia)
GATT	General Agreement on Tariffs and Trade
GDP	Gross domestic product
GMS	Greater Mekong Sub-region
GSP	Generalized System of Preferences
HLTF	High-Level Task Force on ASEAN Economic Integration
IAEA	International Atomic Energy Agency
IAI	Initiative for ASEAN Integration
ICJ	International Court of Justice
ICMI	Ikatan Cendekiawan Muslim se-Indonesia (Association of Indonesian Muslim Intellectuals)
ICT	Information and communications technology
IDPAS	Institutional Development Programme for the ASEAN Secretariat (EU)
ILO	International Labour Organization
IMF	International Monetary Fund
INTELEX	Intelligence exchange (ASEAN)
INTERFET	International Force for East Timor
ISEAS	Institute of Southeast Asian Studies (Singapore)
IT	Information technology
KR	Khmer Rouge
LIPI	Lembaga Ilmu Pengetahuan Indonesia (Indonesian Institute of Sciences)
MAPHILINDO	Malaysia, Philippines and Indonesia
MERCOSUR	Mercado Común del Sur (Common Market of the South)
MFN	Most Favoured Nation
MRA	Mutual Recognition Arrangement

MRC	Mekong River Commission
NAFTA	North American Free Trade Agreement
NAM	Non-Aligned Movement
NGO	Non-governmental organization
NLD	National League for Democracy (Myanmar)
NPT	Nuclear Non-Proliferation Treaty
NZ$	New Zealand dollar
OAS	Organization of American States
ODA	Official Development Assistance
ODP	Orderly Departure Programme
PMC	ASEAN Post-Ministerial Conferences
PMC SOM	Senior Officials Meeting of the Post-Ministerial Conferences
PTA	Preferential Trading Arrangements
REPSF	Regional Economic Policy Support Facility (Australia)
RM	Malaysian ringgit
RMB	Renminbi (People's Money), China's currency
S$	Singapore dollar
SAARC	South Asian Association for Regional Cooperation
SARS	Severe Acute Respiratory Syndrome
SCCAN	Special Coordinating Committee of ASEAN Nations
SEANWFZ	Southeast Asia Nuclear Weapons-Free Zone
SEATO	Southeast Asia Treaty Organization
SEOM	Senior Economic Officials Meeting (ASEAN)
SKRL	Singapore-Kunming Rail Link
SLORC	State Law and Order Restoration Council (Myanmar)
SOM	Senior Officials Meeting
SPDC	State Peace and Development Council (Myanmar)
TAC	Treaty of Amity and Cooperation in Southeast Asia
TIFA	Trade and Investment Framework Agreement (ASEAN-U.S.)
TREATI	Trans-Regional EU-ASEAN Trade Initiative
UMNO	United Malays National Organization (Malaysia)
UN	United Nations
UNCTAD	United Nations Conference on Trade and Development
UNDP	United Nations Development Programme
UNEP	United Nations Environment Programme
UNESCO	United Nations Educational, Scientific and Cultural Organization
UNGA	United Nations General Assembly

UNHCR	United Nations High Commissioner for Refugees
UNICEF	United Nations Children's Fund
UNIDO	United Nations Industrial Development Organization
UNTAC	United Nations Transitional Authority in Cambodia
UNTAET	United Nations Transitional Authority for East Timor
US	United States of America
US$	United States dollar
USSR	Union of Soviet Socialist Republics
USTR	United States Trade Representative
VAP	Vientiane Action Programme
WHO	World Health Organization
WTO	World Trade Organization
ZOPFAN	Zone of Peace, Freedom and Neutrality

1

THE "ASEAN WAY"
Its Nature and Origins

In the early days of August 1967, five men, ministers representing the governments of five Southeast Asian countries, gathered in the beach resort of Bangsaen, less than a hundred kilometres southeast of Bangkok, to play golf and tell stories and jokes. They also went about the serious business of founding a new association for Southeast Asia and arguing over the contents of the declaration that would bring it about.

One of them was Adam Malik, "Presidium Minister for Political Affairs" and Foreign Minister of the New Order in Indonesia under General Soeharto. Soeharto had taken over the presidency from President Sukarno in March 1967. Sukarno had been eased out of actual power the year before, following the coup attempt of September 1965 and the massive bloodbath that ensued. The Sumatran firebrand of the Indonesian revolution, Adam Malik was, with Soeharto and Sultan Hamengku Buwono IX of Yogyakarta, one of the triumvirate at the head of the New Order, and would be the President, in 1971–72, of the United Nations General Assembly.

There was Tun Abdul Razak, then Deputy Prime Minister, Minister for Defence and Minister for National Development, second-in-command to Tunku Abdul Rahman, the father of Malaysia. He was, two years later, to be entrusted with the operation of emergency rule that would be imposed on the country after the race riots of May 1969. In that capacity and, eventually, as the Tunku's successor as Prime Minister, he led the work of laying the foundations for ensuring that such inter-ethnic conflicts would not happen again.

Narciso Ramos, the Secretary of Foreign Affairs of the Philippines, had been a journalist, an anti-Japanese guerrilla fighter, legislator and diplomat (Minister-Counsellor in Washington, D.C., and Ambassador in Buenos Aires,

New Delhi and Taipei). He was the father of Fidel Ramos, then an officer in the Philippine Civic Action Group in Vietnam and, much later, President of the Philippines.

S. Rajaratnam was one of the group of statesmen, led by Lee Kuan Yew, who founded modern Singapore. Born in his parents' native country, then called Ceylon, Rajaratnam grew up in Malaya, went to school in Malaya and Singapore, and studied law at King's College in England. After some years as a fiery editorial writer in several Singapore newspapers, he entered politics, becoming Minister for Culture. He was the first Foreign Minister of independent Singapore, serving as such until 1980, when he was elevated to Deputy Prime Minister.

The fifth was the host, Thanat Khoman, Thailand's long-serving Foreign Minister, diplomat *par excellence*, mentor of a whole generation of Thai diplomats, tireless worker for reconciliation in Southeast Asia, and resolute promoter of Thailand's security and other interests.

On the golf course in Bangsaen and tie-less on easy chairs, the five men engaged in the convivial banter, the jocular repartee and the warm give-and-take that have characterized multilateral diplomacy in Southeast Asia ever since. As Thanat Khoman described it almost 37 years later, they played golf in the morning, had meetings in the afternoon and gathered for informal dinner in the evening.[1] The discussions continued in Thanat's Bangkok residence, where he still lives, now in his nineties. The relaxed atmosphere prevailed even in the storied and elegant setting of Bangkok's Saranrom Palace, until a hushed solemnity descended on the small gathering of diplomats and functionaries, as the five ministers, now in business suits, signed the two-page declaration that is the founding document of the Association of Southeast Asian Nations. It was 8 August 1967.

The warm and congenial interaction among the five men, who had become friends despite their highly disparate personalities, contrasted sharply with — indeed, masked — the tensions that had marked and continued to loom over the relations between their countries. Indonesia had just ended its *konfrontasi* with Malaysia and Singapore over the formation of Malaysia in 1963. Malaysia and Singapore had recently — in 1965 — undergone a bitter separation. The Philippines continued to lay claim to the territory of North Borneo, which, as Sabah, had been incorporated into Malaysia as a component state. Thailand was not involved in any of these disputes, and thus was able to play the role of conciliator. But Thailand felt vulnerable to other threats — the conflicts in neighbouring Vietnam, Laos and Cambodia and a communist insurgency within — threats also felt by all the other countries represented in Bangkok. At the same time,

China posed a broader strategic threat, with the convulsions of the Great Proletarian Cultural Revolution, the Chinese propaganda organs' strident denunciations of the non-communist Southeast Asian regimes, and China's at least verbal support for the communist insurgencies.

The document signed by the ministers of what is sometimes referred to as "maritime Southeast Asia", plus Thailand, was extremely simple.[2] Made up of only two pages, it envisioned joint endeavours "to accelerate economic growth, social progress and cultural development"; "regional peace and stability through abiding respect for justice and the rule of law"; "collaboration and mutual assistance … in the economic, social cultural, technical, scientific and administrative fields … and in "educational, professional, technical and administrative" training and research; some broadly stated forms of economic cooperation; and the promotion of Southeast Asian studies.

To carry this out, the ASEAN Declaration (Bangkok Declaration) sketched out a rudimentary mechanism. The Foreign Ministers were to meet at least once a year, and a Standing Committee to manage the affairs of the association was to be made up of the Foreign Minister of the country hosting the meeting in a particular year as chairman and the ambassadors of the other ASEAN members to that country. Committees of "specialists and officials on specific subjects" were also envisioned. That was it.

The Bangkok Declaration, which is all that ASEAN has by way of a charter, did not have the usual legal formulations — effectivity clauses, ratification requirements, watertight stipulations, provisions for amendments, and so on. It did not set up compliance bodies, any other kind of supranational authority or a dispute-settlement mechanism. For the founding states, the Declaration was essentially an expression of their determination not to allow their disputes to develop into conflict and their resolve to work together for common purposes, purposes that at the time were only vaguely discerned and projected. It also embodied their intention to avoid getting dragged into the quarrels of the great powers then jockeying for position in Southeast Asia, and thus seek to take the regional destiny into their collective hands.

Perhaps because two predecessor-associations — the Association of Southeast Asia, or ASA, and MAPHILINDO — had not had much impact, the media took little notice of the Bangkok event. Perhaps, the media did not expect — and even the founding ministers were not so sure — that the ASEAN Declaration would create a regional organization that was to endure for thirty-eight years, is still going, now embraces all ten countries of Southeast Asia (not counting the new nation of Timor-Leste), and is looked upon, justifiably or not, as some kind of model for the developing world.

Before its 2004 demise as a weekly news magazine, the *Far Eastern Economic Review* was the closest thing that East Asia had to a regional journal of record. The *Review* apparently saw no need to send a correspondent to cover the event. It merely took note of ASEAN's founding in its *Far Eastern Roundup*, a "Weekly Summary of Events in South & East Asia" for 5–11 August 1967, under "Thailand".[3] The same issue, however, had an editorial welcoming, rather perfunctorily, the new association, saying:

> Although the *Review* has editorially lamented the proliferation of economic international organizations in the region, the recent establishment of yet another, the Association of Southeast Asian Nations (ASEAN), must be welcomed. The achievement of the five Foreign Ministers of the key countries involved — Indonesia, Malaysia, the Philippines, Singapore and Thailand — marks not only a joint realization of the need for co-operation in attaining economic and social goals but (as Singapore's representative has noted) a willingness to abandon some of their more extreme nationalistic stances. ...
> The crucial question is of course whether an agreement in principle to co-operate at an economic level can be translated into an agreement in practice — and here the developing countries have shown depressingly little willingness to subordinate immediate national advantage to long-term economic gains. Nevertheless, another declaration of good intent has been made, and another step in the right direction has been taken.[4]

Interestingly, in the next issue of the *Review*, one of its regular commentators at the time, Harvey Stockwin, perspicaciously — and prophetically — observed that "we must not forget that the Bangkok meeting was not produced by direct economic pressures, and therefore could not be expected to produce hard economic results".[5] This was to be true for at least the next twenty-five years.

On the other side of the world, the *New York Times*, too, did not consider the event important enough to cover, but in an editorial the next day, observed that it "fits into a healthy trend in the South Pacific", that is, countries formerly at odds with one another were now intending to cooperate. The editorial declared, "ASEAN holds special promise because it brings Indonesia back into the fold."[6]

SOUTHEAST ASIA IS NOT WESTERN EUROPE

Why did ASEAN take the route that it did, the route of informality, of eschewing legal formulations and legally binding commitments, of avoiding elaborate regional, supranational institutions? After all, Europe, pressed by similar, if much stronger, imperatives of avoiding war and cooperating for the common good, took a very different road. The European enterprise started with a supranational authority, the European Coal and Steel Community, and over the years set up increasingly elaborate and powerful supranational institutions through formal and binding treaties — the European Economic Community, which went into operation in 1958 and merged with the coal and steel and atomic energy communities in 1967 (the year of ASEAN's founding) to form the European Communities; then a Customs Union in 1968; the Single Market in 1992 (the year of the ASEAN Free Trade Area agreement); the decision to have a common foreign and security policy; and the European Union in 1993. Today twelve members of the European Union have a common currency in the euro. The European Central Bank, together with the national central banks of the "euro zone", implements monetary policy for the area. A constitution for the EU has been drafted, although it has floundered on rejections by the French and Dutch electorates. In terms of institutions, apart from the usual inter-governmental bodies, the Union has an elected European Parliament, the power of which, although limited, is increasing; a Court of Justice; and a massive European Commission that employs more than 22,000 persons, including 4,000 interpreters and translators, maintains resident diplomatic missions in many countries, dispenses foreign aid, and negotiates trade agreements with other states. All these are governed by binding treaties and directives that are legally enforced (and funded by an annual budget of over 100 billion euro).[7]

The different approaches of ASEAN and the EU, against which ASEAN is often measured, were dictated by the differences in the nature of the two regions, in the circumstances at the time of the founding of their respective associations, and in the relationships among the founding states.

Europe had just gone through a cataclysmic war, and the issues that set off that conflict had been swept aside by the very upheaval that the region underwent. At the very least, they were overshadowed by the threat from the Soviet Union to the east and the need for Western Europe to anchor itself on an alliance with the United States to the west. The requirements of American support for Western Europe's security and recovery, the need to stand together in the face of the Soviet threat, and the necessity of locking in the western half of a divided Germany to the rest of Western Europe impelled Europe's political and economic integration. Indeed, the need to ensure that the basic tools of war were harnessed only for peaceful purposes required their management by common, supranational bodies — the European Coal and Steel Community, agreed upon in 1951, and, later, in 1957, the European Atomic Energy Community (EURATOM).

On the other hand, the newly independent states of Southeast Asia had not warred against one another, having been under foreign domination for decades or centuries. The many wars between the mainland kingdoms had taken place in pre-colonial times. The disputes that marked the Southeast Asians' relationships as modern independent nations were largely outgrowths of their colonial legacies and the circumstances of their formation as states. Whereas inter-state issues among the Europeans had been largely settled, those among the Southeast Asians were just beginning to rankle.

Western Europe was propelled on the road to regional unity by the determination of its statesmen and peoples to prevent catastrophic wars from devastating the continent again, wars that had ravaged Europe for centuries, but most especially in the twentieth century. (Indeed, as Karoline Postel-Vinay, research director at the Centre for International Studies and Research, National Foundation for Political Science in Paris, has pointed out, the European experience is an example of how past conflict spurs regionalism rather than hinders it.)[8] Those wars were waged by dynasties, later by nation-states, and most recently by regimes driven by millennarian ideologies; but the people of Europe, relatively speaking, remained basically united by a common civilization, culture and religion, religious differences having long before receded as a cause of war. A new Germany and a new Italy emerged from the war and the subsequent occupation in the same political mould as the states that they had warred on. The outcomes of World War II were clear-cut, the issues largely settled and the solutions accepted by all.

On the other hand, the mutual suspicions, tensions and conflicts between the new nations of Southeast Asia — at least the "maritime" parts of it — Indonesia, Malaysia, the Philippines and Singapore — involved the most sensitive and inalienable of human attributes, i.e., race, ethnicity and religion. Dynasties can be overthrown. Ideologies can be abandoned; how quickly, recent history has shown. International relationships shift in accordance with national interests and perceptions of those interests. One cannot change one's race or ethnic character. Religion is an intimate part of one's identity and is only very rarely abjured or replaced.

DIVERSITY AND FRAGILE RELATIONS

The colonial regimes, for the most part, determined the shape of what are today's Southeast Asian nations. Nation-states are supposed to subsume and transcend racial, ethnic and religious groups within their boundaries. But the new nations of Southeast Asia could not do this overnight; even much older nations, in Europe and elsewhere, have difficulty with it. The very newness of Southeast Asia's national experience and the fact that ethno-religious groups straddled national boundaries made the enterprise of nation-building extremely difficult.

Race, ethnicity and religion, as well as territorial disputes, were vital factors in the formation of most of the nations of maritime Southeast Asia and in the relationships among them as they emerged into independent nationhood. Certainly, racial, ethnic and religious proportions and balance were prime considerations in the formation of Malaysia and in Singapore's turbulent role in it — the city-state's membership in and separation from Malaysia. The creation of Malaysia, in turn, triggered Indonesia's *konfrontasi* against the new federation, Jakarta professing to see in the Malaysia project a plot by the West to weaken and even break up the new republic, as the Western powers tried to do at the time of decolonization through to the 1950s. Sabah's inclusion in Malaysia set off a row with the Philippines, which had (and still has, albeit in a dormant state) a claim of sovereignty to the territory. The communist insurgencies in Malaysia and Thailand had a heavy racial content. The Communist Party of Malaya was mostly Chinese in membership. The communist insurgency in northeastern Thailand was heavily ethnic Chinese in participation. The place of ethnic Chinese in Indonesian society has often been a sensitive issue in that country.

Although the change of regime in Indonesia in 1965 paved the way for the end of *konfrontasi*, the mutual suspicions engendered by it carried the potential for renewed conflict with Indonesia's neighbours. In fact, at the time of ASEAN's founding, Indonesia had yet to resume formal diplomatic relations with Malaysia or Singapore, and in a little more than a year Malaysia and the Philippines were to break diplomatic relations yet again. The unresolved issues left over from colonial times and arising from the tangled relations between Malaysia and Singapore are a source of occasional friction to this day. The Philippines' claim to Sabah was intertwined with the problems in the southern Philippines.

In a piece on ASEAN published in the July 2004 issue of the *Asia Europe Journal*, I pointed out:

> Southeast Asians had been interacting with one another through trade, religion, cultural exchanges and human contact long before the West came to colonize them; but they had no experience of inter-state cooperation as modern nation-states. Partly because of the differences in their colonial legacies, partly because of the discrepancies in their perceived interests as new nations, and partly because of their recent history of conflict and continuing potential for conflict, the relations among the Southeast Asian states, even with Indochina excluded, were fragile and delicate at best. The

considerable diversity among them exacerbated the fragility of their relations — the diversity of their historical experiences, cultures, religions and strategic outlooks.[9]

Southeast Asia was, and is, indeed, extremely diverse, much more than is Europe — diverse in race and ethnicity, diverse in the role of religion in political as well as social life, diverse in legal and political systems and modes of governance, diverse in levels of economic development and in approaches to development, diverse in values as well as in historical experience, culture, the practice of religion, and strategic outlook. Moreover, Southeast Asia's peoples hardly knew one another, having been cut off and kept isolated from one another by the colonial powers. On the other hand, Europe's nations and peoples had been interacting with one another through the rise and fall of dynasties and empires and the uninterrupted conduct of intensive trade. More immediately relevant, whereas the present-day countries of Western Europe all saw the Soviet Union as the principal threat and the alliance with the United States as the anchor of their security, the foreign-policy orientations of the five founding states of ASEAN varied widely, particularly with respect to U.S. actions in Indochina, the role of military alliances, and the sources of external threat to their sovereignty.

In fact, despite the relaxed and convivial, even jocular, atmosphere of the Bangsaen and Bangkok talks, the negotiations on the Bangkok Declaration were arduous, according to some recollections of the event. Apparently the most contentious was the statement in the preamble "affirming that all foreign bases are temporary and remain only with the expressed concurrence of the countries concerned and are not intended to be used directly or indirectly to subvert the national independence and freedom of States in the area or prejudice the orderly processes of their national development". As might be expected, it was Indonesia that insisted on a reference to foreign military bases in ASEAN's founding document. Despite the turnaround in much of Indonesia's foreign policy following the change of regime from the Sukarno era to Soeharto's New Order, Indonesians remained extremely sensitive to the presence of such bases in their neighbourhood. After all, Indonesia had evidence of American support for the Outer Islands separatist rebellions in 1958, support launched most prominently from U.S. bases in the Philippines. Indonesia's objections to the formation of Malaysia in 1963 arose at least partly from its fear of having British forces lingering at its doorstep. The attempt by the Dutch, first, to re-occupy Indonesia at the end of World War II and, then, to promote its division, remained fresh in the Indonesian memory. According to the Indonesian scholar Dewi Fortuna Anwar, Jakarta felt compelled to have these concerns reflected in the ASEAN Declaration in order to reassure Indonesians that the new government had not abandoned its "free and active" foreign policy and departed from Indonesia's cherished attachment to non-alignment.[10] The Philippines, with its massive American military bases, and Singapore, with British forces on its soil, were uncomfortable with a bald reference to the "temporary" nature of foreign military bases. The joint statement issued by Presidents Sukarno and Macapagal and Prime Minister Tunku Abdul Rahman in Manila on 5 August 1963, on the occasion of the launching of MAPHILINDO, had this to say:

> The three Heads of Government further agreed that foreign bases — temporary in nature — should not be allowed to be used directly or indirectly to subvert the national independence of any of the three countries. In accordance with the principles enunciated in the Bandung Declaration, the three countries will abstain from the use of arrangements of collective defence to serve the particular interests of any of the big powers.

The original draft of the corresponding paragraph of the ASEAN Declaration of August 1967 was almost identical to this. The qualification that the bases were present with the "expressed concurrence" of the host countries and the dropping of the reference to collective defence arrangements serving big-power interests appeared to be an acceptable compromise. Although Thanat Khoman and some other participants do not recall much controversy over this issue, the fact that the ministers themselves had to spend three days working out the declaration indicated major disagreements that had to be resolved.

It was evidently with this in mind that Secretary Ramos declared in his statement at ASEAN's inaugural meeting:

> The Declaration we have just signed was not easy to come by; it is the result of a long and tedious negotiation which truly taxed the good will, the imagination, the patience and the understanding of the five participating ministers. That the Association of South East Asian Nations has become a reality despite all these difficulties only attests to the fact that ASEAN's foundations have been well and solidly laid.[11]

With the American military no longer in bases in the Philippines, the British having withdrawn their forces "East of Suez", the U.S. no longer so active militarily in the area, the Cold War over, and the configuration of power in East Asia having been transformed, the question of the bases has lost much of its relevance since ASEAN's founding. But at that time, it was a delicate question, highlighting the differences in strategic outlook among ASEAN's founding members and exacerbating the fragility of the relations among them. The Philippines had a formal mutual defence treaty with the United States and hosted the Americans' largest overseas military bases. Thailand based its alliance with the U.S. on the Pacific Pact and allowed U.S. forces to launch offensive military operations in Vietnam from bases in Thailand. Singapore was explicit in its support of the U.S. military presence in East Asia. Malaysia was non-aligned, as was Singapore, but was to be flexible enough to enter, with Singapore, the United Kingdom, Australia and New Zealand, into the Five-Power Defence Arrangement. Indonesia remained resolutely non-aligned, although, in the New Order, not stridently anti-West.

As an ultimate objective, however, all five were united by a common vision. With the United States thrashing around in Vietnam, the spasms of the Great Proletarian Cultural Revolution in China shaking the region, and the Soviet Union seeking to extend its influence, it was the vision of a region free from involvement in the quarrels of the strong — at least as a long-term aspiration.

In an interview with a group of Americans on the day that ASEAN was founded, Thanat Khoman explained the rationale for the new association:

> We want to be free, we do not want to be under the influence of anyone, large or small. We do not want to depend on the outside world, we want to depend on each and everyone of us. In other words, we try to create conditions of mutual help, to ensure our future destiny, we tried to work out our problems among ourselves. We do not want to be dictated (to) from Europe, or from America, or from Moscow, or from Peking, or from anywhere else.[12]

At the ASEAN Ministerial Meeting in 1971, the Philippines' Secretary of Foreign Affairs, Carlos P. Romulo, allowed himself to indulge in some historical speculation:

> In all probability the story of the South East Asia region would not be as it is now if in the sixteenth and nineteenth centuries when foreign powers penetrated into this region we already had a system of consultation — an Asia Forum — and the Philippines would certainly have a different history if the Philippines at the time of their national revolution had been able to ask assistance from a regional organization like the present ASEAN, so that we would not have felt so lonely and solitary as was the case.[13]

This is not an attempt to recount Southeast Asia's or ASEAN's history. It is merely an effort to explain how the diversity within and among the nations of maritime Southeast Asia (plus Thailand), their long isolation from one another, the circumstances of their formation, and the relations among them at the time of ASEAN's creation shaped the characteristics of the association and set what has come to be known as the "ASEAN way".

INFORMALITY AND LOOSE ARRANGEMENTS

What are ASEAN's characteristics, and what is the "ASEAN Way"?

The first characteristic was evident in the circumstances of ASEAN's founding and remains largely true to this day. It is the ASEAN preference, in advancing its causes, for informality and loose arrangements rather than treaties and formal agreements, its dependence on personal relations among leaders, ministers and officials and on peer influence (I hesitate to call it "peer pressure", as pressure is hardly ever exerted in ASEAN) rather than on institutions, and its reliance on consensus and on common interests rather than on binding commitments.

As I recalled earlier, the Bangkok Declaration, ASEAN's founding document, was a simple declaration of intent. It was not couched in legal terms, set up no regional institutions, and was not binding in a legal sense. In contrast, the Organization of American States and the African Union, like the European Union, are much more structured, with a Charter in the case of the OAS and a Constitutive Act in the case of the AU and clear and elaborate rules of procedure in both cases.

My piece in the *Asia Europe Journal* explains, "The delicate nature of the relations among the founding states of ASEAN dictated that the new association proceed very carefully, avoiding occasions for disputation and controversy — including the inherently contentious negotiation — and enforcement — of legally binding agreements."[14]

It was not until 1976 that ASEAN concluded its first formal agreement, when the five ASEAN leaders signed the Treaty of Amity and Cooperation in Southeast Asia.[15] The treaty committed the ASEAN nations to the usual norms of behaviour in the relations among states — national sovereignty and territorial integrity, non-interference in internal affairs, rejection of the use or threat of force, and the peaceful settlement of disputes. It called for economic and other forms of cooperation in rather general terms. The document also provides for a "High Council" of ministers (presumably, foreign ministers) that is to "take cognizance of the existence of disputes or situations likely to disturb regional peace and harmony" and, in case the parties to a dispute fail to settle it through negotiation, make recommendations on "appropriate means of settlement". The High Council may also constitute itself into a committee that is to help the parties arrive at a settlement. In every case, resort to the High Council or any action by it in respect of a dispute needs the consent of the parties to the dispute. Signing on to the treaty has been a requirement for the admission of new members in ASEAN. An amendment in 1987 made it possible for non-regional states to accede to what is known as the TAC, but with no right to participate in the High Council unless the non-regional state concerned is party to a dispute before the Council. Papua New Guinea signed on to the treaty in 1989. China and India acceded to it in October 2003, Japan and Pakistan in July 2004, and South Korea and Russia in November 2004. Mongolia and New Zealand signed the document in July 2005. Australia did so in December 2005.

It is ASEAN's supreme achievement that its members have generally observed the norms for inter-state conduct laid down in the treaty, thus avoiding conflict between them. However, no dispute between ASEAN states has ever been referred to the High Council. It was only in 2001, 25 years after the treaty was signed, that the ASEAN Foreign Ministers finally adopted the rules of procedure of the High Council. It was as if ASEAN had had little expectation that any member-state would invoke the treaty's mechanism anytime soon. To me, this is another manifestation of ASEAN's reluctance to invest the association with anything that may resemble supranational authority or involve it in bilateral disputes. Indeed, some have looked at this as an indication of the efficacy of the "ASEAN Way". Amitav Acharya, Deputy Director and Head of Research at the Institute of Defence and Strategic Studies in Singapore, has pointed out:

> Although this mechanism (the High Council) has never been invoked, this very fact has been cited by ASEAN leaders as indicating an enduring commitment to the non-use of force in intra-regional relations as well as a sign of the grouping's success in intra-mural conflict avoidance and management.[16]

In fact, in the early 1990s Indonesia tried to bring a territorial dispute to the High Council. Indonesia and Malaysia had been arguing since the 1980s over the question of sovereignty over two islets off the east coast of Borneo. Sipadan and Ligitan were under Malaysia's control but claimed by Indonesia. Hasjim Djalal, a former Indonesian ambassador, former director for research and development at the Department of Foreign Affairs, and leading expert on maritime issues, told me that, in talks over 1994 and 1995, Indonesia had suggested referring the dispute to the High Council of the Treaty of Amity and Cooperation. He recalled that the "interlocutors" then were Moerdiono, State Secretary of President Soeharto, and Anwar Ibrahim, then Deputy Prime Minister of Malaysia.[17] Malaysia refused, fearing, senior-level Indonesians involved in the negotiations have said, that the other ASEAN members would be partial towards Indonesia. After all, Malaysia had territorial disputes with all of its immediate neighbours. Kuala Lumpur proposed that the case be brought to the International Court of Justice in The Hague instead, where Indonesia was likely to lose. Recalling this development, Ali Alatas, long-time Indonesian Foreign Minister, told me that, to the dismay of his officials and against their advice, President Soeharto himself eventually decided to agree, on the ground that he did not want to burden "later generations" with this and similar problems.[18] The two countries reached formal agreement on submission to the ICJ in May 1997, the agreement coming into force a year later. The case was submitted to the World Court in November 1998, and in December 2002 the Court ruled in Malaysia's favor.[19] The maritime boundary, however, has not been delimited in accordance with the decision, a circumstance that led to a brief episode of naval sabre-rattling between the two countries in 2005.

Similarly, Malaysia has claimed sovereignty over three maritime features controlled by Singapore. These are Pedra Branca/Pulau Batu Puteh, Middle Rocks and South Ledge, collectively referred to as Pedra Branca in Portuguese and Pulau Batu Puteh in Malay, meaning White Rock. In February 2003, the two ASEAN members agreed to submit the case to the International Court of Justice, which they did in July. Proceedings are continuing.[20] In another case, also in 2003, after Malaysia raised concerns over the environmental impact of Singapore's reclamation activities in the Straits of Johor, the two sides took the matter to the International Tribunal for the Law of the Sea in Hamburg, which issued a ruling that allowed both sides to claim victory. The tribunal did not prohibit Singapore from continuing its reclamation but stressed that it was not to be done in a way "that might cause irreparable prejudice to the rights of Malaysia or serious harm to the marine environment". It also directed Singapore and Malaysia to form an independent group of experts to study the impact of Singapore's land reclamation and propose measures to deal with any adverse effects.[21] In November 2003, Malaysian and Singapore negotiators started discussing the implementation of the Court's directive, and in April 2005 the two parties reached a "full and definitive settlement of the dispute". Under the settlement, Singapore could continue the reclamation works in accordance with the ruling of the International Tribunal on the Law of the Sea but modify the design of part of the shoreline. Singapore gave assurances on "the smooth and safe passage of ships" through the affected areas and agreed to pay compensation amounting to RM374,400, or US$100,000 for Malaysian fishermen's "losses" and the cost of "scour protection" for one Malaysian jetty in the amount of S$300,000, or US$188,000. In this light, the two parties agreed to terminate the case and to "jointly request" the arbitral tribunal constituted in October 2003 to adopt the terms of the settlement agreement.[22]

The irony here is that, apart from Indonesia's failed attempt in the Sipadan-Ligitan case, ASEAN members have so far declined to use what is essentially a political body — the High Council — that would intervene in their disputes, but do so in the "ASEAN Way" — by recommendation, persuasion and friendly advice. And yet, when they are ready and determined to seek a definitive resolution of a dispute, they have gone to global judicial institutions whose decisions are legally binding. Or else, they have tried to do so through bilateral negotiations.

It is interesting to note the spin that Indonesia's Foreign Minister gave to Indonesia and Malaysia's recourse to the ICJ for the settlement of their dispute over Sipadan and Ligitan. In introducing his presentation of the Indonesian case, Minister Hassan Wirajuda told the Court:

> As you are aware, this is the first dispute that has been referred by Special Agreement to the Court by two ASEAN countries. This is a very significant development, Mr. President. The Court will probably be aware that, since the establishment of the Association of Southeast Asian Nations (ASEAN) in 1967, south-east Asian countries have preferred to settle their disputes *en famille*. That method has advantages: these countries were able to solve many, and in some cases even to shelve, disputes amongst them.
>
> However, it is encouraging that two ASEAN countries have shown their confidence in the Court as a fair and impartial arbiter of disputes as well. This reflects a growing maturity in the relations among countries in the region and in their efforts to promote a regional order, peace and stability through abiding respect for justice and the rule of law as stipulated in the ASEAN Declaration of 1967.[23]

Significantly, the minister added, "We hope, and indeed believe, that this step taken by our two countries will provide a precedent that will be followed in the peaceful resolution of similar territorial disputes in the region."[24]

In fact, bilateral disputes between ASEAN members have never been threshed out *en famille*, but, rather, either by bilateral negotiations or, now, by recourse to outside judicial bodies. On 29 January 2003, Cambodian mobs sacked the Thai Embassy and Thai business establishments in Phnom Penh in apparent outrage over the alleged remarks of Thai television actress Suvanant Kongying claiming ownership of Angkor Wat for Thailand, remarks that she subsequently denied making. As relations between the two ASEAN members progressively deteriorated, the ASEAN Secretary-General, Ong Keng Yong, reportedly suggested ASEAN help in cooling things. Cambodia basically told ASEAN to keep out of the quarrel. Phnom Penh eventually apologized to Thailand and agreed to pay compensation.

In the realm of trade, it is interesting to recall that the very first case brought to the World Trade Organization's Dispute Settlement Body involved two ASEAN countries — Singapore's complaint against Malaysia's "prohibition of imports of polyethylene and polypropylene" in 1995.[25] This took place a year before ASEAN agreed on its own dispute-settlement mechanism, although the relevance of this circumstance is doubtful, since, even if the ASEAN mechanism had existed at the time, the two disputants might have ignored it anyway.

Perhaps drawing on his familiarity with European and Latin American systems, the late Raul Manglapus, then Secretary of Foreign Affairs of the Philippines, on 24 July 1990 proposed to the ASEAN Ministerial Meeting in Jakarta the conclusion of an "ASEAN Treaty on Economic Cooperation" that would legally bind the member-states to their commitments on regional economic cooperation. Apparently caught by surprise, the Foreign Ministers, in their joint communiqué, "directed their senior officials, in coordination with senior economic officials and the Directors-General of the ASEAN National Secretariats to consider the setting up of a committee to study the need for a treaty or other framework for ASEAN economic cooperation for submission to the AEM for its consideration".[26] Note the veritable obstacle course: "*consider ... a committee to study* the need for a treaty *or other framework* for ASEAN economic cooperation for" the "*consideration*" of the ASEAN Economic Ministers (emphases mine). Such a pile of cautious conditions could have killed the proposal right there. However, the ASEAN Standing Committee, meeting in Kuala Lumpur in September 1990, requested the Philippines to prepare a concept paper on its proposal and within a month submit it to ASC, which would in turn give it to the Senior Economic Officials.

A draft of the concept paper that I have seen noted the "slow progress in liberalization of intra-ASEAN trade as evidenced by the non-implementation of the Agreement on the Standstill and Roll-back of Non-Tariff Barriers and by the non-adherence to agreed time frames of implementation of commitments under the Preferential Trading Arrangements" and the "lack of significant progress in attempts at greater harmonization of national policies and plans". It cited a similar sluggishness in carrying out the ASEAN Industrial Projects and ASEAN Industrial Joint Ventures schemes. As conceived in the draft, the proposal would create a "cohesive and juridical regional group similar to the European Community", with "supranational institutions similar to the EC Commission and Council", leading to "the adoption of a higher form of regional economic cooperation".[27]

I have been unable to track down the final text of the concept paper, but the joint communiqué of the 1991 ASEAN Ministerial Meeting did note that the Standing Committee, the Senior Officials, the Senior Economic Officials and the Secretary-General had "considered" the proposed economic treaty. The next paragraph stated:

> The Foreign Ministers welcome as a matter for serious consideration the initiative of His Excellency the Prime Minister of Thailand, which was supported by the Honourable Prime Minister of Malaysia, that ASEAN moves towards a Free Trade Area by the turn of the century and agreed that the Senior Officials of ASEAN undertake further study and discussion for submission to the forthcoming ASEAN Summit.[28]

Meanwhile, ASEAN had commissioned, with the support of the United Nations Development Programme, a study on "ASEAN Economic Cooperation for the 1990s". This led directly to the Agreement on the Common Effective Preferential Tariff (CEPT) Scheme for the ASEAN Free Trade Area (AFTA), signed at the ASEAN Summit in Singapore in January 1992.[29] While less comprehensive than the treaty envisioned in the Philippine proposal, the AFTA agreement was perhaps both more practical, being narrower in scope, and more far-reaching, not merely making current commitments legally binding but venturing into new territory, going for across-the-board liberalization of regional trade in goods.

To ASEAN's credit, and with prodding from the ASEAN Secretariat and gentle nudges from one another, ASEAN members have, at least as far as tariff-cutting is concerned, fulfilled their commitments under the agreement by enacting the requisite annual national legislation. Despite the legislation, however, some ASEAN members have complained about the devious ways in which customs authorities in other ASEAN countries have continued to deny AFTA treatment to intra-ASEAN trade. Moreover, little progress is being made in carrying out the commitment under the AFTA agreement to remove non-tariff barriers. (This will be discussed further in Chapter 5.)

Legally binding, too, is the treaty on the Southeast Asia Nuclear Weapons-Free Zone, referred to as SEANWFZ (pronounced shaun fizz), which the Southeast Asian leaders signed on the occasion of the 1995 ASEAN Summit.[30] A commission made up of the signatories' Foreign Ministers is designated to oversee the implementation of and ensure compliance with the treaty. This treaty is interesting in that it departs in two ways from the ASEAN practice of making decisions by consensus. First, the treaty required only seven ratifications for it to enter into force. Thus, for some months, the Philippines, the last of the signatories to ratify the document, sat in on meetings of the SEANWFZ commission only as an observer. The significance of this was merely symbolic, however, since the commission had not, has not, and probably never will, come to the point of making decisions on more than procedural matters. Secondly, the treaty provides for voting by the commission (with a two-thirds majority required) in case consensus cannot be reached, something unheard of in ASEAN bodies until then. It is unlikely, however, that any issue will be brought to such a vote anytime soon.

Another significant binding agreement came in 2002, the ASEAN Agreement on Transboundary Haze Pollution.[31] Apart from the importance and urgency of its subject, it is noteworthy for several reasons. First, it commits member-states to undertake national action to prevent acts in their territories that threaten other member-countries with haze pollution. Secondly, like the SEANWFZ treaty, it needed less than ten ratifications for it to enter into force; six ratifications were enough. I remember the time in 2001, when a ministers-only session of the ASEAN environment ministers was discussing, with some tension, the draft of the proposed haze agreement. The ministers were worried that requiring all ten ASEAN members to ratify the treaty would take too long. After all, the most serious haze-pollution episode had taken place in 1997–98 and could happen again at any time. I then brought up the precedent that the SEANWFZ treaty had set, that of requiring less than ten ratifications. If the environment ministers had insisted on total consensus, ASEAN would today still not have a binding agreement that addresses probably the severest transnational environmental threat ever to face the region. Some people who follow ASEAN affairs point out that the utility of the agreement is vitiated by the fact that Indonesia is not among the seven signatories that have ratified it when the agreement entered into force[32] and is, therefore, not legally and technically bound by it. Yet, Indonesia is the one country that has to comply with its provisions if the agreement is to be effective at all.[33]

ASEAN has other arrangements that are technically binding, like the ASEAN Tourism Agreement of 2002 and a variety of framework agreements; but most of them need implementing agreements to carry out, and few have been concluded or even negotiated.

Thus, ASEAN has had a number of binding agreements, but these are few and far between. Except for the tariff-reduction provisions of the AFTA treaty and some elements of agreements pertaining to customs and product standards, they either have not been carried out, like the ASEAN Tourism Agreement, the ASEAN Framework Agreement on Services, the ASEAN

Framework Agreement on the Facilitation of Goods in Transit, and the ASEAN Investment Area agreement, or have not been invoked, like the High Council of the Treaty of Amity and Cooperation and the dispute-settlement mechanism for the economic agreements.

ASEAN has no formal charter. As pointed out earlier, the association's founding document is merely a two-page declaration. ASEAN Secretary-General Ong Keng Yong has lamented that, because of this, member-states cannot extend tax privileges to private donations to ASEAN or its Secretariat; ASEAN and the Secretariat, therefore, have not been able to resort to private funding to augment the association's finances.[34] In 1974, the Philippines proposed a "charter" for ASEAN, which the ministers promptly consigned to the ASEAN Standing Committee. Thirty years later, at the June 2004 ASEAN Ministerial Meeting, work on an ASEAN charter moved forward, with the Foreign Ministers calling for the "development of an ASEAN Charter".[35] The next year, the ministers approved the draft of a declaration, which the ASEAN leaders issued at the December 2005 ASEAN Summit.[36] The declaration sketched out some elements for the charter and created an Eminent Persons Group that is to draw up recommendations for "the directions and nature of the ASEAN Charter".[37] The leaders would then "consider their recommendations at our subsequent meetings". As discussed in Chapter 8, the charter could be an opportunity to expand ASEAN's formal rules and strengthen its institutions, as well as set its future direction and, as indicated in the leaders' Kuala Lumpur declaration, even define the principles for which it stands.

"A PACE COMFORTABLE TO ALL"

The relative rarity of legally binding agreements in ASEAN is a product of the member-states' preference for caution and gradualism in developing regional institutions. "At a pace comfortable to all" is a favourite phrase in ASEAN documents, which means advancing as fast, or as slowly, as the most reluctant or least confident member allows. It was nine years after its founding that ASEAN held its first summit meeting, when in February 1976 President Soeharto hosted the four other ASEAN leaders in Bali — Hussein Onn of Malaysia, Ferdinand Marcos of the Philippines, Lee Kuan Yew of Singapore, and Kukrit Pramoj of Thailand. Another summit took place in Kuala Lumpur in 1977 for the ostensible purpose of commemorating the tenth anniversary of ASEAN's founding. No summit meeting was convened until 1987; some say it was partly the member-states' reluctance to send their leaders to the country whose turn it was to host the next summit according to the alphabetical order. The third summit took place only after Ferdinand Marcos had been deposed and Corazon Aquino had taken over the Philippine presidency. At the Manila meeting, the ASEAN leaders agreed to convene "every three to five years, if necessary". In fact, the next summit took place in Singapore five years later, when the leaders decided to "meet formally every three years with informal meetings in between". Thus, they met again, in Bangkok, in 1995 and, informally, in Jakarta in 1996 and Kuala Lumpur in 1997. They convened "formally" in Hanoi in 1998 and "informally" in Manila in 1999 and Singapore in 2000. Finally, ASEAN realized that the distinction between "formal" and "informal" summits had become blurred, caused unending confusion, and no longer made any sense. Thus, starting with the 2001 Bandar Seri Begawan meeting, designated as the Seventh ASEAN Summit, there would no longer be such distinctions.

The point of narrating the sequence of ASEAN summit meetings is to illustrate the slow pace of ASEAN's institutional development. After all, in the history of regional associations, it is summit meetings that have usually driven the process of regionalism. ASEAN did not meet at the summit until nine years after its founding. Ten years intervened between the second and the third summits. Another five years were to pass before the fourth summit was convened. It was not until three years after that that the ASEAN leaders began to meet regularly every year. Thanks to the activism of Singapore and Thailand, the ASEAN leaders have, in addition, been gathering in special meetings to address certain urgent issues — East Timor in 1999, SARS in 2003 and the Indian Ocean tsunamis in 2005 — as well as summits with the UN Secretary-General in 2000 and 2005.

This leisurely pace is a manifestation of ASEAN's cautious and deliberate — and slow — approach to building regional institutions and to regionalism in general. Another is the fact that ASEAN did not have a central secretariat until nine years after its founding, when the ASEAN leaders, at their very first summit, the same summit where they signed ASEAN's first formal agreement, created the ASEAN Secretariat and laid down its structure and mandate. However, this does not mean that ASEAN's leaders did not envision a central secretariat early in the association's existence. Tunku Abdul Rahman, Malaysia's first Prime Minister, said in opening the third ASEAN Ministerial Meeting in the Cameron Highlands in December 1969, "It is also my hope and my dream that one day we might put ASEAN on a practical and organized basis by establishing a permanent Secretariat."

As a junior officer on the Thai delegation at Bangsaen and Bangkok, Pracha Guna-Kasem was present at ASEAN's birth. He was to move on to be Thailand's Permanent Representative to the United Nations, Ambassador to France, Permanent Secretary of the Ministry of Foreign Affairs and other diplomatic positions, and, having tried his hand in politics as a member of parliament for a Bangkok district, is now adviser to the governing Thai Rak Thai party. He says that it may have been helpful if a central secretariat had been set up from the start, even if a very small one to begin with. However, he acknowledges that trying to create a secretariat at ASEAN's delicate beginning might have set off a ruinous competition over its location.[38] Whatever the considerations, and whatever the leaders' dreams, the fact is that ASEAN did not have a central secretariat in its first nine years and strengthened it only after another sixteen.

It was only in 1973 that ASEAN began seriously considering such a central secretariat. At the 1973 ASEAN Ministerial Meeting, Malaysia's Deputy Prime Minister Tun Dr Ismail bin Datuk Abdul Rahman declared:

> ASEAN today is a mature and stable organization devoting its energies to a multitude of cooperative projects. The volume of activity has grown and will continue to grow with the admission of the northern States of Southeast Asia. This calls for a revision of our approach towards the question of establishing a permanent Central Secretariat. ... My delegation feels that the time is ripe for us to give serious consideration to the establishment of a permanent Central Secretariat for ASEAN so that our organization may conduct its cooperation more systematically.[39]

The joint communiqué of that meeting announced the decision of the ministers to establish a secretariat and appoint the heads of the ASEAN National Secretariats to study the matter and submit their recommendations to the ministers. The communiqué also noted Indonesia's offer to host the proposed secretariat "provided there was no such offer from other ASEAN member countries".[40] Apparently, the Philippines had made such an offer, as the joint communiqué of the 1974 ASEAN Ministerial Meeting had recorded the Philippines' withdrawal of its bid in favour of Indonesia and the ministers' decision to locate the secretariat in Jakarta.[41]

As created in 1976, the Secretariat was a body extremely modest in nature, size and function. According to the Agreement on the Establishment of the ASEAN Secretariat, signed at the first ASEAN summit in Bali in February 1976,[42] the "Secretary-General of the ASEAN Secretariat" (not of ASEAN) was to be nominated by member-states in alphabetical order for a term of two years (lengthened to three years in 1985). He was to serve mainly as "the channel for formal communications" between ASEAN bodies and between ASEAN and other organizations and governments — like a post office — and otherwise do what he was told. The agreement prescribed seven officers for the Secretariat and their respective areas of responsibility, each to be nominated by a member-state on rotation for three-year terms. An amendment in 1983 allowed for the addition of an unspecified number of officers.[43] In 1989, the position of Deputy Secretary-General was created, appointment to which was by government nomination in alphabetical rotation, and the functions of the three bureau directors were specified — one each to take care of economic, science and technology, and social and cultural matters.[44]

The Secretariat was expanded and strengthened to more or less its present form only in 1992, or 16 years after its creation, mainly to be able to manage the implementation of AFTA. Following the decision laid down in the Singapore Declaration,[45] which the ASEAN leaders issued in January 1992, the head of the Secretariat is now called the Secretary-General of ASEAN rather than the Secretary-General of the ASEAN Secretariat. He (so far it has always been a he) is nominated by the ASEAN Ministerial Meeting, formally appointed by the heads of government and "accorded ministerial status". On paper, he is supposed to be recruited openly, on the basis of merit, but in practice the post has, so far, been filled on the basis of alphabetical rotation among the member-countries. This is entirely consistent with ASEAN's determination to avoid even the possibility of contention. The Secretary-General was given an "enlarged mandate to initiate, advise, coordinate and implement ASEAN activities". This laid the basis for greater activism on the part of the Secretariat and the Secretary-General, which, however, has remained subject to case-by-case limits imposed partly by the member-states and partly by bureaucratic inertia. The leaders agreed to transform the international professional staff from persons nominated by their governments — and thus beholden to them — to officials "openly" recruited on merit and thus expected to be objective and loyal only to the organization. In my time as Secretary-General, we found it difficult to recruit qualified professional staff from several countries. Bruneians did not care to work outside their country. Singaporeans, like the Bruneians, generally did not find the salary scales at the Secretariat attractive, at least until the economic downturn in their country towards the end of the 1990s. There was an informal understanding that the governments of the four newer members could nominate two officers each to the Secretariat, at least for an initial term of three years, in order to ensure those countries' representation, presumably while they developed the capacity of their people to compete openly for Secretariat positions. However, partly because of continuing limitations on their human resources and partly because of their political systems, the practice of the governments of the newer members nominating their officials has persisted, with the partial exception of Vietnam. Needless to say, while politically convenient, this is a most unsatisfactory arrangement from the point of view of developing an independent, competent and professional secretariat.

Meeting in Manila five months after the Singapore summit, the ASEAN Foreign Ministers adopted a protocol formalizing the leaders' decisions on the re-structuring of the Secretariat, lengthening the Secretary-General's tenure to five years, and expanding the size of the professional staff at each level.[46] Interestingly, the protocol provides, "The Deputy Secretary-General shall be appointed by the Secretary-General, following open recruitment and selection by a panel, comprising of representatives of the Contracting Parties, under the Chairmanship of the Secretary-General."

Five years later, however, at a special meeting of Foreign Ministers in Kuala Lumpur on 31 May 1997, the member-states decided to add a second Deputy Secretary-General to the Secretariat roster, despite the misgivings of several of them. In so doing, ASEAN reverted to the old, overly politicized system of having the member-states nominate the Deputy Secretaries-General by alphabetical rotation. (A country one of whose nationals happens to be the Secretary-General has to defer its turn for a deputy position.)[47] Later, during a review of the "role and functions of the ASEAN Secretariat" that the ASEAN Standing Committee undertook in 1999 with the help of PriceWaterhouseCoopers, I sought to have the Deputy Secretaries-General selected by open recruitment and on merit, as the position was envisioned in 1992. One politically appointed official, the Secretary-General, was enough for such a small secretariat, I argued. The newer members resisted this proposal, evidently convinced that the present system was, until far into the future, their only chance of getting their people appointed to high-level positions in the Secretariat. In his farewell statement in 2002, Suthad Setboonsarng, outgoing Deputy Secretary-General, appealed to the ASEAN Economic Ministers to "professionalize the ASEAN Secretariat", meaning his position. However, it was not, and is not, for the Economic Ministers to decide these things but the Foreign Ministers.

(Meanwhile, the composition of the ASEAN Standing Committee, the body that oversees the administration of the association, its "functional cooperation" activities and external relations, had been changed by the 1992 Singapore summit. The Standing Committee no longer consists of the ambassadors to the host-country of the next ASEAN ministerial meeting but the directors-general of the ASEAN National Secretariats and the ASEAN Secretary-General, with the Foreign Minister of the host-country as nominal chairman.)

This narration of the evolution of the ASEAN Secretariat shows ASEAN's willingness to change, particularly in institutional terms, but in slow and gradual steps.

INSTITUTIONS FOLLOWING SUBSTANCE

Something significant is to be noted here. There have been periodic attempts over the years to build new ASEAN institutions and processes or to change existing ones. In 1982–83, a task force recommended the consolidation of ASEAN ministerial bodies, the replacement of the ASEAN Standing Committee with a Jakarta-based Committee of Permanent Representatives, and the establishment of an Advisory Committee on Policy Studies. In 1991–92, a five-man panel headed by Tan Sri Ghazali Shafie, former Foreign Minister of Malaysia, sought to organize ASEAN's heads of government into the Supreme Council of ASEAN. It repeated the recommendation for a Committee of Permanent Representatives, this time to be headed by the ASEAN Secretary-General and not necessarily to be based in Jakarta. In 1998, an Eminent Persons Group proposed that the heads of government take hands-on charge of ASEAN operations and stressed the importance of involving civil society and the business sector in ASEAN's work. In 1999, PriceWaterhouseCoopers drew up a set of elaborate recommendations to make the ASEAN Secretariat more effective.

All of these studies and recommendations made eminent sense and could be considered necessary from a logical point of view. They were all meant to strengthen and facilitate ASEAN cooperation and integration. The problem was that few of the proposals were eventually adopted. This was because the process had it all backwards. At least in ASEAN, institutions are built in order to support measures previously agreed upon for the attainment of common objectives. Usually, but not always, their creation does not lead to the adoption of such measures. In the history of ASEAN institutions, there have been a few landmarks. Most of them were the results of decisions, previously agreed upon, to take steps towards greater cooperation and deeper integration, often in response to changing strategic and economic conditions. Creating or changing institutions did not lead to such measures; it was the other way around, although the institutions may have subsequently influenced ASEAN's future course.

ASEAN's leaders met for the first time in 1976 in order to strengthen political solidarity and consolidate and advance economic cooperation, and for this purpose created the ASEAN Secretariat. In 1992, they decided to set up the ASEAN Free Trade Area; to administer it, they enlarged and strengthened the Secretariat. The end of the Cold War and the ensuing fluidity in the configuration of power in East Asia led to the creation of the ASEAN Regional Forum. It was in response to the shifts in regional economic power, in the global strategic situation, and in inter-state relations in East Asia that ASEAN initiated the ASEAN+3 process, to which the 1997–98 financial crisis gave further momentum. It was also the financial crisis that gave life to ASEAN and ASEAN+3 forums of Finance Ministers and central banks and impelled ASEAN and East Asian cooperation in finance. The High-Level Task Force on ASEAN Economic Integration in 2003 made some significant recommendations of an institutional nature, including the setting up of compliance bodies and a more independent dispute-settlement mechanism, but these were supporting components for the ASEAN Economic Community that was being envisioned. This followed the ASEAN Competitiveness Study by McKinsey & Co., which had called for the considerable strengthening of regional institutions in order better to support the deeper integration that it urged. Nevertheless, new institutions can lead to further developments in ASEAN's character and direction. It is to be assumed that the Eminent Persons Group on the ASEAN Charter, the officials who will draft it and, eventually, the ASEAN leaders will take these dynamics into account.

VULNERABILITY AND MUTUAL SUSPICIONS

In a conference in Paris, Delfin Colomé, a Spanish diplomat who was at the time Executive Director of the Asia-Europe Foundation, remarked that ASEAN's highly personal leadership had damaged its capacity for institution building.[48] That may be true; but it is also true that ASEAN's cautious approach to regional institution building and hence its reliance on personal relationships have arisen from the member-states' sense of fragility and weakness and from lingering suspicions of one another. Member-states invoke national sovereignty almost by reflex when they resist substantive measures or institutions in support of greater regional integration. The question of sovereignty, however, is, to me, a false issue. After all, any decision to adopt such measures or accede to such institutions is a voluntary sovereign act. Rather, I believe, resistance to more rapid and deeper integration and institutionalization has stemmed from a feeling of vulnerability to outside intervention and to possible external pressure to do things that may turn out to be contrary to the perceived interests of the state or its leaders. These are intervention and pressure that may come from fellow-members or from outside powers.

This sense of fragility, weakness and vulnerability has been particularly palpable in the period immediately following the birth of the nation or the installation of a new regime up to the early years of ASEAN membership. Singapore is an affluent but small city-state, a largely Chinese island in a sea of Malays, whose destiny is inextricably intertwined with that of Malaysia but which could not remain part of it. Malaysia was cobbled together from multi-ethnic, multi-racial components and from two territorial wings separated by the South China Sea, its creation initially opposed by two of its immediate neighbours, its relations with Singapore complicated by many complex factors. Indonesia emerged into independent nationhood dedicated to consolidating its "unity in diversity". By far the largest of the Southeast Asian states, Indonesia felt, particularly in its early years, vulnerable to centrifugal pressures, with the Dutch seeking first to reoccupy their former possession and then to foster its disunity. Covert support for separatism later came from the United States. Indonesia subsequently suffered the separation of East Timor and has been bothered by secessionist movements of varying strengths particularly in Aceh and Papua. The Philippines was closely involved militarily with the United States and, on that account, held in suspicion by Indonesia. For its part, the Philippines cast a wary eye on the growing influence of Indonesia's massive communist party. Brunei Darussalam, tiny in area and population, its territory split by a sliver of Malaysian soil, and immensely wealthy from oil and gas exports, had every reason to feel vulnerable.

Thanks partly to their rapid growth, partly to political change within them, partly to shifts in the global and regional strategic environment, and partly to their membership in ASEAN, the first six ASEAN members — Brunei Darussalam, Indonesia, Malaysia, the Philippines, Singapore and Thailand — have gained in self-confidence and in trust in one another — as well as consolidated their sovereignty and nationhood — although not sufficiently as to entrust their interests to regional institutions at more than a snail's pace. However, the four new members — Cambodia, Laos, Myanmar and Vietnam — now seem to be where the older six were in ASEAN's early years. In the years and decades before it joined ASEAN, Vietnam had been under occupation by or in conflict with far stronger powers — the French, the Japanese, the Americans, and, in different periods, the Chinese. ASEAN itself had opposed Vietnam's incursion into Cambodia in the 1980s, a step that Vietnam had presented as an act of self-defence. Cambodia and Laos had felt themselves squeezed between their stronger neighbours, Thailand and Vietnam. From the beginning, Myanmar had had trouble keeping the country together, with its hundred "nationalities" and ethnic groups; added to this in recent years have been pressures from the West and others in the international community, and even from within ASEAN itself, on the ruling military to relax, if not remove, its grip on power. All the newer members, as well as five of the six older members, had been, shortly before their ASEAN membership, under colonialism, the extreme form of interference in nations' domestic affairs.

All this probably explains the sensitivity not just of the newer members of ASEAN, but the older members as well, to the possibility of outside interference in their internal affairs to the detriment of the regime, if not of the country as a whole. The issue of non-intervention or non-interference, so often raised against ASEAN, is discussed in Chapter 3. The prospect of anything approaching supranational institutions is largely related to ASEAN members' sensitivity to this issue.

WHO IS ASEAN'S LEADER?[49]

This sensitivity to a possible erosion of the individual member-states' freedom of action, in turn, illuminates ASEAN's careful avoidance of real or apparent domination by any one member or group of members. This is related to the question of leadership in ASEAN. The question can be broken down into several: Has ASEAN had a leader? Who was it? Does it have one now? Who is it? Or is ASEAN leaderless? Has it always been? Is the question of leadership important? If so, how? How much of an impact does leadership — or the lack of it — have on the nature of ASEAN's objectives and on the direction and pace of ASEAN's progress towards them?

Since ASEAN's founding, and for thirty years thereafter, many commentators considered Indonesia as ASEAN's leader. In reaction to the change of regime in Indonesia in 1998, it was said that the removal of President Soeharto had deprived ASEAN of leadership. When Malaysia's Prime Minister, Dr Mahathir Mohamad, stepped down in October 2003, it was observed that "one of ASEAN's leaders" had departed. Now, it is said that ASEAN is leaderless.

In *The New Shorter Oxford English Dictionary*, 1993 edition, I looked up the definitions of leadership that seem most applicable in the ASEAN context. Here they are:

> Lead, transitive verb: Cause to go along with oneself; guide by persuasion as contrasted with commands or threats; guide with reference to action or

opinion; bring by persuasion or counsel to or into a condition; bring by argument etc. to a conclusion; induce to do.

Leader: A person who guides others in action or opinion; a person who takes the lead in a business, enterprise or movement; a person of eminent position or influence.

Let us see how these definitions help in identifying who or which country has been the leader in ASEAN. Let us go back to the beginning. ASEAN was conceived on an occasion when Thanat Khoman, the Foreign Minister of Thailand, was trying to broker reconciliation among Indonesia, Malaysia and the Philippines in April and May 1966. ASEAN's founding document, the Bangkok Declaration of 8 August 1967, was drafted largely by Thai diplomats. In this sense, Thailand was the leader in ASEAN's founding.

However, Indonesia could be said to be ASEAN's leader, too. It was Adam Malik and other Indonesian diplomats who were asked to draw up the concept paper for the new association. It was they who went around Southeast Asian capitals — Bangkok, Yangon, Phnom Penh and Manila — selling the idea of ASEAN. Adam Malik gave ASEAN its name. The other countries looked to Indonesia for leadership. It was not only the largest and most populous country in the region but had also been the most active in international affairs — convenor of the Asia-Africa summit in Bandung in 1955, a leader and founder of the Non-Aligned Movement, often speaking on behalf of the non-aligned and the developing countries on global issues, including high-profile disarmament questions. Indonesia's stature was such that it could not have just joined the Association of Southeast Asia, or ASA, which had been set up by Malaysia, the Philippines and Thailand in 1961; it had to be a founding member of a new organization. (It is interesting to recall that on 31 July 1967, just a week before ASEAN's founding, the sixth anniversary of ASA was reported as being ceremonially observed in Manila.[50] By 28–29 August, the foreign ministers of Malaysia, the Philippines and Thailand were meeting in Kuala Lumpur and agreeing to dissolve ASA and to turn over its projects to the three-week-old ASEAN.[51])

The leadership of Indonesia was evident in more subtle ways. It was, above all, President Soeharto's policies that enabled Indonesia to take this role. ASEAN would not have been formed with Indonesia in it had Soeharto not decided to end the Sukarno regime's confrontational stance in foreign affairs and instead seek good relations with the rest of the world, including the West, and particularly with its neighbours. Indonesia's transformation — domestically and in its foreign policy — made ASEAN possible. Later, ASEAN's efforts at economic cooperation and integration would not have gotten off the ground if Indonesia had not made its economy more open.

In fact, despite being the least industrialized among the ASEAN members at that time, Indonesia led the way in enlarging the margins of preference and broadening the coverage of the ASEAN Preferential Trading Arrangements in the early 1980s.

An important factor in ASEAN's success was another Soeharto decision, the decision not to throw Indonesia's weight around, not to be seen as seeking to dominate the region. Indonesia was able to exercise its leadership by not seeming to do so. Nana Sutresna, former Director-General for Political Affairs of the Department of Foreign Affairs of Indonesia, former Permanent Representative to the UN, then adviser to President Megawati Soekarnoputri, recalled how President Soeharto refused to be named as the "Father of ASEAN", which one of the member-states had proposed.[52]

On the other hand, Indonesia had to give way to Thailand and Singapore when ASEAN opposed the Vietnamese incursion into and military presence in Cambodia in the late 1970s and the 1980s. Indonesia had tried to moderate ASEAN's opposition both because of its sympathy for Vietnam's resistance to U.S. military intervention and because Indonesia considered China to be a bigger threat than Vietnam. In this case, Thailand, as "frontline state", with strong backing from Singapore, was clearly the leader of ASEAN.

However, Indonesia took the leadership in ASEAN's effort to seek a settlement of the Cambodian problem. It convened the "cocktail parties" among the four Cambodian factions. It hosted the Jakarta Informal Meetings. It co-chaired, with France, the Paris conferences that led to a settlement. ASEAN entrusted Indonesia with leadership in this case precisely because of its strong links with Vietnam. On the other hand, Indonesia was able to exercise this leadership because it had gone along with the others in diplomatically standing up to the Vietnamese in the name of ASEAN solidarity.

Another instance of Indonesia's leadership was the decision to push through with the third ASEAN Summit in Manila. A few months before the summit, a series of attempted coups d'état against the Aquino administration had made ASEAN governments nervous about sending their leaders to supposedly unsafe Manila. It was Soeharto's decisive position in favour of going ahead with the summit that swung ASEAN around. A more negative instance of Indonesian leadership was President Soeharto saying no to Prime Minister Mahathir's 1990 proposal for an East Asian Economic Group. Whatever Soeharto's reasons for doing so, failing to consult him beforehand certainly did not help.

Malaysia, too, has had moments of leadership. The declaration on the Zone of Peace, Freedom and Neutrality was adopted upon Malaysia's initiative and under its chairmanship of an ASEAN Foreign Ministers' meeting in 1971. The term ASEAN Vision 2020, adopted at the ASEAN Summit in Kuala Lumpur in 1997, is an echo of Malaysia's Wawasan 2020. The EAEG proposal, later softened to EAEC (East Asian Economic Caucus), has metamorphosed into "ASEAN+3", now a going concern, with annual summits since the 1997 summit meeting (which Malaysia chaired and hosted) and a growing number of ASEAN+3 ministerial and sub-ministerial forums. It was also in 1997 that Malaysia pushed for the admission of Cambodia, Laos and Myanmar to complete Southeast Asian membership in ASEAN. Upon Malaysia's suggestion, the 2001 ASEAN Summit devoted a session to the problem of HIV/AIDS in Southeast Asia.

Among the newer members, Cambodia took the lead in pushing the landmark ASEAN Tourism Agreement during its hosting of the 2002 summit. Prime Minister Hun Sen has also been at the forefront in the calls for greater coherence among the numerous programmes for the development of the Mekong Basin.

On the economic front, it was Thai Prime Minister Anand Panyarachun, who, in 1991, formally proposed, with the encouragement and support of Singapore's Goh Chok Tong and Malaysia's Mahathir Mohamad, that ASEAN enter into a free trade area, thus initiating the current stage of regional economic integration. With economic integration rising in the ASEAN agenda, particularly after the fourth summit in Singapore in 1992, Singapore seems to have steadily taken leadership in the association. Since then, almost all major initiatives in ASEAN have come from Singapore. It initiated the Asia-Europe Meeting, the Forum for East Asia-Latin America Cooperation and the ASEAN-India Summit. It took the ASEAN lead in moving for a free trade area between AFTA and the Closer Economic Relations of Australia and New Zealand, a project that was watered down to a "Closer Economic Partnership" but has now been revived in the form of an ASEAN-Australia and New Zealand free trade area. Singapore spearheaded the positive ASEAN response to the proposal for a free trade area between ASEAN and China. It introduced the concept of e-ASEAN, an initiative for using information and communications technology as both an object and an instrument of ASEAN's integration and for narrowing the digital divide between and within ASEAN countries. It was Singapore that gave the name Initiative for ASEAN Integration to the association's programme of assisting the newer members to close the development gap between them and the older members. Singapore drove the ASEAN decision to commission a study of ASEAN's competitiveness in the face of the growing competition from China and India and from other regional groups. It proposed the ASEAN Economic

Community as the envisioned next stage of regional economic integration. And it was Singapore that called for quick summit meetings among ASEAN leaders and with China's Premier to deal with the SARS outbreak in East Asia, a successful collective response to a regional emergency. Again, when the 26 December 2004 tsunamis wrought death and destruction in parts of Southeast and South Asia, it was the new Singapore Prime Minister, Lee Hsien Loong, who initiated a summit meeting that was billed as the "Special ASEAN Leaders' Meeting on Aftermath of Earthquake and Tsunami" but involved heads of government or ministers not only of the ASEAN countries but of most of its Dialogue Partners, other donor countries, and other victim countries as well.

Singapore's then Foreign Minister and now Deputy Prime Minister, Professor S. Jayakumar, explained to me that his country placed such high importance on ASEAN because, on account of its small size, anything that happened in the region affected Singapore and perceptions of Singapore, a condition that was less true of the larger ASEAN members. This is why, he said, before every ASEAN Summit, the Prime Minister would brainstorm with officials, primarily from the ministries of foreign affairs and trade and industry, on ways to make the summit a success and further advance the association's interests.[53]

As it hosted the 2003 summit, Indonesia again seized the initiative, with its idea of an ASEAN Security Community, partly in an attempt to balance off the Singapore-initiated ASEAN Economic Community. Subsequently, Indonesia led the drafting of the Plan of Action for the ASEAN Security Community, which the Foreign Ministers endorsed at their regular meeting in Jakarta in June 2004 and the leaders adopted at their summit in Vientiane in November. I understand that Indonesia was quite bold in some of its original proposals both for the elements of the ASEAN Security Community and for its Plan of Action. The Plan of Action approved at the summit is a bit disappointing, but Indonesia should get some credit for taking the leadership in this matter. This is discussed further in Chapter 7.

However, these days, the real test of leadership seems to lie in the move towards regional economic integration. Singapore has been at the forefront of this move — with ideas, drive, determination and interest. But it is deliberately taking a low profile lest its leadership be seen as blatantly self-serving. Thailand, too, regards regional integration to be in its interest. But its search for economic linkages nowadays seems to bypass ASEAN and reach out elsewhere — the Bangladesh-India-Myanmar-Sri Lanka-Thailand Economic Cooperation project, the Asian Cooperation Dialogue, the Ayeyawady-Chao Phraya-Mekong Economic Cooperation Strategy, the Asian

Bond Market initiative — all of them spearheaded by Thailand, all of them outside ASEAN and, indeed, with hardly any reference to it. Moreover, it is hard for Bangkok to exercise overt leadership in ASEAN in the face of the ambivalence of its immediate neighbours towards Thailand's role.

Indonesia seems to be best positioned to take the leadership in the drive toward ASEAN economic integration — not because it is ASEAN's "natural leader". Rather, it is because Indonesia's leadership cannot be said to be self-serving. It has its vast market to offer and open up. However, Indonesia does not seem to be confident of its ability to be competitive even within ASEAN — whether for investments or for markets. Particularly after Soeharto, Indonesia has seemed to be hesitant about regional economic integration. In his time, Soeharto sometimes transcended short-term interests, even going against the counsel of his advisers, for the sake of longer-term and larger purposes — for example, the improvement of the Preferential Trading Arrangements, the third ASEAN Summit in Manila, the Sipadan-Ligitan case, and the long deferment of the normalization of Indonesia's diplomatic relations with China.[54] Today, it depends on President Susilo Bambang Yudhoyono whether Indonesia can lead ASEAN on the road to regional economic integration, this time within the more constraining conditions of democracy and despite enormous domestic economic difficulties. This is important, not least because, on account of its size and prominence, Indonesia's stance on the regional economy heavily influences investor perceptions of the region as a whole.

So far, apart from Singapore, which is, however, understandably diffident, no leader has been pushing Southeast Asian economic integration. Because of the slow progress towards integration, ASEAN has agreed, with increasing determination, to move ahead on an "ASEAN Minus X" basis. The "ASEAN Minus X" formula is based on the principle laid down in the Framework Agreement on Enhancing ASEAN Economic Cooperation, which the ASEAN leaders signed in Singapore on 28 January 1992:

> All Member States shall participate in intra ASEAN economic arrangements. However, in the implementation of these economic arrangements, two or more Member States may proceed first if other Member States are not ready to implement these arrangements.[55]

Outside the economic realm, two important ASEAN agreements follow this principle, as observed above. These are the treaty on the Southeast Asian Nuclear Weapons-Free Zone, which required only seven ratifications for it to take effect, and the Agreement on Transboundary Haze Pollution, which needed only six ratifications to enter into force. While the ASEAN Tourism

Agreement requires ratification by all member-states, the implementing agreements may be concluded by only two or more — and not necessarily all ten — of them. In the same spirit, the ASEAN-Korea Framework Agreement on Comprehensive Economic Cooperation, signed in December 2005, goes into effect upon ratification by Seoul and by only one ASEAN party.

ASEAN is increasingly inclined to resort to the ASEAN Minus X device, so that progress, particularly towards regional economic integration, is no longer held to the pace of the slowest member. If ASEAN applies it in a substantive and extensive way, particularly in integrating markets for some or all of the eleven priority sectors that the ASEAN leaders at their 2003 summit singled out for integration, leadership of ASEAN will, *de facto*, be assumed by the countries at the vanguard of integration. These will probably be any combination of Singapore, Brunei Darussalam, Thailand, Malaysia and Cambodia, if not all of them. They are the ASEAN members most committed to economic integration or at least have little problem with it.

In sum, leadership in ASEAN has alternated, depending on the sector. On the whole, Indonesia seems to take the political leadership — less so these days, although the 2003 Bali Summit saw an attempt by Indonesia to assume it again. Singapore has of late taken the lead in economic integration, albeit in a restrained way. We have yet to see the ASEAN equivalent of the Franco-German leadership of European integration in its early days, or of a Jean Monnet or a Robert Schumann driven by a regional vision and driving its realization. Perhaps, this is not in the ASEAN style; but then the lack of clear and vigorous leadership, whether by member-countries or by individual statesmen, could perpetuate the slow pace of ASEAN's development.

A QUESTION OF EQUALITY

As we have seen, the delicate nature of the ASEAN countries' relations with one another has resulted in a conscious avoidance of the exertion of overt or forceful leadership on behalf of more rapid progress in economic integration and institution-building. Another consequence is the scrupulous observance of the sovereign equality of the member-states. The emphasis on equality is made in spite of the previously noted diversity among the ASEAN countries, including the wide gaps in their levels of development. Looked at another way, sovereign equality has been stressed and insisted upon precisely *because* of this diversity. The members that feel vulnerable in one sense or another seek refuge in statutory equality within the association in order to avoid being dominated by those that are perceived to be stronger.

One result of this preoccupation with equality has been a little-known ASEAN phenomenon: that of member-states contributing exactly the same amounts to the ASEAN Fund and to ASEAN's operational budget, whether Indonesia or Laos, whether Singapore and Brunei Darussalam or Cambodia and Myanmar. This is certainly not the case in the European Union, the Organization of American States, the African Union, the South Asia Association for Regional Cooperation, the Andean Community, the Pacific Islands Forum, or most other regional associations.

In December 1969, the third ASEAN Ministerial Meeting in the Cameron Highlands in Malaysia established an ASEAN Fund to finance projects of a "strategic" nature that the association might agree upon. Each ASEAN country would contribute US$1 million to the fund.[56] Thirty-six years later, with ten members, the national contributions remain at US$1 million each; in the light of the system of equal financial responsibility, any increase is evidently held back by the willingness — or unwillingness — of the least able to contribute. In July 2005, the ASEAN Fund was converted into the ASEAN Development Fund, with expanded terms of reference that would allow its use for counterpart financing for projects undertaken with funding sources outside ASEAN.

Contributions to the ASEAN Science Fund, which finances science and technology projects, are also equal for all members, but the newer members are on a supposedly easier instalment plan. In August 2004, the ASEAN Telecommunications and IT Ministers decided to set up a US$5-million ASEAN ICT Fund, again with member-states pitching in with equal contributions. ASEAN members contribute equal shares also to the ASEAN Centre for Energy. The November 2004 ASEAN Protocol on Enhanced Dispute Settlement Mechanism set up an ASEAN DSM Fund, "a revolving fund, separate from ASEAN Secretariat's regular budget". Like the other funds, the initial contributions to it are to be equal for all ASEAN members. However, parties to a dispute, including third parties, are to replenish any "drawdown" from the fund, presumably for expenses incurred for the panel and the Appellate Body in connection with the dispute.

In the case of the ASEAN Secretariat's operational budget, the rapidly growing range of cooperative activities and sectoral forums and, now, the recommended compliance and dispute-settlement bodies for ASEAN economic agreements have demanded a corresponding expansion of the Secretariat. Yet, such an expansion is restricted by the available funding, which, in turn, is limited by the ability of the poorest members to contribute. Occasionally, there have been polite suggestions from the newer members for a change in the financial arrangements, from one of equal contributions to some kind of scale of assessments based on ability to pay, as measured by an agreed set of criteria, similar to the practice in other regional associations. Invariably, however, such suggestions have been met with counter-proposals for weighted voting based on the level of contributions. It is of some interest that, at the ASEAN Ministerial Meeting in 1976, Singapore's Foreign Minister, S. Rajaratnam, proposed that from the second year of the ASEAN Secretariat's operations contributions to its recurrent expenditures be based on "the Asian Development Bank formula".

Some schemes have been informally put forward to augment financing for ASEAN while skirting the conundrum of equal contributions — a tax on commercial transactions under AFTA, a levy on international airfares into, out of and/or within ASEAN. However, such schemes do not seem to have been taken seriously. Nevertheless, there have been instances of graduated contributions. One of them was the funding of the ASEAN Competitiveness Study, commissioned by the ASEAN Economic Ministers soon after the turn of the century, to which member-states made voluntary contributions of different amounts. However, this was a rare exception.

THE WAY OF CONSENSUS

Another characteristic of the "ASEAN Way" is the consensus method of decision-making. Many commentators have blamed this insistence on consensus for the failure of ASEAN to arrive at quick decisions or to do what they, the commentators, think ASEAN ought to do.

Let us take a look at what consensus means in the ASEAN context. On the basis of what I have seen, consensus in ASEAN does not necessarily require unanimity, although many ASEAN decisions are arrived at on the strength of genuine unanimity. Consensus on a proposal is reached when enough members support it — six, seven, eight or nine, no document specifies how many — even when one or more have misgivings about it, but do not feel strongly enough about the issue to block action on it. Not all need to agree explicitly. A consensus is blocked only when one or more members perceive the proposal to be sufficiently injurious to their national interests for them to oppose it outright.

Actually, other inter-governmental organizations operate in this way in practice, including the UN General Assembly and other UN bodies. However, the charters of many such international organizations provide for clear voting procedures in case consensus fails. According to the UN Charter, the UN General Assembly decides by simple-majority vote, except for certain specified "important questions", which require a two-thirds majority. The Council of the European Union decides by simple majority on procedural issues and by weighted voting on the basis of population size on questions pertaining to the internal market, economic affairs and trade. Unanimity, not just consensus, is required for matters related to foreign policy, defence, judicial and police cooperation, and taxation. The Charter of the OAS requires a simple majority for most decisions, but a two-thirds majority for the admission and suspension of members. According to the Constitutive Act of the African Union, the Assembly (of heads of state or government) or the Executive Council (of foreign ministers) needs a "consensus" or a two-thirds majority (if voting is resorted to) for non-procedural decisions. ASEAN, on the other hand, has no provisions for voting except in the previously cited case of the SEANWFZ Commission, which has, in fact, not resorted to a vote. ASEAN flirted with the notion of majority voting in the 1996 Protocol on Dispute Settlement Mechanism for ASEAN economic agreements. However, before it could be tested, it was superseded by another protocol in 2004, which reverted to decision by consensus.

When commentators criticize ASEAN's decision-making by consensus, what they are really saying is that the organization should resort to voting. Especially for sensitive political issues, the question is: would voting really be a more effective way than consultation, persuasion and consensus? In an association of only ten members, would imposing the will of six or seven members on the other four or three really bear more fruitful results?

FRUITS OF THE ASEAN WAY

We have seen the elements of the so-called "ASEAN Way". The preference for informality and loose arrangements over legal instruments and binding agreements. The greater reliance on personal relations than on institutions. The measured pace of institution-building. The invocation of national sovereignty as a way to ward off anticipated pressures restricting freedom of action and choice. The avoidance of the exercise of overt leadership. The emphasis on the sovereign equality of members. Decision-making by consensus. We have also seen how historical forces, national circumstances and inter-state relationships together shaped ASEAN as an association and set the "ASEAN Way".

This is neither to apologize for nor to criticize the "ASEAN Way". It is simply to try to explain how and why ASEAN developed certain of its characteristics and ways of doing things. For almost forty years, these traits and ways have served ASEAN well. It is generally agreed that ASEAN has been a force for peace and stability in East Asia. The categorical adoption of the non-use of force and other norms of inter-state relations, the avoidance, at the same time, of legally binding agreements (unless absolutely necessary) and of divisive ways of decision-making, a developing sense of regional solidarity (at least among the leadership classes), the network of personal relationships among decision-makers across the region, the expanding fabric of cooperation (even if many specific activities have not produced concrete, significant results), and the mutual confidence thus promoted — these have helped to make a "security community" out of Southeast Asia, a security community in the sense in which Amitav Acharya lucidly applies the concept to ASEAN.[57] This has, in turn, prevented disputes between ASEAN members from developing into inter-state conflicts; it has often been observed that no two ASEAN members have ever gone to war with each other despite the many disagreements left over from history or arising from conflicting interests. (This fact, however, can also be attributed to the contemporary trend that has made inter-state warfare less and less viable or desirable as an option for nations.)

Through ASEAN, Southeast Asian countries have attained a degree of solidarity that was impossible to imagine at the time of ASEAN's founding and during its early years and in the period when Southeast Asia was divided between those within the association and those outside it. This solidarity has magnified ASEAN's influence in the world to an extent that would not be possible for each individual member acting alone. ASEAN's influence was at its most prominent in the group's handling of the Vietnamese incursion into and presence in Cambodia in the 1980s. Despite the genocidal nature of the regime that the Vietnamese had driven out of Phnom Penh and the misgivings of some ASEAN members, ASEAN led the international effort to keep Cambodia's UN seat for the coalition opposed to the Vietnamese-installed regime and prevented that regime from gaining international support until the Paris conferences, in which ASEAN had a leadership role, worked out an acceptable settlement. Thanat Khoman has claimed with pride that ASEAN managed to get the Vietnamese out of Cambodia "without firing a shot".[58] To be sure, the Khmers Rouges received arms and other material support from China and other countries, including probably some in ASEAN. I am told that Thailand sent two young military officers to China to coordinate military assistance to the Khmers Rouges. However, ASEAN itself undertook no military action but used diplomatic skills and its solidarity and prestige — with the indispensable support, of course, of the permanent members of the UN Security Council — to bring about a settlement from which emerged an independent Cambodia.

ASEAN solidarity and persistence transformed the situation in the South China Sea from one of tension and occasional confrontation to, at least so far, a quiescent *status quo*. Although Brunei Darussalam, Malaysia, the Philippines and Vietnam have conflicting claims to parts of the South China Sea, they and the rest of ASEAN maintained a united front to get China to deal with them as an association with respect to this issue, a no small factor in calming the situation.

It was ASEAN's leadership that made possible the establishment of the ASEAN Regional Forum, the only venue for dialogue and consultation on political and security issues in East Asia. Similarly, the ASEAN+3 process has provided an additional and convenient forum for China, Japan and the Republic of Korea to deal not only with ASEAN but also with one another, a development of some significance for the strategic situation in East Asia as well as for the regional economy.

Slowly, in the "ASEAN Way", various "framework agreements" — on services, investments, goods-in-transit, customs coordination, product standards, mutual recognition arrangements, information and communications technology, tourism, and so on — have been put in place, laying the foundations for the integration of the regional economy. And ASEAN, by working together, often with others, has managed to deal with common problems — the SARS outbreak among others.

ASEAN has addressed even those problems and projects that, strictly speaking, directly involve only a few member-countries, like the haze pollution, crimes and other problems of a maritime nature, terrorism, the ASEAN highway and rail link, and measures to facilitate trade across land borders. Even in these cases, ASEAN has played a useful role by placing the political weight of the entire group behind programmes to deal with them and including them in ASEAN's joint projects with other countries and agencies. ASEAN has served as a venue for discussion, contact and networking for undertaking these sub-regional endeavours.

TIME FOR CHANGE?

These are no mean achievements. But ASEAN is almost forty years old, and both the region and the world have undergone immense change. The "ASEAN Way" has to change with them, not all of it, or even most of it, as some theoreticians would like to see — for, as pointed out above, the "ASEAN Way" has served ASEAN well in the past — but in ways that respond to the needs of ASEAN's people today.

In Chapter 8, I indicate the directions that those changes might realistically take.

Notes

1. Interview with Thanat Khoman, Bangkok, 1 June 2004.
2. See Appendix A.
3. *Far Eastern Economic Review*, 17 August 1967, p. 312.
4. Ibid., p. 311.
5. *Far Eastern Economic Review*, 24 August 1967, p. 380.
6. *New York Times*, 9 August 1967.
7. A convenient summary of the development of European integration is provided by *The Process of European Integration and the Draft European Constitution*, a presentation before the Research Commission on the Constitution of the House of Representatives of Japan by Ambassador Bernhard Zepter, Head of Delegation of the European Commission in Japan, Tokyo, 4 March 2004.
8. Intervention at the conference on East Asia and Europe: Experimenting with Region-Building, sponsored by Centre Asie of the Institut Français des Relations Internationales, the Asia-Europe Foundation and De La Salle University of the Philippines, with support from the French Ministry of Foreign Affairs, Paris, 1–3 October 2003.
9. Rodolfo C. Severino. "Will There be a New ASEAN in the 21st Century?", *Asia Europe Journal* 2, no. 2 (July 2004): 180.
10. The Bandung Declaration was issued by the Afro-Asian Conference in Bandung, Indonesia, in April 1955, which laid the foundation for the Non-Aligned Movement.
11. Verbatim Record of the Inaugural Meeting of ASEAN, Ministry of Foreign Affairs, Bangkok, 8 August 1967 (ASEAN/DOC/3).
12. *Collected Interviews of Foreign Minister Thanat Khoman* (Bangkok: Department of Information, Ministry of Foreign Affairs, 1967), p. 50.
13. Quoted in Adam Malik. *In the Service of the Republic* (Singapore: PT Gunung Agung, 1980), p. 274.
14. Severino, op. cit., p. 180.
15. See Appendix B.
16. Amitav Acharya, *Constructing a Security Community in Southeast Asia: ASEAN and the Problem of Regional Order* (London and New York: Routledge, 2001), p. 51.
17. Interview with Hasjim Djalal, Jakarta, 21 November 2003.
18. Interview with Ali Alatas, Jakarta, 21 November 2003.
19. International Court of Justice: Judgment in the Case Concerning Sovereignty Over Pulau Ligitan and Pulau Sipadan (Indonesia/Malaysia), The Hague, 17 December 2002.
20. http://www.icj-cij.org/icjwww/idocket/imasi/imasiframe.htm.
21. http://www.itlos.org/start2_en.html.
22. *Settlement Agreement: Case Concerning Land Reclamation by Singapore in and*

Around the Straits of Johor (Malaysia v Singapore) (http://www.mfa.gov.sg/internet/press/land/Settlement_Agreement.pdf).
23. International Court of Justice: Verbatim Record of the Public Sitting in the Case Concerning Sovereignty Over Pulau Ligitan and Pulau Sipadan (Indonesia/Malaysia), The Hague, 3 June 2002, p. 14.
24. Ibid.
25. http://www.wto.org/english/tratop_e/dispu_e/dispu_status_e.htm#1995.
26. http://www.aseansec.org/3669.htm.
27. I am grateful to Sonia C. Brady, Undersecretary for Foreign Affairs of the Philippines, for bringing the draft to my attention, June 2004.
28. http://www.aseansec.org/3668.htm, paras. 53–54.
29. See Appendix C.
30. http://www.aseansec.org/3636.htm.
31. http://www.aseansec.org/agr_haze.pdf.
32. The agreement entered into force in November 2003, having been ratified by Brunei Darussalam, Malaysia, Myanmar, Singapore, Thailand, and Vietnam. Laos has ratified the agreement since then.
33. See Chapter 3.
34. Keynote address at the ASEAN Community Roundtable, Institute of Southeast Asian Studies, Singapore, 4 June 2004.
35. Joint Communique of the 37th ASEAN Ministerial Meeting, Jakarta, 29–30 June 2004 (http://www.aseansec.org/16192.htm), para. 6.
36. http://www.aseansec.org/18030.htm.
37. The eminent persons are Pehin Dato Lim Jock Seng, Minister for Foreign Affairs and Trade II of Brunei Darussalam; Aun Porn Moniroth, Advisor to the Prime Minister and Chairman of the Supreme National Economic Council of Cambodia; Ali Alatas, former Minister for Foreign Affairs of Indonesia; Khamphan Simmalavong, former Deputy Minister of Laos; Tan Sri Musa Hitam (Chairman), former Deputy Prime Minister of Malaysia; Than Nyun, Chairman of the Civil Service Selection and Training Board of Myanmar; Fidel V. Ramos, former President of the Philippines; S. Jayakumar, Deputy Prime Minister, Coordinating Minister for National Security and Minister for Law of Singapore; Kasemsamosorn Kasemsri, former Deputy Prime Minister and Minister for Foreign Affairs of Thailand; and Nguyen Manh Cam, former Deputy Prime Minister and Minister for Foreign Affairs of Vietnam.
38. Interview with Pracha Guna-Kasem, Bangkok, 2 June 2004.
39. Opening statement at the 6th ASEAN Ministerial Meeting, Pattaya, Thailand, 16 April 1973.
40. http://www.aseansec.org/3686.htm, para. 8.
41. http://www.aseansec.org/3685.htm, para. 8.
42. http://www.aseansec.org/1265.htm.
43. Protocol Amending the Agreement on the Establishment of the ASEAN

Secretariat (Economic Officers), Bangkok, 27 January 1983 (http://www.aseansec.org/1266.htm).
44. Protocol Amending the Agreement on the Establishment of the ASEAN Secretariat, Bandar Seri Begawan, 4 July 1989 (http://www.aseansec.org/847.htm).
45. http://www.aseansec.org/5120.htm.
46. Protocol Amending the Agreement on the Establishment of the ASEAN Secretariat, Manila, 22 July 1992 (http://www.aseansec.org/1198.htm).
47. Protocol Amending the Agreement on the Establishment of the ASEAN Secretariat, Subang Jaya, Malaysia, 23 July 1997 (http://www.aseansec.org/1878.htm).
48. Intervention at the conference on East Asia and Europe: Experimenting with Region-Building, sponsored by Centre Asie of the Institut Français des Relations Internationales, the Asia-Europe Foundation and De La Salle University of the Philippines, with support from the French Ministry of Foreign Affairs, Paris, 1–3 October 2003.
49. Much of this section is excerpted and adapted from a talk given by the author at the Institute of Defence and Strategic Studies, Singapore, 6 February 2004.
50. *New York Times*, 1 August 1967.
51. *New York Times*, 30 August 1967.
52. Interview with Nana Sutresna, Jakarta, 21 November 2003.
53. Interview with Professor S. Jayakumar, Singapore, 19 August 2003.
54. I am indebted to Leo Suryadinata of the Institute of Southeast Asian Studies in Singapore for his insight on the last point.
55. http://www.aseansec.org/5125.htm, Art. I, para. 3.
56. http://www.aseansec.org/1213.htm.
57. Amitav Acharya, *Constructing a Security Community in Southeast Asia: ASEAN and the Problem of Regional Order* (London and New York: Routledge, 2001).
58. Interview with Thanat Khoman, Bangkok, 1 June 2004.

2

WHO BELONGS IN ASEAN?
The Question of Membership

The 1967 ASEAN Declaration states that "the Association is open for participation to all States in the South-East Asian Region subscribing to the aforementioned aims, principles and purposes". While the declaration does not say that ASEAN *must* include all of Southeast Asia but is merely *open* to all states in it, this statement has been taken, as we shall see, as the founding members' "vision" for the ultimate composition of the association.

This raises the question: what precisely is Southeast Asia? Which countries does the "South-East Asian Region" encompass? Several academics have traced the definition of Southeast Asia to Western scholarly works and to the application of military strategy — for example, the creation of Lord Mountbatten's Southeast Asia Command during World War II (headquartered in Colombo) — and to the interaction between them, particularly in relation to the United States' war in Vietnam. Philip Charrier, an assistant professor of history at the University of Regina in Canada, has written a comprehensive and insightful review of the evolution of the concept of Southeast Asia.[1]

One way of defining Southeast Asia, as the concept has evolved, is in terms of what it is not. It does not include China, Japan and Korea. Not Australia and New Zealand. Not India, or Bangladesh, which, until 1971, was part of Pakistan. Thus, one can conceive of Southeast Asia as being the area bounded by China (including Hong Kong and Taiwan), Japan and Korea in the north, Australia in the south, and Bangladesh and India in the west. In the east, while there were questions in the past about where Papua New Guinea belongs, both ASEAN and PNG have settled those questions by taking the official position that PNG is a "non-regional state" for purposes of the Treaty of Amity and Cooperation in Southeast Asia. As for Palau, also in the east, its possible ASEAN membership has never been taken into consideration by anyone, as far as I know. As I will go into later, there was the curious case of Sri Lanka, which once considered itself as having links, geographic, cultural, and commercial, with Southeast Asia but is now definitively regarded by all, including Sri Lanka itself as well as ASEAN, as part of South Asia rather than Southeast Asia.

Within the limits described above, ultimately Southeast Asia, for purposes of membership in ASEAN, is what the decision-makers of the ASEAN members say it is. The joint communiqué of the ASEAN Ministerial Meeting of 22–23 July 1994 in Bangkok stated:

> The Foreign Ministers noted the significance of the 27th ASEAN Ministerial Meeting (AMM) as it was the first time that the Foreign Ministers of all ten Southeast Asian countries were present. They hoped that relation (sic) of ASEAN with the four other Southeast Asian states would further intensify, and reiterated their commitment to building a Southeast Asian community through common membership in ASEAN.[2]

At that meeting, Roberto Romulo, the Philippines' Secretary of Foreign Affairs, declared, "We look forward to the day when Laos, Cambodia, and Myanmar, too, become members of ASEAN. On that day, ASEAN will finally encompass all of Southeast Asia, as ASEAN's founding fathers envisioned it in 1967."[3] His successor, Domingo Siazon, said at the ASEAN Ministerial Meeting in July 1995, "The evolving realization of a community of all ten Southeast Asian countries is being nurtured by the intensifying sense of common purpose among them, and the growing complementarity of their economies."[4]

In his keynote speech at the 1995 ministerial meeting, Sultan Hassanal Bolkiah of Brunei Darussalam stressed, "We must aim gradually to move towards an ASEAN community of ten."[5] At the fifth ASEAN Summit in Bangkok in December 1995, President Fidel V. Ramos of the Philippines observed, "The signing of the Treaty [on the Southeast Asia Nuclear Weapons-Free Zone] by the heads of government of all ten Southeast Asian states is a moment of great significance in regional history. So is our meeting with the three other leaders of Southeast Asia tomorrow."[6] On behalf of Myanmar, then not yet a member of ASEAN but participating in the 1995 summit, Senior General Than Shwe, then Prime Minister as well as Chairman of the State Law and Order Restoration Council, said, "It is our hope that a genuinely harmonious, peaceful and prosperous Southeast Asia — ten under one roof — will come into existence."[7]

While the Bangkok Summit Declaration of 1995 referred only to an "ASEAN comprising all countries in Southeast Asia" as the association's objective, not specifying how many, the press statement of the "informal" summit in Jakarta in November 1996 said, "The Heads of Government reaffirmed their strong commitment to the speedy realization of an ASEAN comprising *all ten* Southeast Asian countries [italics mine]."[8] The joint communiqué of the ASEAN Ministerial Meeting of July 1996 stated, "The Foreign Ministers accepted the formal applications of Cambodia and Laos to become members of ASEAN in 1997; they also granted Observer status of ASEAN to Myanmar; thereby, the vision of ASEAN's founders of all ten Southeast Asian countries living in harmony under a single roof come [sic] closer to realization."[9]

The 26 August 1996 letter of Myanmar's then Foreign Minister, U Ohn Gyaw, seeking Myanmar's admission into ASEAN stated his government's belief "that the integration of Myanmar into ASEAN at the forthcoming thirtieth Anniversary of the Founding of ASEAN will be both timely and appropriate and will also mean the fulfillment of the vision of the founding fathers of the Association since all ten Southeast Asian nations would be part of the ASEAN family."[10] Welcoming Cambodia's admission as ASEAN's tenth member, the joint communiqué of the July 1999 ASEAN Ministerial Meeting declared, "All Southeast Asians are now part of a single community."[11]

The repeated references to "all ten Southeast Asian" countries mean that, as far as the state leaders of ASEAN are concerned, Southeast Asia is made up of Brunei Darussalam, Cambodia, Indonesia, Malaysia, Laos, Myanmar, the Philippines, Singapore, Thailand and Vietnam. ASEAN made this formally explicit in the Second Protocol Amending the Treaty of Amity and Cooperation in Southeast Asia, concluded in July 1998, which declares:

> States outside Southeast Asia may also accede to this Treaty with the consent of all the States in Southeast Asia, namely, Brunei Darussalam, the Kingdom of Cambodia, the Republic of Indonesia, the Lao People's Democratic Republic, Malaysia, the Union of Myanmar, the Republic of the Philippines, the Republic of Singapore, the Kingdom of Thailand and the Socialist Republic of Vietnam.[12]

BURMESE AND CAMBODIAN REFUSAL

ASEAN's founders sought to bring in as many Southeast Asian countries as was thought possible at the time. One of them, Thanat Khoman, the Thai Foreign Minister at ASEAN's founding, was to recall in 1992:

> At the banquet marking the reconciliation between the three disputants, I broached the idea of forming another organization for regional cooperation

with Adam Malik.... Malik agreed without hesitation but asked for time to talk with the powerful military circle of his government and also to normalize relations with Malaysia now that the confrontation was over. Meanwhile, the Thai Foreign Office prepared a draft charter of the new institution. Within a few months, everything was ready. I therefore invited the two former ASA members, Malaysia and the Philippines, and Indonesia, a key member, to a meeting in Bangkok. In addition, Singapore sent S. Rajaratnam, then Foreign Minister, to see me about joining the new set-up. Although the new organization was planned to comprise only the former ASA members plus Indonesia, Singapore's request was favorably considered.[13]

As noted in Chapter 1, two attempts at regional association in Southeast Asia had been made — ASA and MAPHILINDO.[14] However, these consisted of only three members each and thus were hardly representative of the region, among other weaknesses. As the new association was being organized, Adam Malik and his team went around the region with the intention of seeking members beyond the five that Thanat Khoman referred to in the paragraph quoted above. They went to Yangon and Phnom Penh in May 1967, as well as to Bangkok and Manila. The neutralist postures of Burma, as Myanmar was then named, and Cambodia would have served to overcome perceptions of the future ASEAN as a pro-Western alliance.

Burma demurred, however, apparently determined to maintain the international isolation that the five-year-old Ne Win regime had imposed on the country. This, in turn, arose from Burma's resolve to stay non-aligned; after all, the country was squeezed between the two Asian giants, China and India, and two of the countries organizing the new association, the Philippines and Thailand, hosted military bases from which the United States was launching operations against Vietnam. U Ohn Gyaw, who was Foreign Minister at the time of Myanmar's entry into ASEAN, recalled to me that, in 1967, his country had been suspicious of the association and wary of its possible development into a defence alliance.[15] In 2004, the then Prime Minister, General Khin Nyunt, cited domestic conditions:

> Myanmar was compelled to decline the offer [of ASEAN membership] due to the then conditions in the country and the priorities of the Government. At that time, the nation faced insurgencies in many parts of the country and the economy was also encountering much difficulty. Moreover, national unity was also very weak. Under such circumstances, the existing Government had to focus all its attention to the domestic issues.[16]

For many years, Burma continued to keep ASEAN at arm's length; after all, in the 1970s, said U Ohn Gyaw, ASEAN was not doing well economically and was riven by bilateral disputes.[17] Burma was so sensitive about its neutrality that it even left the Non-Aligned Movement, when, at the NAM summit in Havana in 1979, Burma thought the movement was leaning too far to the Soviet bloc. By the early 1990s, shortly after the State Law and Order Restoration Council took over the leadership of Myanmar, the Soviet Union had broken up and the Cold War had ended. Under these circumstances, Myanmar felt itself ready to re-join NAM, which it did at its 1992 summit in Jakarta, and became receptive to ASEAN membership. According to U Tin Winn, the Minister for International Economic Cooperation and Minister for Labour when I interviewed him, Myanmar saw that ASEAN was a success and had shown itself to be committed to peace and non-alignment.[18]

In Cambodia's case, Norodom Sihanouk, who, as Prince and not as King (his father, King Norodom Suramarit, had died in 1960), ruled as well as reigned over Cambodia at that time, recalled to me that he had refused to participate in ASEAN so as to preserve his vision of his country as the "Switzerland of Asia" and maintain its non-aligned status, telling Adam Malik that he preferred being a "friend of ASEAN" to being a member. As the King remembered it, ASEAN "did not appreciate" that decision. He told me in December 2003 that he continued to be "one whose mind is not pro-ASEAN". However, he stressed that he was "not unhappy" with Prime Minister Hun Sen's decision to join the association and saw the need for Cambodia to join a regional group.[19]

Sihanouk's determined neutralist stance in 1967 was, of course, not based on a whimsical conception of Cambodia's place in the world or on an ideological attachment to non-alignment. It was part of his desperate effort to keep his country from being sucked into the Vietnam maelstrom and from having its borders violated by Thailand and/or Vietnam. To ward off pressures from the United States, Thailand and South Vietnam, he felt that he had to seek support from China and North Vietnam and thus eschewed membership in an association that included Thailand and other supporters of the U.S. ventures in Indochina. By the 1990s, the strategic situation in Southeast Asia had changed, and Sihanouk could admit, as he did to me, that Cambodia was "happy to be within ASEAN", although he himself preferred what he called a "Cambodian Cambodia".[20]

SRI LANKA'S BID FOR INCLUSION

While Southeast Asia was moving towards forming the new association, Sri Lanka, then called Ceylon, made a short-lived attempt to be part of it.

According to notes by a Sri Lankan diplomat dated 6 November 1996 (the diplomat is unnamed, but I am certain of the document's authenticity) the Ceylonese Embassy in Bangkok reported the flurry of activities related to the founding of a new regional association. Upon instructions from Colombo, the embassy sought to ascertain from Foreign Minister Thanat Khoman whether the states involved would accept Ceylon as a founding member of the group. The notes report that Thanat "was obviously happy" about the inquiry but would have to consult the other Foreign Ministers. The same evening, the diplomat recalled, the Thai minister told the Ceylonese embassy's chargé d'affaires that "the Foreign Ministers of the associating states were most happy to receive Sri Lanka as a Founding Member" and asked Colombo to communicate its request for membership in writing. The communication never came and, supposedly after a day's delay, the five foreign ministers issued the Bangkok Declaration without Ceylon. Nevertheless, Colombo is said to have been advised that "should Sri Lanka make up its mind any time thereafter, it would be welcomed but not as a Founding Member in view of the circumstances".

The unnamed Sri Lankan diplomat attributed this failure to the opposition of the Left, led by the Sri Lanka Freedom Party under Sirimavo Bandaranaike, and to pressures from several quarters: the Soviet Union and China, which at the time considered the proposed Southeast Asian association to be a tool of the United States; India, which "saw its sphere of influence and its claim to hegemony being eroded"; and "many of the non-aligned community" concerned with the presumed implications of ASEAN membership for Ceylon's non-aligned status.

The Sri Lankan diplomat's notes blame, above all, Prime Minister Dudley Senanayake's failure of will and lament: "Sri Lanka's hope of breaking away from its moorings in South Asia and becoming a trading nation with links to Southeast and East Asian nations as well as to all of littoral Asia was lost. The country continued its inward-looking strategies although its location on sea lanes across the Indo-Pacific made outward-looking strategies the most natural course."

In 1972, according to the diplomat, Sri Lanka proposed to ASEAN that "its application for Asean membership be pigeon-holed for the time being.... It has not since then seen the light of day and Sri Lanka continues to be imprisoned in a South Asian setting with its opportunity of linking its destinies to the fast-moving maritime-centred economies of East and South East Asia lost for the foreseeable future." That was, of course, written before the reforms of the Indian economy in the 1990s took hold.

When I mentioned this episode to some personalities involved in ASEAN's founding, including Thanat Khoman, they dismissed it by pointing out that Sri Lanka is in South Asia and not in Southeast Asia, as if the idea of Sri Lankan membership had never been considered. In fact, Sri Lanka revived its bid for membership in 1981 in a May letter from its Foreign Minister to the chairman of the ASEAN Standing Committee. The ASEAN foreign ministers asked the senior officials to study the matter. There it seemed to have died a natural death. In their initial discussions, the senior officials referred to "the talks" on Ceylon's membership just before ASEAN's birth in August 1967. Although they are now but a footnote, albeit an interesting one, in ASEAN's history, Sri Lanka's attempts to be part of ASEAN indicate a prescient appreciation, as early as 1967, of the association's potential.

OPENING TO INDOCHINA

Thus, ASEAN's founding members were limited to the four independent maritime Southeast Asian nations plus Thailand. The statement in the Bangkok Declaration that "the Association is open for participation to all States in the South-East Asian Region" could refer only to ASEAN's receptivity to the membership of Burma and Cambodia, should they change their minds in the future — as they eventually did — and the two other countries of the former Indochina, i.e., Laos and Vietnam. Brunei Darussalam, of course, was not yet an independent country, but it was definitely in Southeast Asia and thus eligible for eventual membership; moreover, from both ASEAN's and Brunei Darussalam's point of view, it was unthinkable for the sultanate to remain outside the association for any length of time after independence.

Tun Abdul Razak, Malaysia's Deputy Prime Minister, Minister for Defence and Minister for National Development, declared at the inaugural meeting of ASEAN as head of the Malaysian delegation:

> ASEAN has a membership of 5 countries. Although ASEAN represents the majority of the people of this region we as members must once again admit that it is not fully representative of South East Asia. Mr. Chairman, let us therefore in the coming months and in the coming years so direct our activities in the true spirit of ASEAN, to strengthen goodwill, understanding and friendship and to show concrete and tangible results for the welfare and happiness of our people. In this way, we may be able to show to our friends who are not here with us today that despite initial difficulties and hesitations they may have, this association of ours is truly beneficial to our region of South East Asia.[21]

Vietnam was then divided into North and South, and Laos had been dragged into the conflict there. Nevertheless, the Kingdom of Laos, whose capital was then in right-wing hands, and the Republic of Vietnam, that is, South Vietnam, were present at the third ASEAN Ministerial Meeting, in 1969, in the Cameron Highlands as guests of Malaysia. Similarly represented at the fourth ASEAN Ministerial Meeting, in 1971, were the Republic of Vietnam and the new Khmer Republic, which had been established in 1970 upon the ouster of Prince Sihanouk by General Lon Nol, the Prime Minister and commander of the Army. Interestingly, the joint communiqué of that meeting stressed that "the Representatives of the Khmer Republic and the Republic of Vietnam *who had formally requested to attend the Meeting* [italics mine], were present during the Open Session as Guests of the Government of the Republic of the Philippines."[22] The Ambassador of the Khmer Republic and the Consul General of the Republic of Vietnam in Singapore were similarly present at the 1972 meeting, also upon their request. The Secretary of State of Community Development of the Khmer Republic and the ambassador of Laos were in attendance at the 1973 meeting in Pattaya, Thailand, and ambassadors of the two countries were on hand at the meeting the next year in Jakarta, but (North) Vietnam rejected ASEAN's invitation.[23] Myanmar, apparently, was not in the equation at the time.

In 1973, as the process of politically settling the Vietnam conflict was going on, Tun Dr Ismail bin Datuk Abdul Rahman, Deputy Prime Minister of Malaysia, told the sixth ASEAN Ministerial Meeting in Pattaya:

> When the Foreign Ministers of ASEAN states met in Kuala Lumpur in February, they agreed that membership of ASEAN should be expanded at the opportune time to embrace the whole of Southeast Asia. My delegation feels that such a move will certainly engender a higher degree of strength, solidarity and close relationship amongst the nations of the region and lead to a situation whereby no country in the region need feel that it is in a hostile environment. Towards the latter end, my delegation feels that we should make every effort to promote interlocking relationships amongst the nations of the region.

As for the Democratic Republic of Vietnam, that is, the then North Vietnam, Luu Doan Huynh, a fellow at the Institute of International Relations in Hanoi, has this to say:

> Hanoi mistakenly thought ASEAN was just SEATO (the Southeast Asia Treaty Organization) in disguise. This assessment, which was not in keeping with the real policy evolution of ASEAN countries since 1967, was ideologically comforting and seemed plausible to Vietnam because, since

the mid-1960s, Thailand and the Philippines had participated in the American war by sending troops to South Vietnam and allowing the USA to use their bases for the war. But the gap became larger in the early 1970s when Thailand and the Philippines started withdrawing their troops from South Vietnam (March 1973), Thailand refrained from giving direct assistance to the Lon Nol regime, ASEAN started to distance itself from the Indochina War and began to work out a post-war policy vis-à-vis Vietnam, Laos and Cambodia, taking into account the possibility of the latter's victories. While agreeing to establish diplomatic relations with Malaysia (March 1973) and Singapore (August 1974), Vietnam rejected the repeated invitations for a Vietnamese observer to attend the 1973 and 1974 ASEAN foreign ministers meetings and did not respond to other overtures from ASEAN, including the ZOPFAN (Southeast Asian Zone of Peace, Freedom and Neutrality) initiative. This ran counter to a 1972 report of the Foreign Ministry of Vietnam on relations with ASEAN countries which said that 'Developing relations with neighbouring countries is a diplomatic task of primary importance for any state, as its security and development are bound to be deeply affected by the former. For Vietnam, this task is even more urgent.' Presumably this dichotomy shows that there were different views within the leadership.[24]

In 1975, Vietnam was reunited, the Lao People's Revolutionary Party took over the government of a unified Laos and abolished the monarchy, and the Khmers Rouges seized power in Cambodia. ASEAN's member-states, displaying the pragmatism for which the association is well known, immediately stepped up their overtures to the new governments, particularly to that of Vietnam. Although in February 1976 Vietnam reacted harshly to the conclusion of the Treaty of Amity and Cooperation and ASEAN's invitation for Vietnam to accede to it, Hanoi soon extended its hand by sending high-level officials to ASEAN countries, culminating in a round of visits by Prime Minister Pham Van Dong to the ASEAN capitals in 1978 and the establishment of diplomatic relations with them. Opening the ASEAN Ministerial Meeting in 1977, Prime Minister Lee Kuan Yew of Singapore urged the ASEAN countries, in the light of the changed political situation in Southeast Asia, "to build their relations with Vietnam, Laos and Kampuchea on a constructive and productive basis". The joint communiqué of that meeting cited "the desire of ASEAN countries to promote peaceful and mutually beneficial relations with all countries, including Kampuchea, Laos and Vietnam".[25]

This reaching-out process was interrupted by Vietnam's December 1978 incursion into and subsequent stay in Cambodia and ASEAN's opposition to these developments. It resumed only upon the settlement of the Cambodian problem in 1991, but, in ASEAN's pragmatic spirit, quickly gathered pace thereafter. Even before the general elections in Cambodia, which were part of the settlement, the Vietnamese and Lao Foreign Ministers, Nguyen Manh Cam and Phoun Sipraseuth, took their places at the opening ceremonies of the July 1992 ASEAN Ministerial Meeting, which then approved the two countries' status as observers, both having acceded to the Treaty of Amity and Cooperation in Southeast Asia. In July 1994, the Foreign Ministers of Cambodia (which had just installed a new government) and Myanmar joined the eight others on the occasion of the ASEAN Ministerial Meeting, whose joint communiqué noted the significance of the fact that "it was the first time that the Foreign Ministers of all ten Southeast Asian countries were present" and expressed the association's readiness to admit Vietnam to membership.[26] After what I am told was some resistance from "hardliners" in the Communist Party, Vietnam submitted its formal application for membership on 17 October 1994 and was admitted in 1995. In January 1995, Cambodia acceded to the Treaty of Amity and Cooperation and was granted observer status that same year, having been guest of the hosts at the 1993 and 1994 ASEAN Ministerial Meetings. Towards the end of the year, the ten Southeast Asian countries met at the summit for the first time, in Bangkok. There they signed the treaty on the Southeast Asia Nuclear Weapons-Free Zone. The next year, 1996, the foreign ministers agreed to admit Cambodia and Laos to membership in 1997 and accorded observer status to Myanmar, which had acceded to the Treaty of Amity and Cooperation in 1995. In November 1996, as in Bangkok the year before, Prince Norodom Ranariddh and Hun Sen, co-Prime Ministers of Cambodia, Lao Prime Minister Khamtay Siphandone, and Senior General Than Shwe, Myanmar's Prime Minister, joined the seven heads of state or government of ASEAN immediately after the "informal" summit in Jakarta. As it turned out, Laos and Myanmar did become members in 1997, but, on account of the political turmoil in that country, Cambodia's membership was delayed until 1999.

UNCONDITIONAL MEMBERSHIP

According to the ASEAN Declaration of 1967, the only conditions for "participation" in ASEAN were location in "the South-East Asian Region" and adherence to the "aforementioned aims, principles and purposes", which were stated as:

1. To accelerate the economic growth, social progress and cultural development in the region through joint endeavours in the spirit of

equality and partnership in order to strengthen the foundation for a prosperous and peaceful community of South-East Asian Nations;
2. To promote regional peace and stability through abiding respect for justice and the rule of law in the relationship among countries of the region and adherence to the principles of the United Nations Charter;
3. To promote active collaboration and mutual assistance on matters of common interest in the economic, social, cultural, technical, scientific and administrative fields;
4. To provide assistance to each other in the form of training and research facilities in the educational, professional, technical and administrative spheres;
5. To collaborate more effectively for the greater utilization of their agriculture and industries, the expansion of their trade, including the study of the problems of international commodity trade, the improvement of their transportation and communications facilities and the raising of the living standards of their peoples.
6. To promote South-East Asian Studies;
7. To maintain close and beneficial cooperation with existing international and regional organizations with similar aims and purposes, and explore all avenues for even closer cooperation among themselves.[27]

Basically, the commitments pertain to the principles of the UN Charter, respect for justice and the rule of law in international relations, and regional cooperation in a variety of practical areas. After the admission of Brunei Darussalam, an implicit condition for membership has been accession to the Treaty of Amity and Cooperation, which has to do exclusively with inter-state relations, and other ASEAN agreements, all of which are of an economic, technical or administrative nature. There are no other conditions for membership, certainly none in terms of the behaviour of states towards their citizens and other people in their territories, none in terms of political or social systems, and none in terms of economic policy other than those pertaining to regional economic integration and cooperation. This is why, when people ask why ASEAN accepted Myanmar and the three other newer members, the question may be posed in riposte: on what grounds should ASEAN have rejected them? This is quite apart from the strategic benefits that ASEAN saw in their membership.

In contrast, the Constitutive Act of the African Union, in addition to the usual principles pertaining to inter-state relations — sovereign equality, respect for borders, the peaceful resolution of conflicts, the prohibition of the use of force or threat to use force, peaceful co-existence, non-interference in internal affairs — lays down other norms for member-states to observe.

These give the Union the right to intervene in a member-state in case of "war crimes, genocide and crimes against humanity". They also encompass gender equality, respect for democratic principles, human rights, the rule of law and good governance, social justice, respect for human life, and rejection of political assassination, terrorism, subversive activities and unconstitutional changes of government. Indeed, the Union may suspend a government that comes to power through unconstitutional means.

The Charter of the Organization of American States considers "respect for the personality, sovereignty, and independence of States, and the faithful fulfillment of obligations derived from treaties and other sources of international law" as the basis of international order. However, while affirming the unacceptability of external intervention or interference in one another's affairs, the Charter asserts that "the effective exercise of representative democracy" is essential for the purposes of the solidarity of the American states. It proclaims "the fundamental rights of the individual without distinction as to race, nationality, creed, or sex" and declares social justice and social security to be the "bases of lasting peace," thus linking domestic conditions to the maintenance of peace.

On the other hand, the ASEAN Declaration lays down no conditions for membership other than location in Southeast Asia and the usual principles of inter-state relations. Some observers, from within and outside ASEAN, have offered the view that admitting the four new members at the time that ASEAN did, in the latter half of the 1990s, may not have been warranted. Amitav Acharya, Deputy Director and Head of Research at the Institute of Defence and Strategic Studies in Singapore, for example, has told me that admitting the four newer members without having norms for admission may have been a mistake. He cites in particular the case of Myanmar, which he thinks should not have been admitted as a full member pending political reforms in the country. In Acharya's view, it may have been better for the newer members to be allowed to participate in the economic arrangements but not in the political decisions.[28] Whether this would have been acceptable to the four is another question. A former minister of one of the ASEAN-6 countries has asserted that ASEAN's expansion was a mistake, the "systems" of Cambodia, Laos and Vietnam, according to him, being much too different from those of the ASEAN-6 and Myanmar being "a complete misfit". A serving minister has said that the mistake was in bringing them in "so quickly" in the light of their much lower levels of development. These comments raise the question: should not ASEAN at least have certain minimum standards, to be observed before and after admission, even as conditions for admission, not only with respect to inter-state relations but also in terms of the behaviour of states towards their own people and of basic economic and social policies — in other words, certain common values? Without such standards, ASEAN can serve as a useful mechanism for keeping the peace among its members and acting together on certain international issues, as it has done, but it can never be a true community. Only a sense of community can ensure broad support for political solidarity and economic integration.

All of this, of course, is said in retrospect. On membership criteria, the opposite view has already prevailed.

THE ADMISSION OF NEW MEMBERS

In the case of Brunei Darussalam, the process of membership was extremely smooth and uncomplicated. Prince Mohamed Bolkiah attended ASEAN ministerial meetings as an observer in 1981, 1982 and 1983, when he conveyed his country's intention to apply for membership upon attaining independence the next year. On the first day of January 1984, Brunei Darussalam became an independent nation, having declined to join Malaysia in 1963. Six days later, it was admitted into ASEAN. In the instrument of admission, Brunei Darussalam agreed to subscribe or accede "to all the Declarations or Treaties of ASEAN". This meant that Brunei Darussalam had to join one treaty of a political nature, the Treaty of Amity and Cooperation, to which it acceded in June 1987, and two agreements of an administrative character — on the ASEAN Secretariat and on the ASEAN Fund. It also involved two economic agreements (on the preferential trading arrangements and on the food security reserve) and two agreements of a social nature (on the abuse of narcotic drugs and on the environment). The ASEAN-Canada and the ASEAN-European Communities cooperation agreements had to be extended to include the new ASEAN member. Brunei Darussalam also had to accept the ZOPFAN Declaration of 1971 and the Declaration of ASEAN Concord of 1976.

By the time Vietnam was admitted in 1995, however, ASEAN had already concluded the Framework Agreement on Enhancing ASEAN Economic Cooperation, which committed the ASEAN countries to establish the ASEAN Free Trade Area and embark on other forms of economic cooperation, and the Common Effective Preferential Tariff Scheme for AFTA. Vietnam had to accede to these agreements, which required rather intricate negotiations. The protocols of accession to the two agreements, which Prime Minister Vo Van Kiet signed for Vietnam in December 1995, and the letters conveyed by Foreign Minister Nguyen Manh Cam and Trade Minister Le Van Triet laid down detailed commitments on AFTA and

Vietnam's economic relations with the rest of ASEAN and precise schedules for its participation in AFTA.

In a conversation that I had with him in Hanoi, Vu Khoan, Deputy Prime Minister, former Minister for Trade and former Deputy Foreign Minister, explained Vietnam's reasons for wanting to join ASEAN. He said that Vietnam had always, since independence, placed great importance on relations with neighbouring countries, invoking a saying that neighbours are more important than relatives who live far away. With the re-structuring of the Russian economy and the break-up of the Soviet Union, Vietnam saw the loss of much of its market, the old COMECON having accounted for 70 per cent of Vietnam's total trade, and concluded that it would need Southeast Asia as a market and as a source of technology. For this, Vietnam needed peace and cooperation with its neighbours. Vu Khoan stressed that Vietnam did not seek ASEAN membership as a way of "balancing" China.[29] Trinh Quang Thanh, Director-General of the Institute of International Relations at Vietnam's Ministry of Foreign Affairs, put it in a political context, recalling that Vietnam sought ASEAN membership after finding itself without allies when the Soviet Union disintegrated and the Cold War ended.[30] His colleague, Luu Doan Huynh, observed that "by 1992, Vietnam was both free and without allies, with a deep sense of freedom coupled with something like 'a crisis of identity'". To him, Vietnam's membership in ASEAN "would signify a return of Vietnam to its place of origin".[31]

After Vietnam's admission, the process of completing Southeast Asian membership in ASEAN seemed inexorable. The Bangkok Declaration issued by the fifth ASEAN Summit in December 1995 proclaimed the ASEAN leaders' confidence "in the early realization of the ASEAN vision of embracing the whole of Southeast Asia" and asserted, "ASEAN shall work towards the speedy realization of an ASEAN comprising all Southeast Asian countries as it enters the 21st century." Elsewhere in the document, the leaders declared, "ASEAN Member States shall facilitate and expedite the realization of an ASEAN comprising all countries in Southeast Asia.... This historic Meeting of the Heads of State and Government of the ten Southeast Asian countries in Bangkok marked a significant step forward towards the realization of this vision."[32]

In the meantime, as in the case of Vietnam, the work of preparing Cambodia, Laos and Myanmar for membership gathered momentum. With a mandate to ascertain the technical readiness of the prospective members, the then ASEAN Secretary-General, Ajit Singh, visited Cambodia in December 1994 and Myanmar in November 1996, consulting with leaders and officials. Within the parameters of his mandate, he found them ready.

Officials of member-states and officers of the ASEAN Secretariat made several visits to the three countries for consultations and briefings, including discussions on the intricacies of the ASEAN Free Trade Area. Officials of the prospective members went in batches through three to five weeks of orientation at the ASEAN Secretariat in Jakarta. Ministers and senior officials sat in as observers at ASEAN meetings.

The press statement issued by the informal ASEAN summit in Jakarta in November 1996 stated:

> The Heads of Government reaffirmed their strong commitment to the speedy realization of an ASEAN comprising all ten Southeast Asian countries. They agreed that Cambodia, Laos and Myanmar be [sic] admitted as ASEAN members *simultaneously* [italics mine].... As to the actual timing of the admission of the three countries, this will be announced in due time.[33]

This, however, was not to be. At a special meeting in Kuala Lumpur on 10 July 1997 to review the situation in Cambodia, then in turmoil as a result of the fighting between the forces of the co-Prime Ministers, Prince Norodom Ranariddh and Samdech Hun Sen, the ASEAN Foreign Ministers decided, according to their joint statement, that "the wisest course of action is to delay the admission of Cambodia into ASEAN until a later date". They also "agreed that the admission of Laos and Myanmar will proceed as scheduled".[34]

LAOS AND MYANMAR

Thus, on 23 July, on the occasion of the ASEAN Ministerial Meeting in Malaysia, Laos and Myanmar were admitted into ASEAN. With the agreements with Vietnam as a precedent, the negotiations on the accession of Laos and Myanmar to ASEAN agreements had been easier, faster and neater. The 1997 declarations admitting the two countries into ASEAN had identical provisions, both of them patterned after the declaration for Vietnam. All singled out the Framework Agreement on Enhancing ASEAN Economic Cooperation and the agreement on CEPT for AFTA among the agreements to which the new members had to accede. Laos and Myanmar each committed itself to inform the other ASEAN states of its laws, regulations and requirements that affected intra-ASEAN trade. Each had to sign two protocols of accession containing lists of the agreements to which they were acceding and accepting the conditions governing their accessions to some of those agreements. In the case of Vietnam, the corresponding accessions were embodied in the letters of Ministers Cam and Triet.

ASEAN was criticized by some Western governments and by the media, both in the West and within ASEAN, for admitting Myanmar without conditions as to its domestic policies. ASEAN's rationale for taking in Myanmar and its implications and impact are discussed in Chapter 3. For their part, when asked about Myanmar's motives for joining ASEAN when it did, Myanmar's leaders proudly stress that Yangon sought membership in ASEAN not for any direct advantage that it might derive from the association but out of a desire to make a contribution to the region. Then Prime Minister Khin Nyunt declared to me that Myanmar did not join ASEAN for the benefits that it expected but in order to participate in the "Southeast Asian consensus".[35] The Myanmar leaders point to the country's abundance of natural resources and its strategic location between China and India and as a link between South and Southeast Asia. However, then Foreign Minister U Win Aung, over a lunch that he hosted for me, asserted that Myanmar was "not playing geopolitical games", but was simply placing importance on having good relations with all, especially with China and India.[36] Nevertheless, the fact is that Myanmar's membership in ASEAN helped to confer on the regime the legitimacy that some countries outside ASEAN had been questioning by virtue of the manner in which the military held on to power in 1988–90.

In August 2004, I had dinner in Vientiane's Lao Plaza Hotel with Somsavat Lengsavad, Deputy Prime Minister and Foreign Minister, Bounkeut Sangsomsak, Deputy Foreign Minister, and Sayakane Sisouvong, Director-General for ASEAN Affairs at the Ministry of Foreign Affairs of Laos. Somsavat told me that there had been no serious opposition within the country to Laos' membership in ASEAN but some officials had questioned its benefits for the nation. To these officials, he had replied that it would be better to belong to the association than to be isolated in the region. The three officials at our dinner were of the view that ASEAN membership was a stimulus to economic reform and, incidentally, a spur for Lao to learn English. Bounkeut added that ASEAN was one big confidence-building mechanism and served Laos well in that respect.

In his book, *The Evolution of the Lao State*, Phongsavath Boupha, Vice Minister for Foreign Affairs, said:

> The Lao PDR recognized that accession to ASEAN would not only be in line with its foreign policy of peace but in keeping with current global trends to create a favourable environment for national development while enabling it to ensure its independence and sovereignty after a long history of being under foreign rule and facing external aggression and interference. Moreover

accession to ASEAN would be in line with the foreign policy of broadening external relations which would enable it to work together with other ASEAN countries and to strengthen their political, economic and trade bargaining power *vis-à-vis* other countries outside the region. As a member of ASEAN, the Lao PDR could integrate its economy with ASEAN economies and have access to the immense markets both inside and outside ASEAN.[37]

DELAY IN CAMBODIA'S ADMISSION

As noted above, the ASEAN leaders, at their summit of November 1996, declared their agreement on the simultaneous admission of Cambodia, Laos and Myanmar into ASEAN, leaving their ministers to determine the date. At a special meeting in Kuala Lumpur on 31 May 1997, the ASEAN foreign ministers agreed to admit the three countries at their annual meeting two months thence. However, the international community was becoming anxious about the uncertainty of the date of the 1998 Cambodian elections.

Starting on 2 July, Ung Huot, then Minister for Foreign Affairs and International Cooperation, and Keat Chhon, Minister for Economy and Finance, were in Paris attending the meeting of the Consultative Group for Cambodia and assuring the aid donors assembled there about the date of the elections. As Ung Huot recalls it, on 5 July, he and Keat Chhon were surprised to see news of fierce fighting in Cambodia on CNN in their hotel rooms. Ung Huot called his wife in Phnom Penh, and she advised him not to return to the country, as it was too dangerous. A few days later, he flew to Bangkok, where his wife eventually joined him. Meanwhile, Prince Ranariddh had fled the country.[38]

On 8 July, Malaysia's Foreign Minister Abdullah Badawi (now Prime Minister) issued a statement on behalf of ASEAN in his capacity as chairman of the ASEAN Standing Committee:

> ASEAN is dismayed by and deeply regrets the unfortunate turn of events in Cambodia, resulting in the loss of innocent lives, both of Cambodian citizens and of foreigners. ASEAN calls for an immediate ceasefire. ASEAN also calls upon the Government of Cambodia to take immediate steps to ensure the safety of foreign nationals and provide protection to their properties in that country.
>
> ASEAN further calls on the two co-Prime Ministers, the 1st Prime Minister Prince Ranariddh and the 2nd Prime Minister Hun Sen, to resolve their differences peacefully. The Cambodian people have suffered from conflicts for the past two decades. It would be tragic for the conflict to re-ignite in

a country that has long suffered from war. ASEAN calls upon the 1st Prime Minister Prince Ranariddh and 2nd Prime Minister Hun Sen to abide by the terms of the Paris Peace Accords.

ASEAN will monitor carefully the situation in Cambodia and convene a Special Meeting of ASEAN Foreign Ministers on 10th July 1997 in Kuala Lumpur to review the situation in all its aspects.[39]

At the special meeting on 10 July, the ASEAN foreign ministers reiterated the statement of their chairman and, as related above, decided to delay Cambodia's admission indefinitely. In their discussions, those who favoured the delay argued that the situation in Cambodia had changed since November 1996, when the ASEAN heads of government decided on the simultaneous admission of Cambodia, Laos and Myanmar. They pointed out that the events in Cambodia had a great impact on regional peace and stability and that ASEAN had a special stake in the political arrangements in Cambodia, arrangements provided for in the Paris Peace Accords, in which ASEAN had played a leading role. They asserted that if ASEAN were to admit Cambodia two weeks later, as scheduled, such a move would undermine the association's credibility, open the way for intervention by others, and lead to the perception of ASEAN as a club without standards. What those standards were was apparently left unsaid. Despite the misgivings of Malaysia and Vietnam over the delay, the majority's decision carried the day. It was ASEAN consensus-making at work.

The ASEAN ministers also decided to send a delegation to Cambodia to help find a solution to the problem, forming a "troika" of Secretary of Foreign Affairs Domingo Siazon of the Philippines, the incoming chairman of the ASEAN Standing Committee, Foreign Minister Prachuab Chaiyasarn of Thailand, Cambodia's neighbour, and Indonesian Foreign Minister Ali Alatas, the most experienced of the ministers in working on Cambodian questions. (I find the use of the term "troika" unfortunate, since it evoked analogies with the EU Troika, which is an official and institutionalized body, while the informal, *ad hoc* ASEAN group had a much more limited character and mandate. In July 2000, the ASEAN Foreign Ministers adopted the ASEAN troika's terms of reference in an attempt to institutionalize it somewhat and, on the part of some members, to circumscribe it. The "troika" has not been convened since Cambodia's admission into ASEAN.)

Resuming his narrative over lunch in Phnom Penh's Cambodiana Hotel, Ung Huot recalled that, on 14 July, he returned to Phnom Penh and went directly to the French Embassy for the Bastille Day reception. There, the Japanese Ambassador warned him that trouble was brewing, as Hun Sen was about to name the Governor of Siem Reap, a military man, as co-Prime Minister in replacement of Prince Ranariddh, an act that would contravene the constitutional provision requiring a Prime Minister to be an elected member of the National Assembly. When Ung Huot rushed to point this out to Hun Sen, the latter indicated his readiness to nominate him, Ung Huot, to be First Prime Minister, since "no other FUNCINPEC leader was willing to take the position".[40] When Ung Huot demurred, Hun Sen threatened to rule alone. At that point, according to Ung Huot, he relented.[41]

On 19 July, after having called on King Sihanouk in Beijing, the "troika" made its first trip to Cambodia to speak to Hun Sen and help find a way out of the difficult and dangerous situation. Hun Sen was reported to have reacted negatively to the attempt, declaring that ASEAN had no role to play in the Cambodian situation, which needed no outside intervention, and that ASEAN's decision to delay Cambodia's admission was unjustified and further complicated the "reconciliation" process. He added that, if ASEAN's position would not change, Cambodia might have to reconsider its move to seek ASEAN membership; after all, Cambodia had survived without ASEAN all this time. To this, Ali Alatas was supposed to have sarcastically retorted that ASEAN had survived for thirty years without Cambodia. The day before, in Bangkok, the "troika" had met with Prince Ranariddh, who asked ASEAN not to give recognition to the new set-up in Phnom Penh and not to accept the Cambodian observer delegation to the ASEAN Ministerial Meeting that was to take place in a few days. Needless to say, the two co-Prime Ministers gave the "troika" widely different explanations of the month's events in Cambodia.

On the evening of 23 July, the eve of the ministerial meeting in Subang Jaya, Malaysia, the ASEAN ministers decided to stand by their 10 July decision on Cambodia's membership and to allow Ung Huot to represent Cambodia as observer at the ASEAN Ministerial Meeting, but in his capacity as foreign minister and not as a "candidate" First Prime Minister. The ministers conveyed these decisions to Ung Huot, who was already at the meeting venue, and ascertained from him whether Cambodia was still committed to joining ASEAN and whether Hun Sen and his government saw a role for ASEAN in the Cambodian peace process. Ung Huot affirmed that these were Hun Sen's positions.

Thus, at the ASEAN Ministerial Meeting, Ung Huot represented Cambodia as observer; but he had to do more than sit at the opening ceremonies as a symbolic presence. The day before the meeting started, Prince Ranariddh had written to the ASEAN Foreign Ministers thanking them for delaying Cambodia's admission and, in Ung Huot's word, "disauthorizing" the foreign minister.[42] In his statement at the meeting, Ung Huot reaffirmed

Cambodia's desire to join ASEAN. He stressed that the fighting in Cambodia was not between the Cambodian People's Party of Hun Sen and FUNCINPEC or a coup d'état; it was "legitimate action to prevent Cambodia from slipping into anarchy and a possible second genocide". He assured the gathering that the situation had returned to normal, that all state institutions were "in place", and that Cambodia would respect all its international agreements, including the Paris accords of 1991.[43]

Speaking after the Cambodian observer, Indonesia's Foreign Minister, Ali Alatas, reported:

> [T]he regrettable turn of events in Cambodia ... significantly changed the governmental set-up and political situation in that country brought about, unfortunately, by the use of armed force. We have joined the other ASEAN nations in expressing our profound dismay over these events and in calling on the two Co-Prime Ministers of Cambodia to resolve their differences peacefully. The Foreign Ministers of the Philippines, Thailand and Indonesia have just completed a mission — as mandated by the ASEAN Foreign Ministers at our Special Meeting on 10 July 1997 — to meet with His Majesty King Sihanouk, H.R.H. Prince Ranariddh and H.E. Mr. Hun Sen and convey the readiness of ASEAN to contribute its efforts to the peaceful resolution of the situation in Cambodia.
>
> While ASEAN's mission received support from His Majesty King Sihanouk and Prince Ranariddh, we were initially not able to get the same support from H.E. Mr Hun Sen who clearly stated that ASEAN must not play any role in resolving the situation in Cambodia since, in his view, it is an internal matter of Cambodia and he could and would solve it in accordance with the Constitution and relevant laws of Cambodia. Failing this, he would then turn to His Majesty King Sihanouk, as the Head of State, for a solution. However, in a subsequent message conveyed through Foreign Minister Ung Huot, it appears that H.E. Mr. Hun Sen has instructed His Foreign Minister to continue cooperating with ASEAN and stated that Cambodia now does not reject ASEAN's role in helping to restore political stability in Cambodia and that Cambodia remains firm and unchanged in its desire to join ASEAN as a full member as soon as possible.[44]

The meeting's joint communiqué "took note of the new position" of Hun Sen, as conveyed by Ung Huot, "that Cambodia welcomes ASEAN's role in helping to restore political stability in the country". The communiqué went on:

> The Foreign Ministers agreed that, upon reconfirmation of this new position, the ASEAN Ministerial delegation comprising the Minister for Foreign Affairs of Indonesia, the Secretary of Foreign Affairs of the Philippines and the Minister of Foreign Affairs of Thailand would continue

with its efforts to assist Cambodia to find a peaceful resolution of the situation in that country. The Foreign Ministers stressed ASEAN's commitment to the principle of non-interference in the internal affairs of other countries. They noted that ASEAN had offered its good offices to Cambodia in the light of the recent unfortunate developments and in view of Cambodia's interest in joining ASEAN. They expressed the hope that the situation in the country would return to normalcy and that a solution could be found in the spirit of the Paris Peace Accords. Recalling the decision of the first ASEAN Informal Summit in Jakarta in 1996, the Foreign Ministers also expressed regret that Cambodia could not be admitted into ASEAN due to the present circumstances in the country, while reaffirming that Cambodia's Observer status at the AMM remains unchanged. They expressed the hope that a peaceful solution would soon be found so that Cambodia would be able to join ASEAN and fulfill the vision of an ASEAN community of 10 as envisaged by the Founding Fathers of ASEAN.[45]

In less than a week, Ung Huot, writing explicitly on behalf of Hun Sen and confirming that "Cambodia welcomes ASEAN role in helping to restore political stability in the country," invited the "troika" to come to Cambodia, "if possible this week". On 2 August, ASEAN's three-man ministerial delegation visited Phnom Penh again and held talks with Hun Sen and Ung Huot. In those talks, Hun Sen said that the timing of Cambodia's membership was up to ASEAN, but stressed that delaying it too long would not be good for either ASEAN or Cambodia.

Nine days later, the ASEAN Foreign Ministers met in Singapore to receive a briefing from the delegation and assess the situation. According to the joint statement of the special meeting, they agreed that "ASEAN will remain engaged in its effort to help restore political stability in Cambodia". The ministers "stressed the importance of the holding of free and fair elections in Cambodia as scheduled in May 1998" and "reaffirmed the necessity for all political parties to participate fully in the elections". This last statement was a reiteration of ASEAN's consistent insistence on the inclusion of FUNCINPEC in the political process. Indicating continuing disagreement on the timing of Cambodia's admission into ASEAN, the joint statement emphasized that that subject "was not on the agenda of the Meeting".[46] In September, the ASEAN "troika" met separately with Hun Sen and Ung Huot in New York on the occasion of the regular session of the UN General Assembly. At the beginning of the session, the Assembly's Credentials Committee had rejected the credentials of the Cambodian delegation, in effect declaring the Cambodian seat vacant.

Reflecting the persistence of the disagreement within ASEAN on the timing of Cambodia's admission, the press statement of the ASEAN Summit in Kuala Lumpur in December 1997 carefully formulated the leaders' combined position: that "consultations should be intensified so as to enable Cambodia to join ASEAN as soon as possible, preferably before the next ASEAN Summit".[47] The insertion of the word "preferably" was evidently a compromise between the member-states that wanted to pin down the date of admission to December 1998 or before and those that preferred to keep their options open.

A flurry of consultations and other activities followed the Kuala Lumpur summit. Japan put forward a four-point peace proposal: cessation of cooperation between Prince Ranariddh's forces and the Khmers Rouges, a ceasefire and the integration of the royalist forces in the Royal Cambodian Armed Forces, Prince Ranariddh's trial *in absentia* and, in case of conviction, pardon by the King, and a guarantee by Hun Sen of Ranariddh's safe return and participation in the elections. Although the King had misgivings about the arrangement regarding his son's trial, conviction and pardon, Hun Sen eventually accepted the Japanese proposal. Several times, in January in New York, February and March in Manila, and April and June in Bangkok, the members of the ASEAN "troika" met among themselves and, the day after, with the "Friends of Cambodia", an informal, *ad hoc* group made up of Australia, Canada, China, the European Union, Japan, New Zealand, Russia and the United States, to exchange assessments and work on possible solutions. The major concerns were the cessation of violence, the fate of Ranariddh, the holding of free and fair elections, and the participation of all parties in those elections.

Meanwhile, in late January 1998, Ranariddh met in Bangkok with the ambassadors of the ASEAN "troika" and then with Surin Pitsuwan, who had replaced Prachuab as Foreign Minister with the change of government in Thailand. The "troika" called on King Sihanouk in Siem Reap in April and again in June, when they also met, separately, with Hun Sen and Ranariddh in Phnom Penh. This time, all talk was about the coming elections and the circumstances surrounding them; apparently, no reference was made to Cambodia's ASEAN membership.

The elections took place on 26 July 1998, the day after the ASEAN Ministerial Meeting in Manila, with 75 observers from ASEAN joining more than 700 others from the international community and, according to Hun Sen, the participation of 39 political parties and a voter turnout of 93.7 per cent. Hun Sen's CPP won by a wide margin but fell short of the two-thirds majority needed to form a government by itself; indeed, it won only 41 per cent of the vote. Without going into the Byzantine manœuvering over the formation of a coalition, I just note that the resulting arrangement was that Hun Sen would be the sole Prime Minister, as against the previous government's unusual set-up of having two, Ranariddh would preside over the National Assembly, and Chea Sim, the president of CPP and chairman of the National Assembly, would head a new Senate, which had yet to be created. Hun Sen had insisted that a Senate be formed with Chea Sim at its head, so that, in Sihanouk's absence, which was frequent in view of his illness, Hun Sen's ally Chea Sim would be the acting head of state and not Ranariddh. After all, the head of state or acting head of state would have to approve senior appointments and other major decisions of the government.

With the leadership preoccupied with the elections and the political bargaining that followed, Cambodia, as observer, was represented at the ASEAN Ministerial Meeting by a special envoy, Chem Widhya, Permanent Secretary of the Ministry of Foreign Affairs and International Cooperation. In his statement at the meeting's opening, he affirmed, "Cambodia remains committed to its declared intention to join ASEAN.... Cambodia will be Member of ASEAN the day the Association so decides."[48] In their joint communiqué, the foreign ministers "recalled that the ASEAN Heads of State/Government at the Second ASEAN Informal Summit called for the intensification of consultations with Cambodia to facilitate its admission into ASEAN",[49] omitting the leaders' stated preference for the admission to take place before the ASEAN Summit in Hanoi, a compromise formulation, as I have noted.

Hun Sen was invited to that summit on 15–16 December 1998, not merely to be present but to give a speech just like the ASEAN leaders. According to Harish and Julie Mehta, in their biography of Hun Sen, the Prime Minister "was confident that Cambodia would become a member of Asean in December 1998." They continued:

> "I will travel to Hanoi with two options: the first possibility is that, after being officially admitted, we will participate officially in the summit. The second possibility is that we would travel there to be officially admitted," he said.
> Sensing a breakthrough was close at hand Hun Sen wrote to Thailand's Prime Minister Chuan Leekpai on August 31, requesting membership of Asean. In his letter, Hun Sen said: "Cambodia has always had a strong commitment for Asean membership to achieve Asean's founding vision of all Asean nations in one Asean family."[50]

With the power-sharing arrangement worked out in Phnom Penh, ASEAN had no choice but to agree on Cambodia's admission. However, it was still divided on when the admission should take place — at the Hanoi summit or later. Harish and Julie Mehta say that Vietnam, Malaysia, Indonesia and Myanmar favoured Cambodia's immediate admission at the Hanoi summit, while the Philippines, Singapore and Thailand preferred to wait.[51] Surin Pitsuwan, the Thai Foreign Minister at that time, has said on several occasions that Thailand, and presumably the other two, had wanted to wait for the Senate to be created, as agreed upon by the Cambodians. The formation of the Senate, however, would require an amendment to the 1993 constitution. Over lunch in Phnom Penh in May 2003, Ung Huot told me that the real reason was that accepting Cambodia at the summit in Hanoi, the capital of its strongest backer, would have been "too much" for some ASEAN members. On the eve of their summit, the ASEAN leaders went into a huddle in a room in the Daewoo Hotel in Hanoi and hammered out a clever compromise — defer the admission of Cambodia to a later date, but hold the ceremonies in Hanoi.

Hun Sen was resigned to the arrangement. In his public speech on 15 December, he declared:

> We have met all the requirements given by ASEAN. Therefore, we feel greatly encouraged by the decision of the ASEAN Heads of State and Government at its Sixth Summit to admit the Kingdom of Cambodia as the tenth member of ASEAN in Hanoi and to organize an official admission ceremony as soon as possible.[52]

Those ceremonies, among foreign ministers, at which I was present as Secretary-General, took place at the Daewoo Hotel on 30 April 1999. The declaration on the admission of Cambodia was identical to those for Laos and Myanmar. On the same day, Cambodia acceded, in a single protocol, to the same 20 agreements that Myanmar had signed, plus seven that had been concluded since the admission of Laos and Myanmar, including the framework agreements on the ASEAN Investment Area, mutual recognition arrangements, and the facilitation of goods in transit. Cambodia attended the ASEAN Ministerial Meeting in July as a full member.

Kao Kim Hourn, Executive Director of the Cambodian Institute for Cooperation and Peace and now Secretary of State at the Ministry of Foreign Affairs and International Cooperation, rather dryly accused ASEAN of "changing the 'goal posts' for Cambodia in its quest for membership." He recalled that "some ... ASEAN leaders stated publicly that Cambodia's membership in the regional grouping was dependent on the July 1998 elections in Cambodia. Despite some problems in the post-election period, all in all the elections went well. ASEAN member countries actually sent their own observers to participating (sic) in the monitoring of the Cambodian elections. Contrary to what ASEAN leaders said about the Cambodian elections, at the end of the day ASEAN was still not committed to Cambodia, and Cambodia continued to remain outside of the Southeast Asian family." He went on:

> [O]nce again ASEAN changed its position when it argued that Cambodia's entry into the association was dependent on the formation of the new coalition government in Phnom Penh.... By late November 1998, the new coalition government was finally set up, as the two major political parties compromised on power sharing.... (A)gain ASEAN insisted that the political process in Cambodia must be completed before it could become a full member. This time ASEAN insisted that the Senate must be established. Setting up the Senate requires major amendments to the Constitution of Cambodia which will essentially rewrite Cambodia's political system.... At the Sixth ASEAN Summit in Hanoi in December 1998, Cambodia tried hard to convince the leaders of ASEAN to admit Phnom Penh as expeditiously as possible. Because of the slow process of the establishment of the Senate, ASEAN decided to admit Cambodia but delayed the official induction ceremony to a later date.[53]

Kao Kim Hourn was right in his facts, except that the changing conditions imposed on Cambodia's ASEAN membership arose not from the positions taken by ASEAN as a whole but from the reasons given by those members that favored delaying Cambodia's admission. The resulting decisions — and thus the moving goal posts — were the products of back-room compromises. They exemplified ASEAN consensus-making at work and ASEAN's way of papering over disagreements in public. These methods, however, are characteristic not just of the "ASEAN Way" but of international diplomacy generally.

Domingo Siazon, the Philippines' Secretary of Foreign Affairs at that time, disputes Kao Kim Hourn's assertion that ASEAN moved the goal posts in Cambodia's quest for membership. He stresses that, for those who argued for the establishment of the Senate before Cambodia's admission, the overriding consideration was the political stability of Cambodia. He says that "that (the holding of free and fair elections) alone would not have restored political stability in Cambodia. The establishment of the Senate had to be completed to restore political equilibrium in Cambodia at least for a reasonable period of time." The allusion seems to be that the Senate was part of the delicate state structure agreed upon in the settlement between the CPP and FUNCINPEC. In an aside, Siazon gives Ung Huot credit for convincing Hun Sen to reverse himself and accept ASEAN's help in restoring political stability in Cambodia.[54]

Two important observations are to be made in this regard. First, it was the first time that ASEAN conditioned membership — or at least its timing —

on the domestic situation in the prospective member. While in general the concern was over the country's political stability, conditions for membership were actually imposed in terms of elections, the participation of certain parties and even of individuals in those elections, coalitions, legislative institutions, and power-sharing arrangements. A second, related question is whether ASEAN's actions did not constitute interference in a country's internal affairs. ASEAN officials have argued that ASEAN was intervening not in a member-state but in a country still outside the association and that ASEAN had the right to do so in Cambodia's case, because the association had had a key role in bringing about the political settlement in Cambodia in 1991 and thus bore a responsibility for ensuring that it held. Nevertheless, the apparent contrast between ASEAN's treatment of Cambodia's membership and its approach to, say, Myanmar's has been pointed out.

In a speech at a reception in Phnom Penh on 5 May 1999 celebrating Cambodia's entry into ASEAN, Prime Minister Hun Sen cited four qualities of ASEAN that attracted his country. First was the "regional environment of security, peace and stability, allowing this region to prosper ... (and) achieved through a framework of efficient cooperation and consultation based on the main principles of the 1967 Bangkok Declaration, especially the principle of non-interference in each other's internal affairs." The second was the "consensus-building principle in making decisions within ASEAN." He mentioned as the third of ASEAN's "strengths" the region's reputation for "strong economic growth," noting the "positive signs of economic recovery" from the financial crisis that had had the regional economies reeling. The fourth was ASEAN's role as "a major international gateway" through which to conduct relations with the rest of the world. At the same time, Hun Sen stressed Cambodia's own contribution to ASEAN — "the commitment to democracy, the respect for human rights, the prevalence of peace and national reconciliation in the country, the dismantling of the political and military organization of the Khmer Rouge."[55]

Foreign affairs and economic officials of Cambodia diverge somewhat in their valuation of the country's membership in ASEAN. Prince Norodom Sirivudh, half-brother of former King Sihanouk, foreign minister in 1993–94 and now co-Minister of Interior, pointed out that Cambodia could not afford to be isolated in Southeast Asia. ASEAN could be a useful channel for Phnom Penh's relations with the rest of the world and, at the same time, help "loosen up Cambodian thinking and style." He also hoped that Cambodia could get help from ASEAN and its members in developing its human resources. But, first, he stressed, Cambodia had to put its house in order. "It cannot go to a well-dressed party in rags, unbathed and slovenly," he said.⁵⁶ Hor Namhong, Minister of Foreign Affairs and International Cooperation since 1998, and now Deputy Prime Minister as well, recalled that, after 1993, it was "necessary politically and economically" for Cambodia to join ASEAN. He would like to see ASEAN move "from an association to an organization," building the ASEAN Economic Community and strengthening the authority of the ASEAN Secretariat. This would also mean, he said, that the older members had to extend substantial assistance to the newer members, similar to the European Union's support for its less-developed members, like Ireland, Portugal, Greece and Spain, at the early stages of their membership.⁵⁷

On the other hand, the economic officials see little economic benefit from Cambodia's membership in ASEAN. In the view of Cham Prasidh, the Minister of Commerce, only the ASEAN-6 would benefit from regional economic integration. Nevertheless, he stressed, Cambodia's trade and investment regime was already quite "liberal," and his ministry would like to accelerate Cambodia's CEPT schedule and its abolition of tariffs. For Cambodia, he said, the Generalized System of Preferences of the developed countries was much more important than the regional market. As it was, Cambodia was "disappointed" with the implementation of the system of trade preferences that the ASEAN-6 were supposed to extend to the newer members as part of the effort to narrow the development gap between the six and the four.⁵⁸

A TWO-TIER ASEAN?

The admission of Cambodia and the consequent completion of Southeast Asian membership in ASEAN have raised questions about the difficulties arising from a "two-tier ASEAN" — the presumed division between the six older, more-developed members and the four newer, less-developed ones. My replies to such questions, in the run-up to and after the admission of the four, have been consistent: worse than a two-tier ASEAN would be a two-tier Southeast Asia, one group in ASEAN and the other outside it. The alternative to an ASEAN embracing all of Southeast Asia would be an ASEAN limited to six members, with the other four either individually linking up with other countries or groups of countries or forming their own group apart from and in competition with ASEAN. This situation would have Southeast Asia not in solidarity but in division. To me at least, ASEAN membership of all ten Southeast Asian countries is the preferable alternative.

In any case, the divide between the ASEAN-6 and the ASEAN-4 may not be as clear-cut as many commentaries, including statements by ASEAN members themselves, make it out to be. Table 2.1, which comes from the ASEAN Secretariat, compares the gross domestic products and the per capita GDP of the ten ASEAN countries in 2003. The *average* GDP per capita of the ASEAN-6 is more than five times that of the ASEAN-4. However, this apparent divide becomes less meaningful when one considers that the gaps *within* the ASEAN-6 are even wider. Singapore's per capita GDP is more than twenty times that of Indonesia or the Philippines, Brunei Darussalam's almost thirteen times, and Malaysia's more than four times. On the other hand, the per capita GDP of Indonesia or the Philippines is only twice that of Vietnam, a gap less than the difference between Thailand's GDP per capita and that of either Indonesia or the Philippines. This is admittedly an oversimplification, as there are many other factors to consider, but the point is that, at least in terms of GDP per capita, the divide between the older and the newer members may not be all that stark.

It has also been said that the progress of ASEAN's economic integration has been hampered by the admission of the four new members. I fail to see how this is so. If the four had not been admitted into ASEAN, the ASEAN Free Trade Area, for example, would have included only the six older members. However, what has been retarding integration among the six is not the accession of the four, but policy positions and implementation delays largely on the part of the six themselves, including those involving the dismantling of non-tariff barriers, the negotiations on trade in services, the implementation of the agreement on goods in transit, compliance with

TABLE 2.1
GDP of ASEAN Member-Countries, 2003

Country	GDP (in US dollars)	Population	GDP per capita (in US dollars)
Brunei Darussalam	4,715,085,078	363,450	12,973
Cambodia	4,214,899,907	13,798,000	305
Indonesia	208,625,321,605	213,494,000	977
Lao PDR	2,043,163,868	5,618,000	364
Malaysia	103,736,842,105	25,050,000	4,141
Myanmar	9,605,000,000	53,514,512	179
Philippines	79,270,199,255	81,081,000	978
Singapore	91,355,476,919	4,185,000	21,829
Thailand	143,303,334,373	63,950,000	2,241
Vietnam	39,021,400,599	81,185,000	481
ASEAN	685,890,723,710	542,238, 962	1,265

Source: ASEAN Finance and Macroeconomic Surveillance Unit Database.[59]

the tourism agreement, the harmonization of product standards, the coordination of customs procedures, and so on. Doing by far the most trading within the region, the ASEAN-6 have the main responsibility for regional market integration.

In the light of their small share in intra-ASEAN trade and in investments in ASEAN, the ASEAN-4 cannot be the obstacle to ASEAN's progress that they are sometimes accused of being. In fact, the accession of the ASEAN-4 to the AFTA and related agreements has, at least theoretically, given investors a wider choice of where to place their investments in the free-trade area according to the availability and cost of the required labour, the accessibility and cost of other resources, the effectiveness and enforcement of the legal and policy regime, the overall investment climate, and so on. These are all subject to national measures, policies and decisions, and shortcomings in them cannot be said to retard regional economic integration just because of the membership of the ASEAN-4.

More real is the so-called digital divide between the older members and the newer members of ASEAN. A study done by the consultancy services of IBM for the ASEAN Secretariat in 2001 confirmed that divide. The study found that, according to a number of criteria laid down by ASEAN, the ASEAN-4 are indeed behind the rest in the development and use of information and communications technology, with Singapore at the head of the entire pack, and Malaysia coming in second. Again, however, there are wide differences among the ASEAN-6 in particular elements of information and communications technology.

Among the IBM study's recommendations are the adoption of policy and administrative measures by each ASEAN country, including free trade in ICT goods, the formulation of a national master plan for the development and use of information technology, a cabinet-level national body to implement the plan, a competitive environment for ICT service providers, the designation of an independent regulatory body for Internet service providers, the development of plans for national capacity building, the enactment of laws to govern e-commerce, and so on. Unfortunately, many of the suggested measures run counter to the current policies of some ASEAN members. This is an illustration of how the requirements for narrowing the digital divide or even the development gap in ASEAN sometimes clash with the restrictive measures that some ASEAN governments think are necessary to advance certain national or leadership interests.

Another area where there is a gap between the older and the newer members is that of economic policy, with the ASEAN-4's economies still negotiating the transition from centrally planned to market-driven. This is evidently the rationale for the later deadlines conceded to the ASEAN-4 in the ASEAN Free Trade Area and the longer timetables granted them in the 2004 ASEAN-China agreement on trade in goods and the 2003 Framework Agreement on Comprehensive Economic Cooperation between ASEAN and India, as well as the ASEAN Investment Area. I have asked officials in Vietnam and Cambodia why they need to have later deadlines for the regional market-integration schemes: if they believe that being integrated with the ASEAN regional economy is good for them, why delay the process? The answers indicated disagreements within the cabinets of the two countries, with the trade ministries advocating faster liberalization and the finance ministries favouring a more cautious approach.

Some officials of the newer ASEAN members are apprehensive that regional economic integration would somehow place their countries at a disadvantage on account of the relative backwardness of their economies. The fear seems to be that, with regional economic integration, the markets of the newer members would be flooded by goods imported from the older and more advanced members. However, regional trade liberalization works both ways. Assuming that the investment climate is right, investors could take advantage of the lower wages and other costs in the newer members to produce goods for export to an integrated ASEAN market. Moreover, there is much more to economic integration than cutting tariffs. The newer members could benefit from the other elements of integration as much as the older members, elements like smoother transportation and communications links, the harmonization of product standards, better coordinated and more efficient customs procedures, less expensive and better supporting services, and so on.

In any case, the projection of a divide between the older and the newer members of ASEAN is a political reality. The ASEAN advocates in the newer members apparently need to show that ASEAN is helping the country catch up with the older members so as to overcome the misgivings of their more conservative and skeptical colleagues about joining the association. Emphasizing the gap may also be useful in gaining not only trade concessions from the older members but an added avenue for acquiring development assistance from the developed countries and the international financial institutions.

INTEGRATING THE NEWER MEMBERS

Thus, the phrase "narrowing the development gap" entered ASEAN's vocabulary, and the ASEAN leaders, at their summit meeting in 2000 in

Singapore, decided to launch a special programme for this purpose. Upon Singapore Prime Minister Goh Chok Tong's suggestion, the programme was called the Initiative for ASEAN Integration, or IAI. The use of the word "integration" served to stress ASEAN's continuing commitment to regional economic integration, assure the people in the newer member-countries that ASEAN's integration schemes would not exclude them from the benefits of such schemes, and affirm the importance of integrating the newer members into the ASEAN mainstream. The summit chairman's statement explained, "The IAI is to narrow the divide within ASEAN and enhance ASEAN's competitiveness as a region.... The IAI will focus on education, skills development and worker training. These will be key factors of competitiveness in the New Economy."[60]

Eight months later, the 2001 ASEAN Ministerial Meeting issued the Hanoi Declaration on Narrowing the Development Gap for Closer ASEAN Integration. The declaration laid down the components of the IAI — infrastructure, human resource development, information and communications technology, and regional economic integration — and established a special IAI unit in the Secretariat to manage the programme.[61] Subsequently, a workshop was convened, with Japanese funding, to draw up a six-year (2002–08) plan of action for the IAI. The workshop, in which all ASEAN countries, as well as the Secretariat, took part, split up into four groups, one for each of the areas designated by the ministers. The human resource component was handled by foreign ministry officials; the rest by experts in the fields concerned.

The projects that went into the plan of action were based on what the ASEAN-4, also known as CLMV, thought was both needed and possible to carry out in an ASEAN context. Most of the projects were for studies, training, plans and policy measures — areas that were considered as accounting for some of the development gap and that a programme like IAI could handle. The construction of hard infrastructure, for example, like dams, roads and railroads, was largely left to the private sector, to bilateral arrangements with other countries, or to international financial institutions like the World Bank and the Asian Development Bank. Where IAI could help best would be in "soft" infrastructure. The work plan is subject to periodic adjustment according to changing needs and the availability of funding.

Studies, for example, were prescribed for inland waterways and for the feasibility of the missing links and spur lines of the Singapore-Kunming Rail Link. In the infrastructure component, training would be undertaken in such areas as inland waterways, multimodal transport, power transmission, solar energy, and so on. For the development of human resources, CLMV personnel would be trained in HRD planning and labour market monitoring, the training of workers in new skills, higher education management, and overseas employment administration. Training would be undertaken in various aspects of information and communications technology. The CLMV countries' capacity for regional economic integration would be strengthened through capacity-building in such areas as customs valuation and management, the setting of product standards and metrology. In all four areas, training and studies predominate among the projects agreed upon in the IAI work plan.

Just as or even more important are the national measures and policies that the CLMV countries themselves have committed to adopt. Clearly, narrowing the development gap depends more on domestic reforms than on regional cooperation; indeed, many regional cooperation projects are possible only with domestic reforms. For example, the CLMV countries committed themselves in the work plan to streamlining customs and immigration procedures as part of the effort to improve air and river transportation. They acknowledged the need for national legislation to support training activities. Nowhere are domestic measures more necessary than in the area of information and communications technology; examples are telecommunications policy, regulatory frameworks, national master plans for ICT development and use, the establishment of national ICT bodies, intellectual property legislation, regulations on cyber crimes and security, and policies on e-commerce and e-government.

The IAI projects and policy measures were designed to fill gaps in national planning and policy-making, institution-building, technical studies, and the development of human resources, precisely the areas in which the ASEAN-4 were considered to be behind the rest, behind even those that had the lowest economic levels among the ASEAN-6.

The ASEAN Foreign Ministers adopted the work plan at their meeting in July 2002. An IAI Task Force was set up, composed of the ASEAN-4 and the ASEAN Secretariat, to exercise ownership and leadership of the programme. In August 2002, the Secretariat organized a forum to brief potential donors on the work plan and to sound them out on the projects they were willing to support. While the initial response was rather tepid, partly because many of the representatives at the forum were not authorized to make financial commitments for their governments or agencies, it turned quite positive as the projects became clearer as to their nature and scope and, in some cases, were adjusted to donors' abilities and priorities. In a way, the IAI has revitalized development cooperation between ASEAN and its Dialogue Partners and international agencies at a time when the latter had developed misgivings over assistance to a group of countries perceived to have achieved remarkable economic growth and to be no longer short of resources.

According to the Secretariat, the number of projects in the work plan had grown from the initial forty-eight to seventy-six in January 2004 and to 129 by February 2006. One hundred and eight projects had received funding, with sixty-six completed, twenty-one in the course of implementation, and the other eighteen at the planning stage. In the case of four other projects, only some components had received funding; the funded components are being implemented, while the others continue to await funds. Financing for another six was being negotiated. Eleven of the projects had attracted no funding at all. The leading donors have been the Republic of Korea, Japan, India, Norway through the UN Industrial Development Organization, and the European Union.[62]

One notable element in the IAI is the responsibility taken on by the ASEAN-6 to do their part in helping their fellow-members of ASEAN rather than leaving it, as before, to others. Indeed, the chairman's statement of the 2000 ASEAN Summit defines the IAI as "essentially" providing "a framework for regional cooperation through which the more developed ASEAN members could help those member countries that most need it."[63] Malaysia has undertaken or plans to carry out training programmes in oil and gas production and refining, information and communications technology, product standards, trade policy, customs and irrigation; Indonesia in renewable energy and railways; Singapore in ICT, English communications, and curriculum development for vocational education; Thailand in ICT, civil service development, the power industry, and multimodal transport; Brunei Darussalam in information technology, the civil service, and higher education management; and the Philippines in overseas employment administration and technical vocational education. Some of these programmes have had the collaboration of Japan, Australia, the European Commission, India, Korea, Denmark and UNDP. Unfortunately, many of the projects were proposed rather haphazardly by the ASEAN-6 at the expense of a desirable degree of coherence.

The ASEAN-6 have also been conducting similar assistance programmes outside the IAI. Singapore, in fact, has put up and funds a training centre in the capital of each of the newer members, where it runs training programmes with resource persons largely from Singapore. Designed in consultation with the authorities of the host country, the programmes cover a wide variety of subjects, like the English language, tourism management and communications, trade issues and trade negotiating skills, and information technology. All of the ASEAN-6 conduct training courses, some of them for the newer members alone, others for all the ten ASEAN countries. They also offer scholarships for study in their learning institutions. Even Vietnam has begun to share its own knowledge and experience.

In September 2001, upon my recommendation, the ASEAN Economic Ministers agreed that the ASEAN-6 would extend tariff preferences to their imports from the ASEAN-4. Noordin Azhari, at that time the ASEAN Secretariat's assistant director for trade, had suggested this to me. As the system was eventually worked out, each of the CLMV countries was asked to submit a list of products of export interest to it, and the importing country decided which goods would enjoy the preferences. I have been given three reasons for the selective, instead of across-the-board, application of trade preferences. One was the fact that some of the ASEAN-6 themselves continued to be accorded GSP privileges by developed countries and granting similar privileges to others might jeopardize their status as developing countries. Another reason was that only a relatively few products were being exported or had the potential to be exported by the ASEAN-4 to the ASEAN-6. The third was that some exports of the CLMV countries had already achieved significant market share in some of the ASEAN-6. As I have noted elsewhere, some of the CLMV countries have privately expressed their disappointment in the more restricted application of trade preferences than initially expected.

On the basis of data provided by the ASEAN Secretariat, Table 2.2 indicates the number of CLMV export items given preferences by Brunei Darussalam, Indonesia, Malaysia, the Philippines and Thailand, Singapore being a virtually duty-free economy.

Inevitably, there have been some overlaps between the IAI, the ASEAN Mekong Basin Development Cooperation scheme, in which the ASEAN countries and China participate, the ADB's Greater Mekong Sub-region programme, which involves the six Mekong riparian countries, including China, the Mekong River Commission, and the UN ESCAP's Mekong-related programmes. At a meeting of ASEAN leaders on the occasion of UNCTAD

TABLE 2.2
Status of ASEAN Integration System of Preferences

Effectivity and tariff level	Cambodia	Lao PDR	Myanmar	Vietnam
Brunei (from 1 January 2002) — 0%	8	14	79	1
Indonesia (from 1 Jan. 2002) — 0-5%	25	0 request	228	50
Malaysia (from 1 January 2002) — 0%	89	12	282	170
Philippines — 0%	2	2	69	12
Thailand (from 1 January 2004)	309	187	460	34

X in Bangkok in 2000, Prime Minister Hun Sen of Cambodia complained about the confusion surrounding these overlapping programmes and urged better coordination among them. While his observation and plea were eminently sensible, considerations of turf and differences in focus and approach make a measure of overlap and confusion almost unavoidable. Nevertheless, it is clear that the IAI work plan could stand improvement in such matters as breadth and depth of impact, sustainability and follow-through, relevance to broader ASEAN programmes, position in national development plans, ownership by the beneficiary countries, and the ability to attract funding.

In any case, the IAI is a continuing process, with measures and projects being added as needs develop. A mid-term review has been conducted to assess the impact of the projects, the effectiveness of the monitoring mechanism, the need to adjust projects and draw up additional ones, and ways to raise more funding. The review was expected also to address problems related to control and reporting, inter-agency coordination within the CLMV countries, coordination with other development programmes in the Mekong Basin, and follow-through and implementation. It would also make recommendations for filling gaps in the work plan, like those pertaining to the investment climate, barriers to trade and investment between the ASEAN-6 and the ASEAN-4, the services sectors, and the environment and the quality of urban life.

WHAT ABOUT TIMOR-LESTE?

As discussed above, with the settlement of the Cambodian conflict in 1991, the prospects of an ASEAN made up of "all ten Southeast Asian countries" began to get real. Although delayed by two years, the admission of Cambodia in 1999 was supposed to complete Southeast Asian membership in ASEAN. Little did ASEAN's leaders, ministers and officials expect that, soon after that milestone in ASEAN history was reached, another country would emerge in Southeast Asia — the eleventh — presenting ASEAN with another membership decision. That country was, of course, East Timor or, to call it by its Portuguese name, Timor-Leste.

The events leading to the independence of East Timor on 20 May 2002 have been extensively discussed elsewhere. The United Nations Web site conveniently presents a backgrounder and a chronology from the UN viewpoint.[64] ASEAN's involvement in those events since 1975 is examined in Chapter 3. Here, I will deal with the prospects of Timor-Leste's membership and other forms of participation in ASEAN.

An AFP dispatch that appeared in the *Jakarta Post* of 22 July 2000 quoted José Ramos-Horta, who was to be the country's foreign minister and, later, Prime Minister, as expressing East Timor's intention to seek membership in both ASEAN and the South Pacific Forum (renamed in October 2000 as the Pacific Islands Forum) upon gaining its independence. ASEAN countries professed to be confused, wondering how a country could be a member of those two regional organizations at the same time. In fact, the late Sergio Vieira de Mello, who was the UN Secretary-General's Special Representative and head of the UN Transitional Administration in East Timor, favoured membership in ASEAN all along, according to Vieira de Mello's chief of staff, Dato N. Parameswaran, now Malaysia's ambassador to Singapore.[65]

As agreed to by the ASEAN Foreign Ministers, an UNTAET delegation was present at the ASEAN Ministerial Meeting on 24–25 July 2000 as guests of the host, Thailand. On that occasion, Vieira de Mello and his delegation, which included East Timorese leaders Xanana Gusmão, Ramos-Horta and Mario Carrascalão, as well as Parameswaran, met with me to indicate East Timor's interest in its eventual membership in ASEAN. The delegation also had individual meetings with some, if not all, of the Foreign Ministers.

Late in 2001, Ramos-Horta formally made known East Timor's interest in ASEAN membership, its hope to be invited at the next ASEAN Ministerial Meeting in Bandar Seri Begawan in July 2002, that is, after its attainment of independence, and its desire to accede to the Treaty of Amity and Cooperation in Southeast Asia. In an "exclusive interview" with the *Asahi Shimbun* in December 2001, Ramos-Horta acknowledged that he had indeed written to Prince Mohamed Bolkiah, Brunei Foreign Minister and chair of the ASEAN Standing Committee, requesting "observer status in ASEAN as a step toward gaining membership". The *Asahi* story quoted Ramos-Horta as saying, "We will go slowly. Step one is observer status. There are obvious political reasons (in joining ASEAN), but there are also practical costs, in terms of finances and human resources."[66]

The ASEAN ministers and officials, as well as the Secretariat and I, discussed the East Timorese moves extensively. The Secretariat commissioned studies and sent officers to Dili. It was generally agreed that East Timor is geographically in Southeast Asia; it is, after all, hemmed in on the north, the east and the west by Indonesian territory. Several ministers, however, raised the question: but will East Timor be in Southeast Asia "politically"? What the question really meant was whether East Timor would not be too heavily influenced by Australia or Portugal or both. The ministers, therefore, decided to "wait and see".

The lack of consensus on the question of Timor-Leste's membership has prevented ASEAN from arriving at decisions on what seem to be straightforward issues but in reality are complicated ones — ASEAN observer status for Timor-Leste and its accession to the Treaty of Amity and Cooperation. If Timor-Leste were to sign the treaty, would it do so as a regional or a non-regional state? The question is not an idle one, for the treaty makes clear distinctions between the rights of regional and non-regional signatories. If Timor-Leste were to accede to the treaty as a regional state, it would mean acknowledging it as a Southeast Asian country and, therefore, eligible for membership (provided it was deemed to be capable of fulfilling the obligations of membership). Moreover, adding Timor-Leste to the regional signatories would require the amendment again of the treaty itself, whose Second Protocol says:

> States outside Southeast Asia may also accede to this Treaty with the consent of all the States in Southeast Asia, namely, Brunei Darussalam, the Kingdom of Cambodia, the Republic of Indonesia, the Lao People's Democratic Republic, Malaysia, the Union of Myanmar, the Republic of the Philippines, the Republic of Singapore, the Kingdom of Thailand and the Socialist Republic of Vietnam.

The lengthy amendment process, requiring ratification by all the Southeast Asian signatories, would have delayed the signatures of some non-regional states whose accessions ASEAN eagerly wanted. If, however, Timor-Leste were to sign the treaty as a non-regional state, that would mean that the country was not in Southeast Asia for purposes of the treaty and of ASEAN and thus — at least in theory — be excluded forever from ASEAN membership. This conundrum was evidently behind the fact that, while in the joint communiqué issued at their annual meeting in July 2005 the ASEAN foreign ministers welcomed the accessions of the Republic of Korea, Russia, New Zealand and Mongolia to the treaty and Australia's intention to accede to it shortly, they merely "appreciated" East Timor's "interest" in doing so.[67]

The other issue pertained to Timor-Leste's desire for observer status. In our discussions, the question was posed: what kind of observer? The ASEAN senior officials had agreed in 1983 that observer status "should be granted only to potential members of ASEAN who satisfy the criteria set for ASEAN membership". One of the criteria stated, "Only states in the South East Asia region may join ASEAN." Thus, Brunei Darussalam, Cambodia, Laos, Myanmar and Vietnam, being in Southeast Asia, were accorded observer status as a step leading to full membership. Papua New Guinea had been granted observer status although it was considered to be outside Southeast Asia, but this was in 1976, well before the 1983 decision. Thus, giving Timor-Leste observer status would commit ASEAN to admitting it to full membership at some point. The alternative, of course, is to change the senior officials' decision and grant Timor-Leste observer status similar to Papua New Guinea's, in which case ASEAN would, again, at least theoretically, be excluding Dili from membership forever.

The real issue for ASEAN, then, is not giving Timor-Leste observer status or consenting to its accession to the Treaty of Amity and Cooperation, but whether to commit itself to Timor-Leste's eventual membership, no matter how far into the future. This is precisely what some ASEAN countries have difficulty with. One factor has already been mentioned: that of Timor-Leste's foreign-policy orientation, including the alleged presence of Portuguese functionaries all over the Timorese Government. Another is Myanmar's objection to media articles by Timorese personalities supportive of the National League for Democracy of Myanmar. Some member-states are concerned that, having experienced the entry of four relatively underdeveloped members, ASEAN would be admitting an even poorer one.

Thus, in April 2002, Timor-Leste was informed that ASEAN would continue discussing Dili's desire to obtain observer status and accede to the treaty. Brunei Foreign Minister Prince Mohamed Bolkiah, on behalf of the ASEAN Standing Committee, invited East Timor to attend the ASEAN Ministerial Meeting in July as guest of Brunei Darussalam. The joint communiqué of that meeting had this to say about East Timor:

> We welcomed the Democratic Republic of East Timor as a new member of the international community and were prepared to engage East Timor in the long-term. We had invited East Timor to the 35th AMM and agreed to extend similar invitation for future AMMs. We noted East Timor's intention to become observer to ASEAN and to accede to the TAC. We would continue to consult with East Timor on this matter.[68]

Knowing where it stood, Timor-Leste turned its attention to the possibility of participating in the ASEAN Regional Forum, in which Mongolia, North Korea, and Pakistan were taking part despite not being ASEAN members, observers or Dialogue Partners. Emphasizing that the issue of ARF participation was not linked to the question pertaining to observer status or accession to the Treaty of Amity and Cooperation, several ASEAN ministers declared themselves not opposed to Timor-Leste being in the ARF, but apparently no one was actively pushing its cause. Others contended, however, that, in the light of its physical location in Southeast Asia, Timor-Leste's ARF participation might be seen as a prelude to ASEAN membership, on which there was no ASEAN consensus.

Ramos-Horta, representing Timor-Leste, was at the ASEAN Ministerial Meeting in Phnom Penh in June 2003 as guest of the chairman of the ASEAN Standing Committee. That meeting decided to lift the three-year moratorium on new admissions into the ARF and to accept Pakistan, which had been knocking on the ARF's door for years, as its twenty-fourth participant — but not Timor-Leste. On that occasion, I ran into Ramos-Horta at the riverside Foreign Correspondents Club in Phnom Penh. He sadly expressed to me his disappointment and exasperation over this development.

I next saw Ramos-Horta in Jakarta, where he attended the public sessions of the ASEAN Ministerial Meeting in June 2004, again as guest of the chairman of the ASEAN Standing Committee. This time, he contemplated his country's relationship with ASEAN with a mixture of resignation, defiance and optimism. He understood that obtaining ASEAN membership was a "long-term process" and that Timor-Leste's accession to the Treaty of Amity and Cooperation as a regional state might require an amendment to the treaty. In any case, he acknowledged, Timor-Leste lacked the financial and human resources to participate substantively in ASEAN activities. Yet, he could not understand why the idea of Timor-Leste's membership should be such a problem for some ASEAN members or why Timor-Leste could not be admitted into the ARF when it was clearly in Southeast Asia and the non-ASEAN participants and most ASEAN members supported its admission. He pointed out that it was the only member of the Southwest Pacific Forum, which also includes Australia, Indonesia, Papua New Guinea, the Philippines and New Zealand, that was not part of the ARF. Dili was being patient now, he said, but it would soon be more forceful. He asserted that in five years Timor Leste would be in a "very good position"; it was already an oil exporter and in two years would be a "major gas producer." He said darkly that Timor-Leste might develop relations that would "make some in ASEAN nervous." He claimed that China was a major investor in the energy sector, with a Chinese-Saudi joint venture in Timor-Leste to refine Saudi Arabian oil for export to China.[69]

In July 2005, ASEAN finally "agreed to invite Timor-Leste to attend the 12th ARF as the 25th participating country in the ARF and believed that Timor Leste's participation in the ARF would contribute to further enhance [sic] political and security dialogue and cooperation in the region."[70] However, Timor-Leste's membership in ASEAN itself still hangs in the air.

A DIVERSITY OF MEMBERS

The subject of ASEAN membership has to be considered in the light of the region's immense and persistent diversity, as discussed in Chapter 1, and of the association's core objectives, namely, to prevent conflict among Southeast Asian states and together use political and diplomatic means to promote the security and stability of the region. In this light, it made sense for all of Southeast Asia to be brought into the ASEAN fold with only two conditions — location in Southeast Asia and subscription to ASEAN's norms for inter-state relations. Later, accession to ASEAN agreements, all of an economic, technical or administrative nature, was added as a requirement for membership.

ASEAN has no membership criteria related to the character of the political regime, ideological system and orientation, economic policy, or level of development. If there were such criteria for membership, a regional association would not be possible in Southeast Asia, given its diversity. Indeed, three of ASEAN's original members underwent substantial changes in their political regimes subsequent to the association's founding — the Philippines in 1972 and 1986, Thailand in 1991–92 and Indonesia in 1998. One could say that the ASEAN record has demonstrated that the Southeast Asian nations' very diversity made common membership in one association not only possible but necessary. One could, in fact, say that this consideration is closely related to ASEAN's core objectives. ASEAN enables its members to manage their diversity so as to be able to pursue common purposes despite their differences. In a paper presented at the Asia-Pacific Roundtable in Kuala Lumpur in June 1999, Termsak Chalermpalanupap, political officer at the ASEAN Secretariat and special assistant to the Secretary-General, said:

> With or without ASEAN, the diversities in Southeast Asia exist and will continue to exist.... Having included all the 10 Southeast Asian nations in its membership ... represents a historic achievement of ASEAN as a confidence-building mechanism in the region. The fact that its members have different political systems — including some with opposite ideologies — makes the achievement even more remarkable. ASEAN appears to be the only regional organization with such political diversity.... (N)either the Treaty (of Amity and Cooperation) nor any other ASEAN agreements require ASEAN members to change their political systems into any specific homogenized system. ASEAN has never assigned itself the mission of transforming its members into any uniform political system. ASEAN did not set any political criterion for its prospective members to fulfill before admission, unlike in the EU where a prospective member must first meet all the criteria of democratic pluralism.[71]

As noted earlier, almost as soon as Vietnamese forces withdrew from Cambodia in 1989 and especially after a political settlement on Cambodia was arrived at in 1991, ASEAN reached out to Vietnam and Laos. Nothing in ASEAN's rules or practice barred the membership of countries ruled by communist parties or of other one-party states (or of no-party states, for that matter). Indeed, ASEAN was convinced that such a diversity of states needed to be brought together for the sake of its core objectives. As for Myanmar, again nothing in ASEAN's rules or practice said that the association could not accept members that were ruled by the military. After all, Thailand was governed by an essentially military regime for many of the years of its membership in ASEAN. Indonesia's military had a leading role in the country's governance for decades. The Philippines was under martial law for a dozen or so years while remaining a member in good standing.

In the case of Cambodia, the argument was not ostensibly about its membership but about the timing of its admission. The violent falling out between Hun Sen and Ranariddh took place less than three weeks before the ASEAN Ministerial Meeting that was scheduled to bring in Cambodia. However, key ASEAN members were clearly uneasy over the admission of a state the future of which had been rendered uncertain by internal turmoil. For the first time, domestic developments in a Southeast Asian country had become a factor in its admission into ASEAN. Indeed, Cambodia gained entry into the association only after it had settled its internal troubles to an acceptable extent.

I now return to the issue of Timor-Leste's prospective membership. As recalled above, various ASEAN members, more or less publicly, posed three objections in the way of Timor-Leste's membership — its possible foreign-policy orientation, the negative public commentaries of some of the Timorese leadership about one of the member-states, and the country's low level of development. However, a prospective member's foreign-policy stance has never been a test for ASEAN membership. As pointed out in Chapter 1, ASEAN members, at least in the early years of the association, were widely diverse in their foreign-policy leanings and strategic outlooks. ASEAN membership could, in fact, influence the member's foreign-policy posture, as it has done. ASEAN has never lacked bilateral disputes, many of them more serious than negative commentaries of one member about another. In the case of Timor-Leste, its differences with current ASEAN members might be worked out before admission. As stated earlier in this chapter, a country's level of development should not be an obstacle to ASEAN membership or its participation in ASEAN activities. In fact, the presence of three least-developed countries in ASEAN, all of them on the Mekong basin, has rekindled the interest of certain Dialogue Partners in assisting ASEAN as an association. Timor-Leste's capacity to carry out its ASEAN obligations would be assessed jointly by its officials and those of the member-states and the ASEAN Secretariat, as was done in the cases of Cambodia, Laos, Myanmar and Vietnam. However, the political turmoil that started to roil Timor-Leste again in March 2006 may have raised the obstacles to the country's ASEAN membership. Having clouded Dili's political future, the crisis has given additional arguments to those already disinclined towards Timor-Leste's acceptance by ASEAN and thus set back any prospects of membership, already meager to begin with, that Dili might have had before.

Notes

1. Philip Charrier, "ASEAN's Inheritance: The Regionalization of Southeast Asia, 1941–61", *The Pacific Review* 14, no. 3 (2001): 313–38.
2. http://www.aseansec.org/2086.htm, para. 3.
3. Quoted in an unclassified report of the Office of Asian and Pacific Affairs, Department of Foreign Affairs of the Philippines, to Undersecretary of Foreign Affairs, Rodolfo C. Severino, Manila, 14 May 1997.
4. Ibid.
5. Ibid.
6. http://www.aseansec.org/5141.htm.
7. Quoted by Prime Minister Khin Nyunt in a written answer to the author's question, Yangon, 27 July 2004.
8. http://www.aseansec.org/5206.htm, para. 6.
9. http://www.aseansec.org/1824.htm, para. 3.
10. Quoted in an unclassified report of the Office of Asian and Pacific Affairs, Department of Foreign Affairs of the Philippines, to Undersecretary of Foreign Affairs, Rodolfo C. Severino, Manila, 14 May 1997.
11. http://www.aseansec.org/3845.htm, para. 2.
12. http://www.aseansec.org/702.htm. Also see Appendix B.
13. Thanat Khoman, "ASEAN: Conception and Evolution" in *The ASEAN Reader*, compiled by K.S. Sandhu, et al. (Singapore: Institute of Southeast Asian Studies, 1992), p. xviii.
14. ASA stands for the Association of Southeast Asia, and MAPHILINDO for Malaysia, the Philippines and Indonesia.
15. Interview with former Minister U Ohn Gyaw, Yangon, 25 July 2004.
16. Written reply to the author's question, Yangon, 27 July 2004.
17. Interview with former Minister U Ohn Gyaw, Yangon, 25 July 2004.
18. Interview with Minister U Tin Winn, Yangon, 26 July 2004.
19. Interview with King Norodom Sihanouk, Phnom Penh, 10 December 2003.

20. Ibid.
21. Verbatim Record of the Inaugural Meeting of ASEAN, Ministry of Foreign Affairs, Bangkok, 8 August 1967 (ASEAN/DOC/3).
22. http://www.aseansec.org/1234.htm, para. 2.
23. See Chapter 4.
24. Luu Doan Huynh, "Vietnam-ASEAN Relations in Retrospect: A Few Thoughts in Dialogue and Cooperation", in *Peace and Reconciliation: Success Stories and Lessons from Asia and Europe*, edited by Bertrand Fort and Norbert von Hofmann (Singapore: Asia-Europe Foundation and Friedrich Ebert Stiftung Office for Regional Cooperation in Southeast Asia, 2004), pp. 25–26.
25. http://www.aseansec.org/1240.htm, para. 19.
26. http://www.aseansec.org/2086.htm, para. 3.
27. See Appendix A.
28. Interview with Amitav Acharya, Singapore, 18 August 2003.
29. Interview with Deputy Prime Minister Vu Khoan, Hanoi, 21 October 2003.
30. Trinh Quang Thanh's presentation at the third Asia-Europe Roundtable: Peace and Reconciliation: Success Stories and Lessons in Asia and Europe, Hanoi, 20 October 2003.
31. Luu Doan Huynh, op. cit., p. 35.
32. http://www.aseansec.org/5189.htm.
33. http://www.aseansec.org/1820.htm, para. 6.
34. http://www.aseansec.org/1826.htm.
35. Interview with Prime Minister Khin Nyunt, Yangon, 27 July 2004.
36. Interview with Minister U Win Aung, Yangon, 27 July 2004.
37. Phongsavath Boupha, *The Evolution of the Lao State* (Delhi: Konark Publishers PVT Ltd., 2002), p. 163.
38. Interview with Ung Huot, Phnom Penh, 27 May 2003.
39. Document in author's possession.
40. FUNCINPEC or Front Uni National pour un Cambodge Indépendant, Neutre, Pacifique et Coopératif.
41. Interview with Ung Huot, Phnom Penh, 27 May 2003.
42. Ibid.
43. http://www.aseansec.org/3996.htm; also compiled in Kao Kim Hourn: *Cambodia's Foreign Policy and ASEAN: From Nonalignment to Engagement* (Phnom Penh: Cambodian Institute for Cooperation and Peace, 2002), pp. 497–503.
44. http://www.aseansec.org/3997.htm.
45. http://www.aseansec.org/1825.htm, para. 15.
46. Joint Press Statement of the Special Meeting of the ASEAN Foreign Ministers, Singapore, 11 August 1997.
47. http://www.aseansec.org/1816.htm.
48. http://www.aseansec.org/3918.htm.

49. http://www.aseansec.org/3933.htm, para. 14.
50. Harish C. Mehta and Julie B. Mehta, *Hun Sen, Strongman of Cambodia* (Singapore: Graham Brash, 1999), p. 252.
51. Ibid., p. 257.
52. Statement at the ASEAN-Cambodia meeting, Hanoi, 15 December 1998, in *Sixth ASEAN Summit* (Jakarta: ASEAN Secretariat, 1999).
53. Kao Kim Hourn, *Flexible Engagement vs. Non-Interference: ASEAN and Cambodia* in *Principles Under Pressure: Cambodia and ASEAN's Non-Interference Policy*, edited by Kao Kim Hourn and Jeffrey A. Kaplan (Phnom Penh: Cambodian Institute for Cooperation and Peace, 1999), pp. 67–70.
54. Domingo Siazon's letter to the author, 12 August 2004.
55. Compiled in Kao Kim Hourn, *Cambodia's Foreign Policy and ASEAN: From Nonalignment to Engagement* (Phnom Penh: Cambodian Institute for Cooperation and Peace, 2002), pp. 531–33.
56. Interview with Prince Norodom Sirivudh, Secretary-General of FUNCINPEC, Phnom Penh, 7 June 2003.
57. Interview with Minister Hor Namhong, Phnom Penh, 27 June 2003.
58. Interview with Minister Cham Prasidh, Phnom Penh, 12 May 2003.
59. Reproduced in *ASEAN: Narrowing the Development Gap* (Jakarta: ASEAN Secretariat, 2004), p. 12.
60. http://www.aseansec.org/5310.htm.
61. http://www.aseansec.org/3717.htm.
62. http://www.aseansec.org/17947.doc: *Progress of IAI Work Plan: Status Update — as of 10 February 2006.*
63. http://www.aseansec.org/5310.htm, para. 1.
64. http://www.un.org/peace/etimor/UntaetB.htm and http://www.un.org/peace/etimor/Untaetchrono.html.
65. Interview with Ambassador N. Parameswaran, Singapore, 10 August 2004.
66. http://www.asahi.com/english/international/K2001120400600.html.
67. http://www.aseansec.org/17592.htm, para. 12.
68. http://www.aseansec.org/4070.htm, para. 44.
69. Interview with Minister José Ramos-Horta, Jakarta, 29 June 2004.
70. http://www.aseansec.org/17592.htm, para. 24.
71. http://www.aseansec.org/2833.htm, paras. 4, 5 and 22.

3

THE ISSUE OF NON-INTERFERENCE

Perhaps, the most prominent issue raised by the media, some politicians and other public commentators against the Association of Southeast Asian Nations has been its policy and practice of not interfering in its members' internal affairs. Some have even called it a "doctrine", something ideological and, therefore, to be adhered to at all cost and under all circumstances. The frequent implication is that the "doctrine", policy or practice is peculiar to ASEAN, as if the association had invented it. Sometimes, the criticism amounts to heckling or jeering. The public complaints have arisen in recent years, most of them in commentaries about certain events or situations in Southeast Asia. The leading issues have been East Timor, the haze arising from land and forest fires in Indonesia, the financial crisis of 1997–98, and, above all, Myanmar and the question of human rights in general. Most of the commentaries do not specify what precisely ASEAN as an association or its member-states should have done about these situations; they have generally been appeals simply to "do something" about the problem, blaming ASEAN's failure to act on the member-states' rigid adherence to the principle of non-interference. There seems to be an element of frustration in this, in the face of the international community's apparent helplessness or the region's inaction. The frustration is vented on the most visible entity in the area, ASEAN itself. In the light of this, let us examine each of the events and situations cited above and what, if anything, ASEAN did about them or could have done about them. But, first, a few facts.

The "doctrine" of non-interference or, more precisely, the policy and practice of states committing themselves to refrain from interfering in one another's internal affairs has been around for a long time, long before ASEAN was born — or conceived. It has, in fact, been the underpinning of the entire system of inter-state relations since the 1648 Treaty of Westphalia. After four years of negotiations, that voluminous treaty put an end to the Eighty Years' War between the Dutch and the Spanish. What is more significant for the future of international relations and, thus, of mankind is that it conferred sovereignty on the nations of Europe over their respective territories, largely freeing them from the Holy Roman Empire, although the latter continued to exist in one form or another until 1806. It also guaranteed in much of the continent religious liberty and tolerance, at least for the three major branches of Christianity — the Roman Catholic, the Lutheran and the Calvinist.

The sovereignty of nation-states, which encompasses the idea of non-interference in their internal affairs, has governed the relations among nations since then. At its most basic level, it is easy to see the chaos that would engulf the international system if one state, especially a powerful one, were allowed to interfere in another nation's internal affairs. Indeed, such interference has been the cause of many wars and injustices in the world. Interference in a state's internal affairs would strike at the very essence of national sovereignty. This is why countries like the United States have such stringent laws against foreign involvement in, for example, their domestic politics. And this is why most, if not all, significant international associations have in their charters commitments by the parties not to interfere in one another's internal affairs.

The Constitutive Act of the African Union (AU), signed on 11 July 2000, has among its principles "non-interference by any Member State in the internal affairs of another" (Article 4 [g]). Signed on 25 May 1963, the Charter of the Organization of African Unity, the African Union's predecessor, laid down as one of its principles "non-interference in the internal affairs of States" (Article III [2]). The Charter of the South Asian Association for Regional Cooperation (SAARC), adopted on 8 December 1985, states in its Article II, "Cooperation within the framework of the ASSOCIATION shall be based on respect for the principles of sovereign equality, territorial integrity, political independence, non-interference in the internal affairs of other States and mutual benefit." The Charter of the Organization of American States (OAS), signed in 1948, has a similar principle in its Article 3: "Every State has the right to choose, without external interference, its political, economic, and social system and to organize itself in the way best suited to it, and has the duty to abstain from intervening in the affairs of another State."

In December 1965, the United Nations General Assembly issued the Declaration on the Inadmissibility of Intervention in the Domestic Affairs of States and the Protection of Their Independence and Sovereignty. Expressing its concern over "the increasing threat to universal peace due to armed intervention and other direct or indirect forms of interference threatening the sovereign personality and the political independence of States", the Assembly reaffirmed the principle of non-intervention, explicitly citing the charters of the OAS, the Organization of African Unity and the Arab League, and their affirmation by various conferences, including those of the Non-Aligned Movement. It condemned "armed intervention and all other forms of interference or attempted threats against the personality of the State or against its political, economic and cultural elements". It declared that "the practice of any form of intervention not only violates the spirit and letter of the Charter of the United Nations but also leads to the creation of situations which threaten international peace and security".

As the Australian scholar John Funston, writing as a Senior Fellow at the Institute of Southeast Asian Studies in Singapore, pointed out:

> There is ... nothing particularly Asian about the principle of non-interference or, as it is also called, non-intervention. The principle is of Western origin, arising out of the Westphalia agreement of 1648, which laid the foundation for the European order of sovereign states. Non-intervention, sovereignty and the legal equality of states, have traditionally been regarded as the three basic rules specifying "the accepted and expected forms of behavior in relations between states". They are at the center of several United Nations doctrines, which were also largely prepared by Western nations.... It is hardly surprising that those most recently deprived of sovereignty should be amongst the strongest supporters of the principle.... As K. J. Holsti observes, if non-intervention, sovereignty and the legal equality of states "were not observed with reasonable consistency, the structure of the system and the nature of interstate relations would change radically."[1]

Thus, ASEAN was not departing from generally accepted principles when it proclaimed in the preamble of the 1967 ASEAN Declaration the determination of the countries of Southeast Asia "to ensure their stability and security from external interference in any form or manifestation in order to preserve their national identities in accordance with the ideals and aspirations of their peoples". The preamble of the 1971 Zone of Peace, Freedom and Neutrality Declaration reiterated this. Article 2 of the 1976 Treaty of Amity and Cooperation in Southeast Asia committed the signatories to certain "fundamental principles", including "non-interference in the internal affairs of one another". Although the 1976 Declaration of ASEAN Concord made no mention of this principle, the second Declaration of ASEAN Concord, issued in October 2003, emphasized it, reaffirming "the fundamental importance of adhering to the principle of non-interference and consensus in ASEAN cooperation" and proclaiming the member-countries' determination to "exercise their rights to lead their national existence free from outside interference in their internal affairs" and "uphold ASEAN's principles of non-interference, consensus-based decision-making, national and regional resilience, respect for national sovereignty, the renunciation of the threat or the use of force, and peaceful settlement of differences and disputes".

The ASEAN case, however, is different from the AU and the OAS — but not from SAARC — in one important respect. ASEAN, SAARC, the AU and the OAS, as well as the UN General Assembly, are all committed, as we have seen, to the policy of non-interference and other principles governing inter-state relations. However, in addition to this, both the AU and the OAS, according to their respective charters, adhere to certain common values, including those pertaining to the political and social arrangements *within* the member-nations, a provision that allows the possibility of intervention in case of significant violations of those values.

Included among the principles laid down in the AU's Constitutive Act are "gender equality ... respect for democratic principles, human rights, the rule of law and good governance ... social justice ... respect for the sanctity of human life, condemnation and rejection of impunity and political assassination, acts of terrorism and subversive activities", and "condemnation and rejection of unconstitutional changes of governments". Indeed, very explicitly, the same statement of principles affirms "the right of the Union to intervene in a Member State pursuant to a decision of the Assembly in respect of grave circumstances, namely: war crimes, genocide and crimes against humanity".

As an example of the AU's activism in response to developments inside member-states, the Communiqué on the Conflict Situations in Africa issued by the AU's summit-level Peace and Security Council on 25 May 2004 made pointed and specific comments and recommendations on the civil conflicts in Angola, Sierra Leone, the Comoros, the Sudan, Burundi, the Democratic Republic of the Congo, the Central African Republic, Somalia, Côte d'Ivoire and Rwanda and on the continuing tension between Ethiopia and Eritrea. The communiqué laid down the specific measures that the Union itself was to take in order to help in the resolution of some of these national problems in the region.

The day after President Gnassingbé Eyadéma of Togo suddenly died on 5 February 2005, the Togolese military installed his son, Faure E. Gnassingbé, as his successor, ramming through a constitutional amendment to legitimize the move. A spokesman for the president of the African Union Commission, Alpha Omar Konaré, promptly declared, "The African Union cannot accept this situation of *fait accompli* in Lomé. Not only is it a violation of the Togolese Constitution, it is a violation of our Constitution. The AU rejects any power deriving from a *coup d'état*."[2] Subsequently, the AU exerted increasing pressure on Togo, seeking to persuade it to return to constitutional rule by threatening a travel ban, trade sanctions and possible military action. Finally, on 25 February, Gnassingbé stepped down. Mohamed ibn Chambas, executive secretary of the Economic Community of West African States, was quoted as saying, "We have spoken with one voice, we have been clear about the principle and we have insisted that there is a minimum bar for governance, and when it is not met we will not tolerate it."[3] Still, Togo is among the smallest of the African Union's many members, fifty-three of them; it remains to be seen whether the AU is equally capable of acting in the case of unconstitutional change in one of the larger or more powerful states or against acts by a long-established regime that violate the union's stated norms. As it turned out, Gnassingbé regained the presidency as a result of elections in April 2005, with the AU attempting to play a role in the process.

The Charter of the OAS declares, "Social justice and social security are bases of lasting peace." As pointed out in Chapter 2 of this book, domestic conditions are thereby linked to the maintenance of peace and could, therefore, be of concern to the organization. The Charter also says, "The American States proclaim the fundamental rights of the individual without distinction as to race, nationality, creed, or sex." Going further, it stresses, "The solidarity of the American States and the high aims which are sought through it require the political organization of those States on the basis of the effective exercise of representative democracy.... The elimination of extreme poverty is an essential part of the promotion and consolidation of representative democracy and is the common and shared responsibility of the American States."

Institutionally, the OAS has a Convention on Human Rights, the Inter-American Commission on Human Rights, and an Inter-American Court of Human Rights. It has a unit for the promotion of democracy, an Inter-American Democratic Charter and a set of procedures for reacting to threats to democracy in the region. In 1997, a protocol went into effect establishing the organization's right to suspend a member-state whose democratically elected government is overthrown by force. The OAS has intervened in the affairs of Haiti, Peru, Venezuela and others, including the human rights situation and the conduct of elections and referendums, through collective reviews of the situation, official statements, reports, OAS observer-teams, and recommendations, all having to do with the internal affairs of the member-countries concerned — and with their consent.

To be sure, the principles pertaining to democracy, human rights, and racial, religious and gender equality enshrined in the AU and OAS charters and in their other documents may be, in the words of Shakespeare's Hamlet to his friend Horatio, "More honour'd in the breach than the observance".[4] Still, the existence of such agreed principles lays open the possibility of — and legitimizes — intervention by the association in matters that in ASEAN would be considered as the internal affairs of its members. Indeed, it can be argued that such intervention in or intrusion into the domestic situation of a member-state cannot be considered as interference, since it is related to compliance with principles and norms freely agreed upon and is carried out with the member-state's consent. Thus, it does not contradict the principle of non-interference to which the AU and the OAS adhere.

Unlike the AU and the OAS, ASEAN has no agreed norms pertaining to the political arrangements within its member-states or to the behaviour of those states towards their citizens and thus no grounds for intervening in one another's "internal affairs" except in clear cases of events in one country having an adverse impact on two or more of its neighbours and, therefore, calling for a collective response. There are two basic reasons why ASEAN has carefully kept away from even attempting to achieve a common set of norms other than those having to do with the relations between states. One is the considerable diversity within and among the Southeast Asian nations. The other is their fairly recent experience with colonialism and Western intervention and with their relations with one another as well as the current state of those relations. Underlying these, of course, is the reality that an ASEAN country would not want to interfere in the internal affairs of another lest others interfere in its own. It is a matter of national self-interest rather than a mindless adherence to a doctrine or dogma. These reasons have to be viewed in the light of ASEAN's original and still primary objectives — to manage contentious situations and prevent them from developing into conflict and to achieve a certain degree of solidarity in relating to vital international issues.

I need not dwell at length on the diversity among the countries of Southeast Asia — in race, ethnic make-up, religion, culture, and historical experience. They are obvious enough. It may be useful, however, briefly to consider in particular the current political arrangements in each of the ASEAN countries, which, taken together, manifest the region's diversity. Brunei Darussalam is an absolute monarchy that is generally considered as benign, with the unelected Legislative Council recently revived and future elections in prospect. Cambodia has a multi-party political system with periodic elections, but with a strong leader controlling most of the levers of state power and a monarchy that has influence and enormous popular respect but little formal political power. Indonesia has emerged from strongman rule to a multi-party democracy, with the nature of the parties, and thus of the political system, still evolving. Laos is a one-party state that is gradually opening up its economy. Malaysia is a multi-ethnic society and has a multi-party political system. The parties have fairly strong roots in the population, with a coalition of largely ethnic-based parties, led by the Malay party, dominating state power. Myanmar is ruled by the military, which maintains tight control over the state and continues to be bedeviled by the delicate and difficult relationship between the central government and the armed groups holding sway over the vast ethnic territories. The Philippines has all the trappings of a democracy, with periodic elections, a bill of rights, separation of powers, free speech and so on, but is controlled by a conservative oligarchy of which the nominal parties are mere factions in temporary alliances. Singapore is a multi-ethnic society and virtually a one-party state, which tightly manages the economy and society, but does it so well and to such great benefit to the economy that there seems to be little discontent. Thailand is a constitutional monarchy with a recently instituted democratic system, which, however, continues to be vulnerable, albeit less so than in the past, to the exercise of unrestrained executive power. Vietnam is a one-party state that brooks little open dissent but with a system of widespread consultation that results in usually effective, if slow, responses to the needs of the economy.

This sketchy summary is, of course, an oversimplification and is open to argument on all sorts of grounds. Nevertheless, it does give a sense of the political diversity of the region. The differences in levels of development and economic structures have not even been cited. Moreover, the diversity *among* the countries of Southeast Asia is compounded by the diversity *within* them. Brunei Darussalam is a basically Malay sultanate, with an economically prominent Chinese community and a substantial expatriate population, including Indonesians, Malaysians and Filipinos. Cambodia's largely Khmer society includes a significant Muslim population, Vietnamese along the common border, and a substantial number of Chinese, some assimilated, others not. Indonesia is almost 90 per cent Muslim, albeit of different forms, and is tolerant of other religions. It has a small — in proportion to total population — but economically powerful Chinese community. Its people are united by one language but speak many different languages as well, languages that reflect the diversity of other cultural traits. Although the ethnic Lao are dominant in Laos, the country is also populated by many tribal groups. Malaysia and Singapore are each made up of a delicate mix of Malays, Chinese and Indians but in widely different proportions, with the two countries dealing with the mixture in different ways. Myanmar is politically dominated by the Bamars, but Yangon has not quite arrived at a stable relationship with the large ethnic groups that control the territories bearing their names, speak their own languages, and profess a variety of religions. There is a strong Chinese presence of diverse persuasions. The Philippines and Thailand are predominantly Christian and Theravada Buddhist, respectively, but both have significant and restive Muslim populations in their southern regions, which abut Muslim-populated ASEAN countries. Both of them are blessed with a variety of minority tribes. Both also have Chinese populations in various degrees of assimilation. In addition, Filipinos speak a number of different but mostly related languages. Vietnam is relatively homogenous but with several minority groups, including Chinese, Khmer and scattered tribes.

Complicating the delicate nature of racial and ethnic relations within most of the Southeast Asian nations is the fact that many ethnic groups straddle national boundaries — those between Thailand and Myanmar, Thailand and Laos, the Philippines and Malaysia, Malaysia and Indonesia, Thailand and Malaysia, Vietnam and Cambodia, and, of course, Singapore and Malaysia, not to mention southern China on one side and Myanmar, Laos, and Vietnam on the other and, beyond them, Thailand. Muslim populations live in the border areas between the Philippines and Malaysia and Indonesia and between Thailand and Malaysia. And then there are the sensitivities left over from history, the ebb and flow of ancient kingdoms, the wars between Thailand and Myanmar, between Thailand and Laos, and between Thailand and Cambodia, and the merger and bitter separation of Malaysia and Singapore.

With such a complex mixture of races, tribes, religions and cultures transcending national boundaries, and the sensitivity of certain aspects of history, Southeast Asian countries are extraordinarily wary of the very possibility of interference by neighbours in one's internal affairs, and the possible use, deliberate or inadvertent, of the explosive amalgam of race, religion and culture in their interaction with their neighbours and in their internal politics. Indeed, one of the reasons why Southeast Asian states value ASEAN is precisely the mutual commitment of its members to non-interference, which, to some extent, assures them that the incendiary elements of race, religion and culture will not be used in the disputes between them and that no country will seek to promote its own value system to influence those of its neighbours. It is a mutual commitment that contributes a significant measure of stability to the relations among the Southeast Asian states and thus to that of the region as a whole, considerations that are at the heart of ASEAN's core purposes.

Southeast Asians are sensitive to the possibility of interference not only from neighbours; they have also been conditioned by the interference that they experienced from outside the region. All except Thailand fell under Western colonialism, that extreme form of interference in a society's internal affairs. Even Thailand had to employ all the wiles and wisdom at its command in order to keep itself from succumbing to British or French colonialism or both. Even so, King Mongkut caved in to British pressure to allow opium into the kingdom for the consumption of the Siamese people and the profit of British traders, as the Chinese did at the point of a gun and the Burmese did by dint of colonialism. The Dutch tried to thwart Indonesia's drive for independence after World War II by seeking, by military means, to reoccupy the archipelago and, when that failed, to keep it divided. The United States abetted the separatist movements in Indonesia in the 1950s out of its bases in the Philippines. Indonesian leaders professed to see in the creation of Malaysia a Western plot to encircle their country. In the Philippines, even after formal independence in 1946, large tracts of land were reserved for American military bases and a one-sided economic agreement was imposed on the country in Philippine-American versions of "unequal treaties". American meddling in Philippine political processes was widely perceived. Vietnam suffered from attempts by the French to reoccupy it after its declaration of independence and by the Americans to keep it divided, as well as from China's seizure of the Paracels in 1974 and border attacks in 1979. Cambodia and Laos were subjected to severe, often violent, American pressure to get them on the American side in the Indochina war. All, again except Thailand, suffered from invasion and occupation by Japanese forces during World War II.

In the light of the Southeast Asian countries' colonial and post-colonial experience, the immense diversity among them, the make-up of their populations, the still-delicate state of their relations, and their conceptions of their respective interests, it is difficult to see why ASEAN's policy and practice of non-interference in members' internal affairs should be the object of wonder or derision. It is even more difficult to understand when one considers that the policy and practice of non-interference are neither ASEAN's invention nor its monopoly. It is, on the other hand, easy to see why ASEAN finds it difficult — indeed, it does not even try — to arrive at common norms the egregious violation of which would be grounds for intervention by the association in one way or another — norms like those in the OAS and AU charters having to do with democracy, human rights, and other political and social arrangements of a domestic nature within member-states. Thus, contrary to the impression sometimes given by commentators, non-interference is not a doctrine that is adhered to and applied on dogmatic or ideological grounds. It springs from a practical need to prevent external pressure from being exerted against the perceived national interest — or the interest of the regime.

Essentially arising from pragmatic considerations, ASEAN's practice of non-interference has not been absolute. Inter-governmental associations like ASEAN tend to intervene in members' "internal affairs" in two types of circumstances — one, in situations in one country that have adverse effects on two or more of the other member-countries and, two, in case of substantial departures from common norms and values agreed upon. As we have seen, ASEAN does not intervene in the second type of situation, simply because it has not agreed on common norms and values other than those governing relations between them as states; among the principles governing inter-state relations is, precisely, non-interference in one another's internal affairs. On the other hand, ASEAN has intervened in some domestic situations that were perceived to be affecting the other member-countries and the association itself.

ASEAN's position on the Philippine situation in 1986 was one such instance. On 23 February 1986, two days before the ejection of Ferdinand Marcos from the presidency, the ASEAN foreign ministers issued an "ASEAN joint statement" on the situation in the Philippines:

1. As member states of ASEAN, Brunei Darussalam, Indonesia, Malaysia, Singapore and Thailand have followed with increasing concern the trend of events following the presidential election in the Philippines.
2. A critical situation has emerged which portends bloodshed and civil war. The crisis can be resolved without widespread carnage and political turmoil. We call on all parties to restore unity and solidarity so as to maintain national resilience.
3. There is still time to act with restraint and bring about peaceful resolution. We hope that all Filipino leaders will join efforts to pave the way for a peaceful solution to the crisis.[5]

This statement was issued without the participation of the Philippines, having been made outside a formal ASEAN meeting and at a time when the Philippine political situation was already in disarray.

Eleven years later, as discussed at length in Chapter 2, ASEAN intervened, rather forcefully, in Cambodian politics, issuing a strong statement through the chair of the ASEAN Standing Committee on the clashes between the forces of then Second Prime Minister Hun Sen and those of the First Prime Minister, Prince Norodom Ranariddh, and sending three foreign ministers several times to seek explanations and possible solutions for those events. However, Cambodia was not yet an ASEAN member at that time; indeed, Cambodia's entry into the association had been deferred because of the country's unsettled political situation in 1997. Moreover, ASEAN justified its intervention by pointing out that the group had certain responsibilities for the political arrangements in Cambodia, having been the prime mover of the political settlement that brought them about.

In 2003, the ASEAN foreign ministers commented, politely but pointedly, on the situation in Myanmar, with Yangon's participation:

> We discussed the recent political developments in Myanmar, particularly the incident of 30 May 2003. We noted the efforts of the Government of Myanmar to promote peace and development. In this connection, we urged Myanmar to resume its efforts of national reconciliation and dialogue among all parties concerned leading to a peaceful transition to democracy. We welcomed the assurances given by Myanmar that the measures taken following the incident were temporary and looked forward to the early lifting of restrictions placed on Daw Aung San Suu Kyi and the NLD members. We also reaffirmed our continued support for the efforts of the UNSG Special Representative Tan Sri Razali Ismail.[6]

The joint communiqué of the June 2004 ASEAN Ministerial Meeting reiterated this, with some updating and, significantly, in juxtaposition with comments on the "free and peaceful elections" in Malaysia, Indonesia and the Philippines as contributing to "the attainment of a just, democratic and harmonious Southeast Asia":

> 13. We discussed a wide range of issues of ASEAN political cooperation with due regard to the cardinal principle of non-interference within the spirit of an ASEAN family.
> 14. We congratulated Malaysia, Indonesia and the Philippines for their success in holding free and peaceful elections. We believed that these elections have contributed to the attainment of a just, democratic and harmonious Southeast Asia as called for in the Declaration of ASEAN Concord II. We looked forward to a similarly successful round of Indonesia's coming first direct presidential elections.
> 15. We noted the briefing given by Myanmar on the reconvening of its National Convention and the development thereon. We acknowledged the potential of the Convention in paving the way for new constitution and the holding of elections in keeping with it. We recalled and emphasized the continued relevance of the Joint Communique of the 36th AMM and the Chairman's Press Statement of the 9th ASEAN Summit. In this regard, we underlined the need for the involvement

of all strata of Myanmar society in the on-going National Convention. We encouraged all concerned parties in Myanmar to continue their efforts to effect a smooth transition to democracy. We recognized the role of the Special Representative of the United Nations Secretary-General in assisting Myanmar to achieve this goal.[7]

In fact, the ASEAN foreign ministers, during their "retreats", regularly discuss the situation in Myanmar, with the Myanmar minister taking part. However, they have, as a group, done little more than that. We will take a brief look at ASEAN's stance on Myanmar later in this chapter.

ASEAN has intervened, on the side of the government, when the administration of Philippine President Corazon Aquino was being besieged by several coup attempts in 1987–89 and in supporting Indonesia's territorial integrity in the face of separatist movements in East Timor, Aceh, and elsewhere. However, as stated above, ASEAN has been criticized mainly for its perceived inaction on the 1997–98 financial crisis, the haze that periodically arises from land and forest fires in Indonesia, East Timor, the situation in Myanmar, and human rights generally. Let us take them one by one and look at the facts.

THE FINANCIAL CRISIS 1997–98

In the eyes of the media, academic observers, foreign governments, investors, and, not least, Southeast Asia's own people, the financial crisis transformed the image of ASEAN, as well as the lives of many of the region's people. In 1999, the Australian economics professor, Hal Hill, wrote:

> What a difference a year can make! In 1996, ASEAN's prospects looked so rosy. For the first time in its recorded history, all six major economies (that is, Indonesia, Malaysia, Philippines, Singapore, Thailand, and Vietnam) were growing strongly, at 5% or more.... Stock markets were booming, business was confident, and broad-based improvements in living standards were everywhere apparent.
>
> By early 1998, a dramatic reversal in fortunes had occurred. The region's dominant power, Indonesia, was in a terrible economic mess. In 1998, the decline in its GDP will be similar to that which occurred *in total* during the worst of the Depression years (1929–32) in the United Kingdom.... Private capital has fled from much of the region. Whereas there was a net capital *inflow* to the five worst affected East Asian economies (Indonesia, Korea, Malaysia, Philippines, and Thailand) of US$93 billion in 1996, in 1997 there was a net *outflow* of US$12 billion. Everywhere, a loss of confidence is now evident: in the international financial architecture, in

international and regional organizations (ranging from the IMF to APEC and ASEAN), in governments' capacity to protect their citizens from international shocks, in immediate business prospects, and even (in some countries) continued community and ethnic harmony.[8]

In the same year, Karl Jackson, the American Asianist who has been doing the familiar shuttle between academia and senior positions in the U.S. government, said about East Asia:

> In mid-summer 1997, a half-century of economic progress came to a crashing halt. In direct contradiction to conventional wisdom, several Asian economies previously praised for balanced budgets, high savings and investment rates, low inflation and openness to the world marketplace, went into free fall. What became a region-wide panic struck first in Thailand before spreading to Malaysia, the Philippines, Indonesia, and eventually to Korea. Stock markets and currencies plummeted, prompting central banks to mount expensive currency defenses through buying forwards, raising interest rates to unprecedented levels, or both. The magnitude and volatility of the crisis dealt a sharp blow to fragile and over-extended banking systems, while devastating those manufacturing establishments dependent on cheap capital and foreign inputs for their production. During the first year of the crisis, the currencies of the five affected countries depreciated by 35–80 per cent, diminishing substantially the wealth of the five miracle economies.[9]

He went on to describe the human and political impact of the economic crisis.

Some of the effects of the crisis were salutary in that it induced reforms in several national economies and polities, improvements in financial practices, increased attention to raising incomes in the countryside, a greater degree of humility on the part of international financial institutions, sharper questioning of the soundness of the "international financial architecture", closer regional consultation and cooperation on financial matters in East Asia, and a keener awareness, at least at the rhetorical level, of the need for deeper and faster regional economic integration in ASEAN. At the same time, most East Asian economies went on the road to recovery more quickly than most people expected. One of the few who predicted a rapid recovery was the American economist, Paul Krugman, now a columnist for the *New York Times*, whom I quoted in June 1998 as saying in March of that year, "Three years from now, it won't be a surprise to talk about growth of beyond five per cent" in East Asia's economies.[10] However, ASEAN's image had been irreversibly altered.

The financial crisis has been ascribed to many causes, at all levels, national and international, as well as regional: wrong government policies, the failure of the "international financial architecture", predatory speculation, "crony capitalism", national financial systems and practices, the state of the global economy, the spectacular increase in the mobility, and therefore volatility, of international capital movements that was made possible both by information technology and by government policy, and even, at one end, capitalist conspiracies and, at the other, the cultural traits of East Asians. Discounting the last two, it is generally agreed that these factors were not mutually exclusive; indeed, for the most part, they were mutually reinforcing.

At the level of policy, many observers have pointed out, in books, academic papers, speeches and media commentaries, that most governments had liberalized the domestic financial system and opened the capital account without putting the necessary regulatory mechanisms in place beforehand. The governments also generally maintained more or less fixed exchange rates for their currencies, while at the same time giving guarantees, implicit or explicit, for the entry and withdrawal of investments. This enabled and encouraged people to borrow money, short-term, in unhedged hard currencies for long-term investments in local currencies, mostly for real estate and other speculative purposes, confident in the fixed nature of the exchange rate and unhindered by adequate regulation. The results were massive pressure on currencies, the build-up of non-performing loans and the crumbling of financial systems. Meanwhile, the global economy was slowing down, particularly the market for electronics products, which had become the main exports of the leading Southeast Asian economies. When, as this situation was reaching a critical point, the Thai Government tried and eventually failed to defend the baht, the short-term investors, domestic and foreign, pulled out their money not only from Thailand but also from other countries, including South Korea. Attention was then called to the failings of those countries, failings that had been overlooked in the past — crony capitalism and the resulting misallocation of investments, bad governance, lack of transparency, the politicization of the financial system, the undercapitalization of the banks, poor economic policies, ineffective government leadership, and so on. The International Monetary Fund came in for criticism as well, for bad diagnoses and bad prescriptions, as did the international financial system as a whole.

Of course, not all these factors were true of all East Asian countries, and they were present in different combinations and in varying degrees, but it is a measure of how far the economies of ASEAN had coalesced, at least in people's perceptions, that investors lumped them together when making investment — or disinvestment — decisions. Perhaps because of this, some commentators blamed ASEAN, including its "principle of non-intervention", either for not anticipating the crisis and preventing it or, when the crisis struck, for not doing anything effective to contain and repair the damage. For example, the late Michael Leifer of the London School of Economics and Political Science declared in 2000, "ASEAN has been largely irrelevant in the economic crisis.... ASEAN's feebleness and disarray have diminished its international standing."[11]

The Indonesian economist, Hadi Soesastro, Executive Director of the Center for Strategic and International Studies in Jakarta, wrote in 1999:

> There has been much soul-searching in ASEAN during the past year that coincided with the onset of the crisis. Until then ASEAN was still in a state of euphoria due to the region's remarkable record of rapid economic growth, the near completion of the One Southeast Asia enterprise, and its paramount role in the creation of the wider regional co-operative structures by virtue of being a co-pilot in APEC (Asia-Pacific Economic Cooperation) and occupying the driver's seat in the ARF (ASEAN Regional Forum). This position crumbled almost overnight with the financial meltdown. ASEAN's future relevance to its members and to the region suddenly becomes a relevant question in many quarters, even within the ASEAN officialdom. ASEAN, some have argued, cannot maintain its relevance if it continues to be inhibited by the principle of non-intervention that it has held sacrosanct.[12]

In the same year, Stuart Harris of the Australian National University wrote along similar lines:

> The crisis has opened up more directly the already difficult subject of the principle of non-intervention in the affairs of other members. The economic crisis convinced some members that it was not possible to continue strictly adhering to this principle. That, however, has been strongly resisted by, in particular, the new members, notably Myanmar and Cambodia, who would feel vulnerable in those circumstances. Without some compromise on that principle, however, the influence of ASEAN internationally is likely to diminish.[13]

Also in 1999, T. J. Pempel, professor of international studies at the University of Washington, said:

> During the crisis, ASEAN struggled to play a role, but it was not equipped institutionally to do so without the voluntary cooperation of its members. Most governments resisted any surrender of their independence or any modification of the ASEAN principle of noninterference in domestic affairs.[14]

The first question is: could ASEAN have anticipated the crisis as it was building up if only the member-countries had not, in the name of non-interference, refrained from looking too closely into the economic policies of one another? Considered with the benefit of hindsight, the answer may be maybe. To a conference of editors from ASEAN countries in Jakarta in April 1999, I observed:

> The financial crisis that started in East Asia, in ASEAN, caught almost everyone by surprise, including most of the world's most brilliant economists. And it quickly spread. Because of inadequate consultations among ASEAN members, no ASEAN country was sufficiently aware of the problems building up in others or of the imminent impact of those problems on themselves. There was no institutionalized mechanism for ASEAN members to compare notes on developments in their economies, particularly in their financial sectors, but in the real economy as well. There was no formal forum for the finance ministers to consult on what to do about impending or fundamental problems that they may see.[15]

Writing in 1998, when the crisis was already full-blown, and looking to the future, the Filipino economist Manuel Montes said, as one of his prescriptions:

> These events suggest the indispensability of closer consultation among ASEAN countries. As explained above, one of the institutional realities of the new international financial market is that these markets tend to lump projects in one country into one, and, with a little bit of adjustment, countries in one region into one. Prior private notice of intended drastic policy changes among central banks in the region seems to be critical. Increased frequency of meetings among central bank and treasury officials will establish the confidence to underpin these prior notice arrangements.[16]

That was for the future. As the crisis was gathering pace, hardly anyone noticed the signs enough to prevent governments and the international financial community from being caught by surprise. In the preface to the book that he edited, *Asian Contagion*, Karl Jackson asserts that he and his group, over 1994–96, saw telltale signs of a financial crisis in the making, particularly in Thailand, but nobody in Bangkok listened to them.[17] As I pointed out in 1999, it seems that just about everybody else did not anticipate the crisis. Not the IMF. Not the World Bank. Not the Asian Development Bank. Paul Krugman, in his famous article, "The Myth of Asia's Miracle", in the November–December 1994 issue of *Foreign Affairs*, saw the weaknesses in East Asia's remarkable growth but predicted only that the region's economies would slow down, not that they would crash in an economic, social and political disaster. Referring to that piece in a March 1998 speech in Hong Kong, Krugman stressed, "One thing I did not do, however, was predict the current crisis. In fact, I went out of my way to avoid predicting any imminent crisis."[18] In January 1998, he had said, "It seems safe to say that nobody anticipated anything like the current crisis in Asia."[19] Apparently, not even the credit rating agencies, which get paid to analyse these things, saw the crisis coming. In a study that he did for the World Institute for Development Economics Research of the United Nations University in 1999, Abdur Chowdhury of Marquette University in Wisconsin writes:

> One important question is: did the market predict the downturn in these economies? Credit rating agencies provide an ongoing assessment of credit risk in the emerging markets. Any expectation of a financial crisis in a specific country would be recognized by these agencies and would lead to a decline in its credit ratings.... Comparing the ratings (of Moody's) from December 1996 with those in June 1997 would show that none of the countries (Indonesia, Malaysia, the Philippines, South Korea and Thailand) experienced a decline in their ratings prior to the crisis.[20]

As if they had a premonition of the disaster to come, the ASEAN finance ministers, in March 1997, met for the first time as a regular forum, outside the IMF/World Bank and Asian Development Bank meetings. Their joint communiqué, however, gave no indication that they had an inkling of the impending crisis, saying, "The Ministers expressed their optimism regarding the continuing favourable outlook for the region in 1997 given the expectation of improving exports, supportive international environment, healthy levels of FDI flows and strong domestic demand." The IMF apparently had no inkling either. The joint communiqué reported, "The Ministers had a useful exchange of views with the Managing Director of the International Monetary Fund, Mr. Michel Camdessus, on global and regional economic developments, and avenues for enhancing financial cooperation. The Ministers and the Managing Director were in agreement that the economic fundamentals for the ASEAN's continued sustainable growth remain strong."[21] Perhaps, the ministers and the IMF were trying to shore up market confidence at a time, four months before the onset of the crisis, when the Thai baht was already under massive speculative attack and non-performing loans were rapidly piling up in the Thai financial system. If that was the intention, it was too little and too late and, obviously, it did not work. In any case, it may be too much to expect ASEAN to have anticipated the crisis; practically no one else did. The more pertinent questions are: did ASEAN respond effectively to the crisis as it hit the member-countries, and is the response so far likely to improve the region's capacity to prevent similar crises in the future? In an early assessment, Hadi Soesastro did not think so. He wrote in 1999:

> Since the regional impact of the crisis is so pronounced, it would be logical to expect ASEAN to be in the forefront of regional and international responses to the crisis. In the public's view this is one of the most important reasons for having ASEAN and for promoting ASEAN economic cooperation.... The public has been largely disappointed with ASEAN. Its perception is that of a helpless ASEAN, an ASEAN that cannot move decisively, an ASEAN that is trapped under its organizational and bureaucratic weight, and an ASEAN that fails to respond to real, current problems and challenges.[22]

That was the drift of much media commentary.

However, as I indicated above, the crisis sprang from many causes; therefore, it called for multiple responses. I pointed out in June 1998 that the ASEAN response had been at four levels — national, bilateral, regional and international.[23] The national response was reform of the financial systems and the strengthening of financial laws and regulations, in different combinations and with varying degrees of effectiveness. The bilateral measures took the form of rice and medicine, credit guarantees, and standby credit, mostly in emergency assistance to Indonesia. These were palliative gestures, meant to express neighbourly sympathy, but with little substantive or long-term economic effect.

In April 1999, the ASEAN Finance Ministers issued the Common ASEAN Position on Reforming the International Financial Architecture. The statement assertively — some would say defensively — laid emphasis on the diversity of the individual economies and thus on the need for flexible solutions; the necessity of the participation of all countries in the reform of the international financial architecture and the need to take their interests into account; the protection of "the poor and (the) most vulnerable segments of society"; a review of the roles of the international financial institutions; the application of standards of transparency and disclosure to the private as well as the public sectors; greater transparency in the operations of rating agencies; closer and more coordinated monitoring of short-term capital flows; and the right of countries to adopt their own exchange-rate regimes.[24] Clearly, this was intended to make sure that responsibility for the crisis and for the prevention of its recurrence was placed not on the ASEAN countries alone or on the association as a group but also on the international financial system, the private money managers, and the credit rating agencies. More importantly — and this is relevant to the issue of non-interference — the statement was an assertion of the autonomy of individual ASEAN countries in terms of their economic conditions and their financial policies; there were to be no one-size-fits-all solutions and none that were to be externally imposed.

Yet, at the same time, the ASEAN countries recognized the need for frequent consultations on the condition of their economies so that they would not again be caught unawares by a developing crisis. The joint communiqué of the first ASEAN finance ministers meeting had stressed "the importance of having regular consultations on macroeconomic and financial matters to better follow changes in the global economy and to exchange views on sound policies in response to the challenges and opportunities brought about by these changes".[25] That March 1997 meeting, however, failed to anticipate the crisis, as noted above, but as the crisis gathered force, the finance ministers began to meet often as a regular practice, more frequently, it turned out, than any other ASEAN ministerial forum. Aside from their regular meetings, their gatherings on the occasion of the IMF/World Bank and ADB meetings were no longer devoted solely to issues before the international financial institutions but also to consultations on the regional economic situation and such issues as the monitoring of short-term capital flows. The ASEAN ministers are joined by their colleagues from China, Japan and the Republic of Korea with increasing regularity. Convened even more frequently is the forum of senior officials of ministries of finance and central banks, in which their counterparts from China, Japan and Korea often take part.

The centerpiece of the ministerial consultations has been the "peer review", in which the ministers discuss economic developments in the region and in their individual countries, including policy measures taken, in the context of current global economic conditions. The discussions are based on "surveillance" reports prepared by the ASEAN Secretariat, with technical and financial support from the ADB, and reviewed and amended by the senior finance and central bank officials. Largely for this purpose, a special unit was set up at the ASEAN Secretariat. A counterpart outfit was organized at the ADB to extend technical support, provide some funding, undertake special studies, and train finance and central bank officials for surveillance.

The surveillance reports, put out and subjected to ministerial review twice a year, analyse developments in the global and regional economy, presenting a variety of economic indicators, and make short-term projections for the region. They then go into country-by-country analyses and projections, reviews of the economic policies adopted and carried out, and assessments of their impact. The peer review is meant to alert the finance ministers to possible trouble that could spread contagion to their economies. Just as important, it is intended to encourage governments to implement politically difficult policies. How trenchant the confidential discussions are depends to some extent on the skills and inclination of the meeting's chairman. At one of the first peer-review exercises, I privately suggested to one of the more progressive finance ministers that the process could be more incisive in discussing one another's national policies. He recoiled as if in horror. I am told that the peer review has now become more trenchant and more focused. In view of the secretive culture of finance ministries, I have not been able to determine whether the peer-review process has had any influence on any member-state's economic and financial policies, which, after all, have to be decided at the national level. The exercise may be useful in illuminating the nooks and crannies of policy and providing mutual encouragement, but ultimately the decisions belong to national governments.

Because the vital decisions are made by national governments, part of the ASEAN-ADB programme has been the training of officials from the member-countries in the art and techniques of economic surveillance. As of September 2005, 143 officials had gone through three- to six-month training programmes at the ADB.

In May 2000, the ASEAN+3 (the three being China, Japan and South Korea) finance ministers, meeting in Chiangmai, Thailand, adopted what they called the Chiangmai Initiative. The initiative has two components. One is an "economic and financial monitoring system in East Asia" made up of "a network of contact persons to facilitate regional surveillance". The other consists of the expansion of the then 23-year-old ASEAN Swap Arrangement to include all ten ASEAN members, the increase in the amount involved to US$1 billion, and, far more importantly, a set of bilateral "swap and repurchase agreement facilities" among the thirteen East Asian countries, through which one of the two signatories to such an agreement would provide "liquidity support" to the other should the latter run into balance-of-payments difficulties.[26] These arrangements are meant to discourage speculative attacks on any of the region's currencies. By December 2005, sixteen bilateral swap and repurchase agreements had been concluded, with a total value of the equivalent of US$58.5 billion, which, by May 2006, had expanded to US$75 billion.

Gathering on the occasion of the Asian Development Bank's annual meeting in Istanbul in May 2005, the ASEAN+3 finance ministers decided to strengthen the Chiangmai Initiative. In place of the bilateral mechanisms, they agreed to devise a collective decision-making mechanism for the activation of the swap and repurchase arrangements and asked the deputies to study the precise modalities for it. They decided substantially to increase the amounts involved in the swaps. The existing arrangements would be increased; the suggestion was to double their size. The ministers called for the conclusion of new bilateral arrangements, particularly between ASEAN countries. They also urged the conversion of one-way swaps into two-way arrangements. The ASEAN Swap Arrangement was increased further from US$1 billion to US$2 billion. The ministers also decided to increase from 10 to 20 per cent the percentage of the swap amounts that could be drawn down without being subject to IMF conditionalities.[27]

At a similar meeting in Hyderabad in May 2006, the ASEAN+3 Finance Ministers decided: "All swop providing countries can simultaneously and promptly provide liquidity support to any parties involved in bilateral swap arrangements (BSA) at times of emergency.[28]

Not the least of ASEAN's responses to the 1997–98 financial crisis, and contrary to the expectations of the commenting class, was its decision to accelerate the implementation of the ASEAN Free Trade Area. When the financial crisis hit, the "analysts" usually quoted by the media immediately predicted that the ASEAN countries would retreat into their national shells and go into an "inward-looking" mode. Specifically, they were sure that AFTA was dead. I could never understand why these supposedly astute and normally well-informed analysts would make such predictions. In my view, those instant conclusions flew in the face of logic and the facts. Since ASEAN's objective was to bolster investor confidence and keep investments from further fleeing the region in panic, it made no sense for ASEAN to appear to stumble on the road to regional economic integration. In fact, what ASEAN did was accelerate AFTA's timetable. At the December 1995 summit, ASEAN had agreed to advance to 2003 the deadline for the first six signatories to the AFTA agreement[29] to lower their tariffs on intra-ASEAN trade to 0–5 per cent. In 1998, clearly in response to the crisis, the economic ministers decided to accelerate the timing further, to the beginning of 2002, a decision ratified by the December 1998 Hanoi summit. So much for AFTA's death.

In one sense, but only in that limited sense, the doomsayers were proved right. This was Malaysia's insistence on delaying to 2005 the inclusion in the AFTA scheme of finished or ready-to-assemble motor vehicles (not vehicle parts, as often erroneously reported), demand for which had collapsed on account of the crisis, followed by a similar move by the Philippines for the deferment of certain petrochemical products. When it was proposed, Malaysia's deferment would have contravened Kuala Lumpur's commitment under AFTA. However, ASEAN accommodated Malaysia, with great reluctance on the part of Thailand, the region's biggest supplier of vehicles. To keep Malaysia from being in violation of its AFTA commitments, ASEAN, after much heated argument, adopted in November 2000 a protocol allowing an AFTA signatory, under certain conditions, "to temporarily delay the transfer of a product from its TEL (Temporary Exclusion List) into the Inclusion List (IL), or to temporarily suspend its concession on a product already transferred into the IL, if such a transfer or concession would cause or have caused real problems".[30] This was patterned after Article XXVIII of the General Agreement on Tariffs and Trade (GATT), the WTO's predecessor, and was thus consistent with international practice. The Philippines subsequently invoked the protocol to seek a delay in the inclusion of some petrochemical items in the AFTA scheme. In every other respect, ASEAN stepped up the pace, at least on paper, of regional economic integration, not only by accelerating AFTA, but also by concluding in 1998 agreements on investments, goods in transit, and mutual recognition arrangements and in 2000 on information and communications technology, in addition to others that were already in place. At the 1998 Hanoi summit, the ASEAN countries agreed to adopt what they called "bold measures" to make them and the region more attractive to investments, including the further acceleration of AFTA.[31] At the ASEAN Summit in Vientiane in November 2004, the ASEAN leaders adopted the action plan for the ASEAN Economic Community, the name given to the next stage of regional economic integration. ASEAN economic integration will be discussed further in Chapter 5, and the ASEAN Economic Community in Chapter 7.

It is, however, one thing for the ASEAN countries to agree on individual and collective measures meant to deal with the financial crisis; it is another thing to determine whether such measures have been effective or whether agreed expressions of resolve are likely to be carried out at all. As I have noted, ASEAN failed to see the looming financial crisis, but neither did the international financial institutions, most leading economists, and the scholars who have been ASEAN's most vociferous critics on this count. Would closer, more rigorous and objective — and more intrusive — collective examination of the economic situation have enabled regional ministers and central banks to foresee the crisis? A more practical and less speculative question is whether the current system of surveillance and peer review, billed in ASEAN circles as an early warning system, will render the association more capable of anticipating future crises and preventing them. Perhaps; but, thankfully, it has not been tested. Will the network of bilateral currency swap and repurchase arrangements enable ASEAN+3 to ward off speculative attacks against their currencies? The Thai economist Chalongphob Sussangkarn does not think so, pointing out that the amounts involved are too small to defend a currency from a massive attack.[32] However, the system's very existence, involving Japan and China, with their enormous reserves, could help stave off speculative currency attacks as it is intended to do. Not being tested may mean that the system has worked so far.

Moves to deepen regional economic integration, like the acceleration of AFTA, may not be directly effective in preventing future crises, but, indirectly, a show of solidarity and closer cooperation within both ASEAN and East Asia could help. The more effective defences lie in domestic policy, including political and economic reforms, and in the international financial system. At the regional level, unless ASEAN changes its fundamental nature and becomes a supranational authority, ASEAN cannot bear much of the responsibility for more accurate and timely forecasting of financial crises and their prevention. The association just does not have the authority or the resources for that. In any event, within its limits, ASEAN probably has done more than any other regional association, except for the European Union, would or could have. As pointed out above, the financial crisis had many causes, in various combinations. Blame for them cannot be fairly placed entirely, or even largely, at ASEAN's doorstep. Nor can the responsibility for the solution. Nevertheless, ASEAN did take some steps on a regional scale, by itself and with the rest of East Asia. Perhaps, they are not enough, but it cannot be justly said that ASEAN responded to the crisis in "disarray" or that the region found itself in crisis simply because of a mindless adherence to the principle of non-interference.

HAZE AND SARS

There have been, in recent years, two classic instances of a problem in one or more ASEAN countries seriously affecting other ASEAN countries. One was the devastating haze pollution caused by land and forest fires, mostly in Indonesian territory on Borneo and Sumatra. The other was the Severe Acute Respiratory Syndrome epidemic, or SARS. Both had region-wide, or at least sub-regional, impact, in recognition of which ASEAN sought to address both crises on a regional scale. For reasons that we shall see, the two efforts had different degrees of success.

The worst of the haze problem took place in the El Niño year of 1997–98, coinciding, to ASEAN's misfortune, with the financial crisis. The haze arose largely from fires in the forests and peat lands of Indonesia. Forest fires are, of course, not unique to Indonesia. Massive fires have swept millions of hectares of forest, grassland and even national parks in Australia, the southern and western United States, the Asian part of Russia, China, South America, parts of Africa and, fairly recently, Portugal and Spain. Indeed, bush and forest fires have ignited on Brunei, Malaysian and Singaporean soil, albeit on a much smaller scale. The difference is that, in Indonesia, as in the Amazon area of Brazil, the burning has been sparked not only by accident, by human carelessness or by acts of nature; much of it has also been deliberately started by plantation owners, often large corporations, seeking to clear forests for commercial use, largely as oil palm or timber plantations, or by small farmers carrying out slash-and-burn agriculture. Another difference is that, unlike those of the vast land masses mentioned above, the fires in Indonesia have severely affected its neighbours.

In times of drought, fires easily spread, consuming huge areas of forest and casting a pall of haze over the region. Especially in dry weather, with the forest cover thinned out and the swamps drained for rice cultivation, the peat just beneath the surface of Indonesian soil also catches fire, adding to the smoke and haze. The damage is often enormous. In 2001, I wrote:

> The pernicious practice of burning forests to clear land for commercial purposes and the unusually dry weather that caused even the earth to catch fire combined to produce a pall of catastrophic proportions. The loss in terms of agricultural production, transportation, tourism, and other economic endeavours has been estimated at more than $9 billion. The cost to human health, loss of biodiversity, destruction of forests, and general environmental degradation is immeasurable.[33]

Two years earlier, the ADB had published estimates of the losses incurred by Indonesia alone, shown in Table 3.1. These figures do not include the damage inflicted on neighbouring countries, particularly Brunei Darussalam, Malaysia and Singapore. I tried to capture this at an ASEAN-ADB workshop on "transboundary atmospheric pollution" by citing some graphic estimates of the World Wide Fund for Nature:

> According to the World Wide Fund for Nature (WWF), the land and forest fires in 1997 cost US$494 million in timber losses, US$470 million in losses to agriculture, US$1.8 billion in lost direct and indirect forest benefits, US$30 million in the loss of capturable biodiversity, US$25 million for fire-fighting, and US$272 million in carbon releases. It also caused US$941 million in short-term damage to health. It set back tourism by US$256 million. It inflicted US$24.7 million in losses on airports and airlines. It damaged industrial production by US$157 million and fisheries by US$16 million.
>
> WWF calculates that Indonesia could have used its lost resources to provide basic sanitation, water and sewage services for 40 million people, or one-third of its rural poor. WWF estimates that the losses suffered by Singapore tourism alone could have fully funded the Community Chest in that country, which comprises fifty charities and benefits 180,000 people,

for three years. Malaysia could have financed all of the federal government's social programmes for the last three years out of the resources that it lost to the fires and haze.[34]

Indonesia's Fires and Haze: The Cost of Catastrophe gives some very detailed estimates of the damage caused by the fires and haze and the costs that they inflicted on Indonesia, Malaysia and Singapore, analyses the problem, and concludes with some policy recommendations.[35] According to a media release of the United Nations Environment Programme on 25 November 2003 welcoming the entry into force of the ASEAN Agreement on Transboundary Haze Pollution:

> About 10 million hectares of Indonesia's forests, one of the world's centres of biodiversity, were destroyed in 1997–98 in fires started mainly on oil palm plantations and agricultural and forestry holdings on the islands of Sumatra and Kalimantan. The blazes were fanned by hot, dry conditions caused by the El Niño weather phenomena. More than 20 million people

TABLE 3.1
Summary of Costs of the 1997–98 Fires in Indonesia
Estimated Economic Losses (in US$ millions)

Sector	Minimum	Maximum	Mean
Agriculture			
Farm Crops	2,431	2,431	2,431
Plantation Crops	319	319	319
Forestry			
Timber from Natural Forests	1,461	2,165	1,813
Lost Growth in Natural Forest	256	377	316
Timber from Plantations	94	94	94
Non-wood Forest Products	586	586	586
Flood Protection	404	404	404
Erosion and Siltation	1,586	1,586	1,586
Carbon Sink	1,446	1,446	1,446
Health	145	145	145
Transmigration, Buildings and Property	1	1	1
Transportation	18	49	33
Tourism	111	111	111
Firefighting Costs	12	11	12
Total	8,870	9,726	9,298

Source: S. Tahir Qadri, ed., *Fire, Smoke, and the Haze: The ASEAN Response Strategy* (Manila: Asian Development Bank, 2001), p. 55.

were exposed to breathing extremely high levels of pollutants known to cause both acute and long-term health effects, airports in Singapore and neighbouring countries were closed by thick smog, and total economic losses across the region were estimated at around US$9.3 billion.

I remember being in Bandar Seri Begawan in April 1998, at the height of the haze, to attend, ironically, a meeting of the ASEAN environment ministers. On that day, and on several days afterwards, children in Brunei Darussalam had to stay indoors and miss school because of the threat to their health; this was undoubtedly true also of children elsewhere on Borneo. Tourism around the region was badly hurt. Air and sea transportation was disrupted for days at a time. It is not surprising that relations between Indonesia on one side and Brunei Darussalam, Malaysia and Singapore on the other were strained. At the ministerial meeting in the Brunei capital, the ministers charged, with rare candor, explicitly and officially, but not publicly, that much of the burning was being caused by the land-clearing activities of the plantation companies, which they branded as socially irresponsible and deserving of punishment. In opening the ASEAN Ministerial Meeting on the Environment in Jakarta in September 1997, President Soeharto had made the remarkable gesture of apologizing for the harm done by the haze. "To the communities of neighbouring countries who have been disturbed by the fires in our territory," he declared, "Indonesia offers its most sincere apologies." However, he was careful to blame the "sheer vastness of our bushes and forests, and the prolonged drought" as "insurmountable obstacles in the efforts to prevent and put the fires under control". He did not mention the human instigators of those fires, much less the punishment that they deserved, or the obstacles that were *not* "insurmountable".

One of the problems in enforcing environmental laws in Indonesia is that the highest government body charged with environmental matters, the one with the institutional interest in protecting the environment, is a "ministry of state", the State Ministry for the Environment. It is a "staff" agency and, as such, does not have "line" functions. Wielding effective influence are the ministries of agriculture and forestry and the law-enforcement agencies. With the move to decentralize governmental functions, the local governments, mainly the provinces and districts, now also have a say in the matter, although some of them have gone on record as blaming the national government for this particular problem. Thus, when the ASEAN environment ministers met to deal with the haze crisis, the Indonesian minister at that time, Sarwono Kusumaatmadja, plaintively acknowledged that he had little authority to enforce laws and government decisions. Some other ASEAN ministers retorted with the suggestion that, in that case, it might be a good idea to bring into the meeting the ministers who had effective responsibility for the situation. Because there are several agencies dealing with the issue, coordination becomes a problem, even if nominally the Ministry of Forestry and Estate Crops has been designated as the lead agency for purposes of controlling the haze-producing fires. The study cited above, which was published under the auspices of the Asian Development Bank and the ASEAN Secretariat, declared:

> Indonesia's institutional framework for addressing fires and haze is too fragmented to be effective. No fewer than 24 different government agencies are responsible for controlling land and forest fires and haze. With responsibility so widely scattered, effective control is an organizational nightmare. The existing legal instruments are without adequate capability to enforce compliance.[36]

More than the institutional difficulties, the most intractable obstacle to the avoidance of haze has been the clash between the need to prevent fires on the one hand and, on the other, the national policies that encourage the conversion of forests into oil palm and tree plantations and agricultural land and burning as the least expensive means of land clearance.

Even before the 1997–98 crisis, ASEAN was aware of the haze problem as a regional concern. An international conference on "land and forest fire hazards" in Kuala Lumpur in June 2002 recalled, "There have been five major fire outbreaks in Southeast Asia, with small fires occurring almost annually."[37] Serious haze episodes had taken place in 1982–83, 1987, 1991 and 1994. The declaration issued by the 1992 ASEAN Summit cited forest fires in its call for closer ASEAN cooperation on the environment.[38] The resolution that the ASEAN environment ministers agreed on three weeks later listed "haze caused by forest fires" among the areas in which cooperative programmes were to be carried out.[39] However, in these documents, the haze problem was considered as only one of many environmental issues calling for ASEAN cooperation. Indeed, neither the environment ministers' Resolution on Environment and Development of April 1994[40] nor their Strategic Plan of Action on the Environment 1994–98[41] mentioned the haze issue or forest fires at all. It was only in 1995 that ASEAN began to focus on the haze and forest fires as a matter for concentrated attention. Pursuant to the ministers' directive the year before, the ASEAN Cooperation Plan on Transboundary Pollution was drawn up, covering atmospheric pollution, the movement of hazardous wastes, and ship-borne pollution.[42]

The "cooperation plan" was hardly a plan, being largely a listing of rather general actions that governments ought to take to prevent forest fires and, if these should occur, mitigate their effects. The regional cooperation that the plan called for was limited to strengthening the ASEAN Specialized Meteorological Centre, which is basically a Singapore facility; the development of a common air quality index and a fire danger rating system; and the exchange of knowledge and technology. The senior officials dealing with the environment organized the Haze Technical Task Force to work on ways to carry out the plan. It was made up of senior officials from Brunei Darussalam, Indonesia, Malaysia and Singapore, the countries seriously affected by the haze, with Indonesia as chair. The task force met for the first time in October 1995.

During the severe haze episodes of 1997–98, ASEAN set up the ASEAN Ministerial Meeting on Haze, which, although made up of the environment ministers, is a body apart from the regular Ministers of Environment forum. That body and the Haze Technical Task Force met as frequently as every two months at the height of the crisis. As part of their efforts to deal with the problem, they produced the Haze Regional Action Plan, which the ministers approved in December 1997. The plan is important because of its operational focus. It has three components: prevention, monitoring and mitigation. The prevention portion calls on the member-states to develop national plans for preventing land and forest fires and mitigating their effects, with some suggestions for the contents of those plans. The monitoring element basically calls for the strengthening of the ASEAN Specialised Meteorological Centre in Singapore, including an Intranet within ASEAN and workshops among experts. The plan envisions the upgrading of the member-countries' fire-fighting capabilities, beginning with an inventory of their available equipment and expertise. It was generally agreed that policies to encourage mechanical land-clearing methods, instead of burning, were to be put in place.

From early 1998, the ASEAN Secretariat and the ADB began their formal collaboration on the problem, with ADB providing technical support and financing, largely from a Japanese special fund, and the Secretariat contributing staff, office space and other facilities. The principal aims of the collaboration were to put the Haze Regional Action Plan into operation, set up or strengthen institutions to implement it, and build their capacity to do so. The teaming-up of the ADB and the Secretariat also helped mobilize funding from a large number of countries and UN and other international agencies. The primary product of the project was the Operationalized Regional Haze Action Plan, a very detailed set of measures for preventing land and forest fires and the haze that they produce, mitigating their effects, and monitoring. In April 1998, the ASEAN Ministerial Meeting on Haze approved the establishment of Sub-regional Fire-fighting Arrangements, one for Borneo and another for Sumatra, which would institutionalize the collaborative operation of national fire-fighting capabilities. During the period of ADB assistance to the ASEAN Secretariat, a Program Management Unit (PMU) administered the technical assistance. At the end of the arrangement, in October 1999, the PMU was renamed the Coordination and Support Unit, which would coordinate the implementation of the Operationalized Regional Haze Action Plan, serve as a clearing house for assistance and information, conduct simulation exercises, organize community meetings, and so on.

In order to formalize and strengthen their commitment to prevent haze, the Ministers of Environment decided in October 2000 to negotiate the ASEAN Agreement on Transboundary Haze Pollution. Drafted with the help of the UN Environment Programme, the agreement was signed on 10 June 2002. As they entered the final stages of negotiation, the ministers had become worried about the length of time for the agreement to take effect if it had to be ratified by all ten ASEAN governments. Invoking the example of the Southeast Asia Nuclear Weapons-Free Zone treaty, which required only seven ratifications, I suggested that the haze agreement enter into force upon the ratification of only six governments. That suggestion was put in the text. The agreement became effective on 25 November 2003, two months after Thailand submitted its instrument of ratification, bringing to the required six the number of ratifications. Singapore, Malaysia, Myanmar, Brunei Darussalam, and Vietnam had earlier ratified the agreement, in that order, and Laos subsequently did so. The agreement is being considered in the legislatures of Cambodia and the Philippines. However, Indonesia, the key state involved, has not ratified the agreement and has asked for more time for domestic consultations.

The agreement commits each of the parties to ensure that no activity in its territory damages the environment and harms human health *beyond its national jurisdiction* and to "take precautionary measures to anticipate, prevent and monitor transboundary haze pollution as a result of land and/or forest fires...." Each party is to monitor all land and forest fires, the haze that they cause, and the conditions that could give rise to them. It is to take "immediate action to control or to put out the fires". The agreement specifies certain measures for the parties to take in order to prevent and control activities that could cause land and forest fires and the haze pollution that results from them. In general, the parties are bound to manage and use their natural resources, including forest and land resources, "in an ecologically sound and sustainable manner". At the regional level, the party where haze originates is committed to furnish information to the affected countries upon request. The agreement also provides for mutual assistance: a party asked to give assistance is to notify the requesting party whether it can do so, and a party offered assistance is to say whether it will accept it. It makes it clear that authority over the assistance rests with the receiving party. The agreement calls for the establishment of a Coordinating Centre, a fund to support the agreement's implementation, and a conference of the parties to ensure that the agreement is carried out and to perform other functions related to it.[43]

These are, on the surface, weighty and significant obligations. Upon its entry into force in November 2003, UNEP hailed the agreement as a pioneering achievement that "could become a global model for the tackling of transboundary issues". However, there is no assurance that the commitments will be carried out, no external tool for promoting compliance other than peer pressure, which is no match for the powerful interests that profit from burning forests. The ADB-ASEAN study cited above, which was issued before the conclusion of the haze agreement, observed, "ASEAN's current legal and institutional framework is weak." It pointed out that, with respect to transboundary pollution, the legal regimes in ASEAN impose no sanctions for non-compliance, commit the parties to no specific action, and contain "no operational details".[44] The haze agreement, while an improvement, suffers essentially from the same weaknesses.

With particular reference to Indonesia, the study said:

> At the national level, policy and legal instruments relating to the use of fire for land-clearing purposes is in a state of disarray. MOFEC (Ministry of Forestry and Estate Crops) has issued a directive that all land will be cleared using mechanical means, and that the use of fire to clear land is therefore illegal and will not be tolerated. At the same time, there exists a directive that allows open burning, so long as a permit has been granted, but no procedure for obtaining such a permit has yet been put in place.
>
> None of the directives, decrees, legislation, or policies at the national level have much impact at the provincial level where actual land clearing takes place.
>
> Operationally, plantation firms are free to use open burning to clear land with impunity. In the few instances in which firms using open burning to clear land have been brought to the court, none has been convicted.[45]

That was in 2001. More recently, Indonesia has been able to prosecute one company in Riau for intentionally clearing land by burning. Similar offenses by other plantation companies are being investigated. According to media reports, President Susilo Bambang Yudhoyono of Indonesia and Malaysia's Prime Minister Abdullah Badawi agreed at a bilateral meeting in January 2006 to take "stern measures" against companies, some of which are

Malaysian, that "do not follow legal land-clearing procedures". What those measures will be and how they are carried out bear watching.

ASEAN itself has taken important measures, measures that it is able to take as an association. A regional action plan, as well as national action plans, has been adopted. Detailed operational procedures have been laid down for monitoring, assessment and joint emergency response. National focal points have been designated to form a regional network. A monitoring system, an inventory of fire-fighting resources, and training mechanisms are in place. Simulation exercises have been conducted to ensure the adequacy of coordination and communication among member-countries in jointly responding to emergencies. Guidelines for "zero-burning" have been developed, and workshops and dialogues have been carried out for plantation companies and timber concessionaires. Manuals have been put together on controlled burning for the benefit of smallholders, farmers and shifting cultivators, and demonstration sites for the purpose are being established. The ASEAN Peatland Management Initiative is being carried out.

The ASEAN Specialized Meteorological Centre and other monitoring facilities have extended their coverage and are working effectively enough. If you go to the website of Singapore's National Environment Agency, http://app.nea.gov.sg, download "meteorological services", and click on "haze monitoring", or consult the ASEAN Secretariat's http://www.haze-online.or.id, you can see in satellite photographs where in the region the haze, fires and "hot spots" are on any given day. Together with what is obtained by observers and monitoring equipment on the ground, this information is supposed to give local communities, national governments and the ASEAN bodies basis for taking action if necessary. An Intranet system links the haze monitors in the ASEAN countries together. The ASEAN Secretariat has carried out coordinating functions, including those of the envisioned Coordinating Centre pending the latter's establishment. Financial rules for the haze fund have been developed. Several countries, the European Union, a number of UN agencies, and the ADB have provided supporting resources. A formal agreement has been entered into.

Despite the agreements concluded, the declarations issued, the national and regional policies adopted, including the zero-burning policy, the institutional preparations, the operational planning, the exercises, the consciousness-raising, and the early warning that is now possible, some ASEAN officials point out that the practice of setting fire to forests continues. They note that neither the ASEAN haze agreement nor the regional action plan makes any reference to the culpability of plantation owners, a compliance mechanism, or sanctions for states' non-compliance with their commitments.

The system that ASEAN had put in place was tested with a particularly severe haze episode in August 2005, which, although not as widespread or as long-lasting as the one in 1997–98, affected Kuala Lumpur as well as parts of southern Thailand. According to a press release issued at the meeting of the ASEAN Senior Officials on the Environment on 17 August, Indonesia mobilized more than 1,000 personnel to fight the fires, while Malaysia harnessed about 100 firefighters and their equipment. Singapore sent satellite photographs to help locate the fires precisely. Thailand and Vietnam expressed their readiness to help.

The principal factor in the effectiveness or ineffectiveness of an ASEAN response to the haze problem is not any ASEAN "doctrine" of non-interference. The crucial factor is the ability of governments to face down the powerful interests responsible for the burning of forests and their willingness to acknowledge their need for their neighbours' help in this regard. In the end, preventing forest fires rests not on whether ASEAN members are willing to interfere in member-states' internal affairs but on the ability and willingness of countries to enforce their laws and enact new ones if necessary and to carry out their international obligations. Beyond that, it also depends on voluntary cooperation all around in accordance with arrangements previously agreed upon. And this is so, because ASEAN agreements and plans embody no enforcement provisions and carry no sanctions and because ASEAN has no central authority to ensure compliance with its agreements and decisions. These, in turn, result from the ASEAN member-states' reluctance to entrust supranational institutions and mechanisms with the authority to make sure that agreements are complied with rather than from some ideological attachment to non-interference as dogma.

On the other hand, the ASEAN response to the SARS epidemic of 2002–03 encountered few political obstacles. In the case of SARS, no powerful interests stood to gain from the spread of the disease. On the contrary, all governments and their peoples felt threatened by it and realized the absolute necessity of regional cooperation to arrest and ultimately end it. Thus, ASEAN cooperation on SARS was effective even in the absence of formal agreements.

The first case of SARS took place in November 2002 in Foshan in China's Guangdong province. However, it was not until three months later, when the disease had spread elsewhere in the country, including the military hospital in Beijing, that the World Health Organization received a report on the subject from China's health authorities. Apparently out of their concern over the possible repercussions on tourism and the economy, authorities in China sought to downplay or even cover up the existence of the problem. For this, in April, the minister of health and the mayor of Beijing were removed from their posts in the government and the Communist Party. The spread of the strange new disease was most prevalent in Guangdong province and nearby Hong Kong. Among the first persons infected outside the Chinese mainland were those who had stayed on the ninth floor of Hong Kong's Metropole Hotel in the period 21–25 February 2003.

SARS's first appearance in ASEAN was in Hanoi. The victim was a Chinese-American who had travelled to Guangdong, Macao and Hong Kong, where he occupied a room on the ninth floor of the Metropole Hotel. Dr Carlo Urbani, a WHO official based in Vietnam, took care of the Chinese-American, and then caught the disease himself, together with other healthcare workers. Dr Urbani eventually died on 29 March 2003. Earlier in March, the first case appeared in Singapore, that of a woman who had stayed on the ninth floor of the Metropole in that fateful week in February. The deadly infection then leaped from person to person, from hospital to hospital and from country to country. Many of those infected were healthcare workers who had come into contact with SARS patients.

By early April, six ASEAN countries — Indonesia, Malaysia, the Philippines, Singapore, Thailand and Vietnam — had reported SARS cases. The great majority of them took place in Singapore, followed far behind by Vietnam. Yet, the others, too, including the four member-countries that had no infections at all, felt gravely threatened in view of the rapidity of the transmission of the disease through international travel. Moreover, the entire region was suffering from the sharp drop in tourism and business travel. A touching and sober but colourfully presented account published in 2004 takes a look back at Singapore's experience with SARS. Aside from telling the human dimension of that story, the booklet attempts an estimate of the economic cost of the crisis. Tourist arrivals in Singapore in the last week of March dropped by 41,456, a plunge of 28 per cent from the same period the year before; the drop in May was 74 per cent. At least six carriers stopped flying to Changi Airport, and thirty-four reduced the frequency of their flights. Singapore Airlines cut down its flights by about 200 from around 600 a week, with a dive in the value of the airline's shares as the predictable result. One estimate placed a figure of S$23 million on losses *every week* from tourist spending and cancelled flights alone while the SARS crisis lasted. Hotel occupancy sank from 75 per cent in February to 20–30 per cent in April. Restaurants, retail shops and taxi fleets were, of course, badly hit.[46] Although not as severely affected by the epidemic as Singapore, the other ASEAN countries suffered, too, as tourists and business travellers shunned the region altogether.

By 10 April, according to WHO figures, there were 2,781 SARS cases, including 111 deaths due to the disease, in fifteen countries plus Hong Kong and Taiwan.[47] As the seriousness of the crisis and the need for a regional response became increasingly evident, Singapore Prime Minister Goh Chok Tong called his Thai counterpart, Thaksin Shinawatra, to propose an emergency ASEAN summit on the problem. The summit, later joined by Chinese Premier Wen Jiabao and Hong Kong's then Chief Executive, Tung Chee Hwa, convened in Bangkok on 29 April. Three days before that, the health ministers of the ASEAN+3 countries — ASEAN members and China, Japan and South Korea — had gathered in Kuala Lumpur in a previously scheduled special meeting on SARS. By the time the leaders met in Bangkok, the number of reported SARS cases had escalated to 5,462, with 353 deaths, in twenty-seven countries plus Hong Kong and Taiwan. Most of the cases and deaths were in China and Hong Kong. There were 282 cases, with thirty-five deaths, in six ASEAN countries, the bulk of the cases and deaths being in Singapore, followed by Vietnam.[48]

The ASEAN+3 health ministers emphasized the importance of engaging all agencies and sectors in the fight against SARS and proposed the formation of national "multi-sectoral" task forces "with real power of enforcement". They agreed on very specific actions involving a "hotline" network among designated contact points, the quick sharing of information according to a prescribed format, stringent pre-departure screening, health declaration forms, the management of suspected cases while in flight, close surveillance, disinfecting aircraft, coordinated procedures at land and sea borders, and the measures recommended by the WHO for travel to and from countries affected by SARS.[49] At their 29 April meeting, the ASEAN leaders endorsed the health ministers' decisions. The endorsement was important, because the counter-measures agreed upon required the cooperation of sectors other than health, specifically immigration, customs, tourism, trade and industry, transportation, law enforcement, foreign affairs and public information. The leaders stressed information sharing, common protocols for air, land and sea travel, and public education.[50] At the ASEAN-China summit on the same day, Premier Wen Jiabao associated China with the ASEAN declaration and pledged RMB10 million for ASEAN-China cooperation programmes to control and prevent SARS and deal with its impact.[51] Ministerial and senior officials forums were subsequently convened, among ASEAN countries and with China, Japan and Korea, in several sectors, including civil aviation, tourism and labour, as well as health.

The key to the effectiveness of the actions agreed upon was the assiduousness with which each country carried them out; indeed, they had already been taking stringent — one might say, draconian — measures on their own and bilaterally, as in the case of Singapore-Malaysia coordination. There were no legally binding agreements, just declarations recording the leaders' and ministers' joint decisions. Yet, all countries gave them effect, because they saw that it was in their immediate interest to do so.

In the view of Lee Chiong Giam and Robert Chua, officials at the Ministry of Foreign Affairs of Singapore, especially important were the strict quarantine measures instituted by the ASEAN countries, the thermal screening installed at entry and exit points (the equipment and technology having been shared by Singapore), and the personal networks that made quick information sharing possible. Not least, the summit's decisions were strictly carried out.[52]

The day before the summit, the WHO removed Vietnam from the list of areas with recent local transmission, the first country to contain the epidemic. The onset of Vietnam's last known SARS case was on 14 April. At the end of May, Singapore was similarly taken out of the list. On 10–11 June 2003, the ASEAN+3 health ministers met again, in Siem Reap, with Canada (which had also been hit by SARS), Mongolia and the WHO as observers. The ministers declared, "The region is now free of local transmission and ASEAN is a SARS-free region," the last SARS case in ASEAN having been isolated on 11 May. Nevertheless, the ministers stressed the "need to remain vigilant and committed to ensure that there is no let up in implementing the preventive and control measures that have been put in place". Shigeru Omi, Director of the Western Pacific Regional Office of the WHO, was reported to have said at the meeting, "Thanks to the commitment of the governments of the region to fight SARS and the implementation of aggressive and prompt control measures, the SARS epidemic appears to be under control."[53]

Dr Omi was all praises for what ASEAN did on SARS. As he pointed out to me, the special summits demonstrated in a "timely" manner the commitment of the leaders of ASEAN, China and Hong Kong to work together against SARS, citing especially the coordinated measures on people's entry into and exit from the ASEAN countries. However, he was worried about the possible spread of avian influenza in Southeast Asia, which could be a much bigger disaster than SARS. He cited the need for long-term regional planning. He also mentioned the difficulty of persuading pharmaceutical companies to invest heavily in the production of vaccines for an emergency that may or may not take place.[54]

The first known human infection by the avian flu was in 1997, in Hong Kong, where eighteen cases were reported, six of them fatal. To control the spread of the disease, Hong Kong's entire poultry population, 1.5 million birds, was destroyed. Early in January 2004, people and poultry in Vietnam — and Japan — were hit by the avian flu. Later that month, the first human case was reported in Thailand, with 11 million birds in thirty-two Thai provinces affected. By the end of January, reports of infections came from Cambodia, Indonesia and Laos, as well as China. Led by the WHO, in cooperation with the World Organization for Animal Health and the UN Food and Agriculture Organization, a massive effort to control the disease was undertaken through compulsory vaccination and other measures. The first phase of the epidemic was considered closed when the last human case took place in mid-March, in Vietnam. However, in July, there were fresh outbreaks in Cambodia, China, Indonesia, Thailand and Vietnam. This time, Malaysia, too, was hit, albeit on a smaller scale. A WHO publication issued in January 2005 warned that "further evolution of the situation in early 2005 can be anticipated".[55] Indeed, in December, Vietnam had reported large outbreaks in poultry and shortly afterwards in humans, especially children, with cases, including deaths, being reported well into 2005.

In an encouraging sign, the ASEAN bodies dealing with health and agriculture have been working together. Indeed, ASEAN+3 ministers of health and agriculture (plus the United States, but without Brunei Darussalam, Myanmar and the Philippines) met jointly in January 2004 to address the "current poultry disease situation".[56] Several ASEAN forums have been convened to devise cooperative measures for dealing with the avian flu, with Japan, with China, and with international organizations, particularly the WHO, the World Organization for Animal Health and FAO. An ASEAN task force on the avian influenza set up by the ASEAN ministers of agriculture met for the first time in Singapore in December 2004. An ASEAN+3 Emerging Infectious Diseases Programmeme, with Australian support for some ASEAN members, focuses on information-sharing and public awareness, laboratory diagnosis capacity, and epidemiological surveillance. In May 2006, the Japan-ASEAN Initiative to Combat Pandemic Influenza was launched at the ASEAN Secretariat. On that occasion, 500,000 courses of the anti-influenza drug Tamiflu and 700,000 sets of personal protective equipment were symbolically turned over to the Secretariat for stockpiling in Singapore. Valued at US$30 million, funding for the drugs and equipment was to be taken from the new US$70 million Japan-ASEAN Integration Fund. It remains to be seen whether the ASEAN reaction to the avian flu will be as coordinated and as effective as its response to SARS.

This comparison of ASEAN's responses to two crises — the haze in 1997–98 and SARS in 2003 — illuminates the factors that make the difference between effectiveness and hesitancy. For a response to be successful, the ASEAN countries most involved have to see individual as well as common action on a regional problem to be in the national interest. More to the point, none of the ASEAN countries, or, more precisely, their ruling elites, should feel that the actions required of it threaten its interests. The 1997–98 haze affected Jakarta and other densely populated areas of Indonesia less than the neighbouring countries, whereas there was no telling where and when SARS would strike. Taking action against forest fires ran counter to short-term considerations of economic growth and the narrow interests of politically and economically potent forces allied to those in power. On the other hand, nobody had any interest in obstructing cooperative action against SARS; indeed, all felt threatened by the disease. The other factor is engagement at the highest level. ASEAN's national leaders have to be actively and personally engaged in the collective response to big crises, particularly since dealing with most crises requires many agencies and sectors to act in a coordinated manner for a common purpose. ASEAN's leaders were not collectively engaged in confronting the haze crisis; they were in the case of SARS. It is these factors rather than a doctrinaire adherence to non-interference that spell the difference in the levels of effectiveness in ASEAN's responses to the two crises.

This difference, in fact, constitutes a test for the efficacy of a regional association in dealing with common problems — whether it is effective enough to compel states to act for the common good even against potent political forces within the nation. In this, all regional organizations fall short. Even the EU cannot give up agricultural export subsidies over the objections of a tiny sector in a tiny minority of member-states, a circumstance that might be construed as non-interference on a European scale.

EAST TIMOR

ASEAN came in for sharp criticism when it was accused of doing nothing about the 1991 Santa Cruz massacre in East Timor, the 1999 Liquiça killings, or the militia rampage that left a scene of death and destruction in the tiny territory preceding and following the 1999 consultations on its status. Again, ASEAN's policy of non-interference was blamed. For example, Felix Soh, then Foreign Editor and now Deputy Editor of the *Straits Times* of Singapore, wrote on 10 September 1999:

> Asean has not come out smelling good either. Even as the human tragedy is unfolding right in its own backyard, it has not taken any initiative because of its non-interventionist principle.

He could have been writing about Santa Cruz or Liquiça, too.

East Timor was a Portuguese colony for 400 years. After the 1974 military coup ended the long dictatorship of Antonio de Oliveira Salazar and his successor, Marcelo Caetano, Portugal acknowledged the right of its colonies, East Timor among them, to self-determination, including the possibility of independence. In the midst of fighting between East Timorese groups, the Portuguese in 1975 abruptly abandoned the territory. East Timorese independence was declared on 28 November 1975 by FRETILIN,[57] an anti-colonial, guerrilla movement that had prevailed in violent clashes over more conservative rivals. FRETILIN was perceived, not least by Indonesia and the United States, as being heavily influenced by communist ideas and supported by the communist powers. It must be remembered that this was happening right after the victory of North Vietnam and its South Vietnamese partners over the United States and its South Vietnamese allies, with the consequent fear of dominoes falling to communism all over Southeast Asia. Apparently alarmed by the possibility of a communist-ruled enclave in their midst, the Indonesians moved troops into East Timor nine days after the proclamation of independence. In July 1976, Indonesia incorporated East Timor as its twenty-seventh province.

Months before East Timor's declaration of independence, U.S. President Gerald Ford and his Secretary of State, Henry Kissinger, had made it clear that Washington was interposing no objection to Indonesian intervention in East Timor. President Soeharto had discussed with them the possibility of such an intervention during his July 1975 visit to the United States. According to declassified State Department records, the American ambassador, John Newsom, had in August 1975 articulated U.S. policy: if Indonesia were to invade East Timor, it should do so "effectively, quickly, and not use our equipment".[58]

In a forum in Hanoi in October 2003, Wiryono Sastrohandoyo, former Indonesian ambassador in Canberra and several other major posts, stated that President Soeharto, eager to distinguish his rule from the aggressive international policies of Sukarno, had been reluctant to have Indonesia move in to fill the vacuum in East Timor, but was encouraged to do so by Ford and Kissinger, who were wary of a takeover by FRETILIN, with its leftist, and therefore undesirable, orientation.[59] In the same forum in Hanoi, Ana Gomes, former Portuguese chargé d'affaires, later ambassador, in Jakarta, said that the Indonesian takeover of East Timor could take place only because Portugal had a new and weak government, while Indonesia had a strong government (a "dictatorship"), and because the invasion had the acquiescence of the United States and the encouragement of Australia. On the other hand, the Portuguese felt obligated to act on behalf of East Timor's independence;

for one thing, the 1976 post-Salazar Portuguese constitution, in Article 293, stated, "Portugal remains bound by her responsibilities under international law to promote and safeguard the right to self-determination and independence of East Timor." Portugal thus led the international campaign to oppose East Timor's incorporation into Indonesia. "For 24 years," however, Gomes said, Portugal "oscillated" on East Timor, with some policy-makers resigned to the territory's "inevitable" integration into Indonesia. Those twenty-four years, she stated, were marked by "miscommunication and misperception", as Indonesia and Portugal each rejected positions just because the other had proposed them.[60]

Soon after Indonesia's takeover in 1975, ASEAN was content to let Indonesia and Portugal argue out the East Timor issue at the United Nations and other international venues, while generally sympathizing with the Indonesian position. However, Portugal seemed to be more effective in marshaling international support for its stand, particularly among its former colonies in Africa and other newly independent states. At the UN General Assembly, vote after vote went in Portugal's favour during the seven years since Indonesia's annexation of East Timor. The UN never recognized that annexation. In 1976, the UNGA affirmed the right to self-determination and independence of the people of East Timor, rejected the territory's integration in Indonesia, deplored Indonesia's non-compliance with resolutions of the UN Security Council, and demanded the withdrawal of Indonesian troops from East Timor. In December 1975, the Security Council, in Resolution 384, had demanded that Indonesia withdraw its forces "without delay", that Portugal cooperate with the UN to enable the East Timorese to exercise their right to self-determination, and that all states and other parties concerned help the UN find a peaceful solution and decolonize the territory. The Council reiterated these demands in Resolution 389 in 1976. That same year, the ASEAN Ministerial Meeting's joint communiqué quoted the Indonesian foreign minister (Adam Malik) as asserting that "recent developments in East Timor correspond with the provisions of the United Nations Security Council Resolutions No. 384 of 22 December 1975 and No. 389 of 22 April 1976". The communiqué then declared that "the future of East Timor remains, in the final analysis, in the hands of the people of East Timor".[61] Since then, except when compelled to defend ASEAN or Indonesia, the ASEAN foreign ministers as a group fell largely silent on the East Timor question until after the territory had opted for independence in 1999. The ASEAN Regional Forum, from its first meeting in 1994, assumed the same posture.

Hasjim Djalal, the veteran Indonesian diplomat and authority on maritime law, has observed that Indonesia failed to mobilize support from

ASEAN, the Non-Aligned Movement or the Organization of Islamic Conference, whereas Portugal succeeded in getting the European Union, which it joined in 1986 — and, I might add, its former African colonies — behind it on the East Timor issue.[62]

At the UN General Assembly, from 1978 to 1982, Portugal and its allies marshaled majorities behind resolutions affirming the East Timorese people's right to self-determination and independence, expressing concern at their "suffering," and urging international assistance to them. The 1982 resolution added a request to the UN Secretary-General to initiate consultations with all parties concerned with a view to a "comprehensive settlement", evidently the result of an understanding among Indonesia, Portugal and the UN. Almost immediately, Kurt Waldheim, the Secretary-General at that time, started informal consultations with Indonesia and Portugal. The UNGA thereafter stopped adopting resolutions on the issue, allowing the consultations to take their course without hindrance from the Assembly.

While talks continued between Indonesia and Portugal under UN auspices, things took a turn for the worse when, on 12 November 1991, thousands of East Timorese gathered at Santa Cruz cemetery in Dili, East Timor's capital, to mourn the death of Sebastião Gomes, a young man who had been shot to death by Indonesian forces on 28 October. For one reason or another, Indonesian soldiers fired into the crowd. Estimates of the number killed range widely, some as high as 200 or more. What is internationally significant is that the violence was captured on film and witnessed by the journalists covering the event. According to Ana Gomes, international interest in East Timor, even among Portuguese, had been waning. However, images of people praying at the cemetery — in Portuguese — were beamed to Portugal, arousing emotions in the former colonial power. Moreover, a New Zealand journalist was shot to death covering the Santa Cruz killings. U.S. and other journalists were present and gave testimony of the events. Still, Gomes said, "some high officials" in the Portuguese foreign ministry continued to be indifferent to East Timor. Others in Europe were more intent on pursuing their business interests in Indonesia and preferred to have nothing to do with the East Timor problem, she recalled.[63] Nevertheless, thanks to Portugal's efforts, the problem got so much international attention that it could no longer be ignored. It also intruded into the relations between ASEAN and the European Union. Starting in Manila in 1992, the ASEAN-EU Ministerial Meetings were marked by debates between Indonesia and Portugal over the East Timor issue. The Europeans and the Australians repeatedly raised it at the ASEAN Regional Forum, although those discussions were never reflected in the ARF's public statements.

ASEAN was particularly exercised by the EU's tendency to be led by Portugal on the issue. The press statement of the "informal" ASEAN Summit in November 1996 in Jakarta forcefully declared:

> While recognizing the importance of ASEAN-EU relations which have developed over the past two decades, the ASEAN Heads of Government noted with increasing concern the efforts of one member country of the EU to introduce extraneous issues such as the question of East Timor in the economic cooperation and interaction between ASEAN and the EU. They believed that the introduction of such an extraneous issue would only lead to unwarranted aggravation in ASEAN-EU relations, while at the same time jeopardizing the tripartite process on East Timor presently taking place under the auspices of the UN Secretary-General. The Heads of Government reiterated their full support for the Indonesian position on East Timor and rejected the introduction of such an extraneous issue into ASEAN-EU relations by a certain member of EU.[64]

On 27 January 1999, Indonesia stunned the world by announcing that President B. J. Habibie and his cabinet had decided to allow the people of East Timor to express their views on whether they accepted an arrangement under which they would enjoy "autonomy" within Indonesia. If they rejected the arrangement, East Timor would be let go as an independent state. According to many accounts, the immediate trigger for the decision was Australian Prime Minister John Howard's December 1998 letter to Habibie urging him to act on the situation in East Timor. Howard proposed a solution akin to the Martineau settlement under which France resolved its New Caledonia problem. According to Ana Gomes, Habibie was "incensed" by the letter, since it implied that Indonesia was East Timor's colonial ruler, as France was New Caledonia's. She claimed that even Australia's ambassador to Indonesia, John McCarthy, was "outraged". According to her, at the meeting of the Indonesian cabinet that preceded the 27 January announcement, a "riot" erupted over the Howard letter, the Indonesians feeling that Australia had betrayed them in a way that, Gomes said, Portugal had not. For their part, the Portuguese suspected an Indonesian "trick" at first, but ultimately agreed to look seriously at Jakarta's proposal.

Dewi Fortuna Anwar, deputy chair for the social sciences and humanities of LIPI (Indonesian Institute of Science), was Habibie's foreign policy adviser. As she recounted it, Habibie sent Howard's letter to the Coordinating Minister for Political and Security Affairs, Faisal Tanjung, the chief of the armed forces, Wiranto, and the foreign minister, Ali Alatas. On 26 January, the group met and recommended offering East Timor autonomy; if a referendum rejected this course, independence would be granted immediately. The next day, the full cabinet approved the recommendation. Wiranto laid down one condition: there would be no admission that the Indonesian takeover of East Timor was a mistake, as such an admission would imply that the soldiers killed in the territory had died in vain.[65] José Ramos-Horta, East Timor's international spokesman, who would become its foreign minister, sought a ten-year transition period should independence be the people's choice. Habibie rejected this proposal, refusing to continue pouring Indonesian resources into an East Timor that was to leave Indonesia anyway. Alatas and Jaime Gama, Portugal's foreign minister, then proceeded to discuss the modalities of the consultation.

The decision to give the East Timorese the autonomy-or-independence option was not as precipitate as the reaction to the Howard letter would seem to indicate. In June 1998, just a month after taking over the presidency upon Soeharto's resignation, Habibie announced an offer to grant to East Timor a "special status" involving wide autonomy within Indonesia. East Timorese resistance leaders rejected the proposal. Portugal had earlier proposed, through the United Nations, a measure of autonomy for East Timor without prejudging the East Timorese's ultimate decision, but enticing the Indonesians with the idea that, if autonomy succeeded over a fairly lengthy transition period, the East Timorese would, in the end, likely opt for integration with Indonesia. Alatas, who had been negotiating with Portugal on East Timor since 1982, had also been advocating some kind of autonomy for years. In fact, Indonesians who followed these events were dismayed by the Habibie decision, which was made at a time when Indonesia and Portugal seemed to be nearing agreement. In August 1998, the two countries had agreed to negotiate "under the auspices of the [UN] Secretary-General" on "wide-ranging autonomy for East Timor". At that stage, the positions of Jakarta and Lisbon remained apart on the final status of the territory, with Indonesia insisting on its sovereignty and Portugal standing on self-determination for the East Timorese. Portugal accepted the idea of autonomy, but as a transition to full independence after ten years should the East Timorese so decide. On the other hand, Indonesia envisioned only a "review" after ten years. Nevertheless, both agreed on autonomy for East Timor and further negotiations.

The principal negotiator for Indonesia at that stage, Nugroho Wisnumurti, director-general for political affairs at the Department of Foreign Affairs, had known about the Habibie plan by the time, in January 1999, he was about to leave for New York (the negotiations being under UN auspices) for talks with the Portuguese, but he was surprised by the abrupt timing of the public announcement, as were the Portuguese. According to Nugroho,

Habibie did not seem to take into account the developments on the diplomatic front but considered only his inner circle's advice to get rid of East Timor.[66]

Before becoming President, Habibie was a driving force of ICMI, the Association of Indonesian Muslim Intellectuals. Some members of the association, I am told, had taken the position that Indonesia should no longer be burdened politically or financially by "a bunch of Catholics". In fact, as early as two years before Habibie's decision, some in ICMI had privately proposed getting rid of the Catholic enclave in the light of the international pressure, the drain on Indonesia's resources, and the resentment of other provinces, like neighbouring East Nusa Tenggara, of East Timor's undue share of those resources. (According to UNDP, the average annual economic growth rate of East Timor from 1953 to 1962 was two per cent, while, under Indonesia, between 1983 and 1997, it was six per cent. Nevertheless, East Timor emerged into independent nationhood as the poorest country in Asia. Jakarta has claimed that, in twenty-four years, it poured into the development of East Timor more than Portugal had spent in 400 years of colonialism, but some Portuguese charge that something like half of that amount went into the pockets of military officers in power in the territory.)

However, some well-placed Indonesians have told me that, even as Habibie presented the East Timorese with a choice between autonomy and independence, he directed certain officials to make sure that the vote for autonomy carried the day. The Indonesian military, Ana Gomes claimed, tried to ensure this through intimidation, as exemplified by the Liquiça massacre of April 1999, in which Indonesian troops were reported to have attacked a number of pro-independence East Timorese who had clashed with a pro-integration group. Gomes blames Faisal Tanjung and Zaki Anwar, chief of intelligence in East Timor, for masterminding the campaign of intimidation. The alleged determination on the part of Habibie to hold on to East Timor at any cost, of course, contradicts the claim that he supported ICMI members' call for getting rid of it.

Whatever the case, following the Habibie decision, the New York negotiations turned on the modalities of the consultations that were to determine the preference of the East Timorese people. On 5 May 1999, with the UN's Kofi Annan as witness, Indonesia's Alatas and Portugal's Gama signed an agreement on the purpose and terms of the consultations, which the UN would conduct. Under the agreement, Indonesia was to be "responsible for maintaining peace and security in East Timor in order to ensure that the popular consultation is carried out in a fair and peaceful way in an atmosphere free of intimidation, violence or interference from any side".[67]

Instead of abating, however, the violence in East Timor escalated, leading Kofi Annan to delay the consultations from 8 August to 30 August. According to the UN, at least 95 per cent of registered voters cast their ballots, and on 4 September the UN announced that 78.2 per cent of the vote had gone against the autonomy proposal, in effect for independence. A background paper issued by the UN Transitional Administration in East Timor states, "Following the announcement of the result, pro-integration militias, at times with the support of elements of the Indonesian security forces, launched a campaign of violence, looting and arson throughout the entire territory.... Many East Timorese were killed and as many as 500,000 were displaced from their homes, about half leaving the territory, in some cases by force." The paper continues:

> The Secretary-General and the Security Council undertook strenuous diplomatic efforts to halt the violence, pressing Indonesia to meet its responsibility to maintain security and order in the territory. A Security Council mission visited Jakarta and Dili, and the Secretary-General worked to rally support among Governments for a multinational force authorized by the Security Council to bring the situation under control. As the Council mission concluded its visit to Jakarta on 12 September 1999, the Government of Indonesia agreed to accept the offer of assistance from the international community.[68]

On the same day, thirteen days after the consultations in East Timor and eight days after the escalation of violence there, Prime Minister Chuan Leekpai of Thailand, chair-country of the ASEAN Standing Committee, convened a meeting of the seven ASEAN leaders attending the APEC Economic Leaders Meeting in Auckland, New Zealand. Ginandjar Kartasasmita, then Coordinating Minister for Economy, Finance and Industry, representing President Habibie, appealed for prominent ASEAN participation in the International Force for East Timor, which the UN was putting together under Australian command. His appeal was met with a positive response. Three days earlier, ministers or officials from the sovereign states belonging to APEC (that is, excluding Taiwan and Hong Kong) had met to discuss the crisis in East Timor. Formally upon Indonesian request, the UN Security Council on 15 September authorized the establishment of a multinational force under a unified command "to restore peace and security in East Timor".[69]

Southeast Asian participation in the UN operation would not be by ASEAN as an association but by individual countries. ASEAN members differed greatly in their capacities for and attitudes towards peacekeeping operations in general. Most importantly, ASEAN was not, and is not, organized for joint military or police action. Nevertheless, some ASEAN countries did respond to the Indonesian appeal at a meeting convened in an ASEAN context. Two ASEAN lieutenant-generals — starting January 2000, Jaime de los Santos of the Philippines and, after six months, Boonsrang Niumpradit of Thailand — took command of the military component of the UN Transitional Authority for East Timor, thus highlighting the ASEAN profile in the operation. Among Southeast Asian countries, Thailand and the Philippines contributed the most troops, with additional elements from Singapore and Malaysia. The ASEAN countries received high praise for their contributions.

Aside from calling a summit meeting eight days after the surge in violence in East Timor, a meeting which, in any case, was attended by only seven of the ten ASEAN countries, the other three not being APEC members, what else could ASEAN have done as an association to help deal with the crisis in East Timor? What should ASEAN have done in response to the growing problems in the territory?

A month before Indonesia's formal annexation of East Timor, ASEAN was obviously concerned about what had happened in the territory. The joint communiqué of the June 1976 ASEAN Ministerial Meeting[70] reported that the ministers had "heard with appreciation the explanation given by the Foreign Minister of Indonesia on the question of East Timor that recent developments in East Timor correspond with the provisions of the United Nations Security Council Resolutions No. 384 of 22 December 1975, and No. 389 of 22 April 1976". The joint communiqué urged the UN Secretary-General's special envoy, Vittorio Winspeare Guicciardi, to "complete" the mission given him by the resolutions. That mission was basically to "ensure the implementation" of the Security Council resolutions, which called for respect for East Timor's territorial integrity and the right of its people to self-determination, the withdrawal of Indonesian forces from the territory, and Portugal's cooperation in enabling the East Timorese to exercise their right to self-determination. The ASEAN ministers' communiqué then "reaffirmed the view that the future of East Timor remains, in the final analysis, in the hands of the people of East Timor", a position that Indonesia itself had professed to espouse in its interventions in the Security Council debates.

However, ASEAN met Indonesia's formal annexation of East Timor in July 1976 with silence and thereafter increasingly regarded the situation in the territory as Indonesia's internal affair. The international dimensions of the problem were being dealt with at the United Nations, and ASEAN was happy to leave it there. That was, of course, also how Portugal, as well as Indonesia, felt. Moreover, as East Timor became a matter internal to Indonesia, any move to separate it from Indonesia was increasingly looked upon as secession, something regarded in ASEAN as destabilizing to the region.

As violence surged following the 30 August 1999 consultations, members of the Security Council are quoted as warning that "if the security situation in East Timor does not improve within a very short period of time, they will have to consider further action to help the Indonesian Government resolve the present crisis in the Territory". This was on 8 September. Two days later, the Secretary-General is said to have urged Indonesia "to accept the offer of assistance from several Governments, including Australia, New Zealand, the Philippines and Malaysia, without further delay" and threatened that if Indonesia refused to do so, "it cannot escape responsibility for what could amount, according to reports reaching us, to crimes against humanity".[71]

Confronted with the inevitable, Indonesia wanted an ASEAN face to any foreign force that, for the first time since the departure of the Dutch, would set foot on Indonesian soil. In fact, Alatas has told me, Indonesia wanted to see an ASEAN peacekeeping force, but other ASEAN members were not ready for it.[72] Nor were they ready to respond quickly to the crisis in East Timor with their own national forces. Malaysia, the Philippines, Singapore and Thailand, as well as Indonesia itself, had some experience in international peacekeeping operations, but none could afford a contribution of enough substance for the requirements of the East Timor situation, certainly not at such short notice, an undertaking, in any case, that would have been prohibitively expensive. The UN thus had to turn to Australia, which had forces ready and waiting, had extensive experience in foreign conflict, was endowed with the resources to support those forces, and, not least, was eager — some say too eager — to go into East Timor.

In summary, once East Timor was firmly in Indonesian hands, ASEAN considered the problem to be an Indonesian one, despite its earlier support for UN calls for self-determination for the people of East Timor. This was not so much on account of the principle of non-interference. It was, above all, because the other ASEAN countries regarded any hint at secessionism, which, from the ASEAN point of view, the East Timorese struggle had become, as destabilizing to themselves and to the region as a whole. Moreover, the issue was being dealt with between Indonesia and Portugal at the UN, as all parties preferred. In any case, ASEAN was not and is not set up for resolving conflicts of this nature. As it turned out, it could not respond even if in 1999 Indonesia itself was urging it to. Some commentators have said that ASEAN might have taken the lead in organizing the international force authorized by the UN Security Council; but ASEAN was not ready for that, again not so much because of its policy of non-interference as because of its member-states' aversion to investing the association with any kind of supranational power, particularly one involving military force.

The most, or perhaps the least, that ASEAN could have done when things were getting out of hand, and people were being killed and maimed and buildings and property were being destroyed, was to raise a sharp voice of concern. It could have done so as early as the Santa Cruz massacre. This would not have been interference, just as the 1986 ASEAN statement on the events in the Philippines was never construed as interference. Provided Indonesia was responsive to it, an ASEAN call might, in fact, have helped avert the massive international intervention that eventually took place.

With the political crisis that erupted in violence in Timor-Leste in March 2006, ASEAN's capacity to respond effectively to critical events in its neighbourhood was tested once again.

MYANMAR

Much of the criticism of ASEAN's policy of non-interference has been directed at the association's handling — or non-handling — of Myanmar both before its admission in 1997 and afterwards. While ASEAN was being formed, its core founders were eager to bring into the new association as much of Southeast Asia as possible, so that it would acquire sufficient political weight to influence regional affairs and be able to promote reconciliation, regional solidarity and stability over as wide an area as possible. Thus, Adam Malik went to Yangon and Phnom Penh, as well as to Bangkok and Manila, in drumming up membership for the group-in-the-making.

However, both Yangon and Phnom Penh eyed the projected organization with suspicion, seeing it as a likely surrogate for SEATO, the American-led anti-communist Southeast Asia Treaty Organization, a suspicion strengthened by the anti-communist stances of its core founding members. Intent on preserving their neutrality, Burma and Cambodia declined the Malik overtures. In the case of Burma, it did so in spite — or, perhaps, because — of the fact that Burmese-Chinese relations were, in 1967, at their nadir on account of the excesses of the Great Proletarian Cultural Revolution, excesses that spilled over into Burma and evoked a strong reaction from the Burmese in the form of anti-Chinese demonstrations.

Obviously, in inviting Burma to membership, the core ASEAN founders took no account of the fact that Yangon was in the hands of a military regime, led by General Ne Win, that had taken over, five years before, from the elected U Nu government. After all, the New Order in Indonesia was led largely by the armed forces, and the military held sway in Thailand. ASEAN did not have any criteria for membership other than geographical location in Southeast Asia and adherence to ASEAN's norms for inter-state relations.

Until the early 1990s, Burma stayed aloof from ASEAN as an association, although it maintained cordial enough relations with its Southeast Asian neighbours. Indeed, it stayed out of most other international organizations, even pulling out, in 1979, from the Non-Aligned Movement on the grounds that the NAM was leaning too much towards the Soviet Union. At the same time, Burma was undergoing internal upheavals, beset by the continuing insurrection of the Communist Party of Burma, the rebellions of most of the non-Bamar nationalities, the activities of the Nationalist Chinese contingent that had fled the victorious communist armies on the Chinese mainland, conflicts over narcotics and other rackets, and an economic breakdown under the "Burmese Way to Socialism" that ultimately led to Burma's humiliating designation by the United Nations in December 1987 as a least-developed country.

The worsening conditions gave rise to a surge in public unrest, which developed into a protest movement against the government and its ruinous economic policies. The movement found its most organized expression in the National League for Democracy, formed in the aftermath of the collapse of the "socialist" government. In July 1988, General Ne Win, the strongman who had ruled Burma since 1962, stepped down from all his official positions. Later in the year, the military took complete control of the government and announced the formation of the State Law and Order Restoration Council (SLORC) as the ruling organ. In July 1989, the regime placed Daw Aung San Suu Kyi, the NLD's General Secretary, under house arrest and imprisoned other NLD leaders. The daughter of Aung San, the assassinated leader of Burma's drive for independence, Suu Kyi had the year before returned to Burma from England, where she had been living with her British husband and their two sons, to attend to her ailing mother.

Inexplicably, the leadership called for elections, which took place in May 1990. It apparently overestimated its popular support or its ability to control the conduct and outcome of the ballot, much as Marcos did in calling the 1986 "snap elections" in the Philippines. As it turned out, the NLD won 392 out of the 485 seats contested (elections for the seven other seats could not be conducted), with 62 per cent of the vote. The National Unity Party,[73] although winning 25 per cent of the vote, took only ten seats. As the outcome became clear, however, the SLORC asserted that the elections had been for a constituent assembly, not for a parliament, and, on those grounds, barred the NLD from forming a government. The SLORC thus stayed in power.

Burma's Southeast Asian neighbours, except possibly Thailand, took little notice of all this. In 1992, however, Brunei Darussalam, Indonesia, Malaysia and Singapore, four ASEAN countries with proportionately sizeable Muslim populations, as well as Saudi Arabia, did take notice and protested when Burma, whose name the SLORC had changed to Myanmar[74] in 1989, cracked down on the Muslim population that inhabited Myanmar territory lying next to Bangladesh and whose legal status was uncertain. The crackdown drove some 200,000 of them to flee to Bangladesh. The SLORC claimed that the Rohingyas, as the Muslims are called, were not Myanmar citizens, although they and their ancestors had lived in the country for generations. Something similar had happened in 1978.

Meanwhile, the settlement of the Cambodian problem was arrived at with the withdrawal of Vietnamese forces in 1989, the conclusion of the Paris accords of 1991, and the establishment of an elected government in Cambodia in 1993. The ASEAN door was now open to Cambodia, Laos and Vietnam, which were to reach the conclusion that ASEAN membership would be to their benefit. The vision of ASEAN encompassing all of Southeast Asia seemed within reach. Questions, however, were raised about Myanmar, by Americans and Europeans, and even by some within ASEAN, specifically about the denial of power to the victorious party in the 1990 elections, alleged human rights abuses by the military, the claimed use of forced labour and child soldiers, and the regime's perceived tolerance of, if not involvement in, drug-trafficking. On the other hand, some steps were being taken to open the Myanmar economy. (One of the most important foreign investments has been that of Total of France, in which Unocal of the United States and the Petroleum Authority of Thailand also have significant interests, to exploit the Yadana offshore natural gas fields and sell the gas to Thailand. The Yetagun gas field is also being developed by Premier Oil, Petronas of Malaysia and PTT of Thailand.) Starting in 1989, ceasefires were being concluded with the major ethnic rebel groups, so that by 1995 all of them, except the Karen National Union, were back in the "legal fold". Things looked somewhat promising. In the meantime, Myanmar-China ties were deepening and expanding.

The question before ASEAN was: What would be better for ASEAN — Myanmar in as a member, or Myanmar out as the lone Southeast Asian country outside ASEAN? Would it be better for the region if Myanmar were to be part of the regional association or if it were to continue going it alone, fending for itself? For the people of Myanmar, would it be better if their country were admitted into ASEAN or if it were kept out? These questions were debated among policy-makers within ASEAN countries, among ASEAN governments, and between North American and European countries and individual ASEAN members.

In the end, ASEAN easily came down on the side of admitting Myanmar — for both strategic and tactical reasons. Strategic considerations had to do with the perceived need to channel Myanmar's relations with its giant neighbours, China and India, at least partly within an ASEAN framework. Tactically, ASEAN believed that engaging Myanmar, rather than isolating it, would be the more effective approach to whatever problems Yangon posed for its people, for the region and for others in the international community, as well as to the region's broader and longer-term interests. Unlike the stance of some distant countries, ASEAN felt that it was not in its interest to cut itself off from Yangon, although, with the benefit of hindsight, some personalities in ASEAN now feel that Myanmar's admission was premature, considering the country as a "misfit" in the association. In any case, in 1995, according to then Prime Minister Khin Nyunt, then Thai Prime Minister Banharn Silpa-Archa visited Myanmar and invited it to join ASEAN.[75]

At a conference in Paris, Domingo Siazon, the Philippines' Ambassador to Japan and, at the time of Myanmar's admission, Secretary of Foreign Affairs, explained ASEAN's rationale:

1. Myanmar is clearly in the geographic footprint of Southeast Asia.
2. For the first time in its long existence, it had taken a decision to be aligned, in this case, with ASEAN.
3. Myanmar is a relatively large country, bigger than France, with some 52 million people, and very strategically located between China, Thailand, India, Bangladesh and Laos. Its land border with China is 2,185 kilometres long; with Thailand, 1,800 kilometres; and with India, 1,463 kilometres. Its total land border is 5,876 kilometres or twice the land border of France, which is 2,889 kilometres. France's land border with Germany is only 451 kilometres long; yet, three major wars were fought between them from 1870 to 1945. It is clear that Myanmar's territorial integrity and political stability are critical to its neighbouring countries and to ASEAN.
4. Myanmar is also located in the Golden Triangle and is the largest producer of poppy seeds in that region.
5. If Myanmar were a member of ASEAN, there would be better opportunities to influence Myanmar to adjust its internal policies and move toward national reconciliation.

In short, ASEAN determined that Myanmar's admission served the interest of long-term security and political stability of Southeast Asia.[76]

In July 1996, Myanmar, like Laos and Vietnam in 1992 and Cambodia in 1995, was accorded observer status in ASEAN as a step to membership and promptly took its seat in the ASEAN Regional Forum. The year before, the junta had released Daw Aung San Suu Kyi from six years of house arrest. With Malaysia eager for ASEAN to complete Southeast Asian membership during its chairmanship, Laos and Myanmar were admitted to membership at the ASEAN Ministerial Meeting in Kuala Lumpur in 1997, Vietnam having become a member in 1995. However, as we saw in Chapter 2, Cambodia's admission was delayed by two years on account of the political turmoil there. Four months after Myanmar's admission into ASEAN, the junta changed its name from SLORC to the State Peace and Development Council.

As mentioned earlier, it was politically and strategically important for ASEAN to have Myanmar in its fold. Since ASEAN has no criteria for membership other than geographical location, accession to ASEAN agreements, and adherence to certain principles governing inter-state relations, there were no grounds for excluding Myanmar indefinitely even if the ASEAN countries had been so inclined. Beyond the fact of membership, which is important in itself, having Myanmar in ASEAN has enabled the other member-countries to question and seek explanations from Myanmar about developments in the country. Myanmar's participation in the ARF has compelled, as well as given an opportunity for, its foreign minister to respond to criticisms aired and questions raised by other ministers; not even North Korea's internal situation has been subjected to such scrutiny in the ARF.

There are, however, limits to this. For instance, after the sudden sacking of the Prime Minister, General Khin Nyunt, and other senior officials in October 2004, a minister of one of the other ASEAN countries said something like this to me: "Here we are, defending them before the world, and they would not even brief us on this important development." Later, some ASEAN officials professed to resent the fact that Myanmar had not bothered to inform them of the government's move to a new capital inland, near Pyinmana, publicly acknowledged in late 2005.

On the economic side, because of the poor state and inward-looking orientation of Myanmar's economy, its membership has had little impact on the association's economic-integration schemes one way or the other. On the other hand, attempts by China and, more recently and on a smaller scale, India to expand their economic as well as strategic relationship with Myanmar have evoked deep interest within ASEAN.

Myanmar's membership has had some effect on some of ASEAN's external relations, although not as much as sections of the Western media make it seem. Two projects that the ASEAN Secretariat was to carry out with the support of the International Labour Organization, on human resource development planning and on industrial relations, could not proceed because of a resolution approved by the International Labour Conference in June 1999 prohibiting ILO technical assistance from benefiting Myanmar. The resolution was in response to what it claimed was Myanmar's continuing practice of forced labour.[77] The ASEAN labour ministers backed Myanmar, citing the steps that its government had supposedly taken in ensuring the cessation of the practice; for example, the May 1999 directive, announced at the ASEAN Ministers of Labour Meeting in Yangon, to stop the implementation of the British-era Towns Act and Villages Act, both of 1907, which required people to do "community labour". The ASEAN ministers instead promoted dialogue between Myanmar and the ILO and, in 2002, welcomed the agreement on the appointment of an ILO liaison officer in Yangon.

Australia, Japan, New Zealand, and, at one time, India, like the Western Dialogue Partners, have sharply criticized Myanmar in the ARF, but their apparent distaste for the regime in Yangon has had little effect on their policies towards ASEAN as a whole. In terms of actual policy, only Canada, the United States and the European Union have taken concrete measures by way of sanctions against Myanmar. Such measures include the suspension of development assistance, but not of "humanitarian" aid, bans on the issuance of visas to members of the SPDC, senior members of the government and their families, the cessation of military sales to Myanmar, and the control of exports to that country. Canada, the United States and the EU have withheld the trade preferences that Myanmar would otherwise enjoy as a least-developed country. Indeed, the United States has imposed an outright ban on imports from targeted persons and entities in Myanmar and on *new* American investments in that country (being careful not to order Unocal to cease operations there). The United States and the EU have imposed a freeze on the assets of SPDC members and of senior cabinet ministers.

ASEAN-Canada cooperation stalled after Myanmar's admission. However, the two sides have been in frequent discussions lately to work around this difficulty. In March 2004, the regular dialogue was resumed, in Bandar Seri Begawan. In February 2005, a symposium took place in the same city to examine ways of revitalizing the relationship, and in April the next dialogue took place in Vancouver with Myanmar's participation. Canada has proposed extending assistance to ASEAN again, but only to Cambodia, Laos and Vietnam.

ASEAN-EU relations are anchored on the cooperation agreement that dates back to 1980. Vietnam, Laos and Cambodia acceded to the agreement shortly after they were admitted to ASEAN membership in 1995, 1997 and 1999, respectively. However, the EU has refused to conclude a protocol of accession with Myanmar, which joined ASEAN in 1997. As a consequence, because ASEAN would not agree to the exclusion of Myanmar from any

ASEAN-EU meetings, the two sides had to go into diplomatic contortions to satisfy both; at meetings involving the cooperation agreement, Myanmar would be present, but there would be no country name plates, no individual country flags on display, and so on, so that Myanmar's presence would not be so visible. Myanmar could not speak unless it was directly referred to.

Proposed by Singapore, with the strong support of France, the Asia-Europe Meeting, which had its inaugural summit in 1996, is another venue for conducting the relations between ASEAN and EU member-countries. The European countries participating in ASEM were limited to members of the EU, while Asian participation consisted of the seven ASEAN members at the time of ASEM's founding, and China, Japan and South Korea. When it admitted Laos, Myanmar and Cambodia, ASEAN argued for their participation in ASEM, a proposal blocked by the European side on account of its objections to Myanmar. With the enlargement of the EU in May 2004, the Europeans insisted that the ten new members be automatically admitted into the ASEM process. ASEAN riposted that, if new members of the EU had the right to take part in ASEM by virtue of their EU membership, the new ASEAN members ought to have the same right. Thus caught in a bind, the EU had to agree to the participation of Myanmar, as well as of Cambodia and Laos, in the ASEM in Hanoi in October 2004, but on the understanding that Myanmar would be represented at lower than head-of-government level. Accordingly, Myanmar was represented at the Hanoi gathering by U Tin Winn, Minister for Labour, who also served briefly as ASEAN Economic Minister, among other duties, until he was removed from office a month after the ouster of Prime Minister Khin Nyunt and other senior officials.

Although ASEM participation is supposed to be by individual countries, the EU itself, just before the summit, issued a news release that included the following reference to Myanmar's participation:

> The European Union (EU) has accepted the participation of Burma/Myanmar in the expectation that the participation of the Burmese government at the ASEM Summit will be lower than at Head of State/Government level. At the same time, the EU has made clear that if there has been no movement by the authorities in Burma/Myanmar by the time of the summit, to release Daw Aung San Suu Kyi and to allow a genuine and open National Convention, the EU will strengthen the existing targeted sanctions against the Burmese regime. In addition, the Europeans with (sic) take the opportunity at the Summit, to discuss the human rights situation and the need for democratic reforms in Burma/Myanmar with Asian partners as well as making the European position clear to the Burmese representative present.[78]

In September 2005, ASEAN's foreign ministers, meeting in New York, requested their economic ministers not to take part in an ASEM economic ministers' meeting scheduled for that month in Rotterdam, because The Netherlands had refused to issue a visa to Myanmar's minister. The ASEAN ministers were represented by their senior officials at that meeting.

In fact, despite the appearance of unanimity on this and other EU declarations and measures on Myanmar, the EU's Myanmar policy has been driven largely by the United Kingdom, where Aung San Suu Kyi's late husband, Michael Aris, was a citizen, and for a while by Denmark, whose honorary consul in Yangon died while in Myanmar custody. Many of the rest, particularly some of the bigger countries, have been quite exasperated by the EU's hard-line stance. However, the EU members' positions converged somewhat when, on 30 May 2003, Aung San Suu Kyi's motorcade was attacked by mobs widely considered as instigated, if not organized, by the authorities, and she was returned to house arrest and other NLD leaders to prison.

The United States' sanctions on Myanmar have had little direct impact on ASEAN as a group except on its image in the eyes of a few members of Congress and the media. The sanctions are mandated by laws in which only a handful of Congress members and their staffs have any interest; the rest have little knowledge of or interest in Myanmar, but passively go along with the proposals of the few. I once asked a former official who had had an important role in shaping the U.S. Government's Asia policy why the United States seemed to be singling out Myanmar for criticism and sanctions. The former official replied by citing two factors. One was the fact that Myanmar had little leverage and was of little strategic importance to the United States. The calculation seemed to be that the U.S. government could afford to posture for domestic political gain at little cost to itself. The other factor was the presence of a Nobel Prize-winning "icon" in Aung San Suu Kyi; supporting her was thought to be a popular thing to do. (In this context, one might recall that, at the height of the Vietnam war, the United States extended economic and military support, albeit in small magnitudes, to Burma under Ne Win and welcomed the Burmese strongman to Washington in 1966.)

In view of all this, it would be quite misleading to project the sanctions imposed by Canada, the EU and the United States on Myanmar as reflecting the position of the "international community" or to label Myanmar as being "isolated" and a "pariah state". Nevertheless, the hard line taken by the developed West has to be taken seriously in view of its international influence.

It is partly in this light that the ASEAN foreign ministers have sought from their Myanmar colleague explanations of the internal situation in his country. These discussions normally take place in the "retreats" that were initiated at the 1999 ASEAN Ministerial Meeting in Singapore. These are closed-door meetings in which only the ministers and the Secretary-General take part. They take place in conjunction with the regular ministerial meetings and, starting in Yangon in 2001, on separate occasions once a year as well. The joint communiqué of the 2001 AMM "noted encouraging developments in the Union of Myanmar and appreciated the efforts of the Government of Myanmar towards these developments and reiterated our support to the on-going process of national reconciliation in this country".[79] Just a little over two weeks after the renewed detention of Aung San Suu Kyi and her followers on 30 May 2003, the ASEAN foreign ministers, at their "retreat" in Phnom Penh, asked the Myanmar minister about the developments in the country. Their joint communiqué reported:

> We discussed the recent political developments in Myanmar, particularly the incident of 30 May 2003. We noted the efforts of the Government of Myanmar to promote peace and development. In this connection, we urged Myanmar to resume its efforts of national reconciliation and dialogue among all parties concerned leading to a peaceful transition to democracy. We welcomed the assurances given by Myanmar that the measures taken following the incident were temporary and looked forward to the early lifting of restrictions placed on Daw Aung San Suu Kyi and the NLD members. We also reaffirmed our continued support for the efforts of the UNSG Special Representative Tan Sri Razali Ismail.[80]

The 2004 communiqué stated:

> We noted the briefing given by Myanmar on the reconvening of its National Convention and the development thereon. We acknowledged the potential of the Convention in paving the way for new constitution and the holding of elections in keeping with it. We recalled and emphasized the continued relevance of the Joint Communique of the 36th AMM and the Chairman's Press Statement of the 9th ASEAN Summit. In this regard, we underlined the need for the involvement of all strata of Myanmar society in the on-going National Convention. We encouraged all concerned parties in Myanmar to continue their efforts to effect a smooth transition to democracy. We recognized the role of the Special Representative of the United Nations Secretary-General in assisting Myanmar to achieve this goal.[81]

The statement issued in the name of President Megawati Sukarnoputri as chairman of the October 2003 ASEAN Summit in Bali had reported:

> The Leaders welcomed the recent positive developments in Myanmar and the Government's pledge to bring about a transition to democracy through dialogue and reconciliation. The roadmap as outlined by the Prime Minister

of Myanmar that would involve all strata of Myanmar society is a pragmatic approach and deserves understanding and support. The Leaders also agree that sanctions are not helpful in promoting peace and stability essential for democracy to take root.[82]

These statements, evidently negotiated painstakingly between the Myanmar delegation and those of other member-states, put a positive spin on Myanmar's efforts and, at the same time, prodded Yangon to make a "transition to democracy" through "dialogue" and "national reconciliation", involving "all strata of Myanmar society", presumably including the participation of the NLD and the "nationalities". The ministers called for "the early lifting of restrictions placed on Daw Aung San Suu Kyi and the NLD members". On the other hand, the leaders stressed the futility of sanctions "in promoting peace and stability". This was apparently the most that ASEAN could do as an association.

However, as the time approached for Myanmar to assume the chairmanship of the ASEAN Standing Committee, the association came under pressure to deny it that position. When ASEAN admitted Myanmar as a member in 1997, little thought was given to the situation that might arise from that country's assumption of the chairmanship according to the association's normal alphabetical rotation. Myanmar, together with Laos, was admitted under Malaysia's chairmanship. The Philippines had already been designated as the next chairman, in 1997–98. With the delay in Cambodia's membership not expected to be long, Myanmar's turn in the chairmanship would not come until 2006–07, or nine years later. By then, the situation in Myanmar might have changed, or so it was tacitly hoped. As it turned out, the situation did not much improve; in some ways, the signs of internal tensions — the sudden changes in the leadership, bombings in Yangon, the continued detention of opposition political figures, the slow pace toward the drafting of a constitution, the deterioration of the economy, even the transfer to a new capital — got worse.

Thus, with the approach of the July 2005 ASEAN Ministerial Meeting, when the 2006–07 chairmanship would be announced, pressure mounted on ASEAN — and on Myanmar itself — to deal with the prospect of an unchanged Myanmar taking over the chairmanship. The pressure came largely from the possibility of an American boycott of the 2007 Post-Ministerial Conferences and ASEAN Regional Forum and of a somewhat less likely European one. Pressure also came from the group formed by politicians from Cambodia, Indonesia, Malaysia, the Philippines, Singapore and Thailand to deal with the Myanmar issue. Calling itself the ASEAN Inter-Parliamentary

Caucus, the group was led by Zaid Ibrahim, who belonged to the United Malays National Organization (UMNO), the dominant party in the ruling coalition in Malaysia, but most of the other participants were legislators in the formal or *de facto* opposition. The caucus, which started meeting in Kuala Lumpur in November 2004, aimed principally at preventing Myanmar from chairing ASEAN after Malaysia.

However, the matter was not as simple as ASEAN voting against Myanmar taking the chairmanship. Such things are not decided by a vote. In any case, ASEAN could not be seen as succumbing to pressure from the West. More importantly, the foreign ministers must have been wary of setting a precedent for future pressure from outside to alter the association's internal arrangements.

The Foreign Ministers discussed the issue extensively at their April 2005 "retreat" in Cebu in the Philippines. Singapore's George Yeo gave an account of the discussions to the media, as officially transcribed by his staff:

> This issue was discussed during an extended coffee break. It was conducted as an intimate and private discussion among close family members on a sensitive matter.
>
> ASEAN ministers expressed their frank views on the issue. We re-affirmed that ASEAN cannot interfere in the domestic affairs of Myanmar. Indeed, whatever steps Myanmar decides to take, it will be the Myanmars themselves who will bear the consequences, be they good or bad. On ASEAN's part, there is great reluctance to take away Myanmar's Chairmanship as this will set a bad precedent. However, ASEAN is in danger of being dragged into Myanmar's internal politics because of the Chairmanship issue which in turn could complicate Myanmar's internal political situation. It would be best to decouple the two issues. The Myanmar Foreign Minister listened carefully and said that he would convey these views back to Yangon. We realize that this is a tough decision for Myanmar to make. We hope that Myanmar would make the decision on this soon.
>
> I am not unhopeful. During PM Lee's recent visit to Myanmar, he had met with the top Myanmar leadership. They had expressed to PM Lee that Myanmar was not a "selfish" country and would take into account ASEAN's views and consider ASEAN's interests.

The issue was resolved at the July 2005 ASEAN Ministerial Meeting, with Myanmar voluntarily passing up the chairmanship on the stated ground that its government wished to devote "full attention" to the "national reconciliation and democratization process". The ministers agreed that Myanmar would take the chair when it was "ready" to do so. The decision was announced in a statement that the ministers issued on 26 July and were to include in their joint communiqué the next day:

> We the foreign ministers of ASEAN have been informed by our colleague, Foreign Minister Nyan Win of Myanmar, that the government of Myanmar had decided to relinquish its turn to be the chair of ASEAN in 2006 because it would want to focus its attention on the ongoing national reconciliation and democratization process. Our colleague from Myanmar has explained to us that 2006 will be a critical year and that the government of Myanmar wants to give its full attention to the process.
>
> We would like to express our complete understanding of the decision by the government of Myanmar. We also express our sincere appreciation to the government of Myanmar for not allowing its national preoccupation to affect ASEAN's solidarity and cohesiveness. The government of Myanmar has shown its commitment to the well-being of ASEAN and its goal of advancing the interests of all member countries.
>
> We agreed that once Myanmar is ready to take its turn to be the ASEAN chair it can do so.[83]

It turned out, in my view, to be a masterstroke on the part of Myanmar. Yangon came across as magnanimous, for which the official ASEAN statement fairly dripped with appreciation and praise. Indeed, the 2005 joint communiqué omitted all references, contained in previous such documents, to national reconciliation and dialogue, transition to democracy, the lifting of restrictions on Aung San Suu Kyi and NLD members, or support for the UN Secretary-General's special representative for Myanmar. A few ASEAN countries must have felt relieved at being gotten off two hooks — the threat of an American boycott of the 2007 Post-Ministerial Conferences and ASEAN Regional Forum if they were to take place in Yangon, and the pressure of some of their own parliamentarians. Thus, Myanmar rose in stature in the association and lost little in return. The military leadership could continue to manage the writing of a new constitution as it had in the past few years, whether at the same measured pace or not. Not having to bother with hosting a series of high-profile international meetings would leave it free to go about its business undisturbed.

If Myanmar were to chair the ASEAN Standing Committee in the normal alphabetical rotation, the Myanmar minister would preside over an informal lunch meeting of the ASEAN foreign ministers in New York in September 2006. Yangon would host and chair an ASEAN Standing Committee and a Senior Officials Meeting in the latter half of that year. Senior General Than Shwe would then, late in the year, preside over the annual ASEAN Summit, the ASEAN leaders' usual meetings with those of China, Japan, South Korea and India, and the East Asia Summit. These would not cause much of a problem. Myanmar has hosted a number of ASEAN and ASEAN+3 (China, Japan and Korea) ministerial meetings in the past with no trouble. China and India have large stakes in Myanmar, strategic and economic, as well as in ASEAN, and would be happy to take part in the summits as scheduled. Korea has given no sign of harbouring any misgivings about sending its President or Prime Minister to an ASEAN meeting in Yangon. Under pressure from the United States and possibly from its own non-governmental organizations and parliamentary opposition, Japan might pronounce itself on the Myanmar situation, but ultimately the ASEAN+3 summit would take place without a hitch. As a region, Northeast Asia, as well as India, is much too close geographically to Myanmar and has too much at stake in Southeast Asia to allow its relationship with ASEAN to be held hostage to the Myanmar question. It is not clear whether Australia, under domestic and U.S. pressure, would balk at taking part in an East Asia Summit in Yangon.

In May 2007 or thereabouts, it would be Myanmar's turn to host and chair the ASEAN Regional Forum's Senior Officials' Meeting, which normally sets the agenda for the ARF ministerial meeting in the middle of the year. The United States, the European Union and/or Canada might boycott the senior officials' meeting or send low-level representatives. Any such gesture would not have much impact, since the media do not normally give those gatherings much attention. In any case, a boycott or low-level representation by any or all of those three participants would leave China, India, Japan, Australia, New Zealand, Pakistan and the two Koreas, as well as ASEAN, to negotiate the course of the ARF.

The crunch might come in June or July 2007, when Myanmar would host the ASEAN Ministerial Meeting, the Post-Ministerial Conferences (PMC) and the ASEAN Regional Forum. Canada, the EU, and the United States would come under domestic pressure to boycott the meetings. Canada's absence or lower-level participation would not matter too much, ASEAN-Canada relations not being very active in recent years and Ottawa not having a strategic role in East Asia. Much of the EU's relationship with ASEAN is carried out through forums other than the PMC — the ASEAN-EU Ministerial Meeting, the regular consultations between the ASEAN Economic Ministers and the European Trade Commissioner, the biennial Asia-Europe Meeting, and the cooperation between the European Commission and the ASEAN Secretariat, each of which has its own dynamic and none of which, except for ASEM, as discussed above, is affected by some European countries' problems with Myanmar. Perhaps it is because its presence in the PMC and ARF events is not considered crucial that the

EU would not want to stay away. In any case, there are indications that the EU is reviewing its overall stance on Myanmar. It is an American boycott of the PMC and ARF that would deal a blow, although most likely a temporary one, to ASEAN's external relations and its standing in the world by virtue of Washington's superpower status and strategic importance to ASEAN as a group and to many of its members.

The United States could, for domestic political reasons, boycott the event entirely. Or it could send a substitute for the Secretary of State. In the latter case, it would be nothing new, since Condoleezza Rice had also stayed away from a similar occasion in Laos in 2005. Either way, there would be much media attention, even a deluge of foreign journalists into Yangon. A media horde usually follows the Secretary of State wherever he or she goes. If the U.S. skipped the meetings in Myanmar altogether, journalists might still flock there to see how ASEAN coped with the absence of its U.S. partner, how Myanmar handled the meetings, and how the Western attendees dealt with Myanmar's chairmanship. By giving up the chairmanship, Myanmar has spared itself the unwanted attention of an army of journalists who might have been tempted to make unauthorized sorties to the countryside or ask questions about the media icon, Aung San Suu Kyi, as well as the trouble and expense of dealing with the huge entourages of major powers. At the same time, the gesture has not disturbed Yangon's political timetable one bit. Nor has Myanmar given up much in foregoing the chores of the chairmanship. Indeed, as noted above, Yangon gained ASEAN's appreciation — and, in its own way, China's. Without waiting for the ASEAN Regional Forum, Chinese Foreign Minister Li Zhaoxing flew to Yangon right after the ASEAN+3 foreign ministers' July 2005 meeting in Vientiane.

As for ASEAN, by stressing the voluntary nature of Myanmar's decision in their public statement, the foreign ministers once again demonstrated the association's creativity in avoiding either horn of a dilemma and coming out with ASEAN and every state and political group involved a winner — in this case, the ASEAN member-states, some of which have been gotten off the hook, the Western countries uneasy with the prospect of Myanmar's chairmanship of the PMC and the ARF, the ASEAN parliamentarians demanding that Yangon give up the chairmanship, and, not least, the Myanmar leadership itself.

On the other hand, if Yangon had taken the chairmanship as scheduled, the regime might loosen up a bit in order to make possible full participation in the 2007 PMC and ARF. The measures that it took might constitute the sort of progress that would give the United States a public justification for being represented — whether by the Secretary of State or a lower-level official is another question — at the ASEAN meetings even if they were hosted by Myanmar. In the run-up to mid-2007, the other ASEAN members, individually or collectively, could play a useful advisory role in Myanmar's political evolution. This would give substance to ASEAN's policy of engagement; it would not be interference, as it would involve Myanmar's hosting of an important ASEAN event.

This is now all speculation, of course. In any event, even with the issue of Myanmar's chairmanship out of the way, ASEAN again felt pressure to do something about that country. At their summit in December 2005, the ASEAN leaders had to pronounce themselves again on the internal situation in Myanmar. The chairman's statement of that summit said:

> We noted the increased interest of the international community on developments in Myanmar. In this context, we took note of the briefing by Myanmar on the latest developments in the implementation of its Roadmap to Democracy. We encouraged Myanmar to expedite the process and welcomed the invitation by Myanmar to the Foreign Minister of Malaysia in his capacity as Chairman of the ASEAN Standing Committee to visit Myanmar to learn first-hand of the progress. We also called for the release of those placed under detention.[84]

Perhaps unconsciously, the leaders hinted that ASEAN took this step in response to concerns outside the region by acknowledging that the leaders adverted to the situation in Myanmar in the "context" of "the increased interest of the international community (in) developments in Myanmar". Their reference to a proposed visit by the Malaysian Foreign Minister in his capacity as chairman of the ASEAN Standing Committee signaled ASEAN's willingness to be more active with respect to the Myanmar issue. So did the clear allusion to Daw Aung San Suu Kyi in the call for "the release of those placed under detention", although, unlike the Foreign Ministers' 2003 communiqué, the summit chairman's statement did not mention her or her group by name.

After some delay, Malaysian Foreign Minister Syed Hamid Albar did visit Myanmar late in March 2006. He was received by Prime Minister Soe Win and had talks and dinner with Foreign Minister Nyan Win, but did not get to see Senior Minister Than Shwe, as a person of Syed Hamid's rank would normally have done, or Aung San Suu Kyi. The official Myanmar media stressed that the minister had gone to Myanmar on a "goodwill visit" at "the invitation of the Government of Myanmar" rather than as chairman of the

ASEAN Standing Committee asked by ASEAN's leaders "to learn first-hand of the progress" in the implementation of the Road Map to Democracy. The Malaysian foreign ministry had announced that the visit would take place from 23 to 25 March, but, having arrived at 5:00 p.m. on 23 March, the Malaysian minister left for home in the evening of the 24th, abruptly cutting short his visit without any public explanation. The Malaysian foreign ministry did not issue any press release on the results of the visit. Neither did the ASEAN Secretariat. Syed Hamid, however, was supposed to have briefed the ASEAN Foreign Ministers on his mission at their "retreat" in April.

Just how all this political manœuvering will benefit ASEAN or the cause of Myanmar's national unity or the people of Myanmar is not clear. The proponents of sanctions charge that ASEAN's policy of engaging Myanmar has not been effective in improving the lives of Myanmar's people. However, ASEAN engagement cannot improve lives in Myanmar all by itself. ASEAN countries have little official development assistance to dispense. Their capacity to invest in the Myanmar economy is limited. ASEAN represents a relatively small market for Myanmar's main exports — agricultural and forestry products, tourism and garments, as well as natural gas. ASEAN countries do not have well-endowed non-governmental organizations to deploy.

Contrary to the prescriptions of a few Western countries, some sectors in the media, a number of NGOs and the Burmese exile community, as well as the NLD, what ASEAN could do to bring about some improvement in living standards is to seek openly to persuade the developed countries to open their markets to Myanmar's products, encourage investments in that country, promote international NGO activities there, and stop blocking UN agencies and other international institutions from helping the people of Myanmar. The Western embargo on imports from Myanmar has been particularly harmful to its people. Morten B. Pederson of the Australian National University, a senior analyst for the International Crisis Group, writes:

> It is necessary also to re-examine the broader sanctions regime, and in particular the use of trade and investment sanctions. Since the mid 1990s, factory closures and production cut-backs resulting from consumer campaigns against U.S. and European companies sourcing from Myanmar have cost tens of thousands of jobs in Yangon and other cities. The July 2003 U.S. import ban may have cost another 30,000 to 50,000 jobs, mainly for unskilled young women in the garment sector and associated industries. Many of these women were the principal breadwinners in their families, which now are struggling to put food on the table and have had to take the children out of school or borrow from local moneylenders at exorbitant rates that push them further into poverty. Proponents of these and similar

measures may feel that they are "striking a blow" for democracy, but they do so at the expense of Myanmar workers and their families who are losing their jobs and losing hope.[85]

In a footnote citing "a confidential survey by an independent consulting company in Yangon", Pedersen says, "[A]round 30,000 workers in the garment industry were laid off between July and November 2003 as a direct result of new U.S. sanctions, while an undetermined number stayed on at greatly reduced salaries. Another survey by World Vision found that sixty factories had closed at the cost of 40,000 to 60,000 jobs and with serious spin-off effects for support industries including vendors and hostels."[86]

At the same time, ASEAN could be more active and direct in helping — or offering to help — Myanmar to acquire the capacity to benefit from closer economic integration within ASEAN and from the strengthening economic links between ASEAN on the one hand and China, Japan, Korea, India and Australia and New Zealand on the other. In the same spirit, ASEAN and its member-states could also help Myanmar in tapping the external financing that its economy so badly needs. This would mean that the sources of development finance and their constituencies must abandon the posture that the way to help the people of Myanmar is to avoid contact with their government. Such a posture, sometimes referred to as "feel-good diplomacy", is ineffectual at best and counter-productive at worst.

Of course, Myanmar must consent to such help and cooperate with the rest of ASEAN. The SPDC must do its part in improving the country's domestic economic climate and legal regime, above all for the sake of its own people. It could be more forthcoming in sharing information with its ASEAN partners. It might ease restrictions on the flow of information in general, including access to the Internet. It could adopt more effective economic policies. It could release more political prisoners, as it has occasionally done. Real progress must be seen to take place in the writing of the constitution and in expanding and elevating civilian participation in the government. However, the SPDC cannot be expected to do anything that would lead to the break-up of the country into its ethnic parts, threaten the regime's hold on the country or endanger the lives of its leaders.

More active engagement by ASEAN with Myanmar will not directly or immediately lead to regime change, as some people profess to want. Neither will a policy of sanctions and boycotts, which history has shown to be ineffectual in changing political systems, with the possible exception of apartheid South Africa and its very special circumstances. Unlike sanctions and boycotts, engagement by developed countries could at least improve the lives of some of Myanmar's people in terms of jobs, healthcare and education and perhaps even allow them to have some influence on the junta, while the internal political dynamics of the country work themselves out.

If ASEAN were to intervene at all in Myanmar, it would not be on the basis of the issues that ostensibly concern the United States, Canada and some European countries — human rights, democracy, and so on. For ASEAN, and for Myanmar's other close neighbours, strategic considerations trump these issues. The United States should understand this on the basis of its own history and current policy. If ASEAN were to intervene in Myanmar, it would be on account of situations that have an impact on neighbouring states. One such situation might be the flow of illicit drugs from Myanmar to other Southeast Asian countries. Another might be the burden of refugees fleeing pressures in Myanmar. In either case, ASEAN would have to take its signals from Thailand, the country that bears the brunt of Myanmar-related drug and refugee flows. So far, Thailand has sent no such signals and seems inclined to deal with Myanmar bilaterally on both issues and to keep the rest of ASEAN out of them.

Otherwise, despite pressures from a few Dialogue Partners, ASEAN is unlikely to intervene, in any effective way, in Myanmar's internal affairs — not because of any "doctrine" of non-interference. It is because the other ASEAN members reject the possibility of interference in their own internal affairs and because they consider engagement and good relations with Myanmar as important to themselves as well as to the people of that country. Moreover, as I have pointed out, ASEAN has no formal norms governing the internal arrangements in or the domestic behaviour of member-states and, therefore, no grounds for intervening in case of violations of such norms.

HUMAN RIGHTS

The controversy over Myanmar is generally couched in terms of human rights, and human rights are a prominent element in the issue of non-interference in ASEAN. Commentators and organizations within and outside Southeast Asia have urged ASEAN intervention in cases of human rights violations in a member-country notwithstanding the ASEAN policy of non-interference.

The first time that the question of human rights was addressed squarely and extensively in ASEAN was at the 1993 ASEAN Ministerial Meeting in Singapore, which had this to say in its joint communiqué under the heading "Human Rights":

16. The Foreign Ministers welcomed the international consensus achieved during the World Conference on Human Rights in Vienna, 14–25 June 1993, and reaffirmed ASEAN's commitment to and respect for human rights and fundamental freedoms as set out in the Vienna Declaration of 25 June 1993. They stressed that human rights are interrelated and indivisible comprising civil, political, economic, social and cultural rights. These rights are of equal importance. They should be addressed in a balanced and integrated manner and protected and promoted with due regard for specific cultural, social, economic and political circumstances. They emphasized that the promotion and protection of human rights should not be politicized.

17. The Foreign Ministers agreed that ASEAN should coordinate a common approach on human rights and actively participate and contribute to the application, promotion and protection of human rights. They noted that the UN Charter had placed the question of universal observance and promotion of human rights within the context of international cooperation. They stressed that development is an inalienable right and that the use of human rights as a conditionality for economic cooperation and development assistance is detrimental to international cooperation and could undermine an international consensus on human rights. They emphasized that the protection and promotion of human rights in the international community should take cognizance of the principles of respect for national sovereignty, territorial integrity and non-interference in the internal affairs of states. They were convinced that freedom, progress and national stability are promoted by a balance between the rights of the individual and those of the community, through which many individual rights are realized, as provided for in the Universal Declaration of Human Rights.

18. The Foreign Ministers reviewed with satisfaction the considerable and continuing progress of ASEAN in freeing its peoples from fear and want, enabling them to live in dignity. They stressed that the violations of basic human rights must be redressed and should not be tolerated under any pretext. They further stressed the importance of strengthening international cooperation on all aspects of human rights and that all governments should uphold humane standards and respect human dignity. In this regard and in support of the Vienna Declaration and Programme of Action of 25 June 1993, they agreed that ASEAN should also consider the establishment of an appropriate regional mechanism on human rights.[87]

The international discourse on human rights has been driven largely by the West's almost-exclusive emphasis on civil and political and individual rights that are universal in applicability. The carefully crafted 1993 ASEAN position, on the other hand, stressed the equal importance of economic, social and cultural rights, the inalienability of the "right to development", and the need to protect the rights of the community as well as those of the individual. The statement also called for "due regard for specific cultural, social, economic and political circumstances" in the protection and promotion of human rights and, in the international realm, for "cognizance of the principles of respect for national sovereignty, territorial integrity and non-interference in the internal affairs of states". In other words, for some countries, because of their specific circumstances, more stringent rules, closer guidance by the state and the curtailment of some civil liberties may be necessary for citizens to attain a better standard of living and, therefore, greater dignity as human beings, and others should not interfere in this process.

The ASEAN insistence on considering human rights in the light of "specific cultural, social, economic and political circumstances" arises partly from differences between, say, the ASEAN countries and the European Union on the specifics of certain human rights issues. The death penalty, for example, is provided for in the criminal laws of all ASEAN countries (as well as of most, if not all, states of the United States), while it is outlawed in the EU as a violation of human rights. Caning is mandated for certain offences in some ASEAN countries, whereas it is not practised in Europe or the United States. The ASEAN position on the relative applicability of human rights is also a defence against the use of human rights by some states to influence policy in ASEAN countries. The ASEAN communiqué took a swipe at the politicization of human rights protection and promotion, that is, the use of human rights issues in the pursuit of the political agendas of the countries raising them, particularly in the form of "conditionalities" tied to economic cooperation and assistance.

Apparently taking into account the belief of some ASEAN delegations in the universality of "basic human rights", the joint communiqué affirmed the intolerability of violations of "basic human rights … under any pretext" and the obligation of governments to "uphold humane standards and human dignity". However, the foreign ministers made clear where ASEAN has made "considerable and continuing progress" — in the realm of economic rights, in freeing its peoples from "fear and want", thus "enabling them to live in dignity".

At the time the communiqué was issued, ASEAN had only six member-countries, and the impressive rise of the living standards of people in those countries seemed to justify the primacy that ASEAN gave to economic and social rights and to the rights of the community. The subsequent deterioration of the living standards of the people of the Philippines, the ASEAN country with the strongest and broadest paper guarantees of such civil and political rights as freedom of speech, the press and assembly, has appeared to validate further the ASEAN position in the eyes of its advocates. Unfortunately, the emphasis on economic, social and community rights can be used as an argument to justify a degree of repression in some countries that makes impossible both individual freedom and national prosperity.

The entry of the four newer members and the progressive opening of Indonesian society have increased the diversity in the ASEAN countries' approaches to the question of human rights, particularly in their concepts of the right balance between civil and political rights on the one hand and economic and social rights on the other. No ASEAN country — no country, for that matter — has achieved a degree of protection and guarantee of all these human rights in equal measure. Different countries have sought to arrive at different proportions of these rights in accordance with how leaderships perceive the needs of their societies or what it takes for them to stay in power or both.

In ASEAN, for example, some members of the Filipino elite may denigrate the restrictions on the rights of assembly and free speech imposed on the people of Singapore. On the other hand, many Singaporeans are appalled by the inability of the Philippine political system to deliver a better standard of life and social justice for the Filipino people. Under the stringent rule of the Vietnamese communist party, the average Vietnamese is now increasingly regarded — whether accurately remains to be seen — as having better prospects of a higher standard of living than the average Filipino or the average Indonesian, who, unlike the Vietnamese, enjoys the right to demonstrate on the streets and write freely in the newspapers.

In the face of such wide divergences in the situations and conceptions of human rights among ASEAN countries, it is hardly feasible for ASEAN to construct a system for intervening in one another's affairs on the grounds of violations of human rights. Attempts to do so on those grounds could throw the region into instability and turmoil, although a case could be made for a more active ASEAN posture on egregious, specific and proven violations of the more basic human rights. Short of this, what ASEAN can do is focus on specific human concerns that all can share, or at least none can publicly reject, like the protection of minorities, women and children, and the right to the innocent practice of religion. After all, all ASEAN countries are parties to the Convention on the Rights of the Child and all, except Brunei Darussalam, have ratified the Convention on the Elimination of All Forms of Discrimination Against Women. Six of them[88] have ratified the International Labour Organization's 1999 Worst Forms of Child Labour

Convention. Regional cooperation in capacity building for the development and enforcement of norms in these areas should help and be acceptable.

Intensifying collective attention to and cooperation on these common concerns would promote the habit of sharing, within ASEAN, problems that arise or prevail in one country but have a significant impact on others. It would foster a measure of regional accountability and transparency. This would certainly take time — and I doubt whether ASEAN will take even these modest steps anytime soon — but it would be more realistic and effective than trying to impose, as a matter of policy, one or two countries' concepts of the appropriate combination of individual and community rights and obligations on others or, worse, posturing for public consumption. Sanctions normally do not work, and countries in the region cannot afford the feel-good diplomacy that those situated farther away can indulge in.

If ASEAN countries approach issues of human rights from different directions and on the basis of different backgrounds and needs, they are firmly united in dealing with one issue related to human rights — the question of labour standards. Since as early as 1980, the ASEAN Labour Ministers Meeting, one of the oldest ASEAN ministerial forums, has grappled with this issue. Under pressure from its government, corporate and labour-union members from the developed world, the International Labour Organization has espoused the strict application of ILO conventions that mandate, in rather fine detail, certain standards in the treatment of workers. These include conventions on hours of work, night work, workers' insurance, social security, holidays with pay, and the forty-hour work week. ASEAN has professed support for these conventions; indeed, ASEAN member-states are signatories to most of them. However, ASEAN has urged that the conventions, some of which date back to the 1920s, be reviewed and, if necessary, updated and, in any case, be applied to the developing countries with a flexibility that takes into account their levels of development. ASEAN has adopted the position that the ILO should promote compliance with labour standards by assisting the developing countries in building their capacity to comply with them rather than by coercive and punitive measures.

ASEAN has taken its strongest position against what it perceives as the cynical use by the developed countries of labour conventions for trade protectionism, as an effort on their part to eviscerate the comparative advantage that developing countries, including most of ASEAN, have in international trade, their advantage in the cost and flexibility of labour. Accordingly, ASEAN has vehemently opposed the inclusion in trade negotiations, including those in the World Trade Organization and GATT, its predecessor, of labour-related issues, which ASEAN deems to be more appropriately dealt with in the ILO.

The joint communiqué of the 1993 ASEAN Ministerial Meeting also stated that ASEAN should "consider the establishment of an appropriate regional mechanism on human rights". It has been pointed out that Europe, the Americas and Africa have such regional mechanisms but not Asia or East Asia or Southeast Asia. Taking their cue from this portion of the 1993 joint communiqué, human rights bodies of Cambodia, Indonesia, Malaysia, the Philippines and Thailand met as a group with a number of ASEAN ministers and officials in 1996. They have had discussions with the ASEAN senior officials every year thereafter on the occasion of the ASEAN Ministerial Meetings. The main object of the human rights bodies, organized and named as the Working Group for an ASEAN Human Rights Mechanism, was to push for progress in the formation of the contemplated mechanism. While the annual consultations have become routine and ritualistic, workshops were organized in 2001 and 2002 on the subject. The ASEAN Institutes of Strategic and International Studies, which ASEAN had asked to study the matter, organized a colloquium in 2002 for the same purpose.

The annual meetings of the working group with the ASEAN senior officials and their promotional activities are mentioned approvingly in the joint communiqués of the ASEAN Ministerial Meetings. They help to raise consciousness and keep alive the idea of a regional human rights mechanism. However, it is not likely that an ASEAN-wide mechanism will be set up anytime soon. The ASEAN member-nations' concepts of and approaches to human rights and their practices with respect to them are much too diverse. Indeed, less than half of the member-states have official human rights agencies.

When I was ASEAN Secretary-General taking part in the annual consultations, I informally gave the working group two pieces of advice. The first was that, in addition to meeting the ASEAN officials annually *en banc*, each national human rights body should work more closely with its own government delegation so as to influence, or at least be informed of, the current country position on the proposed regional mechanism and on human rights in general. The other piece of advice was that, if they really wanted a regional mechanism, the existing human rights bodies ought to form a network among themselves and work together for common purposes. For this, they need not await the formation of official human rights bodies in all ASEAN countries or seek the permission of other regional authorities. I do not know how closely each of the human rights groups is working with its government today, but the annex to the ASEAN Security

Community Plan of Action adopted by the ASEAN leaders in Vientiane in November 2004 lists among the activities under "Promotion of human rights and obligations" an item calling for the establishment of "a network among existing human rights mechanisms". Such a network, restricted though its scope might be, could be the embryo of a regional human rights mechanism in the future.

"A COMMUNITY OF CARING SOCIETIES"

As pointed out at the beginning of this chapter, the principle of non-interference by states in one another's internal affairs is neither ASEAN's invention nor its monopoly. It is the foundation of the entire inter-state system up until today. It is enshrined in the charters of most regional organizations and in resolutions of the UN General Assembly. It can be abandoned only at the peril of international or regional stability. This is especially so in Southeast Asia, where ethnic balances within and between nations, political systems, historical experiences, and strategic outlooks are extraordinarily diverse and where mutual suspicions linger as a result of this diversity and as a legacy of history, ancient and recent. John Funston ends his paper:

> [T]he principle of non-intervention cannot be abandoned. It remains essential to ensure that smaller states are not brushed aside by big states, and is particularly important for ASEAN at a time when it has just expanded to take in former political rivals. The principle helped bring disparate states together when ASEAN started out thirty two years ago, and it can still play this role today.[89]

However, increasingly, certain events in one country tend deeply to affect neighbouring ones, if not the region as a whole, and, therefore, cannot be considered as affairs entirely internal to the country in which the events take place. This tendency arises from two trends.

The first is that, on account of the advances in transportation, communications and information technology and the growing contact between people across national boundaries that these advances make possible, people are made aware of events beyond their national boundaries more than ever before. With the rise in the activism of non-governmental organizations, certain values tend to converge and be shared, whether these pertain to human rights, systems of government, economic philosophies or religious identities. Segments of the population in one country can thus be more easily outraged today than ever before by events in another. If a group is articulate enough and influential enough and its abhorrence is felt strongly enough, it could put pressure on its government to do something about the object of its indignation. This is true to the extent that governments are susceptible to "civil-society" and media pressure.

In response to this, it may be time, as discussed in Chapters 7 and 8, for ASEAN to consider adopting certain norms rejecting and renouncing conditions that are particularly abhorrent to the people of all the member-countries. Such norms might include strictures against genocide, the use of rape as an instrument of state power or as a weapon of war, the worst forms of child labour as defined by the International Labour Organization, the deployment of child soldiers, trafficking in illicit drugs, and the curtailment of the freedom to practice one's religion in a way that is not offensive to others. Mutual assurances on the fair treatment of minorities could remove a sensitive source of tension between countries. These are norms that no government could possibly reject openly. An ASEAN charter, which the leaders decided on at the 2005 ASEAN Summit, could be the instrument for codifying these norms of domestic behaviour.

To be sure, the norms are embodied in UN conventions and resolutions, including the Universal Declaration of Human Rights, to which most, if not all, ASEAN members are party, but agreeing to apply them specifically to Southeast Asia would place ASEAN firmly in the mainstream of universal values, in much the same way as the proclamation of those values in the charters of the OAS, the AU and other regional associations. By making these unexceptionable commitments, ASEAN would not be abandoning the policy and practice of non-interference, but it would give ASEAN something to invoke in applying peer pressure for compliance with those commitments on the ground that their violation affected the association and region as a whole. Still, much work has to be done to persuade ASEAN members that the possibility of such peer pressure will not be used as a pretext for an ASEAN state to intervene in a neighbouring country on behalf of its own national agenda.

The second trend pertains to the fact that certain problems have a way of easily becoming transnational in nature and impact. Massive fires in one country can blanket its neighbours with severely injurious haze. Pollution in one country's territorial sea can spread to the waters of others. Alterations in the ecology of one country can adversely affect another's. Civil conflicts can drive refugees across national boundaries. Natural disasters sometimes know no such boundaries. Illicit drugs and human beings are trafficked between or among nations. Crimes at sea disrupt commerce between countries. International terrorism requires a broad range of responses that are international in nature and scope. Because of the greatly increased mobility of people, communicable diseases like HIV/AIDS, SARS and avian influenza are transnational in impact. In Southeast Asia, it has been tragically demonstrated that one country's economic troubles can quickly spread to others.

In every one of these areas, except the one on civil conflicts, ASEAN has had a history of cooperation — in some longer than in others. These efforts have to be stepped up and invested with sharper focus, heightened activism, greater intensity and pragmatism, like ASEAN cooperation in response to the SARS crisis. Such cooperation would in itself be called for and be extremely helpful, even indispensable, in dealing with the transnational problems involved; but its salutary effects would go beyond its immediate efficacy. Intensified and more purposeful cooperation would help in law enforcement, aid in building capacity and, incidentally, strengthen the hand of those segments of the elite that are serious about solving the problems from the standpoint of the national interest, as against narrow vested interests. Yet, more active regional cooperation on transnational problems could not be considered as interference, being carried out with common consent. It would be motivated by mutual help and informed by the spirit of caring for one another's institutions and people. This would obviously require cooperative commitment and leadership at the very top.

In any event, unless ASEAN goes in this direction, it cannot be said to be developing into a genuine community, a community that does not interfere in members' internal affairs but cares for their welfare and that of the people in them — in the words of ASEAN itself, "a community of caring societies". It might be worth quoting the passages from *ASEAN Vision 2020* that embody the ASEAN leaders' vision of such a community:

> We see vibrant and open ASEAN societies consistent with their respective national identities, where all people enjoy equitable access to opportunities for total human development regardless of gender, race, religion, language, or social and cultural background.
>
> We envision a socially cohesive and caring ASEAN where hunger, malnutrition, deprivation and poverty are no longer basic problems, where strong families as the basic units of society tend to their members particularly the children, youth, women and elderly; and where the civil society is empowered and gives special attention to the disadvantaged, disabled and marginalized and where social justice and the rule of law reign.
>
> We see well before 2020 a Southeast Asia free of illicit drugs, free of their production, processing, trafficking and use… .
>
> We envision a clean and green ASEAN with fully established mechanisms for sustainable development to ensure the protection of the

region's environment, the sustainability of its natural resources, and the high quality of life of its peoples.

We envision the evolution in Southeast Asia of agreed rules of behaviour and cooperative measures to deal with problems that can be met only on a regional scale, including environmental pollution and degradation, drug trafficking, trafficking in women and children, and other transnational crimes.

We envision our nations being governed with the consent and greater participation of the people with its focus on the welfare and dignity of the human person and the good of the community.[90]

What ASEAN needs to do is to take effective cooperative measures to bring this vision closer to reality. The vision was not regarded as entailing interference in internal affairs in 1997. It should not be so regarded today. Indeed, the obstacles to the attainment of the vision lie not in any "doctrine" of non-interference peculiar to ASEAN and dogmatically adhered to by its governments but in the mutual suspicion that continues to linger, the lack of mutual trust among its component states, and the still-weak sense of regional identity among its peoples. These are what need to be overcome if ASEAN is to become a genuine community and a truly effective one.

Notes

1. John Funston, *ASEAN and the Principle of Non-Intervention: Practice and Prospects*, Trends in Southeast Asia series, March 2000, pp. 1–2 (Singapore: Institute of Southeast Asian Studies). The quotations are from K.J. Holsti, *International Politics: A Framework for Analysis* (Englewood Cliffs: Prentice-Hall International Edition, 1988), p. 81.
2. Quoted in *New York Times*, 7 February 2005.
3. Quoted in *New York Times*, 27 February 2005.
4. William Shakespeare, *Hamlet*, Act I, Scene 4.
5. http://www.aseansec.org/4997.htm.
6. http://www.aseansec.org/14833.htm, para. 18.
7. http://www.aseansec.org/16192.htm.
8. Hal Hill, "An Overview of the Issues", in *Southeast Asia's Economic Crisis: Origins, Lessons, and the Way Forward*, edited by H.W. Arndt and Hal Hill (Singapore: Institute of Southeast Asian Studies, 1999), pp. 1–2.
9. Karl D. Jackson, "Introduction: The Roots of the Crisis", in *Asian Contagion: The Causes and Consequences of a Financial Crisis*, edited by Karl D. Jackson (Singapore: Institute of Southeast Asian Studies, 1999), pp. 1–2.
10. Rodolfo C. Severino Jr., "Weathering the Storm: ASEAN's Response to the Crisis", in Severino, *ASEAN Today and Tomorrow* (Jakarta: The ASEAN Secretariat, 2002), p. 161. Also in http://www.aseansec.org/3269.htm.

11. Michael Leifer, "Regional Solutions to Regional Problems?", in *Towards Recovery in Pacific Asia*, edited by Gerald Segal and David S.G. Goodman (London and New York: Routledge, 2000), p. 109.
12. Hadi Soesastro, "ASEAN During the Crisis", in *Southeast Asia's Economic Crisis: Origins, Lessons, and the Way Forward*, edited by H. W. Arndt and Hal Hill (Singapore: Institute of Southeast Asian Studies, 1999), p. 159.
13. Stuart Harris, *The Asian Regional Response to Its Economic Crisis and the Global Implications* (Canberra: Department of International Relations, Research School of Pacific and Asian Studies, Australian National University, 1999), p. 12.
14. T. J. Pempel, *Regional Ups, Regional Downs* in *The Politics of the Asian Economic Crisis*, edited by Pempel (Ithaca and London: Cornell University Press, 1999), p. 73.
15. Rodolfo C. Severino Jr., "The Impact of the Economic Crisis on ASEAN: A Blessing in Disguise?", in *ASEAN Today and Tomorrow*, edited by Severino (Jakarta: The ASEAN Secretariat, 2002), p. 148. Also in http://www.aseansec.org/3343.htm.
16. Manuel F. Montes, *The Currency Crisis in Southeast Asia* (Singapore: Institute of Southeast Asian Studies, 1998), p. 47.
17. Karl D. Jackson, op. cit., pp. xi–xiv.
18. http://web.mit.edu/krugman/www/suisse.html.
19. http://web.mit.edu/krugman/www/DISINTER.html.
20. Abdur R. Chowdhury, *The Asian Currency Crisis: Origins, Lessons, and Future Outlook* (Helsinki: United Nations University World Institute for Development Economics Research, 1999), pp. 24–25.
21. http://www.aseansec.org/6331.htm.
22. Hadi Soesastro, op. cit., pp. 158–59.
23. Severino, op. cit., pp. 152–54.
24. http://www.aseansec.org/6347.htm.
25. http://www.aseansec.org/6331.htm, para. 4.
26. http://www.aseansec.org/6312.htm.
27. http://www.aseansec.org/17448.htm.
28. http://www.aseansec.org/18390.htm.
29. Brunei Darussalam, Indonesia, Malaysia, the Philippines, Singapore, and Thailand.
30. http://www.aseansec.org/12365.htm.
31. http://www.aseansec.org/8756.htm.
32. Presentation at the Regional Outlook Forum 2006 of the Institute of Southeast Asian Studies, Singapore, 5 January 2006.
33. Rodolfo C. Severino Jr., "Message", in *Fire, Smoke, and Haze: The ASEAN Response Strategy*, edited by S. Tahir Qadri (Manila: Asian Development Bank, 2001), p. vi.
34. Rodolfo C. Severino Jr., "Fighting the Haze: A Regional and Global Responsibility", in *ASEAN Today and Tomorrow*, edited by Severino (Jakarta: The

ASEAN Secretariat, 2002), pp. 201–2. Also in http://www.aseansec.org/3328.htm.
35. David Glover and Timothy Jessup, eds., *Indonesia's Fires and Haze: The Cost of Catastrophe* (Singapore: Institute of Southeast Asian Studies and Canada: International Development Research Centre, 1999).
36. S. Tahir Qadri, ed. *Fire, Smoke, and Haze: The ASEAN Response Strategy* (Manila: Asian Development Bank, 2001), p. 162.
37. Statement to the World Summit on Sustainable Development: Recommendations of the World Land and Forest Fire Hazards 2002: Internationial Conference and Exhibition, 10–12 June 2002, Kuala Lumpur.
38. http://www.aseansec.org/5120.htm, para. 7.
39. http://www.aseansec.org/6083.htm, para. 3.
40. http://www.aseansec.org/6084.htm.
41. http://www.aseansec.org/8950.htm.
42. http://www.aseansec.org/8938.htm.
43. http://www.aseansec.org/agr_haze.pdf.
44. S. Tahir Qadri, ed., op. cit., p. 163.
45. Ibid., pp. 161–62.
46. Chua Mui Hoong, *A Defining Moment: How Singapore Beat SARS* (Singapore: Ministry of Information, Culture and the Arts, 2004), pp. 92–95.
47. http://www.who.int/csr/sars/country/2003_04_10/en/.
48. http://www.who.int/csr/sars/country/2003_04_29/en/.
49. http://www.aseansec.org/14745.htm.
50. http://www.aseansec.org/14749.htm.
51. http://www.aseansec.org/14751.htm.
52. Interview with Lee Chiong Giam and Robert Chua, Singapore, 20 October 2004.
53. http://www.aseansec.org/14823.htm, para. 4.
54. Interview with Dr Shigeru Omi, Manila, 8 October 2004.
55. World Health Organization, *Avian Influenza: Assessing the Pandemic Threat* (Geneva: WHO, January 2005), page 18. Much of the data in the paragraph was obtained from this publication.
56. http://www.aseansec.org/15977.htm.
57. Frente Revolucionária de Timor Leste Independente.
58. This and related documents are in the Gerald R. Ford Library and are available also in http://www2.gwu.edu/~nsarchiv/NSAEBB/NSAEBB62/
59. Statement at the Third Asia-Europe Roundtable, Hanoi, 20 October 2003.
60. Idem.
61. http://www.aseansec.org/3683.htm, para. 23.
62. Interview with Hasjim Djalal, Jakarta, 21 November 2003.
63. Interview with Ana Gomes, Hanoi, 21 October 2003.
64. http://www.aseansec.org/5206.htm, para. 8.
65. Interview with Dewi Fortuna Anwar, Paris, 3 October 2003.

66. Interview with Nugroho Wisnumurti, Singapore, 30 August 2004.
67. http://www.un.org/peace/etimor99/agreement/agreeFrame_Eng01.html.
68. http://www.un.org/peace/etimor/UntaetB.htm.
69. UN Security Council Resolution 1264, 15 September 1999.
70. http://www.aseansec.org/3683.htm, para. 23.
71. http://www.un.org/peace/etimor/Untaetchrono.html.
72. Interview with Ali Alatas, former foreign minister of Indonesia, Jakarta, 21 November 2003.
73. Opponents of SPDC claim that the NUP was "pro-government" and a stalking horse for the junta. Others believe that SPDC, then named SLORC, was deeply suspicious of it.
74. Myanmar is arguably the more appropriate name for the country, and that is how it is known in the United Nations, ASEAN and other international organizations of which it is a member. However, many of those who disapprove of SPDC, including some governments, have insisted on continuing to call it Burma as a rather petty manifestation of their displeasure with the regime.
75. Interview with Prime Minister Khin Nyunt, Yangon, 27 July 2004.
76. Domingo L. Siazon Jr., "No New Walls", keynote address at the 4th European Association for Southeast Asian Studies (EUROSEAS) Conference, Paris, 1 September 2004.
77. http://www.ilo.org/public/english/standards/relm/ilc/ilc87/com-myan.htm.
78. http://europa.eu.int/comm/external_relations/asem/asem_summits/asem5/news/ip04_1178.htm.
79. http://www.aseansec.org/3716.htm, para. 17.
80. http://www.aseansec.org/14833.htm, para. 18.
81. http://www.aseansec.org/16192.htm, para. 15.
82. http://www.aseansec.org/15259.htm, para. 25.
83. http://www.aseansec.org/17589.htm.
84. http://www.aseansec.org/18039.htm, para. 34.
85. Morton B. Pedersen, "The Challenges of Transition in Myanmar", in *Myanmar: Beyond Politics to Social Imperatives*, edited by Kyaw Yin Hlaing, Robert H. Taylor, and Tin Maung Maung Than (Singapore: Institute of Southeast Asian Studies, 2005), p. 178.
86. Ibid., p. 182.
87. http://www.aseansec.org/3666.htm.
88. Indonesia, Malaysia, the Philippines, Singapore, Thailand and Vietnam.
89. John Funston, op. cit., p. 14.
90. See Appendix D.

4

REGIONAL SECURITY
The ASEAN Role[1]

Many people have come to assume that, from the beginning, the Association of Southeast Asian Nations has been devoted principally to economic, social and cultural cooperation. In fact, ASEAN itself has often, deliberately or unwittingly, given that impression. In substance, however, security has been and largely remains at the core of ASEAN's existence; indeed, in today's comprehensive concept of security, as well as in the original conception of ASEAN, regional economic cooperation and integration is seen as part of the endeavour to bolster regional security through economic development, even as security is regarded as an essential condition for development.

The text of the ASEAN Declaration[2] that founded the association places heavy emphasis on economic, social and cultural cooperation. Five of the seven "aims and purposes" laid down by the Declaration for the new association refer to cooperation in economic, trade, social, cultural, professional, educational, technical, agricultural, industrial, transportation, communications, and administrative matters. Another objective urges "cooperation with existing international and regional organizations with similar aims and purposes". The reference to regional security was deliberately muted in order to dispel the notion that ASEAN was intended to be some kind of defence pact or military alliance, even a replacement or surrogate for the Southeast Asia Treaty Organization, or SEATO, as the Soviets and the Chinese were to charge and as the association's founding members, particularly Indonesia, wanted precisely to avoid. The lone item in the ASEAN Declaration's "aims and purposes" that refers to regional security calls only for the promotion of "regional peace and stability", not through any kind of cooperation or joint action, but "through abiding respect for justice and the rule of law in the relationship among countries of the region and adherence to the principles of the United Nations Charter".

Nevertheless, it is clear from the circumstances at the time and the statements of the founding statesmen that their central pre-occupation was regional security even if only as a condition for development — and vice versa. When after the massive upheaval in Indonesia in 1965–66 General Soeharto took over the country's leadership from President Sukarno, the New Order had two basic objectives — the development of Indonesia's ravaged economy and the end of the confrontational stance and policies in its foreign relations. The second objective, which was considered to be essential for the first, necessarily included ending the *konfrontasi* with Malaysia and otherwise solidifying good relations with the country's neighbours. Thus, ASEAN was partly intended to set the regional context and, to some extent, the justification, for the termination of Indonesia's policy of *konfrontasi*. At the same time, it was considered necessary to defuse the dispute between Malaysia and the Philippines over Sabah within a regional framework, as the Association of Southeast Asia (ASA) and MAPHILINDO had been meant to do. It was no coincidence that the idea of a new regional association was first broached, by Thai Foreign Minister Thanat Khoman, during an effort by Thailand to broker reconciliation among Indonesia, Malaysia and the Philippines in April and May 1966. Meanwhile, the United States' war in Vietnam was floundering and U.S. policy in Asia went in flux; the countries of Southeast Asia were resolved to band together against the uncertainties engendered by the events in Indochina and, more broadly, the ebb and flow of the Cold War.

Seven years after ASEAN's founding, Indonesian Foreign Minister Adam Malik was to say:

> Although from the outset ASEAN was conceived as an organization for economic, social, and cultural cooperation, and although considerations in these fields were no doubt central, it was the fact that there was a convergence in the political outlook of the five prospective member-nations ... which provided the main stimulus to join together in ASEAN.... There was early recognition that meaningful progress could only be achieved by giving first priority to the task of overall and rapid economic development. It was also realized that, to this end, policies should be consciously geared towards safeguarding that priority objective, not only in purely economic terms but simultaneously also to secure the essential conditions of peace and stability, both domestically and internationally in the surrounding region.[3]

Jusuf Wanandi, publisher of the *Jakarta Post*, chairman of the Supervisory Board of the Center for Strategic and International Studies in Jakarta and long-time observer of ASEAN, said in 1979:

> Although ASEAN was set up as an organization for regional cooperation in the economic, cultural and scientific fields, the pressures and situations that led to its creation actually consisted of defence and security considerations made in anticipation of and out of concern for the outcome of the war in Indochina.[4]

Speaking at a conference on ASEAN economic cooperation in 1987, Malaysia's then Prime Minister, Mahathir Mohamad, declared:

> You will agree with me that in its first 20 years, the main thrust of Asean has been political. This is as it should be and we have no need for regrets. We should remember that it was political problems between us as neighbours that first brought us together.[5]

Later, another of ASEAN's founding ministers, Thanat Khoman, recalled the reasons for creating ASEAN. "The most important of them," he declared, "was the fact that, with the withdrawal of the colonial powers, there would have been a power vacuum which could have attracted outsiders to step in for political gains."[6]

Stuart Harris of the Australian National University asserts:

> ASEAN's objectives were never primarily economic ... but involved security and then political influence.... As a confidence building measure to facilitate avoidance of conflict among its members ... and then encouraging peaceful settlement of disputes and developing confidence building more widely in the region, it has been a singular success.[7]

Former Indonesian Foreign Minister Ali Alatas has pointed out:

> The truth is that politics attended ASEAN at its birth. It was the convergence in political outlook among the five original members, their shared convictions on national priority objectives and on how best to secure these objectives in the evolving strategic environment of East Asia which impelled them to form ASEAN.[8]

Lee Kuan Yew, former Singapore Prime Minister and now Minister Mentor, said in his memoirs, "While Asean's declared objectives were economic, social and cultural, all knew that progress in economic cooperation would be slow. We were banding together more for political objectives, stability and security."[9]

Malaysian Prime Minister Abdullah Badawi has referred to "the understanding within ASEAN based on the original reasons for its inception in bringing peace, stability and neutrality to the region".[10]

Thus, without being named as such until Indonesia proposed it in 2003, an ASEAN Security Community has been ASEAN's central purpose from the beginning. Then, as now, ASEAN's core objectives were to provide a regional framework for the member-states to manage their disputes peacefully and prevent them from erupting into conflict, to free the region from continuing to be an arena for the strategic rivalries of the big powers while actively engaging them for constructive ends, and to attain a certain degree of solidarity in dealing with vital international issues. It is now widely accepted that ASEAN's supreme achievement lies in these areas. The ASEAN Security Community is, of course, a work in progress, but its foundations were laid in 1967. Since then, even before a name was given to the edifice, building blocks have been added over the years.

THE SABAH QUESTION

Very early in its existence, ASEAN was shaken, like the Association of Southeast Asia before it, by the Philippines' pursuit of its claim to Sabah, which had become a component of Malaysia. This time, tensions were revived, and Philippine-Malaysian relations were plunged into crisis with the exposure, in March 1968, just seven months after ASEAN's founding, of a mutiny on Corregidor island, at the mouth of Manila Bay, by a group of mostly Muslim trainees, a number of whom had been killed. Although the Philippine Government insisted that the training was for operations in Sulu, one of the trainees testified before a Philippine congressional committee that the clandestine activities on Corregidor were actually for the purpose of infiltrating commandos into Sabah. Tensions between Malaysia and the Philippines proceeded to escalate, with mutual recriminations and accusations, diplomatic protests and counter-protests, "popular" demonstrations and counter-demonstrations, flag desecrations, threatening military manœuvres, and, finally, the suspension of diplomatic relations late in the year, relations that had been "normalized" only in 1966. Philippine participants in ASEAN and other meetings were instructed to register explicit reservations over the Malaysian delegates' authority to represent the territory of Sabah.

As might be expected, ASEAN's member-states were deeply concerned over what the quarrel between two founding members would do to the young association. The course that the ASEAN members followed was to keep the bilateral dispute officially out of ASEAN in order to protect it, although the Philippines attempted to get the association involved in one way or another, as it sought to internationalize the issue by bringing it to the United Nations and other multilateral forums. At the same time, also out of their concern for the association, the other ASEAN members tried to defuse the tensions through active behind-the-scenes diplomacy. For their part, the Malaysians publicly invoked this concern — and laid the blame on the Philippines for any damage to or even the destruction of ASEAN as a result of its actions on Sabah.

The second ASEAN Ministerial Meeting was held, as scheduled, in August 1968 in Jakarta, with Malaysia and the Philippines in attendance. By previous understanding, the Sabah issue was not raised officially at that meeting. However, on the same occasion, but outside the meeting, Malaysia and the Philippines, presumably at the urging of the three others, agreed on a "cooling-off" period. Yet, this did not prevent the further escalation of tensions, with the Philippines' maritime baselines law being amended so as to include a reference to Philippine sovereignty over Sabah, Malaysia suspending diplomatic relations with and withdrawing its ambassador from Manila, and the Philippines following suit a few months later. In December of that year, the ASEAN foreign ministers made it a point to attend a meeting of the UN Economic Commission for Asia and the Far East (ECAFE, later renamed Economic and Social Commission for Asia and the Pacific, or ESCAP) in Bangkok. They convened on the sidelines of that meeting to deal with the Sabah problem, with the Malaysian, Philippine and Thai ministers later repairing to the Thai resort of Bangsaen for further talks. The result was a Malaysian-Philippine agreement on another "cooling-off" period and on their continued attendance at ASEAN meetings. This was followed by an announcement by President Ferdinand E. Marcos that the Philippines was "temporarily calling off the Sabah claim".[11]

Following further diplomatic efforts, on 16 December 1969, Tunku Abdul Rahman, Malaysia's first Prime Minister, in the middle of his address opening the third ASEAN Ministerial Meeting in the Cameron Highlands, dramatically announced the resumption of normal diplomatic relations between Malaysia and the Philippines:

> Let me therefore say frankly that the atmosphere of suspicion and mistrust which clouded our relations with the Philippines last year unfortunately resulted in the suspension of the activities of ASEAN. It is now my pleasure and privilege to announce that as a result of discussions with General Romulo,[12] it is agreed that in the spirit of goodwill and friendship diplomatic relations between Malaysia and the Philippines will be normalized forthwith (applause) and our respective Ambassadors appointed. *This shows the great value that we place on ASEAN and what we think it can do for the good of our countries and peoples* (italics mine). It is my earnest hope that we have

now permanently succeeded in overcoming whatever problems we may have so that we can now embark on a fresh start and forge ahead with our various plans and programmes in regional cooperation.

This was duly highlighted in the joint communiqué of that meeting.[13]

In his public statement at the second ASEAN Summit, in Kuala Lumpur in 1977, President Marcos declared:

> As a contribution, therefore, I say in earnest to the future of ASEAN, I wish to announce that the Government of the Republic of the Philippines is therefore taking definite steps to eliminate one of the burdens of ASEAN — the claim of the Philippine Republic to Sabah. It is our hope that this will be a permanent contribution to the unity, the strength and prosperity of all of ASEAN.

Largely because of domestic political pressures, the Philippines never quite took the "definite steps to eliminate" its Sabah claim to Malaysia's satisfaction; the administration of President Corazon Aquino made attempts to do so, which were, however, blocked in the Philippine Senate. Nevertheless, with President Fidel Ramos finally making a state visit to Malaysia in January 1993 and Prime Minister Mahathir returning it in February 1994, the relations between the two ASEAN members have been, for all practical purposes, normalized.

The ASEAN factor was, of course, not the only force that brought about this improvement in a crisis-ridden relationship between two members, but it was helped by the desire of the members to keep the Sabah dispute from destroying ASEAN, even as ASEAN meetings were used as convenient venues for informal talks. ASEAN's role in that dispute pointed the way to what would be the association's stance — stay away from internal problems of member-countries and leave bilateral disputes between member-states to bilateral handling unless such problems or disputes threaten the association itself. The problem lies in determining the existence and extent of the threat to the organization. In any case, ASEAN has, since then, proven its worth, often just by being there, as a useful instrument for the management of potential conflict and the building of mutual confidence and thus, directly or indirectly, helping to keep the peace.

ZONE OF PEACE, FREEDOM AND NEUTRALITY

Just a little over four years after ASEAN's establishment, the ASEAN foreign ministers found themselves "convinced that the time is propitious for *joint action* to give effective expression to the deeply felt desire of the peoples of

South East Asia to ensure *the conditions of peace and stability* (italics mine) indispensable to their independence and their economic and social well-being". They then expressed their determination "to exert initially necessary efforts to secure recognition of, and respect for, South East Asia as a Zone of Peace, Freedom and Neutrality, free from any form or manner of interference by outside Powers". This is the well-known ZOPFAN Declaration.[14] Early in the association's existence, it explicitly pledged ASEAN to cooperate in security matters, specifically in order to keep the region insulated, to the extent possible, from big-power conflicts, such as the then still-raging war in Indochina, and from the machinations of one big power or another, such as the U.S.' support for the 1958 rebellions in Indonesia and China's spasmodic international behaviour in the earlier stages of the Great Proletarian Cultural Revolution. In the view of Indonesia in particular, interference by one or another of the powerful countries was the principal threat to the peace and security of the region. (Indeed, the last paragraph in the preamble of the 1967 ASEAN Declaration emphatically affirmed, evidently on the insistence of Indonesia and apparently after being watered down somewhat at the Philippines' behest, that "all foreign bases are temporary and remain only with the expressed concurrence of the countries concerned and are not intended to be used directly or indirectly to subvert the national independence and freedom of States in the area or prejudice the orderly processes of their national development".) Where the ASEAN members differed was on the timeframe in which ZOPFAN was to be realized. Nevertheless, the ZOPFAN Declaration provided a general sense of ASEAN's stance and that of its member-states in regional and world affairs.

TREATY OF AMITY AND COOPERATION

At the first ASEAN Summit, in February 1976, the ASEAN leaders signed the Treaty of Amity and Cooperation in Southeast Asia (TAC), which reaffirmed their countries' commitment to ASEAN's political principles, including the peaceful settlement of disputes and non-interference in internal affairs. It also set up a High Council of ministerial-level representatives not, as some suppose, as a judicial dispute-settlement mechanism like a regional court but, more realistically, to "take cognizance of the existence of disputes or situations likely to disturb regional peace and harmony" and "recommend to the parties in dispute appropriate means of settlement such as good offices, mediation, inquiry or conciliation".[15] The treaty's dispute-settlement component has never been used; the rules of procedure of the High Council were adopted only in 2001. The only time that resort to the dispute-settlement provisions of the TAC was ever considered was in the mid-1990s, when Indonesia proposed using the TAC's High Council to help resolve its dispute with Malaysia over ownership of the Sipadan and Ligitan islands. Malaysia declined the proposal. Instead, Kuala Lumpur preferred, and President Soeharto eventually agreed, to take the dispute to the International Court of Justice in The Hague, which has since ruled in Malaysia's favour.[16] Nevertheless, the TAC has served as an authoritative affirmation of ASEAN's principles and policies on inter-state behaviour. By amending the treaty in 1987 to allow non-Southeast Asian states to accede to it, ASEAN extended those principles to encompass the conduct in Southeast Asia of states outside of it. Papua New Guinea signed the treaty in August 1989. After the ASEAN foreign ministers adopted the rules of procedure for the High Council in 2001, China and India acceded to the treaty in October 2003, Japan and Pakistan in July 2004, and South Korea and Russia in November 2004.

At ASEAN's summit meeting with Australia and New Zealand in November 2004, the first in twenty-seven years, ASEAN "encouraged" Australia and New Zealand to sign on to the treaty. The eagerness of some ASEAN members apparently stemmed from a desire to forestall Australia's willingness, previously articulated by Prime Minister John Howard, to launch pre-emptive action against a threatened terrorist attack from a neighbouring territory. Pressure on Australia and New Zealand was ratcheted up when the ASEAN foreign ministers, at their April 2005 "retreat", made signature on the treaty, as well as "substantive" relations with ASEAN, a condition for participation by Dialogue Partners in the East Asia Summit scheduled for December 2005. New Zealand signed the treaty on 28 July 2005, as did Mongolia, at the time of the ASEAN Post-Ministerial Conferences and the ASEAN Regional Forum in Vientiane. On the same occasion, Australia announced its intention to do so later in the year. Faced with exclusion from the East Asia Summit, Australia had done an embarrassing policy turn-around after initially refusing to accede to the treaty. The Australian foreign minister signed Canberra's accession four days before the EAS in Kuala Lumpur. Australia's position is discussed in further detail in Chapter 6.

As of this writing, France is the latest to signify its intention to accede to the TAC.

A NUCLEAR WEAPONS-FREE ZONE

ASEAN started actively exploring the concept of Southeast Asia as a nuclear weapons-free zone in the mid-1980s. Before that, an international treaty declaring Antarctica to be nuclear-free had been concluded in 1959, and the

Treaty of Tlatelolco prohibiting nuclear weapons in Latin America and the Caribbean had been signed in 1967. In 1986, the Rarotonga Treaty on the South Pacific Nuclear-Free Zone entered into force. Under consideration since at least the mid-1960s, the Treaty of Pelindaba on the African Nuclear Weapons-Free Zone was signed in 1996. For twenty-three years, from 1974 to 1997, the United Nations General Assembly, every single year, called for a nuclear weapons-free South Asia in resolutions sponsored mainly by Pakistan, supported by overwhelming majorities, and opposed principally by India. The resolutions went unheeded until, in 1998, both India and Pakistan conducted nuclear test explosions, definitively dooming the proposal.

As is true of most international agreements, various interests converged in bringing about the idea of a Southeast Asia nuclear weapons-free zone. One was the assurance that the member-states would give to one another that none of them would acquire nuclear weapons in the future. Another motive was to keep nuclear-weapon states from introducing such weapons into Southeast Asia, although, as a concession to members that had military or ship-servicing arrangements with the United States, the treaty would allow each signatory to decide on visits or transit by foreign vessels or aircraft. Declaring Southeast Asia a nuclear-weapons free zone would be ASEAN's contribution to the international non-proliferation regime, as well as to the region's stability, thus enhancing the association's international prestige. It was only in December 1995 that ASEAN's leaders finally signed the treaty formalizing their countries' undertakings in this regard, the treaty entering into force in March 1997. It has a protocol through which the five powers officially recognized as nuclear-weapon states are to undertake obligations under the treaty. However, four[17] of the five have found it difficult to accede to the protocol mainly because of their concerns over the treaty's area of application, specifically the inclusion of the continental shelf and the 200-mile Exclusive Economic Zone, the "negative security assurances" in the protocol, and other issues. I sometimes regret that ASEAN did not negotiate the protocol with the nuclear-weapon states before finalizing it; after all, it was the five that had to sign it. I bear some responsibility for this, as I had supervision over the Philippine negotiators at the time. In any case, some ASEAN member-states had been unwilling to accept any compromise on the provisions to which the nuclear-weapon states objected, particularly on the zone of application. Nevertheless, the treaty, as signed, is binding on all ASEAN states and, to that extent, is an important component of the global non-proliferation regime, of ZOPFAN and of ASEAN's broader structure of political and security cooperation.

OPPOSING VIETNAM

ASEAN achieved remarkable solidarity in opposing Vietnam's incursion into and prolonged stay in Cambodia even at the cost of being associated with the odious and brutal Khmers Rouges and despite the misgivings of powerful quarters in Indonesia. Vietnam's stated motive was to protect its people from depredations by the Khmers Rouges in the border areas and to liberate Cambodia from the genocidal regime. As the conflict wore on, the reason given for Vietnam's continued military presence was that a premature withdrawal would result in the return of the hated Khmers Rouges. A more strategic motivation was to be acknowledged only later — Vietnam's determination to avoid being threatened by China from the north and by a China-allied Khmer Rouge regime from the south at the same time. On the other hand, ASEAN presented itself as defending the principle of the inviolability of a nation's sovereignty and territorial integrity and the unacceptability of regime change being effected by external force, no matter how odious the ruling group. (The United States' support for this position contrasts sharply with the rationale that Washington has given for invading Iraq in 2003, forcibly replacing its leadership and occupying the country for years — another example of *realpolitik* trumping high-minded rationalizations.) The real, geo-strategic motive was to prevent Vietnam from dominating all of Indochina and extending its presence to the Thai border, thus, as feared at that stage in the Cold War, threatening Thailand with subversion and destabilizing the entire region. This concern was particularly acute in the light of the perceived Soviet support for Vietnam, which had just joined COMECON and entered into what amounted to a treaty of mutual defence with Moscow. Cham Prasidh, Cambodia's Minister for Trade, asserted that ASEAN's stand was influenced by U.S. opposition to what Washington considered as "Vietnamese expansionism" and by Thailand's perceived need for Cambodia to serve as a buffer against Vietnam.[18] On the part of China, Beijing was evidently concerned that Soviet influence would substantially extend over Southeast Asia through the expansion of Vietnamese power. Prince Norodom Sirivudh, uncle of Cambodia's King Norodom Sihamoni, former foreign minister and now co-Minister for the Interior, as well as Deputy Prime Minister, recalled what he referred to as Ho Chi Minh's vision of three countries — Vietnam, Laos and Cambodia — and one state. He compared Vietnam to the Soviet Union, which, after liberating Poland from the Germans, stayed on in that country. Even after Vietnam withdrew its troops in 1989, he said, its intelligence services continued to operate in Cambodia.[19] On the other hand, a senior Cambodian official asserted that, if Vietnam had not intervened, he and his family would have all been killed.

On 9 January 1979, shortly after the incursion of Vietnamese forces into Cambodia, Mochtar Kusumaatmadja, the foreign minister of Indonesia and Chairman of the ASEAN Standing Committee, issued a statement expressing ASEAN's alarm over Vietnam's action. Three days later the five ASEAN foreign ministers met in Bangkok to discuss the situation. At the end of the meeting, they released a joint statement deploring the "armed intervention against ... Kampuchea" and calling for "the immediate and total withdrawal of the foreign forces from Kampuchean territory". Since then, ASEAN diplomacy was almost totally consumed by Vietnam's actions in Cambodia and the problem of the massive numbers of Indochinese "asylum-seekers" stranded in the ASEAN countries. The position that it steadfastly took on these issues and the collective diplomacy that it pursued on them firmly established ASEAN as a political entity and as a major actor in East Asian affairs. Nevertheless, the ASEAN countries never closed the door to constructive relations with Hanoi and its allies in Cambodia.

Nor was ASEAN spared agonizing dilemmas, as its policy entailed supporting the murderous Khmers Rouges. These dilemmas were poignantly, if rather flamboyantly, manifested at one of the annual receptions that ASEAN hosted for the leaders of the Coalition Government of Democratic Kampuchea (CGDK) in the 1980s on the occasion of the regular session of the UN General Assembly in New York. After 1982, then Prince Norodom Sihanouk of FUNCINPEC,[20] Son Sann of the Kampuchean People's National Liberation Front, and Khieu Samphan of the Khmers Rouges would regularly represent Cambodia, or Kampuchea, as it was then called, at the UN sessions, thanks to the successful efforts of ASEAN and its allies to maintain the Cambodian seat for the CGDK and deny it to the government actually in control of the capital. At one of the receptions, the Philippines' Secretary of Foreign Affairs, Carlos P. Romulo, stood on the receiving line as the CGDK leaders filed past and refused to shake the hand of Khieu Samphan on the grounds that the hand had blood on it. Yet, ASEAN as a group had to support the Khmers Rouges' participation in the CGDK, knowing that it was only their brutal forces that had the military capacity to resist Vietnamese power in Cambodia. For its own strategic reasons, Indonesia, too, had misgivings about the Sihanouk-Khmers Rouges alliance. Nevertheless, both Indonesia and the Philippines went along with the ASEAN consensus. To do otherwise would have been to disregard Thailand's and Singapore's strategic concerns, and thus seriously undermine ASEAN solidarity. It was ASEAN consensus-making, as well as *realpolitik*, at work.

At one stage, I am told, as the CGDK was being cobbled together, S. Rajaratnam, Singapore's foreign minister, charged that, because of his participation in the Khmer Rouge atrocities, Ieng Sary, the KR foreign minister, was a hundred times worse than Hitler, at which Ieng Thirith, Ieng Sary's wife, walked out in rage. Yet, Singapore was, together with Thailand, the firmest in ASEAN in promoting Khmer Rouge resistance to Vietnam. Prince Sirivudh called this a dilemma of "morality versus realism".

The same cold-blooded calculation had prompted Sihanouk himself to join forces with the Khmers Rouges, who when they were in power in Phnom Penh had slaughtered four of Sihanouk's twelve then-surviving children and several of his grandchildren. Some ASEAN policy-makers have pointed out that Sihanouk had no choice. According to them, in the light of his importance to the legitimacy of the resistance to Vietnam's actions in Cambodia and the regime that it had installed in Phnom Penh, for Sihanouk to refuse to cooperate with the Khmers Rouges might very well have led to Cambodia's disappearance as an independent country, a prospect with fundamental repercussions for the geopolitical situation in Southeast Asia and possibly beyond. Moreover, Sihanouk was needed to receive assistance for the coalition from donor-countries that were squeamish about giving it directly to the Khmers Rouges. When he was still King, Sihanouk recalled to me that, despite Chinese "pressure", he had refused to join the Khmers Rouges in the resistance because they had killed "two million" Cambodians (not mentioning that his children and grandchildren were among them) — stressing, "not less than two million" — thus leaving only the Khmer Rouge forces to oppose the Vietnamese and the Heng Samrin regime. The King recounted that Air Chief Marshal Siddhi Savetsila, the Thai foreign minister at the time, visited him in Paris to try to persuade him to assume the leadership of the resistance in order to bolster its legitimacy. (According to Prince Sirivudh, the Chinese had, as early as 1979, tried to get Sihanouk, his half-brother, to lead the opposition to Vietnam, but Sihanouk refused.[21]) Sihanouk finally agreed to lead the CGDK in 1982. Before that, he told me, he had, between 1979 and 1981, been writing to Vietnamese Prime Minister Pham Van Dong, with whom he said he had worked "against U.S. imperialism", asking in at least three letters for "the return to Cambodia of the right of self-determination" and for Vietnam's withdrawal from Cambodia.[22]

Luu Doan Huynh, a senior Vietnamese scholar, writes that, because during their many years of fighting Vietnamese policy-makers were cut off from accurate information about what was going on in the world, they repeatedly misread the shifts in the stances of their Southeast Asian neighbours, as well as the changes in the world at large. He says:

> From 1975, in the absence of a new post-victory foreign policy, Vietnam was bound to use old recipes to deal with new issues. And its inflexible

understanding of the changing world and ASEAN, which was further compounded by the euphoria and hubris of victory, was bound to produce disastrous results.[23]

Huynh observes that, even after their victory, their perceptions having been shaped during the war, "Vietnamese leaders underestimated the nationalist credentials of ASEAN countries, refusing to consider them as independent and neutral." He attributes this to their "information gap and long-standing ideological blinkers". He recalls that Hanoi turned down ASEAN's invitations to be present as observer at the 1973 and 1974 ASEAN Ministerial Meetings, extended even before the war had actually ended, and "did not respond to other overtures from ASEAN, including the ZOPFAN (Southeast Asian Zone of Peace, Freedom and Neutrality) initiative". It rejected ASEAN's invitation to Vietnam to sign the Treaty of Amity and Cooperation in 1976 (a rejection accompanied by diatribes against ASEAN in *Nhan Dan*).[24] Just three months before Vietnam's military incursion into Cambodia, Pham Van Dong went on a round of visits to the five ASEAN countries but did not consult or even warn any of them about Vietnam's intentions, evoking a sense of betrayal among ASEAN's leaders. For one, according to Eric Teo, former diplomat, business consultant and Council Secretary of the Singapore Institute of International Affairs, then Prime Minister Lee Kuan Yew felt betrayed by Pham Van Dong.[25]

Huynh suggests that much grief might have been avoided if Vietnam had consulted the ASEAN countries "on how to deal with Pol Pot". As the Cambodian conflict went on, according to him, Vietnamese diplomats and policy-makers held numerous discussions with ASEAN countries, thus developing a clearer idea of their interests and concerns and of their openness to friendly relations with Hanoi after a settlement in Cambodia.[26] On the other hand, Hor Namhong, Cambodia's Minister for Foreign Affairs and International Cooperation, stressed that it was necessary for Vietnam to intervene in Cambodia in order to rid the country of the Khmers Rouges. Otherwise, he said, millions more would have died in addition to the two million whom the Khmers Rouges had already killed. His view was that ASEAN should have talked to Vietnam first before opposing the Vietnamese actions, opposition that he said was based on a "misperception" on the part of ASEAN.[27]

ASEAN not only led the diplomatic opposition to Vietnam's moves in Cambodia; it also actively engaged, under Indonesia's leadership, in the diplomacy that led to the political settlement of the conflict, including the "cocktail parties", the Jakarta Informal Meetings, consultations with the five permanent members of the UN Security Council, and the Paris Conference on Cambodia. Helped by a growing *rapprochement* between Beijing and Moscow (as well as between Beijing and Washington), by, reportedly, a Sino-Soviet deal specific to Cambodia, and finally by the collapse of the Soviet Union,[28] the settlement, concluded in 1991, resulted in a Vietnamese disengagement from Cambodia, Vietnam having withdrawn the bulk of its forces in 1989; the reduction of the Khmers Rouges to an eventually failed insurgency, the group having boycotted the 1993 elections; a constitution and UN-administered elections; and a reasonably viable and independent Cambodia. It was probably the best outcome for Cambodia and the rest of Southeast Asia that was possible under the circumstances. Now that Vietnam, Cambodia and Laos, as well as Myanmar, are part of ASEAN, the likelihood is much better that any disputes, anxieties and suspicions among the Southeast Asian countries, particularly those on the mainland, will be managed more amicably and more effectively, in a way that would make resort to armed force politically costly as well as unnecessary.

THE INDOCHINESE ASYLUM-SEEKERS

ASEAN demonstrated remarkable solidarity also in handling the problem of the Indochinese "asylum-seekers," although, individually, they had different situations, outlooks and methods. After the reunification of Vietnam and the communist takeover in Cambodia and Laos in 1975, people began to flee the three countries in swelling numbers, fearing what was to come. The Vietnamese stole away by stealth or bribery. At one stage, they, especially the ethnic Chinese among them, are said to have been deliberately pushed out by the Vietnamese authorities.[29] On the other hand, Lee Kuan Yew recounts in his memoirs that an "arrogant and objectionable" Pham Van Dong, then Prime Minister of Vietnam, visited Singapore on 16 October 1978 and "claimed that Beijing had instigated 140,000 to 150,000 ethnic Chinese in the north to leave Vietnam and return to China across the border". Lee continues his account of Dong's version:

> They could not understand why. The root cause was China's policy towards Vietnam after Vietnam's victory over the Americans. China had continued its expansionist policy against Vietnam. Beijing had made use of Khmer leaders to launch attacks into Vietnamese territory to commit atrocious crimes. China had caused the Hoa people to leave through a campaign launched by their embassy in Hanoi to train those who returned in order to send them back to Vietnam. The overseas Chinese had always been attached to their fatherland, feelings that were genuine and respectable. Beijing had exploited such sentiments.[30]

Extreme hardships brought about in the South by the forced adjustment to the new system, the mandated relocation from the cities to the countryside, the "re-education" campaign, and general economic distress added to the pressures on large numbers of Vietnamese to get out by any means. The traffic in human beings became a large-scale industry in Vietnam, with the government (for a time), individual bureaucrats, organizers and brokers sharing the profits, boat-makers and -operators and other ancillary enterprises flourishing, and the would-be asylum-seekers stripped of their worldly possessions. Border skirmishes between Chinese and Vietnamese forces starting in 1977 and the overall deterioration in Chinese-Vietnamese relations drove ethnic Chinese to leave Vietnam, a process aggravated by the closure of many private businesses in the South in 1978 and, at one stage, as stated above, the deliberate encouragement by the Vietnamese authorities. Meanwhile, the atrocities of the Pol Pot regime sent many Cambodians fleeing overland to Vietnam and Thailand. Before that, ethnic Vietnamese were being slaughtered in Cambodia, and ethnic Khmers being killed in Vietnam. The Hmong, many of whom had fought for the Americans in the clandestine war in Laos, had to cross the Mekong in large numbers, as the Pathet Lao triumphed in the civil conflict in that country.

The unimaginable misery visited by these events on the peoples of Indochina resulted in what the journalist Barry Wain called "one of the great human dramas of the generation" and "one of the great population shifts in history".[31] Many of them fled in boats of all sizes and materials and in various degrees of seaworthiness — from rusting freighters to barges to wooden junks and fishing boats and all manner of "floating coffins" in between — which earned them the sobriquet of "boat people". They were exposed, and often succumbed, to grave peril from typhoons, rough seas, the miserable state of the boats in which they fled, the inhuman conditions in those vessels, and the barbarities committed against them by mostly Thai pirates, including murder and rape, as well as robbery. Less well-known was the overland flight of large numbers of Indochinese, mostly to Thailand and China.

According to the records of the office of the United Nations High Commissioner for Refugees, the arrivals of "boat people" in East and Southeast Asia from Vietnam alone from 1975 to 1995 had a cumulative total of 796,310, including a massive spike of more than 200,000 in 1979, mostly in the first half, 54,000 in June alone. Of the total, 195,833 landed in Hong Kong, most of the rest in Malaysia (254,495), Indonesia (121,708), Thailand (117,321), the Philippines (51,722), and Singapore (32,457), with much smaller numbers in a few other countries and territories. There was also the enormous overland exodus into Thailand of Cambodians (237,398),

Laotians (359,930) and Vietnamese (42,918).³² These numbers are massive enough; yet they are obviously an understatement, since they do not include the arrivals that were not registered with the UNHCR. Nor do they include the untold numbers of those who perished in the process of flight. One gets an idea of the magnitude of the overland refugee population from an earlier report's estimate that, following the conclusion of the 1991 Paris accords, "[b]etween 30 March 1992 and 30 April 1993, more than 365,000 Cambodians returned home — a rate of nearly 1,000 a day". Most of them, the report notes, had spent from ten to 14 years in refugee camps in Thailand, variously dominated by the Khmers Rouges, the Khmer People's National Liberation Front of Son Sann, and the royalist FUNCINPEC, camps under the administration of the UNHCR, other UN agencies, or the Thai Government directly.³³ No doubt relying on Thai figures, the joint communiqué of the 1983 ASEAN Ministerial Meeting cited the "heavy burden (Thailand) was shouldering in providing temporary refuge to close to 170,000 Indochinese refugees" as well as noted that "close to 200,000 Thai villagers along the Thai-Laos and Thai-Kampuchean borders had been seriously affected and uprooted by the heavy influx of Indochinese refugees".³⁴ The joint communiqué of the 1984 meeting gave 150,000 as the number of refugees that had fled the fighting in Cambodia since 1978 while alluding to the "some 200,000 Thai villagers along the Thai-Kampuchean border who had already been affected and had had to be relocated".³⁵

In his landmark account of the Indochinese exodus, W. Courtland Robinson calculated from UNHCR statistics and other figures that, from 1975 to mid-1997, 1,440,000 Vietnamese, Cambodians and Laotians had arrived in UNHCR-assisted camps. In addition, about 390,000 other Cambodians fled into Thailand but were not registered as UNHCR arrivals. (Of the total, 1,315,000 were eventually resettled in third countries, and 525,000 returned home under UNHCR auspices.)³⁶

The ASEAN countries regarded these waves of humanity fleeing from their communist-ruled neighbours as primarily a security concern. In a 1983 working paper for the Department of International Relations of the Australian National University, Tim Huxley analysed this aspect of the Indochinese refugee phenomenon, summarizing the elements of ASEAN's concern as: "the impact of the influx on relations with the Indochinese countries; the danger of subversion; and the socioeconomic burden, which included a particularly strong ethnic dimension."³⁷

The arrival or attempted landing of the "boat people" in the ASEAN countries immediately following the communist takeover of all of Vietnam, and in Cambodia and Laos, elicited expressions of concern from ASEAN leaders and officials about the potential for communist subversion by agents smuggled among the refugees. Possible attempts by groups of refugees to destabilize the regimes of the three Indochinese countries could invite armed retaliation from those regimes. Indeed, after 1978, Vietnamese forces launched sporadic attacks on the Thai side of the border with Cambodia, which the Khmers Rouges and other resistance forces were using as a haven from Vietnamese pressure. There was also ASEAN's anger at the perceived complicity of the Vietnamese Government in — or, at least, its inaction on — the outflow of "boat people". This anger was later directed at Vietnam's refusal to accept the "boat people's" repatriation. All these complicated the ASEAN countries' efforts to put their relations with Vietnam on a normal footing and ease tensions with it. Of course, after 1978, the refugee issue got all tied up with the problem of Vietnam's presence in Cambodia. As Tim Huxley observed in concluding his working paper, "By 1981, any lasting end to the Indochinese refugee problem as a security concern of the ASEAN states seemed unlikely except in the case of a resolution … of the Cambodian imbroglio, and a lessening of tension between Hanoi and Beijing."[38]

Although the financial burden of sustaining the refugees in the camps was borne largely by UNHCR, international non-governmental organizations, and the governments of some developed countries, the ASEAN countries worried about the social impact of the presence of so many foreign migrants in the midst of their populations — Malaysia and Thailand, above all, but also Indonesia and the Philippines in varying degrees. International spending on the refugees fuelled inflation in the localities of the refugee camps. It highlighted disparities between the living standards of the refugees and those of the surrounding communities, exacerbating social discontents and, in some cases, exploited as a domestic political issue. After the eruption of Mount Pinatubo in 1991 sent many Filipino villagers fleeing to refugee camps that had been hastily set up, some in the Philippines complained about the Vietnamese "boat people" getting better treatment than the Filipino victims of the volcanic eruption. For Malaysia, the heavy proportion of ethnic Chinese among the Vietnamese refugees added a potential threat to the delicate ethnic balance of its society. For Indonesia, the ethnic-Chinese issue was also a sensitive political concern. In his account, W. Courtland Robinson observed, "The fact that Vietnam seemed to be engaged in the wholesale export of its ethnic Chinese population set off alarms throughout the region, especially Malaysia and Indonesia, whose ethnic balances were a matter of profound political sensitivity."[39]

The ASEAN Ministerial Meeting in 1978 referred to the refugee presence as a "heavy burden on ASEAN countries".[40] A special ASEAN foreign ministers meeting in January 1979 stressed that the refugee influx was causing "severe economic, social, political and security problems", particularly for Malaysia and Thailand, and linked the situation to "regional peace and harmony".[41] Later that year, President Soeharto said that ASEAN had hardened its position on "further assistance" to the refugees "for the sake of preserving peace and stability of the region." He called for Vietnam's cooperation "in order to maintain harmonious relations between ASEAN member states and Vietnam".[42]

These concerns varied from country to country and from period to period in terms of severity, proportions and responses. The problem was much more severe in Malaysia and Thailand, and more threatening to Singapore, than it was for Indonesia or the Philippines. Nevertheless, the ASEAN countries recognized that, despite these differences, they had to take common positions internationally and act in solidarity if they were to deal with the refugee problem with any effectiveness, indeed if ASEAN was to be taken seriously. The validity of ASEAN as an association would have been called into question if each member had gone its own way.

For the almost twenty years that it was faced with the refugee problem, ASEAN as a group maintained a basically constant position. While the ASEAN countries were willing, for "humanitarian considerations", to give temporary shelter and assistance to the refugees as "countries of first asylum", they ruled out granting them permanent settlement. Nevertheless, Malaysia was to resettle some 10,000 Khmer Muslims and, subsequently, after much internal wrangling, the Philippines agreed to admit 2,500 screened-out Vietnamese boat people, while Thailand continued to host tens of thousands of "residual" Cambodian refugees; but all these countries have insisted that they made these accommodations as voluntary decisions and not as a matter of international obligation. Indeed, ASEAN regarded the migrants as "asylum-seekers" rather than as refugees as the term is understood in international conventions, since the ASEAN countries were not willing to undertake the responsibility of nations, under the conventions, to give shelter to genuine refugees. In fact, when the Indochinese refugee problem started in 1975, none of the ASEAN countries had ratified the 1951 refugee convention or its 1967 protocol. According to the ASEAN position, the responsibility for the settlement of the people in flight lay with the international community, specifically the developed countries, and with the Indochinese countries themselves, above all Vietnam. While the asylum-seekers were in their temporary accommodations in the ASEAN countries, the United Nations, that is, UNHCR, and the developed countries had an obligation to ensure their maintenance and the upkeep of the refugee camps. Through its statements and its diplomacy and the actions of its individual members — for example, the deliberately harsh treatment of would-be asylum-seekers — ASEAN applied constant pressure, directly or in cooperation with UNHCR, on the developed countries for the speedy intake of the refugees for permanent settlement and on Vietnam for "tackling the problem at source". In 1988, ASEAN explicitly asked Vietnam "to discourage the illegal outflow of its people; to accept the return of those who do not meet international criteria for refugee status; and to expand the Orderly Departure Programme".[43] In December, Vietnam and UNHCR agreed in a memorandum of understanding to accelerate the ODP.

In May 1979, under ASEAN and international pressure, Vietnam had agreed with UNHCR on the ODP, under which Vietnam, the resettlement countries and UNHCR worked together to enable Vietnamese to emigrate without having to undergo the rigors and dangers of escape or other irregular ways of leaving. The rate of resettlement also accelerated, but never fast enough for ASEAN. By the late 1980s, faced with the prospect of holding the bag with "residuals", that is, refugees who were neither resettled in the developed countries nor accepted for repatriation by their countries of origin, ASEAN had shifted its position on repatriation, from one adhering to voluntary repatriation, as provided for in international covenants, to one resorting to involuntary repatriation, a shift apparently sanctioned in the Comprehensive Plan of Action adopted in Geneva in 1989. In the same year, Indonesia, Malaysia, the Philippines and Thailand set the middle of March as the cut-off date after which they would screen the arrivals for eligibility for resettlement in third countries as refugees; the rest would be deported as illegal immigrants — or pushed back to the sea.

Thus, from the beginning, having ruled out local settlement, the ASEAN position envisioned only two alternatives as possible solutions to the intolerable numbers of refugees and asylum-seekers in the ASEAN countries, short of the inhumane one of pushing the boat people back to drift or perish at sea or the land migrants back to Cambodia and Laos. The alternatives were, one, resettlement in third countries and, two, repatriation — whether voluntary or, eventually, involuntary. This position led to unintended contradictions. The prospect of resettlement provided an incentive for more departures by any means. The pressure on Vietnam to stop encouraging irregular departures eventually compelled Hanoi to resort to harsher measures, which in turn pushed people to leave illegally. A third alternative, of course, was an effective ODP. ASEAN welcomed and encouraged this scheme, but it was essentially a matter between Vietnam and UNHCR and the resettlement countries concerned, in which ASEAN was not directly involved but in which it had a deep interest. By making possible safe emigration from Vietnam directly to the countries of resettlement, led by the United States, the ODP ultimately reduced the flow of illegal departures for the first-asylum countries in Southeast Asia.[44] Nevertheless, even with a successful ODP, there was still the problem of the multitudes remaining in the first-asylum camps, and the prospect of large numbers of "residuals" continued to loom.

The ultimate solution was obviously the stabilization of the situation in the Indochinese countries, as eventually happened in Vietnam and Laos and, after the installation of a new regime in 1993 under the Paris accords, in Cambodia. By this time, ASEAN considered the refugee problem as all but over, calling only for the faster resettlement of the remaining refugees and asylum-seekers and being positively amicable with Vietnam. (According to UNHCR, from 1975 to 1995, 1,311,183 Indochinese refugees were resettled in several developed countries, led by the United States, Australia, Canada and France.[45] This figure excludes those admitted to the United States under Vietnam's Orderly Departure Programme, on which the two countries, not having diplomatic relations, had a separate, informal understanding. In addition, the 2000 UNHCR report notes that by the end of 1979, 250,000 people from Vietnam had taken refuge in China, the only country in Asia that granted not only first asylum but permanent settlement to Indochinese refugees from the start.[46]) The last time that ASEAN referred to the problem in a joint communiqué of the ASEAN Ministerial Meeting was in 1993. In a paragraph in the section on the "International and Regional Situation" rather than, as previously, in a separate section entitled "Indochinese Asylum-Seekers", the communiqué said:

> The Foreign Ministers called for a faster pace of resettlement of Indochinese refugees and asylum-seekers. They also called for the expeditious repatriations (sic) of those Vietnamese "screened-out" as non-refugees. In this context, they welcomed Viet Nam's commitment to the "Orderly Repatriation Programme" for Vietnamese boat people and appealed to the international community to finance the programme for Vietnamese boat people. They called on the resettlement countries to facilitate an early resolution of the problem.[47]

At that same meeting, Vietnam had been accorded observer status in ASEAN and was but two years away from full membership.

THE SOUTH CHINA SEA

ASEAN's collective dealings with China on the South China Sea issue, in addition to the bilateral interaction of each claimant-state with Beijing, are among the most significant manifestations of ASEAN solidarity and cooperation in a matter of vital security concern. I will not treat this subject in much depth or detail, as this has been done extensively in other publications and monographs. Here, I will simply sketch out ASEAN's initiatives on the South China Sea and its collective responses to Chinese moves in the area, despite the conflicting claims among four of its members. As will be discussed below, as a result of ASEAN's collective persistence, China has shifted its stance on South China Sea discussions with ASEAN from one of insistence on bilateral dealings alone to willingness to participate in talks not just with individual Southeast Asian countries, not even with the other claimant-states as a group, but with ASEAN as an association.

Apart from nationalist sentiments and the historical and legal arguments usually put forward in support of territorial and maritime claims, the positions of China (and Taiwan), Vietnam, the Philippines, Malaysia and Brunei Darussalam on the South China Sea are evidently driven by strategic considerations and expectations of the area's fisheries resources and estimated hydrocarbon deposits. China, as well as Taiwan, claims the South China Sea on historical grounds without as yet clearly defining the extent or precise legal nature of the claim. Vietnam's position is similar but is even less legally clear. Brunei Darussalam has a claim to an exclusive economic zone and a continental shelf that overlap with those of its neighbours. The Philippines invokes the fact that, in stripping Japan of the Paracels and the Spratlys, the 1951 San Francisco Peace Treaty did not specify to whom they were to revert, in effect declaring them *res nullius*, belonging to no one. On this premise, Manila asserts its sovereignty over features closest to the Philippines, which it claims are not part of the Spratlys, by virtue of discovery, proximity, strategic considerations, occupation, and a succession of legal enactments in the 1970s. The claim, however, is less than clear in terms of its consistency with international law. Malaysia enacted a continental shelf law in 1966, and has laid claim to and occupied islands and reefs on the declared continental shelf.

The Nationalist Chinese first occupied Itu Aba or Tai Ping in 1947, abandoned it in 1950 as they concentrated on the defence of Taiwan, and reoccupied it in 1956, remaining there ever since. On the strength of previous French claims, the (South) Vietnamese began occupying some of the Paracels in the 1960s and some of the Spratlys in the early 1970s, all the while laying legal claim to them. After China's eviction of the Vietnamese from the Paracels, the reunified Vietnam took over the South's outposts in the Spratlys in 1975, reinforcing them in 1987–88, actions that led to the Chinese-Vietnamese clash of 1988. Malaysia occupied Terumbu Layang-Layang (Swallow Reef) in 1983, Ardasier and Dallas Reefs in 1986, and Mariveles

Reef in 1987. At the same time, the Southeast Asian claimants, as well as China, made other moves to reinforce their claims, including the passage of legislation and the granting of hydrocarbon exploration permits to foreign firms. Fishing disputes took place with increasing frequency.

In the face of moves by Southeast Asian claimants, including physical occupation, China moved into the South China Sea to prevent Vietnam, Malaysia and the Philippines from creating *faits accomplis* in an area that the Chinese considered as historically theirs. In the last few centuries, China had felt vulnerable to pressure, if not invasion, through ill-defended border areas, primarily by Japan, the European colonial powers and, eventually, the United States. In the Korean War, the United States had threatened to cross the Yalu River into China. In the same period, the United States had interposed its forces in the Chinese civil war, that is, between Taiwan and the mainland. The United States was to intervene in Vietnam, bombing places close to the Chinese border. China had fought a war with India on their common border. Later, it engaged in a series of border skirmishes and exchanges of dire threats with the Soviet Union. To the south and east, the People's Republic was confronted with U.S. defence alliances with Japan, South Korea, the Philippines and Thailand, as well as a U.S. military presence in Indochina and an American commitment to Taiwan's defence. In the early 1970s, while the Philippines and South Vietnam were extending their presence in the South China Sea and Malaysia was staking its own claim to jurisdiction in the area, China was without much of a physical presence there.

In 1974, evidently in anticipation of Vietnam's reunification under Hanoi and apparently eager to avoid a military confrontation with a reunified communist Vietnam, Chinese forces evicted South Vietnamese troops from the Paracels. Still, this left China without a permanent foothold in the Spratlys. In 1988, the Chinese Navy battled the Vietnamese in the Spratlys, sinking three Vietnamese vessels, killing seventy-two personnel, and proceeding to occupy eight reefs, cays and islets in the area. This cost China little. Soviet support for Vietnam, under Mikhail Gorbachev, was fraying and Sino-Soviet relations were improving; in any event, the Vietnamese defeat in the Spratlys elicited no reaction from Moscow. Vietnam had no friends in non-communist Southeast Asia, having been isolated by its actions in Cambodia. However, Vietnam was in the process of withdrawing its forces from Cambodia and was talking to ASEAN and the major powers about a settlement of the Cambodian problem. Before these could happen, the 1988 clash with Vietnam took place. That same year, the Chinese began putting up structures on several reefs in the Spratlys.

Indonesia is not a claimant to any of the land features in the Spratlys, although the notorious nine bars drawn around the South China Sea on Chinese maps, whose nature remains undefined, encroach on Indonesia's exclusive economic zone and continental shelf. Because of its archipelagic nature, however, and its stake in regional stability, Indonesia takes a deep interest in maritime issues in the region. On the basis of its unique position, Indonesia, specifically Ambassador Hasjim Djalal, the foremost authority on maritime law and politics in Indonesian diplomacy, initiated a series of "Workshops for Managing Potential Conflict in the South China Sea" with financial support from Canada and in cooperation with the University of British Columbia in Vancouver. The first workshop took place in Bali in 1990, with the participation only of the then-six ASEAN members, which agreed that China — and Taiwan and Vietnam — had to be involved if the workshops were to have any meaning and effect. Up to then, China had resisted efforts to "internationalize" discussions on the South China Sea, preferring bilateral talks, and was initially reluctant to take part in the workshops. However, by the second workshop, in 1991, China, faced with exclusion from a regional forum on a subject of vital importance to it, but not willing to take a confrontational stance towards Southeast Asia, agreed to participate, together with Taiwan and Vietnam, plus Laos. To keep tensions down and foster mutual confidence, and to afford China the pretext that the South China Sea issue was not being "internationalized", the workshops were billed as non-official, and the participants went to them ostensibly in their "individual, private capacity". Although the series, technically speaking, was not an ASEAN undertaking, it had an ASEAN aura to it, as all Southeast Asian countries, except Myanmar, were eventually to take part, including landlocked Laos, together with both China and Taiwan, with Canada as observer. Quite unusual was the presence of Taiwan together with China in discussions that were ostensibly technical as well as non-official but were actually highly political in nature. In fact, the delegations to the workshops were heavily laden with foreign ministry and defence officials. The unofficial façade of the workshops allowed not only freer discussion, but also the participation of representatives from Taiwan, whose forces were the first to occupy a land feature in the South China Sea — Itu Aba or Tai Ping — as well as those of the People's Republic, which was then still resisting official multilateral discussions on the South China Sea. I remember presiding over a meeting of the workshop's Technical Working Group on Marine Scientific Research in 1993 in Manila, at which the flow of the discussions was interrupted a number of times by the Taiwan delegates raising Beijing-Taipei issues.

Specific tasks that the workshops decided on were carried out by subsidiary bodies, which eventually added up to Technical Working Groups on marine scientific research, marine environmental protection, resource assessment, safety of navigation, shipping and communication, and legal matters. The Technical Working Groups in turn spawned Groups of Experts and Study Groups. Twelve workshops were held in one or another site in Indonesia every year, except 2000, with an additional, special meeting in 2001. The subsidiary bodies met in other countries. The last workshop took place in Jakarta in October 2002, after Canada had decided to cease funding the series the year before.[48]

For several years, China resisted the official "internationalization" of the South China Sea issue. However, in a number of international forums, the ASEAN countries, working together, succeeded in getting support for the ASEAN positions, specifically the 1992 ASEAN Declaration on the South China Sea and the 1995 ASEAN statement on Recent Developments in the South China Sea, which pertained to Chinese actions on Mischief Reef, events that will be discussed below. The forums included the Non-Aligned Movement at its 1992 and 1995 summits, as well as the ASEAN Regional Forum, despite vigorous lobbying by China, which did not even belong to NAM. Without taking positions on the jurisdictional questions, the European Union and several countries, including Australia and the United States, also gave their support to the provisions of the ASEAN statements.

The Declaration on the South China Sea that the ASEAN foreign ministers issued in July 1992 gave notice of the association's solidarity behind peaceful and constructive approaches to the problem of the South China Sea. It called for the peaceful resolution of sovereignty and jurisdictional issues without resort to force, the exercise of restraint, possible cooperation in maritime safety, environmental protection, search and rescue, and action against piracy, robbery at sea and drug-trafficking, and the application of the principles of the Treaty of Amity and Cooperation as the basis for a code of conduct for the South China Sea.[49] The adoption of the declaration closely followed China's promulgation in February of its Law on the Territorial Sea and Contiguous Zone. The law explicitly asserts the Chinese claim to the Spratlys (Nansha), the Paracels (Xisha), and Diaoyutai, which Japan occupies and calls Senkaku, as well as to Taiwan and the Pescadores (Penghu) and Pratas (Dongsha) islands. The Chinese triumph over Vietnam in their naval skirmish in the Spratlys in 1988 was still fresh in ASEAN's collective memory. China's then foreign minister, Qian Qichen, was at the ASEAN Ministerial Meeting in Manila when the ASEAN Declaration on the South China Sea was issued, and the then-six members of ASEAN pressed him to associate China with the document. After consulting Beijing, Qian stated that, while China agreed with the "principles" underlying the declaration, it could not adhere to it, as the document was an ASEAN statement, in the drafting of which China was not involved.

The declaration was put to a test when in February 1995 the Philippines discovered pre-fabricated metal structures on Mischief Reef, which is well within the country's 200-mile exclusive economic zone and just a little over a hundred nautical miles west of the large island of Palawan. The structures were complete with living quarters, satellite dishes, and Chinese flags. I remember clearly the forceful stance that my colleagues, the ASEAN Senior Officials, took when we discussed the statement that the ASEAN foreign ministers were to issue on that disturbing development. Adopted on 18 March, the statement urged "all concerned to remain faithful to the letter and spirit of the Manila Declaration on the South China Sea which we issued in July 1992". It then said, "We specifically call for the early resolution of the problems caused by recent developments in Mischief Reef."[50]

It so happened that the political consultations between ASEAN and Chinese senior officials that I had proposed took place for the first time, in Hangzhou, in April 1995, just two months after the discovery of the Chinese presence on Mischief Reef. At those initial consultations, the Chinese, led by Vice Foreign Minister Tang Jiaxuan, who was later to become Foreign Minister and is now State Councilor, refused to have South China Sea questions on the agenda or to discuss them in the formal meetings. This was in line with China's position at the time that the South China Sea issue should be dealt with bilaterally rather than between China and ASEAN as a group. Upon ASEAN's insistence, however, the Chinese, with great reluctance, agreed in Hangzhou to talk about the South China Sea, but informally and after the welcoming dinner deep into the night. The tension was almost palpable as the ASEAN officials threw question after question at the Chinese, mostly about Mischief Reef, its implications and Chinese intentions. Questions were also raised about the recently promulgated Law on the Territorial Sea and Contiguous Zone and about the meaning of the nine bars around all of the South China Sea on Chinese maps. In subsequent consultations, however, the South China Sea was taken up as a matter of course, not to resolve the jurisdictional questions but to make sure that conflict did not erupt in the area and that the situation would not be complicated further by stealthy moves like those on Mischief Reef. The Chinese position on discussing the South China Sea similarly evolved in the ARF, where the subject was at first talked about "informally" after dinner but was openly discussed in succeeding meetings. Ironically, but not surprisingly, after China finally agreed to deal with ASEAN as a group on the South China Sea question and acquiesced in open ARF discussions on the matter, ASEAN stopped bringing it up as a contentious issue in international forums.

ASEAN's united posture in discussions with China on the South China Sea question was a further manifestation of political solidarity on regional-security issues and eventually made possible the conclusion, in November 2002, of the ASEAN-China Declaration on the Conduct of Parties in the South China Sea. To reduce tensions arising from the Mischief Reef row, Wang Yingfan, then Assistant Foreign Minister in charge of Asian affairs, and I negotiated, in August 1995, a bilateral code of conduct for the South China Sea, the Philippine objective being to obtain a Chinese commitment not to pull another Mischief Reef. The Philippines and Vietnam later concluded their own bilateral code of conduct. The next stage was a code of conduct for the whole region, that is, between ASEAN and China, an idea that the ASEAN foreign ministers endorsed at their annual meeting in July 1996. ASEAN and Chinese senior officials formally met several times to negotiate the code of conduct, starting in March 2000. A number of issues, including disagreements among ASEAN countries, held up the conclusion of the code and were resolved only at a closed meeting among ASEAN senior officials in Phnom Penh virtually at the last minute, just before the ASEAN-China summit in that city. The first issue was the specific inclusion of the Paracels in the coverage of the code. Vietnam had insisted on it, but China objected to any mention of the Paracels. Finally, the document merely referred to the South China Sea in general without specifying its extent. Another, related issue was the character of the agreement. Without the identification of the geographic extent of the South China Sea, Malaysia found itself in difficulty with the possible implications of a legally binding "code" for its jurisdictional claims, arguing that it could not legally bind itself to a "code" without knowing just where it applied. On the other hand, Vietnam strongly favoured a code. In the end, the document was called a Declaration on the Conduct of Parties in the South China Sea, an unwieldy title that identified it as a political declaration rather than a binding agreement. To address Vietnam's concerns, the last paragraph reads, "The Parties concerned reaffirm that the adoption of a code of conduct in the South China Sea would further promote peace and stability in the region and agree to work, on the basis of consensus, towards the eventual attainment of this objective." To me, however, there is little practical difference between the two nomenclatures in terms of the commitments involved and their enforceability. A third issue was the Philippine desire for a pledge of "no new occupation", which eventually came out as "refraining from action of inhabiting on (sic) the presently uninhabited islands, reefs, shoals, cays, and other features". The Chinese had balked at the use of the word "occupation", the Chinese term for which was supposed to denote that their current "occupations" were something illegal.[51]

The declaration, signed by the foreign ministers of ASEAN and China on the day of the ASEAN Summit and the ASEAN-China summit in Phnom Penh, commits the parties to the peaceful settlement of disputes in accordance with international law, including the 1982 UN Convention on the Law of the Sea, to freedom of lawful navigation and overflight in the area, to "self-restraint", to refraining from "inhabiting" currently uninhabited features, to certain specified confidence-building measures, and to cooperation in a number of stated areas, as well as to the eventual conclusion of a code of conduct.[52] The areas of cooperation listed in the declaration — environmental protection, scientific research, safety of navigation and communication, search and rescue, and transnational crime — seem innocuous enough, but the question of jurisdiction and legal regime could still get in the way of cooperation. For example, in the late 1980s, Razali Ismail, then Deputy Secretary-General of Malaysia's Ministry of Foreign Affairs, who was to serve as President of the United Nations General Assembly in 1996–97 and later as the UN Secretary-General's Special Representative for Myanmar, and I tried to negotiate bilateral arrangements for fisheries cooperation in an area in the South China Sea where the Philippine and Malaysian claims overlapped. However, the effort foundered on the question of which country's laws would govern fishing activities in the disputed area. Under Philippine laws, the government could not enter into any agreement allowing foreigners to fish in Philippine territorial waters or exclusive economic zone. At the same time, the Philippines wanted its fishing fleets to be able to operate in the disputed area without risk of apprehension by the Malaysians. Perhaps, this is why, in the Declaration on the Conduct of Parties in the South China Sea, such potentially controversial areas as fishing and mineral exploration were omitted from the list of sectors for cooperation. In implementing cooperative activities as called for in the declaration, care must be taken that such activities, meant to build confidence, do not, instead, provoke further contention. On the other hand, contention might put pressure on the claimants to resolve some of the jurisdictional issues, although this is highly unlikely at this time. Presumably, the ASEAN-China Working Group set up to "incrementally implement" the declaration is addressing the deceptively simple, but actually complex matter of cooperation in the contested areas. Presumably also, the group is working out ways of ensuring that the assurances and constraints embodied in the declaration are complied with.

A certain fragile stability has descended on the South China Sea since the issuance of the declaration. Its assurance of the parties' "respect for and commitment to the freedom of navigation in and overflight above the South China Sea" has enabled the United States, Japan and the Europeans to maintain their posture of neutrality. (However, China's Law on the Territorial Sea and Contiguous Zone is not clear on the physical extent of the sea and the zone, although it is quite clear in asserting China's sovereignty over the territorial sea and the air space above it, with specific reference to foreign vessels and aircraft.) The parties' stated commitment to the peaceful settlement of their disputes and to the principles of the UN Charter and the Treaty of Amity and Cooperation in Southeast Asia has helped to calm the situation. More importantly, China has become so enmeshed with the world and the global trading and financial system and in its expanding network of relationships with ASEAN and its members that it can less afford to endanger its growing stake in regional and international stability by rash acts in the South China Sea. Although four ASEAN members have conflicting claims to all or parts of the South China Sea, ASEAN has developed a united posture in dealing with China on the matter, strengthening the positions not only of the ASEAN claimants but, apparently, also of those elements in the Chinese Government that favour greater flexibility in relating to Southeast Asia.

While the South China Sea as an issue between ASEAN and China had been less active since the adoption of the 2002 declaration, things were stirred up again when, in early September 2004, Philippine President Gloria Macapagal-Arroyo went on a hurried visit to China. On that visit, the usual raft of agreements was ceremonially signed. Among them was an "Agreement for Seismic Undertaking for Certain Areas in the South China Sea By and Between China National Offshore Oil Corporation and Philippine National Oil Company". The text of the agreement was not made public, but a summary issued by the Philippine Government said:

> PNOC and CNOOC will undertake a joint seismic study of an agreed area in the South China Sea for three years to gather and process data on stratigraphy, tectonics and structural fabric of the subsurface of the area. The agreement has no reference to petroleum exploration and production. The agreement provides for the participation of the national oil company of a third country.[53]

While the Philippine announcement stressed that the agreement was *not* about "petroleum exploration and production", the Philippine move, on which Manila did not consult its ASEAN partners beforehand, upset Vietnam and puzzled other ASEAN countries. If the seismic study was not for the purpose of exploration and production, they asked, what was it for? And why the participation of a third-country *oil* company? Perhaps seeking to make the best out of an unsatisfactory situation, the Vietnamese in March 2005 announced their participation in the China-Philippines arrangement, which was modified and renamed the Tripartite Agreement for Joint Marine Seismic Undertaking in the Agreement Area in the South China Sea. Where that area is has not been publicly spelled out. As for Mischief Reef, the Chinese structures are still there and are reportedly being constantly expanded and strengthened, with Chinese warships visiting regularly. On a broader scale, ASEAN countries continue to worry about the stepped-up activities of Chinese fishing boats in areas claimed by one or another of them.

Thus, despite the quiescent atmosphere, the situation remains fragile. It will stay that way while the jurisdictional issues remain unsettled, and there seems to be no way that they will be settled anytime soon. They are much too complex and their implications are much too great for the vital national interests of the countries involved. In the longer term, as shortages — actual or anticipated — of energy and fish become more and more acute, any moves by any of the claimants, or even by a non-claimant, could become more and more sensitive and could agitate the area once again. Meanwhile, even as China yielded to the ASEAN states and consented to deal with them as a group, Beijing managed, by that very concession, to get the United States, Japan and everyone else out of the multilateral discussions on the South China Sea and the whole issue out of the ASEAN Regional Forum.

THE ASEAN REGIONAL FORUM

In May 1993, senior officials of the foreign ministries of ASEAN and its Dialogue Partners met in Singapore to engage for the first time in discussions on political and security matters. This followed the ASEAN leaders' 1992 summit meeting, which issued a declaration calling on ASEAN, among other things, to "intensify its external dialogues in political and security matters by using the ASEAN Post Ministerial Conferences" between ASEAN and its Dialogue Partners.[54] Not only had the conflict in Cambodia been settled; the Cold War had ended. A new security configuration was emerging in Southeast Asia, as it was in the world at large. Countries in the region and those with interests in it should have a forum for political consultations on the new security situation in Southeast Asia and in the context of that new situation. At that meeting in Singapore, called PMC SOM (for Senior Officials Meeting of the Post-Ministerial Conferences), it became immediately apparent that regional peace and security could not be productively discussed without the participation of China and Russia — and Vietnam. Representing the Philippines, I was one of those who pointed this out in private talks as well as in open meeting. It was thus quickly decided that ASEAN's "consultative partners" (China and Russia) and observers (Papua New Guinea, Laos and Vietnam) should be part of the new forum, to be called the ASEAN Regional Forum. The ARF met at the level of foreign ministers for the first time in Bangkok in 1994 and has been convened annually ever since, in conjunction with the annual ASEAN Ministerial Meeting. It has proved its usefulness as a forum for consultation and confidence building, the only Asia-Pacific-wide, and therefore indispensable, venue for regional-security discussions, another building block for ASEAN's security edifice. For obvious reasons, it was never meant to be a defence alliance or any kind of military organization, so that its management by foreign ministers is entirely appropriate, and the absence of top defence and military officials from it is not the critical shortcoming that the ARF is sometimes said to suffer from. In any case, senior defence, military and national-security officers serve on most ARF delegations and meet on their own, usually over lunch.

Media commentators often dismiss the ARF as a "talk shop". However, I see nothing wrong with "talk shops"; indeed, they are extremely useful in dealing with sensitive regional-security issues. How else can one promote mutual understanding, create channels of communication, build confidence and, as the Chinese say, "expand common ground", unless governments, as well as people, talk — not only in pairs but also in a broader regional setting? In fact, the very first of the ARF's purposes is to build mutual understanding and mutual trust. The ARF's way of doing this includes several things. The forum's centrepiece is the annual ministerial meeting that takes place on the occasion of the ASEAN Ministerial Meeting and Post-Ministerial Conferences; most ARF participants are either ASEAN members or Dialogue Partners. ARF senior officials also meet annually, usually in May, to conduct their own discussions and prepare for the meeting of their ministers. Between ministerial meetings, the ARF conducts what are called "intersessional" activities in specific areas, which, aside from developing the capacity to work together in practical endeavours, serve to promote the cause of mutual confidence and the related aim of networking among professionals in their fields. Activities so far undertaken have had to do with peacekeeping operations, search and rescue, disaster relief, counter-terrorism, transnational crime, and maritime matters, including maritime security and the management of shipboard-generated waste. Among defence-related confidence-building measures have been meetings of the heads of defence colleges, the exchange of policy documents, and seminars and workshops on laws on armed conflict, the conversion of defence industries to civilian purposes, logistics outsourcing, and civilian-military relations.

In ASEAN and ARF parlance, Track II refers to forums of academic institutions and think-tanks dealing with subjects similar to those taken up in the official forums (Track I) but presumably in a manner that is less constrained by official commitments and strictures. The degree of official control over the conduct and positions of the participating think-tanks, of course, varies from country to country — from none to total. For the ARF, the main Track II forum is the Council for Security Cooperation in the Asia Pacific (CSCAP). ASEAN-ISIS, a network of institutes of strategic and international studies in the ASEAN countries, has also contributed to ARF thinking. CSCAP actually antedates the ARF, having been established in 1992 by think-tanks from ten countries. It once included a research centre from Taiwan, but that centre had to leave the Council when China joined CSCAP in 1996. Taiwan, however, continues to participate in subsidiary bodies of the Council. All ARF members, except Laos, Myanmar, Pakistan and Timor-Leste, are represented in CSCAP, which often replicates the ARF in its processes and subjects of concern and gives it intellectual support. The ARF, for example, has openly acknowledged that the principles of preventive diplomacy that it adopted in 2001 came directly from CSCAP. The Council has also given recommendations on how to improve interaction between Track I and Track II. However, ARF-recognized Track II activities include those that are organized by think-tanks, one ASEAN and one non-ASEAN, that are not necessarily CSCAP components.

In terms of process, the ARF has faced three issues — ASEAN's role as "driver" of the ARF, the stages in the ARF's progression, and ARF membership.

Both the successes and shortcomings of the ARF have been attributed to ASEAN's role as the "driver" of the process, something that ASEAN insists upon and non-ASEAN participants accept. ASEAN's place at the core of the ARF was established from the beginning. The forum had its origin in the mandate of the 1992 ASEAN Summit in Singapore that "ASEAN should intensify its external dialogues in political and security matters by using the ASEAN Post-Ministerial Conferences (PMC)" and that, in this context, having "made major strides in building cooperative ties with states of the Asia-Pacific region", ASEAN "shall continue to accord them a high priority".[55] It was in pursuit of that mandate that ASEAN convened the May 1993 PMC SOM referred to above. At the second ARF, in Bandar Seri Begawan in 1995, the chairman's statement cleverly reflected the delicate balance between the prerogatives of the non-ASEAN participants and ASEAN's leading role. It said, "A successful ARF requires the active, full and equal participation and cooperation of all participants. However, ASEAN undertakes the obligation to be the primary driving force." To affirm the ASEAN role, the statement declared that the ARF should take place annually "in the context of the ASEAN Ministerial Meeting and Post Ministerial Conferences" and that its participants would be "ASEAN Member States, Observers, Consultative and Dialogue Partners of ASEAN", with the door left open for membership applications from other states. The ARF's "method and approach" was clearly patterned after ASEAN's, with the support of most of the other Asian members and the realistic recognition by the rest that, in view of the great diversity in the strategic outlooks of ARF participants, the "ASEAN Way" was the only feasible one for the ARF. Thus, the Bandar Seri Begawan chairman's statement said, "The ARF process shall move at a pace comfortable to all participants.... The approach shall be evolutionary.... Decisions of the ARF shall be made through consensus after careful and extensive consultations among all participants."[56]

The concept paper that ASEAN officials drafted and the ARF adopted in 1995 commends "ASEAN's experience, which provides a valuable and proven guide for the ARF". It continues:

> ASEAN has succeeded in reducing tensions among its member states, promoting regional cooperation and creating a regional climate conducive to peace and prosperity.... ASEAN's well established practices of consultation and consensus (musyawarah and mufakat) have ... effectively developed into a preventive diplomacy channel. In the Asian context, there is some merit to the ASEAN approach. It emphasises the need to develop trust and confidence among neighbouring states.[57]

In the early years of the ARF, some Western participating states chafed at the ASEAN monopoly of the forum's chairmanship, informally suggesting co-chairmanship or alternating chairmanships between ASEAN and non-ASEAN participants. However, this seemed to be a minority opinion, and a tentative one even among its proponents. For most ARF participants, and as ASEAN has insisted, there seems to be no better alternative to ASEAN leadership of the ARF.

The second Declaration of ASEAN Concord, issued in Bali in October 2003, or Bali Concord II (BCII), affirms the ARF's role as "the main forum for regional security dialogue, with ASEAN as the primary driving force". As noted earlier, ASEAN was the ARF's driving force in laying the foundations for the forum's methods, approach, organization and direction. It was the driving force in putting together the concept paper on which the ARF's development has been based. From the beginning, it has managed the preparations for and the conduct of the forum. It has chaired its ministerial and senior officials meetings. The chairmanship, always an ASEAN country, has ably handled the delicate task of crafting the chairman's statement issued after every ministerial meeting. Officially, the chairman's statement is his sole responsibility, but in practice it has to take into account the interests of all. It is not formally negotiated but is subject to consultation, and ASEAN has done commendably in reconciling sometimes widely divergent positions. ASEAN has closed ranks in blunting the attacks of some non-ASEAN ARF participants on the behaviour of the regime in Myanmar and on Indonesia's handling of East Timor. However, important as they are, these are largely administrative, procedural or defensive undertakings. Most of the substantive initiatives for advancing the ARF's purposes have come from the non-ASEAN participants. It is a matter of some embarrassment, for example, that only three ASEAN countries[58] contributed to the ARF's Annual Security Outlook in 2005, three[59] in 2004, three[60] in 2003, four[61] in 2002, five[62] in 2001, and two[63] in 2000, the first year that the compilation was published.

The rather passive intellectual role of ASEAN participants in the ARF and their failure to advance solid ideas for confidence building have been attributed to their lack of resources, human or financial or both. Some key ASEAN personalities have asserted that there is no need for activism in the ARF, as it is merely a forum for discussion. However, if ASEAN is to serve as the ARF's "driving force", as it has always insisted upon and as its leaders again called for in Bali in October 2003, if ASEAN is to do so in actuality rather than merely in form, it has to be more proactive than it has been. Indeed, Bali Concord II hinted at ASEAN's shortcomings in this regard when it stated, "ASEAN shall *enhance* (italics mine) its role in further advancing the stages of cooperation within the ARF", and that the ASEAN Security Community "shall enable ASEAN to demonstrate a *greater* (italics mine) capacity and responsibility of (sic) being the primary driving force of the ARF".[64]

Perhaps, ASEAN could begin by seeking to redirect the focus of the ARF's aspirations in preventive diplomacy. The 1995 ARF concept paper envisioned three stages in the ARF's progression — the "promotion of confidence-building measures", the "development of preventive-diplomacy mechanisms", and the "development of conflict-resolution mechanisms". The formulation of the conflict-resolution stage was soon watered down to "the elaboration of approaches to conflict" as a result of some participants' concern that the ARF's involvement in conflict resolution could "internationalize" disputes that they would like to confine as narrowly as possible. As early as 1997, other participants began urging the ARF to start thinking about going beyond confidence building and moving to the preventive-diplomacy stage. In 2001, the ARF ministers adopted a paper on the "Concept and Principles of Preventive Diplomacy", which had been largely drafted by Singapore. Acknowledging that the very definition of preventive diplomacy was "controversial", the paper stressed that preventive diplomacy "is consensual diplomatic and political action taken by sovereign states with the consent of all directly involved parties". The emphasis on sovereignty and consent served to give the assurance that acts of preventive diplomacy would not forcibly intrude into the internal affairs of individual states. The paper proceeded to define the objectives of preventive diplomacy in the ARF context: "to prevent disputes/conflicts between states from emerging, to prevent such disputes/conflicts from escalating into armed confrontation, and to prevent such disputes and conflicts from spreading. Some measures could be taken even before a crisis has actually arisen".[65]

The next year, reflecting the continuing disagreements on the pace of the ARF's development, the supposed advance from confidence building to preventive diplomacy was reduced to identifying four measures straddling the two stages — the "enhanced role of the ARF chair", the register of experts and eminent persons, the Annual Security Outlook, and voluntary background briefings on regional security issues.[66]

This extreme caution on moving from the first ARF stage to the second and the contortions that the ARF is undergoing in order to give the appearance of progress seem to me to be the result of two realities. One is the reluctance of ARF states, including those in ASEAN, to open bilateral disputes to any kind of multilateral intervention. The other is the fact that the major subjects of ARF discussion so far — the Korean peninsula, the Taiwan Straits, and the South China Sea, aside from nuclear proliferation — are flashpoints for conventional conflict. However, these issues are non-starters for ARF preventive diplomacy, since the main protagonists in each of them, realistically enough, choose to deal actively with the problem in smaller forums than the ARF — the Korean peninsula in the Six-Party Talks, the South China Sea between ASEAN and China, and the Taiwan Straits between Beijing and Taipei, with the U.S. presence looming large. Nuclear proliferation questions are, on the other hand, addressed in the broader settings of the United Nations and its subsidiary bodies. Instead, ASEAN might identify those problems that all ARF participants could consider to be *common* threats. International terrorism, including maritime terrorism, piracy at sea, drug trafficking, and transnational crime could be some of those problems. In fact, a Track II seminar on preventive diplomacy in 1997 recommended for the ARF's consideration "[m]ultilaterial co-operation as a form of Prevention Diplomacy on trans-national issues such as drug trafficking; shipment, storage and disposal of nuclear waste; major movements of population etc, where directly linked to security".[67] ASEAN could then propose modalities for ARF diplomacy to act on them, possibly beginning with an Intersessional Group on Preventive Diplomacy focused on the common threats. To be sure, the original division of agenda between the ARF and the ASEAN Post-Ministerial Conferences was that the ARF would cover what were referred to as "traditional" security issues in the forum's "geographical footprint", while the PMC would deal with transnational issues and with political questions outside the "footprint". However, "non-traditional" security issues have increasingly been regarded as proper subjects for the ARF, with the acceptance of such transnational problems as drug trafficking, people smuggling, piracy, terrorism and transnational crime as belonging to the concept of "comprehensive security". The ARF participants, of course, should continue to conduct their very useful exchange of views on the whole range of live security issues and carry out the equally useful confidence-building activities.

The third issue related to the ARF process is the question of participation. As we have seen, the ARF started out as a forum among ASEAN countries, then six, and its Dialogue Partners, "consultative partners" (China and Russia), and observers (Papua New Guinea, Laos and Vietnam). Thus, Cambodia and Myanmar joined the ARF in 1995 and 1996, respectively, when they became observers in ASEAN as a step to full membership in the association. India was admitted in 1996, when it became an ASEAN Dialogue Partner. However, the ARF was open to the possible entry of others. The second ARF, in 1995, decided to adopt criteria for the admission of states that were not ASEAN members, observers or Dialogue Partners, and asked the senior officials to develop such criteria. At their third meeting, in 1996 in Jakarta, the ARF ministers adopted the criteria worked out by the senior officials.[68] ARF participants must be sovereign states, which, at China's behest, was evidently meant to exclude Taiwan. (One wonders, though, if the European Union would have qualified if it had not been a founding member.) They must "abide by and respect fully the decisions and statements already made by the ARF". The criteria stress that ASEAN members "automatically" take part in the ARF. This condition was apparently aimed at ensuring, in the light of some Western participants' hostility to Myanmar, that the ARF would be open to Yangon's participation. All seven ASEAN members, plus Laos and Cambodia, were already part of the ARF by the time the criteria were drawn up by the senior officials in May 1996. In July, Myanmar became an ASEAN observer and, according to the criteria, was admitted into the ARF. Myanmar's admission created an opportunity to raise questions in a multilateral setting about the situation in that country — and to hear Yangon's side. Subsequently, the critical criterion has been that the applicant must demonstrate that "it has an impact on the peace and security of the 'geographical footprint' " of the ARF, defining that "footprint" as Northeast Asia, Southeast Asia and Oceania. All decisions on membership must be decided by consensus. Mongolia came in without a problem in 1999. North Korea did so in 2000.

Pakistan had a harder time. Pakistan had always sought closer relations with ASEAN, particularly since ASEAN-India relations gathered pace. When I became Undersecretary of Foreign Affairs of the Philippines in September 1992, the first top envoy in Manila to talk to me was the ambassador of Pakistan, who proposed the establishment of some kind of dialogue relationship between ASEAN and his country. This was soon after India became what is called a Sectoral Dialogue Partner of ASEAN; that is, the relationship was not a comprehensive one but involved only certain sectors, like trade and investments and science and technology. Pakistan vigorously pursued its goal until in 1993 the ASEAN foreign ministers agreed to confer on it the status of Sectoral Dialogue Partner. In 1997, ASEAN and Pakistani officials worked out the terms of the Sectoral Dialogue, with the ASEAN-Pakistan Joint Sectoral Cooperation Committee holding uneventful meetings in Bali in 1999 and in Islamabad in 2001. However, by this time, Pakistan was obviously interested mainly in the ARF, to which India had been admitted in 1996, fearing that India-Pakistan and other South Asian issues would be taken up in the forum behind its back. In fact, India never raised any of these issues in the ARF. This is to India's credit, but it is also consistent with Delhi's position of keeping the Kashmir issue from being "internationalized".

For a while, ASEAN was divided on Pakistan's participation in the forum. Some ASEAN members argued that Pakistan's foreign-policy orientation was towards West Asia rather than East Asia and that including it in the ARF might lead to the forum being unduly sidetracked by India-Pakistan contention. Other ASEAN members thought that Pakistan ought to take part in the ARF because of its growing interest in East Asia and, perhaps, precisely because India was in it. Pakistan's acquisition of a nuclear-weapons capability was a factor in the consideration of its ARF participation — both for and against. For years, and almost to the last, India and a few other ARF participants opposed Pakistan's membership. However, with the improvement in India-Pakistan relations and, presumably, its critical role in the anti-terrorism struggle, Pakistan was finally admitted into the ARF in Jakarta in 2004, with Indian Foreign Minister K.

Natwar Singh the first to welcome it, and promptly acceded to the Treaty of Amity and Cooperation in Southeast Asia.

As of this writing, Timor-Leste is the latest to be let into the ARF. In Chapter 2, I recounted the disappointment of José Ramos-Horta, Timor-Leste's foreign minister, after the 2002 ARF meeting in Phnom Penh decided to admit Pakistan but not Timor-Leste. Having resigned itself to a long delay in its ASEAN membership, Timor-Leste had focused its attention on ARF participation. After all, Mongolia, North Korea and now Pakistan had been admitted into the ARF, although none of them was an ASEAN member, Dialogue Partner or observer, whereas, unlike them, Timor-Leste was in Southeast Asia. Ramos-Horta also pointed out that Timor-Leste was the only member of the Southwest Pacific Forum — the others being Australia, Indonesia, Papua New Guinea, the Philippines and New Zealand — that was not an ARF participant.[69] At the time, however, no ASEAN member was advocating Timor-Leste's ARF participation zealously enough. Indeed, some members had misgivings about it, fearing that admitting Timor-Leste into the ARF might be construed as preparatory to ASEAN membership, something that they were not ready for. In July 2005, Timor-Leste was finally admitted into the forum, and Ramos-Horta participated fully in it.

For a time, France and the United Kingdom sought to participate in the ARF as individual countries, separately from the European Union, by virtue of their permanent membership in the UN Security Council, their status as recognized nuclear powers, their claimed strategic interests in the Asia-Pacific, and their colonial possessions in the South Pacific and, at that time, Hong Kong, respectively. Britain also invoked its membership in the Five-Power Defence Arrangement with Australia, Malaysia, New Zealand and Singapore. However, the perceived conflict between their individual memberships and that of the European Union, of which they were a part, could not be resolved.

As a forum for East Asian countries and other powers with security interests in the region, the ARF has, since 1994, proven its usefulness for confidence building and networking among foreign ministers and other shapers of regional-security policy. Secondarily, it has served as a venue for informal consultations among two or more participants on security issues of particular interest to them. It is the only Asia-Pacific-wide forum of this kind and is, therefore, virtually indispensable. Because of the dynamics of the security relationships among the major powers, there seems to be no substitute for ASEAN leadership of the ARF and the application of the "ASEAN Way" to its processes. To be even more useful, the ARF ought to concentrate more and more on the "non-traditional" security problems that all participants consider as common threats, even as it continues to serve as a forum for confidence building, which in itself is a contribution to the prevention of inter-state conflict in general.

INTERNATIONAL TERRORISM

Even before the current global alarm over international terrorism, ASEAN had made clear its concern over this phenomenon. For example, at their first meeting, in December 1997, the ministers in charge of law enforcement, one of the newer ASEAN bodies, identified terrorism as one of the transnational crimes against which they would cooperate.

Since the 11 September 2001 attacks on the United States, ASEAN has repeatedly expressed its condemnation of and opposition to terrorism, including the international variety, by itself and jointly with others. When the airborne terrorists hit the two towers of the World Trade Centre in New York and the Pentagon in Virginia, the ASEAN Economic Ministers were in Hanoi for their annual regular meeting. As we were having dinner, the Thai Minister for Commerce, Adisai Bodharamik, who was two seats away from me, received a call on his mobile telephone informing him of the first attack. The offices of the Thai Consulate General in New York were in one of the towers. The next day, 12 September 2001, but still 11 September in the Western Hemisphere, the ASEAN Economic Ministers, together with Pascal Lamy, then the Trade Commissioner of the European Commission, who was having his normal consultations with them, issued a joint statement condemning the terror assaults on the United States.[70] Prince Mohamed Bolkiah, foreign minister of Brunei Darussalam and, at the time, chairman of the ASEAN Standing Committee, followed this with a letter to U.S. Secretary of State Colin Powell conveying ASEAN's sympathies, condemning "all acts of terror", and expressing ASEAN's desire for "closer cooperation with the United States and all other countries to combat them."[71] He later issued a statement on behalf of the ARF condemning the attacks,[72] as Hor Namhong, foreign minister of Cambodia, was to do in response to the October 2002 terrorist bombing that took more than 200 lives in Bali.[73] ASEAN's leaders adopted their own declaration at their summit in November 2001 calling for the ratification by ASEAN members of UN anti-terrorism conventions, for closer cooperation among their law-enforcement agencies, and for exchanges of information and intelligence on terrorism.[74]

At the 2002 summit in Phnom Penh, the ASEAN leaders again denounced the use of terror, particularly in relation to bombings in Bali and in the Philippines. They resolved "to intensify our efforts, collectively and individually, to prevent, counter and suppress the activities of terrorist groups in the region. The ASEAN countries shall continue with practical cooperative measures among ourselves and with the international community." They directed their law-enforcement authorities to step up their cooperation. At the same time, they deplored "the tendency in some quarters to identify terrorism with particular religions or ethnic groups", and they called on countries — unnamed but the reference is clear — "to avoid indiscriminately advising their citizens to refrain from visiting or otherwise dealing with our countries, in the absence of established evidence to substantiate rumours of possible terrorist attacks, as such measures could help achieve the objectives of the terrorists".[75] The ASEAN foreign ministers, through the joint communiqués of their annual meetings in 2002, 2003, 2004 and 2005, added their political weight to these positions and sentiments. The Vientiane Action Programme and the Plan of Action for the ASEAN Security Community adopted by the 2004 ASEAN Summit called for the formation of a working group to draft an ASEAN convention on counter-terrorism.

In May 2002, in Kuala Lumpur, the ASEAN ministers responsible for combating transnational crime convened a special meeting on terrorism. They endorsed a work programme to carry out the plan of action that they had adopted in 1999. The programme involved information exchange, legal measures, law enforcement, training, institution building, and cooperation with other countries and forums.[76] Since then, anti-terrorism has taken a central place in the discussions of the ministers and their senior officials. ASEANAPOL, the long-established association of ASEAN police chiefs, has been a venue for intensified law-enforcement cooperation against terrorism. In January 2003, the ASEAN chiefs of police conducted a three-day workshop in Jakarta to work out cooperative ways of tackling terrorism and other transnational crimes in the region.

ASEAN has stepped up anti-terrorist cooperation with others. The ARF issued statements on terrorist financing (2002), on border security (2003), and on transport security (2004), specifying certain collaborative measures. In March 2002, Malaysia and the United States co-hosted an ARF workshop in Honolulu to deal with the issue of terrorist financing. The next month, Thailand and Australia organized another ARF workshop, in Bangkok, to draw up recommendations for more effective cooperation against terrorism. In March 2003, in Sabah, Malaysia and the United States co-chaired an Intersessional Meeting on Counter-Terrorism and Transnational Crime. The meeting addressed matters relating to the movement of people, the movement of goods, and document security and identity fraud, calling for international cooperation, the sharing of information and intelligence within and between countries, and mutual technical assistance. An ARF workshop on "managing the consequences of a major terrorist attack" was organized in June 2003 in Darwin under the co-chairmanship of Singapore and Australia. It recommended practical measures for cooperation, including those dealing with the effects of chemical, biological and radiological attacks.

For the first time, in January 2004, ministers of China, Japan and Korea joined the ASEAN Ministerial Meeting on Transnational Crime in an ASEAN+3 setting. Terrorism was high on the agenda. Their senior officials have met twice since June 2003.

At the level of foreign ministers, ASEAN issued joint statements on terrorism with the United States in 2002, India in 2003, Australia, Russia and Japan in 2004, and the Republic of Korea, Pakistan and New Zealand in 2005. They all pledged to take measures to strengthen cooperation among law-enforcement agencies, intensify the exchange of information and intelligence, and help one another improve their human and institutional capacity, placing particular emphasis on questions having to do with transport, borders and documents. The declaration issued at the ASEAN-EU Ministerial Meeting in Brussels in January 2003 singled out interaction between EUROPOL and ASEANAPOL. The ASEAN-China document, adopted in November 2002, placed anti-terrorism cooperation in the broader context of cooperation against transnational crime.

These meetings, declarations and statements are important, because they make clear ASEAN's opposition to and condemnation of terrorism. They call on the law-enforcement agencies in the region to cooperate closely in combating terrorism. They state the readiness of ASEAN and its partners to collaborate in practical ways, including information and intelligence exchanges and mutual training and technical assistance. At the same time, they affirm that terrorism should not be identified with any religion, race, culture or nationality.

However, at the operational level, cooperative action is taken outside ASEAN, since not all ASEAN countries are involved in terrorism in its international dimension in the same ways or to the same extent. In Cambodia, Laos, Myanmar and Vietnam, the relatively rare violent manifestations of terrorism are acts of dissidence against the ruling regimes. Those in Thailand are fairly recent; while involving Islamic communities, they are basically part of a domestic insurgency. Southeast Asian ties to Al-Qaeda have been most visible in terrorist operations in or threats to Indonesia, Malaysia, the Philippines and Singapore. Even in Indonesia, Islamist threats to the polity as a whole are decades old, acquiring international links only fairly recently. Similarly, the so-called Muslim problem in the Philippines — involving issues like political autonomy, land, cultural identity, ethnicity, lawlessness, crime, and local power struggles — dates back to Spanish times.

In this light, much of the Southeast Asian anti-terrorist cooperation on the ground is carried out bilaterally and out of public view. Even the Agreement on Information Exchange and Establishment of Communication Procedures initiated by Malaysia, Indonesia and the Philippines, although repeatedly endorsed by ASEAN, involves only the parties to it. Thailand, Cambodia and Brunei Darussalam have acceded to the arrangement since its adoption in May 2002. The four other ASEAN countries have not.

Similarly, the three ASEAN states flanking the Straits of Malacca and Singapore — Indonesia, Malaysia and Singapore — have stepped up their cooperation in dealing with the actual problem of armed robbery at sea and the potential one of maritime terrorism. This is a vital responsibility, as the straits are among the busiest sea lanes in the world. Through them pass some 60,000 vessels a year bearing 30 per cent of world trade and 50 per cent of global energy supplies. While careful not to compromise their national sovereignty over those narrow waterways, the littoral states cooperate closely with the major user-states, particularly in terms of capacity-building and intelligence and information exchange as well as of certain operational matters. The effort encompasses not only maritime security but also safety of navigation and environmental protection.

What seems clear is that, in recent years, the prevention of certain planned terrorist acts in some ASEAN countries and the arrests of purported terrorists have been made possible by cooperation between two or more ASEAN countries or between individual ASEAN members and countries such as Australia and the United States. These cooperative actions were facilitated, encouraged and sanctioned by ASEAN-level public declarations and workshops.

THE NEW MEMBERS AND REGIONAL SECURITY

ASEAN's decision to admit the four new members in the latter half of the 1990s was at least partly motivated by security concerns. Certainly, ASEAN was not obliged to take in all of them. The 1967 ASEAN Declaration merely states that "the Association *is open* (italics mine) for participation to all States in the South-East Asian Region subscribing to the aforementioned aims, principles and purposes". Clearly, ASEAN's intention in deciding to admit the rest of Southeast Asia was partly to seal the healing of the divisions in the region, divisions opened by ideological differences, prevailing geopolitical and strategic considerations, the conflicts in Indochina, and the clash over the Vietnamese incursion into and occupation of Cambodia. It was also partly to ensure that, with the settlement of the Cambodian problem, no part of Southeast Asia would be subjected to conflict, whether between regional states or as an arena of big-power rivalry. With the help of hindsight, some personalities in Southeast Asia have expressed doubts about the wisdom of ASEAN in admitting the four new members, particularly Myanmar, at the time that it did. However, the decision on their admission was impelled almost entirely by politico-strategic concerns, concerns that were also the leading considerations on the part of the new members themselves. As noted in Chapter 2, the newer members, like the older ones, sought membership in ASEAN not for economic gain but in order to foster a sense of belonging, in which all of them, old or new, have a deep interest.

By taking in Myanmar, ASEAN could have a voice in, if not help mitigate, the potential rivalry between China and India over that strategically placed country. The membership of Myanmar gave ASEAN and India a land border between them, while those of Vietnam and Laos, as well as Myanmar, got ASEAN land borders with China. Whether the latter will prove to be an advantage or a disadvantage for ASEAN would depend on China's policies and actions, on the perceptions of Laos, Myanmar and Vietnam — and Thailand — of their respective strategic interests, and on the ability of ASEAN as a group to manage its relations with China for mutual benefit.

By admitting Laos, Myanmar and Vietnam, as well as Cambodia, ASEAN clearly calculated that, on balance, the inclusion of all of Southeast Asia would foster good and stable relations among the states of the region, help to prevent conflict among them, and serve its strategic interests, particularly with respect to its relations with China. However, as noted in Chapter 3, the inclusion of Myanmar has affected to some extent the association's dealings with the European Union, the United States and Canada, which, largely for domestic political reasons, would rather not have highly visible or substantive dealings with the government in that country.

ASEAN+3, ASEAN PLUS INDIA, AND THE EAST ASIA SUMMIT

We have seen how ASEAN has sought to contribute to the security and stability of Southeast Asia and of East Asia as a whole by engaging the major powers in regular consultations and dialogues and through networks of relationships revolving around the association. On top of the dialogue system and the ASEAN Regional Forum, ASEAN has initiated the ASEAN+3 process, in which ASEAN relates to its three economically weighty neighbours to the north, together and individually, in deeper and more intensive ways than in the regular dialogues. As originally envisioned in 1990 by then Prime Minister Mahathir Mohamad of Malaysia, this setting was to develop into an East Asian community, with a growing sense of regional identity. Since the first ASEAN+3 Summit in Kuala Lumpur in 1997, the process has gathered momentum in a widening range of endeavours, with an increasing number of ASEAN+3 ministerial and senior-officials forums and incipient networks among business leaders. This is discussed further in Chapter 6. It is probably in terms of regional security and stability that ASEAN+3 has its greatest value. The forum has provided a framework for pursuing free trade areas or other close economic relationships between ASEAN and China, Japan and South Korea. There is even a proposal for a vast East Asian free trade area. ASEAN+3 has offered an additional setting for ASEAN members to acquire training and technology and other resources from the Northeast Asian economies. However, pending a greater degree of integration of the ASEAN economies, it is the individual ASEAN countries that ultimately relate to the Northeast Asian countries in terms of trade, investments, tourism and development cooperation. On the other hand, in the realm of regional security and stability, ASEAN has to act as a group; the individual members would not carry enough weight to deal with the Northeast Asian countries separately. It is ASEAN's expectation that closer and more intensive relationships with its neighbours to the north would substantially contribute to the stability of the region.

At the same time, the ASEAN+3 process gives the three Northeast Asian countries a convenient venue for fostering mutual understanding, conducting consultations, and improving relations among themselves, as well as strengthening ties with ASEAN. The leaders of China, Japan and South Korea met over breakfast on the occasion of the ASEAN+3 Summit in Manila in 1999. A potentially significant, if little-noticed, outcome of the 2003 ASEAN+3 Summit in Bali was the declaration that they issued committing their countries, in some detail, to cooperation in a broad range of areas on a tripartite basis. It remains to be seen how much of this pledge will be actually carried out, but the very issuance of the declaration has important, if still potential, implications for regional stability and would probably not have been possible — at least not at this time — without the ASEAN+3 process. The heads of government of the three Northeast Asian countries met again on the occasion of the 2004 ASEAN Summit in Vientiane. This time, they did not adopt any public document, but what is important is that they met. Unfortunately, China and South Korea refused a similar meeting with Japan at the time of the December 2005 ASEAN+3 Summit as a gesture of protest against the visit, again, by Prime Minister Junichiro Koizumi to the Yasukuni Shrine in Tokyo.

It is becoming increasingly clear that the defining factor in the security situation in East Asia is the relationship between China and Japan, as well as the relations of each with the United States. The triangular relations among China, Japan and Korea are acquiring a life of their own, but if the ASEAN+3 process helps in the constructive management of those relations, ASEAN will have contributed to the stability of the region. Perhaps, the Northeast Asians might in time have developed a forum of their own by themselves; but the effort would probably have been more difficult and taken much longer.

As in the case of ASEAN+3, ASEAN believes that its rapidly growing linkages with India in an expanding range of areas contribute to regional stability and security. Prime Minister Goh Chok Tong explained it with an aviation analogy. Imagine a jet plane, he told a gathering of ASEAN leaders: ASEAN is the fuselage, the Northeast Asians are one wing, and India has to be the other wing. No aircraft can fly with only one wing. In other words, ASEAN needed to balance Northeast Asia with India, not in any simplistic balance-of-power sense, but out of the strategic necessity of engaging closely all major neighbours with substantial interests and capabilities in the region. India, of course, shared this view.

I concluded my lecture in the India-ASEAN Eminent Persons Lecture Series in New Delhi on 9 January 2001:

> I am confident that I speak for ASEAN when I say that ASEAN values immensely India's strategic engagement in our part of the world. I am sure that India will also find its involvement with Southeast Asia useful to itself. This is both because of Southeast Asia's inherent value and because such an involvement will help to strengthen and enlarge India's ties to East Asia, a part of the world that is of great strategic and economic importance to it.
>
> For both sides, this is the ultimate significance of the ASEAN-India dialogue partnership.[77]

As recalled in Chapter 6, the ASEAN+3 Summit in December 2004 decided to convene the East Asia Summit the next year, much earlier than envisioned by the ministers, officials and counsellors and, previously, by the leaders themselves. Subsequently, ASEAN, with the consent of its partners, expanded EAS participation so as to encompass Australia, India and New Zealand, thus broadening the geo-strategic considerations behind ASEAN+3. To take place annually under the chairmanship of an ASEAN member-country, the EAS is being institutionalized as a venue for top-level networking, confidence building, and strategic dialogue and consultation — on a broader, but still manageable, scale than East Asia as strictly construed. The hope is that the EAS will thus serve as a further, more broadly based contribution to regional stability and, conceivably, as a framework for cooperation in economic and other practical areas. For some, the presence of other influential parties could to some extent dilute the China-Japan relationship as a key factor in regional stability and cooperation. The East Asia Summit is treated in some detail in Chapter 6.

FORUM OF DEFENCE MINISTERS

In May 2006, ASEAN made a breakthrough of sorts in the area of defence and security when the ASEAN Defence Ministers met formally for the first time, the newest of ASEAN's ministerial forums. The ministers' press announcement was deliberately bland about the significance of the event, expressing their intention merely to "contribute to the establishment of an ASEAN Security Community" and "complement the overall ASEAN process".[78] The ASEAN leaders' mandate for the meeting had been equally cautious, presented merely as one of the security activities of the ASEAN Security Community Plan of Action: "Working towards convening … an annual ASEAN Defence Ministers Meeting."[79] Nevertheless, the inauguration of a ministerial forum on defence and the ministers' agreement "to establish an ASEAN Defence Senior Officials' Meeting" marked a historic departure from ASEAN's erstwhile coyness about formal, region-wide cooperation on defence and military matters.

As the beginning of this chapter recalls, ASEAN's principal aim when it was founded was to promote peace and stability among its members and in Southeast Asia as a region. Yet, the association found it necessary at the time to disguise this intent by publicly placing economic, social and cultural cooperation at the top of its objectives. For many years, ASEAN's overt efforts in advancing regional peace and stability were limited to the political and the diplomatic. Defence and military institutions refrained from meeting officially or engaging in any formal arrangements among themselves. The reason for this was clear. ASEAN was determined to avoid being perceived as a defence alliance or as a surrogate for the anti-communist Southeast Asia Treaty Organization. Indeed, Beijing, Moscow and Hanoi denounced it as such when ASEAN was set up.

Yet, as the years went by, contacts and cooperation among defence, military and national-security officials became necessary and inevitable in response to the evolving needs of the region, particularly in the light of the changes in the configuration of power in East Asia and in the nature of the security challenges in the region. The Cold War ended. The foreign-policy stances of the major powers shifted. Strategic partnerships were conducted in fluid combinations. Common threats arose in the form, among others, of international terrorism, piracy, transnational crime and risks to commercial transport, and potential inter-state conflicts diminished in relative importance.

In the midst of all this, ASEAN defence, military and national-security officials have engaged in bilateral and region-wide networking and cooperation on their own. They form part of their country delegations to the ASEAN Regional Forum and meet informally among themselves and their non-ASEAN colleagues at ARF gatherings. The Special ASEAN Senior Officials Meeting was organized precisely to allow the participation of the defence, military and national-security establishments in intra-ASEAN security consultations. ASEAN's chiefs of defence forces and the heads of its armies, navies, air forces, and military intelligence units have developed their own informal networking mechanisms. ASEAN intelligence chiefs meet regularly in an annual forum called INTELEX. In a sense, the establishment of the defence ministers' meeting as an official forum can be considered merely as the formalization of a process that has been unfolding for a number of years, even as ASEAN remains careful to stress that it is not going into the defence-alliance business. Indeed, the 2003 Bali Concord II makes it explicitly clear that the envisioned ASEAN Security Community would not lead "to a defence pact, military alliance or a joint foreign policy".

The formal existence of an ASEAN forum of defence ministers, however, could be useful to ASEAN's purposes under today's regional circumstances. It could strengthen the institutional framework for building confidence among ASEAN states, and eventually with others in East Asia, defence and security being a key area in which mutual confidence is vital. It could provide a venue for the sharing — and, hopefully, the harmonization — of threat perceptionsn. It could elevate and formalize the process of intelligence exchange within ASEAN. Finally, it could facilitate more effective operational coordination in such matters as search and rescue, disaster response, counter-terrorism, anti-piracy, combating transnational crime, and the protection of sea lanes and transportation links.

THE ASEAN SECURITY COMMUNITY

We have seen how ASEAN has agreed on certain decisions and taken certain collective steps related to regional security in response to what it perceives to be the needs of the times. What is clear through the entire process is that, for ASEAN, cooperation for security purposes is essentially and necessarily political in nature; there is no question of ASEAN going into the defence-pact or military-alliance business. What it does is foster mutual understanding, build confidence, dissipate suspicions, and provide, not a mechanism, but a setting for the peaceful management of disputes. It has also laid down certain principles to govern the relations among its members which it keeps repeating like a mantra — respect for sovereignty and territorial integrity, the peaceful settlement of disputes, non-interference in the internal affairs of nations, decisions by consensus, equality of status, and so on — principles that have generally been respected and served ASEAN well thus far. ASEAN has extended these principles and the ASEAN approach to regional security, through engagement, consultation and dialogue, to East Asia as a whole and the wider Asia-Pacific region. It has done this through accessions to the Treaty of Amity and Cooperation, the ARF, the ASEAN+3 process, the East Asia Summit, and joint declarations and other statements. The Declaration of ASEAN Concord, which the ASEAN leaders issued at the 1976 Summit in Bali, had only a one-phrase reference to security cooperation, mentioning, with exceeding caution, "Continuation of cooperation on a non-ASEAN basis between the member states in security matters in accordance with their mutual needs and interests". On the other hand, the second Declaration of ASEAN Concord, adopted by ASEAN's leaders, again in Bali, in October 2003, has a rather lengthy section expressing the intention to establish an ASEAN Security Community, the name given to the next stage of ASEAN cooperation in political and security matters.

The ASEAN Security Community as embodied in Bali Concord II and the Plan of Action adopted for it in Vientiane on 29 November 2004 not only gives this process and its goal a name; it seeks to give a measure of coherence and structure to ASEAN political cooperation on behalf of regional security. Above all, it specifies the next steps in the process, the priority items in today's ASEAN security agenda, potentially expanding it. We shall return to this later.

In the meantime, ASEAN has advanced its security interests, in certain critical areas, through its solidarity and cooperation much more effectively than the individual countries could have done by themselves. The ASEAN context has helped defuse tensions between Malaysia and the Philippines regarding Sabah and provided an additional incentive for its peaceful management. The principles for inter-state relations embodied in the Treaty of Amity and Cooperation and their acceptance by others have served ASEAN well. ASEAN exercised collective diplomacy in pursuing its common positions on the Vietnamese incursion into Cambodia and the

Indochinese refugee situation as security issues and rallying most of the international community behind those positions. It has sought to engage China in a broad range of areas for cooperation as its way of managing its most critical security relationship, while at the same time presenting China with a common stance on the question of the South China Sea. It has exercised leadership in the ASEAN Regional Forum, with the "ASEAN Way" serving as the template for its processes, and has, through the ARF, the ASEAN Dialogue system, and other forums, successfully kept the major powers engaged in East Asian affairs in a constructive way. The completion of the membership of all of Southeast Asia — Timor-Leste aside — in ASEAN has helped in the quick healing of the divisions in the region and fostered regional stability. The ASEAN+3 process, the ASEAN-India linkage, and now the East Asia Summit contribute to stability and cooperation in East Asia, as do ASEAN's relations with the United States, the European Union, Russia, and other individual partners.

Some critics have asserted that ASEAN has been ineffective in promoting peace and stability because it has not been able to prevent bilateral disputes between its members. Recent examples cited are the border skirmishes between Thailand and Myanmar, the violence committed against the Thai Embassy and Thai businesses in Phnom Penh in 2003, the tensions between Malaysia and Thailand related to the brutalities taking place in southern Thailand, and the deployment of Indonesian and Malaysian warships to disputed waters off the coast of Borneo in 2005. Yet, these situations either have been quickly defused or are being managed so as to contain them. This fact could be at least partly attributed to the culture of non-resort to force that ASEAN has cultivated, to the personal ties developed between the leaders concerned, and to the value that ASEAN members place on good relations among themselves. In any case, hardly any regional association of states is without bilateral disputes between members. The important thing is that those in Southeast Asia have been managed and contained.

Clearly, it is in the political and security area, with its ever-stronger impact on global and regional economic relations, that ASEAN has proven its greatest worth. The concept of the ASEAN Security Community now points the way to the next stage of ASEAN security cooperation. How successfully ASEAN goes in that direction remains to be seen.

Notes

1. Some of this chapter is derived, with updating, from the author's paper, *Towards an ASEAN Security Community*, published as part of the Trends in Southeast Asia Series (Singapore: Institute of Southeast Asian Studies, 2004).

2. See Appendix A.
3. Quoted in Roger Irvine, "The Formative Years of ASEAN: 1967–75", in *Understanding ASEAN*, edited by Alison Broinowski (London: MacMillan Press, Ltd., 1982), p. 14.
4. Jusuf Wanandi, *The Security Dimensions of the Asia-Pacific Region in the 1980s* (Jakarta: Centre for Strategic and International Studies, 1979), pp. 51–52.
5. Mahathir Mohamad, Keynote Address in *ASEAN at the Crossroads*, edited by Noordin Sopiee, Chew Lay See and Lim Siang Jin (Kuala Lumpur: Institute of Strategic and International Studies, 1987), p. 1.
6. Thanat Khoman, "ASEAN: Conception and Evolution", in *The ASEAN Reader* (Singapore: Institute of Southeast Asian Studies, 1992), pp. xvii–xviii.
7. Stuart Harris, *The Asian Regional Response to Its Economic Crisis and the Global Implications* (Canberra: Department of International Relations, Research School of Pacific and Asian Studies, Australian National University, 1999), p. 11.
8. Quoted in http://www.aseansec.org/92.htm.
9. Lee Kuan Yew, *From Third World to First — The Singapore Story: 1965–2000* (Singapore: Times Media Private Limited, 2000), p. 370.
10. The President's Policy Address at the General Assembly of the United Malays National Organization, Kuala Lumpur, as published in *The Star*, Kuala Lumpur, 23 September 2004.
11. Quoted in Donald Tracy Laird, "The Philippines in Southeast Asia: Transactions, Interactions and Conflict with Indonesia, Malaysia, Singapore and Thailand", doctoral dissertation for the University of Michigan, Ann Arbor, Michigan, USA, 1975, p. 253.
12. Carlos P. Romulo, at that time Secretary of Foreign Affairs of the Philippines.
13. http://www.aseansec.org/1233.htm.
14. http://www.aseansec.org/1215.htm.
15. See Appendix B.
16. See Chapter 1.
17. France, Russia, the United Kingdom and the United States. The fifth is China.
18. Interview with Minister Cham Prasidh, Phnom Penh, 12 May 2003.
19. Interview with Prince Norodom Sirivudh, Phnom Penh, 7 June 2003.
20. Front Uni National pour un Cambodge Indépendant, Neutre, Pacifique et Coopératif.
21. Inteview with Prince Norodom Sirivudh, Phnom Penh, 7 June 2003.
22. Interview with King Norodom Sihanouk, Phnom Penh, 10 December 2003.
23. Luu Doan Huynh, "Vietnam-ASEAN Relations in Retrospect: A Few Thoughts", in *Peace and Reconciliation: Success Stories and Lessons from Asia and Europe*, edited by Bertrand Fort and Norbert von Hofmann (Singapore: Asia-Europe Foundation and Friedrich Ebert Stiftung Office for Regional Cooperation in Southeast Asia, 2004), p. 27.
24. Ibid., pp. 25, 26 and 29.
25. Interview with Eric Teo, Phnom Penh, 26 May 2003.
26. Luu Doan Huynh, op. cit., pp. 30–36.

27. Interview with Minister Hor Namhong, 27 June 2003.
28. A brief but useful account of the Sino-Soviet dimension of the Cambodian settlement is found in S.D. Muni, *China's Strategic Engagement with the New ASEAN* (Singapore: Institute of Defence and Strategic Studies, 2002), pp. 8–15.
29. Barry Wain of the *Asian Wall Street Journal* has a very detailed account of the plight of the Indochina asylum-seekers in *The Refused: The Agony of the Indochina Refugees* (New York: Simon and Schuster, 1981). He places particular focus on the alleged complicity of the Vietnamese Government at one stage in the exodus.
30. Lee Kuan Yew, op. cit., pp. 348–49.
31. Barry Wain, op. cit., pp. 35 and 80.
32. United Nations High Commissioner for Refugees, *The State of the World's Refugees 2000 — Fifty Years of Humanitarian Action* (Oxford University Press, 2000), p. 98.
33. United Nations High Commissioner for Refugees, *The State of the World's Refugees 1993* (New York: Penguin Books, 1993), pp. 104–5.
34. http://www.aseansec.org/3676.htm.
35. http://www.aseansec.org/3675.htm.
36. W. Courtland Robinson, *Terms of Refuge: The Indochinese Exodus and the International Response* (London and New York: Zed Books Ltd., 1998), p. 272.
37. Tim Huxley, *Indochinese Refugees as a Security Concern of the ASEAN States, 1975–81* (Canberra: Department of International Relations, Australian National University, 1983), p. 1.
38. Ibid., p. 72.
39. W. Courtland Robinson, op. cit., p. 41.
40. http://www.aseansec.org/1241.htm.
41. http://www.aseansec.org/1258.htm.
42. http://www.aseansec.org/1242.htm.
43. http://www.aseansec.org/5114.htm.
44. W. Courtland Robinson, op. cit., p. 173.
45. United Nations High Commissioner for Refugees, *The State of the World's Refugees 2000 — Fifty Years of Humanitarian Action* (Oxford University Press, 2000), p. 99.
46. Ibid., p. 82.
47. http://www.aseansec.org/3666.htm.
48. Hasjim Djalal, the prime mover of the workshop series, has an extensive and authoritative account of the workshop process and some of the important issues surrounding the South China Sea question in *Preventive Diplomacy in Southeast Asia: Lessons Learned* (Jakarta: The Habibie Center, 2003), pp. 38–140.
49. http://www.aseansec.org/3634.htm.
50. http://www.aseansec.org/5232.htm.
51. I am indebted to two men for illuminating some of these issues for me. One is Lauro S. Baja, my successor as Undersecretary of Foreign Affairs and ASEAN

SOM Leader for the Philippines, and now Philippine Permanent Representative to the United Nations in New York, who responded to my questions by e-mail in November 2004. The other is Tan Sri Ahmad Fuzi Hj. Abdul Razak, Secretary-General of the Ministry of Foreign Affairs and ASEAN SOM Leader for Malaysia, who gave me an interview in Putrajaya, Malaysia, on 2 November 2004.

52. http://www.aseansec.org/13163.htm.
53. http://www.news.ops.gov.ph/archives2004/sect04.htm#summary.
54. http://www.aseansec.org/5120.htm.
55. Ibid.
56. http://www.aseansec.org/3617.htm.
57. http://www.aseansec.org/3618.htm.
58. Indonesia, Singapore and Thailand.
59. Indonesia, Singapore and Thailand.
60. Cambodia, Singapore and Thailand.
61. Brunei Darussalam, Cambodia, Singapore and Thailand.
62. Cambodia, Malaysia, Singapore, Thailand and Vietnam.
63. Singapore and Thailand.
64. http://www.aseansec.org/15159.htm.
65. http://www.aseansec.org/3742.htm.
66. http://www.aseansec.org/12000.htm.
67. http://www.aseansec.org/13230.htm.
68. http://www.aseansec.org/3612.htm.
69. Interview with Minister José Ramos-Horta, Jakarta, 29 June 2004.
70. http://www.aseansec.org/589.htm.
71. http://www.aseansec.org/590.htm.
72. http://www.aseansec.org/16170.htm.
73. http://www.aseansec.org/12968.htm.
74. http://www.aseansec.org/5620.htm.
75. http://www.aseansec.org/13154.htm.
76. http://www.aseansec.org/5616.htm.
77. Rodolfo C. Severino Jr., "ASEAN and India — A Partnership for Our Time", in *India-ASEAN Partnership in an Era of Globalization: Reflections by Eminent Persons* (New Delhi: Research and Information System for the Non-Aligned Countries and Singapore: Institute of Southeast Asian Studies, 2004), p. 156; also in Severino, *ASEAN Today and Tomorrow* (Jakarta: ASEAN Secretariat, 2002), p. 279.
78. http://www.aseansec.org/18412.htm.
79. See Appendix H.

5

INTEGRATING THE REGIONAL ECONOMY

As the previous chapter stressed, the Association of Southeast Asian Nations was founded basically for political and security purposes, to prevent disputes and mutual suspicions from developing into conflict and to strengthen Southeast Asia's influence on regional and international affairs. As has also been noted, this is where ASEAN's supreme achievement lies. Nevertheless, ASEAN's founders felt compelled to highlight its economic, social and cultural purposes partly in order to gain public support for the new association, partly to allay suspicions that ASEAN was to be a military pact or a defence alliance, and partly because they were genuinely convinced that comprehensive development — or, as the Indonesians liked to say, national and regional resilience — was a necessary condition for regional, as well as national, peace and stability.

Thus, the ASEAN Declaration of 8 August 1967 laid down as three of its seven objectives the following:

3. To promote active collaboration and mutual assistance on matters of common interest in the economic, social, cultural, technical, scientific and administrative fields;
4. To provide assistance to each other in the form of training and research facilities in the educational, professional, technical and administrative spheres;
5. To collaborate more effectively for the greater utilization of their agriculture and industries, the expansion of their trade, including the study of the problems of international commodity trade, the improvement of their transportation and communications facilities and the raising of the living standards of their peoples.[1]

One will note that the declaration only called for collaboration and mutual assistance and for the expansion of trade generally, not necessarily among themselves. The declaration also highlighted most of the ASEAN countries' preoccupation with "international commodity trade". Malaysia was a leading exporter of palm oil, natural rubber and tin, the Philippines of copra, coconut oil and sugar, Thailand of rice, tapioca and other agricultural products, and Indonesia of a wide range of agricultural, mineral and forestry products. The main markets for all these were in the developed world rather than within ASEAN, where there was little demand for ASEAN products other than Thai rice. Thus, there was no thought at that time about regional market integration or about the need to attract foreign investments through an integrated regional market.

Nevertheless, it soon became clear that something could be gained by a greater degree of cooperation in the economic area among the members of the new association. The Philippines and Thailand were particularly hard-hit by the energy crunch of 1972–73, while Indonesia and Malaysia were exporters of energy. Some suffered periodic shortages of rice; Thailand was a major exporter. The ASEAN countries felt the need to reduce their dependence on developed-country markets and on a few export commodities, whose prices in the world market tended to fluctuate wildly while the prices of their manufactured imports steadily increased. They saw possibilities in the regional market for large-scale industries in critical sectors as a spur to industrialization. In the light of this, Widjojo Nitisastro, Indonesia's Minister of State for Economic, Financial and Industrial Affairs, and Minister for Trade Radius Prawiro visited the ASEAN capitals early in 1975 to gain support for a meeting of economic ministers. The gathering took place in Jakarta in November and was billed as the Meeting of ASEAN Economic and Planning Ministers, a label reflecting its diverse participation. Opened with much solemnity by President Soeharto, the meeting endorsed the draft of what eventually became the economic component of the Declaration of ASEAN Concord that the first ASEAN Summit issued three months later.

BEFORE AFTA

The first ASEAN Summit, in Bali in February 1976, thus moved economic cooperation firmly onto the ASEAN agenda. The Declaration of ASEAN Concord and the joint communiqué of the summit committed the member-states to give one another priority in the supply of food and energy in "critical circumstances", like natural disasters and other situations that cause shortages.

They called for the establishment of large-scale industrial projects in ASEAN countries that would use available materials, increase food production, augment or save foreign exchange, and create jobs. They suggested urea, superphosphates, potash, petrochemicals, steel, soda ash, newsprint and rubber products. Preferential trading arrangements for the output of the ASEAN industrial projects, and for food and energy products, were to be established in the form of long-term quantity contracts, financing at preferential rates, privileges in government procurement, and tariff preferences.[2]

Of institutional significance was the leaders' statement directing the economic ministers to meet, specifying March 1976, which the ministers, of course, had previously agreed upon, presumably at their 1975 meeting. The ministers met as scheduled, in Kuala Lumpur. The record of their discussions reflects a preoccupation with commodities trade and with access to critical supplies — rice and crude oil, in the first place. The ministers decided on the allocation of the ASEAN industrial projects — a urea fertilizer plant each for Indonesia and Malaysia, superphosphates for the Philippines, diesel engines for Singapore, and soda ash for Thailand. Each of the five projects was estimated to require an investment of US$250 million to US$300 million. At the same time, the ministers agreed to consult one another on any plans to put up integrated steel or basic petrochemical industries with a view to "avoiding unnecessary duplication and competition"! They also proposed dialogues with Australia, New Zealand, Canada, the United States, Japan, West Asian countries, the European Economic Community, COMECON, and other regional groups.[3] In fact, as we shall see in the next chapter, the dialogues with the EEC, Japan, Australia and New Zealand were already in place, and those with Canada and the United States were to be initiated the next year.

From their second meeting on, the forum was to be officially named the ASEAN Economic Ministers, or AEM. Although in ASEAN there was no official appointed as an "economic minister", the generic designation was used because, in the early years of the forum's existence, different ministers represented their countries in it — ministers for trade, ministers for industry, ministers for primary industries, ministers for economic planning, ministers in the Prime Minister's office. Today, however, it is the ministers for trade who represent most countries in the ASEAN Economic Ministers meetings.

According to Widjojo Nitisastro, Indonesia had resisted all notions of trade liberalization and regional economic integration. Indonesia, he said, was more concerned with food, as well as energy, security and with the establishment of large-scale industrial projects. Widjojo believed that, if a country felt that trade liberalization was good for it, it would open up trade unilaterally anyway.[4]

ASEAN did go into "preferential trading arrangements", under which each ASEAN country would grant to imports from other member-countries a discount on most-favoured-nation tariffs, called a margin of preference. However, under the agreement negotiated and initialled by the economic ministers and signed by the foreign ministers in February 1977, and ratified by July, the arrangements had for their main purpose not economic integration but an assured market for the products of the large industrial projects and of the industrial complementation operations that the ASEAN countries were allocating among themselves. In opening the ASEAN Economic Ministers meeting in Pattaya in September 1977, General Boonchai Bamrungphong, deputy prime minister of Thailand, stressed:

> It is fortunate that ASEAN is not poor in resources. What is lack(ing) is that much of these resources have remained unexploited, not because of lack of will, capital nor technology. Rather, the exploitation and productive use of resources require market to absorb the resulting flow of goods and commodities. Yet none of the individual ASEAN countries is large enough to provide market support to make these projects commercially and hence economically viable… .
>
> Already, the vital link between production and market has been forged with the ratification of the Agreement on ASEAN Preferential Trading Agreements (sic). Preferential treatment is assured for the products of these (large-scale industrial) projects.[5]

Vicente Paterno, at that time Secretary of Industry and Chairman of the Board of Investments of the Philippines, confirmed to me that "emphasis in the early days was on industrial complementation".[6]

The PTA agreement would cover "basic commodities", particularly food and energy, the products of the ASEAN Industrial Projects and ASEAN Industrial Complementation schemes, and lists of goods to be negotiated among the parties.[7] Implementation of the PTA started at the beginning of 1978. It initially covered 71 products after much hard bargaining on the 1,700 items that had been considered. By 1986, the number of items covered had grown to 12,700 and, by 1990, to 15,295. The margin of preference was originally an insignificant 10 per cent, but was increased to 20–25 per cent in 1980. The cut-off import value was raised from the original US$50,000 to US$10 million in 1983 until it was in effect abolished in 1984. On the occasion of the 1987 ASEAN Summit, the economic ministers signed a protocol committing the ASEAN countries to place in the PTA within five years (with Indonesia and the Philippines allowed seven years) at least 90 per cent of items traded among them with at least 50 per cent of the value of intra-ASEAN trade. The margin of preference for the new items was increased to 25 per cent and for those already in the PTA to 50 per cent, something that the economic ministers had already agreed upon four years before. The ASEAN content requirement would be reduced in five years from 50 to 35 per cent (42 per cent in the case of Indonesia), but "on a case-by-case basis"; after five years, it could be brought back up to 50 per cent.

Still, intra-ASEAN trade did not grow much. Because the coverage of the PTA was negotiated product by product, the tendency of the ASEAN member-countries, true to the protectionist spirit and import-substitution policies of the time, was to include mostly items that were not likely to be extensively traded. The inclusion of snow ploughs and nuclear reactors became the object of derision within knowing circles. The national exclusion lists were long. In any case, even with a margin of preference of 50 per cent, a PTA tariff would remain high if the most-favoured-nation tariff was set at a lofty level. Tariff rates were not brought down; those ASEAN products that were covered were only given 25- to 50-per cent discounts on high tariffs. At their 1991 meeting, the economic ministers observed that, while intra-ASEAN trade in items covered by the PTA had grown from US$121 million in 1987 to US$578 million in 1989, it accounted for an "insignificant" proportion of total intra-ASEAN trade. A 1983 UNIDO study discussed the underlying difficulties:

> The existing low level of intra-ASEAN trade has always been the rallying point for the "regionalists", who strongly advocate a rapid growth of intraregional trade in order to diversify the region's market base and to reduce its over-dependence on the industrialized countries. However, the intra-ASEAN trade since 1976 has simply failed to take off in real terms and remains stagnant at around the 15 per cent level, despite the implementation of some regional trade liberalization measures. In a sense, the sluggish expansion of intraregional trade in ASEAN brings to the fore the inefficacy, at least in the initial phase, of the technique of trade cooperation adopted by ASEAN. At the same time, the stagnancy of intra-ASEAN trade also reflects the tremendous structural problems and institutional biases operating against intraregional trade. Many of the obstacles standing in the way of intra-ASEAN trade are well known. First, the existing trade and production patterns have allowed only limited absorptive capacity in the ASEAN countries for each other's major exports, such as rubber, tin, timber, palm-oil and coconut products, which are primarily destined to be consumed outside the region. A notable exception

is the Thai export of rice. Secondly, the ASEAN economies at their present stages of development have almost exhausted their commercial capacities in responding to the large and growing export markets of the developed countries during the past two decades. Thirdly, the import-substituting policies together with the balance-of-payments difficulties faced by some ASEAN countries have resulted in certain policies that are inherently biased against regional trade, for example high priority for the import of capital and intermediate goods, which are usually supplied by the developed countries.[8]

One might think that ASEAN would move more vigorously on the allocation and establishment of large industrial projects and operations. However, even here, the schemes floundered on the shoals of competing national interests. In March 1980, the ASEAN foreign ministers signed the Basic Agreement on ASEAN Industrial Projects formalizing the conditions governing the five projects previously agreed upon by the economic ministers and other projects to be allocated in the future. (In those days, only the foreign ministers signed formal ASEAN agreements.) The host country would invest 60 per cent of the equity; the other four member-countries would take the other 40 per cent in equal shares. The investor would be a "shareholder entity" that "enjoys the support and guidance" of its government. The agreement had provisions on taxation, incentives, the repatriation of capital and remittance of profits, the protection of minority shareholders, pricing, and bankruptcy. In 1977, Prime Minister Takeo Fukuda of Japan, in his meeting with the ASEAN heads of government, had offered to extend financing in the form of soft loans up to a total of US$1 billion for the industrial projects provided feasibility studies bore out their viability. Within two years, Japan had extended a loan of ¥33 billion to the urea project in Indonesia.

Among the approved ASEAN Industrial Projects, only the urea fertilizer plants in Aceh in northern Sumatra and Bintulu in central Sarawak have survived as such. No ASEAN country was willing to see curbs on its option to put up industries similar to those allocated to another ASEAN country. In 1979, the Philippines substituted the superphosphate project with one that would produce ammonium sulfate fertilizer, which, in the next year, it replaced in turn with a proposal for a pulp and paper plant. The year after that, the Philippines changed plans again, this time in favour of a copper fabrication plant, which the economic ministers approved in 1982. By that time, Thailand had growing apprehensions about its neighbours' commitment to an exclusive regional market for its projected plant for producing soda ash, an essential raw material in glass, chemicals, detergents, and other important industrial products. In 1983, having discovered natural gas in its territory,

Thailand announced its own plans to produce urea fertilizer, much to the chagrin of Indonesia and Malaysia. Encountering technical problems with the soda ash project, Bangkok in 1986 officially withdrew it from the AIP scheme. Three years later, it proposed the replacement of that project with potash mining, the economic ministers approving the proposal the next year, 1990. The ASEAN countries' lack of enthusiasm for AIPs other than their own was indicated by the fact that Brunei Darussalam and the Philippines, as well as Singapore, were willing to commit only one per cent each of the Thai potash project's equity, with Indonesia and Malaysia taking 13 per cent each. Thailand itself had to contribute the balance of 71 per cent, with the Thai Government taking 20 per cent and the balance of 51 per cent open to the private sector. Agreed upon in ASEAN in 1991, the ASEAN Potash Mining Company was organized in 1993, but it was only in 1997 that the Thai cabinet approved the project. By 2004, or seven years later, the Thai Government had decided to pull out of it, with Minister for Industry, Pinit Jarusombat quoted as saying that "potash mining is the role of the private sector".⁹ Presumably, it had thereby lost its status as an AIP, but it no longer mattered. ASEAN's economic ideology had obviously changed.

In view of its free-market inclinations and policies, Singapore was from the beginning antagonistic to a system of states deciding what industries to put up for a protected and exclusive regional market, arguing that the arrangements were anti-competitive. The futility of the AIP scheme was illustrated by the case of the diesel-engine project that Singapore had proposed for itself. The other countries insisted that Singapore seek their consent before selling to them diesel engines below 200 horsepower, with Indonesia demanding a higher floor of 500 horsepower. Neither Indonesia nor Malaysia nor the Philippines was willing to give up its plans to expand its own production of diesel engines below 200 horsepower, which accounted for the bulk of the ASEAN market, despite certain concessions offered by Singapore. Eventually, in 1984, Singapore gave up the project in favour of hepatitis-B vaccines, a move that the economic ministers approved, although it was of a type not envisioned as an AIP. Despite its misgivings about the AIP scheme, Singapore had put up a nominal one per cent as its "equity" in each of the two urea fertilizer enterprises so as to maintain their character as ASEAN projects and, presumably, their eligibility for the financing offered by Japan. As a result, Malaysia, the Philippines and Thailand had to take 13 per cent each of the Aceh project. Indonesia's and Thailand's shares of the Bintulu project are 13 per cent each, the Philippines' 9.5 per cent, and Malaysia's 63.5 per cent to make up for the Philippine shortfall. In return, the other ASEAN countries, including Brunei Darussalam, which had joined ASEAN in 1984, contributed only a token one per cent each for the Singapore project. Apparently, Singapore did not care, announcing that it did not seek market support for its project just as it did not extend such support to the other AIPs. This, of course, ran counter to the entire concept of AIPs. Singapore declared that it would "encourage" its industries to purchase the products of Thailand's projected soda-ash plant and the Philippines' proposed copper fabrication project, but only if their prices were "internationally competitive". Not surprisingly, Singapore withdrew the hepatitis-B project in 1987. The repeated changes in the AIPs of the Philippines and Thailand exposed a practical weakness of the scheme: projects were decided upon before thorough studies were made of their viability even in a protected regional market. More fundamentally, they underscored the incoherence between ASEAN attempts at a regional industrial policy and the ASEAN countries' basic orientation as free-market economies.

ASEAN ventured into other "industrial complementation" schemes. There was the ASEAN Industrial Complementation, or AIC, a scheme formalized in an agreement signed by the foreign ministers in 1981.[10] The scheme provided for the allocation of "complementary" industrial products for manufacture in at least four ASEAN countries (unless fewer participants were approved by the economic ministers) and to be traded among them. Products of AIC "packages" were to enjoy "exclusivity privileges", that is, no AIC participant could manufacture the same product as the one allocated to another participant. "Exclusivity" for "existing" products was to be for two years, and for "new" products three years. AIC products would qualify for preferences under the PTA, which, as decided by the economic ministers, were to include a 50-per cent tariff margin of preference.

Even before the formal AIC agreement was concluded, the economic ministers had, in 1980, adopted two complementation packages, both involving automotive parts. In 1988, ASEAN entered into an arrangement specifically for the automotive industry called "brand-to-brand complementation". The arrangement granted a 50-per cent margin of tariff preference for specified parts and components of vehicles of a particular brand traded among approved ASEAN participants. Interested countries would negotiate individual packages for the approval of the economic ministers' Committee on Industry, Minerals and Energy. Malaysia, the Philippines and Thailand were the participants in the first Brand-to-Brand Complementation (B-to-B) scheme.[11] Indonesia joined it in 1995. The first B-to-B schemes approved, in 1989, were proposed by Mitsubishi, Volvo and Mercedes-Benz, with proposals from Toyota, Nissan and DAF of Belgium and additional ones from Mitsubishi and Volvo following the next year.

Another arrangement was the ASEAN Industrial Joint Ventures. Under the AIJV agreement signed in November 1983, the products of an AIJV project, which had to have equity participation of at least two ASEAN countries, were to enjoy a 50-per cent margin of tariff preference from the participating countries for the first four years from the start of commercial production and market "exclusivity" for three years, provided they were "new" products. Afterwards, non-participating ASEAN countries had to extend the same margin of preference. Specific products covered had to be approved by the economic ministers *en banc*.[12] In December 1987, the foreign ministers signed a revised AIJV agreement enlarging the margin of preference to 90 per cent and lowering the minimum ASEAN equity required from 51 to 40 per cent.[13] Still, in 1989, six years after the signing of the AIJV agreement, the economic ministers complained of the "slow progress" in the approval of AIJV projects. By 1991, enamel, heavy equipment, aluminum hydroxide, and, most prominently, Nestlé projects had been approved.

That same year, the brand-to-brand complementation scheme was expanded to cover non-automotive items, but by then the industrial complementation schemes were about to be superseded by the Common Effective Preferential Tariff Scheme for the ASEAN Free Trade Area and the ASEAN Industrial Cooperation programme.

It is to be noted that, in the early years of ASEAN economic cooperation, the ASEAN private sector, organized in the ASEAN Chambers of Commerce and Industry, was much more active and prominent than it is today. Proposals for ASEAN industrial complementation schemes were pushed by the ASEAN CCI. The AIC agreement gave the ASEAN CCI the function of identifying products for inclusion in AIC packages. It had the privilege of nominating AIJV products under the AIJV agreement. However, as ASEAN moved away from trying to manage industrialization and towards allowing individual firms, ASEAN or non-ASEAN, to decide their own responses to the market, the ASEAN CCI's role diminished considerably, its meetings with the ASEAN Economic Ministers becoming little more than annual rituals.

Up to the late 1980s, ASEAN economic cooperation was preoccupied with the usual developing-country concerns — access of commodity exports to developed-country markets, the prices and competitiveness of those commodities, assured access of member-countries to critical needs like rice and crude oil, particularly in times of crisis, and an assured regional market for state-designated industrial projects, to be protected from competition. It was all about managed industrialization, commodity exports and the stability of their prices, and economic "cooperation". Talk of regional economic integration was taboo, although as early as March 1971 the records of the fourth ASEAN Ministerial Meeting quoted President Ferdinand Marcos of the Philippines as suggesting in his opening address that the "the ultimate dream of ASEAN countries would be to evolve itself into a Common Market whose benefits would reach the masses of Southeast Asian countries". Opening the ASEAN Economic Ministers meeting in Manila in May 1982, Marcos proposed "ASEAN Free Trade" as "our real goal". He continued:

> If free trade is a goal which commends itself to the other ASEAN member governments, then we should lose no time in so resolving that it is. Establishing a free trade regime is an enormous undertaking, requiring a great deal of preparation and lead time. If we resolve today to establish it, perhaps we should need all of the next ten years to stage it.
>
> In the meantime, a statement of the clear objective would undoubtedly assist our private sectors in making the individual corporate plans and strategies, and our preferential trading arrangement negotiators in deciding when, where and how deeply to cut tariffs in preparation for a free trade regime.[14]

Apparently considered ahead of their time, the proposals, made eleven years apart, were neither responded to nor followed through.

In his 1982 speech, Marcos indicated the premise of the free-trade proposal by observing that the current arrangements were not going very far. He said, "It is too soon to say how much increase in intra-ASEAN trade will actually result from these tariff preferences. Perhaps, as some fear, it will not be overly much, since the products placed under preference so far are not the products traded in substantial volume at the present time."[15] Nine years later, Prime Minister Mahathir Mohamad of Malaysia declared in his usual blunt way, "Unfortunately the record of (ASEAN) achievements, particularly in the field of economic cooperation, has been dismal."[16]

The reasons for the "dismal" showing are not difficult to see with hindsight. ASEAN cooperation in the earlier years rested on two pillars — preferential trading arrangements and industrial complementation — both of which collapsed under the weight of unreconciled national interests. The PTA granted margins of preference on tariffs on lists of products negotiated among the ASEAN members rather than, as later arrangements would, reducing tariffs on all products, with only a few exceptions, to minimal levels or abolishing them altogether. In keeping with the protectionist ideology and the nationalistic sentiments of the time, the member-states made a mockery of the system by throwing into it mostly those products in which they expected little or no intra-ASEAN trade. The industrial complementation schemes provided for the allocation of industries among the ASEAN countries by inter-state agreement. The viability of the allocated industries would, in theory, be assured, as their products would enjoy exclusive rights to the region-wide market and be protected from intra- as well as extra-regional competition. It was industrial policy on a regional scale, with governments even insisting on a say in the prices of AIP products and of their raw materials. It was a system presumably inspired by the national industrial policies of Japan and Korea. The problem, however, was that, in contrast to the highly disciplined and cohesive societies of those nations, the Southeast Asian countries were extremely diverse ethnically and economically and were driven largely by often conflicting national interests, ASEAN being a collection of independent, sovereign states. No regional authority ensured compliance with regional agreements. Whatever sense of region the ASEAN countries had was at best inchoate.

Confronted with these realities and other, mounting challenges, ASEAN in the early 1990s decided to take a different approach. Trade and investment decisions would be determined by private entities on the basis of market considerations, with government agreements limited to making trade and investment freer and easier, with the aim of eventually integrating the regional market rather than forcing certain state-selected industries on it.

THE ASEAN FREE TRADE AREA

By the late 1980s, two trends were gathering momentum in the world economy — globalization and regionalization on parallel tracks. The Treaty of Asunción, which created MERCOSUR,[17] was concluded in March 1991. The Final Act of the Uruguay Round of Multilateral Trade Negotiations was completed in December 1991, and the General Agreement on Tariffs and Trade was being reorganized into the World Trade Organization. The European Union was being created, with the Treaty of Maastricht heading for signature in February 1992. The North American Free Trade Agreement[18] was being negotiated, with the signing to take place in December 1992. Meanwhile, the radical economic reforms in the Chinese economy put in place by Deng Xiaoping were infusing a new dynamism into that economy. The transformation of India's economy — from being largely bureaucracy-guided to being increasingly market-driven — was laying the groundwork for similarly rapid growth.

In the light of these developments, ASEAN seemed convinced that it had to move onto the path of regional economic integration, the path that a unifying Europe, MERCOSUR, North America and other regions were treading, each in its own way. Although there remained impediments to their internal trade, China and India by themselves had massive and increasingly dynamic domestic markets. In the face of these challenges, the ASEAN member-countries' ability to compete effectively for markets and investments would be severely hampered unless they achieved the efficiencies of a large, integrated regional market.

Thus, in 1991, Anand Panyarachun, the Thai Prime Minister, whose career had straddled the worlds of the civil service, diplomacy and business, proposed the establishment of the ASEAN Free Trade Area, an idea that the ASEAN foreign ministers welcomed at their annual meeting in July. In support of the Prime Minister's proposal, Thailand drew up a "discussion paper" outlining the concept and the rationale for it and presented the document to the economic ministers. The paper cited four arguments:

1. Subjecting their industries to regional competition would help prepare ASEAN countries for the more liberal global trading regime being worked out in the Uruguay Round.
2. Freeing trade within ASEAN would attract investments and increase industrial exports, with multinational corporations setting up multi-plant operations in line with the globalization of industrial production.
3. The emerging European Single Market and North American Free Trade Agreement require ASEAN countries to coalesce economically in order to avoid becoming "very insignificant" in international economic negotiations.
4. ASEAN would be participating in APEC and the proposed East Asia Economic Group more effectively if it were to do so "as a strong economic entity".[19]

Meeting in October, the economic ministers considered the AFTA idea as part of "an integrated package towards the creation of a truly liberalized ASEAN market", which would include the "growth triangle" concept, an ASEAN treaty on economic cooperation, as proposed by the Philippines, and improved Preferential Trading Arrangements, as well as a Common Effective Preferential Tariff scheme. The joint statement of that meeting recorded:

> The Ministers, in acknowledging the interrelationship of the new initiatives, agreed that all member countries should subscribe to the establishment of the ASEAN Free Trade Area (AFTA) simultaneously so as to create within the time frame of 15 years a truly liberalized ASEAN market with the Common Effective Preferential Tariff (CEPT) in the range of 0–5 per cent for manufactured products. They also agreed that the AFTA shall be effected mainly through the CEPT scheme, while the improved Preferential Trading Arrangements (PTA) scheme will continue to be applied as a complementary tool... .

The Ministers agreed that the establishment of AFTA with the application of CEPT on a sectoral basis within the definite time-frame would serve the interest of all member countries, accommodate the respective national conditions and requirements, lead to the emergence of the ASEAN region as a truly liberalized market, and maintain ASEAN's relevance in the world at large beyond the 1990's.[20]

The fourth ASEAN Summit, in Singapore in January 1992, put its stamp of approval on the ASEAN Free Trade Area as a separate initiative. Two of its three strongest proponents, Thailand's Anand and Singapore's Goh Chok Tong — the third being Malaysia's Mahathir Mohamad — laid down its rationale. Anand said in his statement at the summit:

> In the short run, it (AFTA) could result in initial losses of government revenue. Inefficient sectors would become vulnerable to competition. Industrial restructuring and readjustment could also lead to temporary unemployment in some countries. I am well aware that all of us are bound to be affected one way or the other. Nevertheless, the overall long-term benefits of AFTA will more than compensate for any short-term loss....
>
> Besides freer flow of trade, AFTA would lead to a larger ASEAN market of 360 million people which would surely be more attractive for investments, both from within and without, than six separate markets. With economy of scale, this would also lead to a rational allocation of resources and increased efficiency in production. ASEAN would be in much better position to attract investment as goods would be produced more economically and sold at a more competitive price.[21]

Goh Chok Tong pointed out:

> The flow of private investments is decided by hard-headed businessmen on the basis of expected returns on capital. They will locate their companies where they assess the companies to enjoy the greatest competitive advantage, i.e. where they can manufacture their products at the lowest cost, enjoy the largest domestic markets, and face the least uncertainty about access to overseas markets.... Unless ASEAN can match the other regions in attractiveness both as a base for investments as well as a market for their products, investments by multinational companies are likely to flow away from our part of the world to the SEM (Single European Market) and NAFTA (North American Free Trade Agreement). If we do not synergise our strengths, ASEAN will risk missing the boat. We will be stranded as we watch others sail by.[22]

On the occasion of the Singapore summit, the economic ministers signed the Agreement on the Common Effective Preferential Tariff (CEPT) Scheme for the ASEAN Free Trade Area (AFTA). The agreement, which went into effect upon signature, required the signatories to drop tariffs on intra-ASEAN trade, in specified stages, to 0–5 per cent by 2008, a deadline that was subsequently advanced twice. The staged reductions in tariffs were to be the subject of annual legislative enactments. For a product to qualify for CEPT treatment, it has to be of ASEAN origin to the extent of at least 40 per cent in content.[23]

I was sometimes asked: if AFTA is to be a true free trade area, why have tariffs at all, even if they are only at five per cent or less; why not abolish tariffs altogether? ASEAN countries had different reasons. Some did not want to lose entirely the revenue from duties on imports from other ASEAN countries. Others, like the Philippines, had minimum tariff levels in their laws to cover the administrative cost of processing imports. The International Monetary Fund has called such minimal levels "nuisance tariffs", revenues from which are less than the cost of administering them.

Not included in the scheme when it was adopted were unprocessed agricultural products; most of them were brought in less than three years later. There were the usual exclusions, mostly having to do with national security, public morals, the protection of human, animal and plant life, and articles of artistic, historic or archaeological value. In AFTA, the "sensitive" and highly sensitive" lists were transparent and relatively short. The parties could temporarily exclude certain products, which, however, had to be brought into the scheme after an agreed period. In contrast to the Preferential Trading Arrangements, which applied only to negotiated lists of specific products, the CEPT scheme covered all intra-ASEAN trade other than goods that were specifically excluded.

The CEPT agreement committed ASEAN member-states not only to drop tariffs to minimal levels; they had to do away with non-tariff barriers as well. Member-countries had to remove all quantitative restrictions on imports of a product immediately upon the application of CEPT concessions for that product; all other non-tariff barriers were to be phased out within five years of the enjoyment of such concessions.[24] Economic integration was no longer taboo as a concept. In fact, the Bangkok Summit Declaration of 1995 affirmed ASEAN's resolve to "move towards greater economic integration" and set an "Agenda for Greater Economic Integration".[25]

The economic ministers made several important decisions at their September 1994 meeting. First, they accelerated the AFTA timetable, advancing its completion from 2008 to 2003, or ten years, instead of the original fifteen years, after the start of the AFTA process. The ASEAN leaders formalized this decision at their summit in 1995 by signing a protocol to amend the 1992 Framework Agreement on Enhancing ASEAN Economic

Cooperation. For those items with rates already below 20 per cent, tariffs would go down to 0–5 per cent by the beginning of 2000. For products on the fast track, the target date for achieving the 0–5 per cent level would also be the beginning of 2000 in the case of items with tariffs above 20 per cent, but the beginning of 1998 in the case of those with tariffs at or below 20 per cent. The ministers decided to include all agricultural products, and not just processed ones, in the CEPT scheme, although some agricultural commodities were kept in the so-called "sensitive lists" of products not subject to the tariff reductions. The ministers agreed to remove the temporary exclusion lists by transferring items in them to the inclusion lists in five equal installments of 20 per cent each year, in effect doing away with the temporary lists by the beginning of 2000. They aligned the conditions for the ASEAN Industrial Joint Ventures with the CEPT requirements by raising the foreign-equity ceiling from 49 to 60 per cent and lowering the ASEAN content required in the rules of origin from 50 to 40 per cent.[26]

The negotiations leading to Vietnam's entry into ASEAN in 1995 were made difficult not by any political conditions but by the arguments over the commitments that Hanoi would have to undertake under the CEPT scheme for AFTA, including the time lag that it insisted upon. Finally, it was agreed that, like the original signatories, Vietnam would have ten years from the effective date of its accession within which to lower its tariffs on imports from other ASEAN countries to 0–5 per cent; that is, until 1 January 2006. The other three new members followed the same pattern: up to 2008 for Laos and Myanmar, which joined ASEAN in 1997, and until 2010 for Cambodia, which was admitted in 1999. When I asked Vietnamese and Cambodian authorities why they insisted on the time lag — if integrating into the regional economy would be good for the country, why delay it, I inquired — the responses indicated more than concern over the loss of revenue from customs duties; it was the uncertainty over the potential political, as well as economic, impact. In any case, trade ministries were normally more willing to liberalize intra-regional trade than the more-cautious finance ministries.

At their summit in Hanoi in December 1998, the ASEAN leaders responded to the 1997–98 financial crisis by taking several steps to lure back investments into ASEAN. Among those steps was to advance by yet another year, to the beginning of 2002, the deadline for the first six AFTA signatories to reduce tariffs on trade under CEPT/AFTA to the 0–5 per cent level. Ninety per cent of total tariff lines, accounting for 90 per cent of the value of intra-ASEAN trade, would be at 0–5 per cent by 2000, with each country having 85 per cent of its tariff lines at that level by 2000 and 90 per cent by 2001.[27] This logical step directly contradicted the speculative assumptions of many media commentators and academic analysts that ASEAN member-countries would retreat into their national shells because of the financial crisis, that AFTA had been derailed, that AFTA, in fact, was dead. Indeed, to ASEAN's credit, despite occasional delays in the legislation of tariff reductions, the ASEAN-6 largely succeeded in reaching AFTA's tariff-cutting goals on time, and the other four members have shown no sign that they would not do so.[28]

AFTA suffered something of a setback when Malaysia, seeking to keep its national car project afloat in the midst of reduced vehicle demand on account of the financial crisis, asked for a delay, until 2005, in the transfer of motor vehicles from the temporary exclusion list to the inclusion list. The request pertained to fully assembled or completely knocked down vehicles, but not to vehicle parts, as was often mistakenly reported. This was followed by a similar move by the Philippines on behalf of the petrochemical industry that it was planning to set up. Knowing that it had little choice, ASEAN decided to go along with Malaysia's petition, with great reluctance especially on the part of Thailand, the region's leading exporter of motor vehicles. So that Kuala Lumpur would not be in violation of its AFTA commitments, the economic ministers, after some heated debate, adopted in November 2000 a protocol allowing an AFTA signatory under certain conditions "to temporarily delay the transfer of a product from its TEL (Temporary Exclusion List) into the Inclusion List (IL), or to temporarily suspend its concession on a product already transferred into the IL, if such a transfer or concession would cause or have caused real problems".[29] This was practically lifted from Article XXVIII of the General Agreement on Tariffs and Trade, the WTO's predecessor. The Philippines subsequently invoked the protocol to seek a delay in the inclusion of some petrochemical products in the AFTA scheme, concluding in August 2003 an agreement with Singapore, the leading ASEAN exporter of petrochemical products, on "compensatory adjustment measures", as provided in the protocol.

In January 2003, the economic ministers agreed that tariffs would be completely abolished on trade among the first six signatories to the AFTA treaty by the beginning of 2010 and, for the four later signatories, by the beginning of 2015, with some exceptions. The duties on those exceptions were to be removed by the beginning of 2018. In November 2004, the target dates for removing tariffs were advanced to the beginning of 2007 and 2010 for the ASEAN-6 and the ASEAN-4, respectively, in the case of the priority sectors that the leaders had designated in Bali in 2003.

A successful ASEAN initiative has been the ASEAN Industrial Cooperation scheme, or AICO, which the ASEAN economic ministers agreed upon in 1996. In this scheme, products traded between companies undertaking related operations in different ASEAN countries were immediately entitled to preferential tariffs between zero and five per cent, that is, the CEPT end-rate. Specific arrangements, to be approved by the governments concerned and certified to by the ASEAN Secretariat, cover what products are to be involved and the exact tariff duty on each. Originally companies had to have at least 30 per cent "national equity" in order to qualify for the scheme. To keep AICO attractive, however, the 1998 ASEAN Summit waived this requirement until the end of 2000. The waiver has been extended yearly thereafter. AICO has superseded the ASEAN Industrial Joint Ventures and the Brand-to-Brand Complementation programmes. Unlike the earlier industrial programmes, in which the ASEAN states collectively decided on product coverage, AICO lets companies decide the products for which to seek the tariff concessions, subject to the approval only of the governments immediately concerned. Moreover, in the case of the earlier programmes, the concessions enjoyed by the products covered were margins of tariff preference, not necessarily low tariffs. Under those programmes, other ASEAN countries were barred from producing the same products as those approved for one participating country under the scheme, unless, in the case of the AIJV, 75 per cent of its production was destined for export outside ASEAN. On the other hand, AICO products enjoy the AFTA tariff end-rates, at present zero. Those products have no "exclusivity" privileges and remain subject to competition. Their AICO status is granted only by the countries involved rather than having to be approved by all of ASEAN.

By 2002–03, the 0–5 per cent tariff level for trade among the ASEAN-6 had been achieved. This rendered inoperative the edge that AICO participants enjoyed. To preserve that edge, and "to maintain the relevance of the AICO Scheme until 2010",[30] the year by which CEPT tariffs will have dropped to zero, the ministers, in April 2004, decided to remove tariffs altogether on all AICO-eligible products, although, as exceptions, the Philippines could charge up to one per cent, Thailand up to three per cent, and Myanmar and Vietnam up to five per cent. These countries had to "work towards reducing" tariffs on AICO imports to zero by the beginning of 2005, except for Vietnam, which had until 1 January 2006 to do so.[31]

As of April 2005, 195 applications for AICO arrangements had been submitted, 129 of which had been approved. The value of the transactions under these arrangements is estimated to total US$1.56 billion a year. Most of them are in the automotive or electronic sector, involving such well-known companies as Denso, Toyota, Honda, Volvo, Sony, Isuzu, Matsushita, Nissan, Ford, Mitsubishi, Yamaha, and Samsung. Only a handful of AICO companies are of apparently ASEAN provenance. Among the ASEAN countries, only Indonesia, Malaysia, the Philippines and Thailand have participated extensively in AICO. Singapore and Vietnam are each involved in three projects, two in electronics and one in automotive components.

A strong endorsement of ASEAN's market-integration initiatives came from a leading multinational corporation. As noted above, the Swiss food products conglomerate, Nestlé, went into the AIJV scheme in 1991. Nine years later, J.B. Santos, then Chairman and Chief Executive Officer of Nestlé Philippines, cited Nestlé's experience in hailing the advantages of ASEAN integration:

> Under the AIJV scheme, Nestlé put up a production plant with regional capacities in each of five ASEAN countries — Indonesia, Malaysia, Singapore, Thailand, and the Philippines. The idea was for each of them to become a production center for a particular product to be distributed within ASEAN and other Asian countries. Brunei, the sixth member of ASEAN, was an equity participant in the project.
>
> And so, Indonesia was tapped to produce soya-based beverages; Malaysia — bouillon, chocolate wafers, and chocolate dragees; Singapore — soya sauce powder; Thailand — non-dairy creamer; and Philippines — breakfast cereals. The products were selected so that the benefits would accrue not only to ASEAN as a whole but to each member country. The location of each of the plants, on the other hand, was determined according to demand patterns based on market knowledge.
>
> After almost ten years in place, I am happy to say that the Nestlé AIJV has successfully achieved the following:
> - Consumers have been provided with a wider choice for products at lower or affordable prices;
> - Substantial economies of scale, as the whole ASEAN region becomes the market place;
> - More competitive pricing within ASEAN compared with those products imported from outside the region;
> - Long-term capital inflow and large savings in foreign exchange for both the host and participating countries;
> - Greater use of local raw materials;
> - Systematic transfer of technology, adding value to products made from indigenous raw materials; and
> - Development of small and medium enterprises....
>
> While it has been rewarding to our company, no doubt our AIJV programme has also stimulated and contributed to the dynamism of the ASEAN region's economy and each of the participating countries. In its own modest way, our AIJV project catalyzed the liberalization of trade practices

within ASEAN. This led to the eventual dismantling of tariff barriers in the region, contributing to the emergence of the borderless economy that is beginning to characterize business in the region....

Encouraged by the success of our AIJV, Nestlé has taken a keen interest in the ASEAN Industrial Cooperation Scheme, or AICO, a new programme to promote industrial complementation in the region through sharing of resources and technology.[32]

Nestlé is now an active participant in the AICO programme.

The AFTA agreement provided not only for the reduction and eventual abolition of tariffs but also for the dismantling of all quantitative restrictions and other non-tariff barriers. Non-tariff barriers to intra-ASEAN imports of a particular product were supposed to have been removed within five years of the enjoyment of tariff concessions on that product. In fact, an agreement signed by the economic ministers on the occasion of the 1987 ASEAN Summit had called for the "standstill and rollback" of non-tariff barriers to intra-ASEAN trade, but nothing effective was done about it. The 1995 summit directed that all quantitative restrictions be removed and that the elimination of non-tariff barriers be scheduled beginning on 1 January 1996. In his 2000 speech, Santos, the Nestlé Philippines CEO, pleaded, "Let us lobby for the removal of all forms of non-tariff barriers in trade. All countries in the ASEAN region must exercise their political will and decisively dismantle these NTBs, since these can negate whatever progress we have made in tariff deregulation." Eleven years after the 1995 directive, fourteen years after the AFTA agreement, and nineteen years after the 1987 decision, the collective process of dismantling non-tariff barriers has not even begun. ASEAN expects shortly to agree on the criteria for defining what NTBs are and has set up a database on them. How soon they will dismantle them, whether unilaterally or by negotiation, is another question.

The ASEAN Secretariat has encouraged traders to file complaints about non-tariff barriers obstructing trade between ASEAN countries. The traders have declined to do so, apparently for fear of the retribution that the authorities complained about may visit upon their future shipments.

I took part in a workshop on Vietnam's participation in the ASEAN Free Trade Area in Ho Chi Minh City in August 2005. At that workshop, Le Phung Hao, vice-director of Kinh Do Company, acknowledged that exports of its food products to other ASEAN countries enjoyed tariff preferences, as did imports of ingredients from ASEAN. However, he complained about a variety of non-tariff barriers that faced its exports, declaring that such barriers should at least be transparent. At a similar workshop in Hanoi two days earlier, Do Quang Hien, General Director of T&T Company, which produces motorcycles, refrigerators and electronic goods, recalled that his company had welcomed the prospective reduction in tariffs on its exports to other ASEAN countries and on its imports from those countries. However, he pointed to the lack of consistency in the treatment by customs authorities of the Form D certificates of origin. Who was authorized to issue the forms was uncertain, he said. Moreover, it often took as long as fifteen days for the form to be issued. Hien found information on the status of tariffs difficult to obtain. Emphasizing the inter-related nature of the measures necessary for the free flow of trade, he cited the complicated payments arrangements with some ASEAN countries and the high cost of transport and telecommunications.

SERVICES

Freeing trade in goods is, of course, not enough to integrate a regional economy. Trade in services has to be freed, too, services like transportation, communications, financial services, the professions, construction, and tourism. This becomes more and more important in ASEAN, as services take a larger share of the member-countries' economies. According to the ASEAN Secretariat, a "typical ASEAN country would generate about 40–50 per cent of its GDP from services", up to about 45 per cent for the Philippines, 50 per cent for Malaysia and as high as 70 per cent for Singapore. ASEAN's total exports of commercial services surged from US$31.8 billion in 1991 to US$87.2 billion in 1997, dipping afterwards, probably on account of the financial crisis. ASEAN's imports of commercial services were of about the same magnitudes.[33] I remember the then trade commissioner of the European Union, Pascal Lamy, telling me that, if he had European economic integration to do all over again, he would start not with a customs union but with "open skies". This is because the free flow of services, like transportation and communications, is vital to easing the flow of goods within a region and to integrating the regional economy in general.

Recognizing this, ASEAN concluded the ASEAN Framework Agreement on Services on the occasion of the ASEAN Summit in December 1995, only three years after the entry into operation of the Common Effective Preferential Tariff Scheme for the ASEAN Free Trade Area, which covers trade in goods. In the agreement on services, the ASEAN members committed themselves to eliminating discriminatory measures, market-access limitations and other restrictions on trade in services among them with a view to improving the efficiency and competitiveness of ASEAN suppliers of services.[34] The catch is that the agreement is not self-executing. Negotiations have to be conducted sector by sector. In their summit declaration, the leaders ordered that the first round of those negotiations begin on 1 January 1996 and conclude by 31 December 1998, with emphasis on financial services, maritime transport, telecommunications, air transport, tourism, construction and business services. Since then, three rounds of negotiations have taken place, producing four "packages" of "commitments". A fourth round was launched in September 2004, and a fifth package has been targeted for completion by August 2006. However, the economic ministers have left financial services to the finance ministries, which have devised a "road map" for liberalizing them, and air services are to remain subject to bilateral negotiations.

Negotiated in the WTO mode of "request and offer", most of the commitments made in the four "packages" are already in the books of the member-states. The commitments that are better than those offered in the General Agreement on Trade in Services negotiations in the WTO are only marginally so. At the same time, it seems to me that, in the ASEAN process, most of the negotiators on services trade behave as if they were bargaining at the WTO or bilaterally with developed countries, holding out for concessions from the other side, using their restrictions as bargaining chips, instead of using the liberalization of trade in services as measures for regional economic integration and for developing a free regional trading regime. Even unilateral steps to liberalize trade in some services would serve not only regional economic integration but the national economy as well. For example, the liberalization of transportation services would help trade and tourism immensely. The improvement of communications facilities through regional competition would facilitate trade and investments. So would the liberalization of business services. The entry of foreign IT service providers would bring in capital and technology. Such steps, even if taken purely as a matter of national policy, would reap benefits for the economy regardless of what neighbours did to liberalize their own services. Minister of Commerce Cham Prasidh declared to me that for a country like Cambodia restrictions on services made no sense, since the country lacked the people to provide the services that the economy and society needed, giving engineers as an example.[35]

I asked Cheah Sin Liang, an official at Singapore's Ministry of Trade and Industry, why it was necessary for ASEAN to negotiate the liberalization of trade in services when this was already being done in the WTO and when each member-state could always liberalize its services sectors unilaterally if it deemed that to be in its national interest. Cheah explained to me the advantages of negotiating services trade on a regional basis. Services are an increasingly important part of the national economies of ASEAN, and integrating the services sector is an essential component of regional

Ministers sign the Bangkok Declaration establishing ASEAN, 8 August 1967; from left, Narciso Ramos of the Philippines, Adam Malik of Indonesia, Thanat Khoman of Thailand, Tun Abdul Razak of Malaysia, and S. Rajaratnam of Singapore. — *Photo courtesy of the ASEAN Secretariat.*

Prime Minister Tun Abdul Razak of Malaysia, Adam Malik of Indonesia (back turned to the camera), Thanat Khoman of Thailand, S. Rajaratnam of Singapore and Carlos P. Romulo of the Philippines confer during an informal ASEAN Foreign Ministers meeting, November 1971. *Photo courtesy of the ASEAN Secretariat*

The headquarters of ASEAN in Jakarta was inaugurated on 9 May 1981. — *Photo courtesy of the ASEAN Secretariat.*

From left, Foreign Minister Surakiart Sathirathai of Thailand, Secretary of State Colin Powell of the United States, a Vietnamese official, ASEAN Secretary-General Rodolfo Severino, Prince Mohamed Bolkiah of Brunei Darussalam, and Foreign Minister Alexander Downer of Australia, together with other foreign ministers of ASEAN and its Dialogue Partners, await questions from the media at the close of the ASEAN Post-Ministerial Conferences in Bandar Seri Begawan on 1 August 2002. — *Photo courtesy of the ASEAN Secretariat.*

Participants in an ASEAN Regional Forum workshop on maritime security gather on board Singapore's RSS Endurance, 3 March 2005. — *Photo courtesy of the ASEAN Secretariat.*

ASEAN Secretary-General Rodolfo Severino is about to hand the flag of Cambodia to the honour guard at the ceremony for the admission of Cambodia into ASEAN, Hanoi, 30 April 1999. Present were all the ASEAN Foreign Ministers: from left, Nguyen Manh Cam of Vietnam, Surin Pitsuwan of Thailand, S. Jayakumar of Singapore, Domingo Siazon of the Philippines, U Win Aung of Myanmar (hidden) Syed Hamid Albar of Malaysia (hidden), Somsavat Lengsavad of the Lao People's Democratic Republic, Ali Alatas of Indonesia, and Hor Namhong of Cambodia. Not seen is Prince Mohamed Bolkiah of Brunei Darussalam. — *Photo courtesy of the ASEAN Secretariat.*

President Fidel V. Ramos of the Philippines presents ASEAN Secretary-General Rodolfo Severino with books for the ASEAN Secretariat library. Looking on are former Indonesian Ambassador to the Philippines Peter Damanik, left, and Indonesian Foreign Minister Ali Alatas. — *Photo courtesy of the ASEAN Secretariat.*

Prime Minister Thaksin Shinawatra of Thailand visits the ASEAN Secretariat, January 2002. — *Photo courtesy of the ASEAN Secretariat.*

economic integration. Even if liberalization measures are already in the books of a member-state, locking them into regional commitments makes it harder for the member-state to repeal those measures. ASEAN-wide understandings set regional goals for services liberalization and define the steps and stages for reaching those goals. The negotiations on services are a useful venue for discussing the benefits of services liberalization, supporting the forces of liberalization within a country against domestic protectionist opposition, and preparing the negotiators for the rigors of global negotiations and those on bilateral free trade agreements, which invariably cover trade in services as well as goods.[36]

The trouble is that substantive progress is quite slow. The ASEAN Economic Ministers, at their September 2005 meeting, declared 2015 as "the end-date for the liberalization of all services sectors", although it is unclear what precisely is to be achieved by that year.[37] Many negotiators are extremely cautious either because of their uncertainty about the impact of liberalization or because of the power of domestic interests that benefit from protection even at the expense of the economy and the population in general. There is also the fear of the loss of regulatory control in some services sectors. Still, Cheah believes that the adoption of the ASEAN Economic Community, with its "road maps" for four "priority" services sectors — air services, tourism, e-ASEAN and health care — will hasten the process. So will, he says, the pressures arising from the negotiations on free trade agreements with Dialogue Partners, processes that include important provisions on trade in services as well as goods.

In December 2005, the ASEAN Economic Ministers signed an agreement on mutual recognition arrangements that would allow an "ASEAN Chartered Professional Engineer" to seek registration in an ASEAN country and work as an engineer "in collaboration with designated Professional Engineers in the Host Country".[38] The ministers had hoped to sign a similar agreement on nursing services, but the work on it was apparently not completed on time.

CUSTOMS

Bad and ineffective customs administration raises business costs, tilts the competitive playing field, and distorts the effects of economic policy. Murky and complicated formulations of customs regulations and their arbitrary application act as substantial barriers to trade and serve as protectionist measures or sources of rent for customs officials and their patrons or both. More to the point in ASEAN, preferential intra-regional trade will not work if the customs authorities in the member-countries are inefficient, their procedures uncoordinated, or their officials corrupt. It will not work if ASEAN customs authorities apply different designations, in terms of tariff nomenclatures, to the same products, and if they have different systems of valuation.

As early as 1983, the customs authorities of the then-five ASEAN members adopted a "code of conduct". The code was revised and expanded in 1995 to take AFTA into account. The ASEAN Agreement on Customs, signed by the finance ministers at their first meeting in March 1997, in effect formalized the code. These documents sought to establish a common system for the valuation of traded goods for customs purposes and one for customs classifications and tariff nomenclatures. They aimed to simplify and harmonize customs procedures. They provided for the right of "affected persons" to appeal decisions by customs authorities. They called for regional cooperation in preventing smuggling and fraud. Their watchwords were transparency, consistency, simplicity, efficiency, cooperation, and the right of appeal.

To carry out these aims, the ASEAN countries decided to adopt the GATT/WTO customs valuation agreement. They agreed on the post-clearance audit system under which cargo would be immediately cleared by customs and audits performed afterwards. They resolved to set up the Green Lane system at customs, through which goods receiving CEPT treatment (expanded in 1998 to cover all imports from ASEAN) are cleared quickly, and the Single Window scheme that would do away with the need for importers to shuttle from office to office seeking approvals for their shipments. Not least, they put together the ASEAN Harmonized Tariff Nomenclatures system, so that all ASEAN countries would classify and designate, for customs purposes, all goods in the same way.

At their meeting in August 2003, the ASEAN finance ministers signed the protocol officially adopting the AHTN scheme. It has been applied since April 2004. Disputes over the application of the system are resolved by a technical committee whose decisions are binding. One advantage is that, in negotiating free trade agreements with such countries as China, India and Australia and New Zealand, ASEAN can now work out of only one set of tariff nomenclatures, making the negotiations easier in that respect. Also in 2003, the ASEAN Customs Valuation Guide and the ASEAN Post-Clearance Audit Manual were completed. These are meant to ensure the consistency of the ASEAN countries' application of these systems. The Green Lane set-up is reported to be in place in almost all member-countries. A common ASEAN customs declaration document is supposed to be ready for use in 2006. In December 2005, the ASEAN Economic Ministers signed an agreement establishing the ASEAN Single Window, which commits all ASEAN countries to set up their National Single Windows by 2008 in the case of the ASEAN-6 and by 2012 in the case of the newer four ASEAN members. Under the Single Window system, there would be only one point where customs data and information are submitted and processed and customs decisions are made. ASEAN bodies, with the support of the Secretariat, are to oversee the operation of the system.[39]

Meanwhile, however, according to the 2003 ASEAN Competitiveness Study, an "executive at a consumer goods company" had told McKinsey & Company that "ASEAN's tariff rates were determined more by the whim of customs officials than by government policy" and a "representative of an electronics company" had noted that "identical parts can take from one day to more than five weeks to clear customs" in ASEAN.[40]

Nevertheless, with the measures taken since then, even officials in Singapore, the ASEAN country with the highest standards of customs administration, have an optimistic outlook. While it may have taken a long time for the cooperative framework to be put in place, they say, now that it is in place, customs reform and cooperation in ASEAN should be gathering momentum. Customs authorities acknowledge their leaders' commitment, expressed in the Vientiane Action Programme and in other ways, to efficiency and coordination in customs procedures in ASEAN. Pressures for reform also come from other points — the forces of globalization, the standards of multinational corporations, and the process of negotiating free trade agreements with ASEAN Dialogue Partners, in which customs matters are invariably an important component.

Tran Dong Phuong, director-general of the Multilateral Trade Policy Department of Vietnam's Ministry of Trade, declared to me his satisfaction with Hanoi's adoption of the ASEAN Harmonized Tariff Nomenclatures scheme and the application of the WTO customs valuation system. He affirmed that the operation of the Single Window agreed upon in ASEAN was "active" in his country. He acknowledged, however, that the decentralized structure of customs administration in Vietnam was vulnerable to the uneven application of the rules.[41]

Indeed, in some respects, the process of customs reform and coordination in ASEAN cannot be hurried. The electronic handling of customs transactions varies from country to country. It takes time to train customs officials in such processes as post-clearance audit and customs valuation and, in some cases, to bring about "culture change" in customs agencies. On the other hand, the competition does not stand still. Moreover, business people and even some government ministers have complained about customs authorities in neighbouring countries deliberately putting up obstacles in the way of the preferential treatment of ASEAN products or circumventing their countries' obligations under the AFTA agreement.

PRODUCT STANDARDS

A regional economy cannot be truly integrated if the same products are subject to different standards in the component national economies. The McKinsey study gave a well-noted example — the difference between the actual weight of a 100-gram bar of soap in Indonesia and that of a 100-gram bar of soap in Thailand. The difference arose from the fact that the weight of one bar in Indonesia was measured at the factory and in Thailand on the grocery shelf. Thailand has corrected this anomaly since then. Another example given by McKinsey was the different product standards for ice cream.[42] As a result, a factory in one ASEAN country cannot produce soap or ice cream for distribution in the entire region, and thus benefit from economies of scale, since the product standards differ among ASEAN countries. Numerous other examples could be cited. The consequent cost can be enormous.

To address this problem, ASEAN in 1997 designated twenty priority products for standards harmonization. They are air conditioners, refrigerators, motors and generators, telephones, radios, television sets, loudspeakers, a number of electronic components, condoms, and medical rubber gloves. ASEAN completed the harmonization of standards for these products in 2003. Pursuant to a 1999 decision, safety standards were aligned for seventy-one electrical appliances for commercial and household use and electromagnetic compatibility standards for ten categories of scientific and other equipment. The standardization was completed in July 2004. These endeavours have all been based on international standards. Still, standards for many other products remain to be harmonized.

An aspect of product standardization is the mutual recognition of product tests; that is, a product tested in one ASEAN country need not be tested in another in order for that product to be sold in the other country. In 1998, ASEAN adopted a "framework agreement" on mutual recognition arrangements.[43] MRAs are aimed at removing an important impediment to trade through the parties' acceptance or recognition of one another's "conformity assessments", like product tests, of certain traded products. Such arrangements would cut down delays and costs by doing away with the costly repetition of product tests or other forms of assessment of a product's compliance with requirements and standards. In 2002, ASEAN reached agreement on the mutual recognition of product tests and certification for electrical and electronic equipment,[44] and in 2003 on the harmonization of regulations and the mutual recognition of registration approvals for cosmetics.⁴⁵ Similar work on pharmaceuticals is going on. In December 2005, the ASEAN Economic Ministers signed the Agreement on Harmonized Regulatory Regime for Electrical and Electronic Equipment, which provides for adherence to standards with respect to such equipment in terms of human health and safety, damage to property, the environment, and electromagnetic disturbances. It calls for the harmonization of conformity assessment procedures and the exchange of information on relevant new laws and technical regulations, as well as the mutual acceptance of test reports and certifications. This would facilitate intra-ASEAN trade in electrical and electronic equipment.⁴⁶ In all, however, progress on the harmonization of product standards has been excruciatingly slow.

TRANSPORT

Transportation is, of course, the indispensable lifeline of trade, and ASEAN has taken steps to make it easier to move goods physically across national boundaries within the region. To link up their physical infrastructure, the ASEAN transport ministers in 1999 formalized their programme of developing the ASEAN Highway Network. They approved its route configuration, with each country agreeing to upgrade to the specified standards the sections running through its territory. They decided to work together in formulating the development plan for the network, which has twenty-three designated routes covering 38,400 kilometres.

ASEAN has also adopted the concept of the Singapore-Kunming Rail Link within the context of the ASEAN Mekong Basin Development Cooperation programme, which includes China. Malaysia's Prime Minister Mahathir Mohamad proposed the concept at the 1995 ASEAN Summit. Malaysia later put up two million Malaysian ringgit to finance the feasibility study, which was completed in 2000. The route subsequently approved would cover 5,382 kilometres, entailing the construction of 431 kilometres of "missing links", the most notable being the 48-kilometre Sisophon-Poipet segment on the Cambodian side of the Cambodia-Thailand border and the sector from Phnom Penh to the Vietnamese border, and 585 kilometres of spur lines into Myanmar and Laos. It would also require the rehabilitation of existing railways. Malaysia has offered to support the Sisophon-Poipet link. In 2002, Myanmar's Deputy Minister for Rail Transportation, Thura U Thaung Lwin, cited a 1997 estimate of US$2.5 billion as the total cost of the SKRL. Aside from helping trade on the Southeast Asian mainland, the rail link will ease the access of the region and China to each other.

It is, of course, not enough to have the physical transport infrastructure in place. Administrative, regulatory and political obstructions have to be removed if goods are to move freely through what is supposed to be a free trade area. For a start, in addition to recognizing one another's driving licences under a 1985 agreement, the ASEAN countries in 1998 agreed that inspection certificates issued by one country for commercial vehicles would be valid in the other countries and in November 2005 signed an agreement on multimodal transport. However, the liberalization of transport services among ASEAN countries has been quite slow. ASEAN has been unable to arrive at an agreement on inter-state transport. Air services remain subject to bilateral agreements.

In 1998, ASEAN managed to conclude a "framework agreement" for the facilitation of transit passage of goods traded in the region. This agreement committed the parties to ensure that goods being transported from one ASEAN country to another through a third would not be subjected to unnecessary delays, restrictions, taxation, or customs inspections in the transit country. The agreement was to be carried out through nine implementing protocols pertaining to:

1. designated transit transport routes;
2. designated frontier posts;
3. types and quantity of road vehicles to be used for transit transport;
4. vehicle dimensions, maximum weights and loads, emission standards, and other specifications;
5. third-party liability insurance;
6. railway border and interchange stations, and types and quality of rolling stock;
7. customs transit system;
8. sanitary and phytosanitary measures; and
9. dangerous goods.[47]

Five of the protocols have been signed. The whole package is stalled, however. Protocols 1, 2, 6 and 7 have not been concluded largely because of the dispute between Malaysia and Singapore over the continued location of the Malaysian customs, immigration and quarantine facilities at the Malaysian railroad's Singapore terminal in Tanjong Pagar, well across the city-state from the common border. A legacy of British colonialism and of the 1965 break-up between Malaysia and Singapore, the problem has festered for many years. Unless this issue is resolved, transit transport routes, frontier posts, railway border stations, and customs transit points, the subjects of the four protocols, cannot be designated at the place where it is most critical — the Malaysia-Singapore border. This point is critical because the largest transit trade in ASEAN is by far between Thailand and Singapore through Malaysia. This is why Thailand was the moving force behind the goods-in-transit agreement. It is one more example of how political disputes get in the way of regional integration measures.

I am told that a way to conclude Protocol 1 may have been found. Taking a page from the ASEAN Agreement on Transboundary Haze Pollution,[48] ASEAN transport authorities have proposed that the protocol would enter into force upon its ratification by six member-countries rather than by all. Bilateral agreements designating transit transport routes, as called for by Protocol 1, could be submitted at the time the instruments of ratification are deposited. Protocols 2 and 7 can be concluded once Protocol 1 is agreed upon. Protocol 6 applies only to railway traffic and thus is not essential for the operation of the goods-in-transit agreement. In this way, even if Malaysia and Singapore remained deadlocked on their dispute, Protocol 1 could go into effect, as could the goods-in-transit agreement itself, upon the protocol's ratification by at least six of the rest. The agreement could operate on Borneo, facilitating trade among Brunei Darussalam, East Malaysia and the Kalimantan provinces of Indonesia, and in the rest of mainland Southeast Asia, hypothetically easing trade between Thailand and Vietnam through Laos. However, since the bulk of the trade involved is between Thailand and Singapore through Malaysia, the operationalization of the agreement would not have much meaning without Malaysia and Singapore being full parties to it. Even if Protocol 1 were to be signed and ratified by six of the parties, neither the protocol nor the agreement itself would be substantially operational unless Malaysia and Singapore came to agreement on the transit routes.

It is important for market integration to free up the flow of transportation within the region, so as to lower the cost of doing trade. However, in addition to the legal obstructions to cross-border transportation, a number of business people have complained about the high cost of land transportation in some ASEAN countries, either on account of extortions by law-enforcement authorities on the highways or arising from the cartelization of land transport companies in those countries.

In 2002, the ASEAN countries agreed to allow one another to deliver air-cargo services to their respective territories involving up to 100 tons a week, not a big amount but a good beginning. However, some countries blunted the agreement's effect by restricting the operation of cargo services from other ASEAN countries. Indonesia omitted its largest transport centres — Jakarta,

Surabaya and Medan — from the list of cities where the agreement would apply. Kuala Lumpur's list did not have Penang or any airport in East Malaysia. Vietnam did not include Ho Chi Minh City, the country's largest.[49] This is an example of how ASEAN states undermine the effectiveness of nice agreements that they sign with much fanfare.

The opening up of air passenger services fares even worse. The Hanoi Plan of Action, which the leaders adopted in 1998, called for the institution of "the policy framework and modalities by the year 2000 for the development of a Competitive Air Services Policy which may be a gradual step towards an Open Sky Policy in ASEAN". Despite the extremely cautious, as well as unwieldy, formulation of this item, there was until the 2004 Vientiane summit no sign of work having begun on the "framework and modalities" for the development of a competitive air services regime other than the 2002 air-cargo agreement, which itself was highly restricted in the case of some countries. The "road map" for the integration of air travel attached to the ASEAN Framework Agreement for the Integration of Priority Sectors prescribes a series of steps, with target years, toward the "full liberalization" of ASEAN airfreight services and the "ASEAN-wide liberalization" of scheduled passenger services. These goals are to be reached at the end of 2008 for cargo and the end of 2010 for passenger services. In the meantime, without ASEAN adopting a liberal region-wide air services regime, the growing activity of budget airlines in Asia is punching widening holes in the walls of protection that have shielded so many national air carriers for so long. Unless held back, the penetration by ASEAN's budget airlines of one another's airports could be a significant step towards a regime of open skies over ASEAN.

TOURISM

An open regime for passenger air services is vital for tourism. It is no coincidence that the countries with the most liberal air services policies also enjoy the greatest benefits from tourism. For most ASEAN countries, tourism is a hugely important component of the economy. It brings in foreign exchange almost instantly, is highly labour-intensive, and spreads its benefits to many parts of the country and to many economic sectors. Beyond economics, if the nation and its leaders are wise, tourism can be an incentive for the protection of the environment and the preservation of the historical and cultural heritage. Tourism, especially intra-ASEAN travel, is a powerful catalyst for mutual understanding and for popular support for international and regional cooperation.

Integrating the Regional Economy

Visitor arrivals in the ASEAN countries hit a record high of 44 million in 2002, plunged the next year, evidently because of the SARS scare, and soared back to the 44-million mark in 2004, exceeding it in 2005.[50] Yet, the scope for much greater increases remains immense, especially in the light of the wide divergences in tourist arrivals among ASEAN countries and the rise of nearby China as a source of visitors.

ASEAN has long recognized the value of regional cooperation in the promotion of tourism. Since 1981, the annual ASEAN Tourism Forum has steadily grown to what it is today — the largest and most successful tourism fair in all of Asia and one of the biggest in the world. Here hundreds of sellers of tourism services from ASEAN and buyers from all over the world exchange notes, update one another and make deals. The 2005 ASEAN Tourism Forum in Langkawi, Malaysia, drew more than 400 buyers and about 940 sellers, with 510 tourism booths set up and 131 media agencies in attendance.[51] Some of these numbers went down slightly at the ATF in Davao, the Philippines, in January 2006, with 369 buyers, 815 sellers, 412 tourism booths, and 171 media agencies.[52] The ATF is one of the most vivid demonstrations of the efficacy of ASEAN cooperation in the common interest; ten separate tourism fairs in Southeast Asia would never work. The ASEAN countries cooperate in other joint promotion campaigns; for example, placing on international television spots advertising ASEAN as a single destination. They have agreed on common competency standards for tourism services.

In order to harness regional cooperation in easing and stimulating the flow of visitors into and within ASEAN, the heads of government themselves signed the ASEAN Tourism Agreement at their summit in Phnom Penh in November 2002. Cambodia spearheaded the work on it not only because the government saw the agreement as a good outcome of the event that it was hosting. Cambodia deeply appreciated the value of tourism. It has the matchless attraction that is Angkor. It had seen how the economic surge of its neighbour, Thailand, was launched in large measure by Bangkok's single-minded attention to tourism. As an example of how the liberalization of air services can be such a boon for a country's tourist trade, I often cite Cambodia's opening its skies, particularly at Siem Reap, to boost tourism, even at the cost of killing the national airline, Royal Air Cambodge. Visitor arrivals in Cambodia rose from 700,000 in 2003 to more than one million in 2004, a rate of increase second in ASEAN only to Malaysia's.

Cambodia's Prime Minister Hun Sen, as well as then Minister of Tourism Veng Sereyvudh, took a personal interest in the tourism agreement. As signed by the ASEAN leaders at their 2002 summit in Phnom Penh, the agreement calls for the abolition of visa requirements and travel taxes for ASEAN nationals travelling within ASEAN. It expresses the intention to harmonize procedures for the issuance of visas to international travellers into ASEAN. It provides for the progressive liberalization of air services and, pursuant to the ASEAN Framework Agreement on Services, of trade in tourism services. The agreement calls for "non-restrictive arrangements to enable ASEAN Member States to make use of professional tourism experts and skilled workers available within the region on the basis of bilateral arrangements". It pledges the parties to protect the environment, preserve the natural, cultural and historical heritage, and take "stern measures" against the tourism-related exploitation of women and children. It urges cooperation and information sharing among law-enforcement agencies for the protection of visitors. The agreement promises to intensify joint promotion and marketing of ASEAN as a tourist destination.[53]

Although the heads of government themselves signed the tourism agreement, it is not self-executing; its various elements have to be given effect by specific agreements or protocols, and most of the subjects are outside the authority of the tourism ministers. In fact, none of the implementing agreements and protocols has been concluded or even negotiated, although as few as two of the parties could enter into them. Without them, the tourism agreement is a mere wish list, a statement of intention by the tourism ministers, who have little formal say in such areas as visas (foreign or home affairs), air services (transport, foreign affairs), employment (manpower, home affairs), and law enforcement (home affairs).

In reality, most ASEAN countries already have visa-free arrangements among themselves, or issue visas on arrival to ASEAN nationals. The outstanding exception is Myanmar. It would at this stage be difficult for ASEAN countries to harmonize their visa requirements for international visitors, as those requirements are widely divergent for security and political reasons. Both the Philippines and Indonesia impose charges on international travel by their nationals, but, among the ASEAN-6, it is only the Philippines that has a real exit tax, since the Indonesian levy is a form of advance payment of the traveler's income tax. The Philippine imposition has long been a sore point in ASEAN tourism circles, but lifting it does not seem to be in prospect. The tourism agreement provides that the employment by ASEAN countries of tourism professionals and skilled workers from other countries would be subject to bilateral arrangements, thus adding nothing to the present situation. It may be of some comfort to the tourism sector to know that it is in tourism services where the negotiations on the liberalization of trade in services appear to have made the most progress.

However, tourism services could just as well be left to countries' unilateral policy decisions rather than be the subject of bargaining.

The Vientiane Action Programme would have been a good opportunity to put flesh on the tourism agreement and push its implementation. The VAP does specify several areas for ASEAN tourism cooperation, with early deadlines, but these are mostly in the form of exhortations, beginning with words like "encourage", "work towards", "facilitate", and "strengthen support for". It calls, in very general terms, for the elimination of "the limitations on market access and national treatment to achieve free flow of trade in tourism sector", but sets a distant deadline of 2010. Absent are most of the other substantive measures provided for in the tourism agreement. Indeed, the VAP does not even mention that agreement at all. On the liberalization of air passenger services, transport officials are said to be working on specific measures and timelines, but full ASEAN-wide liberalization is put off to the end of 2010. Meanwhile, what is to stop an ASEAN country from liberalizing air services, normally a matter of national policy or bilateral negotiations, if it feels that to do so would serve its tourism and other economic interests? It need not wait for all of ASEAN to act.

LABOUR

Other than some general references, ASEAN has not addressed regional economic integration in terms of that important factor of production, labour. Labour, of course, is more than just a factor of production; it involves human beings and, therefore, human dignity and welfare, social implications, cultural sensitivities and political complications. Because of the shortage of labour in Malaysia, hundreds of thousands of Indonesians and Filipinos work there. Similar numbers of Myanmars find employment in Thailand. Yet, no bilateral, much less ASEAN-wide, agreement regulates the flow of ASEAN workers and the terms of their employment other than the one between Malaysia and Vietnam. Workers from other ASEAN countries who are legally employed are treated like any other foreign workers. Those who enter Malaysia or Thailand illegally can be deported or simply pushed across the border at anytime depending on market demand or political exigencies. It cannot be said that a regional market is truly integrated unless, like goods, services and capital, labour moves freely within the region. However, in ASEAN, the political, social, cultural and even religious elements are so sensitive, and the disparities in the labour supply-and-demand situation among the ASEAN countries so great, that the region is highly unlikely to see the free movement of people anytime soon. In the case of the smaller market for professional services, ASEAN has considered proposals for the mutual recognition of professional credentials, but little has actually been done about it, except for the recently signed agreement pertaining to engineers.

INVESTMENTS

As for investments and the free flow of capital within the region, the economic ministers signed in December 1987 an ASEAN agreement on the promotion and protection of investments, which was updated and improved somewhat with a protocol in 1996.[54] In 1998, ASEAN concluded an agreement on the ASEAN Investment Area, under which each ASEAN country would extend national treatment to investors and investments from other member-countries in sectors and industries other than those in the general exception list, the sensitive list or the temporary exclusion list that each country would draw up within six months.[55] However, it was not until 2000 that the lists were published. By 2010, the temporary exclusion lists would have been phased out, except for Vietnam, which would have until 2013, and Laos and Myanmar, which were given until 2015. In addition, an ASEAN country was to grant to all other member-countries, on a most-favoured-nation basis, the investment privileges that it would accord to other parties under agreements that it would conclude in the future. This is significant for the bilateral free-trade agreements that some ASEAN countries have concluded or are negotiating with non-ASEAN countries, agreements that often have a prominent investment component. A 2001 protocol amending the AIA agreement made explicit the coverage of AIA: manufacturing, agriculture, fisheries, forestry and mining, and services "incidental" to those sectors.[56] Pursuant to the protocol, Brunei Darussalam, Indonesia, Myanmar, the Philippines, and Thailand abolished their temporary exclusion lists for the manufacturing sector in January 2003; Malaysia and Singapore had no such lists to begin with. According to the protocol, Cambodia, Laos and Vietnam have until the beginning of 2010 to do so. The temporary exclusion and sensitive lists for services were submitted in 2002.

Originally, non-ASEAN investors would be extended national treatment by 2020. However, in 2001, ASEAN advanced the date for the "full realization of the AIA" to 2010 for the first six ASEAN members and to 2015 for the later four.[57] As others have pointed out, it makes little sense for ASEAN to make a distinction between ASEAN and non-ASEAN investors, with a head start for investors from ASEAN as far as national treatment is concerned; after all, the bulk of foreign direct investments comes from outside ASEAN.

However, the ASEAN Investment Area is about more than national treatment. It is also about improving the investment climate in general. Thus, the AIA agreement calls for the reduction or elimination of "regulations and conditions which may impede investment flows and the operation of investment projects". One of the obligations of the parties is "to ensure transparency and consistency in the application and interpretation of their investment laws, regulations and administrative procedures in order to create and maintain a predictable investment regime". To this end, they are to exchange "individual action plans" detailing how they intend to facilitate, promote and liberalize the flow of investments into their countries and into the region.[58] The first such exchange took place in 2000, with the ASEAN Secretariat publishing the compilation of plans.[59] This exercise and the regular meetings of ministers and officials with responsibility for investments help the ASEAN governments, through peer pressure and mutual encouragement, to develop a policy environment that is increasingly friendly to investments. At the same time, an important part of a more friendly investment environment is an integrated regional market.

STUMBLING ON THE ROAD TO INTEGRATION

ASEAN has made some progress on the road to regional economic integration. The tariff-cutting enterprise is largely on schedule. The delay in the transfer of vehicles, completely knocked down or fully assembled, to Malaysia's CEPT inclusion list is, except in an important symbolic and psychological sense, a minor setback. In any case, vehicles are now on Malaysia's inclusion list. Tariffs on them have been considerably reduced and are coming down according to schedule until they hit the 0–5 per cent level by 2008. Despite the low utilization of the CEPT preferences, AFTA is regarded in some international business circles as a touchstone for regional integration. AICO is a success in terms of its use by companies with multinational operations. The ASEAN Harmonized Tariff Nomenclatures scheme has been adopted. The Green Lane system at customs has been installed. A Single Window system for customs has received region-wide agreement. Standards for the twenty priority products have been harmonized; so have safety standards for seventy-one types of electrical appliances and ten electromagnetic compatibility standards. Some practical arrangements to facilitate cross-border land transport are in effect. An agreement on multimodal transport has been signed. A dispute-settlement mechanism is in place.

The foundations for the other elements of integration have been laid. The removal of non-tariff barriers is mandated by the agreement on CEPT for AFTA. Negotiations on the liberalization of certain services sectors have been conducted in accordance with the framework agreement on services. Commitments on the improvement and coordination of customs procedures have been made in several agreements and understandings, and implementing manuals have been published. The agreement to facilitate the passage of goods in transit has been concluded, and five of its nine implementing protocols have been agreed upon. Master plans for the ASEAN Highway Network and the Singapore-Kunming Rail Link have been drawn up. A comprehensive tourism agreement has been signed, even as the ASEAN Tourism Forum has been a roaring success for more than twenty years. Mutual recognition arrangements for two product groups have been concluded in accordance with the framework agreement on MRAs. The 1998 Hanoi Plan of Action, the 2003 Declaration of ASEAN Concord II and the 2004 Vientiane Action Programme embody many commitments to move forward the integration of the regional economy.

However, as I said in my final report to the ASEAN leaders at their 2002 summit, "Regional economic integration seems to have become stuck in framework agreements, work programmes and master plans."[60] At that time, ASEAN had not adopted common criteria for identifying non-tariff barriers, much less acknowledged such barriers, and still less started dismantling them. The negotiations on trade in services have not gotten very far in substantive terms. Customs processes remain slow and unpredictable, although substantial improvements seem to be in prospect. Customs authorities in some countries continue to put up obstacles to the application of tariff preferences under the CEPT scheme for AFTA. Standards have been harmonized only for very few products. Transportation is key to the movement of trade, but no agreement on inter-state transport has been concluded, and the agreement on goods in transit cannot go into operation because of a dispute between two ASEAN member-states. Moreover, transport costs incurred by the shipment of ASEAN goods through the land territory of some ASEAN countries remain prohibitively high. The state of the liberalization of air services in ASEAN is uneven. The regional movement of labour has been too sensitive to be dealt with regionally.

The fundamental question is this: have the measures that ASEAN has taken to integrate the regional economy worked, particularly in influencing trading practices and investment decisions? In determining the reply, three tests may be applied:

- the utilization of AFTA preferences as measured by the use of Form D, which certifies to the ASEAN origin, as defined by the CEPT agreement, of a product traded within ASEAN;

- the expansion of intra-ASEAN trade; and
- the consideration of the degree of ASEAN market integration in investment decisions.

The rate of utilization of Form D is shockingly low. Some authorities put it as low as five per cent of intra-ASEAN imports. Several reasons have been given for this phenomenon. One is that the CEPT scheme is not sufficiently known among traders. Another is that many business people are reluctant to undergo the administrative trouble and expend the time and money in applying for CEPT treatment for their intra-ASEAN trade, especially as the narrowing of the difference between the CEPT and the most-favoured-nation tariff rates makes the trouble, time and expense less worthwhile. Customs authorities in some importing countries have little trust in the certificates of origin of exporting countries, thus discouraging their use. For this reason, Raymond Yee, a former official of the ASEAN Secretariat in charge of trade facilitation, has suggested that the exporter's government be removed from the process of determining a traded product's eligibility for CEPT treatment; instead, he said, as in NAFTA, the certificate of origin should be a matter between the firm or firms involved and the customs authority of the importing country.[61] There is also a belief that some governments fail to report many Form D transactions to the ASEAN Secretariat, a failure that results in the understatement of the rate of utilization of the CEPT preferences. Nevertheless, whether understated or not, the utilization rate is certainly quite low.

The ASEAN Competitiveness Study of McKinsey & Company points out that the share of intra-ASEAN trade in the region's total trade actually shrank by 19 per cent from 1994 to 2001, whereas the share of intraregional trade in the European Union's total trade expanded by 41 per cent in its first ten years, in the North American Free Trade Agreement by 17 per cent in its first seven years, and in MERCOSUR by 67 per cent in its first nine years.[62] It is easy to see why AFTA has not led to a substantial increase in intra-ASEAN trade. Edsel Custodio, Undersecretary of Foreign Affairs for international economic relations and former ASEAN Senior Economic Official for the Philippines, pointed out to me that the bulk of intra-ASEAN trade in manufactured goods was made up of electronics, which were mostly tariff-free anyway.[63]

At the Institute of Southeast Asian Studies in Singapore, I heard presentations of the results of two separate surveys conducted among business decision-makers on the investment climate in Southeast Asia and on the factors considered to be relevant to decisions to invest in the region.

On both occasions, I asked the persons who made the presentations whether the survey respondents had taken into account the degree of regional market integration in assessing the investment climate or in making investment decisions. In both cases, the response was not only, "No," but that the subject was not even raised.

What little is known of ASEAN economic integration efforts suffers from a lack of credibility. The low utilization rate of tariff preferences under AFTA, understated or not, the stagnant and even shrinking share of intra-ASEAN trade in ASEAN's total trade, and — except for AICO participants — the apparent irrelevance of AFTA in investment decisions show the low credibility of ASEAN integration measures among those who count most — the traders and investors. This is hardly surprising. Despite many commitments to take the right measures for integration, those measures have not been put into effective operation. To be sure, tariffs on intra-ASEAN trade have been reduced to minimal or zero levels pursuant to the CEPT agreement, particularly among ASEAN's leading trading nations, and that is a significant achievement. Tariff-cutting is essential to market integration, but it is far from enough. Market integration is achieved by more than tariff-cutting, and it is in the other measures where ASEAN has fallen short. This, in turn, is due to several reasons.

This is due partly to a lack of knowledge. Despite the fact that AFTA has been around for more than a decade, little is known about it in the international business community. I once visited the Munich headquarters of a large and very well-known German company with global operations, and its top executives and even the officers in charge of Asia knew very little about what ASEAN was doing on the economic front. ASEAN occasionally undertakes joint investment promotion missions to Japan, the United States and Europe. Officials from all ten member-countries and the ASEAN Secretariat constitute these missions. Except for one or two of them and the Secretariat representative, the officials usually engage in "beauty contests", touting the assets of their respective countries rather than the advantages of ASEAN as a region. To make matters worse, they often read, one after another, from prepared texts in somnolent monotones. It would be more effective if ASEAN were to designate a proficient communicator with a mandate to promote the region as a whole.

Among the integration measures, tariff reductions may be the most visible and dramatic; it is also the easiest. The others are much more politically or bureaucratically difficult. Non-tariff barriers are often subtle instruments of protectionism or, in some cases, rent-seeking. They are largely opaque and hard even to identify. As they assume ever-greater importance in ASEAN economies, services are becoming even more sensitive than trade in goods. Transportation is vital to trade and tourism, but liberalizing transportation services would expose national airlines, shipping lines and land transport companies, many of which are state-owned (or crony-owned), to greater competition, which, being used to protection, they may not be able to withstand. As we have seen, transboundary transport arrangements can be held hostage to political disputes or pressures. They can even be manipulated for protectionist purposes. Even as open an economy as Singapore's has had difficulty opening up its financial and telecommunications services. Streamlining customs operations and coordinating them regionally may require the overhaul of entire cultures at some national customs authorities. Regulatory bodies may have to give up a measure of their authority in order to harmonize product standards with other ASEAN countries and give recognition to those countries' certificates of compliance with regulations. Governments will have to ensure that companies adjust to ASEAN norms the standards that they have adhered to for years.

National governments have to overcome all these largely political obstacles basically of their own accord and in recognition of the measures' benefit to themselves. ASEAN has no compliance or enforcement mechanisms, such as those in the European Union. Its agreements carry no sanctions for failures to implement them. The ASEAN Secretariat has no power to enforce agreements or the authority even to expose non-compliance with them. Even so, the Secretariat has managed quietly to cajole member-states into adopting their annual legislative enactments for scheduled tariff reductions, even if some are often late.

A fundamental problem is that most ASEAN governments do not feel a sufficient identification of the national interest with regional economic integration. Most ASEAN companies do not see how their businesses benefit from such integration. James Castle, a long-time consultant in Jakarta, confirmed this to me in the case of most Indonesian firms, which, he said, not only failed to recognize the benefits of an integrated regional market; they lacked confidence in their ability to compete even in their own domestic market.[64] Most firms, and thus national governments, place much more value on their markets in Europe, America, Japan and, now, China than on the regional market. The result is that the governments feel no pressure from ASEAN businesses to move faster on regional economic integration. Indeed, a number of private companies, particularly in Indonesia and the Philippines of late, but also some in Malaysia and Thailand, have made their opposition to faster integration loud and clear, although a few — Indonesia's Indofood is an outstanding example — profit hugely from the regional market. The strongest advocates of ASEAN integration are the business groups of the United States, primarily through the US-ASEAN Business Council, and of Japan, mainly through *Keidanren*, the leading Japanese business association. This reinforces the perception that, more than ASEAN companies, it is the multinationals that benefit from AFTA and other measures to integrate the ASEAN economy. Indeed, only a handful of companies of ASEAN provenance or ownership participate in AICO.

In the light of this, then Senior Minister Lee Kuan Yew, Singapore's founding father, told me that it is for the ASEAN governments to take the lead in regional economic integration. Taking the long view, national leaders, he stressed, have to persuade their people of the benefits of regional integration and not wait for pressure from the private sector. "Unless leaders lead, events will pass ASEAN by," he said.[65]

Still, in most ASEAN governments, there is no sign that ASEAN initiatives are incorporated in national planning or pursued in national legislation other than tariff reductions and the ratification of agreements. Pich Rithi, Deputy Director-General for Trade in Cambodia's Ministry of Commerce and ASEAN Senior Economic Official for his country, explained it to me: most of the member-states do not see clearly the advantages of regional economic integration, each of them thinking that the others gain more from it.[66]

This is where the long-term enterprise of building a genuine ASEAN Community is essential.

ON TO THE ASEAN ECONOMIC COMMUNITY

Building a genuine ASEAN Community is a difficult, long-term endeavour. As ASEAN carries on this tedious and long drawn-out work, the world is not standing still for it. ASEAN's competitors are surging past it. Early in 2002, at my invitation, Singapore's George Yeo, then Minister for Trade and Industry, spoke at a symposium that the ASEAN Secretariat organized to promote AFTA in Jakarta. He pointed out, "In 1990, China accounted for less than 20 per cent of total foreign investments in developing Asia while Southeast Asia took 60 per cent. Today, the numbers are reversed."[67] Tham Siew-Yean, senior research fellow at Universiti Kebangsaan Malaysia, invited the attention of a Singapore audience in August 2003 to the drop of ASEAN's share in foreign direct investment worldwide from an annual average of 7.5 per cent in 1990–95 to 1.8 per cent in 2001 and a plunge of its share in

FDI in the developing world from 22.8 to 6.5 per cent in the same period.[68] Ten new members, most of them emerging economies, eventually joined the EU in May 2004, adding to ASEAN's competition.

Realizing this, ASEAN's leaders decided at their Phnom Penh summit in 2002 to move on to the next stage of regional economic integration. In reality, it was more of a decision to get serious about implementing the measures for integration that had already been agreed upon. In order to convey where it was headed and its seriousness about getting there, ASEAN called this next stage, at Goh Chok Tong's suggestion, the ASEAN Economic Community, a phrase that evokes the European Economic Community. (Incidentally, the report of the ASEAN Economic Ministers meeting in August 1986 quoted José Concepcion, Secretary of Trade and Industry of the Philippines, as proposing in his opening statement that the meeting consider the formation of an ASEAN Economic Community by 2000. The proposal elicited no reaction and, as far as I know, was not followed through.)

In 2003, in Bali, the ASEAN leaders defined, in the Declaration of ASEAN Concord II, the ASEAN Economic Community in terms of the economic goal set by the 1997 ASEAN Vision 2020 — "a stable, prosperous and highly competitive ASEAN economic region in which there is a free flow of goods, services, investment and a freer flow of capital, equitable economic development and reduced poverty and socio-economic disparities in year 2020". This was to be achieved by transforming ASEAN into "a single market and production base" and "a more dynamic and stronger segment of the global supply chain". For this, ASEAN would set up "new mechanisms and measures to strengthen the implementation of its existing economic initiatives", including AFTA, the negotiations on trade in services, and the ASEAN Investment Area. It would "facilitate movement of business persons, skilled labour and talents" and "ensure expeditious and legally binding resolution of any economic disputes". As "a first step," the ASEAN leaders called for the implementation of the recommendations of the High-Level Task Force on ASEAN Economic Integration.[69]

Formed in 2002, the task force set clear deadlines for the integration measures that ASEAN had already agreed upon. It recommended 11 priority sectors — seven involving goods and the other four covering services — in which ASEAN integration measures were to be accelerated. It proposed new institutional mechanisms to assist in ensuring compliance with ASEAN agreements and help resolve disputes arising from the application of those agreements, and a more independent dispute-settlement mechanism whose decisions were to be binding.[70]

Chapter 7 discusses the ASEAN Economic Community at greater length, including the obstacles to its realization and its prospects for achievement.

As has been noted, ASEAN started out as a scheme for the prevention of conflict, the building of mutual confidence and the promotion of political stability, with economic cooperation, at least in part, serving as a cover to dispel notions of ASEAN as a military alliance. However, by the turn of the millennium, ASEAN economic cooperation, with regional economic integration as the stated aim, had acquired a life and an imperative of its own. Indeed, ASEAN's economic component has been increasingly regarded as a vital element in its political cohesion and the stability of the region and ultimately in the creation of an ASEAN Community. In this light, ASEAN has to move more smoothly and more rapidly on the road to regional economic integration, and for this leaders have to lead.

Political leadership is especially important in the light of the fact that ASEAN economic integration is not imposed by a comprehensive, very detailed and legally binding treaty like NAFTA or driven by a supranational authority like the European Commission or pushed by a regional business sector eager for the benefits of a regional market.

ASEAN declarations, joint statements, understandings and agreements can set common goals, establish norms and standards, and even put together mechanisms for compliance. Peer pressure can be applied in a friendly ASEAN context. Mutual assistance and regional cooperation are useful in many capacity-building endeavours. However, without a NAFTA-like treaty or an EC-like authority, compliance with ASEAN commitments and the implementation of ASEAN agreements ultimately depend on voluntary national action.

Tariff-cutting under AFTA has to be sanctioned by domestic law. Common tariff nomenclatures have to be adopted by national legislation. The dismantling of non-tariff barriers has to be the product of national policy decisions, most of which are difficult to apply to intra-ASEAN trade alone. Similarly, it is hard to envision ASEAN countries opening up services like health care, finance, insurance, and tourism to other ASEAN countries alone rather than to the rest of the world as a matter of national policy. Customs reforms will be undertaken for all trade rather than for trade within ASEAN alone. ASEAN countries will take steps to increase tourism not just from other ASEAN countries but from all over the world. As noted above, it makes little sense for ASEAN countries to distinguish between ASEAN and non-ASEAN sources when forming their policies on foreign investments, especially since the bulk of such investments comes from non-ASEAN countries. The protection of intellectual property rights, which is an increasingly important factor in investment decisions, is basically a matter of domestic law enforcement. The use and development of information and communications technology are the subject of national decisions.

In view of this, it seems to me that one of the benefits of ASEAN derives from the convivial setting that it provides and the standards that it sets for encouraging member-states to undertake the domestic economic and trade- and investment-related reforms required by ASEAN integration and cooperation and by an investment-friendly climate. This is, of course, in addition to those areas where regional action and ASEAN agreement have intrinsic value, like coordinated preferential tariff-cutting as in CEPT/ AFTA, industrial arrangements like AICO, the harmonization of tariff nomenclatures, product standardization, mutual recognition arrangements, transportation linkages, and joint investment and tourism promotion. If ASEAN manages to make the planned compliance and dispute-settlement mechanisms work, if domestic reforms are carried out, if effective national policies are adopted and applied, and if the cooperative measures for regional integration are put into operation, ASEAN could be an attractive venue for investments again. The clarification and codification of all these in an ASEAN Charter could help.

Whether these conditions actually happen and whether they are enough are for the investors to judge.

Notes

1. See Appendix A.
2. http://www.aseansec.org/5049.htm and http://www.aseansec.org/5053.htm.
3. http://www.aseansec.org/6105.htm.
4. Interview with Widjojo Nitisastro, Jakarta, 20 November 2003.
5. Opening address by General Boonchai Bamrungphong, Deputy Prime Minister of Thailand, at the fifth meeting of the ASEAN Economic Ministers, Pattaya, 2 September 1977.
6. Interview with Vicente Paterno, Makati, 4 August 2003.
7. http://www.aseansec.org/1376.htm.
8. United Nations Industrial Development Organization, *Regional Industrial Co-operation: Experiences and Perspectives of ASEAN and the Andean Pact* (Vienna: UNIDO, 1986), p. 17. The paper was prepared by John Wong of the National University of Singapore as a UNIDO consultant in cooperation with the staff of UNIDO's Regional and Country Studies Branch and originally issued by UNIDO in August 1983.
9. *Fertilizer Focus* (Hampton Hill, England: FMB Publications, Ltd., September–October 2004).

10. http://www.aseansec.org/6377.htm.
11. http://www.aseansec.org/6382.htm.
12. http://www.aseansec.org/6378.htm.
13. http://www.aseansec.org/6381.htm.
14. Address at the opening of the thirteenth meeting of the ASEAN Economic Ministers, Manila, 20 May 1982.
15. Ibid.
16. Keynote address at the meeting of ASEAN Economic Ministers, Kuala Lumpur, 7 October 1991.
17. A common market among Argentina, Brazil, Paraguay and Uruguay, with Bolivia and Chile associating themselves politically with the group in 1996.
18. Parties to NAFTA are Canada, Mexico and the United States of America.
19. *The ASEAN Free Trade Area: A Proposal* (Thai discussion paper, October 1991).
20. http://www.aseansec.org/6126.htm.
21. *Meeting of the ASEAN Heads of Government: Singapore, 27–28 January 1992* (Jakarta: ASEAN Secretariat, 1992), p. 27.
22. Ibid., p. 31.
23. See Appendix C.
24. Ibid.
25. http://www.aseansec.org/5189.htm.
26. http://www.aseansec.org/7143.htm.
27. The sixth ASEAN Summit, "Statement on Bold Measures", Hanoi, 16 December 1998 (http://www.aseansec.org/8756.htm).
28. The ASEAN response to the financial crisis is discussed at greater length in Chapter 3.
29. http://www.aseansec.org/12365.htm.
30. Media Statement of the Tenth ASEAN Economic Ministers Retreat, Singapore, 21 April 2004 (http://www.aseansec.org/16073.htm).
31. Protocol to Amend the Basic Agreement on the ASEAN Industrial Cooperation Scheme (http://www.aseansec.org/16333.htm).
32. J.B. Santos, "Food Security in the ASEAN: Meeting Socio-Economic, Environmental and Consumer Needs" (speech delivered at the seventh ASEAN Food Conference, Manila, 20 November 2000); text in the author's possession.
33. http://www.aseansec.org/6626.htm.
34. http://www.aseansec.org/6628.htm.
35. Interview with Minister Cham Prasidh, Phnom Penh, 12 May 2003.
36. Interview with Cheah Sin Liang, Singapore, 5 May 2005.
37. http://www.aseansec.org/17778.htm, para. 16.
38. http://www.aseansec.org/18009.htm.
39. http://www.aseansec.org/18005.htm.
40. As summarized in Adam Schwarz and Roland Villinger, "Integrating Southeast Asia's Economies", in *The McKinsey Quarterly*, no. 1 (New York: McKinsey & Company, 2004), p. 41.

41. Interview with Tran Dong Phuong, Hanoi, 19 May 2005.
42. Schwarz and Villinger: op. cit., pp. 40–41.
43. http://www.aseansec.org/6674.htm.
44. http://www.aseansec.org/6677.htm.
45. http://www.aseansec.org/pdf/accsq_3.pdf.
46. http://www.aseansec.org/18012.htm.
47. http://www.aseansec.org/7377.htm.
48. See Chapter 3.
49. http://www.aseansec.org/13144.htm.
50. Statement of the Ninth Meeting of ASEAN Tourism Ministers, para. 2 (http://www.aseansec.org/18184.htm).
51. Joint Media Release of the Eighth Meeting of ASEAN Tourism Ministers (http://www.aseansec.org/17091.htm).
52. Statement of the Ninth Meeting of ASEAN Tourism Ministers, para. 16 (http://www.aseansec.org/18184.htm).
53. http://www.aseansec.org/13157.htm.
54. http://www.aseansec.org/6464.htm and http://www.aseansec.org/6465.htm.
55. http://www.aseansec.org/6466.htm.
56. http://www.aseansec.org/6467.htm.
57. Joint Press Statement of the fourth meeting of the ASEAN Investment Area Ministerial Council, Hanoi, 14 September 2001 (http://www.aseansec.org/6477.htm).
58. http://www.aseansec.org/6466.htm.
59. *Individual Action Plan, ASEAN Investment Area Publication Series, No. 3* (Jakarta: ASEAN Secretariat, October 2000).
60. See Appendix E.
61. Interview with Raymond Yee, Singapore, 19 August 2003.
62. Schwarz and Villinger, op. cit., p. 40.
63. Interview with Edsel Custodio, Manila, 7 October 2004.
64. Interview with James Castle, Jakarta, 9 October 2003.
65. Interview with Senior Minister Lee Kuan Yew, Singapore, 18 August 2003.
66. Interview with Pich Rithi, Phnom Penh, 19 June 2003.
67. Speech at the AFTA Seminar, Jakarta, 31 January 2002.
68. Presentation at the ASEAN Roundtable 2003: Roadmap to an ASEAN Economic Community, sponsored by the Institute of Southeast Asian Studies, Singapore, 21 August 2003.
69. See Appendix F.
70. See Appendix G.

6

ASEAN AND THE WORLD

It is one of ASEAN's strengths that it has kept itself politically and economically open to the rest of the world, even as it promotes Southeast Asian solidarity, seeks to keep itself from being entangled in the quarrels of the strong, and professes to strive for the integration of the regional economy. One estimate has it that, in the 1996–2000 period, foreign trade as a percentage of the gross domestic products of Indonesia, Malaysia, the Philippines, Singapore, Thailand and Vietnam — the region's leading trading nations — averaged 149, ranging from Indonesia's 67 per cent to Singapore's almost 320 per cent. The comparable figure for India was less than 27 per cent.[1] Until today, ASEAN member-countries' trade, investment and other economic relationships have been largely with developed economies. They have substantial economic and financial agreements and arrangements with many countries around the world. They take full part in multilateral trade negotiations and other international economic forums. Eight are members of the World Trade Organization; Laos and Vietnam are trying to get in.

ASEAN members have strong political relations with states outside the region, and some have defence arrangements with external powers. ASEAN as a group has embarked on initiatives like free trade agreements and economic partnerships, as well as development cooperation, with several countries and groups of countries — initiatives with high political significance. ASEAN has involved other powers in taking common action on regional problems. A variety of examples abound — the Vietnam-Cambodia issue of the 1970s and 1980s, the Indochinese asylum-seekers, the Treaty of Amity and Cooperation in Southeast Asia, the Southeast Asia Nuclear Weapons-Free Zone, the Chiangmai Initiative on finance cooperation, the South China Sea issue, the SARS crisis, the response to the aftermath of the 2004 tsunamis. These economic and political linkages find their most visible expressions in the ASEAN dialogue system, the ASEAN Regional Forum, the ASEAN+3 process, the summit meetings that ASEAN convenes annually with the Northeast Asian countries and India and, from time to time, with other neighbouring states, and now the East Asia Summit.

One can trace the start of the ASEAN system of dialogue partnerships to 1972, when ASEAN initiated an "informal dialogue" with the European Economic Community through SCCAN, the Special Coordinating Committee of ASEAN Nations. In April 1973, Singapore's Foreign Minister S. Rajaratnam laid down the rationale for linkages with the developed countries:

> ASEAN is essentially an organization for regional economic co-operation. If our organization is to fulfil its major objectives it requires sustained aid and investment from the developed nations. Without substantial external aid economic growth in the ASEAN region would of necessity be painfully slow. Much as I would like to believe it, I see no prospects of growth within ASEAN purely through the device of regional co-operation. Even if all the South-East Asian countries were brought within the framework of ASEAN, I do not see any immediate prospect of ASEAN nations developing on the basis of their own resources. In theory the ASEAN countries can, of course, develop as an independent and self-contained bloc.... Nevertheless economic realities require that regional co-operation must be wedded to external economic participation if ASEAN is to achieve its objectives. It is not intra-regional trade and investments but extra regional trade and investments which will accelerate ASEAN's economic growth.... If during the past five years ASEAN economic co-operation has not produced dramatic results, it is largely because ASEAN has concentrated on promoting intra-regional co-operation. This is of course necessary and we should continue to explore and expand areas for intra-regional co-operation. But it is also necessary for ASEAN to examine ways and means of attracting extra-regional interest in and involvement with ASEAN. A start has already been made in regard to the European Economic Community through the setting up of SCCAN.[2]

Aside from reflecting an ASEAN stance that has been outward-looking from the beginning, this passage indicates ASEAN's original objectives in seeking dialogue relationships with the developed world: development assistance, investments and market access. On the other hand, Indonesia's Foreign Minister Adam Malik stressed something else about the dialogue — the need for ASEAN to remain united in order to deal effectively with other countries and groups of countries. He held up the incipient dialogue with the EEC "as a concrete illustration that only through joint actions can the ASEAN countries be acknowledged as a noticeable force in dealing with more powerful economic groupings".[3] ASEAN clearly saw the value of linking up with the developed economies as markets and as sources of investment and development assistance. It also viewed the dialogues as an opportunity to raise trade-related problems.

One of the earliest issues that ASEAN raised with Japan was "the indiscriminate production and accelerated exports of synthetic rubber", on which ASEAN's "joint approach" was said to have "resulted in obtaining the Japanese Government's agreement to exercise a restraining influence on the Japanese synthetic rubber industry". These were the words of the joint communiqué of the ASEAN Ministerial Meeting in 1974, the year after the onset of the "informal" ASEAN-Japan dialogue.[4] In 1974, ASEAN and Australia started their dialogue relationship and agreed to cooperate on a number of projects. New Zealand followed in 1975. Canada and the United States formally came into the dialogue system in 1977.

The agendas for the early dialogues were heavily, if not exclusively, devoted to market access, commodities, funding for development and other economic issues. For example, the agenda that ASEAN proposed for the ASEAN-U.S. dialogues in Manila in September 1977 and in Washington, D.C., in September 1978 focused on global economic trends, North-South questions, development cooperation, energy, trade, investments and taxation, and commodities. The actual or threatened unloading of tin from the U.S.' strategic stockpile had for a while been an issue between ASEAN and Washington, with ASEAN supporting Malaysia's position, just as it did other ASEAN countries in issues involving trade in other commodities, like natural rubber, copper and coffee. The first ASEAN-Japan ministerial meeting, in Pattaya in June 1978, seems to have dwelt on the world economy, the ASEAN Industrial Projects, the world market for tin, the Common Fund for commodities, and trade matters. Singapore acknowledged the value of ASEAN support in the resolution of its dispute with Australia over the latter's civil aviation policies, which were deemed to be injurious to Singapore Airlines.

The 1981 ASEAN Ministerial Meeting stressed that the focus of the dialogue relationships should be on shipping, energy and access to markets and reviewed individual projects of technical cooperation with individual Dialogue Partners. In 1985, the Foreign Ministers declared that, in its dialogue relationships, "ASEAN should focus on the important objectives of securing improved market access, ensuring better terms of trade, attracting investment, effecting transfer of technology and promoting cooperation in tourism".[5] In fact, until the late 1980s, the Economic Ministers had much to say about the dialogues and dealt substantively with them. They had a voice in the dialogues' agendas, the projects with Dialogue Partners, the designation of the ASEAN coordinator-countries, reports on the state and progress of the dialogues, cooperation agreements, the joint cooperation committees to oversee the implementation of the agreements, and such things as the ASEAN Promotion Centre in Tokyo. The Foreign Ministers and the ASEAN Directors-General of the foreign ministries eventually took sole control of the dialogue process. By the mid-1980s, the Economic Ministers had stopped their involvement in the process and concentrated on the substantive economic content of the dialogues. Today, they conduct consultations with the three Northeast Asian countries collectively and individually, Australia and New Zealand, the United States Trade Representative, and the European Commission's Trade Commissioner quite independently of the foreign ministries.

For ASEAN, in the early years of the dialogues, market access largely meant entrée into the developed economies for the member-countries' commodity exports. Except for Singapore, the ASEAN countries were then highly dependent on commodities for their exports. Malaysia was particularly skilled and resolute in using the ASEAN dialogues to push its tin, rubber and palm oil in the markets of the world. At the same time, the ASEAN countries needed external funding for infrastructure and technical assistance. At that time, it was only the developed countries that could provide both markets and financing. ASEAN also valued them for their political influence in the world. This was visibly manifested in ASEAN's skilful collaboration with its Dialogue Partners and China in dealing with the Cambodian and refugee problems. Even before that, Indonesia's Foreign Minister Mochtar Kusumaatmadja observed that ASEAN's political role in the world had become "more pronounced" after the first meeting between ASEAN and European Community foreign ministers in November 1978.[6] Thus, until 1991, ASEAN's Dialogue Partners were limited to Australia, Canada, the European Community, Japan, New Zealand and the United States, which then comprised most of the developed world, although, as recalled below, India almost became one in 1980.

To the developed countries, on the other hand, by the mid-1970s, ASEAN seemed to be a going concern. It was strategically located and was beginning to exercise a measure of collective influence in the world. The developed countries saw the importance of political linkages with the association, as well as with its individual members. They found ASEAN's growing economies as promising markets and investment sites. Japan, in particular, saw the ASEAN countries as partners in the re-structuring and relocation of its industries. They thus welcomed, indeed sought, dialogue partnerships with ASEAN.

In 1977, right after their second summit, the ASEAN heads of government met with the Prime Ministers of Japan, Australia and New Zealand. In order to pursue the understandings reached by the heads of government in Kuala Lumpur, the ASEAN Foreign Ministers invited their Japanese counterpart to the ASEAN Ministerial Meeting in Pattaya in 1978. The meeting with Japan was called the Post-Ministerial Conference (PMC). The next year, only the Japanese Foreign Minister was supposed again to be invited. However, with Vietnam having invaded Cambodia and the problem of the Indochinese asylum-seekers getting more critical, the United States, Australia, New Zealand, and the European Community reportedly expressed an interest in consultations with the ASEAN ministers. Since 1980, the annual ASEAN Ministerial Meeting has been followed by the Post-Ministerial Conferences, with the ASEAN ministers meeting those of the Dialogue Partners, first as a group and then separately. This was convenient not only for ASEAN's ministers but for those of the Dialogue Partners as well. Not only would they know the dates of the meetings well in advance; they would also have the opportunity to hold bilateral discussions with one another as well as with individual ASEAN ministers. For ASEAN, it had the added political value of having the foreign ministers of the richest countries of the world come to the region at the same time.

For a number of years, the Post-Ministerial Conferences had a session just among the Asia-Pacific countries, that is, among ASEAN, Australia, Canada, Japan, New Zealand and the United States, without the Europeans. At the time when ASEAN had only six members, this forum was called 6+5+1. It was abandoned after a few years, but it bore within it the seeds of APEC.

By the early 1990s, both ASEAN and the world had changed from what they were 20 years before. The ASEAN countries were no longer just exporters of commodities but also of manufactured goods, processed agricultural products, and eventually knowledge products, particularly those related to information and communications technology. They were rising as providers of services. Acting with closer solidarity, they had exerted their political and diplomatic influence on how the world dealt with the Cambodian conflict and the Indochinese asylum-seekers.[7] As those problems came to an end, the vision of all of Southeast Asia within ASEAN moved much closer to realization. At the same time, the ranks of economic powerhouses were expanding; accordingly, the old distinction and relationship between developed and developing countries were undergoing substantial change. For ASEAN, the dialogue system, which had been based on that distinction and that relationship, had to change and expand. First to be included since 1977 was South Korea, in 1991. Korea then was technically a developing country; only in 1996 would it join the Organization of Economic Cooperation and Development, an association of market-economy democracies, almost all of them developed countries. Then, China and India, as well as Russia, became Dialogue Partners in 1996. With the U.S. debacle in Indochina, the break-up of the Soviet Union, the end of the Cold War, the changes within China and India and in their relations with the world, and eventually the settlement of the Cambodian conflict, the strategic configuration in East Asia had also been transformed.

Accordingly, the agendas of the ASEAN dialogues shifted from a preoccupation with market access for commodity exports, development assistance, and the Cambodian and refugee problems. They came to be dominated by more complex international economic issues and the evolving security situation — security both in its "traditional" meaning, that is, relating to the possibility of armed conflict between states, and in its new, "non-traditional" sense, that is, having to do with the threat of international terrorism, drug-trafficking, trafficking in persons, other transnational crimes, environmental degradation, internal conflict, infectious diseases, economic and social insecurity, and so on. Nevertheless, with the entry of three least-developed countries into ASEAN in 1997 and 1999, development cooperation has continued to figure in the dialogue relations. Moreover, ASEAN as an association continues to need technical assistance for expert studies and for building capacity for regional economic integration.

In the light of the rise of security concerns in the dialogue agendas, the ASEAN leaders at their 1992 summit called for the use of the PMC framework for regional security discussions. However, China and Russia were not Dialogue Partners at that time. Vietnam was not yet an ASEAN member. Yet, their participation was essential to any discussion of regional security. A new forum had to be set up to accommodate them. Thus was born, in 1994, the ASEAN Regional Forum, which would embrace ASEAN and its Dialogue Partners, observers — then Laos and Vietnam, as well as Papua New Guinea — and China and Russia, categorized as "consultative partners". It was later to expand to include Cambodia, Myanmar, India, Mongolia, North Korea, Pakistan, and Timor-Leste.[8]

Inevitably, there developed duplications between the subjects discussed in the PMC and the ARF, as there was a large overlap in their memberships. Early in the ARF's existence, the PMC/ARF foreign ministers met over lunch to seek to reduce the areas of overlap between the two forums. They decided that the ARF would deal with security issues in its "geographical footprint", that is, East Asia and the Pacific. The PMC would discuss economic, social and development issues, and security subjects elsewhere in the world, like the Middle East and disarmament questions. Predictably, some overlaps and repetitions remain.

As the number of Dialogue Partners grew from six to ten, the conferences took their toll on the ASEAN ministers' time and energy. They tried various permutations in scheduling and participation, without completely satisfying everyone. The latest change took place in 2004, when the ASEAN Foreign Ministers decided to meet with their counterparts from those countries that had annual summits with ASEAN on the occasion of those summits rather than at the time of the ASEAN Ministerial Meeting. They would hold individual Post-Ministerial Conferences only with the rest of the Dialogue Partners. Thus, the ASEAN Foreign Ministers conferred singly with Australia, Canada, the European Union, New Zealand, Russia and the United States at the PMC in Jakarta in July 2004, and had their individual meetings with the foreign ministers of China, India, Japan and Korea on the occasion of the summits in Vientiane late in the year. They followed the same pattern at the PMC in Vientiane in July 2005 and on the eve of the ASEAN+3 Summit in Kuala Lumpur in December. However, in Kuala Lumpur, instead of conducting the normal PMC consultations, they found themselves dealing largely with preparations for the summit and distracted by having to assist their leaders. Nevertheless, they decided to maintain the new arrangement for the 2006 PMC.

The ambassadors of the ASEAN countries in the capitals of the Dialogue Partners are constituted into committees for regular consultations and social networking. The committees file reports with the ASEAN Standing Committee through the ASEAN Secretariat.

The Dialogue Partners do not, of course, represent the totality of ASEAN's external relations. Some other regional associations have sought to form ties with it. In the 1980s, the ASEAN Economic Ministers expressed their interest in active relations with the Gulf Cooperation Council of Arab states around the Persian Gulf and with the South Pacific Forum, now the Pacific Islands Forum, which was made up of Australia, New Zealand and the small island states of the Pacific. Taking advantage of the presence of the world's foreign ministers in New York on the occasion of the UN General

Assembly's annual General Debate, ASEAN has had meetings with the South Asian Association for Regional Cooperation, the Gulf Cooperation Council, the Economic Cooperation Organization, and the Rio Group of Latin American countries. However, interest quickly waned, and most of the time only the co-chairmen have participated at the ministerial level. The meetings also are often not sure of what to talk about.

The UN Economic and Social Commission for Asia and the Pacific has been convening meetings every two years among the secretariats of ASEAN, the Pacific Islands Forum and the Economic Cooperation Organization, originally made up of Iran, Pakistan and Turkey and later joined by the newly independent Central Asian republics. These have been useful for networking purposes, but only marginally so in terms of substance. In October 1982, officials of ASEAN and of the Andean Pact exchanged views and experiences in the ASEAN-Andean Pact Conference and Study Tour on Regional Industrial Co-operation. In May 2000, Thailand tried to revive and broaden the process by bringing together the secretariats of ASEAN and the re-named Andean Community in Bangkok. In April 2005, the secretaries-general of ASEAN and of the Shanghai Cooperation Organization of China, Kazakhstan, Kyrgyzstan, Russia, Turkmenistan and Uzbekistan signed a memorandum of understanding on cooperation between the two secretariats. Whether it will fare better than the intended cooperation between ASEAN and the Andean Community remains to be seen. A number of countries from South Asia, the Middle East, North Africa and South America have indicated their interest in dialogue relations with ASEAN, which, however, has been holding them off.

As recounted elsewhere in this book, ASEAN has worked with the Asian Development Bank on a range of endeavours, notably those addressing the haze problem and the financial crisis. It has also cooperated with the World Bank on occasion.

ASEAN has entered into understandings with the World Health Organization, the UN Environment Programme and UNESCO and has conducted activities with them. It has worked with UNAIDS, UNICEF, the International Labour Organization and the UN Office on Drugs and Crime. ASEAN has co-sponsored conferences on security with the UN itself. The UN Development Programme is an ASEAN Dialogue Partner, but it did not attend the Post-Ministerial Conferences until 2001 and 2003, when the UNDP Administrator took part in the development-cooperation portion of the ASEAN+10 conference. In other years, a senior UNDP official met with the ASEAN Directors-General on these occasions. The UNDP has given much valuable support to many ASEAN projects, including studies on re-organizing the association and its Secretariat. Its resident representatives undertake consultations with the ASEAN Standing Committee from time to time.

The rest of this chapter will limit itself to ASEAN's dialogue partnerships with individual countries and the European Union, because they are its most important external relationships. This is why these countries and the EU are Dialogue Partners in the first place. The relationships will be discussed one by one, not in any order of importance or chronological sequence. So as to avoid invidious choices, the treatment will be in the order, more or less, of geographical proximity to Southeast Asia. The account of each dialogue relationship will not attempt to be comprehensive, covering all its aspects, but, for the sake of brevity and, hopefully, maintaining interest, will be limited to what I think are the relationship's most significant and interesting elements. In addition to the individual dialogues, however, there are three sections on ASEAN's relations with groups of countries, namely, ASEAN+3, the East Asia Summit and the Closer Economic Relations of Australia and New Zealand, which are separate configurations through which ASEAN pursues the purposes of the dialogues.

ASEAN+3

With ten Dialogue Partners, it was inevitable that a certain hierarchy in the degree of closeness and intensity of relations would evolve. At the start of the 1990s, with the growing economic links among East Asian countries and the shifts in power relationships in the region, Northeast Asia quickly gained priority in ASEAN's attention. The economies of China, Japan and Korea were being rapidly integrated, with heavy Japanese and Korean investments in China, so rapidly that China has become Japan's largest trading partner and South Korea's leading export market. ASEAN was in danger of being left out. On the other hand, more intensive commercial exchanges and closer economic linkages among the East Asian countries in a common framework could spur the economic growth of all the countries in the region. At the same time, it was clear that some transnational problems could be tackled best on an East Asian scale. However, there was — and is — a certain degree of tension in the relations between Japan on the one hand and China and South Korea on the other. Bad blood over World War II memories and territorial disputes, as well as the strategic rivalry between China and Japan, has kept the Northeast Asian countries from achieving the political cohesion without which true economic integration or close regional cooperation is not possible. With its presence smoothing to some extent the sharp edges of these relationships, ASEAN has carved out a role for itself in maintaining stability in East Asia as a whole, with the ASEAN+3 process helping to promote political goodwill, economic integration and regional cooperation.

The concept of ASEAN+3 had its genesis in the proposal for an "East Asia Economic Group" made in December 1990 by then Prime Minister Mahathir Mohamad at a dinner in honour of China's Premier Li Peng, who was on a visit to Malaysia. As the Philippine Ambassador to Malaysia, I was present at that dinner. An unofficial translation of an abridged *Bahasa Melayu* text (I have not been able to obtain a copy of the official and original English text) presents Mahathir's argument in this way:

> Unfortunately there is an unhealthy trend in that there is a tendency to establish economic blocs. Besides the unification of the European market, the United States has formed a joint market with Canada and now with Mexico as well. The United States is now making efforts to attract the Central and Latin American States so that there will evolve a stronger economic link for North and South America.
>
> Apart from the reunification of Germany, there is a possibility that the East European countries may join the European Economic Community.
>
> On the other hand, as countries in the East are seen by the West to achieve the status of developed nations, various measures are taken by the West to frustrate them.
>
> Malaysia disagrees with the formation of economic blocs. But the fact is that many developed countries in the West have formed economic blocs and are using their economic strength to obstruct fair and free trade.
>
> In such a situation, Malaysia has reexamined her stand and is of the view that for the world to achieve a balanced economic development, the countries of the Asia Pacific region should strengthen further their economic and market ties so that eventually an economic bloc would be formed to countervail the other economic blocs.

Ten months later, Mahathir elaborated on his idea:

> If ASEAN is to have a bigger say in trade negotiation internationally, then it must work together with the East Asian countries. The East Asia Economic Group or EAEG will be sufficiently strong to gain the respect of both the EC and the NAFTA. Even presently the countries of South East and East Asia together form a formidable market. But the potential for growth of the EAEG is far greater than that of the EC and NAFTA. This fact will also increase the clout of the EAEG....
>
> It is important that the EAEG should not be a trade bloc. All the countries of the group should be free to trade with anyone under GATT rules. But when it comes to negotiation to maintain a free trading system for the world then the group should meet to discuss issues and take a

common stand. It would be very difficult for the trading blocs of Europe and America to ignore the common stand of the EAEG. Since the EAEG stands for free trade, its strong influence in the GATT rounds is likely to yield positive results... .

Unless we have this group, ASEAN and everyone will be at the mercy of the trade blocs of Europe and America. There will be so many conditionalities and linkages with non-trade issues that the growth of ASEAN countries will be retarded. We will all remain developing countries forever.[9]

Because the other ASEAN members had not been consulted, it took a while for the idea to take hold. Some ASEAN member-states, particularly Indonesia, were concerned about the lack of previous intra-ASEAN consultations. Others had misgivings about the anti-Western tone of the proposal. In the course of further discussions, the concept was watered down to an "East Asia Economic Caucus". Some, rather disingenuously, presented this as meaning an East Asian caucus within APEC, a pretence that was quickly abandoned. Wags had tagged it acerbically as "a caucus without Caucasians". Finally, in December 1997, Malaysia, as host of the ASEAN "informal" summit, invited the leaders of China, Japan and South Korea to meet with those of ASEAN together and individually. Since then, the East Asian leaders have been meeting every year in the same format on the occasion of the annual ASEAN Summit. The forum became known as ASEAN+3 in order to emphasize the centrality of ASEAN's role, the forum's character as process rather than as institution, and its open nature. For some ASEAN members, it would also dissociate the process from the EAEG concept.

The ASEAN+3 leaders, at their summit in Manila in November 1999, issued the Joint Statement on East Asia Cooperation, laying the conceptual premises for the ASEAN+3 process. Without being specific except in a few places, the statement set forth an almost all-encompassing range of areas for cooperation — economic, monetary and financial, social and human resource development, science and technology, culture and information, and development cooperation. The statement also recorded the leaders' agreement on "continuing dialogue, coordination, and cooperation to increase mutual understanding and trust towards forging lasting peace and stability in East Asia" and their resolve to cooperate on "transnational issues".[10]

In July 1994, the ASEAN+3 foreign ministers had met privately, for the first time, on the sidelines of the PMC in Bangkok. Thereafter, they gathered annually over breakfast or lunch until after the first ASEAN+3 Summit in 1997, when, upon the leaders' official direction, their meetings became more structured and formal. In November 1995, on the occasion of the APEC meeting in Osaka, the ASEAN Economic Ministers for the first time held talks with their counterparts from China, Japan and Korea. However, they did not formally meet until May 2000. The Chiangmai Initiative,[11] with its collective economic surveillance and network of bilateral currency swap arrangements, is essentially an ASEAN+3 endeavour, with the East Asian finance ministers and finance and central bank officials meeting frequently. ASEAN+3 forums at various levels have proliferated in many areas, sixteen at last count — political and security, trade and investment, finance, agriculture, fisheries and forestry, energy, the environment, tourism, transnational crime, health, labour, culture and the arts, science and technology, information and communications technology, social welfare, youth, and rural development. Thirteen of these are at ministerial, as well as senior officials, level. ASEAN+3 also constitutes the Asian side of the Asia-Europe Meeting. Asian officials discuss ASEM issues prior to meetings with the Europeans.

Potentially significant but largely unnoticed have been the meetings of the heads of government of China, Japan and Korea on the fringes of the ASEAN+3 summits. They first met over breakfast in Manila in 1999. The first "institutionalized" meeting could be said to have taken place in Bali in 2003, because there they issued a declaration setting forth a broad range of areas for cooperation among their countries. They met again in 2004, in Vientiane. However, China and South Korea refused to meet with Japan on the occasion of the ASEAN+3 Summit in Kuala Lumpur in December 2005 in order to manifest their objection to the Japanese Prime Minister's insistence on visiting the Yasukuni shrine again, where the remains of convicted war criminals are enshrined along with other war dead. This was unfortunate, especially because the tripartite summit meetings could be an additional venue to thresh out problems, advance cooperation and build mutual confidence without the complications of getting together outside the ASEAN+3 setting. The availability of such an added setting assumes greater significance as China and Japan manœuvre in pursuit of their intensifying political rivalry.

At the suggestion of ROK President Kim Dae Jung at the 1998 ASEAN+3 Summit, an East Asia Vision Group (EAVG) of "eminent intellectuals" from the thirteen East Asian countries was formed, in the words of President Kim, to "study concrete ways to nurture East Asia into a single community of cooperation, serving as the basis for the countries of the region to start the discussion on the related issues in earnest".[12] Under Korean leadership, the EAVG delivered its report to the ASEAN+3 Summit in 2001. The report presented a vision of East Asia as being peaceful, progressive, protective of the environment, and sharing a regional identity. This was to be promoted through regional economic integration, financial coordination, development and technological cooperation, political and security cooperation, and cultural and educational exchanges. Perhaps inevitably in a document of this kind, the recommendations were mostly broad and general and in the nature of exhortations for national or regional action. There were some specific proposals, however, the most notable being:

- the formation of an East Asia Free Trade Area;
- the establishment of an East Asian Investment Information Network;
- the extension of the ASEAN Investment Area to cover all of East Asia;
- the consideration of a regional financing facility;
- a regional mechanism for the coordination of exchange rates; and
- the "evolution" of the ASEAN+3 summits into the East Asia Summit.[13]

Again at President Kim's proposal, the 2000 ASEAN+3 Summit set up an East Asia Study Group (EASG) of senior foreign ministry officials and the ASEAN Secretary-General and gave it the task of assessing the recommendations of the Vision Group and determining which of them should be given priority and would be relatively easy to carry out. In particular, the Study Group was to study the "implications" of the proposed East Asia Summit. The EASG produced a report that Korean Prime Minister Kim Suk Soo presented to the 2002 summit. The report generally supported the underlying principles and directions of the EAVG paper. Out of the EAVG's recommendations, the Study Group proposed seventeen for the "short term", among the more concrete being the formation of an East Asia Business Council, an East Asian Investment Information Network, a network of think-tanks, an East Asia Forum of governmental and non-governmental representatives from various sectors, and the promotion of East Asian studies. For the longer term, the EASG called for the pursuit of nine measures, including the East Asian Free Trade Area, the expansion of the ASEAN Investment Area, a regional financing facility, and a mechanism for closely coordinating exchange rates.[14]

Implementation of some of the short-term measures, like the network of think-tanks and the convening of the East Asia Forum, has started; whether it is sustained, whether anything concrete comes out of it, and whether the other measures are carried out remain to be seen. Scepticism is fed by the fact that ASEAN does have plans and commitments for Southeast Asia similar to many of the actions proposed for the larger East Asia — the ASEAN Free Trade Area, the ASEAN Investment Area, and other measures for regional economic integration, as well as the promotion of Southeast Asian studies;

yet, many ASEAN countries continue to find difficulty in carrying them out. They still have to show whether they are able and willing in an ASEAN+3 context to make the decisions and take the actions that they have not carried out within the smaller ASEAN framework. With respect to the proposed East Asia Business Council, an enduring, active and effective business council does not emerge from an inter-governmental decree but from the recognition by the region's business sectors themselves of the value to them of cooperating for common purposes and in their common interest. This has not happened, either in Southeast Asia or in the larger East Asia. Nevertheless, the political and economic weight of the Northeast Asian countries, and possibly their stronger compulsions, may prod the Southeast Asians to make the necessary decisions on integrating their economies not only in East Asia but more rapidly in ASEAN as well.

In any case, the ASEAN+3 process has been useful both as a forum for top-level discussion of broad issues of concern to East Asia and a measure of confidence building and as a framework for cooperation and networking in a variety of specific fields of endeavour. Indeed, it is necessary in the light of the region's extraordinary diversity, its history of conflict, and the delicate relationships among its component states. For the same reasons, one cannot expect effective institutions, much less an East Asian community, to develop anytime soon.

THE EAST ASIA SUMMIT

As for the East Asia Summit, neither the EAVG, the EASG nor, until late in 2004, the ASEAN+3 Summit itself was in any hurry to convene the EAS. The EAVG called for "the evolution of the annual summit meetings of ASEAN+3 into the East Asian Summit". In endorsing this call, the Study Group placed it in the long-term category. Certainly, it did not recommend the immediate convening of the EAS. Indeed, it emphasized that the "evolution of an EAS should proceed in a gradual and balanced way", that an "EAS is a desirable *long-term* objective, but it must be part of an *evolutionary* (italics mine) process". It asked several sensible questions without answering them: "whether an EAS is the start point or end point of East Asian cooperation; … how the pace and timing of the evolution would relate to the very process that the ASEAN+3 is trying to achieve; … what is the nature of the entity that we want to realize". The Study Group underscored the "Need for clarity of objectives and issues which the EAS should pursue". Not least, it raised the issue of membership — who the members of the EAS would be and the criteria for membership.[15]

The ASEAN+3 leaders at first did not seem to be in much of a hurry, either. The press statement of their 2001 summit in Bandar Seri Begawan reported that they had "considered" the EAVG report and merely noted that Korean President Kim Dae Jung had "highlighted" the "possibility of an East Asian Summit".[16] The statement of the 2002 summit in Phnom Penh sounded almost as hesitant, reporting that the "leaders expressed (their) *willingness to explore the phased evolution* (italics mine) of the ASEAN+3 summit into an East Asian summit" and that they "agreed with the Republic of Korea's vision for ASEAN+3 summits to *evolve in the long term* (italics mine) into East Asian Summits and eventually an East Asian Free Trade Area".[17] Neither were the ASEAN foreign ministers in a rush. At their annual meeting in 2003, the foreign ministers' joint communiqué referred only to the "possibility of an East Asia summit".[18] In 2004, according to their communiqué, the ministers "supported the idea of convening the East Asia Summit *at an appropriate time* (italics mine)".[19]

Later in 2004, however, the ASEAN leaders plunged into a decision to hold the East Asia Summit the next year in Malaysia, host of the 2005 ASEAN and ASEAN+3 Summits (and ASEAN's first summit with Russia), a decision subsequently supported by the three partners. Notwithstanding their adoption of the EASG report in 2002, the leaders made the decision without heeding the EASG's advice to go slowly or resolving the Study Group's questions. Other questions might be threshed out at the EAS itself, but the issue of participation obviously had to be settled in advance. At a briefing at the Institute of Southeast Asian Studies in Singapore in August 2005, Ong Keng Yong, the ASEAN Secretary-General, observed that the East Asia Summit would not have been realized if ASEAN's leaders had followed the cautious path advocated by their bureaucrats.

An interesting sidelight of the November 2004 ASEAN Summit in Vientiane accidentally illuminated a disagreement in ASEAN on the nature of the EAS. At the close of the Vientiane summit, the usual chairman's statement had this to say about the subject: "We agreed to transform the ASEAN+3 Summit into East Asia summit (EAS) and to hold the first EAS in Malaysia in 2005 and in this connection, tasked our Foreign Ministers to work out the details concerning its modality and participation." Very shortly after the statement's release to the media and the public, however, an amended version was issued, stating, "We agreed to hold the first EAS in Malaysia in 2005" and so on.[20] The reference to the "transformation" of the ASEAN+3 Summit into the East Asia Summit was no longer in the text; obviously it had actually not been agreed upon. By leaving out the idea of "transformation", the second, and authoritative, version of the chairman's statement implied that the ASEAN+3 process was not necessarily to be replaced by the East Asia Summit, nor would the East Asia Summit necessarily be ASEAN+3 transformed. Neither would the East Asia Summit have necessarily the same participation as ASEAN+3. Indeed, in both versions, the chairman's statement left undecided the question of participation by leaving it to the foreign ministers to work out.

In answer to a question following his Singapore Lecture on 16 February 2005, President Susilo Bambang Yudhoyono expressed Indonesia's preference for the inclusion of India, Australia and New Zealand in addition to the Southeast Asian and Northeast Asian countries. Singapore is reported to have had a similar position. Japan had proposed the participation of the United States. Malaysia was thought to be insisting on limiting participation in the East Asia Summit to ASEAN+3, the direct descendant of former Prime Minister Mahathir's East Asia Economic Group. However, during his visit to Australia in April 2005, Prime Minister Abdullah Badawi was quoted in Canberra as replying to a question about Australia's attendance at the East Asia Summit, "My policy has been one of inclusiveness and not excluding anybody."[21]

Pursuant to the leaders' directive, the ASEAN Foreign Ministers took up the issue in their annual "retreat" in Cebu, the Philippines, in April 2005. Singapore's Foreign Minister, George Yeo, announced the outcome of the discussion in remarks to the media. The first EAS would, of course, involve ASEAN and its three Northeast Asian partners. However, the ASEAN Foreign Ministers came to an agreement that others could be included if they fulfilled three conditions: substantive relations with ASEAN, full Dialogue Partner status, and accession to the Treaty of Amity and Cooperation in Southeast Asia. Yeo declared that, since India fulfilled all three conditions, it was eligible to participate in the EAS. As for Australia and New Zealand, he expressed the hope that they would accede to the treaty "in the coming months", in which case, "we would welcome them to the EAS in KL (Kuala Lumpur)". According to Yeo, it was agreed that "ASEAN alone" would decide which countries could participate in all subsequent East Asia Summits.[22]

At their meeting in Vientiane on 26 July 2005, the ASEAN Foreign Ministers announced the composition of the East Asia Summit as ASEAN+3, India, Australia and New Zealand. New Zealand's Foreign Minister Phil Goff signed the instrument of accession to the TAC two days later. Foreign Minister Alexander Downer issued a declaration of Australia's intention to do so "upon completion of its necessary domestic procedures". On 10 December, four days before the EAS, Downer signed the instrument of Australia's accession to the TAC.

By opening the East Asia Summit to the participation of India, Australia and New Zealand, ASEAN has done several things. The East Asia Summit will no longer be ASEAN+3 "transformed" or "evolved". It will be additional to the ASEAN+3 process. India's drive to link up with East Asia has made significant political progress, a drive that ASEAN supports. The desire of Australia and New Zealand to be involved in the development of East Asia has received a substantial boost. From the viewpoint of some ASEAN countries, the presence of more large powers may dispel the apprehension about East Asia's development being driven by the Sino-Japanese rivalry and other Northeast Asian concerns. Since President Vladimir Putin had been invited to Kuala Lumpur to meet with ASEAN's leaders for the first time, the Russians tried to get him to participate in the EAS. After all, Russia had been an ASEAN Dialogue Partner since 1996 and signed the TAC in November 2004. Apparently, however, ASEAN did not deem Russia's relations with it to be "substantive" enough for participation in the EAS. Nevertheless, in a typical ASEAN compromise, Putin, whose presence was publicly acknowledged as Malaysia's guest, was invited to give a 15-minute address to the EAS but did not participate in the summit itself. According to the chairman's statement, the EAS participants "welcomed the Russian Federation's expression of interest to participate in the East Asia Summit and agreed to consider its participation in future East Asia Summits based on the criteria established by ASEAN".[23] Apparently, no consensus had been arrived at. Should Russia become a regular participant, that development would make the absence of the United States all the more conspicuous to those who feel that Washington should be part of the East Asian process.

For more than a century, the United States has considered itself to have vital security and economic interests in East Asia and the Pacific. Others in the EAS, including China, recognize those interests. However, three obstacles could, from Washington's standpoint, lie in the way of U.S. participation in the new summit. One would be the U.S. reluctance to have its President engage in discussions with the leader of Myanmar. The second would be Washington's policy of declining to accede to the Treaty of Amity and Cooperation in Southeast Asia, one of ASEAN's requirements for participation in the EAS. The third would be the U.S. President's crowded schedule, which might preclude a trip to Asia in addition to the one that he would be undertaking for APEC in the same season.

With some effort to soften up political opinion at home, the United States could, if it wanted to, overcome the Myanmar hurdle by stressing that the EAS would be a meeting of several important countries, including ASEAN members, just like the ARF, in which states like Myanmar and North Korea, as well as the United States, take part. With respect to the TAC, ASEAN, if it wished to bring the United States into the EAS, could argue that Washington had in a way associated itself with the treaty through the November 2005 Joint Vision Statement on the ASEAN-US Enhanced Partnership, in which ASEAN and the United States, in rather tortured language, "[a]cknowledge that the Treaty of Amity and Cooperation in Southeast Asia (TAC) acts as a code of conduct governing inter-State relations in the region for the promotion of peace and stability, and its role as a unifying concept for ASEAN and respect the spirit and principles of the TAC, in line with the commitment of ASEAN and the United States to enhance their partnership". In the end, on the part of the United States, the biggest barrier to American participation in the EAS could be nothing more than the U.S. President's packed schedule. In any case, the United States has given no public indication of its interest in belonging to the EAS at this time. The public posture that American officials have cultivated in relation to this issue has been one of studied indifference. "The U.S. does not have to be in everything," they shrug. More fundamentally, from ASEAN's standpoint, the presence of the U.S. superpower would alter the character of the whole enterprise. There seems to be as yet no consensus on this issue.

In any case, the first EAS emphasized the fluid nature of participation in it. While it is highly unlikely that any of the participants in the first summit will be excluded from it in the foreseeable future, the forum is open for future participation by others. The Kuala Lumpur Declaration on the East Asia Summit stressed that the EAS would be an "open, inclusive, transparent and outward-looking forum".[24]

In an article on the EAS in the *Straits Times* of Singapore, I wrote:

> In its usual pragmatic way, Asean had decided that a new building block was needed for the regional architecture, a group that would transcend the orthodox definition of East Asia but would reflect certain realities on the ground.
>
> One reality was the growing involvement of India, Australia and New Zealand in the affairs of East Asia.
>
> Another was that, with the World Trade Organization (WTO) bogged down, easing trade and investment flows within an area larger than ASEAN+3 and more manageable than the Apec would benefit everyone.
>
> A third reality was that some transnational problems could be managed better in a larger but fairly compact regional context.
>
> The (EAS) refrained from proclaiming abstract and unrealistic ambitions, such as being the Asian reincarnation of the European Union.

At the same time, it exceeded the sceptics' extremely low expectations of it. The chairman's statement and the adopted declaration made it clear that the EAS would be mainly a forum for the discussion of strategic issues.

Still, the leaders also agreed that, beyond political and security consultations, they would deal cooperatively with economic development and integration, poverty eradication, energy security, cultural understanding, the environment, natural disasters, (and) infectious diseases.

Underlining its urgency, the summit issued a separate declaration on avian influenza, setting directions for national and regional cooperative measures to prevent it from turning into a pandemic.

Significantly, the summit saw itself as striving "to strengthen global norms and universally recognized values."[25]

Not least, the summit affirmed the centrality of ASEAN's role in it. It adopted ASEAN's criteria for participation. Where both the EAS chairman's statement and the Kuala Lumpur Declaration cited community building, the reference was to the ASEAN Community rather than to the more long-term project of an East Asian community. The EAS would be convened regularly on the occasion of the annual ASEAN Summit under the chairmanship of ASEAN's country-chairman. It would thus take place in an ASEAN country every year, with the summit agreeing to meet in Cebu on 13 December 2006. It would be pertinent to recall at this point that China had offered to host the first EAS. When ASEAN insisted that the first summit take place in an ASEAN country, the possibility of China hosting the second was considered. The EAS eventually decided to keep the meetings within ASEAN. True to its general policy of conceding to ASEAN on matters that are not of vital importance to it, China graciously yielded in both instances. Thus, ASEAN's central role in shaping the regional architecture — at least in diplomatic and institutional terms — has been affirmed and recognized once more. The extent to which the nations and peoples of ASEAN benefit from this circumstance will depend on two things: the degree of political solidarity and economic integration that ASEAN achieves and the wisdom of the policies of its individual component states.

CHINA

At the time of ASEAN's founding in 1967, China was, in one way or another, a leading factor in the security calculations of the association as well as of its member-states. Not that a military attack or invasion was ever realistically feared; but, in 1967, China was in the throes of the Great Proletarian Cultural

Revolution, and the radical and volatile, sometimes violent, expressions of Chinese diplomacy, Beijing's virulent broadcasts against the regimes in place in the ASEAN member-countries and against the association itself, and its verbal and material support for communist movements in the ASEAN members and in Myanmar, then called Burma — all these together conveyed an implacable hostility to China's southern neighbours and a threat to their stability. And China had the military power to be perceived as threatening; after all, it had fought the United States and its allies to a standstill in Korea and had, in 1964, tested an atomic weapon for the first time.

Towards the end of the 1960s, however, amid the constant power struggles at many levels of the government and party, the Chinese leadership saw a heightened threat from the Soviet Union, with numerous clashes taking place along the long common border and vitriolic invectives being exchanged between Beijing and Moscow. At the same time, the United States seemed to be genuinely seeking a way out of its misadventure in Vietnam and reaching out to China and could serve as a strategic deterrent to what the Chinese perceived as their greater rival and threat, the USSR. As part of their response to these developments, Beijing felt the need to consolidate normal relations with its non-communist Southeast Asian neighbours. All this induced a shift towards a more pragmatic and more orthodox Chinese foreign policy, a process that culminated in the People's Republic taking China's seat in the United Nations in 1971, the establishment of diplomatic relations with European, Latin American and African countries that had until then withheld recognition from Beijing, Richard Nixon's dramatic visit to China in 1972 and the opening of relations with the United States short only of the diplomatic formalities, and the forging of diplomatic ties with Japan in the same year.

Following the upheaval in Indonesia and the consequent mutual recriminations between Jakarta and Beijing, Indonesia had suspended official relations with China in 1967 amid Indonesian suspicions of Chinese support for the attempted coup by the Indonesian Communist Party on 30 September 1965. However, with the changes in Indochina, the shifts in great-power relationships, and the reorientation of Chinese foreign policy, the other ASEAN countries adjusted their outlooks on the geo-strategic situation in East Asia and China's place in it. Malaysia opened diplomatic relations with the People's Republic in 1974, followed by the Philippines and Thailand the next year. In line with these trends, official Beijing had ceased its verbal assaults on ASEAN and its member-states. (In 1971, Burma and China normalized their relations, which had been ruptured by Chinese provocations at the height of the Cultural Revolution.)

Meanwhile, Deng Xiaoping had been reinstated, in 1973, as vice-premier and, early in 1975, appointed as vice-chairman of the Central Committee of the Chinese Communist Party and a member of the Standing Committee of its Politburo. I was present during the talks between President Ferdinand Marcos and Vice-Premier Deng in June 1975 leading to the establishment of diplomatic relations between the two countries. (The joint communiqué on diplomatic relations was signed by Marcos and Premier Zhou Enlai in the Beijing hospital where the latter was confined with a terminal illness. I remember the limpness in Zhou's handshake, something that was uncharacteristic of such a strong personality and evidence of the gravity of his condition. He was to die seven months later.) Specifically, what the Philippines sought from China were the cessation of China's support for the Philippine communist movement, a reliable supply of crude oil following the global energy crisis of 1973, a time when China was still a net oil exporter, and the peaceful management of the disputes in the South China Sea. What the Philippines was to give Beijing would be diplomatic recognition and normal relations on the basis of one China. Beijing had already stopped its direct support for the Philippine communists and had pledged significant supplies of oil at "friendship prices". As for the South China Sea, Deng Xiaoping proposed that the disputes there be "shelved" indefinitely and "joint development" pursued. More broadly, the Philippines had concluded that China was a huge and growing political, economic and military reality that had to be dealt with in the light of the evolving world situation and the needs of the country. Similar considerations must have motivated Malaysia and Thailand in line with their respective needs and concerns.

However, ASEAN *as an association* did not engage China until Vietnam's incursion into Cambodia towards the end of 1978. After China's attack on Vietnam in February–March 1979 to "teach Hanoi a lesson" (dubbed the "pedagogical war"), ASEAN and the People's Republic found common cause in resisting Vietnam's — and, in their view, Moscow's — perceived intention to alter the strategic situation in mainland Southeast Asia and coordinated their diplomatic moves on the matter, with the ASEAN and Chinese Foreign Ministers meeting annually at UN General Assembly time in New York. Together with ASEAN's diplomatic leadership, Chinese military and political support for the Coalition Government of Democratic Kampuchea made possible an eventual settlement on Cambodia, with the disengagement — and eventual disintegration — of the Soviet Union, Vietnam's principal backer, being an important factor. China's role in the Cambodian situation was an unmistakable indication of China's rising influence in Southeast Asia, in this case wielded on behalf of interests that coincided with those of ASEAN.

At this time, the Chinese leadership was laying the foundations of a market economy and the country's integration into the world economy. As a result, China began to loom even larger in the global and regional security, as well as economic, environment, as manifested in China's ability to maintain rapid economic growth, modernize its armed forces, and exert ever-stronger international influence.

In 1990, Indonesia restored, and then Singapore established, formal diplomatic relations with China, although the two countries, especially Singapore, had already had dealings with the People's Republic even before that. Brunei Darussalam followed suit in 1991. With that, all of ASEAN, indeed all of Southeast Asia, had formal relations with China. Although, with the settlement on Cambodia, the ASEAN and Chinese Foreign Ministers ceased to meet regularly in New York, the ASEAN-China relationship quickly gathered pace. It was time to formalize and strengthen the relationship between China and ASEAN as a group.

The Chinese Foreign Minister and his Russian counterpart were invited as guests of Malaysia at the ASEAN Ministerial Meeting in Kuala Lumpur in July 1991. The next year they were at the Manila meeting a notch higher in standing, as guests of the Chairman of the ASEAN Standing Committee. By 1994, China and Russia had become "consultative partners" of ASEAN, a development that illustrated the association's flexibility in creating new categories of relationships as the need arises. It was in that capacity that China and Russia took part as founding members in the inaugural meeting of the ASEAN Regional Forum on the occasion of the 1994 ASEAN Ministerial Meeting in Bangkok. Indeed, it can be said that the ARF was formed in order to allow China — and Russia and the prospective ASEAN members, Vietnam and Laos — to participate in consultations on regional security. Originally envisioned as a forum for ASEAN and its Dialogue Partners to conduct dialogues on regional security questions, the structure of a consultative mechanism on regional security was expanded in order to engage states that were not in ASEAN or its dialogue system but were of vital significance to the security of the region. In 1996, China, together with Russia and India, became a full Dialogue Partner of ASEAN.

In 1994 (the first year of the ARF), pursuant to an agreement reached the year before on a Chinese proposal, ASEAN and China had established two joint committees — one on trade and economic cooperation, the other on science and technology. In 1997, they formed the ASEAN-China Joint

Cooperation Committee, at director-general level, to coordinate the growing number and variety of cooperative activities, including in the economic and "functional" areas, human resource development, people-to-people contacts, and cultural exchanges. In the same year, they set up a US$5 million ASEAN-China Cooperation Fund, financed entirely by China, which has been used to support projects that promote mutual understanding and networking, like study tours and exchanges of people in a variety of areas. At the 2000 and 2004 summits with ASEAN, China announced additional contributions of US$5 million each to the fund.

In previous memoranda of understanding, ASEAN and China had signified their intention to collaborate on agriculture and on information and communications technology. China hosted an ASEAN-China EXPO in November 2004 in Nanning, the Chinese provincial capital closest to an ASEAN country (Vietnam), with the stated intention of making it an annual event. A second one was organized in October 2005 in the same city. China put on an "ASEAN-China Telecommunications Week" in May 2005 in Beijing, Shanghai and Shenzhen. Since the SARS epidemic wrought disaster on China and on several ASEAN countries, China has worked closely with ASEAN, as well as with the WHO, in dealing with infectious diseases.

In view of China's importance in the regional-security equation and in the light particularly of its extravagant jurisdictional claims to the South China Sea, I proposed in 1994 that ASEAN and China set up a forum for regular political consultations at senior-official level on the premise that it would be useful for Southeast Asia, as a group rather than only on bilateral terms, to discuss political issues in some detail with China. Then on my second tour as ASEAN Senior Official for the Philippines, I made the proposal in Bandar Seri Begawan to Lim Jock Seng, the long-serving Permanent Secretary, now the Second Minister, at the Ministry of Foreign Affairs of Brunei Darussalam, which was chairing the ASEAN Standing Committee. Both of us then put the proposal to Wang Yingfan, at that time China's Assistant Foreign Minister for Asian affairs. He readily agreed, as did the other ASEAN members. Since then, the forum has been meeting annually, alternating between a place in China and one in the ASEAN "coordinator-country" for the People's Republic.

Emphasizing its close empathy with ASEAN, China was the first non-regional state, after Papua New Guinea, to accede to the Treaty of Amity and Cooperation in Southeast Asia, doing so in October 2003. It was a largely symbolic gesture, costing China nothing, but it earned the People's Republic some goodwill in the region for its treaty commitment to resolve disputes peacefully and not to interfere in the other signatories' internal affairs. On

ASEAN's part, the calculation was that it would be useful to get China to sign on to the norms for inter-state conduct that had helped to keep the peace among Southeast Asian countries and foster a sense of stability in the region, norms moreover that dovetailed with the Five Principles of Peaceful Coexistence formulated by China in the 1950s.

Similarly, China has let it be known that, as a nuclear-weapon state, it is ready to sign the protocol to the Southeast Asia Nuclear Weapons-Free Zone treaty at any time. Again, this does not cost Beijing anything, since it knows that there will be no protocol to sign until the four other officially recognized nuclear-weapon states agree to it. Meanwhile, China has earned some goodwill for itself and has put one over the other nuclear powers.

China had not been very active in the ARF in terms of specific initiatives, but in Phnom Penh in June 2003 the Chinese delegation pulled a minor surprise by proposing an annual ARF Security Policy Conference among senior defence and security policy officials, basically as a confidence-building measure. The first conference took place in Beijing under Indonesia's chairmanship on 4–6 November 2004.

The July 2004 ARF had decided that subsequent such conferences would "be convened back-to-back with the annual ARF SOM ... hosted and chaired by the ARF chair country".[26]

Beijing has not confined its security linkage with ASEAN to matters related to inter-state conflict; the two sides have indicated their interest in cooperating in so-called "non-traditional security". With the rise of global alarm over international terrorism as a result of the terrorist attacks on the United States in September 2001, the ASEAN and Chinese leaders issued the Joint Declaration of ASEAN and China on Cooperation in the Field of Non-Traditional Security Issues in November 2002 in Phnom Penh. The declaration went beyond anti-terrorism and covered other transnational crimes — drug-trafficking, people-smuggling, including trafficking in women and children, sea piracy, arms-smuggling, money-laundering, international economic crime and "cyber crime". Cooperation was to be carried out through the exchange of information and personnel, training and capacity-building, and joint research.[27] In January 2004, Secretary-General Ong Keng Yong, on behalf of ASEAN, signed with Tian Qiyu, China's Executive Vice Minister of Public Security, a memorandum of understanding specifying the measures for carrying out the leaders' declaration — the compilation of national laws and regulations and of international conventions and bilateral agreements to which ASEAN countries and China are parties, the exchange of intelligence and information on "special equipment and techniques", personnel exchanges and training, cooperation in law enforcement, and joint research. Whether something concretely productive comes out of this remains to be seen, but it is another link forged between ASEAN and China, this time in the broader concept of security. Beyond its specific intent, I consider this memorandum of understanding to be of some significance in that, for the first time, the ASEAN Secretary-General was authorized to act for the association on matters of security, albeit of the "non-traditional" variety and only by way of implementing measures.[28]

As the headwaters of the Mekong are located in Chinese territory, China is also linked to ASEAN through the ASEAN Mekong Basin Development Cooperation (AMBDC), even as it participates in the Asian Development Bank's Greater Mekong Sub-region (GMS) programme. It is the only non-ASEAN country that shares the waters and the ecology of the world's eighth-largest river and thus the only country outside ASEAN that is a member of the AMBDC, although Japan and Korea have occasionally expressed an interest in participating in it and have been invited to do so in some way.

In addition to the always-critical area of human resource development, for which Beijing has earmarked US$5 million, among other contributions, China has indicated a deep interest in transportation and energy linkages with mainland Southeast Asia. Part of this is the Singapore-Kunming Rail Link, a "flagship project" of AMBDC that aims to construct missing segments and rehabilitate portions in disrepair and thus to complete the railway network from the southern tip of mainland Southeast Asia to the capital of Yunnan, a province that borders three ASEAN countries. Another high-profile endeavour is the envisioned highway network from Bangkok to Kunming, a project of the ADB's GMS programme. At the November 2002 ASEAN-China summit, China announced that it would extend to Laos a loan of US$30 million for the construction of the segment that runs through that country. (A few months earlier, Thailand had agreed to provide a loan of a similar amount for the same purpose.)

Another of China's interests in transportation links with mainland Southeast Asia is the improvement of the Mekong's navigability. In June 2001, the Chinese Government announced on its Website that it would "invest more than 42 million yuan (US$5.06 million) to help Myanmar and Laos dredge a navigation section on the Mekong River". The project would cover 331 kilometres, mostly where the river marks the boundary between Laos and Myanmar. By blasting and dredging rapids, reefs and shoals, the clearing would allow, at the first stage, 100-ton ships to ply that section of the river and, at the second stage, 300-ton vessels by 2007.[29] The plan elicited expressions of concern, primarily from non-governmental organizations, over its expected environmental impact, including on the river's fish life, the supposed inadequacy of the project's environmental impact assessment, and its possible effects on the course of the river and, therefore, on the location of international boundaries.

Even more controversial is China's massive endeavour to build dams on the Lancang Jiang, the section of the Mekong that originates in and flows through Chinese territory. While this is only part of an enormous dam-building enterprise in the southwestern and northern regions of China, it is the only significant such effort that has a serious impact on neighbouring countries. Without consultation with any of the downstream riparian countries, much less with ASEAN, China completed the Manwan dam in 1993, the first on the Lancang/Mekong mainstream, and began operating it in 1995. Another, at Dachaoshan, started operation in 2003. Two other dams, the Xiaowan, one of the world's largest, and the Jinghong, are scheduled for completion before 2013. The construction of another, the Nuozhadu, is expected to take place between 2010 and 2020. When the entire "cascade" is done, there will be seven or eight dams in all. The dams are meant to generate valuable energy for a power-hungry China, and for sale to Thailand at prices expected to be lower than hydropower exported from Laos. They are also expected to help control floods in the rainy season and increase dry-season water supply for irrigation and navigation.

On the other hand, the dams have come under heavy criticism from many quarters on account of the forced relocation of tens of thousands of people from the dam sites and the predicted damage to the ecology, including that in the countries to China's south. Critics point to the reduction in the nutrients and sediments that the river deposits downstream. This would necessitate greater use of chemical fertilizer in affected farms, which would raise farmers' costs. At the same time, the sediments trapped at the dams would reduce the projected span of their productive lives. It has been pointed out that the dams would upset the spawning and feeding habits of the numerous varieties of fish in the river, reducing their number and diversity. The higher water levels in the dry season would destroy the seasonal vegetable farms on the banks and riverbed downstream and weaken the foundations of buildings, bridges and other structures.

China has declined to be a full member of the Mekong River Commission, now headquartered in Vientiane and made up of Cambodia, Laos, Thailand and Vietnam, where these concerns could be threshed out, although, according to the MRC, it "maintains regular dialogue with the two upper states of the Mekong River Basin, China and Myanmar".[30] Both those countries were invited to join the commission when it was established in April 1995 to succeed the old Mekong Committee, which dated back to 1957.

Nor have the complex issues arising from the dams been discussed in AMBDC, as far as I know. Two senior engineers of the Yunnan Provincial Environmental Protection Bureau claim that the recommendations made in the environmental impact assessment of the Manwan and Dachaoshan power projects have been complied with. They assert:

> There is a limited impact of the construction of these cascade power stations on the environment because the dam is located in the valley areas. Plant and animal species living in the submerged areas are spread widely in the Yunnan Province. The construction of the dam will not endanger rare plants or animal species. On the other hand, the construction of large-scale dams on the middle and lower reaches of the Lancang River will play an important role in adjusting downstream flow and increasing waterway flow in the dry season.[31]

Nevertheless, high Cambodian officials have expressed their concerns over the effect of the upstream dams on the water level of the Tonle Sap but apparently have not raised them with the Chinese themselves. When I asked senior Lao officials about similar effects on the river that cuts through their country and forms much of the Laos-Thailand boundary, they shrugged them off, pointing out that much of their part of the river is fed not from sources in Yunnan but from the Mekong's many tributaries in Laos itself. However, Evelyn Goh, assistant professor at the Institute of Defence and Strategic Studies in Singapore, states, "In gross terms, the Lancang contributes 16 per cent of the Mekong's total discharge, but in real terms, it contributes 100 per cent of the flow at the Laos border (with China) and 60 per cent as far downstream as Vientiane...."[32]

Goh suggests that the impact of Chinese dam building on the downstream countries be regarded as a security problem. She cites four reasons:

> First, China's potential control over vital water flows to downstream states may be framed as a challenge to the sovereignty and autonomy of these states. Second, the possible large-scale and adverse impacts on communities within each of these states might affect the popularity and stability of the governing national or local regime, as seen in growing community mobilization challenging the central government's policies and priorities in Thailand. Third, expected problems with demand, supply and pricing (particularly if affected by the reduced lifespan of dams or the impact of environmental factors on electricity supply) when the regional power grid is in place, may lead to diplomatic tension between the riparian states. Fourth, the negative impacts on regional livelihoods and food supply may be vital in terms of the number of people affected, particularly in the absence

of effective alternatives and/or increased empowerment of communities, and may lead to migration and other socio-political instability which may be securitized at national level.[33]

Pursuant to this suggestion, the issue of dams on the upper reaches of the Lancang/Mekong could be regarded as a "non-traditional" security matter. However, in the light of the current attitudes of China and the downstream countries, there is little chance that this will happen anytime soon — whether within ASEAN, in ASEAN-China relations, in AMBDC or in the ARF — although "non-traditional" security issues have of late been receiving emphasis in security discussions between ASEAN and its partners, including China, as well as within ASEAN. For China and ASEAN, the impact of dams on the people of the Mekong is evidently not one of those issues at this time.

To be fair, though, one must say that it is not just China's dams that are a possible threat to the Mekong. Destructive fishing practices south of China and Vietnam's dams on the Sesan River, a tributary of the Mekong, are threatening, too. (Under construction since the early 1990s, the 720-MW Yali Falls dam, 70 kilometres upstream from the Vietnam-Cambodia border, has been in operation since 2001. The construction of another dam, Sesan 3, which is 20 kilometres downstream from the one at Yali Falls, started in June 2002. Cambodian villagers and non-governmental organizations have complained about the unpredictable floods and the erratic rise and fall of water levels and have expressed their alarm over the prospect of more dams on the Sesan.)

The one contentious issue on which ASEAN has striven collectively to engage China is the South China Sea. The overlapping claims of China and at least four ASEAN countries to varying expanses of the South China Sea have made the area a security problem in the region. For a number of years, China insisted on dealing with the other claimants individually rather than collectively and never in a multilateral setting. In 1992, at the ASEAN Ministerial Meeting in Manila, at which the Chinese Foreign Minister was present as guest of the chair, ASEAN issued a declaration calling for the peaceful settlement of disputes in the South China Sea, the exercise of restraint, cooperation in maritime safety, environmental protection and search and rescue, and cooperative action against piracy, robbery at sea and drug-trafficking.[34] ASEAN urged China to associate itself with the declaration. After consulting Beijing, Minister Qian Qichen responded that China supported the principles in the declaration but could not sign on to it because, he argued, China had not been involved in drafting it. The declaration was brought to a test when the Philippines announced, early in 1995, the discovery of Chinese facilities on Mischief Reef, which was threateningly close to the large

Philippine island of Palawan. A few months later, at the first of the annual ASEAN-China senior officials consultations that I had proposed, ASEAN raised the issue of Mischief Reef and probed China's intentions in recently promulgating its Law on the Territorial Sea and Contiguous Zone. Before that, ASEAN's foreign ministers had issued a statement calling for "the early resolution of the problems caused by recent developments in Mischief Reef".[35] China had long resisted "internationalizing" the South China Sea issue and even discussing the matter other than bilaterally with individual ASEAN claimants. However, faced with ASEAN solidarity on the problem, China became more open to discussing it with ASEAN as a group and even in the ARF. This process culminated in the conclusion by ASEAN and China of the Declaration on the Conduct of Parties in the South China Sea, which is something of a code of conduct, although, for a number of reasons, it is not called that. Signed by the Foreign Ministers on the day of the ASEAN Summit in Phnom Penh in 2002, the declaration commits the parties to the peaceful settlement of disputes, to freedom of lawful navigation and overflight in the area, to "self-restraint", to refraining from "inhabiting" currently uninhabited features, to confidence-building measures, to cooperation in a number of specified areas, and to the eventual conclusion of a code of conduct.[36] Because the jurisdictional and sovereignty issues have not been resolved, the South China Sea remains a potential flashpoint for conflict. However, ASEAN and China have managed to keep the area quiescent for now. Chapter 4 has a more extensive discussion of the South China Sea issue as a security concern.

As the 1997–98 financial crisis swept through much of East Asia, Beijing gained favour with ASEAN by emphatically and repeatedly declaring its resolve not to devalue the *renminbi* after the currencies of the older ASEAN members had drastically diminished in value as a result of the crisis. A devaluation of the Chinese currency would have wrought further havoc on the competitive positions of the ASEAN countries and on their monetary situations. China is an active participant in the Chiangmai Initiative, being party to five of the sixteen bilateral currency swap and repurchase agreements. These agreements form a network among ASEAN+3 countries designed to shore up the liquidity of a party that runs into balance-of-payments problems and thus help fend off speculative attacks on its currency.

Since the affected ASEAN economies began to recover from the crisis, it has been the proposed ASEAN-China free trade area that has attracted the most interest, with its much-noted promise of being the largest such arrangement in the world, one of 1.7 billion people and with a total economic output of US$2 trillion by some estimates, a combined gross domestic product that is rapidly rising. Proposed by then Premier Zhu Rongji at the November

2000 ASEAN-China Summit, the free trade area moved quickly in terms of agreements reached and schedules set. The 2001 summit endorsed the study by the joint expert group that had been formed for the purpose, accepting the group's call for the conclusion of an economic-cooperation agreement that would provide for a free trade area within ten years (for the ASEAN-6 and China), with an "early harvest" provision. ASEAN had proposed the "early harvest" as a modality for ASEAN to gain concessions from China without reciprocity. However, during the negotiations, China successfully insisted that the "early harvest" programme be reciprocal and that it involve only agricultural products. In November 2002, the ASEAN and Chinese leaders signed the ASEAN-China Framework Agreement on Comprehensive Economic Cooperation, which called for the elimination of barriers to trade in goods by 2010 for the ASEAN-6 and 2015 for the four newer ASEAN members, the liberalization of trade in services, "a transparent, liberal and facilitative investment regime", and measures to facilitate trade and investment. The framework agreement laid down the elements to be covered by a specific accord on trade in goods and those to be addressed by the negotiations on trade in services and on investments. It listed products excluded by some ASEAN countries from the "early harvest" programme. It also called for the establishment of a dispute-settlement mechanism. After they adopted in October 2003 the rules of origin for goods to be covered by the free trade area, the ASEAN and Chinese Economic Ministers concluded in November 2004 the agreement on trade in goods, which prescribed the modalities for reducing and eventually eliminating barriers to trade. They also reached agreement on a mechanism for settling disputes arising from the application of the framework agreement. ASEAN and China are now working on the agreements on trade in services and on investments.

Even before the formal agreements were arrived at, economic interaction between China and ASEAN countries had been growing rapidly. China's share in ASEAN's exports rose from about 2 per cent in 1993 to 2.7 per cent in 1997, to 3.9 per cent in 2001 and to more than 7 per cent in 2004, while its share in ASEAN's imports expanded from 1.9 to 3.8, 5.5 and 9.4 per cent in those years. To be sure, even in 2003, the percentage share and absolute value of China's trade with ASEAN were still far below those of ASEAN's trade with its traditional partners — the United States, the European Union and Japan.[37] The point, however, is China's growing share and the expectations of a further, accelerated expansion. A "reference paper" drawn up by the ASEAN Secretariat for the ASEAN-China Eminent Persons Group in August 2005 noted, "In 2003, (ASEAN-China trade) grew by 43 per cent to a new high of US$78.2 billion," of which US$47.3 billion was accounted for by

Chinese imports from ASEAN, a 50 per cent increase. China's exports to ASEAN amounted to only US$4.3 billion in 1993 and US$17 billion in 2000, while ASEAN's exports to China were at US$4.5 billion in 1993 and US$12.2 billion in 2000. According to the Secretariat's paper, ASEAN investments in China were valued at US$26.2 billion in 2001, making up 6.6 per cent of total foreign direct investments in China and marking a sharp rise from US$90 million in 1991 and US$4.8 billion in 1998. (On the other hand, China's investments in ASEAN in 2001 were worth only US$1.1 billion, representing 7.7 per cent of its total overseas investments.) The envisioned ASEAN-China free trade area and the services and investment agreements being negotiated, even if they fall short of their ambitions, should give further impetus to this trend. The number of visitors from China to ASEAN is also on the rise, having increased from 818,000 in 1995 to 1.9 million in 1999 and to 2.8 million in 2002, but dropped to less than 2.4 million in 2003 evidently on account of the SARS problem. It exceeded 3 million for the first time in 2004.[38]

In the meantime, China has won ASEAN support for its claim to market-economy status, an important factor in China's enjoyment of certain rights under the WTO, which some leading trading powers are denying China. Article 14 of the agreement on trade in goods between ASEAN and China states:

> Each of the ten ASEAN Member States agrees to recognise China as a full market economy and shall not apply, from the date of the signature of this Agreement, Sections 15 and 16 of the Protocol of Accession of the People's Republic of China to the WTO and Paragraph 242 of the Report of the Working Party on the Accession of China to WTO in relation to the trade between China and each of the ten ASEAN Member States.[39]

Whatever variations there are among Southeast Asian countries in their individual relations with China, whatever the state of their bilateral relationships with the United States, Japan and other powers, for ASEAN, China is, and has been from its inception, a vital security relationship. There is the immutable factor of geographic proximity, with the weight and precise nature of this factor varying from country to country in ASEAN. For the mainland states, there is the strategic and economic linkage with southern China in the context of the Mekong Basin and over land borders, although this, too, has an impact on the maritime part of Southeast Asia. China's participation in the ARF has been essential to that body's effectiveness. The delicate and complex nature of the conflicting claims to the South China Sea, the management of this issue, and ASEAN's solidarity on it have been central to the ASEAN-China security relationship.

ASEAN and China are also important to each other in economic terms, although the degree of that importance varies among ASEAN countries in accordance with the structure and strength of their individual economies. For ASEAN generally, China is a major competitor for markets and investments. At the same time, it is a fast-expanding market for goods and services, a potentially important source of investments, and a growing tourist market. The value of the *renminbi* has an impact on the competitiveness of ASEAN countries. On the other hand, the importance, actual and potential, of Southeast Asia and the South China Sea as critical sources of mineral and energy resources and even food for China is increasingly apparent.

All these elements find expression in a growing number of ASEAN-China agreements, joint declarations and expressions of intent that may or may not bear concrete fruit in themselves but signal the importance that China and ASEAN as an association assign to the relationship between them, a relationship that has a significant impact on the stability of the region. In October 2003, in Bali, the leaders of ASEAN and China put out the Joint Declaration on Strategic Partnership for Peace and Prosperity, which reviewed in very positive terms the state of ASEAN-China relations and contained a catalogue of general intentions in the political, economic, social and security areas. At their summit in Vientiane in 2004, they adopted a Plan of Action for the declaration, a long list of activities and directions in varying degrees of vagueness. Again, while these and most other joint declarations and other statements of intention may not result in concrete action and may wind up as largely ceremonial and symbolic documents, they do project to China's bureaucracy, as well as to the international community, a sense of the strength of China's relations with ASEAN and of the value that Beijing places on them. In this spirit, following the special summit in Tokyo commemorating the thirtieth anniversary of ASEAN-Japan relations, the leaders of ASEAN and China agreed in Kuala Lumpur to have an ASEAN-China commemorative summit in 2006, in Nanning, marking the fifteenth anniversary of the People's Republic's first formal participation in an ASEAN forum.

By virtue of the differences among them in geographical location, historical experience, and cultural outlook, ASEAN countries, of course, differ in their assessment of China's role in their national life, in the specifics of their bilateral relations with Beijing, and in their evaluation of the benefits, costs and prospects of individual components of those relations. However, the ASEAN countries share certain basic understandings with respect to dealing with China. One of their main concerns is the possible evolution of China, their massive next-door neighbour, into a regional hegemon on the strength of its growing economic, political and military power, notwithstanding Beijing's repeated denial of any aspiration to hegemony and its doctrinal opposition to the very concept of hegemony. Another is the danger that the disputes on the South China Sea could actually become the flashpoint that they are often depicted to be, especially in the light of the growing shortages in the resources that the South China Sea is thought to harbour and the fact that the jurisdictional disputes there remain unsettled. All ASEAN countries have an interest in peace and stability in the Taiwan Straits and adhere to the one-China policy. They take seriously China's threat to take military action if the authorities in Taiwan declare independence or make moves towards it, not necessarily because they believe in the likelihood of a Chinese attack but because they are, at the very least, concerned about the destabilizing effect of such moves and the broad range of possible Chinese responses to them. Accordingly, they hope that the Taiwan authorities will desist from taking steps towards formal independence, if not explicitly discourage them from such moves, as Singapore has done. The ASEAN members acknowledge the importance of China's role in global and regional affairs — from the nuclear problem on the Korean peninsula to the stability of the *renminbi*, as well as its permanent membership in the UN Security Council — an importance that continues to grow. The Southeast Asian countries view China's economic surge as at once an attractive opportunity and a competitive threat, the balance between the two depending on the structure and strength of the particular country's economy. China's thirst for energy resources to fuel its rapid economic growth is a matter of great interest, if not concern. The ASEAN states tacitly but clearly agree that the best way — indeed, the only way — of addressing and dealing with these common concerns is to engage China, individually and collectively, in as dense a mesh of relationships as possible.

Prime Minister Abdullah Badawi recalled to me that, when he was Malaysia's Foreign Minister, he had urged ASEAN to pursue a policy of engagement with China for the sake of peace and stability in the region. One of the results of this policy, he said, was ASEAN's success in drawing China into a regional dialogue on the South China Sea despite China's initial insistence on dealing bilaterally with ASEAN claimants.[40]

For all the flurry of activity in ASEAN-China relations in a sprawling range of areas, much confidence building remains to be done between the two sides, precisely because of the growing relationship between them, as well as their geographic proximity and the rapid rise of China's political, economic and military power. China, for example, has to foster among the ASEAN countries a better understanding of its strategic outlook. Included in this would be China's view of its relations with the United States and with Japan. ASEAN has to get a clearer appreciation of China's energy concerns, strategies and policies, a subject of increasing urgency and strategic significance. ASEAN's business communities have to have a sharper and more detailed awareness of the opportunities, and not just the threats, that China's economic surge presents. China's conception of its maritime regime, specifically in the South China Sea, has to be better explained. There could be greater transparency with respect to Chinese intentions on the Mekong River. China could do more to support ASEAN's efforts to integrate the regional economy and assist the newer members to become fully part of the ASEAN economic mainstream. For their part, the ASEAN countries could be more active, even if in private, in discouraging Taiwanese moves towards independence. They have to make clear that those who have defence arrangements with the United States are not party to any endeavour to "contain" China from the south. For the longer term, both sides could do much more in fostering greater mutual understanding, especially among the youth and the mass media, through more intensive exchanges, training programmes, and the establishment of promotion centres.

The whole range of ASEAN-China relations was the subject of deliberations in the ASEAN-China Eminent Persons Group, of which I was the member for the Philippines. Qian Qichen, retired Deputy Premier, former State Councillor and former Foreign Minister, was the member for China. The EPG met twice — in Qingdao in August and in Kuala Lumpur in October 2005. Submitted by Tan Sri Musa Hitam, former Deputy Prime Minister of Malaysia and ASEAN co-chairman of the EPG, to the ASEAN-China Summit in December, the group's report reviewed the considerable growth in ASEAN-China relations in the past fifteen years. It reaffirmed the principles of partnership and openness animating the relationship and stressed the value of the cooperation that had rapidly developed since 1996, when China became an ASEAN Dialogue Partner. With agreements already concluded to ease the flow of trade in goods and to set up a mechanism to settle economic disputes, the EPG urged the two sides to accelerate negotiations on agreements on investments and on liberalizing trade in services, as did the 2005 ASEAN-China Summit. The report called for stepped-up cooperation on a range of transnational issues, including the environment and contagious diseases, an open-skies regime for civil aviation, and intensified people-to-people exchanges. For these purposes, the EPG recommended an ASEAN Centre in China, something like the one that had long operated in Tokyo, an ASEAN-China foundation to fund the exchanges, and a two-way scholarship programme.[41]

These measures, on top of the numerous ones that have been carried out over the past nine years, should, apart from their specific objectives, help build confidence between China and its neighbours to the south and thus contribute to the stability of the region. There remain a number of concerns: the unresolved disputes in the South China Sea, the surge in China's competitive power in the global economy, China's strategic intentions. The dissipation of these concerns would depend to a large extent on the mutual trust that is built between ASEAN and China.

INDIA

Since it adopted its Look East policy in the early 1990s, India has recognized, whatever the party in power in New Delhi, that getting closer to East Asia would serve the country's strategic and economic interests. One way of doing so is by linking up in some way with the ASEAN+3 process. The current Prime Minister, Manmohan Singh, has been pushing the idea of an Asian Economic Community as a larger version of the ASEAN Economic Community and of the proposed East Asia Free Trade Area. Pursuant to this, the Indians — through academics for now — have been promoting the vision of JACIK (Japan, ASEAN, China, India and Korea) as a vehicle for Asian regional cooperation. For example, the Indian think-tank Research and Information System for Developing Countries organized in March 2003 in New Delhi an international conference on "Building a New Asia: Towards an Asian Economic Community".[42] In November 2004, I took part in a "High-Level Conference on Asian Economic Integration: Vision of a New Asia" that RIS put together in Tokyo in collaboration with Japanese, Chinese and Malaysian institutes. India's private sector, particularly the Confederation of Indian Industries, has been active in pushing for linkages with East Asia through conferences and other ways of networking.

In August 1998, the Thai journalist, Kavi Chongkittavorn, gave a talk in New Delhi as part of the India-ASEAN Eminent Persons Lecture Series. In that talk, Kavi recalled the fact, largely forgotten now, that India almost became an ASEAN Dialogue Partner as early as 1980.[43] That year, in May, ASEAN and Indian senior officials met in Kuala Lumpur to explore possible areas for cooperation.[44] In opening the June 1980 ASEAN Ministerial Meeting, Malaysia's Prime Minister Hussein Onn noted:

> ASEAN has entered into dialogue with Japan, United States, Canada, Australia, New Zealand and the EEC. *We have also had dialogue with India* (italics mine).... I am pleased that the Foreign Ministers of Australia, India, Japan, New Zealand and the Secretaries of State of Canada and the United States will be in Kuala Lumpur to continue the dialogue with ASEAN after this meeting.[45]

Indonesian Minister for Foreign Affairs Mochtar Kusumaatmadja observed that the first meeting of the ASEAN-India Dialogue constituted "a landmark in promoting ... collective self-reliance among developing countries". The ministers' joint communiqué reported:

> The Meeting noted with satisfaction that ASEAN has expanded its dialogue to include developing countries as evidenced in the start of the ASEAN-India dialogue.[46]

Had India joined the dialogue system for good at that time, it would have indeed been the first developing country to be an ASEAN Dialogue Partner, a circumstance that might have changed the character of the dialogue system even then. Before that could happen, however, India in effect went on Vietnam's — and, as ASEAN perceived it, Moscow's — side in the Cambodian conflict and recognized the Heng Samrin regime in Phnom Penh. As a result, the dialogue partnership was shelved; it stayed shelved until after the Paris accords of 1991 had settled the Cambodian problem. The early 1990s also saw the acceleration of economic reforms in India, and a closer economic relationship between ASEAN and India started to look promising to both. In 1992, ASEAN took in India as a "Sectoral Dialogue Partner", a partnership limited to specific sectors. India signalled the importance that it placed on relations with ASEAN when, in March 1993, the Minister of External Affairs, Dinesh Singh, himself led the Indian delegation for talks in New Delhi with the ASEAN Secretary-General, Ajit Singh, and the member-states' ASEAN Directors-General.

Singapore's Prime Minister Goh Chok Tong gave the process a push when he made a surprise proposal at the 1995 ASEAN Summit to elevate India to full dialogue partnership. The proposal had not gone through the usual consultations at the senior-official and ministerial levels, but received the consent of all the ASEAN leaders. In 1996, India began participating in the ASEAN Post-Ministerial Conferences and the ASEAN Regional Forum.

Meant to be a highlight of the dialogue, one of the components of the ASEAN-India relationship is the "eminent persons" lecture series, in which prominent personages in India deliver lectures in ASEAN countries and similar ASEAN personalities do so in India. However, the choice of subjects is open-ended rather than concentrated on ASEAN-India relations. For example, there have been lectures on "Building a National Nutrition Security System" (M.S. Swaminathan, Chairman, M.S. Swaminathan Research Foundation, Chennai, in Bangkok, 11 January 2002), on "Space Remote Sensing for Sustainable Development" (U.R. Rao, Space Commission of India, in Kuala Lumpur, 17 July 1998), and on "Problems of Maintaining

Cultural Sovereignty in a Technologically Globalized World" (Juwono Sudarsono, Minister for Education and Culture, Indonesia, in New Delhi, 13 October 1998). As a result, although these subjects may be valuable and interesting in themselves, the lecture series suffers from a lack of focus. The texts of the lectures from December 1996 (Malaysia's Prime Minister Mahathir Mohamad) to April 2002 (N.R. Narayana Murthy, Chairman of Infosys Technologies) and August 2002 (former Indonesian Foreign Minister Ali Alatas) have been compiled, something that I suggested after delivering one of the lectures in New Delhi in January 2001.[47]

In December 1997, the ASEAN+3 process was launched with the first summit in Kuala Lumpur. Evidently, it was initiated for strategic, as well as economic, considerations. It soon became clear to ASEAN that, for similar considerations, India, which now had a land border with ASEAN as a result of Myanmar's membership, had to be handled in a manner similar to the treatment accorded Northeast Asia; India could not just be any other Dialogue Partner, like, say, Canada.

In February 2000, Cambodia's Prime Minister Hun Sen made an official visit to India and, looking forward to the ASEAN and related summits in his capital in 2002, threw his support behind an ASEAN-India summit. However, despite Goh Chok Tong's prodding, ASEAN failed to arrive at a definitive agreement on the matter at its November summit in Singapore. In Bandar Seri Begawan the next year, the ASEAN leaders did reach a consensus on the ASEAN-India summit but left open the question of its frequency, with Cambodia making clear its partiality to an annual event. Thus, Indian Prime Minister Atal Bihari Vajpayee was in Phnom Penh in November 2002 for the first meeting between ASEAN and Indian leaders, who quickly decided to meet every year thereafter. In Bali the next year, India acceded to the Treaty of Amity and Cooperation in Southeast Asia on the same day that China did.

Also at the Bali summit, the ASEAN and Indian leaders agreed to negotiate a so-called "Regional Trade and Investment Area", including a free trade area in goods, services and investments and other forms of economic cooperation. This was to encompass the removal of tariff and non-tariff barriers to trade in goods, the liberalization of trade in services, the simplification of customs procedures, mutual recognition arrangements, and other ways of facilitating trade and investments. According to the agreement, tariffs on trade between India and Brunei Darussalam, Indonesia, Malaysia, Singapore and Thailand were to start coming down from the beginning of 2006 and be removed altogether by the end of 2011. Cambodia, Laos, Myanmar, Vietnam and the Philippines do not have to eliminate tariffs on

Indian goods until the end of 2016. India's tariffs on its imports from Cambodia, Laos, Myanmar and Vietnam, however, should be down to zero by the end of 2011, but by 2016 on Philippine goods. Tariffs on a limited number of "sensitive" products are to be abolished at a later date to be negotiated by the parties. Also to be negotiated are other measures for the liberalization and facilitation of trade in goods and services and of investments. The parties adopted a list of products on which, under an "early harvest" programme, tariffs would start coming down in November 2004 and be eliminated by October 2007 for India and the ASEAN-6 and by October 2010 for the newer ASEAN members. They agreed on interim rules of origin while negotiations were going on. I am given to understand that talks on the permanent rules of origin have been particularly difficult. According to the chairman's statement at the close of the ASEAN-India Summit in Vientiane in November 2004, the leaders were satisfied with the progress thus far in the negotiations on the free trade area. However, in a marked departure from the upbeat formulations usual in such documents, the chairman's statement of the 2005 ASEAN-India Summit recorded the leaders' observation that the FTA negotiations had "not progressed as expeditiously as originally envisaged", indicating significant problems.[48] Evidently, one of those problems was India's proposed exclusion list, which ASEAN considered to be ridiculously lengthy.

At the Vientiane summit, the leaders of ASEAN and India agreed on a "Partnership for Peace, Progress and Shared Prosperity". Its accompanying "plan of action" indicates broad areas for further ASEAN-India cooperation, each of which still needs a specific work programme. Earlier, the dialogue process had produced understandings to cooperate in trade and investment, science and technology, human resource development, tourism, transport and infrastructure, health, small- and medium-scale enterprises, and people-to-people contact. The 2005 ASEAN-India Summit resulted in agreements of a more concrete nature, including those involving cooperation in information technology and biotechnology. The leaders expressed their support for the development of a generic version of drugs to combat avian influenza and the regional stockpiling of such drugs. As part of its assistance programme for the newer members of ASEAN, India announced its intention to set up a permanent Centre for English Language Training in each of them and a "satellite-based network" linking India with those countries for tele-medicine and tele-education. India replenished the ASEAN-India Cooperation Fund by US$2.5 million and pledged a further US$5 million for it plus a US$1 million contribution to the ASEAN Development Fund.

At their retreat in April 2005, the ASEAN Foreign Ministers decided to allow countries outside ASEAN+3 to participate in the East Asia Summit on three conditions: "substantive" relations with ASEAN, full Dialogue Partner status, and accession to the Treaty of Amity and Cooperation in Southeast Asia. Since India had fulfilled all three, its participation in the EAS was assured. This was a significant step in India's drive for stronger linkages with East Asia as well as in ASEAN's effort to have India strategically and economically engaged in the affairs of the region.

The strategic dimension of ASEAN-India relations is discussed in Chapter 4.

JAPAN

Japan has always considered its relations with Southeast Asia as vital to its interests. The first ASEAN-Japan Summit, in 1977, manifested Japan's fundamental decision to seek solid ties with ASEAN as an institution. This relationship has been conducted in three principal modes — trade and investments, development assistance, and political and symbolic gestures. These modes, of course, have been mutually reinforcing. As it emerged from war and occupation, Japan saw Southeast Asia once again as a source of important raw materials, particularly fossil fuels, certain minerals and timber, as well as an export market and, later, as a site for the relocation of Japanese manufacturing industries. To be able to perform these functions, Southeast Asia had to have its purchasing power raised, its people trained, and its infrastructure built. This was the impulse behind Japan's large programme of official development assistance, which, in the case of several Southeast Asian countries, had its beginning in the post-war Japanese reparations programme. Development assistance was meant not only to promote Japanese exports to Southeast Asia but also to increase the region's capacity to absorb Japanese investments, as well as strengthen political links with individual countries in the area. In any case, Japanese ODA was highly concentrated in Southeast Asia. Even in the 1990s and beyond, Southeast Asia accounted for around 30 per cent of Japan's ODA.

Japan's role as a leading market, an important source of investments and technology, and a major financier of cultural and people-to-people exchanges solidified political ties with Southeast Asia, while intergovernmental bonds between them provided a political framework for the conduct and stimulation of trade and investments and the provision of development aid, as well as for cultural exchanges.

At the same time, there were contentious issues that Southeast Asian countries raised with Japan, including those related to commodities vital to the region, such as rubber. There was the problem of the access of Southeast Asia's agricultural (e.g., pineapples and bananas) and manufactured exports to Japan's highly protected market. There was the Southeast Asians' apprehension over the possibility of Japanese economic domination. Not least were the emotions that lingered from their experience with Japan's wartime atrocities.

Southeast Asian fears and grievances burst into the open when Prime Minister Kakuei Tanaka, touring the ASEAN countries in January 1974, was met with anti-Japanese riots in Bangkok and Jakarta. This was particularly worrisome for Japan, since it came soon after the 1973 energy crisis that exposed the country's vulnerability to raw-material shortages. It thus became clear that Japan had to approach its relations with Southeast Asia not only from the standpoint of economic gain but from other angles as well, including the political and the cultural. The approach had to be both comprehensive and integrated. It had to be directed both at individual Southeast Asian countries and, as a matter of deliberate policy, at ASEAN as a group. At the same time, in the wake of the U.S.' ignominious withdrawal from Indochina, Japan had to take a more active political role in regional affairs, a stance that would bring it into closer engagement with ASEAN.

It was, perhaps, no coincidence that the aid arm of Japan's Ministry of Foreign Affairs, the Japan International Cooperation Agency, JICA, was established in 1974. It was also in 1974 that Japan initiated a highly successful programme of gathering some 300 to 350 young (18 to 30 years old) people from Japan and the Southeast Asian countries on board the Nippon Maru, normally a cruise vessel, for around fifty days each year. The participants are encouraged to form friendships and learn about one another's country, people and culture and about the region. The ship docks at several Japanese and Southeast Asian ports, and the participants stay with host families for a few days, immersing themselves in the country's way of life. Although the Ship for Southeast Asian Youth is not, strictly speaking, an ASEAN undertaking, it has taken on the character of an ASEAN-Japan activity on account of the nations involved. I visited the ship a number of times, as ASEAN Senior Official for the Philippines and as ASEAN Secretary-General, and was deeply impressed by the camaraderie that had developed among the young people. Alumni of the cruises have formed national associations, a useful way of networking within the region.

It was in this setting that the Fukuda Doctrine was proclaimed, the first in a series of doctrines, initiatives, frameworks and concepts attributed to Japanese prime ministers that sought to define the conceptual underpinnings of Japan's policy towards Southeast Asia. Domingo Siazon, then Secretary of

Foreign Affairs and now on his second tour as Philippine Ambassador to Japan, recalled at a conference in Tokyo in 2000:

> Japan resolved to be an active partner in the promotion of peace and progress in Southeast Asia. That was the essence of the Fukuda Doctrine, which was enunciated by ... Prime Minister Takeo Fukuda in 1977. ... The development of Southeast Asian economies became a strong Japanese policy objective.[49]

Together with those of Australia and New Zealand, the Prime Minister of Japan was the first head of government to have a summit with ASEAN's leaders as a group, on 7 August 1977 in Kuala Lumpur. At the end of his tour of ASEAN capitals following the Kuala Lumpur summit, Fukuda proclaimed in Manila:

> First, Japan, a nation committed to peace, rejects the role of a military power, and on that basis is resolved to contribute to the peace and prosperity of Southeast Asia, and the world community.
>
> Second, Japan, as a true friend of the countries of Southeast Asia, will do its best in consolidating the relationship of mutual confidence and trust based on "heart-to-heart" understanding with these countries, in wide-ranging fields covering not only political and economic areas but also social and cultural areas.
>
> Third, Japan will be an equal partner of ASEAN and its member countries, and cooperate positively with them in their own efforts to strengthen their solidarity and resilience, together with other nations of the like mind outside the region, while aiming at fostering a relationship based on mutual understanding with the nations of Indochina, and will thus contribute to the building of peace and prosperity throughout Southeast Asia.[50]

The first principle enunciated by Fukuda was clearly meant to reassure ASEAN that Japan would not be a military threat again. The second laid the basis for Japan's resolute sponsorship of cultural and people-to-people exchanges with ASEAN. The third gave the assurance of Japanese economic and financial support for ASEAN as an association, as well as its individual members, while reaching out to the new regimes of Indochina as part of Southeast Asia.

In the joint statement issued after the ASEAN-Japan Summit,[51] Japan had indicated the direction in which the Fukuda Doctrine pointed by announcing some concrete measures for carrying it out. The statement established, as a fundamental policy, Tokyo's recognition of the importance of ASEAN as a regional association and laid down the basic objective of Japan's cooperation with the group — contributing to its self-reliance, resilience and solidarity. It pledged Japan's intention to open its markets to ASEAN's manufactured, semi-manufactured and primary products and its support for "a permanent ASEAN trade and tourism exhibition hall in Tokyo". The statement conveyed Japan's readiness to assist in ASEAN's industrialization by encouraging Japanese investments in the region's industrial sector, foreshadowing the policy, to be adopted some years later, of supporting the relocation of Japanese factories in certain sectors in Southeast Asia. Tokyo also committed itself to contributing a total of US$1 billion, plus technical assistance if requested, to the ASEAN Industrial Projects,[52] provided the particular project was designated as an ASEAN project and found to be economically feasible. Pursuant to this commitment, Japan extended a loan of ¥33 billion to Indonesia's urea project. It announced the doubling of its official development assistance within five years, with the bulk of it going to cooperation with ASEAN. Finally, Japan promised to finance a programme of cultural cooperation that would be the subject of a study proposed by Fukuda.

The Fukuda Doctrine laid the foundation of ASEAN policy that succeeding Japanese leaders were to build upon. Since Fukuda, every new Japanese prime minister has made the rounds of the ASEAN countries in his first or second (after the United States) venture overseas as head of government, although, with ASEAN's expansion to ten members, the high-level tours have become more selective. Each new Japanese leader has proclaimed a new set of policies for Southeast Asia, based on a new "vision" or "doctrine", in most cases named after himself and including the announcement of a fresh financial package for ASEAN. Most of them have invoked the Fukuda Doctrine as their policy fountainhead. Prime Minister Noboru Takeshita met with the six ASEAN heads of government in Manila in December 1987. Before that, Zenko Suzuki had followed in Fukuda's footsteps by making the rounds of the ASEAN countries in 1981, and two years later Yasuhiro Nakasone took his turn. Two years after the Manila summit, Takeshita himself went around the ASEAN countries except for Brunei Darussalam. Following him, Toshiki Kaifu made the ASEAN round in 1991, Kiichi Miyazawa in 1993, Tomiichi Murayama in 1994, and Ryutaro Hashimoto at the beginning of 1997.

Sueo Sudo, professor of international relations at Nanzan University in Nagoya, has observed:

> (O)fficial prime ministerial visits have uniquely characterized Japan's political relations with ASEAN. Even if the frequency of ministerial meetings between Japan and ASEAN does not signify anything unusual — after all ASEAN holds regular meetings with other dialogue partners as well — the

almost *de rigueur* visits to the ASEAN region by Japanese prime ministers would appear to contain special implications. Compared with top-level visits by the other dialogue countries, the difference is underscored by the "closeness" of Japan-ASEAN relations.[53]

Like those of China and South Korea, Japan's government leader has held annual summits with ASEAN as a group since the start, in 1997, of the ASEAN+3 process. At the same time, Japanese prime ministers have continued to visit individual countries on ASEAN swings. Keizo Obuchi visited Cambodia, Laos and Thailand in January 2000, and Junichiro Koizumi toured the Philippines, Malaysia, Thailand, Indonesia and Singapore in January 2002. In an unprecedented gesture, the ASEAN leaders went to Tokyo for a meeting with Koizumi in December 2003 to "commemorate" the thirtieth anniversary of ASEAN's relationship with Japan, the first time that they had met with a Dialogue Partner outside the ASEAN region.

It is interesting that, through this commemoration, ASEAN and Japan dated the start of the dialogue partnership in 1973. In fact, the ASEAN Foreign Ministers had met with their Japanese counterpart in April of that year only for the specific purpose of discussing the competition posed by Japanese synthetic rubber to Southeast Asia's natural rubber. In its relations with Japan and other developed countries at that time, ASEAN was preoccupied with market-access and commodities issues and considered regular, collective consultations as a way of dealing with them. In Japan's case, ASEAN's immediate problem was the "indiscriminate expansion" of Japan's production of synthetic rubber and its depressing effect on the prices of natural rubber, of which Malaysia and also Indonesia and Thailand were major producers. ASEAN first raised the issue formally as a group at its April 1974 meeting with the Japanese foreign minister. At that meeting, the ASEAN Foreign Ministers declared "their satisfaction that the ASEAN joint approach to Japan on the indiscriminate production and accelerated exports of synthetic rubber had resulted in obtaining the Japanese Government's agreement to exercise a restraining influence on the Japanese synthetic rubber industry".[54] In 1976, however, the foreign ministers expressed their disappointment in "the limited results from the ASEAN-Japan forum on synthetic rubber and on canned pineapples".[55] The joint statement of the ASEAN-Japan summit the next year referred to the "noteworthy results" of the forum on synthetic rubber, which had been formally set up in November 1973. The statement explicitly cited Japanese financial assistance for the establishment of testing and development laboratories and the strengthening of rubber research centers in ASEAN. The question of competition between Japanese synthetic and ASEAN natural rubber was apparently sidetracked in favour of Japanese financial and technical assistance to ASEAN in the rubber sector.

In March 1977, the forum was expanded and named the ASEAN-Japan Forum, evidently in preparation for the broader ASEAN-Japan relationship to be explicitly envisioned at the August 1977 summit between the two sides. This is generally considered to have marked the formal start of the ASEAN-Japan dialogue. Held every one or two years, the forum started out as a gathering of foreign ministry officials at the director-general level and mainly covered market-access and other economic issues and development cooperation. In 1993, the forum was elevated to deputy-minister rank on the Japanese side and at senior-official level on the ASEAN side, expanding its coverage to political and security matters.

Other steps were taken to follow through on the Fukuda Doctrine and the discussions at the 1977 summit. Japan was the first of the Dialogue Partners to hold a Post-Ministerial Conference with the ASEAN Foreign Ministers, in Pattaya on 17 June 1978, the day after the annual ASEAN Ministerial Meeting. At that meeting, the Japanese foreign minister "reaffirmed" his government's "readiness" to contribute ¥5 billion, in annual instalments, to the ASEAN Cultural Fund, which ASEAN had agreed to establish, apparently in anticipation of the Japanese contribution. At the exchange rate at the time, that contribution was about US$20 million. The Fund was formally established by an agreement in December 1978, which provided that it would be "administered solely by ASEAN" and that contributions to it "shall belong to ASEAN and shall be held in the custody of the ASEAN Secretariat". Eventually, it was to yield about US$2 million a year, which would be spent on projects basically decided upon by the ASEAN Committee on Culture and Information. The committee had met for the first time two months before the establishment of the Cultural Fund. The Cultural Fund is further touched upon in Chapter 8.

1980 saw the establishment of the Japan Scholarship Fund for ASEAN Youth, worth US$1 million a year, affording numerous ASEAN students the opportunity of pursuing education in Japan in an incredibly varied range of areas. In 1984, pursuant to a proposal made by Prime Minister Nakasone during his ASEAN tour the previous year, Japan initiated the Friendship Programme for the twenty-first Century, in which young people from ASEAN countries were, after a process of application and screening, invited to stay for several weeks in Japan for lectures, study visits, observation tours, home stays, and get-togethers with Japanese youth. From 1984 to 2001, 14,942 young people from ASEAN were recorded as having gone to Japan under the programme. The programme was later expanded to include 120 countries — by 2003, a total of 26,000 youth had participated in it — but the core has remained ASEAN. Indeed, it is often referred to in official documents as the "ASEAN-Japan Youth Friendship Programme". Alumni have organized themselves into national associations, which since 1988 have been networked in the ASEAN-Japan Friendship Association for the 21st Century, or AJAFA-21.

Another significant decision to advance the ASEAN-Japan partnership was the creation of the ASEAN Promotion Centre in Tokyo. A provisional centre to promote Japanese imports from, investments in and tourism to ASEAN was set up in 1979. The permanent centre, officially named the ASEAN-Japan Centre, was formally established in 1981. The centre has an exhibition hall for showing ASEAN goods in its headquarters in the Ginza and joins fairs and shows throughout Japan to promote them. It is a central source of information on ASEAN products for Japanese importers and advises ASEAN exporters on the characteristics and requirements of the Japanese market. The centre organizes investment seminars on individual ASEAN countries and on regional schemes like AFTA and AICO. It provides information to Japan's business community on investment opportunities and conditions in ASEAN. It sends investment missions to the ASEAN countries and advises those countries on effective ways of attracting Japanese investments. The centre helps ASEAN countries promote tourism, distributing slides, videos, posters and publications to travel agencies and the public and organizing promotional trips for media and the travel trade. It sponsors an annual ASEAN tourism festival. The centre's website is a rich source of information on ASEAN for the business community, the media and the public in Japan. Japan contributes 90 per cent of the centre's operational budget, with the balance divided equally among the ASEAN countries. The centre has officers from ASEAN countries working in its trade, investment and tourism sections, but the Secretary-General is always Japanese.

Two strands run through the fabric of ASEAN-Japan economic relations. One is ASEAN's continuing concern with access to the Japanese market of its members' agricultural and, increasingly, manufactured exports. Although Japan's importation of Southeast Asia's manufactured goods has become progressively liberal, and such goods have made up an increasing share in ASEAN exports to Japan, trade in the sensitive agricultural sector remains a problem. In 1985, the ASEAN Economic Ministers said in a joint statement:

> The Ministers ... expressed disappointment over the Japanese so-called "market opening measures," announced in December 1984, for the developing countries. These measures did not address the market opening measures requested by ASEAN and reiterated over the years of dialogue with Japan. The Ministers, therefore, strongly urged Japan to address directly and substantially the market access problem faced by ASEAN exports to the Japanese market.[56]

The other strand is the relocation, starting in the late 1980s, of Japanese factories to Southeast Asia largely as a result of the rise in the yen's value. This form of Japanese support for the region's industrialization has been generally welcomed in ASEAN. In 1988, ASEAN set up the Brand-to-Brand Complementation scheme for the automotive industry within the framework of the Basic Agreement on ASEAN Industrial Complementation of 1981. Under an approved arrangement, parts of a specific vehicle model traded in ASEAN by the brand-owner or "brand-related original equipment manufacturer" and used for the manufacture of "original equipment" products enjoyed a margin of tariff preference of 50 per cent. Malaysia, the Philippines and Thailand were the original participants in the scheme, with Indonesia joining it in 1994. While the programme was clearly aimed at attracting Japanese vehicle manufacturers to set up production facilities in ASEAN, Volvo, Mercedes-Benz and Belgium's DAF, as well as Mitsubishi and Toyota, took part in it. In 1991, its coverage was extended to include non-automotive products. In 1996, ASEAN established the ASEAN Industrial Cooperation scheme, which superseded the Brand-to-Brand Complementation. AICO is different from the previous scheme in that, among other differences, products exchanged under AICO enjoy not margins of preference but specific tariff rates — 0–5 per cent at the beginning, and since 2004 zero per cent (except for Myanmar, Vietnam, Thailand and the Philippines, which have allowed themselves maximum tariffs of one, three or five per cent). Only the countries directly involved in an AICO arrangement, rather than all of ASEAN, need to approve it. Japanese automotive companies continue to dominate the scheme, although it has become progressively diversified.[57]

Frequent missions by Japanese business groups, primarily the *Keidanren*, to Southeast Asia reflect their strong business ties with the region to the south and their deep interest in the economic, investment and trade policies of its governments. The *Keidanren* staff is very knowledgeable about business conditions in ASEAN.

Japan's increasingly close economic connection to Southeast Asia led to its development cooperation programme for that region. Not only did Southeast Asians' purchasing power need to be raised, not only had their capacity to absorb Japanese investments to be increased; political ties and popular goodwill had also to be cultivated. Moreover, ASEAN continued to press Japan to open its market to Southeast Asian exports and, in the late 1980s, to make up in some way for the appreciation of the yen. Assurances of increased development assistance were Japan's response.

On his first overseas trip as Prime Minister, Noboru Takeshita announced at the 1987 ASEAN-Japan Summit in Manila a "new partnership for peace and prosperity" between Japan and Southeast Asia. The partnership would be underpinned by an ASEAN-Japan Development Fund amounting to US$2 billion and the Japan-ASEAN Comprehensive Exchange Plan.

Japan's assistance programmes have undergone several transformations under different names and with different emphases. At the 1997 ASEAN-Japan Summit, Tokyo offered a "comprehensive human resource development" programme for 20,000 persons from ASEAN over five years and committed itself to "facilitating the integration of new ASEAN member states into the mainstream of ASEAN economic development and globalization" and to "promoting and supporting regional and sub-regional programmes, particularly in the Greater Mekong Sub-region". The ASEAN leaders expressed their appreciation for Japan's assistance in response to the economic damage inflicted by the financial crisis on their countries.

Currently, Japan's technical assistance programmes for ASEAN are funded by the Japan-ASEAN Exchange Programme and the Japan-ASEAN General Exchange Fund. How many of those programmes have actually been carried out and how effective they have been are unclear. Japan financed the workshop in 2001 that drew up the work plan for the Initiative for ASEAN Integration and the one in 2002 that processed and approved specific IAI projects. Japan then agreed to fund several of the projects. It assigned experts and deployed equipment to "centres of excellence" in the newer ASEAN members. JETRO's Institute of Developing Economies in 2001 did a study on ASEAN's industrial competitiveness. Japan funded the assignment of a customs expert to the ASEAN Secretariat to help develop the system of post-clearance audit that the ASEAN countries had agreed to adopt in their customs procedures.

In recent years, Japan has channelled some of its assistance to ASEAN through the ASEAN Foundation. Proposed by Indonesia at the 1996 ASEAN Summit in Jakarta, the foundation was established at the December 1997 summit in Kuala Lumpur to promote awareness of ASEAN, interaction among the people of the region, and the development of human resources. The foundation was originally intended to raise funds from non-government sources, such as corporations, individual philanthropists and other foundations, in order to augment resources available for funding "people" cooperation in ASEAN. The board of trustees would be appointed by the ASEAN member-states, while a Council of Advisors would be made up of "prominent individuals of high stature in the region". As it turned out, however, the foundation took on the character of another inter-governmental organization. Eight of the ASEAN countries are represented on the Board of Trustees by their ambassadors to Indonesia, with the ASEAN Director-General sitting for Indonesia. The Singapore trustee is an ambassador-at-large. (At the beginning, the Philippines and Thailand were represented by private individuals, as originally envisioned. However, both of them now have their ambassadors sitting on the board.) Instead of "prominent individuals of high stature", the ASEAN Directors-General of the member-states decided that they themselves would sit on the Council of Advisors. Funding so far has come almost entirely from governments, with the ASEAN member-states voluntarily contributing varying amounts ranging US$100,000 to US$1 million. China donated an amount for initial administrative expenses. South Korea has also made a donation. The largest contribution by far has come from Japan, in the amount of US$20 million. The foundation's projects are largely dependent on this amount, called the Solidarity Fund.

The ASEAN Economic Ministers and the Minister for Economy, Trade and Industry of Japan have their own framework of technical cooperation called AMEICC, for AEM-METI Economic and Industrial Cooperation Committee. Set up in 1998, AMEICC has working groups in such areas as textiles and garments, the automotive and chemical industries, consumer electronics, statistics, the West-East Corridor on the Southeast Asian mainland, small and medium enterprises, human resource development, and, the latest, information technology. There are similar, if less structured, ASEAN-Japan frameworks for transport and energy.

Japan gained points in ASEAN with its response to the 1997–98 financial crisis. According to the Washington, D.C., economist Edith Terry, "during the early months of the crisis Japan had emerged as a hero within Asia".[58] Japan's stature loomed larger particularly in comparison with the perceived slow, hesitant and niggardly response from the United States. Barely a month after the crisis broke out in Thailand, Japan convened a meeting of Asian finance authorities, from which emerged a US$10 billion facility for Thailand, US$4 billion of it from Japan itself. In addition, the Japanese Government persuaded Japanese banks to roll over their Thai loans. Eisuke Sakakibara, then Vice Minister of Finance for International Affairs, proposed the establishment of an Asian Monetary Fund consisting of US$100 billion in standby financing. The United States promptly opposed the idea ostensibly on "moral hazard" grounds. Japan's quick retreat on the issue caused dismay in ASEAN and diminished somewhat the stature that Japan had gained from its early response to the crisis.

However, Japan in 1998 repackaged the proposal as the New Miyazawa Initiative (after Minister for Finance Kiichi Miyazawa), this time with U.S. acquiescence. Under the initiative, US$30 billion would be available in loans at below-market interest rates and few conditions. A ¥2 trillion fund would be set up to guarantee yen-denominated bonds issued by Asia-Pacific economies, encouraging the wider use of the yen as a reserve currency. The next year, Japan set up the US$1-billion Asian Currency Crisis Support Facility at the Asian Development Bank, plus a special yen facility valued at US$6 billion for lending for public works projects on extremely easy terms.

Japan has been a key member of the Manila Framework Group, a gathering of senior finance and central bank officials from 14 economies — the ASEAN-6, Australia, Canada, China, Hong Kong, Korea, New Zealand, and the United States, as well as Japan — set up in November 1997 in Manila to deal with the effects of the financial crisis and seek to prevent its recurrence. Tokyo is a crucial participant in the Chiangmai Initiative, adopted by the ASEAN+3 Finance Ministers in May 2000 in Chiangmai, the core of which is a network of bilateral currency swap and repurchase agreements among the ASEAN+3 countries. Japan is a party to seven of the sixteen agreements currently (as of September 2005) in effect.[59] In addition, Japan has provided funding for critical technical assistance in the financial sector in ASEAN.

The leadership role that Japan took in response to the financial crisis was in keeping not only with its economic power and capacity but also with the rise in its political activism in Southeast Asia. Although Japan was niggardly in taking in refugees from Vietnam and Cambodia, it did play an active role in the search for a political settlement of the Cambodian problem, a role underpinned by Japan's enormous economic capacity. Diplomatically supporting ASEAN's leadership, Tokyo proffered ideas for a settlement and hosted a meeting in 1990 among the four Cambodian factions. After a settlement was reached in 1991, Japan convened an international conference on Cambodia's reconstruction and development, for the first time sent out troops for peacekeeping operations overseas, as well as ceasefire observers, electoral observers and civilian police, and supplied the head of the UN Transitional Authority in Cambodia in the person of Yasushi Akashi. As recounted in Chapter 2, Japan helped to broker the settlement of the 1997 political crisis in Cambodia, which led to that country's membership in ASEAN.

The turn of the century afforded ASEAN and Japan a milestone for reviewing, adjusting and invigorating their relationship. The Japanese have been pointing out that the ASEAN region is now Japan's second largest trading partner as well as the leading recipient of Japan's official development assistance with 30 per cent of total bilateral ODA. Sixty per cent of total assistance from the OECD countries is from Japan. Japanese investments play a crucial role in Southeast Asia's development. Recently, globalization, the changing structures of Southeast Asia's economies, the entry into ASEAN of less advanced members, and, in the background, the rise of China have brought new dimensions to the ASEAN-Japan relationship.

On a visit to Southeast Asia in January 2002, Koizumi announced his Initiative for the Development of East Asia, apparently an attempt to assert a leading Japanese role in the rapid developments in East Asian interaction. An ASEAN-Japan meeting of foreign ministers and development ministers was convened in Tokyo later that year to draw up the broad outlines of ASEAN-Japan cooperation.

Following, but not necessarily in reaction to, the proposal of a free trade area between ASEAN and China in 2000 and the signing of the ASEAN-China Framework Agreement on Comprehensive Economic Cooperation in 2002, the ASEAN-Japan Summit of 2002 issued a joint declaration on a Comprehensive Economic Partnership. The partnership would include "elements of a possible free trade area" and should be concluded within ten years. It would take into account not only the differences in economic levels but also the "sensitive sectors in each country".[60] These extremely cautious formulations clearly reflected the difficulties of dealing with Japan's need to protect its agricultural sector from ASEAN competition, as well as the preoccupations of some ASEAN members, including the newer ones. Thus, the partnership was to begin with trade facilitation rather than liberalization — capacity building, policy dialogue, the mobility of business people, and other trade and investment facilitation measures.

In October 2003, the ASEAN and Japanese leaders signed the "framework" on the CEP. The agreement called for measures to promote and facilitate trade and investments, policy and business dialogues, the mobility of business people, and the exchange of trade statistics and related data. It also provided for cooperation in customs computerization, simplification and harmonization, improvements in the business climate, intellectual property rights, energy, information and communications technology, human resource development, small and medium enterprises, tourism, transport, and standards and conformance and mutual recognition arrangements. The "framework" envisioned the liberalization of trade in both goods and services — in the case of goods, the progressive elimination of duties.

Both the declaration and the "framework" encouraged negotiations on bilateral arrangements in recognition of the divergence of interests among ASEAN countries in their economic relations with Japan. In January 2002, Japan and Singapore concluded a comprehensive agreement grandly labeled as the New Age Economic Partnership. That was relatively easy, since Singapore has no agricultural exports to speak of. It was followed by the start of negotiations with Malaysia, the Philippines and Thailand on similar, but not identical, economic agreements presumably embodying some liberalization of trade in goods and services.

On Japan's proposal, 2003 was designated an ASEAN-Japan exchange year, with each country dedicating a different month for mounting cultural and other public events to observe the thirtieth anniversary of ASEAN-Japan relations, Japan taking the first and the last months. The observance culminated in the commemorative summit in Tokyo on 11–12 December referred to earlier. The summit issued the Tokyo Declaration for the Dynamic and Enduring Japan-ASEAN Partnership in the New Millennium and its plan of action. (As recalled above, China followed suit by proposing an ASEAN-China commemorative summit in 2006.)

Another of those joint statements that lay out common views and stake out areas for cooperation, the declaration states Japan's intention to give priority to ASEAN in its official development assistance, singling out the Initiative for ASEAN Integration and sub-regional development schemes like the Greater Mekong Sub-region and the Brunei-Indonesia-Malaysia-Philippines East ASEAN Growth Area. The plan of action is a sprawling document full of expressions of intent. However, some specifics are worth noting:

- Japan's expectation of devoting US$1.5 billion to the Greater Mekong Sub-region over three years;
- Cooperation in advancing ASEAN countries' competitiveness;
- Cooperation in fighting terrorism, piracy and other transnational crimes;
- Japan's intention to contribute to human resource development in ASEAN in the amount of more than US$1.5 billion over the next three years, with exchange programmes involving some 40,000 people;
- Effort to begin negotiations on the CEP agreement starting at the beginning of 2005;
- Intensification of efforts to complete the network of bilateral swap arrangements under the Chiangmai Initiative;
- Support for the Asian bond market;
- Cooperation in customs, intellectual property rights, standards and conformance, competition policy, small and medium enterprises, the integration of the automobile industry, transport and logistics, and information and communications technology;
- Japan's pledge to host 10,000 youths from ASEAN over the next five years; and
- Continuation of the Ship for Southeast Asian Youth and the Japan-ASEAN Youth Friendship Programme.

From the Fukuda Doctrine to the declaration and plan of action of the commemorative summit, Japan's proclamations of Southeast Asian policy and its joint statements with ASEAN have been meant to dramatize and give a measure of coherence to Japan's programmes for ASEAN. Southeast Asians have looked to Japan as a lucrative market, although they have encountered access problems in that market, particularly for agricultural products. Japan has been a pillar of support for Southeast Asia's drive to industrialize, supplying investments and technology, although there have been complaints about Japan's stinginess in transferring technology. In the case of the Philippines at least, Japan is host to large numbers of workers in the entertainment industry. Nevertheless, Japan's stature of late seems to have been somewhat diminished in Southeast Asian eyes by its long economic stagnation, a condition contrasted with the dynamic surge of China's economy. An assertive China, moreover, has apparently succeeded in putting Japan on the defensive with respect to issues related to World War II and in blocking its bid for a permanent seat on the United Nations Security Council. On the other hand, survey after survey of Japanese opinion has shown Southeast Asians to be low in the regard of the Japanese public. For all their long standing and active state, ASEAN-Japanese relations continue to need intensive cultivation.

KOREA

Among ASEAN's Dialogue Partners, I found the Republic of Korea one of the easiest to deal with in terms of development cooperation, and I am sure my colleagues in the ASEAN Secretariat did, too: focus on small practical projects, not too much argument, expeditious processing. The Koreans did not promise much, but delivered on what they did.

Seoul expressed its interest in "economic and technical cooperation" with ASEAN as early as July 1977 through a letter from the Korean ambassador to Indonesia to the Secretary-General of the ASEAN Secretariat, as that official was then designated. However, it was not until twelve years later, in 1989, that Korea became a "Sectoral Dialogue Partner", ASEAN's first. One might say that ASEAN invented that kind of partnership for Korea. Categorized at that time as a developing country, Korea was not considered as being ripe to be a full Dialogue Partner, although, as we have seen, India almost became one as early as 1980. Korea specifically sought a Dialogue Partnership with ASEAN in 1982, but ASEAN then was divided on the matter.

A Sectoral Dialogue Partnership was supposed to be limited to trade, investments and tourism. However, at the first ASEAN-ROK dialogue meeting, in August 1990, Korea put up a Special Cooperation Fund and sponsored an ASEAN Week in Seoul. A year later it became a full ASEAN Dialogue Partner, the first country to do so since 1977 and the first developing country in the dialogue system. In that capacity, the ROK was a founding participant in the ASEAN Regional Forum.

By the time of the second ASEAN-ROK dialogue in June 1995, twenty projects had been completed under the Special Cooperation Fund, which Korea augmented by an additional US$2 million. By the third dialogue, in 1997, nine more projects had been completed since 1995, two others were being carried out, and another four had been approved. The ROK put up additional funding for so-called Future-Oriented Cooperation Projects, which had to do with youth, media and cultural exchanges. According to the ASEAN Secretariat, over 2000–04, fifty-one projects were completed under both funds, eleven were being carried out, and twenty-one were pending. From 1990 to 2003, the ROK contributed US$17.7 million to the Special Cooperation Fund and US$7 million to the FOCP fund. It pledged an additional US$5 million for projects in the Initiative for ASEAN Integration Work Plan, including feasibility studies for the segments of the Singapore-Kunming Rail Link that run through Cambodia, Laos, Myanmar and Vietnam.[61]

Itself a victim of the 1997–98 financial crisis, Korea is party to six of the sixteen bilateral currency swap and repurchase agreements, a series of arrangements under the Chiangmai Initiative set up to discourage currency speculation by providing a measure of liquidity to a party that encounters balance-of-payments difficulties.

At their November 2004 summit, the ASEAN and ROK leaders issued a Joint Declaration on Comprehensive Cooperation Partnership pledging cooperation in political, security and economic matters, in narrowing the development gap within ASEAN and between ASEAN and the ROK, in education and science and technology, in fostering mutual understanding, and on issues before international economic forums. It called for the negotiation of a framework for an ASEAN-Korea free trade agreement, to start in early 2005 and to be completed in two years. Tariffs on 80 per cent of products traded between ASEAN and Korea would be abolished by 2009, with "special and differential treatment" for the newer members of ASEAN.[62]

At their summit in December 2005, a year earlier than the deadline, the ASEAN leaders and the President of Korea signed the Framework Agreement on Comprehensive Economic Cooperation,[63] pursuant to which their economic ministers, on the same occasion, concluded agreements on trade in goods and a dispute-settlement mechanism as components of the envisioned ASEAN-ROK free trade area. The dispute-settlement mechanism provided for in the agreement is similar to the one that ASEAN had concluded with China. The agreement on trade in goods has not been published. Of political significance is the reference in the summit's chairman's statement to ASEAN's "agreement in principle" to Korea's proposal that products from South Korea's Kaesong Industrial Complex in North Korea be included in the free trade area.[64] The 2005 framework agreement also called for the conclusion of an agreement on the liberalization of trade in services and one on the creation of "a liberal, facilitative, transparent and competitive investment regime", both of them to be negotiated and concluded within 2006. The framework provided for cooperation in a long list of areas, the modalities of cooperation in each area set forth in some detail in an annex.

The ROK acceded to the Treaty of Amity and Cooperation in Southeast Asia on the occasion of the 2004 summit.

The ROK has been an enthusiastic supporter of the ASEAN+3 process ever since the annual ASEAN+3 summit meetings were inaugurated in 1997. Indeed, it took a leadership role in that process during the administration of President Kim Dae Jung, who proposed the formation and mandate of an East Asia Vision Group of "eminent intellectuals" during the 1998 summit. At the 2000 summit, he initiated the establishment of the East Asia Study Group of senior officials and the ASEAN Secretary-General to review the recommendations of the EAVG, which Korea chaired, and to sort them in some order of priority. The EASG was also to assess the implications of the proposed East Asia Summit. Prime Minister Kim Suk Soo presented the EASG report to the 2002 summit. The ASEAN+3 process, including the two reports, is discussed above.

AUSTRALIA

Australia is recognized as the first individual country to become an ASEAN Dialogue Partner. This was in 1974, when the dialogue was conducted twice, at director-general level. Carlos P. Romulo, the Philippines' Secretary of Foreign Affairs, pointed out, at the ASEAN Ministerial Meeting in that year, that the ASEAN-Australia dialogue was the first occasion on which ASEAN discussed economic cooperation projects (as against trade issues alone) with a non-member. According to the joint press statement of the ASEAN-Australia summit meeting of 7 August 1977, the ASEAN and Australian leaders "recalled that Australia had been the first country to establish formal relationships with ASEAN in 1974". The ASEAN website's entry on the ASEAN-Australia Dialogue refers to Australia as "ASEAN's very first Dialogue Partner". Australian government publications make the same point. The ASEAN summit with Australia and New Zealand in November 2004, the second after the one in 1977, was justified as being in commemoration of the thirtieth anniversary of the dialogue relationships, New Zealand having become a Dialogue Partner in 1975. The European Economic Community was actually the first of all Dialogue Partners, but it was not a country.

In terms of institutions, the ASEAN-Australia Dialogue has been conducted in the Post-Ministerial Conferences, which take place between ministers right after the annual ASEAN Ministerial Meetings (starting in 1980), and in the ASEAN-Australia Forum, which has convened every one or two years since the dialogue relationship began in 1974 at the level of Ministry of Foreign Affairs directors-general.

For Australia, relations with ASEAN have been a useful channel for and a highly visible manifestation of its engagement with Southeast Asia as a region. The drive for such an engagement has been motivated by the economic opportunities that Southeast Asia and the rest of East Asia present, by Southeast Asia's strategic location between Australia and the rest of Asia, and by ASEAN's role as the hub of East Asian regionalism. These motivations, when taken together with Australia's close and unwavering relationship with the United States, have been a source of Australia's sometimes ambivalent and fluctuating relationship with Southeast Asia.

For ASEAN, the dialogue in its earlier years served as a forum and a framework for working out essentially bilateral economic issues with Australia and for members, individually as well as collectively, to receive development assistance from Canberra. The economic issues were mainly about access of ASEAN products, principally agricultural, to the Australian market. ASEAN countries perceived Australia's stringent sanitary and phytosanitary requirements for imported agricultural goods as protectionist measures in disguise. With a collective voice, ASEAN also called for improvements in Australia's system of tariff preferences for imports from the region. Singapore benefited from ASEAN support in the 1979 tussle between Singapore Airlines and Qantas over air rights to Europe, which was resolved to Singapore's — and ASEAN's — satisfaction.

Development aid has been a major instrument in Australia's relations with the Southeast Asian countries. Channeling some of it through ASEAN has given the aid programme a regional dimension and image. Until 2004, the bulk of this fell under the ASEAN Australia Economic Cooperation Programme. In the first phase, which covered 1974 to 1989, the AAECP focused on food and nutrition, an area of Australia's strength and ASEAN's concern, with the first projects dealing with such things as soya bean processing, protein-rich foods, the handling and storage of grains, the transport of livestock and other perishable goods, and food technology research and development. In 1986, the scope of the programme was expanded to include tree improvement and microelectronics. Covering 1989–94, Phase II of the AAECP, responding to ASEAN's broadened preoccupations, progressively extended its reach to trade and investment and science and technology, and human resource development in these areas. Phase III, with its ten-year coverage (1994–98, extended to 2004), dealt with more specifically defined concerns, like water supply, eco-tourism, computers for the blind, and livestock health. Since the four newer members came into ASEAN in 1995, 1997 and 1999, the Australian aid programme has taken special account of their needs. The regional dimension of that programme has given it an added measure of efficiency and, more importantly, additional political impact. A beneficial result for both sides has been the networking that has developed among critical focal points within ASEAN as well as between them and their Australian counterparts in a broad range of sectors.

Two years before the 2004 expiration of the AAECP's Phase III, ASEAN and Australia concluded an agreement for the next stage of Australia's regional aid programme, but under another name, the ASEAN Australia Development Cooperation Programme. It has three components. One, called the Programme Stream, has two basic objectives — promoting ASEAN's economic integration and strengthening its competitiveness, reflecting the association's current concerns. The second component, the Regional Partnership Scheme, funds partnerships between ASEAN and Australian institutions in building ASEAN's capacity for regional development and participation in the global economy. The AADCP, like its immediate predecessor, purports to pay special attention to the requirements of Cambodia, Laos, Myanmar and Vietnam. So far, it has extended support to three projects under the work plan of the Initiative for ASEAN Integration. The three projects involve a study on managing revenue losses from participation in the ASEAN Free Trade Area, which is referred to below, national master plans on standards, conformity assessment and accreditation systems, and skills recognition systems.

At their meeting in April 2004, ASEAN's health ministers acknowledged Australia's support, through the AADCP, for the development of the ASEAN+3 Emerging Infectious Diseases Programme, which is meant to carry out the ASEAN+3 Action Plan on Prevention and Control of SARS and Other Infectious Diseases. The action plan, in turn, was a response not only to the SARS crisis but also to the threat of avian influenza in the region. This linkage of Australia to ASEAN+3 has attracted little notice, but it is a remarkable phenomenon; for it seems to be the first time that the ASEAN+3 process has received assistance from an individual country outside of the thirteen.

A novel feature of Australia's current aid programme is the AADCP's third component, called the Regional Economic Policy Support Facility. Early in my term as ASEAN Secretary-General, I observed that ASEAN-commissioned studies were often so late in being launched and so slow in being carried out that, by the time one was completed, the problem had either gone away or had become too far advanced for anything much to be done about it. I, therefore, informally proposed a facility that could act quickly, rapidly commissioning studies that were useful for current ASEAN needs and disbursing funds for them, and that had relatively short deadlines. The inclusion of the REPSF in the AADCP was in part Australia's response to my complaint and proposal.

Upon my urging, one of the earlier studies commissioned by the facility was on managing the possible revenue losses that the newer members of ASEAN might incur as a result of the reduction of their customs duties under the agreement on the Common Effective Preferential Tariff scheme for the ASEAN Free Trade Area. This was one of the concerns expressed by some of the newer members in the run-up to their ASEAN membership. A study was commissioned to validate the concerns and propose several options for managing them. This was the second project. The first one was on a possible set of economic indicators establishing the extent of ASEAN economic integration. Subsequent ones have included studies on negotiations on intra-ASEAN trade in services, negotiations that are still going on; liberalizing financial services and capital movements, a current process; open skies policies, undertaken at the instance of ASEAN's transport officials; the liberalization and harmonization of telecommunications, another current concern; and electricity trading, an area of particular interest to the newer members of ASEAN. The subject of customs valuation policies and practices was examined as ASEAN members began to carry out the WTO customs valuation agreement. Just one month after the adoption of the Vientiane Action Programme, a study on a monitoring and impact-assessment mechanism for the VAP was concluded. Soon after the designation of 11 priority sectors for purposes of economic integration, a REPSF project studied the pattern of intra-ASEAN trade in those sectors. The value of these studies, like the effectiveness of training programmes, will, of course, be determined by how the ASEAN member-states make use of them.

As previously noted, ASEAN started its formal relationship with Australia preoccupied with market access, particularly for its agricultural exports, but also with preferential treatment for its other exports to the Australian market. Since the ASEAN Economic Ministers began regular consultations with their Australian and New Zealand counterparts in 1995, discussions on trade have become both more comprehensive and more pragmatic. ASEAN's moves towards free trade areas with other countries and groups of countries started in 1999 with talks on an ASEAN-CER free trade area. This process will be discussed later in this chapter.

Underlying Australia's relationship with ASEAN has been its apparent ambivalence about the country's place in East Asia. In large measure, this seeming ambivalence is a reflection of the different outlooks of John Howard's Liberal Party and the opposition Labour Party, which tended to be less equivocal in its desire for identification with East Asia. Under either party, Canberra has exerted vigorous efforts to ensure for itself a place at the East Asian table — as an ASEAN Dialogue Partner, as a participant in the ASEAN Regional Forum, as a party, together with New Zealand, to the proposed ASEAN-CER free trade area, in ASEAN's growing summit schedule, which already regularly involves China, India, Japan and Korea, and now at the East Asia Summit. Officially recognized as ASEAN's first Dialogue Partner, Australia has had an effective development cooperation programme with ASEAN that has been regularly reinvigorated over thirty years. It worked with ASEAN in initiating APEC. Canberra is an enthusiastic participant in the ARF. Together with Singapore, it has pushed vigorously for an ASEAN-CER FTA, a project that has now been revived and is moving forward. John Howard himself lobbied hard for an Australia-New Zealand summit with ASEAN. In an unscheduled meeting, he went out of his way to talk to me about it when, as ASEAN Secretary-General, I was on an official visit to Canberra in June 2002. That summit did take place in Vientiane in 2004, the 30th year of Australia's dialogue relationship with ASEAN. Now, Australia is part of the new ASEAN-led East Asia Summit.

There have been bumps along the way. As noted above, ASEAN's agricultural exporters have viewed Australia's strict sanitary and phytosanitary regulations for agricultural imports as disguised protectionism. This perception served — or was used as an excuse — to sidetrack the ASEAN-CER FTA. Early in the ARF's existence, Australia informally sought equal footing in the forum between ASEAN and non-ASEAN members, primarily itself, rubbing ASEAN and some other participants the wrong way. Canberra's perceived eagerness to intervene militarily in East Timor as that territory moved, in a wave of violence, towards separation from Indonesia touched raw nerves in Jakarta, although Australian troops eventually worked quite well under the Philippine and Thai generals who had taken over command of the international force in East Timor. In reply to media questions, John Howard used infelicitous language in talking about possible "pre-emptive" military action in responding to terrorist threats from neighbouring countries. Finally, there was Canberra's very public denigration of the Treaty of Amity and Cooperation in Southeast Asia, a critical pillar in ASEAN's institutional structure, and Australia's initial refusal to accede to it.

Howard was reported to have pointed out that the treaty was an outgrowth of non-alignment and a "relic of the Cold War" and was, therefore, outdated. However, China, Japan, South Korea and Russia had acceded to the treaty, although none of them was technically or historically non-aligned. Australia's neighbour, New Zealand, certainly not a member of the Non-Aligned Movement, signed the treaty in July 2005. Howard invoked Australia's alliance with the United States, although, as media commentators were quick to point out, Japan and South Korea and two ASEAN countries, the Philippines and Thailand, were treaty allies of the U.S. The terms of the treaty that pertain to the settlement of disputes would, according to him, make Australia a "second-class" signatory, although such major powers as China, India, Japan and Russia, as well as South Korea, Pakistan and Papua New Guinea, had signed on those terms, and New Zealand, as well as Mongolia, was to do so. Howard also talked about being constrained, in the name of non-interference, from commenting on other signatories' internal affairs! Yet, after the treaty was amended in 1987 to allow non-Southeast Asian states to accede to it, Australia — under another leadership — was one of the first countries to express an interest in doing so.

On the same day that New Zealand acceded to the treaty, Foreign Minister Alexander Downer issued a declaration of Australia's intention to do the same thing "upon completion of its necessary domestic procedures". Even so, Canberra had made it clear that it was signing the treaty only because accession was a condition for its participation in the East Asia Summit. Such displays of reluctance have exacerbated misgivings about Canberra's motives and intentions in Southeast Asia. Under the TAC, a non-regional party can sit on the High Council only if it is itself a party to the dispute under consideration. Australian leaders have complained that this would make Australia a "second-class" signatory. Yet, one might ask, why would Australia want to sit on the High Council in the event that it discussed disputes between two Southeast Asian countries or between a Southeast Asian country and a non-regional party other than Australia? And why was Canberra having problems with committing itself to non-interference in other signatories' internal affairs? Unfortunately, such misgivings tend to overshadow the excellent cooperation that takes place between Australia and ASEAN and its individual members at the practical, operational level. In a piece in the 10 August 2005 issue of the Australian Internet journal *New Matilda*, I cited the long history of constructive relations between Australia and ASEAN and Southeast Asia and the Howard government's initial resistance to signing the TAC. The piece concluded:

> Under either political party, Australia has long considered close association with ASEAN and with the larger East Asian region to be in its highest interests. Accession to the TAC, as well as participation in the East Asian Summit, will be a highly visible manifestation of this association. All's well than ends well, of course, but a bit more enthusiasm and a bit less reluctance on Canberra's part would have been even better.

NEW ZEALAND

New Zealand was ASEAN's third Dialogue Partner, after the EEC and Australia, entering the partnership in 1975. Two years later, Prime Minister Robert Muldoon, like the Japanese and Australian heads of government, joined the five ASEAN leaders for a summit meeting in Kuala Lumpur, the only solo summit that New Zealand has had with ASEAN.

New Zealand is a small country, with only about four million people, about the same as Singapore's. It has a small economy, although a developed one, with a gross domestic product smaller than the individual GDPs of ASEAN's first five members. Consequently, it is a relatively small market for ASEAN. On the other hand, the first five ASEAN members together account for 7.3 per cent of New Zealand's total exports, ranking among the country's twenty largest export markets. New Zealand is one of the ASEAN countries' major sources of milk and other dairy products and also supplies them meat and wood products. It imports mainly electronic and electrical and other manufactured goods, some fruits and vegetables, and petroleum products from ASEAN countries. In the light of the size of New Zealand's population, its tourism exchanges with ASEAN are surprisingly vigorous, with more than 240,000 New Zealanders visiting ASEAN in 2004 and more than 252,000 people from ASEAN going to New Zealand. More than half of the foreign students in New Zealand are from ASEAN countries.

Despite its small size, New Zealand *is* a developed country, and it has accumulated experience and acquired skills in certain areas of development. It has put these strengths to good use in its development cooperation with

ASEAN. The first five projects pertained to animal husbandry, reforestation and pine forest development, and a survey of the end-uses of timber, as noted in the records of the third ASEAN-New Zealand dialogue in 1977. By the fifth dialogue, in 1981, the coverage of cooperation had expanded to include energy — bio-energy, geothermal power, energy inventory and assessment, and microhydropower — and a seed technology center. The eighth dialogue, in Wellington in 1987, noted NZ$12 million being devoted to New Zealand's official development assistance to ASEAN over the next five years. New Zealand also funded several research fellowships on ASEAN affairs at the Institute of Southeast Asian Studies in Singapore. As a manifestation of the importance given by Wellington to the ASEAN relationship, Prime Minister David Lange personally closed the Wellington dialogue together with Singapore Foreign Minister S. Dhanabalan, who was on a visit to New Zealand. The next year, in Yogyakarta, the ninth dialogue heard New Zealand's decision to fund the Trade and Investment Promotion Programme and linkages between ASEAN and New Zealand professional, academic, commercial and scientific institutions. The fifteenth dialogue, in 2002, instituted the cost-sharing system, under which New Zealand would no longer solely fund ASEAN projects, an acknowledgement of the economic progress that ASEAN countries had achieved. For 2004, the ASEAN-New Zealand Regional Cooperation Programme was budgeted at NZ$1.7 million. New Zealand is the only country outside ASEAN that has contributed to the ASEAN Science Fund. Over 1975–2003, its development assistance to ASEAN amounted to NZ$32.2 million.

As part of the work programme to develop the Closer Economic Partnership between ASEAN and Australia and New Zealand, Wellington initiated studies on non-tariff barriers to trade in seafood, forestry products, electronics and automobiles. New Zealand has been especially supportive of ASEAN's newer members, particularly through the Initiative for ASEAN Integration, the Mekong River Commission and the Mekong Institute, in addition to its bilateral programmes. It is funding two projects in the IAI Work Plan, one pertaining to customs valuation and the other to product standards.

The Philippine Government designated me as Special Envoy to represent the country at the ASEAN Ministerial Meeting in Jakarta in June 2004. The meeting coincided with President Gloria Macapagal-Arroyo's inauguration for a new term, an event that all ministers had to attend, and so none was available to go to Jakarta. With the Philippines as "coordinator-country" for the New Zealand dialogue, I co-chaired with Foreign Minister Phil Goff the ASEAN Post-Ministerial Conference with New Zealand. In my opening statement, after references to economic and development cooperation, I stressed the security outlook that ASEAN and New Zealand shared, including their common aversion to nuclear weaponry, a basis for Wellington's support for the Southeast Asia Nuclear Weapons-Free Zone. Citing New Zealand's active participation in the ARF, particularly in its inter-sessional activities, I reiterated the ASEAN position that New Zealand's accession to the Treaty of Amity and Cooperation in Southeast Asia would be a further expression of Wellington's commitment to peace and stability in Southeast Asia. At the 2004 ASEAN-Australia-New Zealand summit, the ASEAN leaders "encouraged" Australia and New Zealand to accede to the TAC.

On 10 May 2005, the office of Prime Minister Helen Clark issued a news release reporting the announcement by the Prime Minister that New Zealand had "decided in principle" to sign the TAC and that the government would submit the text of the treaty to the New Zealand Parliament. The release quoted Clark as saying:

> Accession to the Treaty would send a signal of New Zealand's commitment to closer engagement with ASEAN and with Asia more generally. In recent years China, Japan, the Republic of Korea, India and other countries have acceded to the Treaty as their own relations with ASEAN have deepened. This year is the 30th anniversary of New Zealand's relations with ASEAN. Accession by New Zealand would be very timely. A careful study has been made of the obligations arising under the Treaty. Accession is not expected to constrain New Zealand in the conduct of its foreign policy.[65]

On 28 July 2005, Foreign Minister Phil Goff signed the TAC in Vientiane. By acceding to the treaty, New Zealand became eligible, according to the conditions that the ASEAN Foreign Ministers had laid down in April, to participate in the first East Asia Summit later that year. Indeed, the day before, the ASEAN Foreign Ministers had already announced that New Zealand would be among the participants in the EAS.

AUSTRALIA-NEW ZEALAND CLOSER ECONOMIC RELATIONS

In the economic realm, much of ASEAN's interaction with Australia and New Zealand is now conducted with both of them together, through the Closer Economic Relations. The CER is a series of agreements and arrangements progressively to integrate the economies of Australia and New Zealand. It started when the Australia-New Zealand CER trade agreement went into effect at the beginning of 1983. Replacing the New Zealand Australia Free Trade Agreement, which had been in force since 1966, the CER covers all trade except for specifically excluded products and services, whereas the NAFTA was applicable only to those items that were specifically included.

Today, under the CER, goods are traded freely between the two parties, unhampered by tariffs or quantitative restrictions. There is free trade in services between them, except only for air services and coastal shipping and, additionally for Australia, broadcasting and television, third-party insurance and postal services. Almost all products and services of Australia and New Zealand enjoy mutual recognition from each other. Australians and New Zealanders can visit and live and work in each other's country without restriction. As a result, Australia-New Zealand trade grew by nine per cent a year over 1992–2002.

The ASEAN Economic Ministers and the trade ministers of the CER had the first of their annual consultations in 1995, deciding to focus their cooperation on customs procedures and standards and conformance. Subsequently, they also addressed impediments to the trade between them, as identified by the private sector. During their consultations in October 1999, the ministers agreed to explore the possibility of free trade between the ASEAN Free Trade Area and the CER. To establish its feasibility, the ministers decided to form a task force headed by the former Philippine Prime Minister and Minister of Finance, Cesar E. A. Virata, then a banker and consultant.

The task force found that a free trade area between AFTA and the CER was "not only feasible but also advisable". It pointed out that such an FTA would strengthen the bargaining positions of the two sides in international negotiations, presumably including the ones addressing the agricultural export subsidies of the United States and the European Union. It would both manifest and promote the component countries' commitments to economic reform. The task force projected that the FTA would double the size of the regional market to one with a combined GDP of US$1 trillion. It recommended that trade liberalization between the two groups proceed at a faster pace than that agreed upon in APEC but no faster than the AFTA commitments of the ASEAN countries. The task force report also proposed that the newer members of ASEAN be extended the required technical assistance. Virata presented the report, subsequently named The Angkor Agenda,[66] to the ASEAN and CER ministers at their October 2000 consultations in Chiangmai.

However, as widely reported in the press, Minister for International Trade and Industry Rafidah Aziz, in tense discussions among the ASEAN ministers, registered Malaysia's objections to a free trade area between ASEAN and the CER. In order nonetheless to keep the momentum of the economic relationship, the ASEAN and CER ministers decided to go ahead with elements of closer economic linkages, in the form largely of trade facilitation measures and technical assistance. The proposals for expeditious trade liberalization between the two regions were dropped, at least for the time being. Naming the package Closer Economic Partnership or CEP, the ministers asked the senior economic officials to flesh it out, taking "into account relevant recommendations" of the Virata task force and paying "particular attention" to "technical assistance and capacity building measures". In their joint press statement, the ministers also referred to "some current trade issues concerning non-tariff barriers such as SPS (sanitary and phytosanitary measures) and technical barriers to trade". Presumably, this was a reference to barriers that, ASEAN countries complained, Australia and New Zealand maintained against their agricultural exports.[67]

The ASEAN and CER ministers, in their consultations in September 2001, endorsed the "framework" for the CEP put together by their officials. Emphasizing the importance of "open, transparent and competitive markets", the "framework" focused on economic cooperation, trade and investment facilitation, business competitiveness, and transparency of regulations. It also cited the needs of ASEAN's newer members. The CEP's initial work programme was to deal with technical and other non-tariff barriers to trade, customs cooperation, trade and investment promotion and facilitation, standards and conformity assessment, electronic commerce, small and medium enterprises, and capacity-building, particularly in the newer ASEAN members and in the CEP's areas of focus. The Ministerial Declaration on the AFTA-CER Closer Economic Partnership that the 12 ministers issued on 14 September 2002 formalized the "framework". The ministers put a working group in charge of carrying out and coordinating the CEP programme. The declaration, like the "framework", was silent on trade and investment liberalization and on tariff reductions, but it did refer to bringing down technical and other non-tariff barriers to trade.[68]

Soon after the change of leadership in Malaysia in October 2003, the idea of a free trade area between ASEAN and Australia and New Zealand was revived and discussion of it resumed. The ASEAN Economic Ministers, at their annual "retreat" in Singapore in April 2004, decided again to promote the idea. Not only that. "In line with" upgrading "economic relations to the next level", they "supported the possibility of convening an ASEAN-CER Commemorative Summit in Vientiane in November 2004", when an ASEAN-CER free trade area might be launched.[69] Australia had been pursuing the idea of a summit with ASEAN member-states with a view to commemorating the thirtieth anniversary of the ASEAN-Australian dialogue. New Zealand had been doing the same thing. Two months later, the

ASEAN Foreign Ministers officially endorsed the Economic Ministers' proposal, stressing that the meeting would be a "commemorative summit", that is, commemorative of the 30th anniversary of the Dialogue Partnerships, a "one-off event".[70]

The summit, on 30 November 2004 in Vientiane, resulted in a joint declaration that pledged the commitment of the ASEAN countries, Australia and New Zealand to cooperate in a number of areas. It stated, "ASEAN Leaders encourage Australia and New Zealand to positively consider acceding to the Treaty (of Amity and Cooperation in Southeast Asia) in the near future in the spirit of the strong trust and friendship between ASEAN and Australia and New Zealand and their common desire to contribute to regional peace and stability."[71] The declaration did not record the response, if any, of Prime Minister John Howard of Australia or Prime Minister Helen Clark of New Zealand. Subsequently, the media quoted Howard's explanation of Australia's unwillingness to accede to the treaty. The explanation is discussed above. New Zealand announced its intention to sign the treaty and did so eight months later.

Most importantly, the summit declaration embodied the leaders' commitment to start negotiations on an "ASEAN-Australia and New Zealand Free Trade Area" in early 2005 and to complete them within two years. This time, the arrangement was no longer for an ASEAN-CER or an AFTA-CER free trade area but for an ASEAN-Australia and New Zealand FTA. The change was made upon the realization that neither AFTA nor the CER was a customs union with common external tariffs; therefore, it was the individual members that had to join the larger FTA. The declaration had an annex containing the "guiding principles" for the negotiations. The basic objective was to deepen economic integration between the two regions through the "progressive elimination of all forms of barriers to trade in goods, services and investment; and through trade and investment facilitation and economic cooperation measures". The guidelines envisioned the FTA to be "fully implemented" within ten years, but with "differentiated timeframes" among Australia and New Zealand, the ASEAN-6 and the newer ASEAN members. They would provide for technical assistance and capacity building to enable all parties to participate in and benefit from the FTA. AFTA and the CER would "continue to exist as distinct, functioning agreements".[72] In all, the situation was a dramatic turnaround from what it had been in 2000.

However, as the negotiations progressed in 2005, they evidently encountered, in the words of the Joint Media Statement of the September 2005 consultations between the ASEAN and CER Economic Ministers, "a number of difficult issues, particularly regarding the coverage and scope of the FTA" in the light of the "broad range of interests and the diverse economic circumstances of the twelve participating countries". Nevertheless, progress was being made not only in the negotiations but also in the understanding of the issues involved.[73]

In practical terms, the future of ASEAN's ties with Australia-New Zealand depends on the state of Australia's relations with Indonesia and Malaysia, which have undergone ups and downs over the years, but have apparently been much improved of late. The imperatives of geography are compelling. Australia and New Zealand together have been involved with Southeast Asia not only in the FTA project but also in a number of other forums and arrangements beyond the economic realm. Together with the United Kingdom, they are part of the Five-Power Defence Arrangement for the defence of Malaysia and Singapore. In the 1950s, they were members of the Southeast Asia Treaty Organization. They were for the most part on the American side in the Indochina conflict of the 1960s and 1970s. Today they participate in the Forum for East Asia Latin America Cooperation on the East Asian side. They are mentioned in the same breath when the expansion of the East Asian component of the Asia-Europe Meeting is discussed. Unlike in 1977, when they met with ASEAN separately, Australia and New Zealand sat together for the thirtieth anniversary "commemorative summit" with ASEAN in 2004, although they became Dialogue Partners in different years. As noted above, with New Zealand and, subsequently, Australia signing the Treaty of Amity and Cooperation in Southeast Asia, the two countries took part in the first East Asia Summit in December 2005.

RUSSIA

During the Cold War, ASEAN countries acknowledged the Union of Soviet Socialist Republics as a superpower with global significance, although, for a while, some withheld diplomatic relations with Moscow for reasons rooted in Cold War considerations. By 1976, almost all Southeast Asian countries had diplomatic relations with the Soviet Union. However, Moscow had minimal relations with ASEAN as a group. At that time, ASEAN's external relations were driven largely by economic considerations — development cooperation, investments and trade. Being a socialist state, the Soviet Union had a centrally planned economy that was striving to be as self-sufficient as possible, an aspiration that seemed plausible by virtue of the country's vast natural resources and technological advances. The USSR, therefore, had little normal economic interaction with Southeast Asia. Exceptions were the extensive Soviet aid to and trade with Vietnam and Indonesia before the end of the Cold War. Moscow also had only bad things to say about ASEAN, which it initially viewed, as China did, as a thinly disguised defence alliance in league with the United States. The ASEAN members in turn looked upon the Soviet Union as a supporter of their communist insurgencies.

Just as non-communist Southeast Asia and the USSR were beginning to warm to each other, Vietnam invaded Cambodia in the last days of 1978, an act that ASEAN vehemently opposed. ASEAN viewed Moscow as a strong backer of Vietnam. Shortly before Vietnam went into Cambodia, it had joined COMECON and entered into what amounted to a mutual defence treaty with the USSR, whose intentions in the region the ASEAN countries regarded with suspicion. Indeed, a strong motivation for ASEAN's opposition to Vietnam's incursion into Cambodia, even if that ended the reign of terror of the Khmers Rouges, was the fear of an expansion of Soviet influence in the region.

In the late 1980s, however, things began to change. Mikhail Gorbachev initiated *glasnost* and *perestroika*, or openness and re-structuring, including steps to liberalize and privatize more and more sectors of the economy. Vietnam withdrew its troops from Cambodia. At the same time, Soviet support for Vietnam was seen to be diminishing. The settlement of the Cambodian situation was making progress, partly as a result of significant improvements in Sino-Soviet relations. Ultimately, the Soviet Union broke up and the Cold War ended, with the Russian Federation taking over most of the former USSR's foreign relations and obligations.

The end of the Cold War resulted in a new security configuration in East Asia. For ASEAN, it was the time to seek stronger engagement with all major powers that had interests in or a role to play in East Asia's security. For ASEAN, Russia clearly had such interests and such a role. Like China, as well as the United States, it was a permanent member of the UN Security Council, a recognized nuclear-weapon state, and a leading conventional military power. In recognition of their strategic importance, Russia and China were invited to the 1991 ASEAN Ministerial Meeting as guests of the host, Malaysia. The next year, both were in attendance at the Manila meeting a degree higher in status, as guests of the chair of the ASEAN Standing Committee, the Philippines. In January 1992, the ASEAN Summit directed the use of the Post-Ministerial Conferences as a framework for dealing with regional security issues. In compliance with that directive, a PMC Senior Officials Meeting was convened in Singapore in 1993. There the ASEAN Regional Forum was agreed on — to include not only ASEAN and its Dialogue Partners, but also the then observers, Vietnam, Laos and Papua New Guinea, and the "consultative partners", Russia and China.[74] As part of the process of engaging Russia, ASEAN took it in, together with China and India, as a Dialogue Partner in 1996. Since 1999, Russia has been pushing for the conclusion of an Asia-Pacific Concord in the ARF.

In institutional terms, Russia is linked to ASEAN through the Post-Ministerial Conferences, the ASEAN Regional Forum, the annual ASEAN-Russia senior officials' political consultations, and the Joint Cooperation Committee and its subsidiaries — the Joint Planning and Management Committee and the working groups on trade and economic cooperation and on science and technology. Regular consultations between senior economic officials have been proposed.

ASEAN's interest in a relationship with Russia arose, above all, from strategic considerations, both geopolitical and economic. It certainly was not for official development assistance, although some in ASEAN insisted on the usual "entrance fee" from Russia for the dialogue relationship. The "entrance fee" concept may have been valid in the 1970s, when ASEAN depended on and expected technical and financial assistance from its Dialogue Partners; perhaps, it remains valid today as far as the newer members are concerned. However, as it was undertaking the transition from a centrally planned to a market economy, Russia was having problems getting the necessary funds together. Not that it did not have a few million dollars for the purpose; the problem, rather, was bureaucratic and legal in nature, the Russians pointing out that they did not have any mechanism for financial relationships with groups of countries. Several modalities were tried, including the device of having the private sector serve as a conduit, to no avail. Accordingly, I urged ASEAN not to press the matter but instead focus on the strategic nature and political dimension of the relationship. Russia has proposed an economic and development cooperation agreement with ASEAN, which would supposedly enable Russia's finance ministry to allocate the necessary funds for ASEAN-Russia projects. However, ASEAN and Russia failed to conclude the agreement at their Post-Ministerial Conference in July 2005. The joint declaration issued at the first ASEAN-Russia Summit in December 2005 simply states, "ASEAN welcomes the readiness of the Russian Federation to make voluntary financial contributions to the ASEAN-Russian Federation Dialogue Partnership Financial Fund...."[75] The foreign ministers had agreed to set up the fund, with Russia to decide on the amount of its contribution and the two sides to work out its terms of reference.

Nor is trade ASEAN's overriding concern. After all, its trade with Russia in 2003, which amounted to less than US$4 billion, was dwarfed by that with China, which was valued at US$78.2 billion in the same year. The combined number of visitors from the Commonwealth of Independent

States to ASEAN is far exceeded by those from individual countries in Western Europe and East Asia. Russia, however, remains a potential source of knowledge and training in the basic sciences and applied technology; tapping it for this purpose in an ASEAN framework could have added value, although in substantive terms this will have to be pursued by ASEAN members individually.

In political terms, Russia is an important actor on the world stage. Aside from being a permanent member of the UN Security Council and a nuclear-armed military power, Russia is now a member of the Group of 8 leading economies. Its immense energy resources make Russia a major global power in an age of rapidly rising energy demand. As the leader of the Commonwealth of Independent States of former Soviet Republics, and by virtue of geography, Russia exercises strong influence in Central Asia. It has always been a factor in the Middle East; it is, together with the United States, the European Union and the United Nations, a member of the Quartet on the Israel-Palestine peace process. It participates in the Six-Party Talks on the nuclear problem in North Korea. Bilaterally and through the Shanghai Cooperation Organization, Moscow's relationship with Beijing is strengthening. It has joined, in 2005, the Asian Cooperation Dialogue.

It is largely for these considerations that ASEAN welcomed Russia's accession to the Treaty of Amity and Cooperation in November 2004, when Foreign Minister Sergey Lavrov made a special trip to Vientiane at the time of the ASEAN Summit to sign the instrument of accession. It was also with these in mind that ASEAN agreed to invite President Vladimir Putin to a summit in Kuala Lumpur in December 2005, the first such meeting between ASEAN and Russia. The summit issued a joint declaration, with an accompanying "comprehensive" programme of action, embodying both sides' intention to cooperate in a wide range of areas. In their political portions, the documents emphasized the importance of the role of the United Nations and international law. The agreement on economic and development cooperation that the foreign ministers signed on the same occasion similarly set forth the areas where cooperation was to take place, without saying much by way of specific action. The ASEAN and Russian leaders agreed that their summits would be "regular" without specifying their frequency.

Since Putin would be in Kuala Lumpur, the Russians tried to get him admitted to the EAS. Russia is a full ASEAN Dialogue Partner and a signatory to the Treaty of Amity and Cooperation. Being in the EAS would be an acknowledgement of Russia's "substantive relations" with ASEAN, the last of the three ASEAN criteria for EAS participation. Moreover, meeting with

ASEAN and then being left out of the EAS the next day would have been an embarrassment for the Russian President. In a typical compromise, ASEAN arranged to have Putin speak briefly at the EAS as a "guest" of the Malaysian government but not take part in the summit itself. As recalled above, the EAS chairman's statement noted that the participants "welcomed the Russian Federation's expression of interest to participate in the East Asia Summit and agreed to consider its participation in future East Asia Summits based on the criteria established by ASEAN". Obviously, it was not yet decided whether Russia's relations with ASEAN were "substantive" enough.

THE UNITED STATES

Long after the event, observers were still trying to figure out why Condoleezza Rice had skipped the Post-Ministerial Conferences and the ASEAN Regional Forum in Vientiane in July 2005. Her staff had stated that her engagement with Middle East events prevented her from going to Asia at that time. As far as I can remember from the fourteen ASEAN Ministerial Meetings that I attended as ASEAN Senior Official for the Philippines, as Philippine Ambassador to Malaysia, as ASEAN Secretary-General, or as Philippine Special Envoy, and as far as I can tell from the record, the American Secretary of State had always been present at the Post-Ministerial Conferences except in 1982, when Alexander Haig gave it a miss. Since its founding, the ASEAN Regional Forum had never failed to benefit from the presence of the Secretary of State. He or she took the occasion of the ASEAN meetings to hold bilateral consultations with other foreign ministers in attendance and to make official visits to individual ASEAN and other Asian countries. This consistent participation was meant to manifest Washington's abiding security and economic interests in East Asia and its commitment to the region's stability and progress. For ASEAN, it was a mark of the region's importance and an opportunity to engage the United States as a group. It was also a chance to display ASEAN and its members to the world's media, which are always attracted to the activities and statements of the American Secretary of State.

As a global power, now *the* superpower, and as the world's largest market and leading economy, the United States is naturally counted among the ASEAN countries' most important relationships. It is certainly a vital factor in the security equation in East Asia as well as in the world at large, particularly in terms of both nuclear and conventional military power. By virtue of history, strategic outlook, or diplomatic and commercial interests, or all of these together, some ASEAN countries have a defence relationship with the United States of one sort or another. The Philippines and the United States have a mutual defence treaty that dates back to 1951 and regularly conduct joint military exercises. Similarly, Thailand and the United States embark on regular military exercises as a function of their defence alliance, which is based on the 1954 Southeast Asia Collective Defence Treaty that created the now-defunct SEATO. Two to four other ASEAN countries may have agreed arrangements for the docking or repair of U.S. naval vessels, none of which, however, has been officially and publicly acknowledged. Although the ASEAN countries have widely divergent views of the security role of the United States in the region, all of them, in one way or another, take the United States prominently into account in their strategic and security calculations. For that reason, the United States is a leading participant in the ASEAN Regional Forum.

The United States is the largest export market of the six older ASEAN members, the association's leading trading nations. It is their second biggest source of imports, after Japan. In the period 1995–2003, the cumulative total of U.S. investments in ASEAN was US$35.717 billion, topping Japan's and those of individual EU members.[76] By virtue of its importance as a trading partner and source of investments, it is almost unthinkable for the United States not to be a Dialogue Partner of ASEAN. Indeed, it was one of the first six ASEAN Dialogue Partners, becoming one in 1977.

In one of his early appearances at the ASEAN PMC, Secretary of State Colin Powell circulated to the ASEAN delegations thick sheaves of paper containing lists of projects that the United States had undertaken for Southeast Asia, with their dollar values. Almost all of them, however, were cooperative activities carried out with individual countries rather than with ASEAN *as a group*. It also included work being done by the U.S. private sector, primarily the U.S.-ASEAN Business Council. Despite the importance of the United States to ASEAN and its member-countries and the presumed value of Southeast Asia to Washington, the ASEAN-U.S. relationship today does not have the density of ASEAN's linkages with some of the other Dialogue Partners.

Economic matters are discussed in the sporadic meetings between the ASEAN Economic Ministers and the U.S. Trade Representative. The ASEAN Secretariat has pushed for the involvement of the U.S. Department of Commerce in trade talks, since ASEAN is interested in trade facilitation, which is largely handled by Commerce, as much as in liberalization, dealt with by the USTR. In April 2001, then Secretary of Commerce Donald Evans and I signed a "memorandum of cooperation" on trade-related standards and conformance. Since then, the ASEAN Consultative Committee on Standards and Quality has been meeting regularly with the U.S. Department of Commerce on its implementation. I concluded a similar memorandum with

Secretary of Agriculture Ann Veneman, since then named the new head of UNICEF. Cooperation on the environment has been carried out through the U.S. Asia Environmental Partnership. Particularly useful was the role of the Department of Agriculture's U.S. Forest Service in the ADB-funded project to deal with the haze problem in Southeast Asia.

To be sure, the United States' attendance at the Post-Ministerial Conferences and the ASEAN Regional Forum and the opportunities that it presents for ministerial-level consultations between ASEAN and the U.S. are extremely valuable for political, diplomatic and strategic, as well as symbolic, purposes. The dialogue between ASEAN and U.S. officials, which takes place about once every eighteen months, covers political, security, economic, and social issues and is quite useful for mutual understanding. However, in terms of cooperative projects, in terms of technical assistance and other development cooperation, the relationship between the United States government and ASEAN as an association is rather thin.

The more substantive relationship is actually carried out, on the U.S. side, by the U.S.-ASEAN Business Council. With its membership of well over a hundred of the United States' leading corporations, the council is the single most active and strongest promoter of ASEAN and of ASEAN-U.S. relations in America. It constitutes a powerful lobby group with the U.S. Congress and the executive branch. In the early days of the first administration of President George W. Bush, it sent to the White House a set of recommendations on the policies that the new leadership ought to draw up towards Southeast Asia. The council participates in an appropriate segment of the regular ASEAN-U.S. dialogue, often taking ASEAN's side on certain issues in dispute, such as those pertaining to protectionism and market access.

The council arranges seminars, symposiums and media events promoting ASEAN, including setting up speaking engagements and interviews for ASEAN leaders and ministers and the Secretary-General. For a number of years, it has been sponsoring tours — several states at a time — for ASEAN ambassadors in Washington, D.C., and American ambassadors to the ASEAN countries. Its website is a valuable source of information on the situation in ASEAN and its member-countries, including business developments. The council presents the interests and concerns of American business in regular encounters with the ASEAN trade ministers, starting in October 2000, and subsequently with the finance, transport, telecommunications and other ministers. It has a programme of technical cooperation, which has so far covered seminars, training and study tours on the use of information and communications technology for effective governance, customs best practices, and central banking. The council is also a strong advocate of ASEAN economic integration as something in the interest of the region as well as of the council's members.

Unfortunately for both Southeast Asia and the United States, the U.S. involvement in Southeast Asia has been increasingly limited to security and business matters, with educational and cultural exchanges having progressively diminished for decades. As for ASEAN-U.S. relations, the advent of the Bush Administration saw an increase in official Washington's attention to ASEAN as an association. I expressed ASEAN's appreciation of this to President George W. Bush during an informal meeting between him and the seven ASEAN heads of government attending the APEC Economic Leaders' Meeting in Los Cabos, Mexico, on 26 October 2002. I also remarked on this to Secretary Powell at the ASEAN-U.S. Post-Ministerial Conference earlier that year. The increased attention had been manifested in several ways. In May 1998, it was the U.S.' turn to host the ASEAN-U.S. dialogue. However, not wanting to receive senior Myanmar officials in the United States, the Americans requested that they "host" the meeting in Manila, right after the senior officials meeting of the ARF that was taking place there. On the other hand, in November 2001, not only was the dialogue hosted by the United States in Washington, D.C.; the delegation leaders were engaged by Secretary Powell, Deputy Secretary Richard Armitage and Assistant Secretary James Kelly in discussions at the State Department and by Condoleezza Rice, then National Security Adviser, in the White House. The ASEAN delegation included U Thaung Tun, the director-general for political affairs of the Myanmar foreign ministry. All the ASEAN delegations similarly took part in the June 2005 dialogue in Washington. As Secretary of State, Condoleezza Rice met with the ASEAN Foreign ministers in New York in September, reviving a practice that had been discontinued for many years.

It was at the informal ASEAN-U.S. summit in Los Cabos in 2002 that President Bush announced the Enterprise for ASEAN Initiative. The Deputy U.S. Trade Representative had earlier alerted me to it by telephone. The ASEAN Economic Ministers were similarly alerted. As Bush and his officials described it, the EAI would be the regional framework for the U.S. to negotiate free trade agreements with those ASEAN countries with which the U.S. had Trade and Investment Framework Agreements (TIFA). At that time, Singapore was close to signing a comprehensive economic agreement with the United States, Indonesia, the Philippines and Thailand had TIFAs, and Brunei Darussalam was about to conclude one. Presumably, this arrangement would allow the United States to exclude certain ASEAN countries, Myanmar being under a U.S. trade and investment embargo and Cambodia being denied, until 2004, most-favoured-nation treatment by the United States. The

ASEAN Economic Ministers, however, subsequently insisted that the EAI be discussed with ASEAN as a whole and that a framework be worked out between ASEAN as a group and the United States. Then U.S. Trade Representative Robert Zoellick concurred, but operative agreements, including those on free trade areas, would still be negotiated between the United States and individual ASEAN members. As of November 2005, work on an ASEAN-U.S. framework agreement had not started.

There have been, on the ground, some incremental moves on the part of the United States towards cooperating more closely with ASEAN as an association. USAID has opened a regional development mission in Bangkok, an ASEAN liaison officer has been assigned to the U.S. Embassy in Jakarta, and a U.S. trade specialist has set up shop at the ASEAN Secretariat. At the beginning of the ARF, the United States had insisted on running the ARF website out of the University of Washington. However, the United States has now agreed to the ASEAN Secretariat operating the site and is, indeed, giving it support in terms of its development and the training of its staff.

Bush met again with the seven ASEAN members of APEC on 18 November 2005, on the occasion of the APEC leaders' meeting in Busan, South Korea. The day before, the Joint Vision Statement on the ASEAN-U.S. Enhanced Partnership was issued in Washington, D.C. and in each of the ASEAN capitals, including, I am told, Yangon. The document is largely symbolic, expressing the intention to carry out political and security, economic, and social and development cooperation and affirming certain common principles.

The joint press statement of the June 2005 dialogue hinted at the possibility of an ASEAN-U.S. summit in 2007, but the Joint Vision Statement is silent on it. One opportunity for a summit could be the APEC leaders' meeting in Hanoi in late 2006. The heads of government of Cambodia, Laos and Myanmar, the ASEAN members not included in APEC, could join those of the seven ASEAN members of APEC and the United States for a full ASEAN-U.S. summit meeting. The ASEAN-U.S. TIFA could be announced then. This assumes, of course, that the American President will be willing to sit down with Myanmar's Prime Minister.

THE EUROPEAN UNION

ASEAN's first Dialogue Partner was the European Economic Community. This was probably because ASEAN found it logical at that time to anchor its external relations on its partnership with another regional organization, one that was showing the way to regionalism. The Special Coordinating

Committee of ASEAN Nations, or SCCAN, was formed in 1972 to conduct relations with the EEC. By getting the Europeans to link up with it, ASEAN for the first time won recognition for the association from a major international player. As recalled above, Adam Malik, the Indonesian foreign minister, observed in 1973 that it was ASEAN's solidarity that gained it that recognition.

It was the ASEAN Economic Ministers who first held talks with the EEC, in Brussels in June 1972, next in Bangkok in 1973, and the third time in Jakarta in 1974. The AEM's interlocutor was Sir Christopher Soames, the European Commission's Vice-President and Commissioner for External Relations. The establishment of an ASEAN-EEC Joint Study Group to map out the relationship was agreed upon at the Jakarta meeting.

The ASEAN Economic Ministers' central role in the first six years of the ASEAN-EEC dialogue was a natural reflection of ASEAN's primary concern in the relationship — improvements in the EEC's GSP and access to the European market for the ASEAN members' tropical products and commodity exports. The economic ministers of the two sides met again in 1985. The ASEAN Economic Ministers started consulting regularly with the EU Trade Commissioner in 2000. Dealing with a wide range of issues in free-flowing discussions, the consultations usually take place after the regular ASEAN Economic Ministers meetings, as do those with China, Japan, Korea, Australia and New Zealand, and, sporadically, the United States.

It was not until 1978 that the ASEAN Foreign Ministers met with their counterparts from the European Community's member-states and the leadership of the European Commission. That was to be the first of a series of meetings between foreign ministers of the two groups, called AEMM for ASEAN-EC — later ASEAN-EU — Ministerial Meeting. These have been held every eighteen months or so. Until the ASEAN Foreign Ministers' meetings with those of China, Japan and South Korea became regular, annual affairs, the AEMM was the only forum in which the ASEAN Foreign Ministers met with counterparts from a Dialogue Partner outside the Post-Ministerial Conferences. Indonesia's Foreign Minister, Mochtar Kusumaatmadja, was to observe that ASEAN's political role had become "more pronounced" with the first AEMM in 1978. In 1979, the EC opened a delegation office in Bangkok, the first in Southeast Asia. Today it has delegations in all ASEAN capitals except Bandar Seri Begawan, to which the mission in Jakarta is accredited, and Yangon.

While the ASEAN Economic Ministers continued to object loudly to the EEC's protectionist policies with respect to ASEAN's agricultural and commodity exports, the Foreign Ministers used the AEMM to press the same concerns. At the first AEMM, the Europeans parried ASEAN's complaints by stressing that the protectionist measures were temporary and were meant to address special situations in only a few sectors. However, the AEMM turned increasingly to political issues, as well as development cooperation, even as ASEAN maintained pressure on trade matters. High on the agenda were the Indochinese asylum-seekers, the Vietnamese incursion into Cambodia, and the Soviet occupation of Afghanistan, until the settlement of the Cambodian question and the departure of Soviet forces from Afghanistan in the early 1990s.

The essentially political orientation of the ASEAN-EU dialogue became more pronounced with the initiation in 1995 of the ASEAN-EU Senior Officials Meeting, a forum of high-level diplomats that usually precedes the AEMM by a few months. In the AEMM, East Timor and Myanmar became contentious issues between the two sides. On each issue, the EU's policy was driven by one or two member-states — in the case of East Timor, by Portugal, and in that of Myanmar, by the United Kingdom and Denmark — with some others chafing at the hard line being pursued and seeking more pragmatic approaches. On Myanmar, as early as 1994, the AEMM joint statement indicated the different approaches of the two sides but diplomatically highlighted the complementary relationship between ASEAN's "constructive engagement" and the EU's "critical dialogue". After Myanmar entered ASEAN in 1997, the joint statements issued by the AEMM referred to discussions on the situation in that country and its place in ASEAN-EU relations, sometimes explicitly, at other times obliquely in formulations like "political dialogue through frank discussions of sensitive issues of common concern", a reference not just to Myanmar but to issues of human rights in general.[77]

When Vietnam, Laos and Cambodia joined ASEAN, they had no trouble acceding to the 1980 ASEAN-EC Cooperation Agreement. However, the EU refused to let Myanmar sign the agreement. The result was that, as recounted in Chapter 3, ASEAN and the EU had to go into diplomatic contortions so as to allow Myanmar to be present at the meetings of the Joint Cooperation Committee while enabling EU members to claim that Myanmar was not really participating; there were to be no national flags and no country name plates, and Myanmar representatives could not speak unless their country was directly alluded to.

The EU's outlook on ASEAN and Southeast Asia has been reflected in policy papers that it has published from time to time. They are either focused on ASEAN or Southeast Asia specifically or placed in the larger context of EU-Asia relations. The first of these, in 1994, was *Towards a New Asia Strategy*. The *New Dynamic in EU-ASEAN Relations*, issued in 1996, was specifically on the EU's relations with ASEAN. The 2001 paper, *Europe and Asia: A Strategic Framework for Enhanced Partnerships*, was followed in 2003 by *A New Partnership with South East Asia*.[78] These "communications" from the European Commission all stressed the importance of Asia or Southeast Asia to Europe in the light of the circumstances of the times and proposed areas of focus for the EU's relations with the region in response to those circumstances. In discussing *Towards a New Asia Strategy*, the joint declaration of the landmark Karlsruhe AEMM in 1994 affirmed, "ASEAN should remain a cornerstone of the EU's dialogue with the Asian region." Further on, it stressed that EU-ASEAN cooperation was "a central element in relations between Europe and the Asia-Pacific Region". *A New Partnership with South East Asia* emphasized that, in its cooperation with ASEAN, the EU would give priority to regional stability; human rights, democracy and good governance; "justice and home affairs issues" like crime and migration; trade and investment; and supporting ASEAN's poorer members in health and education. These policy parameters are today supposed to guide the EU's cooperation with ASEAN.

In addition to its efforts to open the European market to ASEAN products, ASEAN has always looked to the EU for development cooperation. The second AEMM, in March 1980 in Kuala Lumpur, saw the signing by the two sides' foreign ministers of the ASEAN-EC Cooperation Agreement. In it, the ASEAN countries and the Community extended most-favoured-nation treatment to one another's goods. It expressed the EC's intention to extend assistance to Southeast Asia's development, including in regional projects and other endeavours related to ASEAN cooperation. A Joint Cooperation Committee was to oversee and monitor the agreement's implementation.

Since then, the EC/EU, through the Commission, has undertaken a number of projects with ASEAN. Some have had to do with facilitating trade in goods — customs, patents and trademarks, and standards and quality assurance. Business exchanges have been promoted. A few ASEAN centres have been set up with EU support. Among these are the ASEAN Timber Industry Research and Development Centre and the ASEAN Customs Institute for Training and Research. An ASEAN-EU Management Centre in Bandar Seri Begawan has been in the works for several years, and the EU is currently helping draw up a business plan for it. An ASEAN Regional Center for Biodiversity Conservation has been set up with EU support. The ASEAN-EC Energy Management Training and Research Centre had been in operation for nearly ten years before it was folded into the ASEAN Centre for Energy in 1999, an ASEAN facility that now coordinates all regional energy activities and continues to receive some EU project support. The EU has for many years been funding technology transfer in the generation of energy through biomass. An 18-million euro ASEAN-EC Energy Facility was launched in 2002.

With ASEAN moving to integrate the regional economy since the decision on AFTA in 1992, regional integration became a natural focus for ASEAN-EU cooperation. The Institutional Development Programme for the ASEAN Secretariat, covering the 1996–98 period, was meant to expose the Secretariat's officers to how the EU and EC function, promote networking between the Secretariat and the Commission, and train the Secretariat officers in regional policy-making. The programme was projected to cover a broad range of areas for integrating the regional economy, including customs, non-tariff barriers, product standards, investments, transport, telecommunications, public information, services, the environment, culture and drugs. IDPAS was succeeded by the ASEAN Programme for Regional Integration Support, or APRIS, covering 2004 and 2005. APRIS is designed to assist ASEAN in policy development and in institutional capacity building for regional integration, going beyond the ASEAN Secretariat to workshops, studies, institution building and training of personnel of the member-states. Among the projects financed by the programme with a grant of four million euro are those dealing with mutual recognition arrangements for standards in services, statistics, customs reform, copyrights, the consultative mechanism for compliance with ASEAN economic agreements, the integration of the agro-based products and textile and apparel sectors, and a study on non-tariff barriers.

Pursuant to *A New Partnership with South East Asia*, the Commission produced, after consultation with the ASEAN Secretariat and Indonesia, the ASEAN coordinator-country for the EU, a "Regional Indicative Programme" for 2005–06.[79] Under the programme, ASEAN-EU cooperation would concentrate on four areas. One is the implementation of APRIS. An interesting step is the Trans-Regional EU-ASEAN Trade Initiative, or TREATI, which would encourage inter-regional dialogue on trade issues with a view to building, in the words of the joint statement of the March 2005 AEMM, "the foundations for a future FTA by sharing knowledge and experience between our different regulatory systems and establishing greater transparency and understanding between the two regions".[80] It has been made clear that the possible free trade area would be "WTO Plus", and thus can be substantively addressed only after the current round of multilateral trade negotiations is concluded. Nevertheless, a joint feasibility study on a possible free trade area and other forms of economic cooperation has been launched. The second area is strengthening ASEAN's regional and national capacity in statistics, particularly in the less-developed ASEAN members. The third has to do with regional cooperation against terrorism, especially through transborder information sharing. The final area is an information and communications campaign to spread knowledge about the EU and its institutions and the merits of regional integration.

ASEAN-EU cooperation is meant to equip ASEAN — the Secretariat and the member-states — with knowledge, insights and expertise in different elements of regional economic integration. ASEAN, of course, does not intend to go the way of the EU all the way, but it can learn many things from the European experience by way of practical measures. It is up to ASEAN's member-states to adapt and apply those measures that are necessary for integrating the Southeast Asian economy.

ASEAN-EU interaction now takes place also in the larger context of a process that brings together the leaders of the EU and not just ASEAN but East Asia. At the 1995 ASEAN Summit in Bangkok, Singapore's Prime Minister Goh Chok Tong proposed regular meetings between the heads of government of East Asia, that is, ASEAN, China, Japan and Korea, and those of Europe, observing that in the trilateral relationship among the three centres of global economic dynamism — East Asia, Europe and North America — the East Asia-Europe leg was the weakest. The ties between Western Europe and North America, he noted, were long established and thriving, and those between East Asia and North America were manifested and fortified in APEC and in the United States' strong relations with many East Asian countries. Relations between Europe and East Asia were not as solid and institutionalized. President Jacques Chirac of France immediately took up the idea and pushed it in the European Union. The first Asia-Europe Meeting took place in Bangkok in March 1996.

Asymmetries in the ASEM process soon became apparent. The Europeans participated in it as the European Union. Non-EU members, like Norway, Iceland or Switzerland, were not to take part, and countries that subsequently joined the union would automatically attend ASEM. The President of the European Commission was also in attendance. On the other hand, the East Asian side took part in ASEM as individual countries. The ASEAN Secretary-General was not invited to the meetings. Until 2004, the Europeans were able to block the countries that joined ASEAN after 1996 — Laos, Myanmar and Cambodia — from admission into ASEM, clearly on account of some

EU members' objections to Myanmar. Another asymmetry had to do with representation. Whereas the East Asians were almost always 100-per cent represented at the leaders' meetings, the extent of European participation at the highest level varied from year to year.

According to an ASEM understanding, Asia or Europe is to propose ASEM participation on its side, subject to approval by the other side. However, as noted above, the EU's position is that EU membership automatically entitles a country to take part in ASEM. On the East Asian side, ASEAN has not been able to arrive at a consensus on the participation of Australia and New Zealand. Moscow has been knocking on ASEM's door almost from the beginning. However, the Europeans have declined to propose Russia for ASEM participation, presumably because it is not a member of the EU, while the feeling in East Asia is that the Russians more appropriately belong to Europe. Nevertheless, that perception may change should Russia, having been recently admitted into the Asian Cooperation Dialogue, succeed in gaining participation in the East Asia Summit.

The necessity of EU approval prevented the participation of Cambodia, Laos and Myanmar in ASEM even after they joined ASEAN. The EU apparently had no problems with Cambodia or Laos but objected strongly to Myanmar. On the other hand, ASEAN insisted on all three joining ASEM at the same time. The deadlock reached a crucial juncture when ten new members were admitted into the EU in May 2004 and the EU demanded that they automatically take part in ASEM. ASEAN countered that, in that case, ASEAN's three new members ought to gain admission, too, implicitly dangling the possibility that otherwise ASEAN would withhold approval of the new EU members' participation in ASEM. The EU was thus forced to accept a compromise in which Myanmar would be admitted into ASEM but would agree to be represented in the October 2004 summit in Hanoi at lower than the level of head of government, a compromise that the EU itself publicly announced. The EU statement also said:

> At the same time, the EU has made clear that if there has been no movement by the authorities in Burma/Myanmar by the time of the summit, to release Daw Aung San Suu Kyi and to allow a genuine and open National Convention, the EU will strengthen the existing targeted sanctions against the Burmese regime. In addition, the Europeans with (sic) take the opportunity at the Summit, to discuss the human rights situation and the need for democratic reforms in Burma/Myanmar with Asian partners as well as making the European position clear to the Burmese representative present.[81]

There is no sign that the EU has made good its threat of strengthened sanctions. However, The Netherlands refused a visa to Myanmar's minister, who was to attend an ASEM economic ministers' meeting in Rotterdam in September 2005, whereupon ASEAN's Foreign Ministers asked their economic ministers not to take part. ASEAN senior officials took their ministers' place.

ASEM is essentially a top-level forum convened every two years for government leaders of Europe and Asia to discuss the great issues of the times, share visions of the future, and give impetus to cooperation between the two regions. The ASEM foreign ministers met for the first time right after the ASEAN-EU Ministerial Meeting in February 1997. Since then, forums have convened among economic, finance and environment ministers. The Asia-Europe Foundation, which is headquartered in Singapore, serves as ASEM's *de facto* executive for cultural, educational, intellectual and people-to-people exchanges. With limited resources, ASEF has sponsored, almost non-stop, an impressive number of imaginative events — colloquiums, symposiums, book- and journal-publishing, cultural festivals — in both Asia and Europe, bringing the peoples of the two regions together, promoting understanding between them. With its 2004 enlargement, ASEM now counts thirty-nine participants, including the European Commission.

CANADA

Never a colonial power, Canada, it can be said, started its involvement in Southeast Asian affairs when, along with India and Poland, it was named to the International Commission for Supervision and Control that oversaw compliance with the 1954 Geneva agreements on Indochina — a nomination "unsought and unwanted", according to Robert Bothwell, a professor of history at the University of Toronto.[82] Canada apparently considers this involvement to be of little significance. An official history of Canada's foreign relations on the website of the country's Department of Foreign Affairs and International Trade does not mention it at all.[83]

Recognized as a major developed country through its admission in 1976 into the group of the world's leading economies (now Group of 8), Canada was brought into the ASEAN dialogue system in 1977. The potential for both trade and development assistance was alluring to ASEAN. Twenty-eight years later, however, the potential for trade has not been realized. As recently as 2002, according to ASEAN Secretariat figures, ASEAN-Canada trade amounted to only about US$5 billion both ways. The level of Canadian investments in ASEAN is low but rising. Development cooperation is founded on the ASEAN-Canada Economic Agreement, which was signed in 1981 and revised in 1993. Canadian assistance has been devoted to forestry, human resource development, fisheries, energy, agriculture, transportation and communications. The Canadian International Development Agency also funded the Indonesia-led series of informal workshops on managing potential conflict in the South China Sea, an undertaking that was technically outside ASEAN but involved all ASEAN countries.

A Joint Cooperation Committee handled ASEAN-Canada cooperation, holding eleven meetings alternately in ASEAN and Canada from 1983 to 1997. Such meetings were suspended after Myanmar joined ASEAN in July 1997, two months after the eleventh JCC meeting, as Canada found itself unable to extend assistance to an association that had Myanmar as one of its members. It also claimed to be constrained by rules of the Organization of Economic Cooperation and Development against giving aid to high-income countries like Brunei Darussalam and Singapore.

Both ASEAN and Canada, however, tried hard to get the dialogue back on track, even as neither side gave way on what each stood on as a matter of principle. I myself suggested to the Canadians a number of formulas that might get the relationship going while papering over the disagreements. After several attempts and much coming and going, the dialogue, at senior officials' level, was finally held at the end of March 2004 in Bandar Seri Begawan, with Brunei Darussalam as co-chair, the first time in seven years. According to the co-chairs' statement issued at the close of the dialogue, Canada fully supported ASEAN's recent endeavours, including the ASEAN Community and the Initiative for ASEAN Integration, and the linkages that the association was forging with neighbouring Dialogue Partners. Canada expressed its hope for expanded exchanges with ASEAN. An interesting initiative that came out of the meeting was the proposal for "trilateral cooperation" involving Canada, one of the older ASEAN members and one of the newer ones, which would enable Canada to extend assistance to Cambodia, Laos and Vietnam without complications. In general, the dialogue seemed to be upbeat and forward-looking. Following an "ASEAN-Canada Partnership Symposium" in Brunei Darussalam, the dialogue resumed in Vancouver in April 2005. The statement issued there was even more optimistic, referring to additional efforts to expand the content of the relationship. A meeting of ASEAN and Canadian senior economic officials and a business forum took place for the first time in Toronto in May.

In June 2006, another Dialogue session, dubbed the third ASEAN-Canada Dialogue, took place in Bandar Seri Begawan. Aside from the usual exchange of views on current international issues, the meeting alluded to the ASEAN-Canada Joint Cooperation Work Plan that was being drawn up as a basis for future cooperation. The participants agreed to meet again in Canada "in early 2007".[84]

Canada being the host and chair of the Group of 7 summit in Halifax in 1995, then Foreign Minister André Ouellet made it a point to invite his ASEAN counterparts to Vancouver beforehand to hear their views on what Canada should raise at the summit. I represented the Philippines at that meeting. As far as I know, it was the only time that a Group of 7 or Group of 8 host has made such a gesture, although Japan, in the ASEAN+3 economic ministers' meeting in May 2000, offered to bring up ASEAN's interests and concerns at the Group of 8 summit in Okinawa that year.

Canada is a founding participant in the ASEAN Regional Forum by virtue of its being an ASEAN Dialogue Partner rather than because it had a strategic role to play in East Asia in the traditional sense. In the ARF, Ottawa has in recent years been promoting the concept of "human security" — according to the Department of Foreign Affairs and International Trade, "a people-centred approach to foreign policy which recognizes that lasting stability cannot be achieved until people are protected from violent threats to their rights, safety or lives".[85] Canada raises issues of human rights in the ARF and in the ASEAN Post-Ministerial Conferences under this rubric and that of states' "responsibility to protect".[86]

Notes

1. An unpublished paper made these calculations from World Bank and IMF statistics.
2. Opening address at the sixth ASEAN Ministerial Meeting, Pattaya, Thailand, 16 April 1973.
3. Opening statement at the sixth ASEAN Ministerial Meeting, Pattaya, Thailand, 16 April 1973.
4. http://www.aseansec.org/3685.htm.
5. http://www.aseansec.org/3674.htm.
6. Speech at the 12th ASEAN Ministerial Meeting, Bali, 28 June 1979.
7. See Chapter 4.
8. The ARF is extensively discussed in Chapter 4.
9. Address at the meeting of the ASEAN Economic Ministers, Kuala Lumpur, 7 October 1991.
10. http://www.aseansec.org/5301.htm.
11. See Chapter 3.
12. Speech at the ASEAN+3 "informal" summit, Manila, 28 November 1999 (http://www.aseansec.org/5289.htm).

13. http://www.aseansec.org/pdf/east_asia_vision.pdf.
14. http://www.aseansec.org/viewpdf.asp?file=/pdf/easg.pdf. A printed version, dated 4 November 2002, was made available at the ASEAN+3 Summit in Phnom Penh.
15. Ibid.
16. http://www.aseansec.org/5317.htm.
17. http://www.aseansec.org/13188.htm.
18. http://www.aseansec.org/14833.htm, para. 38.
19. http://www.aseansec.org/16192.htm, para. 48.
20. http://www.aseansec.org/16631.htm, para. 21.
21. *Asian Wall Street Journal*, 8 April 2005.
22. http://www.mfa.gov.sg/internet/.
23. Chairman's Statement of the First East Asia Summit, Kuala Lumpur, 14 December 2005 (http://www.aseansec.org/18104.htm), para. 11.
24. http://www.aseansec.org/18098.htm.
25. *Straits Times*, 3 January 2006. The article was reprinted in the *Korea Herald*, 4 January 2006.
26. http://www.aseansec.org/16245.htm.
27. http://www.aseansec.org/13185.htm.
28. http://www.aseansec.org/15647.htm.
29. http://www.china.org.cn/english/MATERIAL/15428.htm.
30. http://www.mrcmekong.org/about_us/about_us.htm.
31. Zhou Bo and Yang Weimin, "Priorities of the Greater Mekong Subregion: Issues, Strategies and Realities: Views of China's Yunnan Province", in *The Greater Mekong Subregion and ASEAN: From Backwaters to Headwaters*, edited by Kao Kim Hourn and Jeffrey A. Kaplan (Phnom Penh: Cambodian Institute for Cooperation and Peace, 2000), p. 207.
32. Evelyn Goh, *China in the Mekong River Basin: The Regional Security Implications of Resource Development on the Lancang Jiang* (Singapore: Institute of Defence and Strategic Studies, July 2004), p. 2.
33. Ibid., p. 12.
34. http://www.aseansec.org/3634.htm.
35. http://www.aseansec.org/5232.htm.
36. http://www.aseansec.org/13163.htm.
37. *ASEAN Statistical Yearbook 2005* (Jakarta: ASEAN Secretariat, 2004), Tables V.7 and V.8. The figures do not include those of Laos and Vietnam, which did not make them available to the Secretariat.
38. Ibid., Table VIII.6.
39. http://www.aseansec.org/16646.htm.
40. Interview with Prime Minister Abdullah Badawi, Putrajaya, Malaysia, 3 November 2004.
41. http://www.aseansec.org/ASEAN-China-EPG.pdf.
42. Papers presented at this conference, together with others, are compiled in *Towards an Asian Economic Community: Vision of a New Asia*, edited by Nagesh Kumar

(New Delhi: Research and Information System for Developing Countries and Singapore: Institute of Southeast Asian Studies, 2004).
43. Kavi Chongkittavorn, "Brotherly Engagement: India, China and ASEAN", in *India-ASEAN Partnership in an Era of Globalization: Reflections by Eminent Persons* (New Delhi: Research and Information System for the Non-Aligned and Other Developing Countries and Singapore: Institute of Southeast Asian Studies, 2004), pp. 158–59.
44. Joint Press Statement of the Meeting at Official Level Between ASEAN and India, Kuala Lumpur, 16 May 1980 (http://www.aseansec.org/5733.htm).
45. Opening address at the 13th ASEAN Ministerial Meeting, Kuala Lumpur, 25 June 1980.
46. http://www.aseansec.org/3679.htm.
47. *India-ASEAN Partnership in an Era of Globalization: Reflections by Eminent Persons* (New Delhi: Research and Information System for the Non-Aligned and Other Developing Countries and Singapore: Institute of Southeast Asian Studies, 2004).
48. http://www.aseansec.org/18079.htm, para. 6.
49. Domingo L. Siazon. Remarks at the opening of the ASEAN Promotion Center's symposium on ASEAN-Japan Relations in the 21st Century, Tokyo, 27 September 2000 (http://www.dfa.gov.ph/archive/speech/siazon/sp-asean21st.html).
50. As quoted, in English translation, in Masaharu Kohno, "In Search of Proactive Diplomacy: Increasing Japan's International Role in the 1990s", in *Global Politics* (Washington, D.C.: Brookings Institution, 1999) (http://www.brookings.edu/fp/cnaps/papers/1999_kohno.htm).
51. *Joint Statement of the Meeting of ASEAN Heads of Government and the Prime Minister of Japan, Kuala Lumpur, 7 August 1977.*
52. See Chapter 5.
53. Sueo Sudo, *Evolution of ASEAN-Japan Relations* (Singapore: Institute of Southeast Asian Studies, 2005), p. 35. I am indebted to this work for its account of the visits of Japanese Prime Ministers to ASEAN.
54. http://www.aseansec.org/3685.htm.
55. http://www.aseansec.org/3683.htm.
56. http://www.aseansec.org/6120.htm.
57. See Chapter 5.
58. Edith Terry, *The World Bank and Japan: How Godzilla of the Ginza and King Kong of H Street Got Hitched* (Tokyo: Japan Policy Research Institute Working Paper #70, August 2000). This paper gives a comprehensive account of Japan's role in the 1997–98 Asian financial crisis.
59. The Chiangmai Initiative is more extensively discussed in Chapter 3.
60. http://www.aseansec.org/13190.htm.
61. http://www.aseansec.org/7672.htm.
62. http://www.aseansec.org/16811.htm.
63. http://www.aseansec.org/18063.htm.

64. http://www.aseansec.org/18082.htm, para. 6.
65. http://www.beehive.govt.nz/ViewDocument.aspx?DocumentID=22963.
66. *The Angkor Agenda: Report of the High-Level Task Force on the AFTA-CER Free Trade Area* (http://www.aseansec.org/angkor_agenda.pdf).
67. http://www.aseansec.org/947.htm.
68. http://www.aseansec.org/12780.htm.
69. Media Statement of the Tenth ASEAN Economic Ministers Retreat, Singapore, 21 April 2004.
70. http://www.aseansec.org/16192.htm, para. 51.
71. http://www.aseansec.org/16796.htm.
72. http://www.aseansec.org/16799.htm.
73. http://www.aseansec.org/17792.htm, paras. 4–7.
74. See Chapter 4.
75. http://www.aseansec.org/18070.htm, para. 5.
76. These data are taken from *ASEAN Statistical Pocketbook 2005* (Jakarta: ASEAN Secretariat, 2005), pp. 36 and 56.
77. Joint Declaration of the Twelfth ASEAN-EU Ministerial Meeting, Singapore, 13–14 February 1997 (http://www.aseansec.org/5643.htm).
78. http://europa.eu.int/comm/external_relations/asia/doc/com03_sea.pdf.
79. http://europa.eu.int/comm/external_relations/asean/csp/rip_05-06_en.pdf.
80. http://www.aseansec.org/17354.htm.
81. http://europa.eu.int/comm/external_relations/asem/asem_summits/asem5/news/ip04_1178.htm.
82. Robert Bothwell, "Eyes West: Canada and the Cold War in Asia", in *Canada and the Early Cold War 1943–57*, edited by Greg Donaghy (Ottawa: Canadian Government Publishing, 1998).
83. http://www.dfait-maeci.gc.ca/department/history/canada9-en.asp.
84. http://www.aseansec.org/18485.htm.
85. http://www.humansecurity.gc.ca/menu-en.asp.
86. See International Commission on Intervention and State Sovereignty, *The Responsibility to Protect* (Ottawa: International Development Research Centre, 2001).

7

THE ASEAN COMMUNITY
Is It for Real?

The Declaration of ASEAN Concord II, or Bali Concord II (BCII), which ASEAN's leaders issued at their summit in Bali on 7 October 2003, states in its first operative paragraph:

> An ASEAN Community shall be established comprising three pillars, namely political and security co-operation, economic co-operation, and socio-cultural co-operation that are closely intertwined and mutually reinforcing for the purpose of ensuring durable peace, stability and shared prosperity in the region.[1]

Although BCII is meant to present an integral and coherent vision of an ASEAN "community", with its three components interacting with one another as parts of the whole, "closely intertwined and mutually reinforcing", the document actually treats the three "pillars" highly discretely. This is perhaps inevitable in the light of the fact that different sets of officials drafted the three segments. This compartmentalized division of bureaucratic turf in turn reflects the lack of a body in any of the ASEAN countries that takes charge of ASEAN matters in a comprehensive manner. That lack is one of ASEAN's main institutional weaknesses.

AN ECONOMIC COMMUNITY

The concept of an ASEAN Community as envisioned at the ASEAN Summit in Bali in 2003 had its genesis in the proposal for an ASEAN Economic Community. At the ASEAN Summit in Phnom Penh on 4 November 2002,

Prime Minister Goh Chok Tong of Singapore had proposed that the next stage in regional economic integration be named the ASEAN Economic Community. He and a few other ASEAN leaders were deeply concerned over the weakened ability of the ASEAN countries to attract foreign direct investment, on which all of them depended for sustained economic growth. This development was a consequence of the changes wrought by the Asian financial crisis in investors' perceptions of Southeast Asia's economic prospects. Some of the proverbial "observers" attributed it also to the surge of China and, later, of India as competing destinations for investment. Those ASEAN leaders were convinced that the only way for Southeast Asia to meet these challenges was to deepen the integration of the ASEAN economy in a way that was credible to investors. Investors, within and outside ASEAN, had to be persuaded that ASEAN was serious about regional economic integration, and that ASEAN was clear about its objective and about the steps that it was taking towards it. Specifically, investors had to be convinced that the ASEAN economy, when integrated, would be — or at least had good prospects of being — a veritable "domestic" market almost half the size of China's in terms of population, with a gross "domestic" product approaching the level of magnitude of China's GDP. Holding up the vision of the ASEAN Economic Community as a goal could guide ministers and officials in the steps they were to take towards closer regional economic integration and goad them to move faster towards that goal.

Recognizing the need for regional economic integration, ASEAN had in 1992 entered into an agreement to cut tariffs on intra-ASEAN trade to minimal levels and eventually remove them altogether and to bring down non-tariff barriers to that trade. The ASEAN countries had agreed to harmonize their customs procedures and otherwise get those procedures to facilitate, rather than hinder, trade among them. In 1995, they decided to negotiate the liberalization of trade in services, particularly in seven priority sectors. In 1997, they agreed to harmonize standards for twenty product groups. In 1998, they entered into "framework agreements" on intra-ASEAN investments, mutual recognition arrangements and goods in transit. In 2005, they concluded an agreement on multimodal transport.

ASEAN has largely kept to its tariff-cutting schedule. It has adopted the ASEAN Harmonized Tariff Nomenclatures and agreed on common standards for the twenty product groups. It has strengthened its dispute-settlement mechanism. However, not much substantive progress has been made on most of the other components of economic integration. In my final report to the ASEAN leaders as ASEAN Secretary-General, delivered at the 2002 Phnom Penh summit, I lamented:

However, the process of integration has generally stalled. To be sure, some progress has been made, notably in AFTA, but progress has fallen short of measuring up to the challenges faced by our region and carrying out the leaders' vision and resolve. AFTA has seen little actual use by traders. The other foundations for regional integration have not been built upon. Regional economic integration seems to have become stuck in framework agreements, work programmes and master plans.[2]

By accepting Goh Chok Tong's proposal to use the term ASEAN Economic Community, the ASEAN leaders seemed to want to signal their seriousness about regional integration and the way they intended to go to attain it. The term evokes the European Economic Community, which was created by six European nations in 1957 and evolved into the Single European Market and the European Union. This did not necessarily mean that ASEAN intended to achieve the level of Europe's political and economic integration where it is today; rather, it indicated that ASEAN did seek to project itself as moving towards a degree of market integration that would make that integrated market large enough and diverse enough to be an attractive option for investors, that ASEAN would be proceeding faster on the road to integration than the snail's pace at which it had been moving.

GETTING SERIOUS ABOUT MARKET INTEGRATION?

Two months before the Phnom Penh summit, the ASEAN Economic Ministers agreed to form a High-Level Task Force on ASEAN Economic Integration. Composed of senior economic officials, it was to recommend measures for deepening the region's economic integration beyond AFTA. Its work would thus put flesh on the concept of an economic community. The ministers had earlier commissioned the international consultants, McKinsey & Co., to make a study of the state of ASEAN's competitiveness and draw up recommendations to strengthen it.

The McKinsey study, which was presented at different stages to the relevant ASEAN forums at different levels, including the Phnom Penh summit, observed that ASEAN had great economic promise and a potentially large market, but it was losing out to others as an investment destination largely because it was fragmented as a market. The slowing down of the flow of investments into ASEAN, according to the study, was also eroding the region's export competitiveness. It cited the relatively small share of intra-ASEAN trade as a percentage of the total trade of the ASEAN countries. The study presented some indicators of how far ASEAN still had to go on the road to market integration. It gave several examples of the widely varying prices of the same goods in different ASEAN countries. The study graphically illustrated the lack of common product standards by pointing out the difference in actual weight between a 100-gram bar of soap in Indonesia and a 100-gram bar of soap in Thailand. It also cited the different specifications for ice cream. Such differences stand in the way of market integration, reducing efficiency and raising costs and prices. The McKinsey study observed that customs procedures in ASEAN were applied in "subjective" and unpredictable ways.

To remedy the situation, McKinsey advocated a resolute push for regional economic integration. However, because of many member-states' apprehensions about the negative economic, social and political effects of rapid integration, it recommended that integration measures be applied first to two broad sectors — electronics and consumer goods. It also advised that regional institutions be strengthened so as to enable them to make technical decisions on regional integration issues, monitor the progress of integration independently and publicly, and settle disputes with binding rulings. McKinsey invoked the benefits of deeper integration: faster economic growth, better economic policies, greater efficiency, higher productivity, and lower costs. Politically, economic integration would foster mutual trust, boost ASEAN's international bargaining power, and strengthen its international influence.[3]

In a concept paper on the proposed ASEAN Economic Community, issued in February 2003, the Institute of Southeast Asian Studies in Singapore, after reviewing the steps that had been taken to integrate the ASEAN economy, observed:

> ASEAN needs a higher level of economic integration in order to achieve closer cohesion. Economic integration would, among other things, allow countries to focus on their comparative advantages as well as create an attractive destination for FDI. Deeper economic integration would also benefit the less developed ASEAN countries ... Cambodia, Laos, Myanmar and Vietnam (CLMV).[4]

The concept paper emphasized the need for ASEAN to liberalize trade in services and for its member-states to undertake domestic reforms. It called for a "stronger institutional structure and an effective enforcement mechanism", including a body with "supranational powers" to set policies, coordinate process, and implement and enforce agreements. The paper envisioned as components of the ASEAN Economic Community the free movement of goods, services, investments and capital, an "attractive regional production platform", the free movement of skilled labour and creative talent, the free flow of tourists within ASEAN, the harmonization of customs procedures and the "minimization" of customs requirements, the harmonization of standards consistent with international standards, and a "well-developed" institutional and legal infrastructure.[5]

As finally issued, Bali Concord II invokes the ASEAN vision of "a stable, prosperous and highly competitive ASEAN Economic Region in which there is a free flow of goods, services and investments, a freer flow of capital, equitable economic development and reduced poverty and socio-economic disparities" by 2020.[6] It defines that vision further as "a single market and production base", with "opportunities for business complementation" in "the global supply chain". It points the way to attaining that vision — the implementation of current initiatives, including AFTA, the liberalization of trade in services, and the ASEAN Investment Area; accelerated regional integration in the designated priority sectors; the easier movement of "business people, skilled labour and talents"; and strengthened ASEAN institutions. It takes care to mention the need to integrate the newer members into the ASEAN economy. It prescribes stepped-up cooperation and integration in a menu of areas. The heart of the economic portion of BCII, however, is its wholesale adoption of the High-Level Task Force's recommendations, which are annexed to the document, as "a first step towards the realization of the ASEAN Economic Community".[7]

The task force had recommended the acceleration of current ASEAN economic-integration programmes, laying down clear deadlines for specific measures, in the areas of tariffs, non-tariff measures, customs, standards, services, investments, intellectual property rights, and finance. Another recommendation was the designation of eleven "priority sectors" for accelerated integration — seven in merchandise trade and four in services. These are agro-based products, air transport, automotives, e-ASEAN, electronics, fisheries, health care, rubber-based products, textiles and apparel, tourism, and wood-based products. The idea was to make the process of integration more manageable and, for some countries, less threatening than across-the-board integration. In any case, the coverage of each sector is broad enough to account for a substantial portion of intra-ASEAN trade. According to the ASEAN Secretariat, the 11 sectors together accounted for about half of intra-ASEAN trade in 2003, US$48.4 billion in exports and US$43.4 billion in imports. Others sectors may be added later.

In the seven goods sectors, tariff and other barriers to trade are to be removed, and customs procedures speeded up and simplified. Mutual recognition arrangements are to be concluded and product standards and technical regulations harmonized at a faster pace. The four priority services sectors are to be liberalized by 2010 and mutual recognition arrangements worked out for them. In addition, the movement of people is to be facilitated. Finally, the task force proposed new institutional mechanisms — an advisory mechanism in each ASEAN country to help solve operational problems encountered by business firms and people; a legal unit in the ASEAN Secretariat to help sort out trade disputes; a "compliance monitoring body" for "peer adjudication" of such disputes; and an impartial dispute-settlement mechanism.[8]

On 29 November 2004, the ASEAN leaders adopted the Vientiane Action Programme, laying down the "goals and strategies" for bringing the ASEAN Community to reality.[9] Annexed to the VAP are "programme areas and measures" for each of the three communities. Both the VAP and its annex on the ASEAN Economic Community elaborate on recommendations of the High-Level Task Force. On the same day, the leaders signed the ASEAN Framework Agreement for the Integration of Priority Sectors, which further formalized the measures agreed upon in the VAP.[10] Earlier in the day, the Economic Ministers had signed 11 protocols, one for each of the priority sectors. The protocols form integral parts of the framework agreement. Each of them contains a set of measures common to all the goods sectors or one common to all the services sectors, and another set specific to each goods or services sector.[11] The task force recommendations, the VAP, the framework agreement on the priority sectors, and the protocols are for the most part consistent with one another in terms of the individual measures and their respective deadlines. The following section examines each of the principal recommendations.

CONCRETE MEASURES AND SHORT DEADLINES

In terms of barriers to trade in goods, by the end of 2004, the improvement in the AFTA rules of origin was to be "finalized" and "substantial transformation" adopted as the basis for determining origin. According to an officer of the ASEAN Secretariat, the rules of origin and their operational certification procedures have been under improvement since 2003. Part of the process is the alignment of the AFTA rules of origin with those being worked out in the negotiations on free trade areas between ASEAN and others, like China, Korea and India. ASEAN has adopted "substantial transformation" for determining the origin of textile and wheat-flour imports and is working on the rules for wood-based products, iron and steel, and semi-finished aluminum products. Tariffs on intra-ASEAN trade in the priority sectors are to be abolished by 2007 in the case of the ASEAN-6 and by 2012 in that of the ASEAN-4. A database on non-tariff measures in ASEAN was to have been set up by the middle of 2004. Since July of that year, a database on non-tariff measures of each member-country has been on the ASEAN Secretariat's website. However, the databases list the non-tariff barriers acknowledged by the governments; more meaningful would be those that *business* finds to be obstructive of trade. By the end of 2004, ASEAN countries were to adopt the WTO agreements on technical barriers to trade, sanitary and phytosanitary measures, and import licensing procedures and draw up guidelines for implementing the agreements in ASEAN. All ASEAN members of WTO are now parties to the agreements. ASEAN was to agree on criteria for identifying non-tariff barriers to intra-ASEAN trade by the middle of 2005, a deadline that has apparently been missed. A work programme for the removal of non-tariff barriers was to be drawn up by the end of 2005.

The expeditious processing of commercial documents by the customs authorities is critical to the conduct of trade, including preferential trade. The programme for the ASEAN Economic Community addresses this. By the end of 2004, the Green Lane System for the smooth and timely processing of goods traded under AFTA was to be fully operational, common guidelines for the implementation of the WTO Agreement on Customs Valuation were to have been developed, and a "service commitment" was to have been adopted by each ASEAN customs authority. The Green Lane is said to be operational in all ASEAN countries, the common guidelines have been adopted and published, and most customs authorities have completed their "service charters". By the end of 2005, customs declaration forms in ASEAN were to be simplified, improved and harmonized, and the Single Window system and the electronic processing of documents installed at customs. However, the agreement on the Single Window signed in December 2005 sets its implementation by 2008 for the ASEAN-6 and by 2012 for the CLMV countries. The VAP envisions that, within "the next two years", any container entering any ASEAN port would be released within an average of thirty minutes. The ASEAN Customs Declaration Document was indeed agreed upon in 2005, but has not been used by most member-countries.

Common product standards and the mutual recognition of product tests are crucial to market integration. According to the Vientiane agreements, starting in January 2005, the implementation of the few existing mutual recognition arrangements was to be accelerated, and new ones would be developed where called for, and a common ASEAN policy on standards and conformance would be "explored". By the end of 2005, "clear targets and schedules" were to be set for the harmonization of standards in the priority sectors. Technical regulations are to be harmonized by the end of 2010.

In services, "clear targets and schedules" are to be set for the liberalization of each sector by 2010, with mutual recognition arrangements for "major professional services" adopted by 2008. Such arrangements were formalized for engineering services in December 2005. The High-Level Task Force and the VAP also call for the establishment of a "Professional Exchange" by 2008.

The ASEAN Investment Area, agreed upon in 1998, provides for national treatment of investments from other ASEAN countries. The only exceptions are the sectors in "sensitive lists" or "temporary exclusion lists". The Vientiane agreements urge the transfer of sectors from the sensitive to the temporary exclusion lists beginning in 2005. Starting in 2004, restrictive investment measures were to be progressively removed from the temporary exclusion lists until they are eliminated by the end of 2010 for the ASEAN-6, 2013 for Vietnam, and 2015 for Cambodia, Laos and Myanmar, targets that are in the original AIA agreement. The degree of protection of intellectual property rights is increasingly important in investment decisions. Beyond trademarks and patents, the ASEAN countries were to cooperate, starting at the end of 2004, in copyright information exchange and enforcement.

Tourism, as a services sector, is a key area for integrating a regional economy. The VAP has a long list of measures for cooperation and standardization in tourism, most of them with 2004 or 2005 deadlines. However, all of the Vientiane documents are silent on the ASEAN Tourism Agreement, which the leaders themselves had signed only two years before. That agreement, even in its watered-down final form, contained more-substantive elements than the agreements and programmes arrived at in Vientiane. As recalled in Chapter 5, it would facilitate travel within the region, liberalize air services, allow wider market access to one another's tourism services, preserve the cultural heritage and the natural environment as tourism assets, ensure visitors' safety and security, foster cooperation in human resource development in the tourism industry, and expand the joint promotion of tourism. Yet, in the context of the ASEAN Economic Community, the agreement seems to be all but forgotten. The obstacles in the way of carrying out the tourism agreement are discussed in Chapter 5. The VAP calls for doing away with the limitations on market access and national treatment in the tourism sector so as to free the flow of tourism services, but sets the deadline at a distant 2010.

The harmonization of statistical data is, of course, basic to economic integration. The VAP calls for a "core set of ASEAN Statistical Indicators" (by 2005), "Harmonized statistical classification ... (2008) ... Harmonized merchandise trade statistics (2008) ... Comparable methodology and tools for statistics in International Trade in Services (ITS) (2008)", and "Automated data processing of merchandise trade statistics (2010)".

The VAP also has long lists of measures in transport, telecommunications and information technology, science and technology, energy, and food, agriculture and forestry. Some, particularly those in transport and telecommunications and information technology, have clear target dates, ranging from 2005 to 2010.

What are breathtaking about the Vientiane documents are the extremely short deadlines for carrying out most of the concrete measures to advance market integration. In the light of ASEAN's foot-dragging on most of these measures in the past, this is truly remarkable. Still, it remains to be seen whether the deadlines set in BCII, the VAP and the framework agreement on the priority sectors will be met. So far, as we have seen, the record has been mixed. More importantly, the measures agreed upon have to be complied with and not circumvented. If they are carried out — and carried out on time — they will go a long way towards giving ASEAN the makings of an economic community. Even then, sceptical business people, especially outside investors, have to be convinced that this time it is for real. ASEAN has lost so much time that it will have to work doubly hard to persuade them.

As everywhere else, including in the European Union, fundamental to the achievement of real economic integration in ASEAN are the political considerations. In an article on regional integration for a book published in Spain, I wrote:

> There should be little problem in getting rid of tariffs, although the prospect of liberalization almost invariably strikes a nervous chord in most countries, not just in ASEAN but everywhere. However, as elsewhere, non-tariff barriers are often opaque and versatile instruments for protecting politically powerful special interests and tend to undermine the benefits of reducing or removing tariffs. Or else, some ASEAN countries lack the expertise to manage non-tariff measures with the aim of doing away with them, a process that is much more complicated than cutting tariffs. Liberalizing trade in services is politically sensitive in many countries. Streamlining and harmonizing customs procedures are not only essential for economic integration; they are also of immense value in reducing transaction costs in international trade and in otherwise making trade more efficient and expeditious. Yet, the murky and complicated formulation and application of customs rules and procedures are often another means of protection and a lucrative source of rent income for customs authorities and their patrons. There should be no reason why customs transactions in ASEAN cannot be electronically processed now that we are in the 21st century. As noted earlier, the ASEAN goods-in-transit agreement cannot be carried out because of

bilateral disputes, which are largely political, between two key member-states. ASEAN nationals can now travel without visas to most other ASEAN countries. Myanmar is the outstanding exception. Freeing up intra-ASEAN travel, which would make business transactions quicker, smoother, easier and less expensive, as well as boost tourism, requires a fundamental political decision on the part of the country or countries concerned.

In other words, identifying and removing non-tariff barriers to trade, liberalizing trade in services, streamlining and harmonizing customs procedures, strengthening and clearing transportation and communications links within the region, and opening up borders to neighbors — no less than lowering tariffs — not only have to do with regional economic integration; they are at the heart of economic, and even political, reform within each of the ASEAN countries.[12]

In most cases, the measures required by the commitments in Bali and Vientiane for the ASEAN Economic Community depend for their implementation on national policy decisions and domestic reforms and, occasionally, on the settlement of bilateral problems. One wonders, for example, why customs forms were not simplified and harmonized a long time ago. Customs reform, of course, is basically a national endeavour, its way strewn with domestic obstacles. National legislation had to be enacted for the ASEAN Harmonized Tariff Nomenclatures to take operational effect. Protection of intellectual property rights is essentially a matter of law enforcement at the national level. The development and use of information technology depend in large measure on a government's ability to make hard national decisions. The accuracy of regional statistics is a function of the capacity of each country's personnel and institutions, and the willingness to share statistics is governed by national policies on transparency. As outlined in the VAP, the measures required for the liberalization of air services, which is vital for tourism, trade and investments, depend largely on unilateral policy and bilateral agreements. The VAP calls for the "Operationalization of the ASEAN Framework Agreement on the Facilitation of Goods in Transit" by 2005. However, four of the nine implementing protocols of this agreement cannot be concluded because of disputes between Malaysia and Singapore. The four protocols have to do with transit routes, frontier posts, railway border and interchange stations, and customs, subjects of disagreement between the two countries. The logjam may indeed be removed, albeit, as noted in Chapter 5, by going around the problem rather than resolving it and thus failing to achieve the objectives of the agreement.

It remains to be seen whether the member-states will have the political will to settle their bilateral differences and make the sometimes difficult but necessary decisions at the national level. Nevertheless, the regional goals and norms set in ASEAN agreements and programmes have immense value both in raising standards and in the application of peer pressure for member-states to live up to those standards. Advocates of reform within the member-countries can invoke ASEAN goals and norms as they struggle for change against entrenched forces.

Ironically, without an overarching treaty that is legally binding on the member-states or a supranational authority to ensure compliance with ASEAN agreements, a certain sense of regional community is required to overcome the political obstacles — and the mutual suspicions — that stand in the way of more rapid regional economic integration. At the same time, the agreements arrived at in Bali and Vientiane — if, with strong political leadership, they are carried out as intended and within the timeframes agreed upon — could help in building that sense of community. Moreover, the global competition for markets and investments is inexorably rising, with serious repercussions on economic growth, employment, living standards, and ultimately the political fate of ruling parties and regimes. The recognition of that challenge may serve to prod the hesitant ASEAN states to move more rapidly on integrating the regional economy. The question is: will this consideration be enough for ruling regimes to overcome powerful domestic forces pulling in the opposite direction? The answer, of course, will vary from country to country, but all will have to deal with it.

ASEAN MINUS X AND TWO PLUS X

One thing that ASEAN may have going for it is the decision, as recommended by the High-Level Task Force, to apply the ASEAN Minus X formula in integrating the 11 priority sectors, with services and investments being specifically singled out. ASEAN Minus X is defined and sanctioned in a provision of the 1992 Framework Agreement on Enhancing ASEAN Economic Cooperation, the foundation document of AFTA and other current economic initiatives. That provision states: "All Member States shall participate in intra-ASEAN economic arrangements. However, in the implementation of these economic arrangements, two or more Member States may proceed first if other Member States are not ready to implement these arrangements."[13] The advantage of this device is that the implementation of regional integration arrangements need not proceed at the pace of the slowest or the least willing ASEAN member. The success achieved by the countries that go ahead of the rest would demonstrate to the others the benefits to be gained from integration and reassure them of its non-threatening nature. Some delegations have asserted that the leaders in Bali had actually agreed on a variant of ASEAN Minus X, called Two Plus X, meaning that two or more ASEAN members could enter into any kind of cooperative economic arrangement with or without the consent of the rest. Others contend that such an arrangement could not be considered as an ASEAN activity. My understanding is that ASEAN Minus X pertains to the *implementation* of arrangements agreed upon by all, while Two Plus X refers to agreements worked out by two or more, but not all, ASEAN members. However, whether ASEAN Minus X or Two Plus X, the device ought to be resorted to with care. In practical terms, no one can stop two or more countries from embarking on arrangements on their own; but the device could serve to ease the pressure on members to undertake the necessary reforms, as in the liberalization of services and the enforcement of intellectual property rights, or to resolve their bilateral differences, as in the goods-in-transit agreement. If used indiscriminately, it could also undermine the fragile sense of community in ASEAN.

EMPOWERED REGIONAL INSTITUTIONS

Another positive decision is the one establishing a set of regional institutions that would be empowered to act and decide on problems with or disputes over the application of ASEAN economic agreements. A network of government agencies is to take care of operational problems encountered by business people in availing themselves of ASEAN commitments. The new legal unit in the ASEAN Secretariat is to give advice to parties in a potential dispute and encourage them to deal with the dispute through consultations. The Secretary-General could also help. Members of the compliance monitoring body not parties to a dispute will, upon request, review and issue findings on the case.

On the occasion of the Vientiane summit, the ASEAN Economic Ministers "enhanced" the ASEAN dispute-settlement mechanism, setting up a special fund to support it.[14] Under the protocol that they signed, the DSM is in some ways stronger than the one previously envisioned but in other ways weaker. In 1996, the ASEAN Economic Ministers had agreed to set up a dispute-settlement mechanism for ASEAN economic agreements. Under that protocol, disputes over the implementation of an economic agreement were to be subject to consultations between the parties, failing which the Senior Economic Officials were to form a panel to assess the dispute. The interesting thing is that the Senior Economic Officials, minus the parties to the dispute, were to rule on the findings of the panel by simple majority. The Economic Ministers were to serve as an appeals body that was also to decide by majority vote.[15] The High-Level Task Force on ASEAN Economic Integration recommended a set of compliance bodies and a strengthened dispute-settlement mechanism, a recommendation endorsed by the ASEAN leaders at their summit meeting in October 2003.[16] Under this recommendation, the appeals body would no longer be the Economic Ministers but an independent group of "well-qualified, independent and experienced professionals", as in the World Trade Organization. The possibility of sanctions was also envisioned. However, while "strengthened" and "enhanced" in some ways, the dispute-settlement mechanism appears to have been weakened in other ways. In apparent compliance with the HLTF recommendation, the ASEAN Economic Ministers, in November 2004, concluded the "ASEAN Protocol on Enhanced Dispute Settlement Mechanism"[17] to take the place of the 1996 instrument. Whereas the 1996 agreement provided for SEOM ruling by a simple majority, the new agreement is silent on how the Senior Economic Officials are to adopt a panel report. The presumption is that it will be by consensus, since that is the default mode of decision making in ASEAN. Moreover, the Appellate Body's report is subject to rejection by SEOM. The 1996 protocol on dispute settlement was never resorted to. It remains to be seen whether and how the 2004 protocol will be used and how effective it will be. That would, in the end, be the test of its credibility.

In any case, if these new institutions prove to be effective — and their pragmatic and realistic nature is reassuring in this regard — this one decision, if taken seriously, will be a major step in strengthening the association, intensifying the sense of region among officials and the business sector, and shoring up the credibility of ASEAN's compliance and dispute-settlement institutions. If they work as intended, they will boost the confidence of businessmen and investors in the efficacy of ASEAN economic agreements, a not unimportant factor in the purposes of the ASEAN Economic Community.

AN ASEAN CUSTOMS UNION?

In the literature on regional economic integration, the next stage of such integration after a free trade area is a customs union. At least, this has been the experience of several other regional associations. A customs union means not only duty-free trade within the union but also the adoption of a common set of external tariffs. In ASEAN, Singapore is already duty-free, Brunei

Darussalam virtually so. Creating an ASEAN customs union would require Singapore and Brunei Darussalam to abandon a regime on which their entire economies have been based, something that is possible but highly unlikely. Accordingly, there have been proposals calling for a customs union among Indonesia, Malaysia, the Philippines and Thailand and one among the newer members — Cambodia, Laos, Myanmar and Vietnam. A free trade area would then be formed among these two customs unions, Brunei Darussalam and Singapore. It is an interesting idea that has not been seriously pursued but should probably be looked into.

THE SECURITY COMMUNITY: ITS CONTENTS

When I made my farewell call on him towards the end of 2002, Indonesian Foreign Minister Hassan Wirajuda was already talking about the possible output of the summit that Indonesia would be hosting and chairing in the last quarter of 2003. He was thinking of a document that would hark back to the Declaration of ASEAN Concord issued by the first ASEAN Summit in 1976 in Bali, otherwise known as the Bali Concord. Hassan said that he wanted ASEAN to renew the principles enshrined in the Bali Concord and build on them. When Indonesia took over the chairmanship of the ASEAN Standing Committee in the middle of 2003, it immediately went about preparing for the ASEAN Summit that it would host later that year.

The centrepiece of Jakarta's efforts was to promote the concept of an ASEAN Security Community. Among other considerations, officials at the Department of Foreign Affairs — or DEPLU, its Indonesian acronym — were apparently concerned that economic discussions, particularly on the ASEAN Economic Community, work on which was proceeding inexorably, would dominate the summit unless they were balanced by a political and security component. If the summit discussions were preponderantly economic, the Indonesian role would not be as prominent as befits the summit host, since Jakarta was hesitant about going rapidly into regional economic integration, a stance that reflected its lack of confidence in the competitive ability of its industries. At the same time, without a political and security component in the summit's output, DEPLU and the other ASEAN foreign ministries would risk being marginalized at the event, relegated to handling the administrative chores. More substantively, the Indonesians were reportedly concerned about the flow of arms to Indonesian separatist groups from or through neighbouring countries. In addition, Indonesian diplomats were said to be worried about the lack of coherence in ASEAN's responses to such international developments as the U.S. military action in Iraq. They might also have seen an opportunity to advance the democratic and human rights agenda in ASEAN in the context of an ASEAN Security Community. Thus, Bali Concord II wound up with three "pillars", with the addition, at the Philippines' suggestion, of a socio-cultural component.

The ASEAN Security Community segment of BCII reaffirms the basic principles and policies underlying ASEAN's approach to issues of regional security:

- The peaceful settlement of disputes;
- The renunciation of the use or threat of force in resolving differences;
- Respect for the sovereignty of nations;
- Non-interference in countries' internal affairs;
- The other principles embodied in the Treaty of Amity and Cooperation in Southeast Asia (TAC) and the Declaration on the Zone of Peace, Freedom and Neutrality;
- Consensus-based decision-making;
- The comprehensive nature of security;
- A nuclear weapons-free Southeast Asia;
- The importance of the High Council of the TAC as a reflection of ASEAN's commitment to the peaceful resolution of disputes;
- The primacy of the ASEAN Regional Forum as a venue for enhancing political and security cooperation in the Asia-Pacific; and
- The role of ASEAN as the ARF's primary driving force.

Beyond the reaffirmation of these well-known ASEAN principles, policies and commitments, BCII charts the future direction of ASEAN security cooperation by setting forth the next steps to be taken in this regard. Generally, BCII makes it clear that the contents of the ASEAN Security Community that it prescribes are meant "to bring ASEAN's political and security cooperation to a higher plane". It marks out seven areas where intensified political and security cooperation is to take place:

- Setting values and norms;
- Maritime security;
- Weapons of mass destruction;
- Terrorism and transnational crime;
- Defence cooperation;
- The ASEAN Regional Forum; and
- Cooperation with the UN.

SETTING NEW NORMS

The first is probably the boldest, having the potential to break new ground. It has to do with nurturing "common values" and developing "a set of socio-political values and principles" and with sharing "information on matters of common concern". In February 2004, at the Institute of Southeast Asian Studies in Singapore, I told a seminar on the ASEAN Security Community as envisioned in BCII:

> The leaders, of course, do not specify the nature and content of the values and principles that are to be nurtured and developed; it is up to ministers and officials to do that. If in doing so the ministers and officials merely reiterate the old shibboleths about national sovereignty, non-interference, the non-use of force, the peaceful settlement of disputes, and even the comprehensive nature of security, they will not be advancing the development of an ASEAN Security Community. They will not be adding substance to it; they will appear to be ignoring the leaders' directives. On the other hand, what could those common values and principles be? Whatever they are, they would have to amount to new norms that would govern not just the behavior of member-countries toward one another, which is already covered by the present, oft-repeated norms, but the conduct of states within their own borders or the treatment by states of their own people in a particularly abhorrent way. At the very least, the leaders call for intensified political consultation and exchanges of information, presumably on a more candid basis and on a broader range of subjects than heretofore. Could this be "flexible engagement" or "enhanced interaction" by another name?
>
> In any case, I venture to suggest that consultations ought to be conducted and information exchanged on situations, between states or within them, that could threaten regional peace and stability, the well-being of ASEAN countries or ASEAN's vital purposes. Examples of such situations might be a bilateral dispute or conflict preventing ASEAN agreements from being implemented, internal developments that could impel the massive movement of people into other ASEAN countries, cross-border terrorist activities, maritime terrorism and piracy, environmental disasters causing harm to two or more ASEAN countries, the spread of serious disease across national boundaries, and international events that would call for consultations and mutual assistance among ASEAN governments. Such situations might include the training of persons in one country for terrorist operations in another or the education of nationals from a neighboring country or countries in extreme ideologies that foster terrorism.[18]

Expressing an Indonesian view of this dimension of the ASEAN Security Community, former Foreign Minister Ali Alatas had stated:

Although not expressly mentioned in the text of the Declaration, due to lingering fears on the part of some of the member-countries, it is tacitly understood that the principles of respect for national sovereignty, non-interference and consensus-based decision-making should be applied in a flexible and selective manner. The "enhanced interaction" approach, which ASEAN informally adopted in 1998 to deal with problems internal to one member-country but having a negative impact on other member-countries, should continue to be honoured and further refined. ASEAN should be able to develop an agreed mechanism through which member-states could work together to help a member-country in addressing internal problems with clear external implications.[19]

There is a growing acceptance of the need for ASEAN to concern itself with events in a member-country that have or may have an impact on its neighbours, especially on their security. Indeed, pressure is rising on ASEAN to do so, not only from the Western world but also from within ASEAN itself. There is increasing recognition that the scope of such events is steadily expanding for well-known reasons — the globalization of economic relations, the phenomenal advances in transportation and in information and communications technology, the surge in the threat from international terrorism, the multi-level integration of the region. Chapter 3 recalls how ASEAN dealt with domestic problems of member-countries that had significant effects outside their borders — the Philippines in 1986, Myanmar more recently, the financial crisis, the land and forest fires in Indonesia, and human rights. It has also been recalled that the ASEAN countries worked together and with others to stop the spread of SARS in its tracks.

The questions before ASEAN are: Should it agree beforehand on certain norms for defining the kinds of events that warrant their collective concern and possible intervention, or should it continue to address such events by feel and instinct and in a reactive way, in accordance with the political circumstances of the moment? Should ASEAN continue in its cautious, gingerly and polite manner of dealing with them, or should it be more activist and move more quickly? Should ASEAN responses continue to be *ad hoc*? Or should the association have an "agreed mechanism through which member-states could work together to help a member-country in addressing internal problems with clear external implications", as Alatas suggests? As recounted in Chapter 2, a "troika" was put together to handle the 1997 crisis in Cambodia on ASEAN's behalf. However, the subsequent adoption of "terms of reference" to govern the operation of the "troika" served as an occasion to empty any future "troika" of all effectiveness.[20]

In addition, regional solidarity and mutual confidence could be fostered by the explicit recognition of certain common values pertaining not just to inter-state relations but to domestic arrangements and behaviour as well. Indeed, ASEAN has hinted at such common values in the past. For example, the ASEAN joint statement on the Philippine situation in 1986 cited the need for "restraint" and for "unity and solidarity" and a "peaceful resolution" in dealing with domestic political disputes.[21] In commenting on Myanmar, the joint communiqué of the ASEAN Ministerial Meeting in 2003 called for "national reconciliation and dialogue", "a peaceful transition to democracy", and the "early lifting of restrictions placed on Daw Aung San Suu Kyi and the NLD members".[22] The 2004 joint communiqué, in referring to the recent elections in Malaysia, Indonesia and the Philippines, affirmed that "holding free and peaceful elections" had "contributed to the attainment of a just, democratic and harmonious Southeast Asia". In the very next paragraph, the communiqué reported that the Foreign Ministers had "underlined the need for the involvement of all strata of Myanmar society in the ongoing National Convention" and had "encouraged all concerned parties in Myanmar to continue their efforts to effect a smooth transition to democracy".[23] If these are any indication, ASEAN seems to share, at least for public consumption, certain values in the conduct of domestic political affairs — the peaceful resolution of political disputes through dialogue, free and peaceful elections, democracy as an end-goal of the political process, and broad participation in that process, including the opposition.

However, these values are affirmed with respect to specific situations rather than as normative principles to be universally applied. In Chapter 3, I cite the reasons that militate against the adoption of such universal principles by ASEAN — the vast diversity among the member-countries, their historical experience with external intervention, the mutual suspicions engendered by their diversity and the remaining tensions in their bilateral relations, and the wide gaps in the social values embraced by the ruling elites. Nevertheless, it may be time for certain basic values and norms to be explicitly adopted both as a measure for cultivating a regional identity, without which a genuine ASEAN community would not be possible, and as a manifestation of the ASEAN states' concern for ASEAN's people no matter what their nationality.

ASEAN countries have different concepts of and approaches to democracy and human rights and the timing involved. However, common values and norms might encompass the collective rejection of acts that are generally considered as inhuman and abhorrent — genocide, "ethnic cleansing", torture, the worst forms of child labour, the abuse of children, rape as an instrument of warfare or state power, restrictions on the peaceful practice of religion, denial of healthcare or education by reason of gender, religion, race or ethnicity, and other acts prohibited by existing UN conventions, as well as the overthrow of legitimate governments by military force. Some of the values and norms could derive from such documents as the Universal Declaration of Human Rights and the 1993 Vienna Declaration and Programme of Action. Needless to say, discussions in ASEAN on questions of compliance with or deviation from agreed norms must be motivated by a desire to understand the truth and prevent or mitigate the adverse impact on neighbouring countries or on the region as a whole rather than to interfere in a country's internal affairs or to grandstand for the domestic or Western audience. They must be based on facts and realism and on the recognition of the complexity of the situation rather than on impressions and images purveyed and exploited by the mass media, exile groups, single-issue movements, and other sources.

I understand that, in developing the Plan of Action for the ASEAN Security Community, Indonesia tried to have some of these values embraced by ASEAN. The Plan of Action ultimately adopted by the Vientiane summit in November 2004 does have references to standards of domestic behaviour on the part of the ASEAN members. For example, in the section on Political Development, the Plan of Action states, "ASEAN member countries shall not condone unconstitutional and undemocratic changes of government or the use of their territory for any actions undermining peace, security and stability of other member countries."[24] These are significant commitments, although some might say that they are commitments to the preservation of the status quo. In any case, however, the Plan of Action does not spell out the consequences of a violation of these norms. In the Organization of American States or in the Commonwealth, a coup d'état or other unconstitutional means of changing a government would call for the suspension of the member concerned. In early 2005, the African Union moved against a regime installed in Togo by unconstitutional means.

In the annex enumerating the "activities" to "realize" the ASEAN Security Community, the part on Political Development lists some elements that have to do with states' internal arrangements and behaviour, including strengthening the rule of law and the judicial system, good governance, "effective and efficient civil services", "preventing and combating corruption", promoting "public awareness (of) human rights", and the protection of "vulnerable groups including women, children, people with disabilities, and migrant workers". However, the annex does not answer the questions of how and when. Without specific measures and timelines, the items in it are mere wish lists, things to be aspired for. Nevertheless, the mere mention of such concepts as human rights, the rule of law and governance seems to indicate a new willingness on the part of ASEAN to make such "domestic" matters regional concerns.

Much of the list of "activities" under "Shaping and Sharing of Norms" merely reiterates long-established ASEAN principles for inter-state conduct and relations. However, there are specific references to an ASEAN extradition treaty and an ASEAN treaty of mutual legal assistance. This is not the first time that such treaties are proposed. As early as 1976, the ASEAN leaders were said to have considered "the possibility of an ASEAN Extradition Treaty".[25] The ASEAN Inter-parliamentary Organization is pushing the idea. However, some member-states are reluctant to conclude such treaties even bilaterally with their neighbours. As for mutual legal assistance, even as the ASEAN leaders were meeting in Vientiane and were calling for the "Identification of issues relating to the establishment of an ASEAN MLA Agreement" and committing themselves to "Undertake preparatory steps with a view to concluding an ASEAN Mutual Legal Assistance Agreement", ministers or attorneys-general of eight ASEAN countries were *on the same day* in Kuala Lumpur signing a Treaty on Mutual Legal Assistance in Criminal Matters.[26] (Myanmar and Thailand did not sign, but Thailand gave the assurance that it would accede to the treaty before long, while Myanmar said that it still had to review its laws.) Evidently, the foreign ministries were totally unaware of what their law and justice ministries and attorney-general's chambers were doing!

In general, it remains to be seen whether ASEAN has the will to give flesh to its commitments through specific measures, with timelines, and thereby make them "actionable". On the other hand, seeking to enforce them could, at this stage, be divisive of the association.

MARITIME SECURITY

The second area designated for heightened security cooperation in BCII is that of maritime security. The leaders rightly called on ASEAN to address "maritime issues and concerns" regionally in the light of the fact that they are "transboundary in nature". Presumably, this would encompass such apparently straightforward problems as marine pollution and piracy at sea. It would also have to address the growing threat of maritime terrorism. The journalist Michael Richardson, now a senior fellow at the Institute of

Southeast Asian Studies in Singapore, has warned in a recent book[27] of the heightened danger of maritime terrorism and other crimes at sea. However, if ASEAN is serious about this, it may have to confront such sensitive realities as the involvement of personnel of some national security agencies in either environmental destruction or piracy or both. It could also involve the many unsettled maritime boundaries in the region if only to determine the extent of each country's claims to jurisdiction. Indonesia has sensibly proposed the establishment of a forum and centre to deal with maritime issues and concerns in ASEAN. That proposal raises questions about the forum's structure and level of participation and the functions, staffing and funding of the centre, questions that need to be addressed in a realistic and expeditious way if the leaders' mandate is to be carried out. The Plan of Action, however, alludes to maritime security in a single phrase — "Promoting ASEAN maritime security cooperation". Again, it remains to be seen what ASEAN means to do about this critical security issue.

WEAPONS OF MASS DESTRUCTION

The third area pertains to weapons of mass destruction. BCII directs that the ASEAN Security Community "work to ensure that the Southeast Asian Region remains free of all weapons of mass destruction". The Southeast Asia Nuclear Weapons-Free Zone treaty, signed in December 1995 and in force since March 1997, binds ASEAN members not to "develop, manufacture or otherwise acquire, possess or have control over nuclear weapons, ... station or transport nuclear weapons, ... or test or use nuclear weapons ..." or, with the exception of transport, allow other states to do these things in their respective territories. The treaty also forbids the dumping at sea or the discharge into the atmosphere of radioactive material or wastes or their disposal on land in other states. However, efforts to get the five internationally recognized nuclear-weapon states duty-bound to respect the provisions of the treaty through a special protocol have run into a years-long impasse. While the issues of concern to the nuclear-weapon states are being painstakingly worked out, imaginative ways should be found to get these states committed to the provisions of the treaty without prejudice to their positions on the contentious issues. Meanwhile, ASEAN could step up its consultations with the International Atomic Energy Agency on the enforcement and implementation of the treaty, which it inexplicably neglected to undertake during the drafting. In any case, the ASEAN countries' own pledges to abjure nuclear weapons through the SEANWFZ treaty, as well as the Nuclear

Non-Proliferation Treaty, to which all ASEAN states are parties, are helpful to the goal of keeping the region nuclear weapons-free.

No ASEAN country has embarked on the use of nuclear power for energy generation. In 1986, under severe pressure from political and environmental forces, the new Philippine Government of President Corazon Aquino stopped the already-completed nuclear power plant in Bataan from going into operation, although the Philippine Government continues to pay enormous interest charges on the loan incurred to build it. However, if an ASEAN country decides to do so in the future, as Indonesia seems to have decided and Vietnam is considering, the question of the re-processing of nuclear fuel will have to be addressed with a view to ensuring that the resulting material is not diverted to the manufacture of nuclear weapons. For this purpose, ASEAN countries ought to commit themselves to inform one another early of any plans to harness nuclear power for energy-generation, research or other peaceful pursuits as well as abide by the NPT provisions and IAEA regulations. ASEAN should also take into account not just the production or acquisition of nuclear weapons but also of fissile materials that could be used to build such weapons. The disposal of nuclear waste and the reprocessing of nuclear by-products should be addressed.

At the same time, there are weapons of mass destruction other than nuclear weapons, namely, biological and chemical weapons. In order to carry out the leaders' mandate, ASEAN officials ought to begin working on a treaty or treaties banning chemical and biological weapons. All ASEAN countries have signed the UN's Chemical Weapons Convention and Biological Weapons Convention, although Cambodia and Myanmar have not ratified the CWC and Myanmar has yet to ratify the BWC. As in the SEANWFZ, it would be useful if ASEAN could conclude a treaty or treaties to reinforce at the regional level the member-countries' renunciation of chemical and biological weapons and to make the UN conventions' provisions applicable specifically to Southeast Asia, and if it could get the major powers — the five permanent members of the UN Security Council, to begin with — to associate themselves with that application, carefully avoiding the factors that have snagged the nuclear-weapon states' commitment to the SEANWFZ treaty.

In its single reference to weapons of mass destruction, however, the Plan of Action merely calls for the resolution of "all outstanding issues to ensure early signing of the Nuclear Weapon States to (sic) the Protocol to the SEANWFZ Treaty". This contributes little of value, as the ASEAN officials have been negotiating with their counterparts from the recognized nuclear-weapon states all this time.

TERRORISM AND TRANSNATIONAL CRIME

BCII envisions the ASEAN Security Community as "strengthening national and regional capacities to counter terrorism, drug trafficking, trafficking in persons and other transnational crimes". BCII also stipulates that, in doing so, the ASEAN Security Community "shall fully utilize the existing institutions and mechanisms within ASEAN". These institutions and mechanisms will have to work out ways of dealing with terrorism and so on beyond what they are already doing. BCII serves as a mandate for this purpose. Because ASEAN countries face these problems in varying degrees, cooperative activities at the operational level will have to be undertaken with less than complete ASEAN participation. However, it is important that the full political weight of ASEAN be placed behind such endeavours. The convention on counter-terrorism called for in the Plan of Action would serve this purpose. However, that is all that the Plan of Action has to say about terrorism or other transnational crime that is of any substance.

DEFENCE COOPERATION

BCII refers to "the enhancement of defence cooperation among ASEAN countries" and contemplates "an annual ASEAN Defence Ministers meeting". Pursuant to this, the first ASEAN defence ministers' meeting took place in Kuala Lumpur on 9 May 2006. In fact, the defence ministers have been meeting bilaterally for a number of years. They and the chiefs of ASEAN armed forces and military services carry on the practice of visiting one another upon assuming and leaving office. National-security, defence and military officials are included in many delegations to the ARF ministerial meetings and take part in ARF inter-sessional activities. The Special ASEAN Senior Officials Meeting is designed specifically for the participation of such officials. Military leaders have other settings for networking. These include the gathering of Army commanders at the end of the annual ASEAN Armies Rifle Meet, the biennial ASEAN Navy Interaction, and the ASEAN Military Intelligence Meeting. They, therefore, do not lack venues or opportunities for consultations, bilaterally or as a group. However, they have been careful to emphasize that their meetings are informal and outside the ASEAN context. This is in line with ASEAN's old resolve not to be mistaken for a defence alliance. Apparently, the ASEAN leaders have decided that such misperceptions are no longer of much concern.

In my view, the initial function of the defence forum would be to explore in which defence areas ASEAN can profitably cooperate. Some of these areas might be sharing of threat perceptions, training for peacekeeping operations, defence procurement, interoperability of military equipment, communications linkages, border patrols, search and rescue, disaster relief, regularization of joint military exercises, joint training, intensification of intelligence exchanges, and networking among defence colleges. The forum would serve consultative and confidence-building purposes for ASEAN as a whole. However, because of the differences in defence outlooks, capabilities and circumstances among ASEAN states, operational activities would likely have to continue to be conducted by two or more, rather than necessarily all, ASEAN countries.

BCII makes it explicitly clear that the defence cooperation that it advocates does not mean any form of defence pact or military alliance. Nevertheless, the mere specification of ASEAN defence cooperation and a defence ministers' forum represents a significant departure from ASEAN's long-standing policy of avoiding such cooperation in any kind of ASEAN context.

The Plan of Action calls for an ASEAN Arms Register. The purpose of this is unclear to me, since both the United Nations and the ARF already have such registers. Also unclear is how seriously the ASEAN members take these existing registers. Similarly, the decision in the Plan of Action to publish an Annual Security Outlook for ASEAN is difficult to understand, since the ARF has been publishing a compilation of the same name since 2000, and, as noted in Chapter 4, only two to five ASEAN countries have been contributing to it.

THE ASEAN REGIONAL FORUM

While the ASEAN Security Community is meant, above all, to foster ASEAN solidarity for the sake of regional security, it is open to — indeed, actively seeks — the collaboration of others on behalf of regional peace and stability. As BCII declares, "The ASEAN Security Community is open and outward looking in respect of actively engaging ASEAN's friends and Dialogue Partners to promote peace and stability in the region." BCII affirms the ARF as "the main forum for regional security dialogue" and "the primary forum in enhancing political and security cooperation in the Asia Pacific region, as well as the pivot in building peace and stability in the region". More particularly, BCII stresses ASEAN's role "as the primary driving force" of the ARF.

The Plan of Action, however, merely prescribes the establishment of an "ARF Unit within the ASEAN Secretariat", which already existed *de facto* during my term as Secretary-General and has been formalized and slightly augmented under my successor. It also calls for the "Enhanced Role of the

ARF Chair", which has already been decided on in the ARF itself, but does not say how that role is to be "enhanced". The rest of its suggestions are already being carried out.

COOPERATING WITH THE UN

BCII directs the ASEAN Security Community to "explore enhanced cooperation with the United Nations ... for the maintenance of international peace and security". In the 1980s and up to the early 1990s, ASEAN cooperated very closely with the UN on the Cambodian problem and on the related one of Indochinese asylum-seekers. Indeed, one could say that both ASEAN and the UN and the cooperation between them were indispensable to the eventual settlement of these problems.[28] Over 1993–94, three international workshops were conducted in Singapore and Thailand on ASEAN-UN cooperation on peace and preventive diplomacy. ASEAN and the UN subsequently held three joint workshops on "conflict prevention, conflict resolution and peace-building", the last one in February 2003. Today, the ASEAN leaders evidently believe that ASEAN-UN cooperation needs to be "enhanced" in the area of peace and security. This might start with consultations between ASEAN and the UN at senior levels on possible modalities for further ASEAN-UN cooperation. Some of these modalities might involve a number of the priority areas designated by the ASEAN leaders for security cooperation, including maritime security, weapons of mass destruction, and transnational crime. However, the Plan of Action merely calls for intensifying "cooperation with the United Nations and other organizations/donor countries" in the context of "Post-conflict Peace Building".

Inevitably, heightened ASEAN-UN contacts will bring up the question of ASEAN's observer status at the UN General Assembly. UN Secretary-General Kofi Annan has raised this question, most notably at the ASEAN-UN summit on the occasion of the UN Conference on Trade and Development (UNCTAD) in Bangkok in February 2000. So have other UN officials. They point out that ASEAN is the only major regional organization that is not an observer at the UNGA. Most member-states support observer status for ASEAN, which, in their view, would cost virtually nothing, would do no harm, and would do some good for both ASEAN and the UN. For some reason unclear to me, the proposal has not gained the ASEAN Foreign Ministers' unanimous assent. However, by 2004, resistance seemed to have weakened, with the ASEAN Ministerial Meeting's joint communiqué stating, "(W)e are actively considering requesting for an observer status in the United

Nations General Assembly. We believed that an institutional relationship with the United Nations would support the realization of ASEAN Community, as well as efforts to strengthen cooperation between ASEAN and the UN as stipulated in United Nations General Assembly Resolution 57/35 of 21 November 2002 on 'Cooperation between the United Nations and the Association of South-East Asian Nations' ".[29]

THE SECURITY COMMUNITY: ITS PROSPECTS

In BCII, ASEAN's leaders have reaffirmed the principles, policies and commitments that have been the building blocks for an ASEAN Security Community, have served ASEAN well in the past, and have contributed much to regional peace and security. They have also charted the direction for the future of the Security Community, prescribing, mostly in general terms, the steps for advancing it further still. They have indicated security-related areas for heightened ASEAN cooperation, including norms-setting, maritime security, weapons of mass destruction, terrorism and transnational crime, and defence cooperation. They have called on ASEAN to discharge its responsibility as the ARF's driving force more effectively and cooperate more closely with the UN.

Should ASEAN succeed in putting together "a set of socio-political values and principles", as its leaders urge, and should those values and principles go beyond those already agreed upon, that would represent a major breakthrough and a substantive advance in expanding ASEAN's value for its peoples. Extending ASEAN's attention to maritime security and defence cooperation would expand ASEAN's scope for political and security cooperation. Strengthening ASEAN cooperation and members' capacities in dealing with terrorism and transnational crime would reinforce the association's usefulness. Reaffirming and, perhaps, expanding in formal and binding terms ASEAN's renunciation of nuclear, chemical and biological weapons would contribute to making Southeast Asia, as well as the world at large, a safer place. Discharging its leadership role and responsibility in the ARF in a more substantive and proactive manner would enhance ASEAN's capacity to shape the security configuration in its part of the world. Working more closely with the UN would elevate ASEAN's international prestige and could bolster its effectiveness.

However, ministers and officials will still have to work out the implementing measures necessary to carry out those steps; for BCII as issued gives few guiding indications of such measures. ASEAN has seen too many instances of its leaders agreeing on far-sighted, even visionary decisions, which officials then fail to follow through and carry out in good time, although it is often those same officials who draw up and recommend the decisions in the first place. Thus, it remains to be seen whether the agreements and decisions embodied in BCII for the ASEAN Security Community are carried out in substantive ways and in a timely manner.

A SOCIO-CULTURAL COMMUNITY: IS IT NECESSARY?

Standing on fundamental premises and taking a long-term perspective, one would say that the core of the ASEAN Community is the Socio-Cultural Community, if one conceived of the Socio-Cultural Community as a vehicle for developing a sense of Southeast Asian identity, building a regional awareness and fostering mutual understanding among the people of ASEAN. That identity, that awareness and that understanding would contribute greatly, indeed would be essential, to the building of a security community in Southeast Asia. They would be necessary for common norms to be adopted and common values to be shared. They would make regional cooperation easier on a broad range of security concerns. They would also smooth the path to regional economic integration by cultivating mutual trust and, thereby, building confidence in regional institutions, arrangements and understandings. Many of the hopes for and obstacles to the ASEAN enterprise lie in the mind, the minds of ASEAN's people.

Unfortunately, among the three components of BCII, the Socio-Cultural Community, including its Plan of Action,[30] is the least developed. It is a hodge-podge of generalities, suffers from a dearth of specifics, has no timelines, and lacks focus. Part of the problem is institutional. With substantial outside advice, one set of officials painstakingly worked on the ASEAN Economic Community. An established, authoritative forum, the Senior Economic Officials, negotiated it, and the ASEAN Economic Ministers cleared it. Similarly, Indonesia's Department of Foreign Affairs vigorously pushed the ASEAN Security Community. The ASEAN Senior Officials Meeting grappled with its contents, and the Foreign Ministers endorsed it. The Socio-Cultural Community, on the other hand, was put together by foreign ministry officials out of a very wide range of social concerns over which the BCII segment and its Plan of Action sprawl — from education to drugs, from health to labour to the environment — and with which the officials had insufficient familiarity. Indeed, each of those concerns was and is being handled by a different set of other ministries and officials.

The Socio-Cultural Community was apparently brought in almost as an afterthought, at the Philippines' suggestion, in the interest of rounding out the concept of a community. It seems to have been partly an effort — with a touch of political correctness — to show the world that ASEAN is not just about politics and security, the concerns of states, politicians and bureaucrats — that it is not just about economics, the business of business and governments (it is often forgotten that economic integration and the economic efficiency that should come from it would also benefit workers and consumers). It presses the point that ASEAN is also about "the people" — their health, education and social security — and their environment and general quality of life, including in particular that of the "marginalized" and "disadvantaged" groups.

The trouble, in the ASEAN context, is that these "people concerns" are functions and responsibilities of individual states, with regional cooperation substantially coming into play only in cases like transboundary atmospheric and marine pollution and contagious diseases. This is why the regional dimension of these social endeavours usually comes in the form of sharing of "best practices", networking and similar activities. The thinking is that compliance is to be encouraged by the distribution of "individual action plans" and a degree of peer pressure. I doubt if it will work; after all, governments regard most social issues as essentially domestic in nature and hardly susceptible to regional treatment. Nevertheless, the point has been made — that ASEAN is addressing "people concerns".

To me, it would have been better if ASEAN had just emphatically affirmed the conviction of its members about the importance of these concerns and the need to address them at the national level, cooperating regionally wherever that would clearly help, and then gone on to put flesh on those elements of a socio-cultural community for which a regional approach would have added value, particularly in terms of creating a true ASEAN Community.

BCII suggests some areas in which regional cooperation would be useful: measures to improve the regional mobility of people, mutual recognition of professional credentials (although this might be more plausibly addressed bilaterally), the prevention and control of infectious diseases, access to affordable medicine, and problems related to the environment and natural disasters. But then the VAP annex and the Plan of Action for the Socio-Cultural Community load the agenda with a smorgasbord of social issues that more properly belong to national policy and responsibility.

At the same time, the VAP and the Plan of Action are woefully thin in the area that *is* critical to the creation of an ASEAN Community, including the Security Community and the Economic Community. This is the endeavour to foster a sense of regional identity and mutual understanding among ASEAN's people. This matter is addressed in the very short sections headed "Promoting an ASEAN Identity" in the VAP annex and "Strengthening the Foundations of Regional Social Cohesion" in the Plan of Action. However, these are mere wish lists, specifying no actions or measures and no timelines, leaving the crucial questions of how and when entirely unanswered.

Needless to say, building a regional identity and mutual understanding is a long-term and never-ending endeavour, involving the education of children and the general public, the transformation of attitudes, and the breaking down of prejudices and mutual suspicions. This is why it is extremely important for ASEAN to begin, now, by agreeing on concrete steps and clear timetables for carrying them out. The Vientiane summit, with its action programme and plans of action, would have been a great opportunity to engage the ASEAN leaders themselves in this vital ASEAN enterprise. In welcoming the decision of the ASEAN Ministers of Education to meet regularly, the December 2005 Kuala Lumpur ASEAN Summit stressed the importance of education in "raising the awareness of ASEAN, instilling the 'we feeling' and creating a sense of belonging to the ASEAN community".[31] The development of textbooks and school and university courses on ASEAN and Southeast Asia for various levels — and ensuring their use — would be a good start. After all, at the very beginning of ASEAN, the ASEAN Declaration laid down as one of the association's seven objectives the promotion of Southeast Asian studies, something that has been generally ignored.

Europe was a socio-cultural community, even if a quarrelsome one, long before it became an economic community and a security community. Latin America is ahead of Southeast Asia as a socio-cultural community. ASEAN, on the other hand, has to build all three communities at the same time; in fact, the socio-cultural community is lagging behind the other two, such as they are. Southeast Asia cannot be an enduring security community or an effective economic community — indeed, it cannot be an ASEAN Community in its truest and deepest sense — without being a socio-cultural community.

Notes

1. See Appendix F.
2. See Appendix E.
3. The ASEAN Competitiveness Study is summarized in Adam Schwarz and Roland Villinger, "Integrating Southeast Asia's Economies", in *The McKinsey Quarterly*, No. 1 (New York: McKinsey & Company, 2004).

4. Institute of Southeast Asian Studies, *Concept Paper on the ASEAN Economic Community* (Singapore, 26 February 2003), p. 4.
5. Ibid., pp. 12, 13, 15 and 18.
6. See Appendix D.
7. See Appendix F.
8. See Appendix G.
9. http://www.aseansec.org/VAP-10th%20ASEAN%20Summit.pdf.
10. http://www.aseansec.org/16656.htm.
11. Ibid.
12. Rodolfo C. Severino, *Integración económica regional en Asia-Pacífico: la experiencia de ASEAN* in *Anuario Asia Pacífico 2004* (Barcelona: Fundación CIDOB, 2005), p. 305.
13. http://www.aseansec.org/5125.htm, Art. I, para. 3.
14. http://www.aseansec.org/4924.htm.
15. http://www.aseansec.org/16654.htm.
16. See Appendix G.
17. http://www.aseansec.org/16754.htm.
18. Rodolfo C. Severino, *Towards an ASEAN Security Community*, Trends in Southeast Asia Series (Singapore: Institute of Southeast Asian Studies, 2004), pp. 10–11. Some of the discussion of the ASEAN Security Community in this chapter is taken from that paper.
19. Ali Alatas, "Some Reflections on ASEAN Concord II", statement at the Regional Outlook Forum of the Institute of Southeast Asian Studies, Singapore, 7 January 2004.
20. http://www.aseansec.org/3637.htm.
21. http://www.aseansec.org/4997.htm.
22. http://www.aseansec.org/14833.htm.
23. http://www.aseansec.org/16192.htm.
24. See Appendix H.
25. Declaration of ASEAN Concord, A.6 (http://www.aseansec.org/5049.htm).
26. http://www.aseansec.org/17363.pdf.
27. Michael Richardson, *A Time Bomb for Global Trade: Maritime-Related Terrorism in an Age of Weapons of Mass Destruction* (Singapore: Institute of Southeast Asian Studies, 2004).
28. See Chapter 4.
29. http://www.aseansec.org/16192.htm, para. 52.
30. See Appendix I.
31. http://www.aseansec.org/18039.htm.

8

WHAT KIND OF FUTURE FOR ASEAN?

The previous chapters have shown that, generally, ASEAN has served its members well. Out of the contention of the past, ASEAN has fashioned a region in which armed conflict between nations is all but unthinkable. As I assert elsewhere in this book, it has been ASEAN's supreme achievement that it has provided a setting for the peaceful management of disputes among its members. The constant interaction and sense of common purpose among the ASEAN members have built mutual confidence and dissipated some of the mutual suspicion that is a legacy of past differences and an outgrowth of current disagreements. A growing sense of community and networks of personal contacts have not only prevented conflict as a solution for disputes but have also fostered cooperation for certain common goals.

The ASEAN countries have worked together to uphold what they perceive as the regional security interest. ASEAN's solidarity helped settle the problems posed in the 1980s by the Cambodian situation and the Indochinese asylum-seekers. After these were resolved, ASEAN moved quickly to heal the division of Southeast Asia by bringing the rest of the region into itself. Through the Southeast Asia Nuclear Weapons-Free Zone, ASEAN has contributed its share to the global non-proliferation regime.

Partly through the Treaty of Amity and Cooperation in Southeast Asia and partly through its own practices, ASEAN has set regional norms for the peaceful relations among states — respect for sovereignty and territorial integrity, the peaceful settlement of disputes, non-interference in the internal affairs of nations, decisions by consensus, equality of status, and so on. It has sought to extend these norms for others' adherence by encouraging non-regional states to accede to the treaty; ten have done so. In the same spirit, ASEAN has initiated forums for consultation, dialogue and confidence building with creativity, flexibility and pragmatism and in a non-confrontational way. Through the system of Dialogue Partners, the ASEAN Regional Forum, ASEAN+3, and now the East Asia Summit, ASEAN engages the major powers and others with interests in the region in confidence building, conflict prevention and cooperation in a wide range of areas. At the same time, it has allowed enough space for its individual members to enter into security arrangements with non-regional powers without threatening fellow-members. It has reached an understanding with China on the South China Sea, even if one that is well short of resolving the jurisdictional issues.

By its example, ASEAN has set certain standards for managing rivalries within the larger region of East Asia. The network of relationships being developed in East Asia through the ASEAN+3 process is contributing in a focused way to the stability of the region. The first East Asia Summit has laid the ground for doing so in a larger but still focused context. Stability for East Asia and for the "East Asia Plus" region seems to be ASEAN's higher vocation. Thus, ASEAN has put in place and continues to develop, by itself and with its partners, systems and practices for managing, in a peaceful way, potential inter-state conflicts and other sources of tension that may destabilize the region.

In ASEAN eyes, the concept of security goes beyond such potential conflicts and tensions. It involves problems that transcend national boundaries and, under today's conditions, are more plausible threats to the region. These have to do with the dangers to the regional environment, piracy, robbery and other crimes at sea, particularly at the straits and choke points, drug trafficking, trafficking in human beings, communicable diseases, natural disasters, and terrorism. The networks that ASEAN has built among authorities — and, in some cases, civic groups — dealing with these questions have provided mechanisms for cooperation.

In the past, the ASEAN countries brought their collective weight to bear on efforts to pry open developed-country markets for their commodity and other exports and to mobilize development assistance from their Dialogue Partners. More recently, they have worked together in dealing with the larger, global economic issues. Above all, they have gone beyond cooperation in economic matters and laid the foundations for regional economic integration. Tariffs on most intra-ASEAN trade have been abolished or are down to minimal levels, and AFTA has become, for some in the investing community, a touchstone for regional economic integration. The ASEAN Industrial

Cooperation scheme is serving its purpose, although only four ASEAN countries are participating extensively in it. The ASEAN countries have adopted a set of harmonized tariff nomenclatures and have agreed to comply with the WTO customs valuation system. They have worked out procedures for the expeditious clearance of ASEAN imports. Standards for twenty priority products have been harmonized and safety and compatibility standards for a number of others have been agreed upon. Two mutual recognition arrangements have been concluded, and one is being worked on. Master plans for the Singapore-Kunming Rail Link, the ASEAN Highway Network, and the Trans-ASEAN Gas Pipeline Network have been drawn up. Negotiations are underway on the liberalization of intra-ASEAN trade in certain services. A tourism agreement has been signed.

These are no mean achievements, and ASEAN should, in fairness, be duly credited with them, more fairly than it often is. However, almost forty years after ASEAN's birth, they fall short of what the people of Southeast Asia today require of a regional association at its present stage of development. They fail to measure up fully to what ASEAN could become and to what it could yet do.

In practice and on the ground, the pace of ASEAN economic integration is at best uneven and at worst excruciatingly slow. Except for the special case of the AICO participants, traders and investors remain sceptical of the extent of ASEAN economic integration. This is partly because most implementing measures have not been decided on and partly because implementing agencies of some ASEAN governments often go around ASEAN integration measures already agreed upon, including the CEPT scheme for AFTA, or do not carry them out at all. One result is that regional schemes are not taken into account in most decisions about investing in Southeast Asia. Indeed, only a very small portion of intra-ASEAN trade takes advantage of the tariff preferences offered by the ASEAN Free Trade Area. The standardization of products, the harmonization of customs procedures, the seamlessness of transportation and communication links, the liberalization of trade in services, and the coordination of regulations and policies — all so necessary for effective economic integration — are proceeding much too slowly.

The record of cooperation in dealing with transnational problems has been spotty. The effectiveness of the cooperative mechanisms in place has been uneven. Regional cooperation has been held back by competing national interests, in some instances by mutual suspicion, and by an apparent lack of faith in the efficacy of regional action. An outstanding example is the problem of transboundary haze pollution. Elaborate mechanisms and processes have been put in place to deal regionally with its regional impact, but their full, effective utilization has been hampered by a failure of will on the part of key actors. The success of the ASEAN response to the SARS problem appears to be an exception.

There seems to be no alternative to the ASEAN role as the "default" hub of regional diplomacy in East Asia. ASEAN has used this situation to claim the "driver's seat" in regional diplomatic processes. However, if ASEAN is actually to drive these processes, instead of merely occupying the driver's seat, instead of merely serving as a hub, it has to take collective action and be capable of doing so.

ASEAN as a group has been able to take effective action in the past. The Cambodian issue of the 1980s, the problem of Indochinese asylum-seekers, and the SARS epidemic are the notable instances. However, in each of those cases, ASEAN was galvanized into common action by what all perceived as manifest and immediate threats to security or human health. Many of today's threats are more intangible and long-term but are no less real — possible regional instability, the threat of economic debility, and the danger to people's health and environment. We now understand that these risks are intertwined in character. In the light of this reality, the approach to them can no longer be disaggregated, in the ASEAN manner, into political and security, economic and "functional".

For example, the ASEAN Regional Forum has been, in a sense, stuck in its first, confidence-building phase. Confidence building is important, and the ARF does this mostly through multilateral dialogues on regional-security issues and cooperative activities. To keep such dialogues from drifting, as they tend to do, ASEAN has to make sure that they are conducted at all levels in pointed and trenchant ways so as to help illuminate great strategic issues, such as China's relations with Japan, India and the United States, on which global and regional security largely rests. However, if the ARF is to move to its second, "preventive-diplomacy" phase, ASEAN ought to seek to turn the ARF's primary attention to the so-called "non-traditional" security problems. Several participants in and observers of the ARF have urged that the forum approach its work on the basis of a "comprehensive" concept of security, by which they mean the inclusion of the "non-traditional" threats to regional security. It would, of course, be important for the traditional issues, that is, problems with the potential to ignite inter-state conflict, to continue to be discussed in the ARF. Such discussions contribute to the clarification of positions and thus to mutual understanding, transparency and mutual confidence. However, those problems, mainly the South China Sea, the Taiwan issue, North Korea's nuclear weapons, and nuclear proliferation in general, are being dealt with more effectively in other venues. The South

China Sea question is being handled between ASEAN and China. The Taiwan situation is considered by China to be its internal affair. The nuclear issue in Korea is the subject of the Six-Party Talks. Nuclear proliferation is addressed in the UN and other disarmament forums. The areas in which the ARF could go beyond dialogue and confidence building and take active cooperative measures are those involving situations that all participants would regard as common security threats. Today, as indicated above, these would include piracy, robbery and other crimes at sea, gunrunning, drug trafficking, trafficking in persons, natural disasters, search and rescue, and terrorism. ARF-sponsored operational plans could be drawn up for combating these threats and joint exercises could be organized to test those plans. It would be in ASEAN's interest and it would be its responsibility to lead this effort. For this, it would have to achieve a greater degree of political solidarity, cohesion and coordination than it has today.

If ASEAN is to discharge this responsibility, it has to strengthen its own intra-association cooperation in what is known in ASEAN parlance as the "functional" sectors. However, focus must be selective so as to avoid dissipating attention and effort. ASEAN has to concentrate on those areas that are transboundary in nature and in which regional cooperation would, therefore, be necessary. In addition to the (non-traditional) security issues listed in the previous paragraph, I would suggest heightened cooperation in the protection of the environment and the prevention of the spread of communicable diseases.

At the same time, ASEAN has to make a reality of regional economic integration, first by putting into operation the integration measures already agreed upon. Integrating the regional economy would not only bolster ASEAN's economic competitiveness as a region; it would, as the European experience instructs, also promote the regional cohesion required for political solidarity and for cooperation in non-economic areas. Political solidarity and "functional" cooperation, in turn, would help to bring down barriers to economic integration.

However, ASEAN's current capacity to cooperate effectively in non-traditional security or in the "functional" areas and to follow through on regional economic integration is suspect. It seems to me that this arises from an insufficient sense of regional identity on the part of leaders, other policy-makers and the populations at large. Few political leaders seem genuinely convinced that deeper integration and closer cooperation are of vital national and political interest.

OF INSTITUTIONS AND VALUES

Some observers have pointed to the feebleness of ASEAN institutions as an obstacle to ASEAN cooperation and a stronger commitment to regional interests. Because ASEAN has few binding agreements and lacks a regional authority to enforce compliance with them, regional economic integration and closer ASEAN cooperation are almost totally dependent on national policy decisions and on the commitment of leaders to the region. Others have maintained that ASEAN's institutional frailty stems precisely from a weak sense of region. To me, both views are right. Institutional strengthening and intensifying a sense of identity with the region are mutually reinforcing and have to be simultaneously pursued.

Strengthening ASEAN institutions primarily means enlarging the functions and authority of the ASEAN Secretariat. In order to promote ASEAN economic integration and other forms of regional cooperation, the Secretariat has to be further empowered and encouraged to take initiatives, for the approval of the member-states, on the basis of studies that it does or commissions. The Secretary-General has to be entrusted with the authority to speak for ASEAN on political, as well as economic, matters. The Secretariat has to be allowed more forcefully to invite the association's attention to the non-compliance of a member-state with its obligations under ASEAN agreements. In order to convince the member-states that the Secretary-General and the Secretariat's staff do not act at the behest of their governments but in the regional interest, they have to be as apolitical and as professional as possible. A couple of steps would help. One is to choose the Secretary-General and his deputy or deputies on the basis of merit rather than by alphabetical rotation and government nomination. This could be done with the help of credible search committees. The other is to do away with the system of the newer members seconding officers to the Secretariat. All should compete for the positions on merit, while the attachment programmes for officers of the newer members could continue as long as necessary.

The recommendations of the High-Level Task Force on ASEAN Economic Integration on compliance bodies and procedures and on a dispute-settlement system for ASEAN economic agreements are certainly in the right direction. If they are carried out, they will substantially help in strengthening ASEAN's institutional capacity and authority. The ASEAN system for settling disputes could cover all agreements and not just the economic ones.

Regional institutions cannot be substantially strengthened unless their financial support is considerably expanded. This cannot be done under the current system of equal contributions by member-states, which are capped by the ability and willingness of the least able and willing. The system will have to give way to some kind of scale of assessments or an independent source of funds or both.

There will be resistance to the strengthening of regional institutions as long as mutual suspicions persist. These can be overcome only with a stronger sense of region, as well as through bilateral efforts. This is a long-term endeavour, but it has to begin. It would require painstaking measures to get the peoples of Southeast Asia to know one another better and to understand better the region as a whole. It has to be done at a very early age in the schools and up to the tertiary level. It has to be carried out through intensive exchanges of scholars, journalists, political leaders, artistic and other exhibitions and cultural performances.

The ASEAN Cultural Fund and the ASEAN Foundation, both largely funded by Japan, are meant to make such exchanges possible. In 1978, the ASEAN Cultural Fund was established with a US$20 million Japanese contribution. The ASEAN Committee on Culture and Information, organized just before the fund was set up, has carefully husbanded the interest proceeds from the Japanese donation. The fund has financed projects to bring ASEAN people together, like youth camps and the exchange of journalists. With its support, ASEAN has put on a modern-dance rendition of the Ramayana epic in Europe, Japan, China, Korea, India and several ASEAN countries and published high-quality books featuring treasures from ASEAN museums and photographs of cultural features of the ten ASEAN countries. The fund has made possible song, film and dance festivals and a region-wide ASEAN quiz and an essay-writing contest. However, some of the money has been dissipated in projects that have little to do with mutual understanding or the promotion of ASEAN awareness but involve activities that could and should be undertaken outside ASEAN, such as study tours by librarians and training courses on pest control for the cultural heritage.

The ASEAN Foundation is another possible source of support for programmes promoting mutual understanding among ASEAN's people and increasing awareness of ASEAN on the part of the world outside of, as well as inside, Southeast Asia. At the 1996 "informal" ASEAN Summit in Jakarta, Indonesia pushed the establishment of the ASEAN Foundation, in the words of the summit's press statement, to "promote ASEAN awareness" and "people-to-people contact", as well as human resource development.[1] According to the memorandum of understanding setting up the foundation, which was signed by the ASEAN Foreign Ministers on the occasion of the ASEAN

Summit in 1997, its first objective is to "promote greater awareness of ASEAN".[2] As originally envisioned, the foundation would raise funds for activities in pursuit of its objectives not only from governments but also from private corporations, other foundations and individual contributors. To help in the fund raising, the foundation would have a Council of Advisors made up of "prominent individuals of high stature in the region" appointed by the Board of Trustees — government representatives — for "non-renewable" terms of three years.[3] As it turned out, however, the ASEAN Foundation became just another inter-governmental body, with an ambassador-at-large of Singapore, Indonesia's ASEAN Director-General and the ambassadors to Indonesia of the eight other member-countries serving on the Board of Trustees and the ASEAN Directors-General of the member-states being appointed to the Council of Advisors. According to the ASEAN Foundation's web page, ASEAN member-states have pledged only US$4.2 million to the foundation, with US$3.7 million remitted.[4] The foundation was actually saved by the contribution by Japan of US$20 million, named the Solidarity Fund. China and Korea have given much smaller sums.

The foundation's projects, mostly involving training, seminars and workshops, do not differ much from those in other ASEAN programmes like the Initiative for ASEAN Integration and Hanoi Plan of Action or those sponsored by the "functional" bodies. The Solidarity Fund has, in effect, merely served as a supplementary source of funding for such programmes.

Ultimately and on a broader scale, a sense of regional identity will not be possible unless it is based on some common values. Thus, the basic documents of the European Union, the Organization of American States, and the African Union all enshrine the values that the members of those regional associations hold in common. On the other hand, because of the great diversity of their historical experiences, political situations and ethnic make-ups, one might think that the notion of common values among and even within ASEAN countries is a bit far-fetched. However, ASEAN *has* pronounced itself on some common values in the past: the peaceful settlement of domestic political disputes (foreign ministers' 1986 statement on the situation in the Philippines[5]), a peaceful transition to democracy (joint communiqué of the 2003 ASEAN Ministerial Meeting[6]), "free and peaceful elections" as the way to "a just, democratic and harmonious Southeast Asia" (joint communiqué of the 2004 ASEAN Ministerial Meeting[7]), the need for the involvement of "all strata" of society in the political process (joint communiqué of the 2004 ASEAN Ministerial Meeting[8]). ASEAN Vision 2020 states:

> We see vibrant and open ASEAN societies consistent with their respective national identities, where all people enjoy equitable access to opportunities for total human development regardless of gender, race, religion, language, or social and cultural background.
>
> We envision a socially cohesive and caring ASEAN where hunger, malnutrition, deprivation and poverty are no longer basic problems, where strong families as the basic units of society tend to their members particularly the children, youth, women and elderly; and where the civil society is empowered and gives special attention to the disadvantaged, disabled and marginalized and where social justice and the rule of law reign. ...
>
> We envision our nations being governed with the consent and greater participation of the people with its focus on the welfare and dignity of the human person and the good of the community.[9]

The joint communiqué of the 1993 ASEAN Ministerial Meeting spelled out the agreed ASEAN position on human rights.[10]

In Chapter 7, I wrote:

> ASEAN countries have different concepts of and approaches to democracy and human rights and the timing involved. However, common values and norms might encompass the collective rejection of acts that are generally considered as inhuman and abhorrent — genocide, "ethnic cleansing," torture, the worst forms of child labor, the abuse of children, rape as an instrument of warfare or state power, restrictions on the peaceful practice of religion, denial of health care or education by reason of gender, religion, race or ethnicity, and other acts prohibited by existing UN conventions, as well as the overthrow of legitimate governments by military force. Some of the values and norms could derive from such documents as the Universal Declaration of Human Rights and the 1993 Vienna Declaration and Programme of Action.

These need not be the last word on what ASEAN would acknowledge as common values, but they could be a start.

Another set of values that ASEAN will have to adopt has to do with Southeast Asia's capacity to integrate the regional economy and pull investments into the region. One of the primary objectives of regional economic integration is to attract investments with a large, integrated market, bigger economies of scale, greater economic efficiency, and higher productivity. However, the region cannot be regarded as an attractive investment destination unless it is perceived to adhere to certain norms in common. These would include the prevalence of the rule of law, the credibility of the judicial system in adjudicating contractual disputes, consistency in the application of economic policy, a willingness to combat and control corruption, and the fair treatment of investors. They, too, are values that ASEAN and its members have to be seen as embracing.

The strengthening of institutions and the codification of values could be embodied in the proposed ASEAN charter.

AN ASEAN CHARTER

It is not clear which member-state or member-states pressed for an ASEAN charter at this time or what its or their objectives were in doing so. What is clear is that at their annual meeting in June 2004 the ASEAN Foreign Ministers "agreed to work towards development of an ASEAN Charter which would, inter alia, reaffirm ASEAN's goals and principles in inter-state relations, in particular the collective responsibilities of all ASEAN Member Countries in ensuring non-aggression and respect for each other's sovereignty and territorial integrity; the promotion and protection of human rights; the maintenance of political stability, regional peace and economic progress; and the establishment of effective and efficient institutional framework for ASEAN".[11] The Vientiane Action Programme adopted by the ASEAN leaders in November 2004 called for "the development of an ASEAN Charter". Meeting in July 2005, the Foreign Ministers approved the draft text of a declaration on the ASEAN charter, including the establishment of an Eminent Persons Group, for adoption by the ASEAN leaders later in the year.[12]

The declaration envisioned the proposed charter as "a legal and institutional framework" to support ASEAN's pursuit of its goals, as conferring "legal personality" on ASEAN, and as defining the functions and "areas of competence of key ASEAN bodies" and the relationships among them. It is interesting that the ASEAN leaders devoted the lengthiest portion of the declaration to the reaffirmation of the "principles, goals and ideals" embodied in ASEAN's "milestone agreements". The declaration proceeded to spell these out. The enumeration is worth quoting in full:

- Promotion of community interest for the benefit of all ASEAN Member Countries;
- Maintaining primary driving force of ASEAN;
- Narrowing the development gaps among Member Countries;
- Adherence to a set of common socio-cultural and political community values and shared norms as contained in the various ASEAN documents;
- Continuing to foster a community of caring societies and promote a common regional identity;
- Effective implementation as well as compliance with ASEAN's agreements;

- Promotion of democracy, human rights and obligations, transparency and good governance and strengthening democratic institutions;
- Ensuring that countries in the region live at peace with one another and with the world at large in a just, democratic and harmonious environment;
- Decision making on the basis of equality, mutual respect and consensus;
- Commitment to strengthen ASEAN's competitiveness, to deepen and broaden ASEAN's internal economic integration and linkages with the world economy;
- Promotion of regional solidarity and cooperation;
- Mutual respect for the independence, sovereignty, equality, territorial integrity and national identity of all nations;
- Renunciation of nuclear weapons and other weapons of mass destruction and avoidance of arms race;
- Renunciation of the use of force and threat to use of force; non-aggression and exclusive reliance on peaceful means for the settlement of differences or disputes;
- Enhancing beneficial relations between ASEAN and its friends and partners;
- Upholding non-discrimination of any ASEAN Member Countries in ASEAN's external relations and cooperative activities;
- Observance of principles of international law concerning friendly relations and cooperation among States; and
- The right of every state to lead its national existence free from external interference, subversion or coercion and non-interference in the internal affairs of one another.[13]

Thus, the charter would place ASEAN on a firm legal footing, define its institutions, and embody its values. Just before the 2005 ASEAN Summit, the Institute of Southeast Asian Studies in Singapore published a booklet *Framing the ASEAN Charter*. In the main article in that publication, I wrote:

> A charter would establish the association as a juridical personality and a legal entity. It would make clear the association's objectives. The charter would enshrine the values and principles to which the association's members adhere and which, in a real sense, define its very nature.... It would establish the organs of the association and delineate their respective functions, responsibilities, rights and limitations, the relationships among the organs, and their decision-making processes....[14]

Apart from these merits, the charter would present an opportunity to project ASEAN's destination as it takes steps on the road of regional economic integration. Does ASEAN mean to construct a customs union? A common market? A single market? Whatever it is, the charter ought to lay the foundations of the institutions that would support it. The same holds true for the areas of ASEAN cooperation that the charter could delineate. Among the issues that those working on the charter could look at are: how much authority and independence to allow the ASEAN Secretariat; the way ASEAN arrives at decisions (for example, what sorts of decisions require unanimity and whether voting, weighted or not, is to be resorted to); whether to set up a dispute-settlement mechanism for political issues and, if so, what kind; the question of whether to keep the present system of equal contributions, to adopt a scale of assessments, or to work out other methods of funding the association.

The leaders' declaration indicated that a core element of the proposed charter — and easily the most delicate one — would be the definition of ASEAN's principles and values. As noted elsewhere in this book, without the adoption of a common set of values, ASEAN could not hold its members to any standards of behaviour freely agreed upon and would find it impossible to promote a sense of community among ASEAN's people. *Framing the ASEAN Charter* points to the many principles and values that ASEAN has affirmed over the years, classifying them into those that pertain to relations among member-states, relations between ASEAN and states outside the region, and standards of behaviour within member-states.[15] However, these are scattered in numerous documents. Codifying them in a legally binding charter would give them an added measure of seriousness and proclaim ASEAN as an association with standards. Some member-states might balk at adopting the principles and values in this manner precisely because of the seriousness and clarity with which they would be imbued.

Thus, the framing of an ASEAN charter would be a golden opportunity for ASEAN to promote Southeast Asia's political cohesion, advance regional economic integration, regularize its decision-making processes on the basis of clear rules, strengthen its institutions, improve the association's financial capacity, adopt common norms, and enhance the sense of regional community among ASEAN's people. Having made rather specific proposals, I wrote:

> The ASEAN Charter would establish ASEAN as a juridical and legal entity. By clearly defining the association's objectives, it would make it easier for ASEAN to advance toward those objectives. By embodying the values that ought to bind ASEAN together, the charter would make clear to the international community and to its own peoples what ASEAN stands for and the member-states' mutual expectations of one another. By setting the association's direction in the integration of the regional economy, that is, toward a customs union and a common market, the charter would be guiding ministers and officials in taking measures in this regard and the

ASEAN and international business sectors in making their investment and other business decisions. The charter would mandate ASEAN cooperation in dealing with the challenges posed by transnational problems.

The charter would help ensure that ASEAN agreements are complied with and implemented. It would make ASEAN institutions more effective by making clearer their functions and responsibilities. It would substantially strengthen the Secretary-General and the Secretariat by enhancing their status, enlarging their independence, and expanding their authority. The Secretariat's capacity for research and analysis would be strengthened. ASEAN's resources would be augmented with the modification of the system of contributions to its budget and the opening of additional methods for raising funds.

Decision-making would be streamlined and expedited by the application of different requirements to different types of decisions — unanimity and weighted voting or simple majority — while consensus would remain the preferred mode. A credible mechanism would be set up to settle disputes not only on the economic agreements but on all.[16]

All this would be true only if the ASEAN member-nations take the substance of the charter to heart and genuinely believe that regionalism is good for them and that the interests of the region are their own. Otherwise, instead of being an opportunity to advance ASEAN's purposes, the making of an ASEAN charter could be an occasion for holding back its progress. It might be pertinent to recall, again, that the ASEAN "troika", which had worked effectively on the Cambodian crisis of 1997, was thoroughly emasculated with the adoption in 2000 of its written "terms of reference".[17] Nor would it do to draft the ASEAN charter merely as an exercise in tinkering with ASEAN's institutions without clarifying and strengthening its nature as a regional entity, as an association of nations, which the institutions would support. It would be even worse if the member-states were to adopt a charter substantially advancing ASEAN as a regional organization on paper only to ignore its provisions in practice.

MOVING ASEAN NOW

None of the measures indicated above for ASEAN's future direction is dramatic or radical or unprecedented. Their merit, I believe, lies in the fact that their aims are in the realm of the possible, albeit not necessarily in terms of the near future. Strengthening the ASEAN Secretariat and other ASEAN institutions, cultivating a sense of regional community, and adopting and internalizing common values and norms — these will take time to take root.

However, they should not wait upon one another. Nor should the integration of the regional economy wait upon them. Neither should closer cooperation on the environment, communicable diseases, and "non-traditional" security issues. All of them are mutually reinforcing. One need not precede another. They should proceed in parallel and do so now.

Notes

1. http://www.aseansec.org/5206.htm, para. 5.
2. http://www.aseansec.org/5217.htm, para. 2a.
3. Ibid., para. 5d.
4. http://www.aseansec.org/99.htm, "Source of Funds."
5. http://www.aseansec.org/4997.htm.
6. http://www.aseansec.org/14833.htm, para. 18.
7. http://www.aseansec.org/16192.htm, para. 14.
8. Ibid., para. 15.
9. See Appendix D.
10. http://www.aseansec.org/3666.htm, paras. 16–18. See also Chapter 3.
11. Joint Communiqué of the 37th ASEAN Ministerial Meeting, Jakarta, 29–30 June 2004 (http://www.aseansec.org/16192.htm), para. 6.
12. Joint Communiqué of the 38th ASEAN Ministerial Meeting, Vientiane, 26 July 2005 (http://www.aseansec.org/17592.htm), para. 6.
13. http://www.aseansec.org/18030.htm.
14. Rodolfo C. Severino, compiler, *Framing the ASEAN Charter* (Singapore: Institute of Southeast Asian Studies, 2005), pp. 7–8.
15. Ibid., pp. 12–19.
16. Ibid., pp. 28–29.
17. http://www.aseansec.org/3637.htm.

APPENDICES

Appendix A

THE ASEAN DECLARATION
(Bangkok Declaration)
Bangkok, 8 August 1967

The Presidium Minister for Political Affairs/Minister for Foreign Affairs of Indonesia, the Deputy Prime Minister of Malaysia, the Secretary of Foreign Affairs of the Philippines, the Minister for Foreign Affairs of Singapore and the Minister of Foreign Affairs of Thailand:

MINDFUL of the existence of mutual interests and common problems among countries of South-East Asia and convinced of the need to strengthen further the existing bonds of regional solidarity and cooperation;

DESIRING to establish a firm foundation for common action to promote regional cooperation in South-East Asia in the spirit of equality and partnership and thereby contribute towards peace, progress and prosperity in the region;

CONSCIOUS that in an increasingly interdependent world, the cherished ideals of peace, freedom, social justice and economic well-being are best attained by fostering good understanding, good neighbourliness and meaningful cooperation among the countries of the region already bound together by ties of history and culture;

CONSIDERING that the countries of South-East Asia share a primary responsibility for strengthening the economic and social stability of the region and ensuring their peacefull and progressive national development, and that they are determined to ensure their stability and security from external interference in any form or manifestation in order to preserve their national identities in accordance with the ideals and aspirations of their peoples;

AFFIRMING that all foreign bases are temporary and remain only with the expressed concurrence of the countries concerned and are not intended to be used directly or indirectly to subvert the national independence and freedom of States in the area or prejudice the orderly processes of their national development;

DO HEREBY DECLARE:

FIRST, the establishment of an Association for Regional Cooperation among the countries of South-East Asia to be known as the Association of South-East Asian Nations (ASEAN).

SECOND, that the aims and purposes of the Association shall be:

1. To accelerate the economic growth, social progress and cultural development in the region through joint endeavours in the spirit of equality and partnership in order to strengthen the foundation for a prosperous and peaceful community of South-East Asian Nations;

2. To promote regional peace and stability through abiding respect for justice and the rule of law in the relationship among countries of the region and adherence to the principles of the United Nations Charter;

3. To promote active collaboration and mutual assistance on matters of common interest in the economic, social, cultural, technical, scientific and administrative fields;

4. To provide assistance to each other in the form of training and research facilities in the educational, professional, technical and administrative spheres;

5. To collaborate more effectively for the greater utilization of their agriculture and industries, the expansion of their trade, including the study of the problems of international commodity trade, the improvement of their transportation and communications facilities and the raising of the living standards of their peoples;

6. To promote South-East Asian studies;

7. To maintain close and beneficial cooperation with existing international and regional organizations with similar aims and purposes, and explore all avenues for even closer cooperation among themselves.

THIRD, that to carry out these aims and purposes, the following machinery shall be established:

(a) Annual Meeting of Foreign Ministers, which shall be by rotation and referred to as ASEAN Ministerial Meeting. Special Meetings of Foreign Ministers may be convened as required.

(b) A Standing committee, under the chairmanship of the Foreign Minister of the host country or his representative and having as its members the accredited Ambassadors of the other member countries, to carry on the work of the Association in between Meetings of Foreign Ministers.

(c) Ad-Hoc Committees and Permanent Committees of specialists and officials on specific subjects.

(d) A National Secretariat in each member country to carry out the work of the Association on behalf of that country and to service the Annual or Special Meetings of Foreign Ministers, the Standing Committee and such other committees as may hereafter be established.

FOURTH, that the Association is open for participation to all States in the South-East Asian Region subscribing to the aforementioned aims, principles and purposes.

FIFTH, that the Association represents the collective will of the nations of South-East Asia to bind themselves together in friendship and cooperation and, through joint efforts and sacrifices, secure for their peoples and for posterity the blessings of peace, freedom and prosperity.

DONE in Bangkok on the Eighth Day of August in the Year One Thousand Nine Hundred and Sixty-Seven.

For the
Republic of Indonesia:

ADAM MALIK
Presidium Minister for
Political Affairs
Minister for Foreign Affairs

For Malaysia:

TUN ABDUL RAZAK
Minister of Defence and
Minister of National Development

For the
Republic of the Philippines:

NARCISO RAMOS
Secretary of Foreign Affairs

For the
Republic of Singapore:

S. RAJARATNAM
Minister of Foreign Affairs

For the
Kingdom of Thailand:

THANAT KHOMAN
Minister of Foreign Affairs

Appendix B

TREATY OF AMITY AND COOPERATION IN SOUTHEAST ASIA
Indonesia, 24 February 1976

The High Contracting Parties:

CONSCIOUS of the existing ties of history, geography and culture, which have bound their peoples together;

ANXIOUS to promote regional peace and stability through abiding respect for justice and the rule or law and enhancing regional resilience in their relations;

DESIRING to enhance peace, friendship and mutual cooperation on matters affecting Southeast Asia consistent with the spirit and principles of the Charter of the United Nations, the Ten Principles adopted by the Asian-African Conference in Bandung on 25 April 1955, the Declaration of the Association of Southeast Asian Nations signed in Bangkok on 8 August 1967, and the Declaration signed in Kuala Lumpur on 27 November 1971;

CONVINCED that the settlement of differences or disputes between their countries should be regulated by rational, effective and sufficiently flexible procedures, avoiding negative aftitudes which might endanger or hinder cooperation;

BELIEVING in the need for cooperation with all peace-loving nations, both within and outside Southeast Asia, in the furtherance of world peace, stability and harmony;

SOLEMNLY AGREE to enter into a Treaty of Amity and Cooperation as follows:

CHAPTER I: PURPOSE AND PRINCIPLES

Article 1
The purpose of this Treaty is to promote perpetual peace, everlasting amity and cooperation among their peoples which would contribute to their strength, solidarity and closer relationship.

Article 2
In their relations with one another, the High Contracting Parties shall be guided by the following fundamental principles:

a. Mutual respect for the independence, sovereignty, equality, territorial integrity and national identity of all nations;

b. The right of every State to lead its national existence free from external interference, subversion or coersion;

c. Non-interference in the internal affairs of one another;

d. Settlement of differences or disputes by peaceful means;

e. Renunciation of the threat or use of force;

f. Effective cooperation among themselves.

CHAPTER II: AMITY

Article 3
In pursuance of the purpose of this Treaty the High Contracting Parties shall endeavour to develop and strengthen the traditional, cultural and historical ties of friendship, good neighbourliness and cooperation which bind them together and shall fulfill in good faith the obligations assumed under this Treaty. In order to promote closer understanding among them, the High Contracting Parties shall encourage and facilitate contact and intercourse among their peoples.

CHAPTER III: COOPERATION

Article 4
The High Contracting Parties shall promote active cooperation in the economic, social, technical, scientific and administrative fields as well as in matters of common ideals and aspirations of international peace and stability in the region and all other matters of common interest.

Article 5
Pursuant to Article 4 the High Contracting Parties shall exert their maximum efforts multilaterally as well as bilaterally on the basis of equality, non-discrimination and mutual benefit.

Article 6
The High Contracting Parties shall collaborate for the acceleration of the economic growth in the region in order to strengthen the foundation for a prosperous and peaceful community of nations in Southeast Asia. To this end, they shall promote the greater utilization of their agriculture and industries, the expansion of their trade and the improvement of their economic infrastructure for the mutual benefit of their peoples. In this regard, they shall continue to explore all avenues for close and beneficial cooperation with other States as well as international and regional organizations outside the region.

Article 7
The High Contracting Parties, in order to achieve social justice and to raise the standards of living of the peoples of the region, shall intensify economic cooperation. For this purpose, they shall adopt appropriate regional strategies for economic development and mutual assistance.

Article 8
The High Contracting Parties shall strive to achieve the closest cooperation on the widest scale and shall seek to provide assistance to one another in the form of training and research facilities in the social, cultural, technical, scientific and administrative fields.

Article 9
The High Contracting Parties shall endeavour to foster cooperation in the furtherance of the cause of peace, harmony, and stability in the region. To this end, the High Contracting Parties shall maintain regular contacts and consultations with one another on international and regional matters with a view to coordinating their views actions and policies.

Article 10
Each High Contracting Party shall not in any manner or form participate in any activity which shall constitute a threat to the political and economic stability, sovereignty, or territorial integrity of another High Contracting Party.

Article 11
The High Contracting Parties shall endeavour to strengthen their respective national resilience in their political, economic, socio-cultural as well as security fields in conformity with their respective ideals and aspirations, free from external interference as well as internal subversive activities in order to preserve their respective national identities.

Article 12
The High Contracting Parties in their efforts to achieve regional prosperity and security, shall endeavour to cooperate in all fields for the promotion of regional resilience, based on the principles of self-confidence, self-reliance, mutual respect, cooperation and solidarity which will constitute the foundation for a strong and viable community of nations in Southeast Asia.

CHAPTER IV: PACIFIC SETTLEMENT OF DISPUTES

Article 13
The High Contracting Parties shall have the determination and good faith to prevent disputes from arising. In case disputes on matters directly affecting them should arise, especially disputes likely to disturb regional peace and harmony, they shall refrain from the threat or use of force and shall at all times settle such disputes among themselves through friendly negotiations.

Article 14
To settle disputes through regional processes, the High Contracting Parties shall constitute, as a continuing body, a High Council comprising a Representative at ministerial level from each of the High Contracting Parties to take cognizance of the existence of disputes or situations likely to disturb regional peace and harmony.

Article 15
In the event no solution is reached through direct negotiations, the High Council shall take cognizance of the dispute or the situation and shall recommend to the parties in dispute appropriate means of settlement such as good offices, mediation, inquiry or conciliation. The High Council may however offer its good offices, or upon agreement of the parties in dispute, constitute itself into a committee of mediation, inquiry or conciliation. When deemed necessary, the High Council shall recommend appropriate measures for the prevention of a deterioration of the dispute or the situation.

Article 16
The foregoing provision of this Chapter shall not apply to a dispute unless all the parties to the dispute agree to their application to that dispute. However, this shall not preclude the other High Contracting Parties not party to the dispute from offering all possible assistance to settle the said dispute. Parties to the dispute should be well disposed towards such offers of assistance.

Article 17
Nothing in this Treaty shall preclude recourse to the modes of peaceful settlement contained in Article 33(l) of the Charter of the United Nations. The High Contracting Parties which are parties to a dispute should be encouraged to take initiatives to solve it by friendly negotiations before resorting to the other procedures provided for in the Charter of the United Nations.

CHAPTER V: GENERAL PROVISION

Article 18
This Treaty shall be signed by the Republic of Indonesia, Malaysia, the Republic of the Philippines, the Republic of Singapore and the Kingdom of Thailand. It shall be ratified in accordance with the constitutional procedures of each signatory State. It shall be open for accession by other States in Southeast Asia.

Article 19
This Treaty shall enter into force on the date of the deposit of the fifth instrument of ratification with the Governments of the signatory States which are designated Depositories of this Treaty and the instruments of ratification or accession.

Article 20
This Treaty is drawn up in the official languages of the High Contracting Parties, all of which are equally authoritative. There shall be an agreed common translation of the texts in the English language. Any divergent interpretation of the common text shall be settled by negotiation.

IN FAITH THEREOF the High Contracting Parties have signed the Treaty and have hereto affixed their Seals.

DONE at Denpasar, Bali, this twenty-fourth day of February in the year one thousand nine hundred and seventy-six.

<table>
<tr><td>For the
Republic of Indonesia:

SOEHARTO
President</td><td>For the
Republic of Singapore:

LEE KUAN YEW
Prime Minister</td></tr>
<tr><td>For Malaysia:

DATUK HUSEIN ONN
Prime Minister</td><td>For the
Kingdom of Thailand:

KUKRIT PRAMOJ
Prime Minister</td></tr>
<tr><td>For the
Republic of the Philippines:

FERDINAND E. MARCOS
President</td><td></td></tr>
</table>

Protocol Amending the Treaty of Amity and Cooperation in Southeast Asia
Philippines, 15 December 1987

The Government of Brunei Darussalam

The Government of the Republic of Indonesia

The Government of Malaysia

The Government of the Republic of the Philippines

The Government of the Republic of Singapore

The Government of the Kingdom of Thailand

DESIRING to further enhance cooperation with all peace-loving nations, both within and outside Southeast Asia and, in particular, neighbouring States of the Southeast Asia region.

CONSIDERING Paragraph 5 of the preamble of the Treaty of Amity and Cooperation in Southeast Asia, done at Denpasar, Bali, on 24 February 1976 (hereinafter referred to as the Treaty of Amity) which refers to the need for cooperation with all peace-loving nations, both within and outside Southeast Asia, in the furtherance of world peace, stability and harmony.

HEREBY AGREE TO THE FOLLOWING:

Article 1
Article 18 of the Treaty of Amity shall be amended to read as follows:

> "This Treaty shall be signed by the Republic of Indonesia, Malaysia, the Republic of the Philippines, the Republic of Singapore and the Kingdom of Thailand. It shall be ratified in accordance with the constitutional procedures of each signatory State.
>
> It shall be open for accession by other States in Southeast Asia.
>
> States outside Southeast Asia may also accede to this Treaty by the consent of all the States in Southeast Asia which are signatories to this Treaty and Brunei Darussalam."

Article 2
Article 14 of the Treaty of Amity shall be amended to read as follows:

> "The settle disputes through regional processes, the High Contracting Parties shall constitute, as a continuing body, a High Council comprising a Representative at ministerial level from each of the High Contracting Parties to take cognizance of the existence of disputes or situations likely to disturb regional peace and harmony.
>
> However, this article shall apply to any of the States outside Southeast Asia which have acceded to the Treaty only in cases where that state is directly involved in the dispute to be settled through the regional processes."

Article 3
This Protocol shall be subject to ratification and shall come into force on the date the last instrument of ratification of the High Contracting Parties is deposited.

DONE at Manila, the fifteenth day of December in the year one thousand nine hundred and eighty-seven.

For Brunei Darussalam:

PRINCE HAJI MOHAMED BOLKIAH
Minister of Foreign Affairs

For the
Republic of Indonesia:

PROF. DR. MOCHTAR KUSUMAATMADJA
Minister of Foreign Affairs

For Malaysia:

DATO HAJI ABU HASAN HAJI OMAR
Minister of Foreign Affairs

For the
Republic of the Philippines:

RAUL S. MANGLAPUS
Secretary for Foreign Affairs

For the
Republic of Singapore:

S. DHANABALAN
Minister of Foreign Affairs

For the
Kingdom of Thailand:

AIR CHIEF MARSHALL SIDDHI SAVETSILA
Minister of Foreign Affairs

Second Protocol Amending the Treaty of Amity and Cooperation in Southeast Asia
Manila, Philippines, 25 July 1998

The Government of Brunei Darussalam

The Government of the Kingdom of Cambodia

The Government of the Republic of Indonesia

The Government of the Lao People's Democratic Republic

The Government of Malaysia

The Government of the Union of Myanmar

The Government of the Republic of the Philippines

The Government of the Republic of Singapore

The Government of the Kingdom of Thailand

The Government of the Socialist Republic of Vietnam

The Government of Papua New Guinea

Hereinafter referred to as the High Contracting Parties:

DESIRING to ensure that there is appropriate enhancement of cooperation with all peace-loving nations, both within and outside Southeast Asia and, in particular, neighbouring States of the Southeast Asia region;

CONSIDERING Paragraph 5 of the preamble of the Treaty of Amity and Cooperation in Southeast Asia, done at Denpasar, Bali, on 24 February 1976 (hereinafter referred to as the Treaty of Amity) which refers to the need for cooperation with all peace-loving nations, both within and outside Southeast Asia, in the furtherance of world peace, stability and harmony.

HEREBY AGREE TO THE FOLLOWING:

Article 1
Article 18, Paragraph 3, of the Treaty of Amity shall be amended to read as follows:

> "States outside Southeast Asia may also accede to this Treaty with the consent of all the States in Southeast Asia, namely, Brunei Darussalam, the Kingdom of Cambodia, the Republic of Indonesia, the Lao People's Democratic Republic, Malaysia, the Union of

Myanmar, the Republic of the Philippines, the Republic of Singapore, the Kingdom of Thailand and the Socialist Republic of Vietnam."

Article 2
This Protocol shall be subject to ratification and shall come into force on the date the last instrument of ratification of the High Contracting Parties is deposited.

DONE at Manila, the twenty-fifth day of July in the year one thousand nine hundred and ninety-eight.

For Brunei Darussalam:

PRINCE MOHAMED BOLKIAH
Minister of Foreign Affairs

For the
Kingdom of Cambodia:

CHEM WIDHYA
Special Envoy of the
Royal Government of Cambodia

For the
Republic of Indonesia:

ALI ALATAS
Minister for Foreign Affairs

For the
Lao People's Democratic Republic:

SOMSAVAT LENGSAVAD
Deputy Prime Minister and
Minister of Foreign Affairs

For Malaysia:

DATUK SERI ABDULLAH
HAJI AHMAD BADAWI
Minister of Foreign Affairs

For the Union of Myanmar:

U OHN GYAW
Minister for Foreign Affairs

For the
Republic of the Philippines:

DOMINGO L SIAZON, JR.
Secretary of Foreign Affairs

For the
Republic of Singapore:

S JAYAKUMAR
Minister for Foreign Affairs

For the
Kingdom of Thailand:

SURIN PITSUWAN
Minister of Foreign Affairs

For the
Socialist Republic of Vietnam:

NGUYEN MANH CAM
Deputy Prime Minister and
Minister of Foreign Affairs

For Papua New Guinea:

ROY YAKI
Minister of Foreign Affairs

Appendix C

AGREEMENT ON THE COMMON EFFECTIVE PREFERENTIAL TARIFF SCHEME FOR THE ASEAN FREE TRADE AREA

The Governments of Brunei Darussalam, the Republic of Indonesia, Malaysia, the Republic of the Philippines, the Republic of Singapore and the Kingdom of Thailand, Member States of the Association of South, East Asian Nations (ASEAN):

MINDFUL of the Declaration of ASEAN Concord signed in Bali, Indonesia on 24 February 1976 which provides that Member States shall cooperate in the field of trade in order to promote development and growth of new production and trade;

RECALLING that the ASEAN Heads of Government, at their Third Summit Meeting held in Manila on 13–15 December 1987, declared that Member States shall strengthen intra-ASEAN economic cooperation to maximize the realization of the region's potential in trade and development;

NOTING that the Agreement on ASEAN Preferential Trading Arrangements (PTA) signed in Manila on 24 February 1977 provides for the adoption of various instruments on trade liberalization on a preferential basis;

ADHERING to the principles, concepts and ideals of the Framework Agreement on Enhancing ASEAN Economic Cooperation signed in Singapore on 28 January 1992;

CONVINCED that preferential trading arrangements among ASEAN Member States will act as a stimulus to the strengthening of national and ASEAN Economic resilience, and the development of the national economies of Member States by expanding investment and production opportunities, trade, and foreign exchange earnings;

DETERMINED to further cooperate in the economic growth of the region by accelerating the liberalization of intra-ASEAN trade and investment with the objective of creating the ASEAN Free Trade Area using the Common Effective Preferential Tariff (CEPT) Scheme;

DESIRING to effect improvements on the ASEAN PTA in consonance with ASEAN's international commitments.

HAVE AGREED AS FOLLOWS:

ARTICLE 1: DEFINITIONS

For the purposes of this Agreement:

1. "*CEPT*" means the Common Effective Preferential Tariff, and it is an agreed effective tariff, preferential to ASEAN, to be applied to goods originating from ASEAN Member States, and which have been identified for inclusion in the CEPT Scheme in accordance with Articles 2 (5) and 3.

2. "*Non-Tariff Barriers*" mean measures other than tariffs which effectively prohibit or restrict import or export of products within Member States.

3. "*Quantitative restrictions*" mean prohibitions or restrictions on trade with other Member States, whether made effective through quotas, licences or other measures with equivalent effect, including administrative measures and requirements which restrict trade.

4. "*Foreign exchange restrictions*" mean measures taken by Member States in the form of restrictions and other administrative procedures in foreign exchange which have the effect of restricting trade.

5. "*PTA*" means ASEAN Preferential Trading Arrangements stipulated in the Agreement on ASEAN Preferential Trading Arrangements, signed in Manila on 24 February 1977, and in the Protocol on Improvements on Extension of Tariff Preferences under the ASEAN Preferential Trading Arrangements (PTA), signed in Manila on 15 December 1987.

6. "*Exclusion List*" means a list containing products that are excluded from the extension of tariff preferences under the CEPT Scheme.

7. *"Agricultural products"* mean:

- (a) agricultural raw materials/unprocessed products covered under Chapters 1–24 of the Harmonized System (HS), and similar agricultural raw materials/unprocessed products in other related HS Headings; and

- (b) products which have undergone simple processing with minimal change in form from the original products.

ARTICLE 2: GENERAL PROVISIONS

1. All Member States shall participate in the CEPT Scheme.

2. Identification of products to be included in the CEPT Scheme shall be on a sectoral basis, i.e., at HS 6-digit level.

3. Exclusions at the HS 8/9 digit level for specific products are permitted for those Member States, which are temporarily not ready to include such products in the CEPT Scheme. For specific products, which are sensitive to a Member State. pursuant to Article 1 (3) of the Framework Agreement on Enhancing ASEAN Economic Cooperation, a Member State may exclude products from the CEPT Scheme, subject to a waiver of any concession herein provided for such products. A review of this Agreement shall be carried out in the eighth year to decide on the final Exclusion List or any amendment to this Agreement.

4. A product shall be deemed to be originating from ASEAN Member States, if at least 40% of its content originates from any Member State.

5. All manufactured products, including capital goods, processed agricultural products and those products falling outside the definition of agricultural products, as set out in this Agreement, shall be in the CEPT Scheme. These products shall automatically be subject to the schedule of tariff reduction, as set out in Article 4 of this Agreement. In respect of PTA items, the schedule of tariff reduction provided for in Article 4 of this Agreement shall be applied, taking into account the tariff rate after

Appendix C

the application of the existing margin of preference (MOP) as at 31 December 1992.

6. All products under the PTA which are not transferred to the CEPT Scheme shall continue to enjoy the MOP existing as at 31 December 1992.

7. Member States, whose tariffs for the agreed products are reduced from 20% and below to 0%–5%, even though granted on an MFN basis, shall still enjoy concessions. Member States with tariff rates at MFN rates of 0%–5% shall be deemed to have satisfied the obligations under this Agreement and shall also enjoy the concessions.

ARTICLE 3: PRODUCT COVERAGE

This Agreement shall apply to all manufactured products, including capital goods, processed agricultural products, and those products failing outside the definition of agricultural products as set out in this Agreement. Agricultural products shall be excluded from the CEPT Scheme.

ARTICLE 4: SCHEDULE OF TARIFF REDUCTION

1. Member States agree to the following schedule of effective preferential tariff reductions:

- (a) The reduction from existing tariff rates to 20% shall be done within a time frame of 5 years to 8 years, from 1 January 1993, subject to a programme of reduction to be decided by each Member State, which shall be announced at the start of the programme. Member States are encouraged to adopt an annual rate of reduction, which shall be (X-20)%/5 or 8, where X equals the existing tariff rates of individual Member States.

- (b) The subsequent reduction of tariff rates from 20% or below shall be done within a time frame of 7 years. The rate of reduction shall be at a minimum of 5% quantum per reduction. A programme of reduction to be decided by each Member State shall be announced at the start of the programme.

- (c) For products with existing tariff rates of 20% or below as at 1 January 1993, Member States shall decide upon a programme of tariff reductions, and announce at the start, the schedule of tariff reductions. Two or more Member States may enter into arrangements for tariff reduction to 0%–5% on specific products at an accelerated pace to be announced at the start of the programme.

2. Subject to Articles 4 (1) (b) and 4 (1) (c) of this Agreement, products which reach, or are at tariff rates of 20% or below, shall automatically enjoy the concessions.

3. The above schedules of tariff reduction shall not prevent Member States from immediately reducing their tariffs to 0%–5% or following an accelerated schedule of tariff reduction.

ARTICLE 5: OTHER PROVISIONS

A. Quantitative Restrictions and Non-Tariff Barriers

1. Member States shall eliminate all quantitative restrictions in respect of products under the CEPT Scheme upon enjoyment of the concessions applicable to those products.

2. Member States shall eliminate other non-tariff barriers on a gradual basis within a period of five years after the enjoyment of concessions applicable to those products.

B. Foreign Exchange Restrictions

Member States shall make exceptions to their foreign exchange restrictions relating to payments for the products under the CEPT Scheme, as well as repatriation of such payments without prejudice to their rights under Article XVIII of the General Agreement on Tariff and Trade (GATT) and relevant provisions of the Articles of Agreement of the International Monetary Fund (IMF).

Appendix C

C. **Other Areas of Cooperation**
Member States shall explore further measures on border and non-border areas of cooperation to supplement and complement the liberalization of trade. These may include, among others, the harmonization of standards, reciprocal recognition of tests and certification of products, removal of barriers to foreign investments, macroeconomic consultations, rules for fair competition, and promotion of venture capital.

D. **Maintenance of Concessions**
Member States shall not nullify or impair any of the concessions as agreed upon through the application of methods of customs valuation, any new charges or measures restricting trade, except in cases provided for in this Agreement.

ARTICLE 6: EMERGENCY MEASURES

1. If, as a result of the implementation of this Agreement, import of a particular product eligible under the CEPT Scheme is increasing in such a manner as to cause or threaten to cause serious injury to sectors producing like or directly competitive products in the importing Member States, the importing Member States may, to the extent and for such time as may be necessary to prevent or to remedy such injury, suspend preferences provisionally and without discrimination, subject to Article 6 (3) of this Agreement. Such suspension of preferences shall be consistent with the GATT.

2. Without prejudice to existing international obligations, a Member State, which finds it necessary to create or intensify quantitative restrictions or other measures limiting imports with a view to forestalling the threat of or stopping a serious decline of its monetary reserves, shall endeavour to do so in a manner, which safeguards the value of the concessions agreed upon.

3. Where emergency measures are taken pursuant to this Article, immediate notice of such action shall be given to the Council referred to in Article 7 of this Agreement, and such action may be the subject of consultation as provided for in Article 8 of this Agreement.

ARTICLE 7: INSTITUITIONAL ARRANGEMENTS

1. The ASEAN Economic Ministers (AEM) shall, for the purposes of this Agreement, establish a ministerial-level Council comprising one nominee from each Member State and the Secretary-General of the ASEAN Secretariat. The ASEAN Secretariat shall provide the support to the ministerial-level Council for supervising, coordinating and reviewing the implementation of this Agreement, and assisting the AEM in all matters relating thereto. In the performance of its functions, the ministerial-level Council shall also be supported by the Senior Economic Officials' Meeting (SEOM).

2. Member States which enter into bilateral arrangements on tariff reductions pursuant to Article 4 of this Agreement shall notify all other Member States and the ASEAN Secretariat of such arrangements.

3. The ASEAN Secretariat shall monitor and report to the SEOM on the implementation of the Agreement pursuant to the Article III (2) (8) of the Agreement on the Establishment of the ASEAN Secretariat. Member States shall cooperate with the ASEAN Secretariat in the performance of its duties.

ARTICLE 8: CONSULTATIONS

1. Member States shall accord adequate opportunity for consultations regarding any representations made by other Member States with respect to any matter affecting the implementation of this Agreement. The Council referred to in Article 7 of this Agreement, may seek guidance from the AEM in respect of any matter for which it has not been possible to find a satisfactory solution during previous consultations.

2. Member States, which consider that any other Member State has not carried out its obligations under this Agreement, resulting in the nullifications or impairment of any benefit accruing to them, may, with a view to achieving satisfactory adjustment of the matter, make representations or proposal to the other Member States concerned, which shall give due consideration to the representations or proposal made to it.

3. Any differences between the Member States concerning the interpretation or application of this Agreement shall, as far as possible, be settled amicably between the parties. If such differences cannot be settled amicably, it shall be submitted to the Council referred to in Article 7 of this Agreement, and if necessary, to the AEM.

ARTICLE 9: GENERAL EXCEPTIONS

Nothing in this Agreement shall prevent any Member State from taking action and adopting measures, which it considers necessary for the protection of its national security, the protection of public morals, the protection of human, animal or plant life and health, and the protection of articles of artistic, historic and archaeological value.

ARTICLE 10: FINAL PROVISIONS

1. The respective Governments of Member States shall undertake the appropriate measures to fulfill the agreed obligations arising from this Agreement.

2. Any amendment to this Agreement shall be made by consensus and shall become effective upon acceptance by all Member States.

3. This Agreement shall be effective upon signing.

4. This Agreement shall be deposited with the Secretary-General of the ASEAN Secretariat, who shall likewise promptly furnish a certified copy thereof to each Member State.

5. No reservation shall be made with respect to any of the provisions of this Agreement. In witness Whereof, the undersigned, being duly authorized thereto by their respective Governments, have signed this Agreement on Common Effective Preferential Tariff (CEPT) Scheme for the Free Trade Area (AFTA).

DONE at Singapore, this 28th day of January, 1992 in a single copy in the English Language.

For the Government
of Brunei Darussalam:

ABDUL RAHMAN TAIB
Minister of Industry and
Primary Resources

For the Government
of the Republic of the Philippines:

PETER D GARRUCHO JR
Secretary of Trade and Industry

For the Government
of the Republic of Indonesia:

DR ARIFIN M SIREGAR
Minister of Trade

For the Government
of the Republic of Singapore:

LEE HSIEN LOONG
Deputy Prime Minister and
Minister for Trade and Industry

For the Government
of Malaysia:

RAFIDAH AZIZ
Minister of International Trade
and Industry

For the Government
of the Kingdom of Thailand:

AMARET SILA-ON
Minister of Commerce

Appendix D
ASEAN VISION 2020

We, the Heads of State/Government of the Association of Southeast Asian Nations, gather today in Kuala Lumpur to reaffirm our commitment to the aims and purposes of the Association as set forth in the Bangkok Declaration of 8 August 1967, in particular to promote regional cooperation in Southeast Asia in the spirit of equality and partnership and thereby contribute towards peace, progress and prosperity in the region.

We in ASEAN have created a community of Southeast Asian nations at peace with one another and at peace with the world, rapidly achieving prosperity for our peoples and steadily improving their lives. Our rich diversity has provided the strength and inspiration to us to help one another foster a strong sense of community.

We are now a market of around 500 million people with a combined gross domestic product of US$600 billion. We have achieved considerable results in the economic field, such as high economic growth, stability and significant poverty alleviation over the past few years. Members have enjoyed substantial trade and investment flows from significant liberalization measures.

We resolve to build upon these achievements.

Now, as we approach the 21st century, thirty years after the birth of ASEAN, we gather to chart a vision for ASEAN on the basis of today's realities and prospects in the decades leading to the Year 2020.

That vision is of ASEAN as a concert of Southeast Asian nations, outward looking, living in peace, stability and prosperity, bonded together in partnership in dynamic development and in a community of caring societies.

A Concert of Southeast Asian Nations

We envision the ASEAN region to be, in 2020, in full reality, a Zone of Peace, Freedom and Neutrality, as envisaged in the Kuala Lumpur Declaration of 1971.

ASEAN shall have, by the year 2020, established a peaceful and stable Southeast Asia where each nation is at peace with itself and where the causes for conflict have been eliminated, through abiding respect for justice and the rule of law and through the strengthening of national and regional resilience.

We envision a Southeast Asia where territorial and other disputes are resolved by peaceful means.

We envision the Treaty of Amity and Cooperation in Southeast Asia functioning fully as a binding code of conduct for our governments and peoples, to which other states with interests in the region adhere.

We envision a Southeast Asia free from nuclear weapons, with all the Nuclear Weapon States committed to the purposes of the Southeast Asia Nuclear Weapons Free Zone Treaty through their adherence to its Protocol. We also envision our region free from all other weapons of mass destruction.

We envision our rich human and natural resources contributing to our development and shared prosperity.

We envision the ASEAN Regional Forum as an established means for confidence-building and preventive diplomacy and for promoting conflict-resolution.

We envision a Southeast Asia where our mountains, rivers and seas no longer divide us but link us together in friendship, cooperation and commerce.

We see ASEAN as an effective force for peace, justice and moderation in the Asia-Pacific and in the world.

A Partnership in Dynamic Development

We resolve to chart a new direction towards the year 2020 called, ASEAN 2020: Partnership in Dynamic Development which will forge closer economic integration within ASEAN.

We reiterate our resolve to enhance ASEAN economic cooperation through economic development strategies, which are in line with the aspiration of our respective peoples, which put emphasis on sustainable and equitable growth, and enhance national as well as regional resilience.

We pledge to sustain ASEAN's high economic performance by building upon the foundation of our existing cooperation efforts, consolidating our achievements, expanding our collective efforts and enhancing mutual assistance.

We commit ourselves to moving towards closer cohesion and economic integration, narrowing the gap in the level of development among Member Countries, ensuring that the multilateral trading system remains fair and open, and achieving global competitiveness.

We will create a stable, prosperous and highly competitive ASEAN Economic Region in which there is a free flow of goods, services and investments, a freer flow of capital, equitable economic development and reduced poverty and socio-economic disparities.

Appendix D

We resolve, inter-alia, to undertake the following:

- maintain regional macroeconomic and financial stability by promoting closer consultations in macroeconomic and financial policies.
- advance economic integration and cooperation by undertaking the following general strategies: fully implement the ASEAN Free Trade Area and accelerate liberalization of trade in services, realize the ASEAN Investment Area by 2010 and free flow of investments by 2020; intensify and expand sub-regional cooperation in existing and new sub-regional growth areas; further consolidate and expand extra-ASEAN regional linkages for mutual benefit cooperate to strengthen the multilateral trading system, and reinforce the role of the business sector as the engine of growth.
- promote a modern and competitive small and medium enterprises (SME) sector in ASEAN which will contribute to the industrial development and efficiency of the region.
- accelerate the free flow of professional and other services in the region.
- promote financial sector liberalization and closer cooperation in money and capital market, tax, insurance and customs matters as well as closer consultations in macroeconomic and financial policies.
- accelerate the development of science and technology including information technology by establishing a regional information technology network and centers of excellence for dissemination of and easy access to data and information.
- establish interconnecting arrangements in the field of energy and utilities for electricity, natural gas and water within ASEAN through the ASEAN Power Grid and a Trans-ASEAN Gas Pipeline and Water Pipeline, and promote cooperation in energy efficiency and conservation, as well as the development of new and renewable energy resources.
- enhance food security and international competitiveness of food, agricultural and forest products, to make ASEAN a leading producer of these products, and promote the forestry sector as a model in forest management, conservation and sustainable development.
- meet the ever increasing demand for improved infrastructure and communications by developing an integrated and harmonized trans-ASEAN transportation network and harnessing technology advances in telecommunication and information technology, especially in linking the planned information highways/multimedia corridors in ASEAN, promoting open sky policy, developing multi-modal transport, facilitating goods in transit and integrating telecommunications networks through

greater interconnectivity, coordination of frequencies and mutual recognition of equipment-type approval procedures.
- enhance human resource development in all sectors of the economy through quality education, upgrading of skills and capabilities and training.
- work towards a world class standards and conformance system that will provide a harmonized system to facilitate the free flow of ASEAN trade while meeting health, safety and environmental needs.
- use the ASEAN Foundation as one of the instruments to address issues of unequal economic development, poverty and socioeconomic disparities.
- promote an ASEAN customs partnership for world class standards and excellence in efficiency, professionalism and service, and uniformity through harmonized procedures, to promote trade and investment and to protect the health and well-being of the ASEAN community,
- enhance intra-ASEAN trade and investment in the mineral sector and to contribute towards a technologically competent ASEAN through closer networking and sharing of information on mineral and geosciences as well as to enhance cooperation and partnership with dialogue partners to facilitate the development and transfer of technology in the mineral sector, particularly in the downstream research and the geosciences and to develop appropriate mechanism for these.

A Community of Caring Societies

We envision the entire Southeast Asia to be, by 2020, an ASEAN community conscious of its ties of history, aware of its cultural heritage and bound by a common regional identity.

We see vibrant and open ASEAN societies consistent with their respective national identities, where all people enjoy equitable access to opportunities for total human development regardless of gender, race, religion, language, or social and cultural background.

We envision a socially cohesive and caring ASEAN where hunger, malnutrition, deprivation and poverty are no longer basic problems, where strong families as the basic units of society tend to their members particularly the children, youth, women and elderly; and where the civil society is empowered and gives special attention to the disadvantaged, disabled and marginalized and where social justice and the rule of law reign.

We see well before 2020 a Southeast Asia free of illicit drugs, free of their production, processing, trafficking and use.

We envision a technologically competitive ASEAN competent in strategic and enabling technologies, with an adequate pool of technologically qualified and trained manpower, and strong networks of scientific and technological institutions and centres of excellence.

We envision a clean and green ASEAN with fully established mechanisms for sustainable development to ensure the protection of the region's environment, the sustainability of its natural resources, and the high quality of life of its peoples.

We envision the evolution in Southeast Asia of agreed rules of behaviour and cooperative measures to deal with problems that can be met only on a regional scale, including environmental pollution and degradation, drug trafficking, trafficking in women and children, and other transnational crimes.

We envision our nations being governed with the consent and greater participation of the people with its focus on the welfare and dignity of the human person and the good of the community.

We resolve to develop and strengthen ASEAN's institutions and mechanisms to enable ASEAN to realize the vision and respond to the challenges of the coming century. We also see the need for a strengthened ASEAN Secretariat with an enhanced role to support the realization of our vision.

An Outward-Looking ASEAN

We see an outward-looking ASEAN playing a pivotal role in the international fora, and advancing ASEAN's common interests. We envision ASEAN having an intensified relationship with its Dialogue Partners and other regional organizations based on equal partnership and mutual respect.

Conclusion

We pledge to our peoples our determination and commitment to bringing this ASEAN Vision for the Year 2020 into reality.

Kuala Lumpur
15 December 1997

Appendix E
ASEAN AT A CROSSROADS

Report of Rodolfo C. Severino, Secretary-General
of the Association of Southeast Asian Nations,
to the 8th ASEAN Summit

Phnom Penh, 4 November 2002

Since this is my last report to Your Majesty and Your Excellencies, I should like, with your indulgence, to take a longer perspective than usual and take a glance at the past five years instead of just the last one. *In any case, the report card for the past year, which Your Majesty and Your Excellencies have directed me to draw up, has been circulated.*

When ASEAN's leaders kindly appointed me to the office of Secretary-General, Southeast Asia was at the height of the financial crisis of 1997–98. ASEAN was in the process of expansion, a process that was projected to place severe strains on the association. The haze from land and forest fires that was enveloping the region was testing the ability of ASEAN to work out regional solutions to regional problems. All this degraded ASEAN's image in the world, affecting the perceptions of investors and ASEAN's influence in international affairs. At the same time, the rise of certain large economies and other regional groups was posing a challenge for ASEAN in the global competition for markets and investments.

ASEAN's responses to these developments have, to some extent, mitigated their adverse impact and the negative perceptions of ASEAN. The Secretariat and other ASEAN bodies managed somewhat to reverse the slide of ASEAN's image. The association continued to help maintain regional peace and stability by sustaining its solidarity, managing the ASEAN Regional Forum, and strengthening the association's linkages with its neighbours, particularly China, Japan and Korea. The negotiations on a declaration on conduct in the South China Sea had a calming effect on this critical area. This process has concluded, and the declaration is ready for signing this afternoon. ASEAN has responded to the surge of international terrorism, adopting strong positions, taking concrete cooperative measures, and working with the international community. The recent terrorist attack in Bali has prodded ASEAN to intensify these efforts.

To deal with the vulnerabilities exposed and exacerbated by the financial crisis, ASEAN has stepped up its cooperation in finance with greater vigor and sharper focus. ASEAN's finance ministers have been undertaking regular reviews of the regional economy to minimize the likelihood of surprises. An early warning system is being developed, and procedures for monitoring short-term capital flows are being put in place. To help ward off speculative currency attacks, eleven bilateral currency swap and re-purchase agreements have been concluded among ASEAN countries, China, Japan and Korea; three more are under negotiation.

The haze from land and forest fires has periodically caused severe damage to the economy, health and environment of several Southeast Asian countries. At the regional level, ASEAN has strengthened its ability to monitor the situation and cooperatively fight fires. It has worked with national governments concerned to prevent fires through education, persuasion and law enforcement. The measures that last year's ASEAN summit adopted to deal with the scourge of HIV/AIDS are being pursued actively at all levels, thanks to the impetus given by the ASEAN leaders themselves. ASEAN has intensified its cooperation in combating transnational crime, including terrorism.

By signing the e-ASEAN Framework Agreement, ASEAN's leaders gave clear direction to ASEAN's commitment to harness information and communications technology for the region's development. The e-ASEAN Task Force has launched several valuable projects to implement that commitment. An e-readiness assessment commissioned by the ASEAN Secretariat gauged the state of ASEAN's readiness for the information age and made several recommendations for ensuring that readiness. Most ASEAN governments have carried out some of those recommendations.

Your Majesty and Your Excellencies have taken it as your personal mission to narrow the development gap between the older and the newer members of ASEAN. A work plan for the Initiative for ASEAN Integration has been drawn up, with financial support from Japan. Made up of some fifty projects, it has been developed largely by the newer members themselves and endorsed by all the ASEAN Foreign Ministers. *The work plan is now before Your Majesty and Your Excellencies for approval.*

In the meantime, the mobilization of resources to support the IAI projects is in full swing. Most of the projects have attracted the interest of governments, foundations, and corporations. I am happy to highlight the fact that the older ASEAN members are marshaling their own technical and financial resources in this endeavour. The IAI is being pursued in coordination with other schemes for the development of the newer members. The Greater Mekong Sub-region programme, which is supported by the Asian Development Bank, has been an effective endeavour. Yesterday, a GMS summit took place for the first time, giving strong impetus to a programme that is most valuable for purposes of the IAI.

Finally, I come to regional economic integration. As early as 1992, ASEAN's leaders have recognized that integrating the ASEAN economy is critical to attracting investments into the region, bolstering ASEAN's competitiveness in the world, and strengthening its international influence. The ASEAN Free Trade Area is basically on track. ASEAN has laid the foundations for the other elements of regional economic integration. Commitments have been made and frameworks have been put in place for the removal of non-tariff barriers, the liberalization of trade in services, the harmonization of product standards, the streamlining of customs procedures, the seamlessness of transportation and communications, the facilitation of tourism, the regionalization of information and communications technology, the formation of an ASEAN power grid and a trans-ASEAN gas pipeline network, and the free flow of investments.

However, the process of integration has generally stalled. To be sure, some progress has been made, notably in AFTA, but progress has fallen short of measuring up to the challenges faced by our region and carrying out the leaders' vision and resolve. AFTA has seen little actual use by traders. The other foundations for regional integration have not been built upon. Regional economic integration seems to have become stuck in framework agreements, work programmes and master plans.

In the face of this situation, the ASEAN Economic Ministers have decided that member-countries that are ready to do so may move ahead in the implementation of collective commitments previously agreed upon; the rest can join in when they are ready. This should help unblock some implementing arrangements that are stalled because one or two member-countries are, for one reason or another, unwilling or unable to carry them out. The Economic Ministers have also proposed to set up a permanent body to help ensure compliance with commitments already made.

Your Majesty and Your Excellencies at your summit last year ordered the drawing up of a Roadmap for the Integration of ASEAN to chart the course of regional economic integration beyond AFTA. Officials have been working on the detailed components of the roadmap. *Your Majesty and Your Excellencies may wish to take note of the matrix mapping the progress of their work.* My reports to ministers this year have given some recommendations for the next, essential steps for deeper integration. The Economic Ministers have commissioned a study on the state of ASEAN's competitiveness. McKinsey & Co. will in a few minutes give a short briefing on their findings thus far.

I venture to suggest that a major reason why ASEAN seems to be bogged down on the road to economic integration beyond tariff-cutting is that it is not clear what the medium-term, much less the long-term, objective is. To be sure, ASEAN Vision 2020 envisages an "ASEAN Economic Region in which there is a free flow of goods, services and investments." But how precisely is this to be achieved? What kind of economic integration should ASEAN strive for? Should ASEAN now aim for a customs union? A common market? A single market? An economic union?

The Economic Ministers have agreed to establish a high-level task force to recommend measures to deepen the region's economic integration beyond AFTA. The work of the task force could encompass the form of economic integration that ASEAN should strive for, taking into account the recommendations in the McKinsey study, the Roadmap, and my report.

For a start, ASEAN could select one industry sector in which all the elements of economic integration could be comprehensively applied. The automotive industry could be one such sector, in which components as well as end products would be freely trade, tests in one country would be recognized in all the others, environmental and safety requirements and other product standards would be harmonized, and so on.

Regional economic integration should involve not only trade and industry but also finance. For next steps, studies are being done on such measures as integrating capital markets, adopting an ASEAN currency unit, liberalizing financial services, and removing restrictions on intra-ASEAN capital-account transactions. Again, some idea of the eventual objective has to take shape.

ASEAN must decide. Having a clear idea of its destination would enable ASEAN to proceed more rapidly and smoothly on the path of economic integration. It is critical for ASEAN to know its destination and which path will take it there at this crossroads in its history.

Appendix F
DECLARATION OF ASEAN CONCORD II
(Bali Concord II)

The Sultan of Brunei Darussalam, the Prime Minister of the Kingdom of Cambodia, the President of the Republic of Indonesia, the Prime Minister of the Lao People's Democratic Republic, the Prime Minister of Malaysia, the Prime Minister of the Union of Myanmar, the President of the Republic of the Philippines, the Prime Minister of the Republic of Singapore, the Prime Minister of the Kingdom of Thailand and the Prime Minister of the Socialist Republic of Viet Nam;

RECALLING the Declaration of ASEAN Concord adopted in this historic place of Bali, Indonesia in 1976, the Leaders of the Association of Southeast Asian Nations (ASEAN) expressed satisfaction with the overall progress made in the region;

NOTING in particular the expansion of ASEAN to ten countries in Southeast Asia, the deepening of regional economic integration and the impending accession to the Treaty of Amity and Cooperation (TAC) by States outside Southeast Asia;

CONSCIOUS of the need to further consolidate and enhance the achievements of ASEAN as a dynamic, resilient, and cohesive regional association for the well being of its member states and people as well as the need to further strengthen the Association's guidelines in achieving a more coherent and clearer path for cooperation between and among them;

REAFFIRMING their commitment to the principles enshrined in the ASEAN Declaration (Bangkok, 1967), the Declaration on Zone of Peace, Freedom, and Neutrality (Kuala Lumpur, 1971), the Treaty of Amity and Cooperation in Southeast Asia (Bali, 1976), the Declaration of ASEAN Concord (Bali, 1976), and the Treaty on the Southeast Asia Nuclear Weapons Free Zone (Bangkok, 1995);

COGNIZANT that the future of ASEAN cooperation is guided by the ASEAN Vision 2020, the Hanoi Plan of Action (1999–2004), and its succeeding Plans of Action, the Initiative for ASEAN Integration (IAI), and the Roadmap for the Integration of ASEAN (RIA);

CONFIRMING further that ASEAN Member Countries share primary responsibility for strengthening the economic and social stability in the region and ensuring their peaceful and progressive national development, and that they are determined to ensure their stability and security from external interference in any form or manner in order to preserve their national interest in accordance with the ideals and aspirations of their peoples;

REAFFIRMING the fundamental importance of adhering to the principle of non-interference and consensus in ASEAN cooperation;

REITERATING that the Treaty of Amity and Cooperation in Southeast Asia (TAC) is an effective code of conduct for relations among governments and peoples;

RECOGNIZING that sustainable economic development requires a secure political environment based on a strong foundation of mutual interests generated by economic cooperation and political solidarity;

COGNIZANT of the interdependence of the ASEAN economies and the need for ASEAN member countries to adopt "Prosper Thy Neighbour" policies in order to ensure the long-term vibrancy and prosperity of the ASEAN region;

REITERATING the importance of rules-based multilateral trading system that is equitable and that contributes towards the pursuit of development;

REAFFIRMING that ASEAN is a concert of Southeast Asian nations, bonded together in partnership in dynamic development and in a community of caring societies, committed to upholding cultural diversity and social harmony;

DO HEREBY DECLARE THAT:

1. An ASEAN Community shall be established comprising three pillars, namely political and security cooperation, economic cooperation, and socio-cultural cooperation that are closely intertwined and mutually

reinforcing for the purpose of ensuring durable peace, stability and shared prosperity in the region;

2. ASEAN shall continue its efforts to ensure closer and mutually beneficial integration among its member states and among their peoples, and to promote regional peace and stability, security, development and prosperity with a view to realizing an ASEAN Community that is open, dynamic and resilient;

3. ASEAN shall respond to the new dynamics within the respective ASEAN Member Countries and shall urgently and effectively address the challenge of translating ASEAN cultural diversities and different economic levels into equitable development opportunity and prosperity, in an environment of solidarity, regional resilience and harmony;

4. ASEAN shall nurture common values, such as habit of consultation to discuss political issues and the willingness to share information on matters of common concern, such as environmental degradation, maritime security cooperation, the enhancement of defence cooperation among ASEAN countries, develop a set of socio-political values and principles, and resolve to settle long-standing disputes through peaceful means;

5. The Treaty of Amity and Cooperation in Southeast Asia (TAC) is the key code of conduct governing relations between states and a diplomatic instrument for the promotion of peace and stability in the region;

6. The ASEAN Regional Forum (ARF) shall remain the primary forum in enhancing political and security cooperation in the Asia Pacific region, as well as the pivot in building peace and stability in the region. ASEAN shall enhance its role in further advancing the stages of cooperation within the ARF to ensure the security of the Asia Pacific region;

7. ASEAN is committed to deepening and broadening its internal economic integration and linkages with the world economy to realize an ASEAN Economic Community through a bold, pragmatic and unified strategy;

8. ASEAN shall further build on the momentum already gained in the ASEAN+3 process so as to further draw synergies through broader and deeper cooperation in various areas;

Appendix F

9. ASEAN shall build upon opportunities for mutually beneficial regional integration arising from its existing initiatives and those with partners, through enhanced trade and investment links as well as through IAI process and the RIA;

10. ASEAN shall continue to foster a community of caring societies and promote a common regional identity;

DO HEREBY ADOPT:

The framework to achieve a dynamic, cohesive, resilient and integrated ASEAN Community:

A. **ASEAN SECURITY COMMUNITY (ASC)**

1. The ASEAN Security Community is envisaged to bring ASEAN's political and security cooperation to a higher plane to ensure that countries in the region live at peace with one another and with the world at large in a just, democratic and harmonious environment. The ASEAN Security Community members shall rely exclusively on peaceful processes in the settlement of intra-regional differences and regard their security as fundamentally linked to one another and bound by geographic location, common vision and objectives.

2. The ASEAN Security Community, recognizing the sovereign right of the member countries to pursue their individual foreign policies and defence arrangements and taking into account the strong interconnections among political, economic and social realities, subscribes to the principle of comprehensive security as having broad political, economic, social and cultural aspects in consonance with the ASEAN Vision 2020 rather than to a defence pact, military alliance or a joint foreign policy.

3. ASEAN shall continue to promote regional solidarity and cooperation. Member Countries shall exercise their rights to lead their national existence free from outside interference in their internal affairs.

4. The ASEAN Security Community shall abide by the UN Charter and other principles of international law and uphold ASEAN's

principles of non-interference, consensus-based decision-making, national and regional resilience, respect for national sovereignty, the renunciation of the threat or the use of force, and peaceful settlement of differences and disputes.

5. Maritime issues and concerns are transboundary in nature, and therefore shall be addressed regionally in holistic, integrated and comprehensive manner. Maritime cooperation between and among ASEAN member countries shall contribute to the evolution of the ASEAN Security Community.

6. Existing ASEAN political instruments such as the Declaration on ZOPFAN, the TAC, and the SEANWFZ Treaty shall continue to play a pivotal role in the area of confidence building measures, preventive diplomacy and the approaches to conflict resolution.

7. The High Council of the TAC shall be the important component in the ASEAN Security Community since it reflects ASEAN's commitment to resolve all differences, disputes and conflicts peacefully.

8. The ASEAN Security Community shall contribute to further promoting peace and security in the wider Asia Pacific region and reflect ASEAN's determination to move forward at a pace comfortable to all. In this regard, the ARF shall remain the main forum for regional security dialogue, with ASEAN as the primary driving force.

9. The ASEAN Security Community is open and outward looking in respect of actively engaging ASEAN's friends and Dialogue Partners to promote peace and stability in the region, and shall build on the ARF to facilitate consultation and cooperation between ASEAN and its friends and Partners on regional security matters.

10. The ASEAN Security Community shall fully utilize the existing institutions and mechanisms within ASEAN with a view to strengthening national and regional capacities to counter terrorism, drug trafficking, trafficking in persons and other transnational crimes; and shall work to ensure that the Southeast Asian Region remains free of all weapons of mass destruction. It shall enable ASEAN to

demonstrate a greater capacity and responsibility of being the primary driving force of the ARF.

11. The ASEAN Security Community shall explore enhanced cooperation with the United Nations as well as other international and regional bodies for the maintenance of international peace and security.

12. ASEAN shall explore innovative ways to increase its security and establish modalities for the ASEAN Security Community, which include, inter alia, the following elements: norms-setting, conflict prevention, approaches to conflict resolution, and post-conflict peace building.

B. **ASEAN ECONOMIC COMMUNITY (AEC)**

1. The ASEAN Economic Community is the realization of the end-goal of economic integration as outlined in the ASEAN Vision 2020, to create a stable, prosperous and highly competitive ASEAN economic region in which there is a free flow of goods, services, investment and a freer flow of capital, equitable economic development and reduced poverty and socio-economic disparities in year 2020.

2. The ASEAN Economic Community is based on a convergence of interests among ASEAN members to deepen and broaden economic integration efforts through existing and new initiatives with clear timelines.

3. The ASEAN Economic Community shall establish ASEAN as a single market and production base, turning the diversity that characterizes the region into opportunities for business complementation making the ASEAN a more dynamic and stronger segment of the global supply chain. ASEAN's strategy shall consist of the integration of ASEAN and enhancing ASEAN's economic competitiveness. In moving towards the ASEAN Economic Community, ASEAN shall, inter alia, institute new mechanisms and measures to strengthen the implementation of its existing economic initiatives including the ASEAN Free Trade Area (AFTA), ASEAN Framework Agreement on Services (AFAS) and ASEAN Investment

Area (AIA); accelerate regional integration in the priority sectors; facilitate movement of business persons, skilled labour and talents; and strengthen the institutional mechanisms of ASEAN, including the improvement of the existing ASEAN Dispute Settlement Mechanism to ensure expeditious and legally binding resolution of any economic disputes. As a first step towards the realization of the ASEAN Economic Community, ASEAN shall implement the recommendations of the **High Level Task Force on ASEAN Economic Integration as annexed.**

4. The ASEAN Economic Community shall ensure that deepening and broadening integration of ASEAN shall be accompanied by technical and development cooperation in order to address the development divide and accelerate the economic integration of Cambodia, Lao PDR, Myanmar and Viet Nam through IAI and RIA so that the benefits of ASEAN integration are shared and enable all ASEAN Member Countries to move forward in a unified manner.

5. The realization of a fully integrated economic community requires implementation of both liberalization and cooperation measures. There is a need to enhance cooperation and integration activities in other areas. These will involve, among others, human resources development and capacity building; recognition of educational qualifications; closer consultation on macroeconomic and financial policies; trade financing measures; enhanced infrastructure and communications connectivity; development of electronic transactions through e-ASEAN; integrating industries across the region to promote regional sourcing; and enhancing private sector involvement.

C. ASEAN SOCIO-CULTURAL COMMUNITY (ASCC)

1. The ASEAN Socio-cultural Community, in consonance with the goal set by ASEAN Vision 2020, envisages a Southeast Asia bonded together in partnership as a community of caring societies.

2. In line with the programme of action set by the 1976 Declaration of ASEAN Concord, the Community shall foster cooperation in social development aimed at raising the standard of living of disadvantaged groups and the rural population, and shall seek the

active involvement of all sectors of society, in particular women, youth, and local communities.

3. ASEAN shall ensure that its work force shall be prepared for, and benefit from, economic integration by investing more resources for basic and higher education, training, science and technology development, job creation, and social protection. The development and enhancement of human resources is a key strategy for employment generation, alleviating poverty and socio-economic disparities, and ensuring economic growth with equity. ASEAN shall continue existing efforts to promote regional mobility and mutual recognition of professional credentials, talents, and skills development.

4. ASEAN shall further intensify cooperation in the area of public health, including in the prevention and control of infectious diseases, such as HIV/AIDS and SARS, and support joint regional actions to increase access to affordable medicines. The security of the Community is enhanced when poverty and diseases are held in check, and the peoples of ASEAN are assured of adequate health care.

5. The Community shall nurture talent and promote interaction among ASEAN scholars, writers, artists and media practitioners to help preserve and promote ASEAN's diverse cultural heritage while fostering regional identity as well as cultivating people's awareness of ASEAN.

6. The Community shall intensify cooperation in addressing problems associated with population growth, unemployment, environmental degradation and transboundary pollution as well as disaster management in the region to enable individual members to fully realize their development potentials and to enhance the mutual ASEAN spirit.

We hereby pledge to our peoples our resolve and commitment to bring the ASEAN Community into reality and, for this purpose, task the concerned Ministers to implement this Declaration.

Done in Bali, Indonesia, on the Seventh Day of October in The Year Two Thousand and Three.

For Brunei Darussalam

HAJI HASSANAL BOLKIAH
Sultan of Brunei Darussalam

For the
Kingdom of Cambodia

SAMDECH HUN SEN
Prime Minister

For the
Republic of Indonesia

MEGAWATI SOEKARNOPUTRI
President

For the
Lao People's Democratic Republic

BOUNNHANG VORACHITH
Prime Minister

For Malaysia

DR. MAHATHIR BIN MOHAMAD
Prime Minister

For the Union of Myanmar

GENERAL KHIN NYUNT
Prime Minister

For the
Republic of the Philippines

GLORIA MACAPAGAL-ARROYO
President

For the
Republic of Singapore

GOH CHOK TONG
Prime Minister

For the
Kingdom of Thailand

DR. THAKSIN SHINAWATRA
Prime Minister

For the
Socialist Republic of Viet Nam

PHAN VAN KHAI
Prime Minister

Appendix G
RECOMMENDATIONS OF THE HIGH-LEVEL TASK FORCE ON ASEAN ECONOMIC INTEGRATION

INTRODUCTION

1. The realization of a fully integrated economic community requires implementation of both liberalization and cooperation measures. The Task Force while focusing its recommendations relating to liberalization and facilitation measures in the area of trade in good, services and investment, acknowledges on the need to enhance cooperation and integration activities in other areas. These will involve among others, human resource development and capacity building; recognition of educational qualifications; closer consultations on macroeconomic and financial policies; trade financing measures; enhanced infrastructure and communications connectivity; development of electronic transactions through e-ASEAN; integrating industries across the region to promote regional sourcing; and enhancing private sector involvement.

ASEAN ECONOMIC COMMUNITY

2. As a step towards the realization of ASEAN Economic Community for trade in goods, services and investment, the HLTF took into account the experience of other Regional Trading Arrangements (RTAs), ASEAN's own experience, the development perspective in ASEAN and also the views contained in the following documents:

   (i) ASEAN Vision 2020, the Hanoi Plan of Action (HPA), and RIA;
   (ii) ASEAN Competitiveness Study;
   (iii) ASEAN Economic Community: Concept Paper by ISEAS; and
   (iv) ASEAN ISIS: Towards an ASEAN Economic Community.

3. The HLTF is of the view that the elements of the AEC in the area of goods, services and investment have been elaborated in ASEAN Vision 2020, HPA and RIA, and recommends that the AEC should be:

   (i) The end-goal of economic integration as outlined in the ASEAN Vision 2020;

(ii) Characterized as a single market and production base, with free flow of goods, services, investment and skilled labour, and freer flow of capital by 2020; and

(iii) Approached on a progressive basis with clear timelines by strengthening existing initiatives and building new initiatives to enhance economic integration.

RECOMMENDATIONS

4. Recognizing that not all ASEAN member countries can meet the recommended deadlines, the HLTF recommends that flexibility be allowed in its implementation to enable those member countries that are ready to proceed first.

I. CURRENT ECONOMIC COOPERATION INITIATIVES

5. The HLTF recommends that cooperation under the current economic initiatives be further strengthened in the following areas:

A. Trade in Goods
(i) By end-2004, finalize the improvement to the CEPT Scheme Rules of Origin (ROO) by:

- Making it more transparent, predictable and standardized and taking into account the best practices of other RTAs including the WTO ROO; and

- Adopting substantial transformation as alternative criteria for conferring origin status.

(ii) Ensure transparency on Non-Tariff Measures (NTMs) and eliminate those that are barriers to trade:

- Establish ASEAN Database of NTMs by mid-2004;

- Set clear criteria to identify measures that are classified as barriers to trade by mid-2005;

- Set a clear and definitive work programme for the removal of the barriers by 2005; and

- Adopt the WTO agreements on Technical Barriers to Trade; Sanitary and Phyto-Sanitary and Import Licensing Procedures and develop implementation guidelines appropriate for ASEAN by end-2004.

Customs
(i) Ensure full implementation of the Green Lane system for CEPT products at entry points of all Member Countries by 2004;

(ii) Adopt WTO agreement on Customs Valuation and develop implementation guidelines appropriate for ASEAN by end-2004;

(iii) Adopt service commitment (client charter) by ASEAN customs authorities; and

(iv) Adopt the Single Window approach including the electronic processing of trade documents at national and regional level.

Standards
(i) Accelerate the completion and implementation of the Mutual Recognition Arrangements (MRAs) for the five identified priority sectors (electrical and electronic equipment, cosmetics, pharmaceuticals, telecommunications equipment and prepared foodstuff) within 2004/2005; and other sectors with significant potential for trade;

(ii) Set specific targets for the harmonization of standards and technical regulations to trade focusing on sectors with significant trade value and those with potential for trade in the future; and

(iii) Develop ASEAN technical regulations, where possible, for national applications.

B. **Trade in Services**
(i) Set clear targets and schedules of services liberalization for each sector and each round towards achieving free flow of trade in services; and AEM to provide specific mandate in every round of services

negotiations. The end date to achieve free flow of trade in services earlier than 2020;

(ii) Accelerate services liberalization in specific sectors earlier than end-date by countries which are ready, through the application of the ASEAN-X formula;

(iii) Complete MRAs for qualifications in major professional services by 2008 to facilitate free movement of professional/skilled labour/talents in ASEAN;

(iv) Promote the use of ASEAN professional services through the establishment of a "Professional Exchange" by 2008;

(v) Recognize the AEM as the coordinator for services liberalization across all sectors; and

(vi) Each country to be represented by senior officials who are authorized to negotiate on behalf of the government.

C. **Investment**
(i) Speed up the opening of sectors currently in the sensitive list to TEL, using the ASEAN-X formula, beginning 2004;

(ii) Encourage and promote companies to relocate within ASEAN and where appropriate, special incentives should be given;

(iii) Institute a mechanism to monitor the specific activities and timelines undertaken by each country vis-à-vis their submitted planned actions/activities on annual basis;

(iv) Establish a network of ASEAN free trade zones (FTZs) so that companies could structure their manufacturing processes across different ASEAN countries to take advantage of their comparative strengths; and in the process increase intra-ASEAN trade and investment. Special marketing efforts should be undertaken for ASEAN-based companies; and

(v) Undertake more effective joint ASEAN facilitation and promotion measures and develop new sources of inward FDI, particularly from potential countries such as China, India and ROK.

D. Intellectual Property Rights (IPRs)

6. ASEAN IPR cooperation beyond trademarks and patents by including cooperation in copyrights information exchange and enforcement by 2004.

E. Capital Mobility

7. To facilitate trade and investment flows, expedite the implementation of the Roadmap for Integration of ASEAN in Finance.

II. NEW INITIATIVES AND MEASURES

Priority Integration Sectors

8. The Special Informal AEM agreed to accelerate 11 priority sectors for integration to be coordinated by the following countries.

 (i) Indonesia: Wood-Based Products and Automotives;
 (ii) Malaysia: Rubber-Based Products; Textiles and Apparels;
 (iii) Myanmar: Agro-Based Products and Fisheries;
 (iv) Philippines: Electronics;
 (v) Singapore: e-ASEAN and Healthcare; and
 (vi) Thailand: Air Travel and Tourism

9. The approach recommended for the integration of these priority sectors be premised on:

 (i) Combine the economic strengths of ASEAN Member Countries for regional advantage;

 (ii) Facilitate and promote intra-ASEAN investments;

 (iii) Improve the condition to attract and retain manufacturing and other economic activities within the region;

 (iv) Promote out-sourcing programme within ASEAN; and

 (v) Promote the development of "Made in ASEAN" products and services.

10. Roadmap should be developed for each of the priority sectors and be implemented with the active involvement of the private sector, beginning 2004.

11. Possible measures proposed for the goods sector:

    (i) Zero internal tariffs;

    (ii) Immediate removal of barriers to trade;

    (iii) Faster customs clearance and simplified customs procedures; and

    (iv) Accelerated development of MRAs and harmonization of products standards and technical regulations.

12. Integration of services sectors be implemented through:

    (i) Accelerated liberalization of these priority sectors by 2010;

    (ii) Accelerated development of MRAs; and

    (iii) Promote joint ventures and cooperation, including in third country markets.

13. Facilitate mobility of business people and tourists through:

    (i) Visa exemption for intra-ASEAN travel by ASEAN nationals by 2005

    (ii) Harmonizing the procedures for issuing visas to international travelers in ASEAN by 2004; and

    (iii) Developing ASEAN agreement to facilitate movement of business persons and skilled labour and talents by 2005.

III. INSTITUTIONAL STRENGTHENING

14. To streamline the decision-making process and ensure effective implementation of all ASEAN economic initiatives, the following measures are recommended:

    (i) Re-affirm the AEM as the coordinator of all ASEAN economic integration and cooperation issues;

(ii) Issues of policy in nature to be resolved by AEM/AFTA Council/ AIA Council;

(iii) Technical/operational issues to be resolved by SEOM and the various committees/working groups;

(iv) Decision-making process by economic bodies to be made by consensus, and where there is no consensus, ASEAN to consider other options with the objective of expediting the decision-making process.

(v) By end-2004, establish an effective system to ensure proper implementation of all economic agreements and expeditious resolution of any disputes. The new system should provide for advisory, consultative, and adjudicatory mechanisms as follows:

- Establish a legal unit within the ASEAN Secretariat;
  (Advisory — the legal unit will provide legal advice on trade disputes)

- Establish the ASEAN Consultation to Solve Trade and Investment Issues (ACT);
  (Consultative — the ACT is the ASEAN equivalent of the EU SOLVIT mechanism to provide quick resolution to operational problems)

- Establish the ASEAN Compliance Body (ACB); and
  (Adjudication — modeled after the WTO Textile Monitoring Body and make use of peer pressure)

- Enhanced ASEAN DSM to make it more practical.
  (Adjudication — amend the ASEAN DSM to ensure expeditious and legally binding decision in resolving trade disputes)

The proposed concept, elements and flow chart of the new system appear as ANNEX 1.

(vi) Enhance the capability of the ASEAN Secretariat to conduct research and analytical studies related to trade, investment and finance.

IV. OUTREACH

15. To promote better appreciation and understanding of ASEAN economic issues among business/investor community and public sector agencies, the HLTF recommends the following:

   (i) Conduct out-reach programmes annually at both national and regional level; and

   (ii) Consult regularly with private sector representatives at national and regional level to address issues of concern/interest relating to the implementation of ASEAN economic initiatives.

V. DEVELOPMENT AND TECHNICAL COOPERATION

16. The recommendations to address the development divide and accelerate economic integration of CLMV:

   (i) Expand the coverage of the AISP products; and

   (ii) Implement IAI projects through mobilization of resources from within ASEAN.

CONCLUSION

17. The HLTF recommends that a review be made after one year of its implementation and the Secretary General of ASEAN to submit an annual progress report of its implementation to the AEM.

Annex 1
MECHANISM OF THE DISPUTE SETTLEMENT SYSTEM

Advisory Mechanism

ASEAN Consultation to Solve Trade and Investment Issues (ACT)

(i) The ACT is adapted from the EU SOLVIT mechanism. It is a network of government agencies (one from each country) to allow the private sector to cut through red tape and achieve speedy resolution of operational problems encountered, thus helping to create a pro-business environment in ASEAN.

(ii) Private individuals and businesses faced with operational problems related to countries' ASEAN commitments, either at home or in other ASEAN countries, can highlight these problems to the ACT in their country (Host ACT). For problems encountered within the home country, the Host ACT will direct the problem to the appropriate government agencies, and ensure that a proposed solution is sent to the individuals/businesses within 30 calendar days.

(iii) For problems encountered in other ASEAN countries, the Host ACT will forward the problem to the other countries' ACT (Lead ACT). The Lead ACT will be responsible for directing the problem to the appropriate government agencies in its country, and ensuring that a proposed solution is sent to the individuals/businesses via the Host ACT within 30 calendar days. To minimize delays, communication between Host and Lead ACTs should be via electronic means, for instance an online database accessible to all member countries.

(iv) If the proposed solution does not resolve the problem highlighted, the private individuals/businesses can request that their government raise this issue to the other dispute settlement mechanisms described below.

ASEAN Legal Unit

(i) The ASEAN Legal Unit will be staffed by qualified lawyers specializing in trade laws employed by the ASEAN Secretariat. The unit will offer legal interpretation/ advice on potential trade dispute issues upon request from countries. The advice is purely advisory and non-binding in nature.

(ii) The ASEAN Legal Unit would play a useful role in screening out issues that are operational/technical in nature which could be resolved through bilateral consultations, rather than being surfaced to the ASEAN Compliance Monitoring Body or the Enhanced ASEAN Dispute Settlement Mechanism. The ASEAN Legal Unit will also be responsible for providing legal advice and secretariat support to the ASEAN Compliance Monitoring Body and enhanced ASEAN Dispute Settlement Mechanism.

Consultative Mechanism

ASEAN Compliance Monitoring Body (ACMB)

(i) The ACMB is modelled after the Textile Monitoring Body of the WTO, and makes use of peer adjudication, which is less legalistic and offers a speedier channel, to help countries resolve their disputes.

(ii) In cases of non-compliance by one or more ASEAN Member Country/Countries in any ASEAN economic integration agreement, ACMB members from countries not involved in the dispute will upon request, review and issue findings on the case within a stipulated timeframe. The case findings of the ACB are not legally-binding. However, any opinion pointing to non-compliance should lead to the offending ASEAN Member Country/Countries to seriously consider measures to rectify the non-compliance. Moreover the ACMB's findings would be tabled as inputs to the DSM should the case be raised to the DSM.

(iii) Subject to agreement by both Parties, Member Countries who do not wish to avail of the ACMB after going through the ACT can go directly to the ASEAN DSM panel.

(iv) AEM had earlier directed SEOM to work out a Terms of Reference for this monitoring body.

Conciliation and mediation processes

(i) Upon mutual voluntary agreement, member countries can at any time, engage in conciliation and mediation procedures to resolve their dispute before it is surfaced for adjudication at the enhanced ASEAN Dispute Settlement Mechanism.

(ii) Proceedings under these conciliation and mediation procedures, including respective positions taken by parties to the dispute during the proceedings, shall be confidential.

(iii) The ASEAN Secretary General may, acting in an ex officio capacity, offer good offices, conciliation and mediation procedures.

Enforcement Mechanism

Enhanced ASEAN Dispute Settlement Mechanism (DSM)

(i) To ensure that binding decisions can be made based solely on legal considerations, changes should be made to the procedures of the existing ASEAN DSM to depoliticize the entire process.

(ii) The enhanced ASEAN DSM would be modeled after the WTO DSM, which have already established a proven track record in resolving trade disputes. It would include the following key features: (i) having panels of three independent professionals from countries not involved in the disputes (including non-ASEAN countries) to rule on the disputes and administer the appellate process. To ensure de-politicization of the processes, ASEAN should replace the AEM with an appellate body comprising of well-qualified, independent and experienced professionals as the appeal body for the panels' decisions, and adopt the existing WTO DSM panel selection procedures, including the listing of qualified individuals who can serve as panelists and members of the appellate body (maintained by the WTO Secretariat); (ii) strict and detailed procedures and timeline governing each stage of the dispute settlement process (adopted from the WTO DSM procedure) to ensure speedy progress towards a fair outcome, and (iii) effective mechanisms, including the possibility of imposing sanctions on non-compliant countries, to ensure full implementation of the DSM rulings.

Appendix H
ASEAN SECURITY COMMUNITY PLAN OF ACTION

Introduction
Leaders at the Ninth ASEAN Summit in Bali adopted the Declaration of ASEAN Concord II (Bali Concord II), which stipulated the establishment of an ASEAN Community resting on three pillars: an ASEAN Security Community, an ASEAN Economic Community and an ASEAN Socio-Cultural Community.

These three pillars shall be developed and implemented in a parallel and balanced manner.

Recognizing the strong interconnections among political, economic and social realities, the ASEAN Security Community acknowledges the principle of comprehensive security, and commits to address the broad political, economic, social and cultural aspects of building an ASEAN Community. It is also acknowledged that political and social stability, economic prosperity, narrowed development gap, poverty alleviation and reduction of social disparity would constitute strong foundation for a sustained ASC given its subscription to the principle of comprehensive security.

The realization of an ASEAN Security Community would ensure that countries in the region live at peace with one another and with the world at large in a just, democratic and harmonious environment. The ASC would be based on shared norms and rules of good conduct in inter-state relations; effective conflict prevention and resolution mechanisms; and post-conflict peace building activities.

The ASC promotes an ASEAN-wide political and security cooperation in consonance with the ASEAN Vision 2020 rather than a defence pact, military alliance or a joint foreign policy. The ASC Plan of Action is mutually-reinforcing with bilateral cooperation between ASEAN Member Countries while recognizing the sovereign rights of the Member Countries to pursue their individual foreign policies and defence arrangements. In addressing future security challenges, ASEAN Member Countries share the responsibility for strengthening peace, stability and security of the region free from foreign military interference in any form or manifestation.

The ASC shall contribute to the further promotion of peace and security in the wider Asia Pacific region. In this regard, the ASC is open and outward looking, engaging ASEAN's friends and Dialogue Partners to promote peace and stability in the region. The ASC will reflect ASEAN's determination to move forward the stages of ASEAN Regional Forum (ARF) at a pace comfortable to all. In this regard, the ASC will strengthen ASEAN's role as the driving force in the ARF.

Since its inception in 1967, ASEAN has developed confidence and maturity to address issues of common concern as one ASEAN family. The ASC process shall therefore be progressive. This process shall be guided by well-established principles of non-interference, consensus based decision-making, national and regional resilience, respect for the national sovereignty, the renunciation of the threat or the use of force, and peaceful settlement of differences and disputes which have served as the foundation of ASEAN cooperation. ASEAN shall strengthen existing initiatives, launch new ones and set appropriate implementation frameworks.

The ASC upholds the existing ASEAN political instruments such as the Declaration on ZOPFAN, the TAC and the SEANWFZ Treaty, which shall play a pivotal role in the area of confidence building measures, preventive diplomacy and the approaches to conflict resolution. It shall abide by the UN Charter and other principles of international law.

ASEAN shall explore innovative ways to implement the Plan of Action which comprises six components, but not limited to, as follows: political development, shaping and sharing of norms, conflict prevention, conflict resolution, post-conflict peace building, and implementing mechanisms. A list of areas of activities, which is non-exhaustive, is provided to ensure a coordinated process of cooperation towards an ASEAN Security Community.

I. **Political Development**
One of the main objectives of the ASEAN Security Community as envisaged in the Bali Concord II is to bring ASEAN's political and security cooperation to a higher plane.

In working towards this objective, ASEAN Member Countries shall promote political development in support of ASEAN Leaders' shared vision and common values to achieve peace, stability, democracy and prosperity in the region. This is the highest political commitment that would serve as the basis for ASEAN political cooperation. In order to better respond to the new dynamics within the respective ASEAN Member Countries, ASEAN shall nurture such common socio-political values and principles. In this context, ASEAN Member Countries shall not condone unconstitutional and undemocratic changes of government or the use of their territory for any actions undermining peace, security and stability of other ASEAN Member Countries.

A conducive political environment will ensure continued peace, security and stability in the region, in which member countries shall rely exclusively on peaceful processes in settling intra-regional differences and disputes and consider their individual security as fundamentally linked together and bound by geographic location, common vision and objectives.

II. Shaping and Sharing of Norms

Shaping and sharing of norms aim at achieving a standard of common adherence to norms of good conduct among members of the ASEAN Community; consolidating and strengthening ASEAN's solidarity, cohesiveness and harmony (the "we feeling"); and contributing to the building of a democratic, tolerant, participatory and transparent community in Southeast Asia.

These norms setting activities shall adhere to the following fundamental principles:

1. Non-alignment;
2. Fostering of peace-oriented attitudes of ASEAN Member Countries;
3. Conflict resolution through non-violent means;
4. Renunciation of nuclear weapons and other weapons of mass destruction and avoidance of arms race in Southeast Asia; and
5. Renunciation of the threat or the use of force.

ASEAN Member Countries shall therefore engage in such activities as strengthening the ASEAN Declaration of 1967, the ZOPFAN, the TAC and the SEANWFZ regimes, developing regional legal frameworks, and establishing a Code of Conduct in the South China Sea.

III. Conflict Prevention

Based on the principles contained in the TAC, which is the key code of conduct governing relations between states and diplomatic instrument for the promotion of peace, security and stability in the region, the objectives of conflict prevention shall be:

1. To strengthen confidence and trust within the Community;
2. To mitigate tensions and prevent disputes from arising between or among member countries as well as between member countries and non-ASEAN countries; and
3. To prevent the escalation of existing disputes.

ASEAN Member Countries shall enhance security cooperation by strengthening confidence building measures; carrying out preventive diplomacy; resolving outstanding regional issues; as well as enhancing cooperation on non-traditional security issues.

IV. Conflict Resolution
It is essential that any disputes and conflicts involving ASEAN Member Countries be resolved in a peaceful way and in the spirit of promoting peace, security and stability in the region. While continuing to use national, bilateral and international mechanisms, ASEAN Member Countries shall endeavour to use the existing regional dispute settlement mechanisms and processes in the political and security areas and work towards innovative modalities including arrangements to maintain regional peace and security so as to better serve theirs as well as collective interests of all members for peace and security.

V. Post-conflict Peace Building
Post-conflict peace building seeks to create the conditions necessary for a sustainable peace in conflict-torn areas and to prevent the resurgence of conflict. It is a process involving broad-based inter-agency cooperation and coordination across a wide range of issues. ASEAN activities related to post-conflict peace building shall include the establishment of appropriate mechanisms and mobilization of resources. As an ASEAN family, members should assist each other in post-conflict peace building efforts, such as humanitarian relief assistance, reconstruction and rehabilitation.

VI. Implementing Mechanisms
To ensure the effective implementation of this Plan of Action, the following measures will be undertaken:

1. The AMM shall take necessary follow-up measures to implement this Plan of Action including consultation and coordination with other

relevant ASEAN ministerial bodies; to set up ad-hoc groups as appropriate; and to report annually the progress of implementation to the ASEAN Summit; as well as to introduce new measures and activities to strengthen the ASEAN Security Community as appropriate;
2. The AMM shall undertake overall review of progress of this Plan of Action. The AMM shall inscribe permanently an agenda item entitled "Implementation of the ASC Plan of Action" in the agenda of its meetings; and
3. The Secretary-General of ASEAN shall assist the ASEAN Chair in monitoring and reviewing the progress of implementation of this Plan of Action.

VII. Areas of Activities

To realize the ASEAN Security Community by 2020, ASEAN shall endeavour to work towards the implementation of the areas of activities in the following **Annex**. It is acknowledged that some of these activities are already ongoing and at various stages of implementation. Additional activities could also be implemented in the future. ASEAN will make every effort to promptly carry out activities which gain consensus support.

ANNEX for ASEAN Security Community Plan of Action

ACTIVITIES

I. Political Development
1. Promotion of a just, democratic and harmonious environment:
    a. Strengthening democratic institutions and popular participation;
    b. Promoting understanding and appreciation of political system, culture and history of ASEAN Member Countries;
    c. Strengthening the rule of law and judiciary systems, legal infrastructure and capacity building;
    d. Promoting free flow of information among and within ASEAN Member Countries;
    e. Enhancing good governance in public and private sectors;
    f. Strengthening effective and efficient civil services; and
    g. Preventing and combating corruption.

2. Promotion of human rights and obligations:
    a. Establishing a network among existing human rights mechanisms;

b. Protecting vulnerable groups including women, children, people with disabilities, and migrant workers; and
c. Promoting education and public awareness on human rights.

3. Promotion of people-to-people contacts:
   a. Encouraging the role of ASEAN Inter-Parliamentary Organization (AIPO) in political and security cooperation;
   b. Promoting public participation and the contribution of the ASEAN People's Assembly (APA) to the ASEAN community building;
   c. Strengthening the role of the ASEAN Foundation;
   d. Encouraging the contribution of ASEAN-ISIS to political development;
   e. Strengthening the role of the ASEAN Business Advisory Council (ABAC); and
   f. Supporting the activities of the ASEAN University Network.

II. Shaping and Sharing of Norms

1. Strengthening the TAC regime:
   a. Accession to the TAC by non-ASEAN countries; and
   b. Periodic assessment of the implementation of the TAC and exploration of ways and means for its effective implementation.

2. Working towards development of an ASEAN Charter which will *inter alia* reaffirm ASEAN's goals and principles in inter-state relations, in particular the collective responsibilities of all ASEAN Member Countries in ensuring non-aggression and respect for each other's sovereignty and territorial integrity; the promotion and protection of human rights; the maintenance of political stability, regional peace and economic progress; and the establishment of effective and efficient institutional framework for ASEAN.

3. Resolving all outstanding issues to ensure early signing of the Nuclear Weapon States to the Protocol to the SEANWFZ Treaty.

4. ASEAN Treaty on Mutual Legal Assistance (MLA) Agreement:
   a. Compilation of existing bilateral MLA Agreements among ASEAN Member Countries and between ASEAN and other countries;
   b. Identification of issues relating to the establishment of an ASEAN MLA Agreement; and
   c. Conclusion of ASEAN MLA Agreement.

5. ASEAN Extradition Treaty as envisaged by the 1976 Declaration of ASEAN Concord:
   a. Identification of ASEAN political decisions to establish Extradition Treaty and bilateral Extradition Treaties between ASEAN Member Countries; and
   b. Establishment of a working group on ASEAN Extradition Treaty under the purview of ASEAN Senior Law Officials Meeting (ASLOM).

6. Ensuring the implementation of the Declaration on the Conduct of Parties in the South China Sea (DOC) through, *inter alia*:
   a. Establishing an ASEAN–China Working Group on the Implementation of the DOC;
   b. Establishing a review mechanism on the implementation of the DOC; and
   c. Working towards the adoption of the Code of Conduct in South China Sea (COC).

7. ASEAN Convention on Counter Terrorism:
   a. Identification and analysis or assessment of documents and relevant instruments related to counter terrorism;
   b. Working towards accession to and ratification of the relevant UN conventions on counter terrorism; and
   c. Preparation, negotiation and conclusion of an ASEAN convention on counter terrorism.

III. Conflict Prevention
1. Strengthening Confidence Building Measures:
   a. Organizing and conducting regional military exchanges among high-ranking officials, military academies, and staff colleges of ASEAN Member Countries, apart from increasing bilateral visits and exchanges;
   b. Periodic publication of strategic assessments on the security environment, defence policies, and other security issues, such as Defence White Papers and equivalent documents;
   c. Working towards convening of an annual ASEAN Defence Ministers Meeting (ADMM);
   d. Promoting exchange of observers at military exercises;
   e. Establishment of an ASEAN Arms Register to be administered by

the ASEAN Secretariat, in line with a similar activity being conducted in the ARF;
   f. Utilizing military and civilian personnel in disaster relief operation;
   g. Promotion of civil-military relations; and
   h. Exploring joint development and sharing of resources.

2. Strengthening Preventive Measures:
   a. Publishing an ASEAN Members Annual Security Outlook;
   b. Voluntary briefing by ASEAN Member Countries on national security issues; and
   c. Developing an ASEAN early warning system based on existing mechanisms to prevent occurrence/escalation of conflicts.

3. Strengthening the ARF process in support of the ASEAN Security Community:
   a. ARF Unit within the ASEAN Secretariat;
   b. Enhanced role of the ARF Chair;
   c. Strengthening ASEAN's role in addressing the four overlapping issues of CBMs and Preventive Diplomacy (Enhanced role of the ARF Chair, Annual Security Outlook, Register of Experts/Eminent Persons, Voluntary Briefing on Regional Issues); and
   d. Moving the ARF to the preventive diplomacy stage and beyond (implementation of the Concept Paper on Preventive Diplomacy, establishment of an Intersessional Support Group on Preventive Diplomacy).

4. Enhancing cooperation on non-traditional security issues:
   a. Combating transnational crimes and other trans-boundary problems, including money laundering, illegal migration, smuggling and illegal trade of natural resources, trafficking in persons, drugs and precursors, as well as communicable diseases;
   b. Promoting ASEAN maritime security cooperation;
   c. Strengthening law enforcement cooperation; and
   d. Promoting cooperation on environmental issues including haze, pollution and floods.

5. Strengthening efforts in maintaining respect for territorial integrity, sovereignty and unity of member countries as stipulated in the Declaration on Principles of International Law Concerning Friendly Relations and Cooperation among States in Accordance with the Charter

of the United Nations:
   a. Strengthening cooperation on the state's obligation not to intervene in the affairs of other neighbouring states, including refraining from the use of military, political, economic or other form of coercion aimed against the political independence or territorial integrity of other neighbouring states;
   b. Enhancing cooperation among ASEAN Member Countries to prevent the organization, instigation, assistance and participation in terrorist acts in other neighbouring ASEAN Member Countries;
   c. Preventing the use of territory of any ASEAN Member Country as base for any activities against security and stability of neighbouring ASEAN Member Countries; and
   d. Strengthening cooperation to address subversive and insurgency activities aimed at neighbouring ASEAN Member Countries.

6. Strengthening cooperation to address threats and challenges posed by separatism.

IV. Conflict Resolution
1. Strengthening Dispute Settlement Mechanisms:
   a. The use of existing modes of pacific settlement of disputes such as negotiations and consultations, good offices, conciliation and mediation by all ASEAN Member Countries, or use of the High Council of the TAC as a preferred option; and
   b. If the High Council so requires, it may establish on an *ad hoc* basis an Experts Advisory Committee (EAC) or an Eminent Persons Group (EPG), which may extend assistance to the High Council to provide advice or counsel on the settlement of disputes upon request, in accordance with the Rules of Procedure of the High Council of TAC.

2. Developing regional cooperation for maintenance of peace and stability:
   a. Promoting technical cooperation with the UN and relevant regional organizations in order to benefit from their expertise and experiences;
   b. Establishing/assigning national focal points for regional cooperation for maintenance of peace and stability;
   c. Utilization of national peace keeping centres which currently exist, or are being planned, in some ASEAN Member Countries to establish regional arrangement for the maintenance of peace and stability; and

d. Establishing a network among existing ASEAN Member Countries' peace keeping centres to conduct joint planning, training, and sharing of experiences, with a view to establishing an ASEAN arrangement for the maintenance of peace and stability.

3. Developing Supporting Initiatives:
   a. Promoting exchange and cooperation among ASEAN centres of excellence on peace, and conflict management and resolution studies; and
   b. Considering the establishment of an ASEAN Institute for Peace and Reconciliation.

V. **Post-conflict Peace Building**
1. Strengthening ASEAN humanitarian assistance:
   a. Providing safe havens in conflict areas;
   b. Ensuring the delivery of basic services or assistance to victims of conflict;
   c. Orderly repatriation of refugees/displaced persons and resettlement of internally displaced persons;
   d. Ensuring safety of humanitarian relief assistance workers;
   e. Promoting the role of humanitarian relief assistance organizations;
   f. Considering the establishment of an ASEAN Humanitarian Assistance Centre; and
   g. Intensifying cooperation with the United Nations and other organizations/donor countries.

2. Developing cooperation in post-conflict reconstruction and rehabilitation in affected areas by:
   a. Undertaking human resources development and capacity building;
   b. Assisting in institutional building and promoting popular participation;
   c. Reducing inter-communal tensions through educational exchanges and curriculum reform; and
   d. Increasing cooperation in reconciliation and promotion of a culture of peace.

3. Establishing a mechanism to mobilize necessary resources to facilitate post-conflict peace building (e.g. a Stability Fund), including through cooperation with donor countries and international institutions.

Appendix I

THE ASEAN SOCIO-CULTURAL COMMUNITY (ASCC) PLAN OF ACTION

INTRODUCTION

The Vision of an ASEAN Socio-Cultural Community

1. Embedded in ASEAN Vision 2020, Declaration of ASEAN Concord I (1976), Declaration of ASEAN Concord II (2003) and the Hanoi Plan of Action (HPA) is ASEAN's goal of a community of cohesive, equitable and harmonious societies, bound together in solidarity for deeper understanding and cooperation. Its key features are:

- Equitable access to opportunities will be universal — rising above the barriers of religion, race, language, gender and social and cultural background;
- Human potentials are nurtured to the fullest, so that all individuals can participate meaningfully in a competitive world in a manner that gives paramount importance to their welfare and dignity;
- Norms of social and distributive justice are upheld by addressing issues of poverty and equity, and special care is given to vulnerable groups — children, youth, women, the elderly, and persons with disabilities — who could be the subject of abuse, neglect and discrimination;
- The environment and natural resources are protected and managed to sustain development and as a legacy for future generations;
- Civil society is engaged in providing inputs for policy choices;
- People are healthy in mind and body and living in harmony in safe environments; and
- ASEAN citizens interact in a community conscious of its ties of history, aware of its cultural heritage and bound by a common regional identity.

The Imperatives of the ASEAN Socio-Cultural Community

2. The ASCC reflects ASEAN's social agenda that is focused on poverty eradication and human development. It is linked inextricably with the economic and security pillars of the ASEAN Community. Social inequities can threaten economic development and in turn undermine

political regimes. Economic instability can exacerbate poverty, unemployment, hunger, illness and disease. Social instability can emerge from environmental scarcity or the inequitable distribution among stakeholders of the use of environmental assets. Failure to address these critical and persistent social issues can further cause both economic and political dislocations.

3. The ASCC will evolve amidst profound changes that are taking place in ASEAN's social landscape. These include: (i) the rise of consumerism and lifestyle changes resulting from rapid economic growth; (ii) increased personal mobility resulting from advances in infrastructure and more open regimes; (iii) transformation of the family roles and structures, with implications on the care of children and the elderly; (iv) the potential of information technology to enhance the speed and quality of learning and development of human skills, thus narrowing the digital divide; (v) the rapid pace of urbanization and its impact on employment and the delivery of basic services; (vi) shifts in the labour market resulting from economic integration; and (vii) unsustainable exploitation of natural resources in the process of meeting developmental needs.

The ASEAN Socio-Cultural Community Plan of Action

4. This ASCC Plan of Action (PoA) will have four core elements:
   - Building a community of caring societies to address issues of poverty, equity and human development;
   - Managing the social impact of economic integration by building a competitive human resource base and adequate systems of social protection;
   - Enhancing environmental sustainability and sound environmental governance; and
   - Strengthening the foundations of regional social cohesion towards an ASEAN Community in 2020.

Building a Community of Caring Societies

5. Poverty alleviation, equity and human development lie at the very core of a strong and resilient ASEAN Socio-Cultural Community. Poverty reduction is fundamental to the development of the human potential, allowing people to participate fully in the mainstream of economic life and contribute to society. A community of caring societies in ASEAN can enhance the potential for production, consumption and wealth

creation, thus ensuring the benefits from economic integration. ASEAN Member Countries will therefore strive, individually and collectively, to build caring societies concerned with, committed to, and capable of addressing fundamental issues of poverty, equity and human development. Governments, private sector and civil society will work in partnership to address these concerns.

6. Under the ASCC PoA, the goal of building an ASEAN community of caring societies will address the following concerns:

- Accelerating the goal of poverty reduction within the framework of the Millennium Development Goals (MDGs);
- Facilitating universal access to education for increased employability, good citizenship, and as a means of empowerment and life-long learning;
- Promoting the welfare of children by safeguarding their rights, ensuring their survival and full development, and protecting them from abuse, neglect and violence;
- Promoting improved standards and access to education through networking and institutional collaboration, using existing regional bodies;
- Enabling youth to have a better future by developing their leadership skills, entrepreneurship, and technical and vocational abilities;
- Promoting equitable participation of women in the development process by eliminating all forms of discrimination against them;
- Ensuring that the elderly are adequately cared for by promoting community-based support systems to supplement the role of the family as primary caregiver;
- Augmenting and supporting the efforts of sectoral bodies to prevent and combat human trafficking, particularly in women and children, through comprehensive policies and measures;
- Strengthening the system of social welfare through the enhancement of national capacities in responding to emerging social issues;
- Promoting health and nutrition, including through advocacy on health-related issues and healthy lifestyles;
- Preventing the spread of HIV/AIDS and other infectious diseases (including SARS and Avian influenza) through, among others, sharing of experiences and best practices and systems of surveillance;
- Ensuring access to safe, quality and affordable medicines by building ASEAN capacity and competitiveness in pharmaceutical as well as

traditional medicines and complementary and alternative medicines;
- Enhancing food security and safety as a fundamental requirement of human security;
- Ensuring a drug-free ASEAN by 2015 through community-based drug prevention, treatment and control of drug abuse in parallel with eliminating drug-trafficking and illicit drug supply through law enforcement and alternative development for the sustainability of drug control; and
- Promoting a culture of science and technology and enhancing cooperation in the utilization of appropriate applied science and technology in socio-economic activities to improve social well-being;
- Establishing efficient and well-functioning regional mechanisms for disaster prevention and relief that are fully compatible with global disaster management systems.

Managing the Social Impact of Economic Integration

7. ASEAN Member Countries, as a community of caring societies, are committed individually and collectively, to address the impact of economic integration to minimize its social costs and ensure its benefits. Domestic policy adjustments and emerging regional production arrangements from economic integration will have profound social impact that will be felt mostly in the labour market.

8. To manage the social impact, the following key goals will be pursued under the ASCC PoA:

- Promoting human resource development to build a competitive labour force, through, among others, closer cooperation among existing regional centres in the area of education;
- Promoting an efficient labour market through mutual skills recognition arrangements to enhance regional mobility so that ASEAN's workforce are prepared for and benefit from economic integration; such efforts would enable labour markets to operate efficiently with appropriate matching of jobs and skills;
- Strengthening systems of social protection at the national level and working towards adoption of appropriate measures at the regional level to provide a minimum uniform coverage for skilled workers in the region;
- Addressing the impact of liberalization in the health sector to meet the needs of ASEAN; and

- Promoting joint certification and accreditation of science and technology at the regional level to improve science and technology competence of ASEAN's human resources.

Enhancing Environmental Sustainability

9. A clean and green ASEAN, with fully developed mechanisms for environmental governance, is both a shared goal and responsibility of ASEAN Member Countries. ASEAN commitments to the Johannesburg Plan of Implementation of the World Summit for Sustainable Development (WSSD) have provided the framework for ASEAN cooperation on the environment which currently focuses on ten priority areas: (i) global environmental issues: (ii) land and forest fires and transboundary haze pollution; (iii) coastal and marine environment; (iv) sustainable forest management; (v) sustainable management of natural parks and protected areas; (vi) freshwater resources; (vii) public awareness and environmental education; (viii) promotion of environmentally sound technologies and cleaner production; (ix) urban environmental management and governance; and (x) sustainable monitoring and reporting, and database harmonization.

10. Under the ASCC PoA, the following goals for promoting environmental sustainability will be pursued:

- Building national capacities to address issues and commitments to multilateral environmental agreements through awareness raising and informed policy choices;
- Effectively managing transboundary haze in accordance with the ASEAN Agreement on Transboundary Haze Pollution;
- Promoting the sustainable use of ASEAN's coastal and marine environment as a source of food supply and natural heritage;
- Conserving ASEAN's rich biological diversity and the fair and equitable sharing of the benefits from these biological and genetic resources;
- Promoting the sustainable management of forest resources and conserving critical ecosystems through the eradication of unsustainable practices and related activities, as well as strengthening preservation and management of ASEAN Heritage Parks;
- Promoting the sustainability of water resources to ensure adequate and quality water supply to meet ASEAN health and food needs;
- Promoting environmental education with the view to developing ASEAN citizens who are environmentally conscious;

- Promoting environmentally-sound technologies in partnership with the private sector;
- Ensuring quality living standards in ASEAN cities and urban areas;
- Augmenting and supporting the efforts of the ASEAN Economic Community through the energy sector in developing alternative fuels in order to prevent environmental devastation and resource exhaustion; and
- Promoting environmentally sound and socially responsible mineral development practices in the sustainable management and optimum utilization of mineral resources.

Strengthening the Foundations of Regional Social Cohesion

11. With globalization, many of the region's traditional societies, with their cherished cultural norms and practices, are facing new challenges .As ASEAN continues in its community-building efforts, the concern is how to fulfill its aspirations for progress and prosperity while at the same time preserving its rich cultural heritage. Thus, the ASEAN Community envisaged to emerge from regional integration by 2020 is where people, amidst the diversity of their historical and cultural experience, are conscious of a common regional identity. This sense of regional identity and solidarity will have been built on years of cumulative interaction in all facets of social and economic life and at all levels — communities, governments and civil society.

12. Under the ASCC PoA, the goal of creating an ASEAN identity involves:

- Mainstreaming the promotion of ASEAN awareness, regional identity and values in national communications plans, educational curricula, people-to-people contact mainly through culture, arts and sports, especially among the youth, and the promotion of ASEAN languages learning through scholarships and exchanges of linguists;
- Preserving and promoting ASEAN cultural heritage and living traditions, as a vehicle to better understand the link between culture and development, and as a source of inspiration for future endeavours;
- Fostering dialogues among civilizations, cultures and religions as a means to foster better understanding, build confidence, and address threats to peace and security; and
- Promoting ASEAN's standing in the international community.

Implementation Modalities

13. Specific measures envisaged under each of the four elements of the ASCC PoA are in **Appendix A**. These measures will be translated into more concrete projects and activities in the Vientiane Action Programme (VAP) covering the medium-term period 2004-2010. In general, ASCC activities fall into three categories: (i) nationally-driven initiatives: (ii) regional activities that enhance or complement national initiatives through sharing of experiences, information and knowledge; establishment of regional networks; and joint regional approaches (e.g. the development of regional work programmes); and (iii) regional activities that involved setting up of regional mechanisms or standards.

14. For nationally-driven initiatives, ASEAN Member Countries shall prepare individual action plans for the period 2005-2010 consistent with their respective national policies and development priorities, and taking into account implementation capacity, including the availability of budgetary resources. Peer review and monitoring of these individual action plans will be done at the level of the relevant ASEAN body, consolidated by the ASEAN Secretariat, and reflected in the Secretary-General's report card to the ASEAN Summit.

15. The AMM shall take necessary follow-up measures to implement this Plan of Action including consultation and coordination with other relevant ASEAN Ministerial bodies; setting up ad-hoc groups as appropriate; reporting annually the progress of implementation to the ASEAN Summit; as well as introducing new measures and activities to strengthen the ASEAN Socio-Cultural Community as appropriate.

16. Self-reliance, shared responsibility and ownership are the principles that will guide the implementation of ASCC projects. The discipline of mainstreaming regional goals and commitments into the national plans and priorities will be of paramount importance in order to secure the resources required for implementation. Regional advocacy can provide the leverage to help drive national level actions and secure the necessary budget resources.

17. For regional level activities, particular attention will be given to activities that are best achieved through regional cooperation because of resulting economies of scale, value-added, or strategic interests. These activities will

be implemented primarily through the relevant ASEAN bodies or through the ASEAN Secretariat.

18. Implementing the ASCC PoA will require intensive and sustained capacity building at the national and regional levels in a wide range of areas. Active participation of various stakeholders in ASCC activities will also be encouraged to draw from their wealth of expertize and experience and to promote a strong sense of commitment and ownership of projects and activities. Building region-wide networks of NGOs, training centres, academic institutions and other ASEAN organizations will gradually weave into the fabric of the ASEAN Community and help to strengthen social cohesion.

19. Mobilization of resources will remain to be a key challenge for implementing various activities under the ASCC PoA. Resource mobilization, however, should increasingly be viewed as a process of mobilizing national, regional and external resources — intellectual, technical and financial — in support of ASEAN priorities.

20. Finally, the ASEAN Foundation, with the full support of the Member Countries, should play a more active role in supporting the implementation of the ASCC PoA. Activities where the ASEAN Foundation could play an active role include: promoting access to ICT resources of differently advantaged groups (youth, women, persons with disabilities, and rural communities); promoting ASEAN awareness through language training and mass media; and youth exchange activities (such as through volunteer programmes and youth camps) with the view to facilitating greater awareness among ASEAN youth of the region's vision of a cohesive community of caring societies.

21. To realize the ASEAN Socio-Cultural Community by 2020, ASEAN shall endeavour to work towards the implementation of the areas of activities in the following Appendix. It is acknowledged that some of these activities are already ongoing and at various stages of implementation. Additional activities could also be implemented in the future. ASEAN will make every effort to promptly carry out activities, which gain consensus support.

Appendix A for ASEAN Socio-Cultural Community (ASCC) Plan of Action

Specific Measures

I. **Building a Community of Caring Societies**
   a) Implement an "MDG Plus" initiative to accelerate poverty reduction in ASEAN;
   b) Facilitate universal access to education for vulnerable groups (youth, women, persons with disabilities) to obtain the skills and knowledge necessary for gainful employment and meaningful participation in society;
   c) Strengthen educational networks and institutional collaboration to improve standards of, and access to, education;
   d) Ensure a better future for children by safeguarding their rights, ensuring their survival and development, and protecting them from abuse, neglect and violence;
   e) Create enabling environments to prepare the youth for their future role as ASEAN citizens equipped with the necessary skills in leadership, entrepreneurship, and technical and vocational abilities;
   f) Promote the equitable and effective participation of women in all fields both as agents and beneficiaries of development;
   g) Promote community-based support systems for the elderly to supplement the role of families as primary caregiver and to build the capacity of health care professionals to address the needs of the elderly;
   h) Ensure access of persons with disabilities to opportunities and protection against all forms of discrimination;
   i) Strengthen social welfare mechanisms to make them more responsive to emerging social issues resulting from globalization as well as demographic shifts;
   j) Strengthen regional mechanisms and networks for combating human trafficking;
   k) Ensure a healthy ASEAN Community living in harmony and safe environments;
   l) Promote an enabling environment for the prevention of HIV/AIDS and for the comprehensive treatment, care and support for people living with HIV/AIDS in ASEAN;

m) Enhance the effectiveness of regional surveillance, preparedness, early warning, and response to emerging and resurging infectious diseases;
n) Ensure access to safe, quality and affordable medicines by building ASEAN capacity and competitiveness in pharmaceuticals as well as traditional medicines/complementary and alternative medicines;
o) Promote an enabling environment that allows ASEAN citizens to make healthy lifestyle choices accessible, affordable and sustainable and consistent with their views, beliefs, and culture in supportive environments;
p) Strengthen food security by enhancing stability in food production and supply and protect the region against fluctuations in production of basic commodities;
q) Strengthen food safety systems to ensure the protection of consumers' health by increasing the level of credibility and competency of regulatory authorities, and enhancing industry and consumer awareness and participation in food safety;
r) Promote activities related to community-based drug prevention aimed at families, schools and youth through publications, campaigns and training;
s) Strengthen cooperation with the private sector, in creating a science and technology community in the region;
t) Promote applied science and technology in socio-economic activities to improve social well-being; and
u) Establish efficient and well-functioning regional mechanisms for disaster prevention and management, including a coordinated response action plan in ASEAN and a network of training institutes.

II. **Managing the Social Impact of Economic Integration**
a) Support the efforts of the ASEAN Economic Community to facilitate the movement of professional and skilled persons, including mutual skills recognition arrangements for qualification in professional services to realize regional economic integration in ASEAN;
b) Develop a well-prepared labour force in ASEAN that would benefit from and cope with the challenges of regional economic integration;
c) Establish a technologically competitive ASEAN, competent in strategic and enabling technologies, with an adequate pool of technically trained manpower, strong networks of scientific and technical institutions and centres of excellence;
d) Strengthen systems of social protection at the national level and work towards adoption of appropriate measures at the regional level to

provide a minimum uniform coverage for skilled workers in the region;
e) Promote sound industrial relations, industrial harmony, high productivity and social practice through tripartite cooperation;
f) Secure the benefits of trade liberalization in healthcare services in terms of increased availability and better accessibility to quality and affordable health-related products and services;
g) Enhance the competitiveness of ASEAN health and related industries;
h) Strengthen regional training on management of innovation and technology, and establish a mechanism for its regional certification and accreditation; and
i) Consider the establishment of centres for training and research to support the development of human resources and institutional capacity in regional as well as international cooperation.

III. Enhancing Environmental Sustainability

a) Effectively address global environmental concerns by building national capacities to address issues and commitments to multilateral environmental agreements through awareness-raising and informed policy choices;
b) Effectively manage transboundary haze pollution resulting from land and/or forest fires through concerted national efforts and intensified regional action and international cooperation in accordance with the provisions of the ASEAN Agreement on Transboundary Haze Pollution (the Haze Agreement), including the operationalization of the ASEAN Centre for Transboundary Haze Pollution Control and the ASEAN Haze Fund;
c) Promote the sustainable use of ASEAN's coastal and marine environment through the implementation of the ASEAN criteria for marine waters, and marine heritage and protected areas;
d) Ensure the conservation of ASEAN's rich biological diversity through the implementation of the ASEAN Framework Agreement on Access to, and Equitable Sharing of Genetic and Biological Resources (expected to be concluded in 2004);
e) Promote the sustainable management of forest resources, which include protection of forests in an ecologically sound and integrated manner by developing and adopting common criteria for sustainable forest management in ASEAN, and eradicating unsustainable practices and related activities;

f) Promote the preservation of ASEAN Heritage Parks through coordinated systems of management;
g) Promote sustainability of water resources to ensure sufficient water quantity of acceptable quality to meet the needs of ASEAN in terms of health, food security and environmental sustainability through among others, the promotion of integrated river basin management and awareness promotion;
h) Promote environmental education through formal and non-formal education systems, capacity building and networking;
i) Promote environmentally-sound technologies in active partnership with the business sector through innovative financial mechanisms and labelling schemes;
j) Promote quality living standards in ASEAN cities/urban areas by achieving standards for environmental pollution reduction, including ensuring good ambient air and water quality, and minimum solid waste disposal;
k) Establish parameters for harmonizing environmental policies, legislation, regulations, standards and databases, and preparing regular state of the environment reports; and
l) Pursue joint research in developing alternative fuels in order to prevent environmental devastation and resource exhaustion.

IV. **Strengthening the Foundations of Regional Social Cohesion**
a) Promote ASEAN awareness with the ultimate goal of fostering an ASEAN regional identity by promoting interactions and exchanges among artists, writers, media practitioners, scholars, students, cultural entrepreneurs, professionals, experts in culture and sports and others;
b) Promote people-to-people contact, especially among the youth through youth volunteer programmes and youth camps;
c) Promote ASEAN languages learning through scholarships and exchange of linguists;
d) Coordinate efforts for the documentation, preservation and safeguarding of national and regional treasures and other properties, antiquities, and works of historic, archaeological, anthropological and scientific significance;
e) Enhance ASEAN cooperation in culture and information to formulate and implement effective and efficient programmes in a concerted manner in order to promote the rich and vast cultures of ASEAN;

f) Promote confidence-building at the national and regional levels by promoting the learning of core values, customs and traditions and integrating multiple perspectives on civilizations through regular dialogue mechanisms; and
g) Promote an image of unity, stability and dynamism of ASEAN by strengthening contacts with mass media, the international fora and other channels of communication.

INTERVIEWS

Interviewee	Position at Time of Interview	Place	Date
Abdullah Badawi	Prime Minister, Malaysia	Putrajaya	3 November 2004
Acharya, Amitav	Deputy Director, IDSS	Singapore, Paris	18 August, 30 September 2003
Ajit Singh	Former ASEAN Secretary-General	Singapore	4 June 2004
Alatas, Ali	Former Foreign Minister, Indonesia	Jakarta	21 November 2003
Anwar, Dewi Fortuna	Scholar, former Presidential Adviser	Singapore, Paris	9 July, 2–3 October 2003
Anwar, Yos Rizal	Business executive	Paris	3 October 2003
Aye Lwin	Former ASEAN Dir.-Gen., Myanmar	Yangon	25 July 2004
Bounkert Sangsomsak	Deputy Foreign Minister, Lao PDR	Vientiane	23 August 2004
Carlos, Meneleo	Business executive	Metro Manila	4 December 2003
Castle, James	Consultant	Jakarta	9 October 2003

Interviewee	Position at Time of Interview	Place	Date
Cham Prasidh	Commerce Minister, Cambodia	Phnom Penh	12 May 2003
Cheah Sin Liang	Ministry of Trade & Industry, Singapore	Singapore	5 May 2005
Chem Widhya	Perm. Sec., MFAIC, Cambodia	Phnom Penh	23, 24 and 28 June 2003
Chin, David	Dir-Gen, Ministry of Trade and Industry	Singapore	24 May 2005
Cho Kah Sin	Asst. Director, ASEAN Secretariat	Jakarta	8 October 2003
Chua, Reginald	Editor, *Asian Wall Street Journal*	Hong Kong	12 June 2004
Chua, Robert	Director, MFA, Singapore	Singapore	20 October 2004
Custodio, Edsel	Foreign Affairs Undersec., Philippines	Metro Manila	7 October 2004
Dhanabalan, S.	Banker, former Foreign Minister	Singapore	18 August 2003
Flores, Jamil Maidan	Adviser, DFA, Indonesia	Singapore	15 July 2004
Fuzi Hj. Abdul Razak	Secretary-General, MFA, Malaysia	Putrajaya	2 November 2004
Goh Chok Tong	Prime Minister, Singapore	Singapore	13 October 2003
Gomes, Ana	Former Ambassador, Portugal	Hanoi	20–21 October 2003
Hadi Soesastro et al.	Center for Strategic and International Studies	Jakarta	8 October 2003
Hamid Albar	Foreign Minister, Malaysia	Putrajaya	2 November 2004
Hasjim Djalal	Former Ambassador, Indonesia	Jakarta	21 November 2003
Hor Namhong	Foreign Minister, Cambodia	Phnom Penh	27 June 2003

Interviews

Interviewee	Position at Time of Interview	Place	Date
Jawhar Hassan, M.	Director-General, ISIS-Malaysia	Kuala Lumpur	3 November 2004
Jayakumar, S.	Foreign Minister, Singapore	Singapore	19 August 2003
Kao Kim Hourn	Foreign Ministry Adviser, Cambodia	Phnom Penh	May 2003
Kavi Chongkittavorn	Journalist	Bangkok	1 June 2004
Khin Maung Win	Deputy Foreign Minister, Myanmar	Yangon	26 July 2004
Khin Nyunt	Prime Minister, Myanmar	Yangon	26 July 2004
Koh, Tommy	Adviser, MFA, Singapore	Singapore	27 January 2004
Kwa Chong Guan	Scholar, IDSS	Phnom Penh	25 May 2003
Lee Chiong Giam	Deputy Perm. Sec., MFA, Singapore	Singapore	20 October 2004
Lee Kuan Yew	Senior Minister, Singapore	Singapore	18 August 2003
Letchumanan, Raman	Asst. Director, ASEAN Secretariat	Jakarta	3 December 2004
Luu Doan Huynh	Fellow, Institute of Intl. Relations	Hanoi	20 October 2003
Mahathir Mohamad	Former Prime Minister, Malaysia	Kuala Lumpur	2 November 2004
Mathews, Verghese	Singapore Ambassador to Cambodia	Phnom Penh	26 June 2003
Moe Thuzar	Asst. Director, ASEAN Secretariat	Jakarta	3 December 2004
Mya Than	Economist, Chulalongkorn University	Singapore	22 December 2003
Narongchai Akrasanee	Business executive	Bangkok	1 June 2004
Nathan, S. R.	President, Singapore	Singapore	14 October 2003
Nguyen Anh Tuan	Foreign Investment Agency, Vietnam	Hanoi	19 May 2005

Interviewee	Position at Time of Interview	Place	Date
Nguyen Dinh Cung	Central Institute for Economic Mgmt.	Hanoi	20 May 2005
Nitisastro, Widjojo	Former Coor. Minister, Indonesia	Jakarta	20 November 2003
Noordin Azhari	Director, ASEAN Secretariat	Singapore, Jakarta	4 June, 3 December 2004
Norodom Sihanouk	King, Cambodia	Phnom Penh	10 December 2003
Norodom Sirivudh	Sec.-Gen., FUNCINPEC	Phnom Penh	7 June 2003
Ohn Gyaw	Former Foreign Minister, Myanmar	Yangon	25 July 2004
Omi Shigeru	Regional Director, WHO	Manila	8 October 2004
Ong Keng Yong	ASEAN Secretary-General	Jakarta	4 December 2004
Ong, Romualdo A.	Former SOM Leader, Philippines	Metro Manila	30 December 2004
Pan Sorasak	Undersecretary of State, Cambodia	Phnom Penh	29 May 2003
Parameswaran, N.	High Commissioner of Malaysia	Singapore	10 August 2004
Paterno, Vicente T.	Former Min. of Industry, Philippines	Metro Manila	4 August 2003
Petrie, Charles	UNDP Resident Representative	Yangon	26 July 2004
Pham The Vinh	Asst. Director, ASEAN Secretariat	Jakarta	8 October 2003
Phongsavath Boupha	Vice Foreign Minister, Lao PDR	Vientiane	24 August 2004
Pich Rithi	Ministry of Commerce, Cambodia	Phnom Penh	19 June 2003
Pola Singh	Senior Officer, ASEAN Secretariat	Jakarta	3 December 2004

Interviews

Interviewee	Position at Time of Interview	Place	Date
Pracha Guna-Kasem	Adviser to the Prime Minister, Thailand	Bangkok	2 June 2004
Ramos-Horta, Jose	Foreign Minister, Timor Leste	Jakarta	29 June 2004
Ridzwan Dzafir	Former Dir.-Gen., TDB, Singapore	Singapore	19 August 2003
Sarasin Viraphol	Business executive	Singapore	15 January 2004
Sastrohandoyo, Wiryono	Former Dir.-Gen., DFA, Indonesia	Jakarta	6 October 2003
Sayakane Sisouvong	ASEAN Dir.-Gen., MFA, Lao PDR	Vientiane	23 August 2004
Schwarz, Adam	Consultant	Singapore	22 August 2003
Siregar, Arifin	Former Minister, Indonesia	Jakarta	9 October 2003
Somsavat Lengsavad	Dep. Prime Minister, For. Min., Laos	Vientiane	23 August 2004
Soulivong Daravong	Minister of Commerce, Lao PDR	Vientiane	24 August 2004
Steinberg, David I.	Professor	Yangon	25 July 2004
Sunoto, Dhannanjaya	Director, ASEAN Secretariat	Jakarta	2 December 2004
Surin Pitsuwan	Former Foreign Minister, Thailand	Paris	8 July 2003
Suryadinata, Leo	Scholar, ISEAS	Singapore	14 July 2004
Suthad Setboonsaarng	Consultant, former ASEAN DSG	Bangkok	2 June 2004
Sutresna, Nana	Presidential Envoy, Indonesia	Jakarta	21 November 2003
Tan Chin Tiong	Perm. Secretary, MFA, Singapore	Singapore	22 August 2003
Teh, Robert	WTO officer; former Dir., ASEAN Sec.	Geneva	4 October 2004
Teo, Eric	Consultant	Phnom Penh	26 May 2003

Interviewee	Position at Time of Interview	Place	Date
Thanat Khoman	Former Foreign Minister, Thailand	Bangkok	1 June 2004
Tin Maung Maung Than	Scholar, ISEAS	Singapore	22 December 2003
Tin Winn	Min. for Int'l. Econ. Coop., Myanmar	Yangon	26 July 2004
Tongzon, Jose	Professor, National Univ. of Singapore	Singapore	1 August 2004
Tran Dong Phuong	Dir.-Gen., Ministry of Trade, Vietnam	Hanoi	19 May 2005
Trinh Quang Thanh	Dir.-Gen., Institute of Intl. Relations	Hanoi	20 October 2003
Trisulo, Bambang	Business executive	Jakarta	9 October 2003
Ung Huot	Senior Minister, Cambodia	Phnom Penh	27 May 2003
Vatikiotis, Michael	Editor, *Far Eastern Economic Review*	Hong Kong	15 June 2004
Virata, Cesar E.A.	Former Prime Minister, Philippines	Metro Manila	1 August 2003
Vriens, Hans	Consultant	Jakarta	8 October 2003
Vu Khoan	Deputy Prime Minister, Vietnam	Hanoi	21 October 2003
Wain, Barry	Correspondent, AWSJ	Singapore	28 October 2004
Wanandi, Jusuf	Chairman, CSIS Indonesia	Singapore	7 and 8 July 2003
Win Aung	Foreign Minister, Myanmar	Yangon	26 July 2004
Wisnumurti, Nugroho	Former Dir.-Gen., DFA, Indonesia	Singapore	30 August 2004
Worapot Manupipatpong	Director, ASEAN Secretariat	Metro Manila	30 July 2003
Yap, Wendy	Senior Officer, ASEAN Secretariat	Jakarta	8 October 2003

Interviewee	Position at Time of Interview	Place	Date
Yee, Raymond	Consultant; former officer, ASEAN	Singapore	19 August 2003
Yeo Yong Boon, George	Trade and Industry Minister, Singapore	Singapore	14 October 2003
Zainal Abidin Sulong	Chairman, MIDA	Kuala Lumpur	3 November 2004

INDEX

A
Abdul Razak, Tun, 1, 47, 463
Abdullah Badawi, 57, 114, 163, 271, 288
Abdul Rahman, Tunku, 19, 165
Abdur Chowdhury, 101
Aceh, 25
Acharya, Amitav, 52, 463
ADB-ASEAN study, 114
ADB's Greater Mekong Sub-Region programme, 74
Adam Malik, 1, 27, 162, 257
Adisai Bodharamik, 198
Advisory Committee on Policy Studies, 23
African Nuclear Weapons-Free Zone, 169
African Union
    Constitutive Act, 51, 86, 88
African Union Commission, 88
AFTA-CER Closer Economic Partnership, 319
Agenda for Greater Economic Integration, 225
Agreement for Seismic Undertaking for Certain Areas in the South China Sea by and Between China National Offshore Oil Corporation and Philippine National Oil Company, 188
Agreement on Information Exchange and Establishment of Communication Procedures, 201
Agreement on the Common Effective Preferential Tariff (CEPT) Scheme, 16, 53, 224, 225, 402–10
    consultations, 408
    definitions, 403, 404
    emergency, measures, 407
    exceptions, 409
    final provisions, 409
    general provisions, of, 404
    institutional arrangements, 408
    other provisions, 406, 407
    products covered, 405
    reason for certain countries to join ASEAN, 55
    schedule of tariff reduction, 405, 406
Agreement on Harmonized Regulatory Regime for Electrical and Electronic Equipment, 237
agreement on services, elimination of discriminatory practices, 231
agro-based products, 346
air transport, 346
Ajit Singh, 463
Al-Qaeda, 200
Ali Alatas, 13, 59, 60, 126, 163, 357, 463
Amitav Archarya, 12, 52, 463
Anand Panyarachun, 29, 223
Annual Security Outlook, 194
anti-terrorism measures, 279
Anwar, Dewi Fortuna, 8, 9, 125, 463

Anwar, Yos Rizal, 463
APEC Economic Leaders' Meeting, 328
apparel, 346
Aquino, Corazon, 166
ARF Security Policy Conference, 279
ASEAN+3, 24, 29, 37, 104, 202–205, 264–69
 finance ministers, 104, 105, 304
 ministerial meetings hosted by Myanmar, 143
 ministers of health and agriculture, 120
 origins, 265, 266
ASEAN+3 Emerging Infectious Diseases Programme, 120
ASEAN+3 process, 257, 290
ASEAN+3 Summits, 270
ASEAN Agreement on Transboundary Haze Pollution, 17, 31, 109, 113, 239
ASEAN at Crossroads, 416–21
ASEAN Australia Development Cooperation Programme, 311
ASEAN Centre for Energy, 33
ASEAN Chambers of Commerce, 220
ASEAN Charter, 18, 253, 381–84
ASEAN Community, 337
 existence of, 342–70
 long term endeavour, 250
ASEAN Competitiveness Study, 34
 McKinsey & Co., 24
ASEAN Competitiveness Study, 235, 247
ASEAN Compliance Monitoring Body (ACMB), 438
ASEAN Consultative Committee on Standards and Quality, 326
ASEAN Cooperation Plan on Transboundary Pollution, 111
ASEAN countries, 242
 frequent consultations, 103
 competitiveness, 287
 diversity of, 213
 lack of interests in AIPs, 218
 main markets for exports, 213
ASEAN Cultural Fund, 378
ASEAN Customs Declaration Document, 348
ASEAN Customs Valuation Guide, 234

ASEAN customs union, 354, 355
ASEAN Declaration, 3, 8, 27, 41, 87, 118, 161, 167, 201, 212, 309–91
 no conditions for membership, 52
ASEAN Declaration on the South China Sea, 184
ASEAN Defence Ministers, 205, 206
ASEAN Deputy Secretary-General, 21
ASEAN Dialogue Partners, 235, 338
ASEAN dialogue system, 257
ASEAN Director-General, 379
ASEAN DSM Fund, 33
ASEAN economic cooperation, 163
ASEAN Economic Community (AEC), 24, 30, 67, 233, 251, 252, 344, 345, 347, 348, 349, 351, 425, 426, 429
 High-Level Task Force, 344
ASEAN Economic Cooperation for the 1990s, study on, 16
ASEAN Economic Ministers (AEM), 74, 214, 215, 221, 233, 318, 326, 353, 354
 central role, 330
 framework of technical cooperation, 303
 joint statement, 300
 regular consultations, 143
ASEAN economies
 integration, 203
ASEAN finance ministers, 102
 meeting outside regular forum, 101
 regular consultations, 103
ASEAN Foundation, 378, 379
ASEAN foreign ministers, 141
 invitation to Japanese counterparts, 260
 protocol on restructuring Secretariat, 22
 retreats, 96
ASEAN forums, 120
ASEAN Framework Agreement for the Integration of Priority Sectors, 240
ASEAN Framework Agreement on the Facilitation of Goods in Transit, 18
ASEAN Framework Agreement on Services, 17, 231, 242
ASEAN Free Trade Area (AFTA), 16, 68, 69, 220, 222–31, 253, 418
 establishment of, 54
 implementation, 21, 105

Index 473

period before, 213–22
tariff-cutting goals, 227
ASEAN Fund
   contribution of member state, 33
ASEAN Harmonized Tariff Nomenclatures
   system (AHTN), 234, 343, 351
ASEAN Highway Network, 237, 246
ASEAN ICT Fund, 33
ASEAN Industrial Complementation
   (AIC), 215, 219
ASEAN Industrial Cooperation, 220, 301
ASEAN Industrial Cooperation Scheme
   (AICO), 227, 253
   participation of Nestle, 230
ASEAN Industrial Joint Ventures, 220, 228
ASEAN Industrial Projects (AIP) scheme,
   215, 258, 297
   allocation of, 214
   futility of, 218
   products, 222
ASEAN Informal Summit, 61
ASEAN integration system of preferences, 74
ASEAN Integration Work Plan, 308
ASEAN Inter-Parliamentary Caucus, 141
ASEAN Investment Area agreement, 18
ASEAN Investment Area (AIA), 70, 244,
   245, 349
ASEAN Labour Ministers Meeting, 152
ASEAN Mekong Basin Development
   Cooperation (AMBDC), 280
ASEAN Mekong Basin Development
   Cooperation Scheme, 74
ASEAN Mekong Basin Development
   Cooperation programme, 237
ASEAN Ministerial Meeting, 15, 18, 177,
   190, 221, 258
   Myanmar passing up chairmanship, 141,
   143
   Pattaya, in, 260
   position on human rights, 380
   second, 165
   Singapore, in, 139
ASEAN Ministerial Meeting on the
   Environment, 110
ASEAN Ministerial Meeting on Haze, 112
ASEAN Ministerial Meeting on
   Transnational Crime, 200

ASEAN Ministers of Labour Meeting, 136
ASEAN Minus X, 31, 32, 352, 353
ASEAN Mutual Legal Assistance
   Agreement, 361
ASEAN Navy Interaction, 364
ASEAN National Secretariat, 22
ASEAN Peatland Management Initiative,
   115
ASEAN plus India, 203–205
ASEAN Post-Clearance Audit Manual, 234
ASEAN Post-Ministerial Conferences, 189,
   191, 195, *see also* Post-Ministerial
   Conference (PMC)
ASEAN Potash Mining Company, 218
ASEAN Preferential Trading Arrangements,
   28
ASEAN Programme for Regional
   Integration Support, 333
ASEAN Promotion Centre, 259
ASEAN Protocol on Enhancing Dispute
   Settlement Mechanism, 33
ASEAN Regional Forum, 123, 134, 143
   Senior Official's meeting, 143
ASEAN Regional Forum, 24, 37, 78, 189–
   98, 202, 206, 208, 257, 261, 291,
   313, 323, 365, 375
   attendance of Timor-Leste, 79
   origins, 190
   subjects discussed, 262
ASEAN Science Fund, 33
ASEAN Secretariat, 20, 21, 23, 67, 74,
   228
   cooperation with European Commission,
   143
   professionalization of, 22
   Program Management Unit, 113
   restructuring of, 22
   surveillance report, 103
ASEAN Secretary-General
   Ong Keng Yong, 14, 18
ASEAN Security Community, 164, 355,
   356, 368
   cooperation with UN, 366, 367
   future prospects, 367
   setting new norms, 357, 358
ASEAN Security Community (ASC), 30,
   193, 199, 206–208, 423–25

ASEAN Security Community Plan of
    Action, 154, 440–44
ASEAN Senior Officials on the
    Environment, 116
ASEAN Single Window, 234
ASEAN Socio-Cultural Community, 450–
    62
    plan of action, 451
    vision of, 450
ASEAN Socio-Cultural Community
    (ASCC), 426, 427
ASEAN Specialized Meteorological Centre,
    112, 115
ASEAN Standing Committee, 22, 23, 94,
    145, 171
ASEAN Summit, 224, 230, 266
    Kuala Lumpur, in, 166
ASEAN Swap Arrangement, 104, 105
ASEAN Tourism Agreement, 17, 29, 241,
    349
ASEAN Tourism Forum, 241, 246
ASEAN Treaty on Economic Cooperation
    proposal, 15
ASEAN "troika", 58
ASEAN Vision 2020, 29, 156, 411–15, 419
    community of caring societies, 414, 415
    concert of Southeast Asian nations, 411,
        412
    outward looking, 415
    partnership in dynamic development,
        412–14
ASEAN Way, 35–37, 208
ASEAN-4
    transition economies, 69
    see also CLMV
ASEAN-6, 52, 73
    average GDP per capita, 68
ASEAN-6, 227, 242
ASEAN-ADB programme, 104
ASEAN-Australia Dialogue, 310
ASEAN-Australia-New Zealand summit,
    317
ASEAN-Canada cooperation, 53, 136
ASEAN-Canada Partnership Symposium,
    337
ASEAN-CER free trade area, 313
ASEAN-China agreement, 70

ASEAN-China Declaration on the
    Conduct of Parties in the South
    China Sea, 186
ASEAN-China Eminent Persons Group,
    285, 289
ASEAN-China Framework Agreement on
    Comprehensive Economic
    Cooperation, 285, 305
ASEAN-China Summit, 118, 186, 187, 289
ASEAN-China Working Group, 187
ASEAN-EC Energy Facility, 333
ASEAN-EEC dialogue, 330, 331
ASEAN-EEC Joint Study Group, 330
ASEAN-EU interaction, 334
ASEAN-EU Ministerial Meeting, 200
ASEAN-EU relations, 136
ASEAN-European Communities
    cooperation agreement, 53
ASEAN-India linkage, 208
ASEAN-Indian Summit, 29, 293
ASEAN-ISIS, 191
ASEAN-Japan Centre, 300
ASEAN-Japan Development Fund, 302
ASEAN-Japan dialogue, 258
ASEAN-Japan exchange, 306
ASEAN-Japan Summit, 294, 296, 301
    declaration on Comprehensive Economic
        Partnership, 305
ASEAN-Japan Youth Friendship
    Programme, 299
ASEAN-Korea Framework Agreement on
    Comprehensive Economic
    Cooperation, 32
ASEAN-ROK dialogue, 307
ASEAN-US dialogue, 258
ASEAN-US Summit, 329
ASEAN-X, 352, 353
ASEANAPOL, 199, 200
Asia-Africa summit, 27
Asia-Europe Meeting (ASEM), 137, 143,
    334, 335
Asian Development Bank (ADB), 71, 111,
    263, 304
    annual meeting, 104
    financial support given, 103
Asian financial crisis, 85, 96–107, 284
Asian Monetary Fund, 303

Index

Asia Europe Journal, 7
Asia-Europe Meeting, 29
Asian Bond Market, 31
Asian Cooperation Dialogue, 30
Asian Development Bank, 34
Association of Indonesian Muslim
    Intellectuals, 127
Association of Southeast Asia (ASA), 3, 27,
    44
Association of Southeast Asian Nations
    (ASEAN)
  admission of new members, 53–55
  admission of Vietnam, 226
  confidence-building mechanism, 56
  criticism from some Western
      governments, 56
  contribution of members, 34
  coverage by media, 4
  diversity, 26
  diversity of members, 80–82
  economic cooperation, 163
  economic integration, *see* economic
      integration
  first instance of conditioned
      membership, 65
  founding document, 2, 8
  future direction, 384, 385
  future of, 372–85
  High Council, 11
  informality and loose arrangements, 11–
      18
  instances of interference, 96
  institutional development, 19
  institutions and values, 377–81
  integration of new members, 70–75
  lack formal norms in internal
      arrangements, 148
  leadership, question of, 26–32
  membership criteria, 80
  members in WTO, 256
  more active engagement with Myanmar,
      147
  non-interference in member's internal
      affairs, 85–157
  objectives, 212
  political arrangements, lack of norms for,
      90
  policy of engaging Myanmar, 146
  proposed dialogues, 214
  refugee problem, 178, 179
  role in regional security, 161–208
  sensitivity of members, 26
  take effective cooperative measures, 157
  two tier, 67–70
  unconditional membership, 50–53
assured markets
  products, for, 215
Atal Bihari Vajpayee, 292
Australia, 309–15
  Treaty of Amity and Cooperation, 168
Australia-New Zealand, closer economic
    relations, 317–21
Australian National University, 146
automotives, 346
Aye Lwin, 463
Ayeyawady-Chao Phraya-Mekong
    Economic Cooperation Strategy, 30
average GDP per capita, ASEAN-6, 68
avian flu, 119
  dealing with, 120

B
Bali, bombings, 198
Bali Concord II, 193, 346, 369
Bambang Trisulo, 468
Bangkok Declaration, 54
Bangkok Summit Declaration, 42
Bangladesh-India-Myanmar-Sri Lanka-
    Thailand Economic Cooperation, 30
banks
  undercapitalization of, 98
Basic Agreement on ASEAN Industrial
    Complementation, 301
Basic Agreement on ASEAN Industrial
    Projects, 217, 253
B.J. Habibie, 125
  leader of ICMI, 127
bilateral disputes, 14
bilateral measures
  Asian financial crisis, 102
boat people, 175, 176
Board of Trustees, 379
Boonchai Bamrungphong, 215
Bounkert Sangsomsak, 463

brand-to-brand complementation, 219, 220, 228, 301
Brunei Darussalam, 25, 47, 90
  admission into ASEAN, 53
  Chinese community in, 91
  legislative council, 90
  Malay sultanate, 91
Burma
  anti-Chinese demonstrations, 131
  leaving NAM, 45
  non-Bamar nationalism, 132
  refusal to join ASEAN, 43–45
  see also Myanmar
  State Law and Order Restoration Council (SLORC), 132
  State Law and Restoration Council, 45
  State Peace and Development Council (SPDC), 135
  withdrawal from NAM, 132

C
Cambodia, intervention by ASEAN, 94–95
Cambodia, 25
  role in ASEAN Tourism Agreement, 29
  sacking of Thai embassy, 14
Cambodia
  admission delayed, 57–67
  admission into ASEAN, 63
  delay in admission, 81
  disappointment with system of trade preferences, 67
  general elections, 50
  Khmer Rouge coming into power, 49
  opening of skies, 241
  refusal to join ASEAN, 43–45
  turmoil in, 55
  valuation of membership in ASEAN, 66
  withdrawal of Vietnamese forces, 81
Cambodian Institute for Cooperation and Peace, 64
Cambodian issue, 261
Cambodian People's Party, 60
Camdessus, Michael, 101
Canada, 336–38
Canadian International Development Agency, 337
capital mobility, 433

Carlos, Meneleo, 463
Castle, James, 249, 463
Central Committee of the Chinese Communist Party, 276
Centre for International Studies and Research, 6
Center for Strategic and International Studies, 99, 163
certificates of origin, 231
Cham Prasidh, 170, 232, 464
Chalongphob Sussangkarn, 106
Charrier, Philip, 41, 82
Charter of the Organization of African Unity, 86
Charter of the Organization of American States, 86, 89
Charter of the South Asian Association for Regional Cooperation, 86
Cheah Sin Liang, 232, 464
Chemical Weapons Convention and Biological Weapons Convention, 363
Chem Widhya, 464
Chiangmai Initiative, 104, 256, 267
Chin, David, 464
China, 274–90
  ASEAN support for market-economy status, 286
  bilateral code of conduct for South China Sea, 186
  border skirmishes with Vietnamese forces, 175
  full dialogue partner of ASEAN, 277
  occupation of Paracels, 181
  permanent membership in UN Security Council, 288
  putting of structures on Spratlys, 182
  relations with Indonesia, 31
  SARS outbreak, 30
  seizure of Paracels, 93
  South China sea, relations over, 182, 373
  South China sea in, 182
  threat from, 3
  Treaty of Amity and Cooperation, 168
Chinese community
  Brunei, in, 91
Cho Kah Sin, 464

Christianity, main branches, 86
Chua, Reginald, 464
Chua, Robert, 119, 464
Chuan Leekpai, 128
CLMV countries
　capacity for economic integration, 72
　list of exports, 74
Closer Economic Partnership (CEP), 319
Closer Economic Relations (CER), 317
Closer Economic Relations of Australia and New Zealand, 29
Coalition Government of Democratic Kampuchea (CGDK), 171
Cold War, end of, 9, 24
Colomé, Delfin, 24
Colonialism, 93
COMECON, 54, 170
Committee of Permanent Representatives, 23
Committee on Industry, Minerals and Energy, 219
Common ASEAN Position on Reforming the International Financial Architecture, 102
Common Effective Preferential Tariff Scheme (CEPT), 220, 223, 226, 231, 253, 312
　end-rate, 228
　preferences, utilization of, 245
common market, 221
communications, advances in, 154
Communist Party of Burma, 132
Communist Party of Malaya, 7
Communists
　takeover of Cambodia and Laos, 174
community of caring societies, 154–57, 451, 452, 458, 459
Competitive Air Services Policy, 240
Comprehensive Plan of Action, 179
concept and principles of preventive diplomacy, 194
conciliation and mediation processes, 438, 439
conflict prevention, 442, 443, 446, 447
conflict resolution, 443, 448, 449
consultations
　need for frequent, 103
consultative mechanism, 438, 439

Convention on the Elimination of All Forms of Discrimination Against Women, 151
Convention on the Rights of the Child, 151
Coordinating Centre, 114, 115
Coordination and Support Unit, 113
Corregidor island
　mutiny, 164
Council for Security Cooperation in the Asia Pacific (CSCAP), 191
Court of Justice, 5
crony capitalism, 98
Custodio, Edsel, 247, 464
custom authorities
　code of conduct, 234
custom procedures
　harmonization, 69
customs, 233–36, 432
customs and immigration procedures
　streamlining of, 72, 249
customs valuation system, 374
cyber crime, 279

D

Daw Aung San Suu Kyi, 132, 135, 138, 142, 359
　lifting of restrictions, 140
Declaration of ASEAN Concord, 87, 192, 207, 213, 246, 251, 420–28
Declaration on the Conduct of Parties in the South China Sea, 284
decision-making
　consensus method, 34
defence cooperation, 364, 365
defence ministers
　forum of, 205, 206
de Mello, Sergio Vieira, 76
Deng Xiaoping, 222
Department of Foreign Affairs, 355
Department of International Relations, Australian National University, 176
development and technical cooperation, 436
Dewi Fortuna Anwar, 8, 9, 125
Dhanabalan, S., 464
Diaoyutai, 184

Dialogue Partner, 277
  EEC, 329
  New Zealand, 315
digital divide, 69
Dongsha islands, 184
Donor
  IAI projects, 73
Downer, Alexander, 271

E
e-ASEAN, 346
e-ASEAN, 233
e-ASEAN Framework Agreement, 417
East Asia
  view of Karl Jackson, 97
East Asia Economic Caucus, 266
East Asian Economic Group (EAEC), 28, 265
East Asia Plus, 373
East Asia Study Group (EASG), 268
East Asia Summit, 204, 208, 257, 269–74, 270
  participation in, 294
East Asian Free Trade Area, 268
East Timor, 25, 121–31, 193
  autonomy, 126
  escalation of violence, 128
  independence, 75
  Indonesia intervention after independence, 122
  Portuguese colony, 122
  see also Timor-Leste
Economic and Social Commission for Asia and the Pacific, 165
economic community, 342–44
Economic Cooperation Organization, 263
economic cooperative initiatives, 430–33
economic integration
  managing social impact of, 453, 454, 459, 460
economic policies
  non-effectiveness, 98
enforcement mechanism, 439
Eighty Years' War, 86
electronics, 346
electronic products
  drop in demand for, 98

Enhanced ASEAN Dispute Settlement Mechanism (DSM), 439
environmental sustainability
  enhancing, 454, 460, 461
European Atomic Energy Community (EURATOM), 5
European Central Bank, 5
European Coal and Steel Community, 5
European Commission, 5
European Commission, cooperation with ASEAN Secretariat, 143
European Economic Community (EEC), 5, 329
  dialogue with, 258
European integration
  development of, 38
European Trade Commissioner, 143
European Union, 11, 73, 231, 249, 329–36, 350
  common currency, 5
  parliament, 5
  views on East Timor, 125
EUROPOL, 200
Exclusive Economic Zone, 169

F
facilitation of transit passage of goods, 238
Faisal Tanjung, 127
Far Eastern Economic Review
  coverage of ASEAN's founding, 4
  demise, 4
financial system
  politicization of, 98
fires
  cause of haze, 155
  transnational impact, 155
fisheries, 346
fisheries cooperation, 187
Five-Power Defence Arrangement, 10, 321
Flores, Jamil Maidan, 464
Ford, Gerald, 122
Form D certificates of origin, 231
  rate of utilization, 247
founding document
  ASEAN, 2
France
  participation of, 197

Framework Agreement on Comprehensive Economic Cooperation between ASEAN and India, 70
Framework Agreement on Enhancing ASEAN Economic Cooperation, 31, 53, 226
Framing the ASEAN Charter, 382, 383
free trade
  ICT, in, 69
frequent consultations
  need for, 103
FRETILIN, 122
Friendship Programme, 299
Fukuda Doctrine, 295, 296, 297, 299, 307
FUNCINPEC, 60, 61, 83
Funston, John, 87, 157
Future-Oriented Cooperation Projects, 308
Fuzi Hj. Abdul Razak, 464

G

General Agreement on Tariffs and Trade (GATT), 106, 227
General Agreement on Trade in Services, 232
Generalized System of Preferences, 67
Ghazali Shafie, Tan Sri, 23
Ginandjar Kartasasmita, 128
glasnost, 322
global economy
  slowing down of, 98
Gloria Macapagal-Arroyo, 188
Gnassingbe Eyadema, President, 88
Goff, Phil, 317
Goh Chok Tong, 29, 71, 118, 204, 224, 251, 291, 292, 343, 344, 464
Gomes, Ana, 122, 124, 464
Gorbachev, Mikhail, 322
governance
  bad, 98
government leadership
  ineffective, 98
Great Proletarian Cultural Revolution, 3, 10, 131, 167
Greater Mekong Sub-region (GMS) programme, 280, 302
Green Lane system, 234, 348

gross domestic products, 68
Groups of Experts, 184
guidelines for zero burning, 115
Gulf Cooperation Council of Arab States, 262
Gusmão, Xanana, 76

H

Hadi Soesastro, 99, 102, 464
Hamid Albar, 464
Hanoi
  first appearance of SARS, 117
Hanoi Declaration on Narrowing the Development Gap for Closer ASEAN Integration, 71
Hanoi Plan of Action, 240, 246
Harris, Stuart, 99, 163, 209
Hasjim Djalal, 12, 123, 183, 210, 464
Hassanal Bolkiah, Sultan, 42
Hassan Wirajuda, 14
haze problem, 85, 107, 111, 416
  ability of governments to face powerful interests, 116
  severely injurious, 155
Haze Regional Action Plan, 112
Haze Technical Task Force, 112
healthcare, 233, 346
healthcare workers
  affected by SARS, 117
hepatitis-B vaccines, 218
High Council
  rules of procedure, 167
High Council of ministerial level representatives, 167
High-Level Task Force on ASEAN Economic Integration, 24, 251, 344, 346, 347, 349, 354
  recommendation of ASEAN Minus X Formula, 352
highway and rail link, 37
Hill, Hal, 96
HIV/AIDS, 417
Hmong, 175
Holy Roman Empire, 86
Hor Namhong, 67, 173, 464
HRD planning, 72
human rights, 148–54

ASEAN's position, 380
basic, 150
degree of protection, 151
establishment of mechanism, 153
in light of circumstances, 150
politicization of, 150
right to development, 150
Hun Sen, 45, 59, 60, 61, 63, 66, 75, 81, 241, 292
Huxley, Tim, 176, 177

I

IAI Task Force, 72
IAI work plan, 75, *see also* Initiative for ASEAN Integration
IBM study
  recommendations, 69
ICT providers
  competitive environment for, 69
Inclusion List (IL), 106
independent regulatory bodies
  internet service providers, for, 69
India, 290–94
  ASEAN dialogue partner, 195, 290
  Treaty of Amity and Cooperation, 168
India-ASEAN Eminent Persons Lecture Series, 204
Indochina
  ASEAN opening up to, 47
  US debacle, 261
Indochinese asylum seekers 171, 174–80, 256, 261
Indochinese refugees, 208
Indonesia, 25
  ASEAN participation in East Timor, 130
  Chinese community, 7, 91
  enforcement of environmental laws, 110
  exporter of minerals and forestry products, 213
  failure to mobilize support, 123
  fires, cost of, 109
  losses caused by haze, 108
  Ministry of Forestry and Estate Crops, 111, 114
  movement of troops into East Timor, 122

objection to formation of Malaysia, 8
prosecution for clearing land by burning, 114
rebellions with US support, 167
relations with China, 31
transformation of, 27
view on formation of Malaysia, 93
industrial complementation, 219, 221
information and communication technology, 69
information technology
  advances in, 154
Initiative for ASEAN Integration (IAI), 29, 71, 306, 311, 316, 417
  donors, 73
  projects, 72
  work plan, 73
Institute of Defence and Strategic Studies, 282
Institute of Developing Economies, 302
Institute of Southeast Asian Studies, 87, 247, 345
  publication of *Framing the ASEAN Charter*, 382
institutional development
  slow pace of, 19
institutional strengthening, 434, 435
integration
  road to, 245–50
INTELEX, 206
intellectual property rights, 433
International Court of Justice in The Hague, 13
International Crisis Group, 146
Inter-American Democratic Charter, 89
international economic crime, 279
international financial architecture
  soundness of, 97
International Force for East Timor, 128
International Labour Conference, 135
  definition of child labour, 155
International Labour Organization (ILO), 263
International Monetary Fund, 98
International Trade in Services (ITS), 350
International Tribunal on the Law of the Sea, 13

Index

Internet service providers, 69
Intersessional Meeting on Counter-Terrorism and Transnational Crime, 199
intra-ASEAN imports, 247
intra-ASEAN trade, 69, 221, 225
  low growth, 216
  tariffs, 343, 347
investments, 244, 245, 432
  misallocation of, 98
Ismail bin Datuk Abdul Rahman, Tun Dr, 48
Itu Aba, 181, 183, *see also* Tai Ping

J
Jackson, Karl, 97, 100
Jakarta Informal Meetings, 28, 173
Japan, 294–307
  China's trading partner, 264
  four-point peace proposal for Cambodia, 62
  official development assistance, 294
  national industrial policies, 7
Japan-ASEAN Comprehensive Exchange Plan, 302
Japan-ASEAN Exchange Programme, 302
Japan-ASEAN General Exchange Fund, 302
Japan-ASEAN Initiative to Combat Pandemic Influenza, 120
Japan-ASEAN Integration Fund, 120
Japan International Cooperation Agency (JICA), 295
Jawhar Hassan, M., 465
Jayakumar, S., 30, 465
Joint Cooperation Committee, 337
Joint Declaration of ASEAN and China on Cooperation in the Field of Non-Traditional Security Issues, 279
Joint Declaration on Comprehensive Cooperation Partnership, 308
Joint Declaration on Strategic Partnership for Peace and Prosperity, 287
Joint Statement on East Asia Cooperation, 266
Junichiro Koizumi, 204, 298
Jusuf Wanandi, 163, 209, 468

K
Kakuei Tanaka, 295
Kao Kim Hourn, 64, 465
Kashmir issue, 196
Kavi Chongkittavorn, 290, 465
Keindanren staff, 301
Keizo Obuchi, 298
Khin Maung Win, 465
Khin Nyunt, 44, 82, 134, 135, 465
Khmer Rouge, 36, 49, 170
Kiichi Miyazawa, 297
Kim Dae Jung, 267, 270, 309
Kissinger, Henry, 122
Koh, Tommy, 465
konfrontasi, 2, 162
Korea, 261, 307–309
  national industrial policies, 222
Korean War
  crossing of Yalu River, 182
Krugman, Paul, 97, 100
Kuala Lumpur Declaration, 274
Kwa Chong Guan, 465

L
labour, 243–44
  regional movement of, 246
labour conventions
  use in trade protectionism, 152
labour standards, 152
lack of transparency, 98
Lamy, Pascal, 198, 231
Lange, David, 316
Laos, 25
  abolition of monarchy, 40
  admission into ASEAN, 55
  one-party state, 91
Law on the Territorial Sea and Contiguous Zone, 184, 185, 188, 284
leadership
  definition of, 26, 27
Lee Chiong Giam, 119, 465
Lee Hsien Loong, 30
Lee Kuan Yew, 49, 163, 173, 174, 209, 465
legally binding agreements
  lack of, 18
Leifer, Michael, 99

Leo Suryadinata, 467
Letchumanan, Raman, 465
Ligitan, 12, 14
losses
  owing to SARS, 117
Liquiça killings, 121
Luu Doan Huynh, 48, 83, 172, 173, 209, 465

M

Mahathir Mohamad, 26, 163, 203, 221, 224, 465
  proposal for EAEC, 28, 265
Malaysia, 25, 91
  AFTA scheme, 105
  CEPT inclusion list, 245
  dispute with Philippines over Sabah, 162
  dispute with Singapore, 238
  exporter of palm oil, 213
  formation, 8
  inclusion of Sabah, 7
  tension with Philippines, 207
  territorial dispute with Singapore, 13
Manglapus, Raul, 15
Manila Framework Group, 304
Manmohan Singh, 290
MAPHILINDO, 3, 44, 162
  launch of, 9
market access
  limitations eliminated, 231
  purpose of dialogues, 259
market integration
  tariff cuts essential, 248
markets
  products, for, 215
maritime security, 361, 362
maritime terrorism, 201
market integration, 344
Marcos
  declaration on claim to Sabah, 166
maritime Southeast Asia, 3
Mathews, Verghese, 465
McCarthy, John, 125
McKinsey & Company, 247, 345
Mekong Basin
  call for development, 29
  development programmes, 75

Mekong Institute, 316
Mekong River Commission, 74, 281, 316
Meeting of ASEAN Economic and Planning Ministers, 213
MERCOSUR
  creation of, 222
Minister for International Trade and Industry, 318
Ministry of Forestry and Estate Crops, Indonesia, 111, 114
Mischief Reef, 184, 185, 189, 284
Mochtar Kusumaatmadja, 259, 291, 330
Moe Thuzar, 465
Mohamed Bolkiah, Prince, 198
Mongkut, King, 93
Mongolia
  Treaty of Amity and Cooperation, 168
Montes, Manual, 100
Mountbatten, Lord, 41
Mount Pinatubo, 177
Multilateral Trade Policy Department (Vietnam), 235
Musa Hitam, Tan Sri, 289
Muslims
  Cambodia, in, 91
  Thailand, in, 92
Myanmar, 25, 91, 131–48, 193
  acceptance into ASEAN, 51
  admission into ASEAN, 55, 134
  advantages of giving up chairmanship, 144
  ASEAN's view of, 95
  benefits of ASEAN membership, 133
  economy, 135
  EU declarations and measures, 138
  membership in ASEAN, 202
  Muslim population, 133
  observer status, 134
  political domination by Bamars, 91, 92
  potential advantages of taking up chairmanship, 144
  question about Chairmanship of ASEAN, 140
  Rohingyas, 133
  trade preferences withheld by other countries, 136
  US sanctions, 138
  western embargo, 146

western hostility towards, 195
see also Burma
Mya Than, 465

N
Nakasone, 299
Nana Sutresna, 28, 467
Nansha, 184
Narongchai Akrasanee, 465
"narrowing the development gap", 70, 71
Nathan, S.R., 465
National Environment Agency, 115
national human rights body, 153
National League for Democracy, 78, 132
National master plan
  development of information technology, 69
national response
  Asian financial crisis, 102
National Single Window, 235
national sovereignty, 35
National Unity Party, 132
Nestlé
  participation in AIP, 230
  production plant, 229
Ne Win, General, 131, 132
New York Times
  report on founding of ASEAN, 4
New Zealand, 315
  Treaty of Amity and Cooperation, 168, 314
New Zealand-Australia Free Trade Agreement
  replaced by CER, 317
Nguyen Anh Tuan, 465
Nguyen Dinh Cung, 466
Nitisastro, Widjojo, 466, *see also* Widjojo Nitisastro
Nixon, Richard, 275
Noboru Takeshita, 301
Non-Aligned Movement (NAM), 27, 124, 132, 314
  Burma's departure, 45
non-interference doctrine, 85–157
non-tariff barriers, 230, 248
non-use of force, 35
Noordin Azhari, 74, 466

norms
  shaping and sharing, 442, 445, 446
Norodom Sihanouk, *see* Sihanouk, Prince Norodom
Norodom Sirivudh, Prince, 66, 170
North American Free Trade Agreement (NAFTA), 222, 224, 254
Northeast Asia, 203
North Vietnam
  reunification with South, 49
  see also Vietnam
Nuclear Non-Proliferation Treaty, 363
nuclear weapons-free zone, 168, 169
Nugroho Wisnummurti, 126, 468
Nyan Win, 145

O
Ohn Gyaw, 466
Omi Shigeru, 466
Ong Keng Yong, 14, 466
Ong, Romualdo A., 466
Operationalization of the ASEAN Framework Agreement on the Facilitation on Goods in Transit, 351
Operationalized Regional Haze Action Plan, 112
Orderly Departure Programme (ODP), 179
  resettlement of refugees, 180
Organization of African Unity, charter of, 86
Organization of American States (OAS), 11
Organization of American States (OAS), charter of, 52, 86
Organization of Islamic Conference, 124
Ouellet, André, 338

P
Pacific Islands Forum, 262, 263
Pacific Pact, 10
Pakistan, 196
Pakistan
  Treaty of Amity and Cooperation, 168
Pan Sorasak, 466
Papua New Guinea, 25
Paracels, 181, 184, 186
  seizure by China, 93
Parameswaran, N., 466
Paris Conference, 173

Paris Peace Accords, 61
Paterno, Vincente, 215, 466
Pathet Lao, 175
Pederson, Morten B., 146
Pedra Branca, 13
peer review, 103, 104
Pempel, T.J., 99
people-smuggling, 279
per capita GDP, 68
perestroika, 322
personal relations
  reliance on, 35
Penghu, 184
Pescadores, 184
Petrie, Charles, 466
petrochemical industry
  Philippines, in, 227
Pham The Vinh, 466
Pham Van Dong, 49, 172, 173
Philippines, 25, 91, 242
  bilateral code of conduct for South China Sea, 186
  bombings in, 198
  claim to Sabah, 7, 164
  deterioration of living standards, 150
  discovery of structures on Mischief Reef, 185
  dispute with Malaysia over Sabah, 162
  ejection of Marcos, 94
  martial law, under, 81
  mutual defence treaty with United States, 10
  predominance of Christianity, 92
  row with Malaysia, 7, 207
  tension with Malaysia, 207
Phnom Penh, 14, 198
  viewed ASEAN with suspicion, 131
Phongsavath Boupha, 466
Pich Rithi, 250, 466
Pinit Jarusombat, 218
piracy
  Straits of Malacca, at, 201
Plan of Action, 199, 368
plantation owners
  slash and burn agriculture, 108
Pola Singh, 466
political arrangements
  lack of norms for ASEAN, 90
political development, 441, 442, 444
political impact
  Asian financial crisis, 97–98
polyethylene
  imports of, 15
polypropylene
  imports of, 15
Portugal, 123, 125
post-conflict peace building, 443, 449
Post-Ministerial Conference (PMC), 260, 325
  subject discussed, 262
Post-Ministerial Meetings, 143
poverty
  elimination of, 89
Pracha Guna-Kasem, 19, 467
Pratas, 184
preferential trading arrangements, 214, 215, 216, 223
  improvement on, 31
preventive diplomacy, 195
priority integration sectors, 433
product standards, 236–37
  harmonization of, 69, 245
Programme Stream, 311
Protocol on Dispute Settlement Mechanism for ASEAN economic agreements, 35
protocols
  implementation of, 238
Pulau Batu Puteh, *see* Pedra Branca
Putin, Vladimir, 272, 324
Pyinmana, 135

Q
Qian Qichen, 283
quarantine measures
  SARS counter measures, 119

R
Radiu Prawiro, 213
Rafidah Aziz, 318
Rajaratnam, S., 2
Ramos, Fidel, 42
Ramos-Horta, Jose, 76, 79, 126, 197, 466
Ramos, Narciso, 1
Ranariddh, Prince, 59, 62, 81

Index   **485**

Rarotonga Treaty, 169
Razali Ismail, 187
ready-to-assemble motor vehicles, 105
real exit tax, 242
realpolitik, 170
Recommendations of High Level Task Force on ASEAN Economic Integration, 429–39
reduction in numbers, 180
refugee convention
 ratification, 178
refugee problem, 178, 261
regional economic integration, 70, 107, 376, 212–53
 push for, 345
Regional Economic Policy Support Facility, 312
regional integration, 418
regional institutions, empowered, 353, 354
Regional Partnership Scheme, 311
regional security, 161–208
 new members, 201, 202
regional social cohesion
 strengthening foundation of, 455, 461, 462
Regional Trade and Investment Area, 292
renminbi
 stability of, 288
 value of, 287
Rice, Condoleeza, 144, 325, 328
Ridzwan Dzafir, 467
right to development, 150
Rio Group of Latin American countries, 263
Road Map to Democracy, 146
Robinson, W. Courtland, 177
Rohingya
 crackdown on, 133
Romulo, Carlos P., 10, 171, 209, 309
Romulo, Roberto, 42
rubber-based products, 346
Russia, 321–25

S
Sabah, 164–66
 cause of dispute between Philippines and Malaysia, 162

 claim by Philippines, 164
 inclusion into Malaysia, 7
Salazar, Antonio de Oliveira, 122
Santa Cruz massacre, 121, 124, 131
Santos, J.B., 229
Sarasin Viraphol, 467
Sarwono Kusumaatmadja, 110
Sastrohandoyo, Wiryono, 467
Sayakane Sisouvong, 467
scholarships, 74
Schwarz, Adam, 467
Sectoral Dialogue Partnership, 307
security community, 36
Senanayake, Dudley, 46
Senior Officials Meeting of the Post-Ministerial Conferences (PMC SOM), 189
Senkaku, 184
Sesan River, 283
Severe Acute Respiratory Syndrome (SARS), 107
 ASEAN cooperation, 116, 156
 counter measures, 118
 death toll, 118
 effect on China, 30
 effect on economy, 117
 end of outbreak, 119
 first appearance, 117
Shanghai Cooperation Organization, 263, 324
Shigeru Omi, 119
Ship for Southeast Asian Youth, 295
Siazon, Domingo, 42, 65, 134
Siddhi Savetsila, 172
Sihanouk, Prince Norodom, 45, 171, 466
 joining forces with Khmer Rouge, 172
Singapore, 25
 activism of, 19
 complaint against Malaysia, 15
 dispute with Malaysia, 238
 effect of SARS, 117, 118
 giving up of AIP, 218
 land reclamation, 13
 National Environment Agency, 115
 occurrence of SARS, 117
 territorial dispute with Malaysia, 13
Singapore Declaration, 21

Singapore-Kunming Rail Link, 71, 237, 246
Single Window system, 245, 348
Sipadan, 12, 14
Siregar, Arifin, 467
Sirivudh, Prince, 172
Sisophon-Poipet link, funding of, 237
Six-Party Talks, 194, 324, 376
slash and burn agriculture, 108
Socio-Cultural Community, 368
    whether necessary, 368, 370
Soeharto, 1, 162, 178
    removal, 26
Soe Win, 145
Solidarity Fund, 303
Somsavat Lengsavad, 467
Soulivong Daravong, 467
Southeast Asia
    definition of, 41
    diversity among countries, 90
    factors for formation of nations, 7
    geographical boundary, 41
    more diversity than Europe, 8
    newly independent states, 6
    role of colonialism, 6
    tensions and conflicts, 6
South Asian Association for Regional Cooperation (SAARC), charter of, 86
South China Sea, 180–89
    understanding with China, 373
Southeast Asia Collective Defence Treaty, 326
Southeast Asian Nuclear Weapons-Free Zone, 31
Southeast Asia Nuclear Weapons-Free Zone (SEANWFZ), 16, 17, 362
    Commission, 35
Southeast Asia Nuclear Weapons-Free Zone Treaty, 113
    signing of, 50
Southeast Asia Treaty Organization (SEATO), 48, 131, 161, 205, 321
South Vietnam, 48
    reunification with North, 49
Southwest Pacific Forum, 197
Soviet Union
    break up of, 54
    principal threat, 8
    support of Vietnam, 182
Special ASEAN Leaders' Meeting on Aftermath of Earthquake and Tsunami, 30
Special Coordinating Committee of ASEAN Nations (SCCAN), 257, 330
Spratlys, 181, 184
    Chinese structures on, 182
Sri Lanka, 42
    bid to join ASEAN, 45–47
Sri Lanka Freedom Party, 46
State Ministry for the Environment (Indonesia), 110
Steinberg, David I., 467
Stockwin, Harvey, 4
Straits of Malacca
    problem of piracy, 201
Sub-regional Fire-fighting Arrangements, 112
Sukarno, 1, 27, 162
Sunoto, Dhannanjaya, 467
Supreme Council of ASEAN, 23
Surin Pitsuwan, 62, 467
Suryadinata, Leo, 467
Susilo Bambang Yudhoyono, 31, 114, 271
Suthad Setboonsaarng, 467
Sutresna, Nana, 467
Syed Hamid Albar, 145

T
Tai Ping, 181, 183
Takeo Fukuda, 217
Tamiflu, 120
Tan Chin Tiong, 467
tariff preferences
    extension of, 74
tariff rates, 216
tariff-reduction
    AFTA treaty, 17
tariffs
    cuts essential for market integration, 248, 252
Technical Working Groups, 184
Teh, Robert, 467
Temporary Exclusion List (TEL), 106, 244
Teo, Eric, 173, 467
Termsak Chalermpalanupap, 80

Index

territorial disputes, 12, 13
terrorism, 198–201, 364
textiles, 346
Thailand, 91
　activism of, 19
　apprehension over ASEAN industrial project, 217
　baht, fall of, 98
　bilateral ties with Myanmar, 148
　exporter of rice, 213
　governed by military regime, 81
　Islamic communities, 200
　Theravada Buddhism, predominance of, 92
Thanat Khoman, 2, 9, 10, 27, 36, 43, 44, 47, 162, 163, 209, 468
Than Shwe, 145
The Evolution of the Lao State
　Phongsavath Boupha, by, 56
Tian Qiyu, 279
Timor-Leste, 75–79, 197
　attendance at ARF, 79
　foreign policy, 78
　membership, 77
　political crisis, 131
　Portuguese functionaries, 78
　prospective membership, 81
　refining of Saudi oil, 79
　see also East Timor
Tin Maung Maung Than, 468
Tin Winn, 468
Togo, 88, 89
Tokyo Declaration for the Dynamic and Enduring Japan-ASEAN Partnership in the New Millennium, 306
Tongzon, Jose, 468
tourism, 110, 240–43, 346
tourism agreement, 69
tourism, effect of SARS, 117
Towns Act and Villages Acts, 136
Track I, 191
Track II, 191
Trade and Investment Framework Agreements (TIFA), 328, 329
Trade and Investment Promotion Programme, 316

trade in goods, 430–33
trade in services, 431, 432
　liberalization of, 232
trade protectionism
　use of labour conventions, 152
Tran Dong Phuong, 235, 468
transit passage of goods
　facilitation, 238
transnational crime, 364
transport, 237–40
transportation
　advances in, 154
　disruption caused by haze, 110
　importance of, 246, 249
Trans-Regional EU-ASEAN Trade Initiative, 333
Treaty of Amity and Cooperation, 11, 12, 41, 50, 78, 167, 168, 184, 188, 207, 256, 271, 273, 292, 294, 309, 314, 372, 392–401
　accession by New Zealand, 314
　amity, 393
　conclusion, 49
　cooperation, 393, 394, 395
　East Timor's interest in acceding to, 76
　general provisions, 396
　implicit condition for joining ASEAN, 51
　protocol amending, 398, 399
　purpose and principles, 392, 393
　second protocol amending, 400, 401
　settlement of disputes, 395, 396
　signing by Brunei, 53
　US refusal to accede to, 272
Treaty of Asuncion, 222
Treaty of Pelindaba, 169
Treaty of Tlatelolco, 169
Treaty of Westphalia, 86
Trinh Quang Thanh, 83, 468
Tripartite Agreement for joint Marine Seismic Undertaking in the Agreement Area in the South China Sea, 189
Trisulo Bambang, 468
tsunami, 30
Tun Abdul Razak, 47

U

UNAIDS, 263
UN Charter, 149, 188
   adherence to principles of 162
UN Convention on the Law of the Sea, 187
UN Economic Commission for Asia and the Far East (ECAFE), 165
   see also Economic and Social Commission for Asia and the Pacific
UN Environment Programme, 263
UNEP, 114
UN ESCAP
   Mekong-related programs, 74
UNESCO, 263
UN General Assembly
   voting for East Timor problem, 123
UN High Commissioner for Refugees (UNHCR), 175
   statistics, 176, 180
UNICEF, 263
UNIDO study, 216
UN Industrial Development Organization, 73
UN Office on Drugs and Crime, 263
UN Security Council, 307
   East Timor problem, 123
UN Transitional Administration in East Timor, 128, 129
UN Transitional Authority (Cambodia), 304
Universal Declaration of Human Rights, 155
United Kingdom
   participation in ASEAN dialogues, 197
Ung Huot, 59, 60, 61, 64, 468
United Malays National Organization (UMNO), 141
United Nations
   cooperation with, 366, 367
United Nations Development Programme, 16
United Nations Environment Programme, 109
United Nations General Assembly
   Declaration on the Inadmissibility of Intervention in the Domestic Affairs of States, 86
United States, 325–29
   alliance with, 8
   defence treaty with Philippines, 10
   military presence, 9
   vital in East Asia and Pacific, 272
Universal Declaration of Human Rights, 360
UNTAET delegation, 76
U Ohn Gyaw, 42, 44
U Tin Winn, 45, 137
urea fertilizer
   approved ASEAN industrial project, 217
Uruguay Round of Multilateral Trade Negotiations, 222
Urbani, Carlo, 117
US-ASEAN Business Council, 250, 327
US-Asia Environmental Partnership, 327
USAID, 329

V

Vatikiotis, Michael, 468
Vienna Declaration and Programme of Action, 149, 360
Vientiane Action Programme, 199, 235, 243, 312, 347
Vietnam, 25, 91
   admission into ASEAN, 53
   border skirmishes with China, 175
   division, 48
   entry into ASEAN, 226
   eviction from Paracels, 181
   first appearance of SARS, 117
   incursion into Cambodia, 28, 170, 171
   opposing, 170–74
   re-education campaign, 175
   refusal to repatriate boat people, 177
   reunification, 49, 174
   Soviet support, 182
   US War in, 162
   withdrawal from Cambodia, 81
   see also South Vietnam
Vietnam-Cambodia issue, 256
Vietnamese communist party, 151
Virata, Cesar, E.A., 468
visa-free arrangements, 242
Vision Group, 268
   lowering of tariffs, 226

Vriens, Hans, 468
Vu Khoan, 468

W

Wain, Barry, 175, 210, 468
Waldheim, Kurt, 124
Wanandi, Jusuf, 468
weapons of mass destruction, 363
Wen Jiabao, 118
Western Colonialism, 93
Western Europe
   regional unity, 6
Widjojo Nitisastro, 213, 214
Win Aung, 468
Wiryono Sastrohandoyo, 122
Wisnumurti, Nugroho, 468
wood-based products, 346
Worapot Manupipatpong, 468
workers
   standards in treatment of, 152
Working Group for an ASEAN Human Rights Mechanism, 153
Workshops for Managing Potential Conflict in the South China Sea, 183
World Conference on Human Rights, 149
World Health Organization (WHO), 116, 263
World Institute for Development Economics Research, 101
World Trade Centre, 198
World Trade Organization (WTO)
   members from ASEAN, 256
World Trade Organization's Dispute Settlement Body, 15
World War Two, 41
World Wide Fund for Nature, 108
Worst Forms of Child Labour Convention, 152
WTO Agreement on Customs Valuation, 348
WTO customs valuation system, 374

X

Xisha, 184

Y

Yadana offshore natural gas fields, 133
Yalu River, 182
Yangon, 131
Yap, Wendy, 468
Yasuhiro Nakasone, 297
Yasukuni Shrine, 204, 267
Yasushi Akashi, 304
Yee, Raymond, 489
Yeo Yong Boon, George, 141, 250, 271, 469
Yetagun gas field, 133
Yunnan Provincial Environmental Protection Bureau, 282

Z

Zaid Ibrahim, 141
Zainal Abidin Sulong, 469
Zaki Anwar, 127
zero burning guidelines, 115
Zhu Rongji, 284
Zone of Peace, Freedom and Neutrality (ZOPFAN), 28, 49, 87, 166, 167
ZOPFAN Declaration, 167
   acceptance by Brunei, 53

Map of Southeast Asia

CHINA

BANGLADESH
- Dhaka

Bay of Bengal

MYANMAR
- Yangon

HONG KONG
- Kowloon

Hainan

LAOS
- Vientiane

VIETNAM
- Hanoi

Gulf of Tongking

Paracel Islands

THAILAND
- Bangkok

CAMBODIA
- Phnom Penh
- Ho Chi Minh City

Andaman Islands

Andaman Sea

Nicobar Islands

Gulf of Siam

South China Sea

Spratly Islands

PALA

Penang

Aceh

Medan

Straits of Malacca

BRUNEI DARUSSALAM
- Bandar Seri Begawan

Kota Kinabalu

SABAH

MALAYSIA
- Kuala Lumpur

SINGAPORE

Riau Archipelago

SARAWAK

Kuching

SUMATRA

Mentawai Islands

KALIMANTAN

INDONESIA

INDIAN OCEAN

Jakarta

JAVA

BALI

SUM